INSIGHT GUIDE
NewEngland

Discovery
CHANNEL

APA PUBLICATIONS

L

Part of the Langenscheidt Publishing Group

ABOUT THIS BOOK

INSIGHT GUIDE New England

Editorial

Project Editor
Susan Gordon
Managing Editor
Emily Hatchwell
Editorial Director
Brian Bell

Distribution

UK & Ireland
GeoCenter International Ltd
The Viables Centre, Harrow Way
Basingstoke, Hants RG22 4BJ
Fax: (44) 1256 817988

United States
Langenscheidt Publishers, Inc.
46–35 54th Road, Maspeth, NY 11378
Fax: (718) 784 0640

Canada
Thomas Allen & Son Ltd
390 Steelcase Road East
Markham, Ontario L3R 1G2
Fax: (1) 905 475 6747

Australia
Universal Press
1 Waterloo Road
Macquarie Park, NSW 2113
Fax: (61) 2 9888 9074

New Zealand
Hema Maps New Zealand Ltd (HNZ)
Unit D, 24 Ra ORA Drive
East Tamaki, Auckland
Fax: (64) 9 273 6479

Worldwide
Apa Publications GmbH & Co.
Verlag KG (Singapore branch)
38 Joo Koon Road, Singapore 628990
Tel: (65) 6 865 1600. Fax: (65) 6 861 6438

Printing

Insight Print Services (Pte) Ltd
38 Joo Koon Road, Singapore 628990
Tel: (65) 6 865 1600. Fax: (65) 6 861 6438

©2002 Apa Publications GmbH & Co.
Verlag KG (Singapore branch)
All Rights Reserved
First Edition 1984
Seventh Edition 1999
Updated 2002(Reprinted 2002)

CONTACTING THE EDITORS
We would appreciate it if readers
would alert us to errors or out-
dated information by writing to:
**Insight Guides, P.O. Box 7910,
London SE1 1WE, England.**
Fax: **(44) 20 7403 0290.**
insight@apaguide.demon.co.uk
NO part of this book may be reproduced,
stored in a retrieval system or transmitted
in any form or means electronic, mech-
anical, photocopying, recording or otherwise, without prior written permission of
Apa Publications. Brief text quotations
with use of photographs are exempted
for book review purposes only. Information has been obtained from sources
believed to be reliable, but its accuracy
and completeness, and the opinions
based thereon, are not guaranteed.

www.insightguides.com

This guidebook combines the interests and enthusiasms of two of the world's best-known information providers: Insight Guides, whose titles have set the standard for visual travel guides since 1970, and Discovery Channel, the world's premier source of nonfiction television programming.

Insight Guides' editors provide practical advice and general understanding about a place's history, culture, institutions and people. Discovery Channel and its extensive web site, www. discovery.com, help millions of viewers explore their world from the comfort of their home and also encourage them to explore it firsthand.

A region with such a rich history and culture as New England lends itself especially well to the approach taken by the 190-title Insight series. In this latest edition, we take you around the region's six states, starting in Boston and journeying to historic towns and pristine clapboard villages, visiting serene lakes, forested mountains, lobster shacks, and the old lighthouses that dot the coast.

EXPLORE YOUR WORLD

Discovery CHANNEL

How to use this book

The book is carefully structured to convey an understanding of New England and its culture and to guide readers through its sights and attractions:

◆ The Features section, with a yellow colour bar, covers the region's history and culture in lively authoritative essays written by specialists.

◆ The Places section, with a blue bar, provides full details of all the sights and areas worth seeing. The chief places of interest are coordinated by number with specially drawn maps.

◆ The Travel Tips section, with an orange bar, at the back of the book, offers a point of reference for information on travel, accommodation, restaurants, and other practicalities. These details may be located quickly using the index printed on the back-cover flap, which also serves as a bookmark.

The contributors

The new edition builds on earlier ones edited by Brian Bell and Jay Itzkowitz. This time the editor was **Sue Gordon**, a partner in OutHouse Publishing Services, author of a guide to Boston and, with **Tim Locke**, co-author of another book on New England. Locke, who has written several travel guides, revised and re-structured parts of this book.

The chief updater and contributor of new material was **Kimberly Grant**, a Boston-based photographer and author. She has written or co-written several guides to New England and a number of her pictures appear in the book.

The writers whose text has been adapted from earlier editions are **Mark Bastian, Marcus Brooke, Tom Brosnahan, Kay Cassill, Inez and Jonathan Keller, Molly Kuntz, Sandy MacDonald, Julie Michaels, Mark Muro, Adam Nossiter, Norman Sibley, Mark Silber, Bryan Simmons**, and **Peter Spiro**. The travel tips were updated by Bill and David Scheller, and the book was indexed by **Lynn Bresler**.

Among the photographers who capture New England's visual splendor are **Carole Allen, Ping Amranand, Marcus Brooke**, and **Stephen Trimble**.

Map Legend

▬ ▪▪	International Boundary
▬ ▬ ▬	State Boundary
▬ ● ▬	National Park/Reserve
▬ ▬ ▬	Ferry Route
🇹	Subway
✈ ✈	Airport: International/Regional
🚌	Bus Station
🅿	Parking
❶	Tourist Information
✉	Post Office
✝ ✝	Church/Ruins
✝	Monastery
☾	Mosque
✡	Synagogue
🏰	Castle/Ruins
∴	Archeological Site
Ω	Cave
⚑	Statue/Monument
★	Place of Interest

The main places of interest in the Places section are coordinated by number with a full-colour map (e.g. ❶), and a symbol at the top of every right-hand page tells you where to find the map.

INSIGHT GUIDE
New England

CONTENTS

Maps

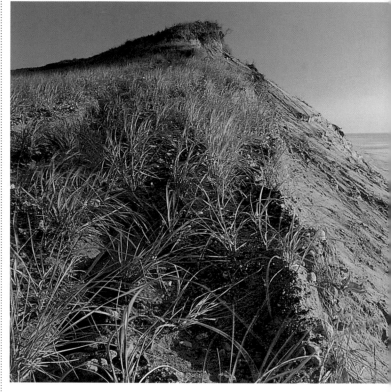

There is a map of New England on the inside front cover and a map of Boston and the MBTA subway on the inside back cover

Introduction

History

Features

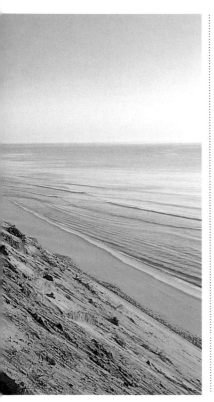

Dune-backed
beach at Truro,
Cape Cod

Insight on....

Information panels

Places

Travel Tips

AMERICA'S ATTIC

The blending of Old England traditions and New World values
created six distinctive states, each with its own character

New England "is a finished place," wrote Bernard DeVoto in 1936. "Its destiny is that of Florence or Venice, not Milan, while the American empire careens onward towards its unpredicted end... It is the first American section to be finished, to achieve stability in its conditions of life. It is the first old civilization, the first permanent civilization in America."

And, as America's first old civilization, New England has a rich endowment of many of the nation's most cherished memories: Paul Revere's midnight ride, the Battle of Bunker Hill, the charisma of the Kennedys. It was here that the first cries of American Independence were heard, here that the movement to abolish slavery found fertile ground, here that education achieved its fullest flowering, here that American art and literature attained their greatest refinement.

This is America's attic, crammed with marvelous antiques of every description. Here are the homes of Hawthorne, Emerson, Dickinson, and Melville; souvenirs of clippers and whaling ships from centuries past; houses and churches in whose gables and steeples can be read a national architectural history. The countryside abounds with inspiring vistas, enchanted with the bright golds and reds of fall, slumbering beneath winter's heavy snows, bursting with the worshipful energy of spring's ritual rebirth, and joyful in summer's ceaseless flowering.

The alluring variety embraces Maine's coast, its rocky promontories pointing to adventure; New Hampshire's lakes, deep with silent wonder; Vermont's mountains, shimmering in spring's verdant cloak and majestic in winter's whiteness; the Berkshires' captivating forests; Connecticut's celebrated colonial heritage; Newport's well-preserved luxury; Cape Cod's charming villages and rolling dunes; Martha's Vineyard's quirky vision of quaintness; and Boston's vibrant cityscape.

If Boston is a state of mind – a remark variously attributed by the city's contentious academics to Mark Twain, Ralph Waldo Emerson, and Thomas G. Appleton – so is New England to an even greater degree. And it is a state of mind well worth embracing.   ❑

PRECEDING PAGES: quintessential fall scenery; sleigh ride on Come Spring Farm, Union, Maine; all the gear for lobstering; sailboats racing on Penobscot Bay.
LEFT: history re-enacted on Hampton Beach, New Hampshire.

NEW ENGL

THE PORTRAICTUER OF CAPTAYNE IOHN SMITH ADMIRALL OF NEW ENGLAND

Æta 37 Aº 1616

The most remarqueable parts thus nam
by the high and mighty Prince CHAR-
nowe King of great Britaine

These are the Lines that shew thy Face: but those
That shew thy Grace and Glory, brighter bee
Thy Faire-Discoueries and Fowle - Overthrowes
Of Salvages, much Civillizd by thee
Best shew thy Spirit; and to it Glory Wyn
So, thou art Brasse without, but Golde within

If so; in Brasse, too soft Smiths Acts to beare
I fix thy Fame, to make Brasse Steele out weare

Thine, as thou art Virtues
John Davies. Here?

SouthHampton

Schooters hill

Sandwich

Dartmouth

Ipswich

Snadoun hill

P. Kent

P. Reeues

Boston

Poynt Dames

Hull

Smith Iles

COGNITA

GENS IN

P. Wynthrop

Cape Anna

Bristow

Salem

Bassable

Talbotts Bay

Fawmouth

Saugus

Charles Towne

Francis Ile

The River CHARLES

Bastable Harbery

Charlton

Winnisime

Dorchester

Claiborns Ils

Medford

London

P. Salthrostale

AND

Aberden

44 ½

Gunnells Ils

Lowmonds

Edenborough

Finis Il

The River Forth

St John Towne   Norwich

44

P. Travers

Martins Ile

Pembrocks Bay

Leth

Gerrards Ils

Hoghton Ils

Willowby Ils

Barty Ils

43

Cape Elizabeth

Paynes Ils

43

SERVIET

42 ½

A Scale of Leagues

Decisive Dates

9000 BC Earliest evidence of human activity in New England, at Shawville, Vermont.
AD 1000 The Viking Leif Erikson discovers Vinland the Good, the location of which remains unknown.
14th–15th centuries The Algonquin Indians arrive in the region.

EARLY COLONISTS

1492 Christopher Columbus reaches America.
1497 John Cabot explores the North American coast.
1524 Giovanni da Verrazano, sailing under the flag of

the French King François I, journeys as far north as Narrangansett Bay.
1602–6 Bartholomew Gosnold, Martin Pring, and George Weymouth lead successful expeditions to the region. Weymouth returns with five Indians abducted from the coast of Maine.
1607 One hundred adventurers, funded by the Plymouth Company, build Fort St George on Parker's Island, Maine, where they spend the winter.
1614 The surveyor John Smith, also commissioned by the Plymouth Company, returns laden with furs and fish from what he calls "New England."
1620 The Plymouth Company finances a group of 66 Puritans to establish a permanent settlement in North America. They leave Plymouth on the *May-*

flower, and sight Cape Cod just over two months later on November 11. In mid-December they found Plymouth Colony.
1630 The Massachusetts Bay Colony is founded by John Winthrop on the Shawmut Peninsula.
1635 The country's first secondary school, the Boston Latin School, is established.
1636 Harvard College is established. Reverend Roger Williams is banished from the Massachusetts Bay Colony and founds Providence, Rhode Island. War erupts with the Pequots.
1639 The first printing press is set up, in Cambridge.
1675–76 King Philip's War sees the demise of Indian society in New England.
1692 The Salem witch trials take place, during which 400 stand accused of sorcery and other crimes. Of the guilty, 19 are hanged.
1701 The Collegiate School (later renamed Yale) is founded.
1712 Captain Christopher Hussey of Nantucket is blown off course and bags the first sperm whale.

ROAD TO INDEPENDENCE

1764 The Revenue Act, imposed by Britain on the colonists, taxes sugar, silk, and some wines.
1765 The Stamp Act is passed, which taxes commercial and legal documents, newspapers, and playing cards. Demonstrations are held throughout New England.
1767 The Townshend Acts place harsh duties on paper, glass, and tea. Two regiments of British troops land at Boston to impose order.
1770 On March 5, five colonists are killed outside the Custom House by Redcoats in what becomes known as the "Boston Massacre."
1773 On December 16, in the "Boston Tea Party," 60 men (disguised as Mohawk Indians and blacks) dump tea over the railings of three ships in Boston Harbor in protest against taxes on tea.
1774 Britain retaliates against the Boston Tea Party by imposing the Coercive Acts, including the Boston Port Act which closes Boston Harbor. On September 5 the First Continental Congress convenes at Philadelphia and starts to organize an army.
1775 On the night of April 18, Paul Revere and William Dawes ride from Boston to warn Minutemen of the impending arrival of 700 British troops sent to destroy an arms depot in Concord. The following day the two sides engage at Lexington in the first battle of the Revolution. On June 17 the British face their first major defeat at Bunker Hill.
1776 On July 4, the Declaration of Independence is adopted.

BOOM AND BUST

1789 Samuel Slater, apprentice to Jedediah Strutt (partner of industrial innovator Richard Arkwright), is engaged by financier Moses Brown to set up a cotton mill at Pawtucket.

1800 Poor working conditions at Pawtucket lead workers to strike in the nation's first industrial action.

1826 The growing community surrounding the Merrimack Manufacturing Company's showpiece cotton mill is renamed Lowell after its founder.

1831 The Abolitionist William Lloyd Garrison founds the weekly *Liberator* newspaper.

1842 The Wadsworth Atheneum is founded in Hartford, Connecticut.

1871 The Museum of Fine Arts opens in Boston.

1880s Irish immigrants start to dominate New England politics.

1885 Debut of the Boston Pops.

1929 The Wall Street Crash and resultant Great Depression hit New England hard.

1936 The Boston Symphony Orchestra's summer festival is inaugurated at Tanglewood.

MODERN EVENTS

1960 John F. Kennedy is elected President of the United States.

1960s–1970s Boston's urban center is transformed in a major renewal project.

1845–50 The Potato Famine in Ireland. More than 1,000 immigrants arrive in Boston each month.

1852 *Uncle Tom's Cabin*, by Harriet Beecher Stowe, encourages the Abolitionist movement.

1854 The Boston Public Library becomes the world's first free municipal library.

1861 Petroleum-derived kerosene, discovered in Pennsylvania, marks the beginning of the end for the whaling industry.

1870 The first race of the America's Cup is held at Newport, Rhode Island.

PRECEDING PAGES: an early English map of the region.
LEFT: Cotton Mather, Puritan preacher and orator.
ABOVE: a harpooned whale overturns a whaleboat.

1980s New England's economy booms with the manufacture of computers and other precision products.

1989 George Bush, originally from Greenwich, Connecticut, and a Yale graduate, is elected President of the United States. He continues to summer at his compound in Kennebunkport, Maine.

1992 The Mashantucket Pequots open Foxwoods High Stakes Bingo and Casino in Connecticut, a highly profitable but controversial operation.

1990s President Clinton and family vacation on Martha's Vineyard, bringing it worldwide attention.

1990s A multi-billion-dollar public works project (the "Big Dig") to depress Boston's Central Artery and add a third harbor tunnel to the airport is the biggest in American history. Completion due 2005. ❑

EARLY DAYS

The first Indians arrived in the region around 12000 BC, but it was the landing

of the Pilgrim Fathers in 1620 that changed the face of America for ever

Acrumbling stone wall in the middle of a forest: this is New England. Separating trees from other trees, this wall stands as a reminder of what man can and cannot do, of what the pioneers accomplished and what nature has reclaimed, of what New England was and what it is. The frontier no longer faces technology, and the scholar to study the lessons of the past and plan for the future.

And so the stone wall stands proud. Its people – the newly arrived and those with centuries of American lineage – embody the strength of diversity. Its history – a long trail of advance and retreat – provides an enduring

the rolling hills and woodlands; the Indians no longer hunt and fish undisturbed; the white man no longer clears the forest to eke out a precarious life. Now, spruces and firs tower over this crumbling stone wall, dwarfing the achievements of those pioneers who toiled so hard in the excitement and uncertainty of a new land.

New England's work, for good or bad, has been done; its limits have been met. But its spirit lives on to grapple with the intricacies of a different age. The same urge that impelled the explorer to chart an unknown land, the freeman to stake his claim, and the immigrant to make his fortune, now lead the politician to guide the nation, the engineer to create new

inspiration. And its landscape – the elegance of time-worn peaks, the tranquility of forests that will never be conquered, the lulling crash of the ocean waves – draws countless visitors.

Lay of the land

As defined today, New England encompasses 66,672 sq. miles (172,680 sq. km) including the states of Massachusetts, Connecticut, Rhode Island, Vermont, New Hampshire, and Maine. It is bounded by Canada to the north, the Atlantic Ocean to the east, Long Island Sound to the south, and New York to the west. Moving inland from the coastal lowlands in the south and east, the terrain gradually rises to forested hills and culminates in the weather-beaten peaks of the Appalachian system, represented by the White Mountains to the north and the Green and Taconic Mountains and Berkshire Hills to the west.

Perhaps 2 billion years ago, a vast ocean trough, under the pressure of more than 500,000 cubic miles (2 million cubic km) of sediment, was convulsed upward by an upheaval of the earth's crust. The mountains thus created were ancestors of the Appalachians. Its foundation a great buckling fold, the chain continued to shift and shudder. The intense heat generated by the formation of these mountains metamorphosed sandstone and limestone deposits into the schists and marble now found in the southeastern lowlands and Berkshire Hills of Massachusetts and in Vermont's Green Mountains. Later, streaks of intrusive rocks formed, represented by the granite of Rhode Island, New Hampshire, and Maine, and the reddish rocks found in the Connecticut River Valley.

About 200 million years ago, the thrusts from below the earth's crust stopped. The geologic revolution complete, the Appalachians towered about 30,000 ft (some 9,000 meters), the Himalayas of another time.

The elements went to work on the jagged landscape, until much of southern and central New England was no more than a featureless plain. Some outcroppings fared better against the wind and rain than others, accounting for the few scattered mounts that stand unescorted out of the lowlands – now called monadnocks after New Hampshire's Mount Monadnock. About 8 million years ago, meanwhile, the rest of the flats were gently folded one final time into the hills we see today.

Legacy of the Ice Age

The marauding glaciers of the Ice Age added the finishing touches to the landscape. About a million years ago, a sudden drop in the world's average summer temperature thickened existing ice masses to 200 ft (60 meters). Under this pressure, their foundations spread outward, grasping for new ground, until the glaciers eventually claimed more than one-third of the globe's total area. Ice swallowed up northeastern America on four different occasions during the

Pleistocene Era, retreating and readvancing over the millennia, finally leaving New England about 10,000 to 12,000 years ago.

This last flooding etched the New England landscape we admire today. Although the glaciers left unchanged the land's basic geologic make-up, they did leave reminders of their former supremacy. Working like steel wool, the glaciers – often more than 2 miles (3 km) deep – rounded out slopes and valleys.

Carving scratches (glacial striations) on exposed rock, the glaciers left behind evidence of the path they traveled. Glacial till, the chaff that the ice scraped off the ground, was carried

LEFT: a prehistoric inhabitant.
RIGHT: primitve tools unearthed in forests.

TRIASSIC PARK

During the Triassic period, the great swamplands that surrounded the Appalachian core and the hot climate created a perfect habitat for dinosaurs, the rulers of the day. Between 200 and 300 million years ago, dinosaurs roamed the Newark Bed, which runs more or less along what is now the Connecticut River Valley. Such primitive dinosaurs as *coelophysia* (an early two-legged herbivore), *rhychosaurus* (a tusked four-legger with an eery rodent look), and more than 150 other species of reptiles and amphibians, left tracks by the thousands in Smith's Ferry and South Hadley in central Massachusetts, and, of course, at Dinosaur State Park in Rocky Hill, Connecticut.

south. As the glaciers receded, this material was left behind; much of New England's bedrock is blanketed with a thin layer of this till, composed of clay, sand, and broken rock. Rounded hills of glacial till, called drumlins, are found scattered throughout New England, with Bunker Hill in Boston the most famous.

A similar process gave birth to Cape Cod, and the islands of Martha's Vineyard and Nantucket. Other dramatic legacies of the Ice Age include glacial cirques (large bowl-shaped

BEACHED WHALE

In 1848, workers laying railroad tracks in Charlotte, Vermont, a distance of over 150 miles (240 km) from the Atlantic Ocean, unearthed the skeleton of an improbable resident: a whale.

the oceans claimed many areas that are landlocked today. In parts of Maine, Atlantic waves crashed against shores up to 75 miles (120 km) inland from the present coastline; Lake Champlain was a sea which transformed northern New England into an Atlantic peninsula. Evidence of marine activity has been found at more than 500 ft (150 meters) above today's sea level. Hundreds of lakes once thrived where there are none now.

The waters gradually evaporated, and New

depressions), glacial erratics (boulders, weighing as much as 5,000 tons, dragged for miles by the moving ice), and kettle lakes (crater-like indentations, of which Walden Pond is a good example). Like the towering Appalachians millions of years ago, many of these features are slowly wearing away. The erosion can only be measured in thousands of years, however, and the distinctiveness these features lend to New England's landscape will survive far into the future.

When the glaciers melted in force, they released a vast amount of water, perhaps as much as 8 million cubic miles (33 million cubic km) worldwide. The floods were great, and

England assumed its present configuration. Tundra plants and (later) trees took hold as the ice and sea receded. A flourishing fauna could live once again on the land but, this time, with a new creature in its midst: man.

Frustrated explorers

History remembers success more kindly than it does failure. Although, as the name suggests, it was the English who sowed the seeds of New England's fortune, they were not the first to gaze on these northern shores. Anthropologists gen-

ABOVE: Viking longboats arrived around AD 1000.
RIGHT: an 1876 painting of a native New Englander.

erally agree that the first pilgrims reached North America overland from Asia via the then-frozen Bering Straits, arriving on the continent between 12,000 and 25,000 years ago.

The oldest fossil finds of human activity in New England, uncovered in Shawville, Vermont, and Wapunucket, Massachusetts, date respectively to 9000 and 4000 BC and include a variety of spear points, knives, pendants, and ancient house floors. These early settlers were to witness the landing of the Vikings, the first documented European visitors to North America. In AD 1000, King Olaf of Norway commissioned young Leif Erikson to bring Christianity to the new Viking settlement in Greenland, founded only 15 years earlier by Eric the Red, Leif's father. Despite the winds that blew his *knarr* (Viking longboat) south of his appointed mission, Leif the Lucky lived up to his name and discovered a new land where grapes and wheat grew wild: Vinland the Good.

A few years later Thorfin Karlsefni set sail with several families and a few cattle, intending to establish a permanent settlement in Vinland. At first, the new frontier treated them well. They were impressed by the fertile land, the fish-filled streams, and the game-packed forests.

VINLAND'S LOCATION

The Vikings' visit to North America is well documented, but precisely where Vinland the Good lies on a contemporary map of North America is a matter of much debate. Some claim the stump of a stone tower in Newport, Rhode Island, marks the southernmost extent of their explorations. Other evidence pointing to an 11th-century visit to New England includes a Viking axe found at Rocky Nook, Massachusetts (near Plymouth Rock); early English accounts of blue-eyed natives; and reports that Karlsefni and his band wintered in a place without much snow. Other historians refuse to believe the Vikings ventured south of Nova Scotia.

The skrellings

But the natives proved too strong for the small band. Initial relations between the two groups were good; a cordial exchange system was established where Viking cloth was traded for local furs. All was well, says one saga, until the *skrellings* (Norse for dwarfs) were startled to martial frenzy by a bellowing Viking bull. A fierce battle ensued in which several Vikings fell (including Leif's brother Thorwald). Concluding that "although the country thereabouts was attractive, their life would be one of constant dread and turmoil" because of the natives, Karlsefni and his followers headed home to Greenland. The Vikings did not return.

The Algonquins

The Algonquins were the Indians of the real Age of Discovery and the Indians who were first befriended and then destroyed by European fortune hunters and refugees. Represented as far west as the Rockies and as far south as the Carolinas, the Algonquin tribes were related to one another approximately as the French are to the Spanish. Although intertribal communication often demanded an interpreter, the two languages shared basic grammatical and phonetic constructions.

The Algonquins seeped into the New England forests probably sometime during the

14th or 15th centuries. They did not come in droves; by 1600, no more than 25,000 Indians populated New England, fewer than one for every 2 sq. miles (5 sq. km). Nor did this population comprise a unified culture: the Algonquins broke down into at least 10 tribal divisions. Tribes included the Narragansetts of present-day Rhode Island, the Abenaki of Maine, the Pennacooks of New Hampshire, and the Massachusetts of their namesake, as well as lesser groups such as the Nipmucs, Nausets, Pocumtucks, and Niantics. Some tribes could boast no more than 200 or 300 members.

Far from being the crazed nomads of later characterizations, the Algonquins were agricultural and semi-sedentary, wandering little more than the fashionable Bostonians who summer on Cape Cod. Tribal communities moved with the seasons, following established routes restricted to particular tribal domains. In the winter they occupied the sheltered valleys of the interior, in the warmer months the fertile coastal areas.

But the Indians had to toil year round to feed and clothe themselves. With an excellent understanding of agricultural techniques, they grew crops such as beans, pumpkins, and tobacco, but relied most heavily on maize, the Indian corn. Meat and fish sufficiently balanced the vegetable fare. Plentiful moose and beaver, turkey and goose, lobsters and clams, salmon and bass, along with other delectables, made for an enviably varied menu.

Politics and state affairs were left in the charge of the *sachem*, a hereditary chief who commanded each tribe in much the same way that monarchs ruled medieval Europe. Although men usually controlled the sachemships, there were many cases of women filling the top posts. Sub-*sachems* and war captains, the Indian equivalents of lords and knights, paid material tribute to these rulers and were nominally subject to their will.

The *powwows*, or medicine men, gained considerable political might as the vicars of Indian religion. They combined healing with religion and enjoined their parishioners in intense mystical rites.

In no sense did the Algonquins comprise a nation in the modern European style. Unlike their Iroquois neighbors to the west, no council, senate, or chief-of-chief disciplined the Algonquin tribes toward unified action. Divided into

A WOMAN'S WORK

Everyone contributed to the efficient workings of the typical Algonquin community. While the men took care of the chase, the women sowed and harvested the fields, tended the children, and maintained the portable family wigwams. The Algonquins were, in fact, dumbfounded by the inequity of European sex roles. As one Englishman reported the Indians' reaction to the white female's social function: "They say *Englishman* much foole, for spoiling good working creature meaning women. And when they see any of our English women sewing with their needles, or working coifes, or such things, they will cry out Lazie *Squaes!*"

sachemships, New England's Indians were not simply disunited; they were constantly at each other's throats. "The savages… for the most part," reported the merchant-adventurer George Peckham, "are at continuall warres with their next adjoyning neighbor." These conflicts could be extremely vicious, typified by the grotesque torture of prisoners and the parading of a slaughtered adversary's head and hands.

Tribal animosities so hardened by generations of battle would later contribute to the Algonquins' downfall by preventing the tribes from unifying against the advancing white settler, a formidable common enemy.

Columbus's countryman Giovanni Caboto (John Cabot), searching for the Northwest Passage to the East, received slightly better treatment from his patron, Henry VII of England. The first European to visit America's northern shores (at Labrador, historians believe) since the Norse, Cabot was blessed with a huge royal pension of £20 a year after his 1497 expedition. It was a good bargain for the Crown, considering that England based its claim to all America east of the Rockies and north of Florida on the extent of Cabot's exploration.

For most of the 16th century, Spanish conquistadors dominated the New World, where

Path to settlement

The early European explorers of North America were not mere adventurers, but determined fortune hunters seeking an easier passage to the Orient and its treasures. When the Genoese sailor Cristoforo Colombo (better known by the latinized Christopher Columbus) was trying to finance his expedition, he spoke of riches and trade. So when he returned with a new continent, but with no gold or spices, he was ridiculed and disgraced.

LEFT: contact is established with the natives.
ABOVE: French explorer Jacques Cartier.
RIGHT: the Italian Giovanni da Verrazano.

they profitably exploited resource-rich Central and South America. After Cabot's venture, the less inviting and accessible north was largely neglected and the Northwest Passage remained no more than a merchant's dream.

Sailing for the French King François I, Giovanni da Verrazano traveled the Atlantic seaboard in his *Dolphin* as far north as Narragansett Bay. Jacques Cartier laid the foundation for what would later become New France by navigating the important St Lawrence River. The Portuguese joined the French in fishing the teeming waters of the Grand Banks. But, as yet, there was very little talk of settling the then unchristened land of New England.

The English take over

In the closing decades of the 16th century, Elizabeth I's England eclipsed Spain as master of the seas. Recognizing conquest and colonization as a path to power, the late-starting English were to take over from the conquistadors as pioneers of the New World.

In 1583, equipped with a royal charter to discover "remote heathen and barbarious land not actually possessed by any Christian prince or people… and to have, hold, occupy and enjoy" such territories, Sir Humphrey Gilbert was the first Englishman to attempt the settlement of North America. Sailing from Plymouth with his flagship *Delight* and three other vessels, Gilbert intended to establish a trading post at the mouth of the Penobscot River. But after reasserting English control of Newfoundland, he sailed south to disaster. The expedition never reached its goal: three out of the four ships sank and Gilbert himself lost his life.

The misfortune of Gilbert proved only a temporary inhibition to other pathmakers. The first years of the 17th century saw a renewed interest in exploration. Between 1602 and 1606, expeditions led by Bartholomew Gosnold, Martin Pring, and George Weymouth went smoothly and, although not ambitious enough to plant settlements, these voyages did discover a commercial lure to New England – plentiful sassafras bark, then considered a powerful cure-all. Weymouth also had another interesting cargo – five Indians abducted from Maine.

In 1606, James I granted charters for two new ventures, the Virginia Companies of London and Plymouth, giving the latter rights to found a colony somewhere between North Carolina and Nova Scotia. Directed by luminaries such as Sir Ferdinando Gorges, Raleigh Gilbert (son of Sir Humphrey), and the veteran Pring, 100 adventurers set out from Plymouth in early 1607. Loaded with the usual arms and foodstuffs, some livestock, and trinkets to trade with the natives, the crew built Fort St George on Parker's Island in Maine. There they wintered but, finding no evidence of precious metals, and the weather "extreme unseasonable and frosty," the group left the following spring.

Recognizing the need to plan more carefully, the Plymouth Company next commissioned the experienced surveyor John Smith to take a critical look at the region's potential for settlement and profit. Smith is credited as the first to give the region its name of "New England."

Answering a higher call

The explorers of the 16th century were driven by the profit motive. Since they discovered neither the coveted Northwest Passage nor gold and diamonds, they couldn't discern the promise of the New World. Decades of work produced no more than a few crude maps and travelogues. The Cabots and Gosnolds and Weymouths were not interested in settling New England; only a higher call would people the new land.

Renaissance Europe could not imagine religious tolerance. Dissent was treason, and heretics mounted the same scaffolds as did traitors. To the Puritans, devotees of more extreme Protestant beliefs, the symbols of papal domination – jeweled miters, elaborate rituals, and power-hungry bishops – were the Devil's work. Satan himself was said to be a representative of the Apostolic See.

Perhaps even more disturbing to the Puritans was the persecution they suffered under Catholic sympathizer James I. The Puritans had enjoyed years of respectability during Elizabeth I's reign. Their followers included highly placed academics and public officials, many merchants, and local clergymen. The

In 1602, a group of several hundred Puritans from Lincolnshire migrated to the college town of Leyden, Holland, but they did not prosper. The exacting Puritans found their travel along the True Path hindered by the fact that "the morals of the people in the Low Countries were loose." And so, the Puritans struck a deal with the Plymouth Company to finance a settlement in the unpopulated north of America. In the early summer of 1620, 66 of the Leyden community sailed with the *Speedwell* to Southampton to prepare for the trials ahead. "They knew they were pilgrims," Bradford wrote, and so they are remembered by history.

shock of disgrace under James I, therefore, was all the more frightful. The new king wasn't lopping off any heads, but harassment went beyond mere inconvenience. "Some were taken, & clapt up in prison, others had their houses besett & watcht night and day, & hardly escaped their lands," related Puritan leader William Bradford in his oft-quoted *History of Plimoth Plantation*, "and ye most were faine too flie & leave their houses & habitations; and the means of their livelihood."

LEFT: eight-year-old Anne Pollard, the first white woman to set foot in Boston (1630).
ABOVE: "Pilgrims" at Plimoth Plantation today.

Leaving from Plymouth on the 180-ton *Mayflower*, the Pilgrims packed everything they needed to start and maintain a self-sufficient community. The trip itself was no luxury cruise, and after more than two months at sea the travelers "were not a little joyful" to sight Cape Cod on November 11. Deciding that the sandy cape was not the best place to till the land, the group dispatched Captain Miles Standish (who was nicknamed "Captain Shrimp" because of his height) to find a more fertile site. In mid-December, the Pilgrims disembarked at Plymouth Rock.

The first winter was a miserable ordeal, testing fully the hardened Puritan will. Scurvy, pneumonia, and other infections killed more than half of the settlers, including Governor John Carver and the wives of Bradford and Standish. At any one time, no more than six or seven remained in good health. But with warmer weather came better times and the critical cooperation of the local Indians.

As luck would have it, Squanto, one of those brought back to England by George Weymouth, had returned to his homeland and was there to greet the Pilgrims. Squanto persuaded Massasoit, the local *sachem*, to help the beleaguered English pioneers. A treaty of friendship was signed.

A PURITAN ACHIEVEMENT

Like the Pilgrim Fathers, the later Puritan arrivals were determined not only to establish themselves permanently in the New World but also to live fully their religious ideals. "For wee must consider that wee shall be as a Citty upon a hill," Governor Winthrop declared. "The eies of all people are upon us; so that if we shall deale falsely with our god in this worke… wee shall shame the faces of many of God's worthy servants, and cause their prayers to be turned into Cursses upon us till wee be consumed out of the good land." Driven by such heavenly aspirations, these religious refugees fared well with their worldly pursuits. The founding of New England was a Puritan achievement.

Heavenly aspirations

Acknowledging the native contribution, the Pilgrims hosted a feast of celebration nearing the first anniversary of their arrival. In this first Thanksgiving, natives and newcomers enjoyed a meal of roasted game (including turkey), eel, fruits, vegetables, and cornbread. A few weeks later, 35 freedom-seekers, well stocked with provisions, joined the *Mayflower* survivors, and by the spring of 1624, Plymouth was a thriving village of more than 30 cottages.

With tracts such as Edward Winslow's *Good Newes From New England* making their way back to the mother country, more settlers overcame an understandable timidity to join the religious migration.

In 1628 another group of Puritans, led by Thomas Dudley, Thomas Leverett, and John Winthrop, obtained a royal charter as the "Company of the Massachusetts Bay in New England." The next summer, 350 hopefuls arrived at Salem, followed by another 1,500 in 1630. Like the Pilgrims before them, these later settlers suffered many casualties during the early days. But they, too, were determined to succeed in order to become an example for the chosen.

As Charles I and Archbishop William Laud tightened the screws of persecution back home, the Massachusetts Bay Colony grew quickly despite primitive conditions. Some 2,000 immigrants joined the settlement each year between 1630 and 1637, and, to accommodate these arrivals, new communities such as Ipswich, Dorchester, Concord (the first inland village), Dedham, and Watertown sprang up.

In 1636, the Puritan clergy established Harvard College to train future ministers. The General Court was formed to manage administrative and judicial affairs, a governor and deputy governor being indirectly chosen by the colony's freeholders (those who owned Bay Company stock). At lower levels of government, the founders of each town ordinarily convened to confront problems of general interest; this was an entirely practical mechanism of administration given that, even as late as 1700, the average town included no more than 200 or 300 families.

Growth was not limited to the area of the first landings on the Massachusetts shore. The reverends Thomas Hooker and Samuel Stone, along with former Bay governor John Haynes, left Cambridge for Connecticut, where they settled the towns of Hartford, Wethersfield, and Windsor. Londoners Theophilus Eaton and John Davenport soon after established themselves at New Haven. The Plymouth Colony had been operating a trading post on Maine's Kennebec River since 1627, and New World magnates John Mason and Sir Ferdinando Gorges tried to develop vast property grants in New Hampshire and Maine, but these ventures were humbled by the region's inhospitability.

Elsewhere, groups of New Englanders helped pave the frontiers outside the region. Puritan communities transplanted to New York, North Carolina, and Georgia maintained ties with

all worldly pursuits, the rigorous Calvinistic standards made the Puritans far less tolerant of social or theological deviation than their oppressors back in England had been. Indeed, in 1661, the king himself intervened to protect Quakers in the Bay Colony after several were hanged publicly on Boston Common. As has often been the case in American history, tragic deeds of injustice belied the ringing slogans of liberty.

Such intolerances did, however, bear an unwanted but ultimately productive child in the new colony of Rhode Island. In the early years of Massachusetts Bay, the Reverend Roger

their old homes. One such group, originally from Westmorland, Connecticut, continued to send representatives to the Connecticut Assembly long after moving to Pennsylvania.

The social satirist and Revolutionary War general Artemus Ward once observed: "The Puritans nobly fled from a land of despotism to a land of freedom, where they could not only enjoy their own religion, but could prevent everybody else from enjoying his." Dictating rules of conduct not just for the church but for

Williams, a graduate of Cambridge University, took it upon himself to condemn the shackles of imposed religion, preaching from his pulpit in Salem that "forced worship stinks in God's nostrils." Williams' compatriots in the General Court banished him from the colony in 1636.

But Williams did not return to England. He turned instead to Canonicus and Miantonomi, the two Narragansett *sachems* whom he had befriended in the course of studying the native population. The chieftains saw fit to grant him, *gratis*, a large tract on the Pawtuxet River. Here, Williams founded Providence. Fellow exiles joined him over the next few years – Anne Hutchinson (mother of 15 children) and

LEFT: Pilgrims give thanks for their safe landing.
ABOVE: early settlers barricading their house against Indian attack.

William Coddington on nearby Rhode Island (so named because someone thought it resembled the Greek island of Rhodes), and Samuel Gorton in Warwick.

Though the new settlement grew slowly – from fewer than 20 families in 1638 to no more than 1,000 individuals three decades later – the Providence and Rhode Island plantations proved an unholy thorn in Massachusetts' underbelly. No kind words here: Hutchinson, with her "very voluble tongue," lambasted her former parish

SANCTUARY FOR ALL

Aside from outcast Puritans, the new community of Rhode Island welcomed New England's first Jewish émigrés in 1662, along with scores of Quakers and French Huguenots.

descended from a lost tribe of Israel), the Puritans soon assumed the task of converting their new-found neighbors from their heathen ways.

Missionary efforts did show some initial promise. The Bible was translated into the Algonquian language. The Reverend John Eliot set up a string of "Praying Towns," along the Connecticut River and near Cape Cod, in which Christian Algonquins had their own preachers, teachers, and magistrates. During the 1660s and early

with "Call it whore and strumpet not a Church of Christ;" while back in Massachusetts, the ordinarily restrained Cotton Mather continually insulted the colony as the "fag end of creation," "the sewer of New England," and, ever so cleverly, "Rogue's Island." But Rhode Island lived up to its intent, and religious freedom was guaranteed by a 1663 royal charter.

A much worse oppression than Williams had suffered was imposed upon the indigenous population. Although the Puritans owed much to the Algonquins for their cooperation in the early days of settlement, and although they professed no racial prejudice against the Indians (one contemporary theory held that they were

1670s, these communities may have accounted for as many as one-fifth of all New England Indians. But the Puritans were looking for more than religious fellow-travelers; they sought to create nothing less than a breed of neo-Englishmen.

As the historian Alden T. Vaughan concluded, the natives would have had to "forsake their theology, their language, their political and economic structures, their habitations and clothing, their social mores, their customs of work and play" – in short, commit cultural suicide – to please the Puritans sufficiently.

Several Algonquins were sent to Harvard for ministerial training, but only Caleb Cheeshahteaumuck graduated. Many natives took to drinking the "strong water" introduced by the English, and were chastised for their supposed indolence, a cardinal Puritan sin. A few might have made the crossing to "civilization," but to expect all to do so was unreasonable and typical of a profound disrespect for a proud society.

Soon empire-building replaced missionary zeal and led to bloodshed. At first, there was plenty of room for the natives and settlers to coexist peacefully. About a third of the Algonquin inhabitants had fallen victim to a great plague in the early 1600s, leaving their lands

Wampanoag forces, nominally led by Philip (whose real name was Metacom), suffered from chronic tribal disunity and were outnumbered by at least five to one. At the "Great Swamp Fight" near present-day South Kingston, Rhode Island, 2,000 Narragansetts were slain (many of them women and children trapped in burning wigwams) in one of the fiercest battles ever fought on New England soil. The Indian will was broken; for them, the war had been a holocaust.

For the settlers, whose initial ascetic zeal had been diluted, politics, not religion, would be the rallying call of a new era. ❏

underpopulated when the *Mayflower* landed. And, as the English pushed south, the Indians realized that the white settlers intended to expand their holdings.

In 1636 war erupted with the Pequots (a fearsome tribe whose name means "destroyer" in Algonquian), and battles at Fort Mystic and Fairfield, Connecticut, saw several hundred lives lost on both sides. It was King Philip's War (1675–76), however, that marked the demise of Indian society in most of New England. The Nipmuc, Narragansett, and

LEFT: Roger Williams, founder of Providence.
ABOVE: King Philip's War broke the Indians' will.

LAST OF THE WAMPANOAGS

Following the Narrangansett massacre at the Great Swamp Fight in December 1675, King Philip and his allies formed raiding parties, looting and burning towns and garrisons. These attacks spread terror across New England until the settlers began to learn the art of forest warfare and Indian tactics.

These new methods, combined with a policy of withholding food supplies from all but friendly Indians, reduced Philip's forces dramatically until only a few weakened warriors remained. Philip himself was captured in July 1676 and beheaded. Wampanoag land was confiscated and the tribe ceased to exist.

BIRTH OF A NATION

The famous "shot heard around the world" signaled the start of the
American Revolution and the fight for independence

Captain Preston, a veteran of the Revolutionary War, was interviewed in 1842 by a certain Mallen Chamberlain:

Q: Were you not oppressed by the Stamp Act?

A: I never saw one of those stamps. I certainly never paid a penny for one of them.

Q: Well, then, what was the matter? And what did you mean in going in the fight?

A: Young man, what we meant in going for those Redcoats was this: we always had governed ourselves, and we always meant to. They didn't mean we should.

Politics were not new to New England. But the northern colonies had, for the most part, been left to their own devices from the first landing at Plymouth until the dramatic Stamp Act crisis of 1765. When the mother country attempted to rein in her distant child, the reaction had been quick and biting, a portent of the more drastic rebellion that lay ahead.

Suffering serious political turmoil in the early 17th century, highlighted by the beheading of Charles I and the subsequent ascendancy of the Great Protector Oliver Cromwell, England had little time to attend to the governing of dissident settlers 3,000 miles from London. The Puritans gladly filled the vacuum and took on the responsibilities of *de facto* autonomy.

Even before reaching their destination, the Pilgrims signed the famous Mayflower Compact, creating a government "to enact, constitute, and frame such just and equal Laws, Ordinances, Acts, Constitutions, and offices, from time to time, as shall be thought most meet and convenient for the general good." John Winthrop and his followers carried with them their royal charter when they sailed to Massachusetts, and in 1631 the freemen of the new colony gave an oath of fidelity not to the king but to the Bay Company and its officers. The settlers agreed that if England tried to impose its own governor on them,

"we ought not to accept him, but defend our lawful possessions."

Dominion days

Fifty-five years later, they were given the chance. In 1686, James II unilaterally revoked the northern colonies' sacred charters and con-

solidated English holdings from Maine to New Jersey into a vast Dominion of New England in America. The monarch justified his decision as a security measure, a benevolent protection from the French and Indians. The colonists knew better: who could presume that the Puritans would kowtow to a royally appointed governor? The king's first envoy, Joseph Dudley, an avid Anglican, was scorned as having "as many virtues as can consist with so great a thirst for honor and power."

His successor, Edmund Andros, was ridiculed as "the greatest tyrant who ever ruled in this country." When the new administration extorted taxes, "ill Methods of Raising money

---

PRECEDING PAGES: a Revolutionary re-enactment.
LEFT: the Battle of Bunker Hill, June 1776.
RIGHT: British colonial governor, General Thomas Gage.

without a General Assembly," the disenfranchised populace grew more incensed.

A strong cue from England itself moved New England to action and revolt. At the "Glorious Revolution" of early 1689, William and Mary, in cahoots with Parliament, seized the throne from James II. New England spontaneously erupted; Andros and his cronies were dragged from state house to jail cell. The old powers of self-government were largely restored, along with a certain mutual respect between Crown

MOB RULE

Many of the demonstrations against the Stamp Act were peaceful, but in Boston, mobs ransacked the houses of stampman Andrew Oliver and Governor Thomas Hutchinson.

ridiculed at mock trials. Liberty was buried in symbolic funerals. Citizens of all stripes throughout New England, both of city and country, gathered to decry the new tax. Parliament, led by commoner William Pitt, took the hint and repealed the Stamp Act in March 1766.

But Britain had not learned a proper lesson. In the summer of 1767, with Prime Minister Charles Townshend boasting before the Commons, "I dare tax America," Parliament passed the Townshend Acts, impos-

and colonies. Though only three years long, the Dominion days had nonetheless decisively molded the New Englanders' political instincts.

But Hanoverian monarch George III would have a prostrate America or none at all. Britain's first *faux pas* on the road to losing its New World empire was the Revenue Act of 1764, which imposed duties on sugar, silk, and certain wines. The tax was duly denounced and boycotts proclaimed.

The infamous Stamp Act followed a year later, requiring that all commercial and legal documents, newspapers, and playing cards be taxed. The measure was fiercely assailed. Stamp distributors were hanged in effigy and

ing harsh duties on such imports as paper, glass, and tea. Two regiments of British troops landed at Boston to put some muscle behind Governor Hutchinson's waning control.

A tea party

The Redcoats were not pleasantly received. On the night of March 5, 1770, a crowd of several hundred rowdy Bostonians gathered to taunt a lone "lobster-back" standing guard outside the customs house on King Street (present-day State Street). When shouts turned to stones and snowballs, seven Redcoats came to aid the sentry. One fired into the melee without orders, others followed, and, after the smoke had cleared, three colonists lay dead (including a black man named Crispus Attucks) and two were mortally wounded. The American revolt had its first martyrs, and the growing anti-British element in New England had a field day with the nocturnal showdown.

Tempers cooled after the Boston Massacre. In the early 1770s, economic prosperity returned to the colonies. A once-again pragmatic Parliament struck down the Townshend Acts – all except one, that is. Just to make sure nobody questioned who was still boss – or king – Britain maintained the tax on East Indian tea, a not insignificant gesture given that tea was about as important as bread to the 18th-century diet.

American addicts turned to smuggled Dutch blends or to "Liberty Tea," a nasty brew made from sage, currant, or plantain leaves. The British responded by subsidizing their brand and, in September 1773, flooded the market with about half a million pounds of the "pestilential herb," with shipments to points all along the eastern seaboard. It didn't work.

Boston emerged once again as the focus of resistance. The Massachusetts Committee of Correspondence, an unofficial legislature, and the local chapter of the Sons of Liberty, a fast-growing secret society at the forefront of revolutionary activism, barred the piers and demanded that Governor Hutchinson send home the tea-laden *Dartmouth*.

When he refused, the protesters' reaction was swift and calculatedly theatrical. On December 16, 60 men (among them Sam Adams and John Hancock) disguised as Mohawk Indians and blacks descended on the *Dartmouth* and two sister ships. Boston Harbor was turned into a giant teapot as they dumped 342 crates over the railings.

The Boston Tea Party, as it came to be called, was a display of profound disrespect to the Londoners. Parliament responded with the so-called Coercive Acts. Most infamously, the Boston Port Act sealed off the city by naval blockade. This time, the colonies had had enough. The First Continental Congress convened in Philadelphia on September 5, 1774. Revolution was at hand.

LEFT: the British Redcoats retreat from Concord, defeated by the Minutemen.
ABOVE: the Battle of Lexington.

A shot heard round the world

An uneasy stalemate prevailed from the fall of 1774 to the spring of 1775. British garrisons controlled only the major towns. The countryside became virtually unpoliceable. New Englanders stockpiled arms and ammunition to prepare for the inevitable conflict.

The rebels didn't have to wait long for war. In early April 1775, London instructed Boston commander General Thomas Gage to quash seditious activities in rural Massachusetts, where a Provincial Congress had assumed de facto governmental control. Late on April 18, Gage accordingly dispatched a contingent of 700

soldiers to destroy a makeshift arms depot in Concord, located 20 miles (32 km) west of Boston. At Lexington 70 ragtag colonial soldiers, the original Minutemen, lay in wait for the British by dawn's light, having been forewarned by the daring early morning rides of patriots Paul Revere and William Dawes.

The two forces met on the town common. A musket was fired. Minutes later, eight Americans lay dead. The unscathed Brits continued on to Concord, where the colonial militia triggered, in Ralph Waldo Emerson's words, "the shot heard round the world." The Minutemen made up for what they lacked in numbers by employing unconventional guerrilla tactics, harassing their enemies with crack sniper fire. By nightfall they had knocked off 273 British soldiers.

Sensational accounts of these skirmishes sent settlers reaching for their rifles. "The devastation committed by the British troops on their retreat," reported one, "is almost beyond description, such as plundering and burning of dwelling houses and other buildings, driving into the street women in child bed, killing old men in their houses unarmed." Among the dead bodies, the card of compromise lay discarded.

PAUL REVERE'S RIDE

Henry Wadsworth Longfellow immortalized Paul Revere's ride in his famous ballad: "Listen, my children, and you shall hear/ Of the midnight ride of Paul Revere…"

supply of ammunition. It was for this reason, and not out of bravery, that Colonel William Prescott issued his famous command: "Don't fire until you see the whites of their eyes, men."

Bunker Hill was a costly victory for the Crown, which suffered over 1,000 casualties. Optimism, seen in remarks like General John Burgoyne's "We'll soon find elbow room," was reduced to the doubting reflections of another British officer: "This victory has cost us very dear indeed… Nor do I see that we enjoy one

The first major engagement of the war, the Battle of Bunker Hill, broke out in June on the Charlestown peninsula, across the Charles River from Boston. To consolidate control of overland access to the port city, Continental Army General Artemus Ward ordered the fortification of Bunker's Hill (as it was then known), although it was actually on adjoining Breed's Hill that the Americans dug in.

The British could not allow such a build-up if they were to entertain even the faintest hope of holding Boston. On June 17, Redcoats scaled Breed's slopes twice but were rebuffed. In a desperate third attempt they succeeded, but only because the colonial force had exhausted its

solid benefit in return, or are likely to reap from it any one advantage whatever." Less than a year later, Gage evacuated his troops to Halifax.

A few months later, on July 4, 1776, the Declaration of Independence was adopted by the Continental Congress. Of the proud signatories, 14 came from the charter states of Massachusetts, Connecticut, New Hampshire, and Rhode Island. Except for Newport, Rhode Island, which was not taken from the British until October 1779, the rest of New England had achieved its independence.

Once the Revolutionary War was over in 1781, the magnates of New England's prosperous cities turned to protect their newly established interests as the 13 independent colonies hammered out an integrated union. Concerned that a centralized federal government would prove as insensitive to local sentiment as had the Crown, revolutionary heroes Sam Adams and John Hancock gave only grudging support to the Constitution. Rhode Island, in more than a dozen votes between 1787 and 1789, voted down the Constitution and only ratified it after the Bill of Rights was added.

The industrial age

New England's leaders became increasingly reactionary as they went about guarding their

seas and on the seas that New England's money was made. Codfish and whale products provided a lucrative export to Catholic Europe. New England was at the pivot of the profitable Triangular Trade: in harbors like Newport, a fleet of 350 ships unloaded West Indian molasses and reloaded with rum. From there, the rum was transported to Africa, where it was traded for slaves who were shipped to the West Indies and, in turn, traded for molasses. New England shipyards gained world fame for crafting swift, easily managed ocean-going vessels, a tradition launched even before Pilgrim settlement with the

economic interests. In Massachusetts, poor hill farmers rose against the state government in Shays' Rebellion of 1786, demonstrating that genuine equality remained a dream. In 1812, fearing the loss of a thriving maritime trade, New England firmly opposed renewed and greater conflict with Great Britain.

When not calling comrades to religious or political barricades, the colonial New Englander attended to the more practical pursuit of commerce: it was both out of the

LEFT: whaling was an early source of wealth.
ABOVE: the 19th century saw improvements in transportation, including the Fall River paddle steamer.

construction of the *Virginia* in the short-lived Popham, Maine, colony in 1607.

Although disrupted by the Revolution, maritime trade bounced back quickly, mining the riches of China and India so coveted by the early American explorers. In 1792, Boston's *Columbia* threaded the Straits of Magellan en route to Canton to trade for tea, spices, silk, and opium. The magnates of rival Salem – Elias Haskett Derby, Joseph Peabody, and Billy Gray – preferred to sail east, skirting the southern tip of Africa on frequent and successful ventures to the Orient.

But, unfortunately, the first two decades of the 19th century demonstrated how vulnerable maritime trade was to the whims of international politics. The Napoleonic Wars, President Thomas Jefferson's Embargo Acts, and the War of 1812 ("Mr Madison's War") severely hampered New England's chase after an honest, apolitical dollar. Recognizing that it is best not to put all one's commercial eggs in one flimsy basket, its merchants turned to the herald of a new industrial age.

In the fall of 1789, a teenage Samuel Slater sailed from England to New York disguised as a common laborer. Slater departed in defiance of British laws forbidding the emigration of skilled mechanics. For seven years Slater had

his knowledge to use. Together, they built America's first successful cotton mill on the Blackstone River at Pawtucket.

With underpaid workers kept at the grind for 70 hours a week, Pawtucket became the site of the nation's first strike in 1800. It was left to Bostonian Francis Cabot Lowell (from the family that would later produce a Harvard president, a celebrated astronomer, and a cigar-smoking poetess) to take a more enlightened approach.

During a two-year visit to England, Lowell became an avid industrial tourist and, on his return to Massachusetts, he was determined to duplicate British weaving feats. Putting up

apprenticed to Jedediah Strutt, a partner of the famed industrial innovator Richard Arkwright, and had carefully memorized the specifications of Arkwright's factory-sized, cotton-spinning machine.

In America, the reduction of raw cotton was still being done by the inefficient "put-out" system, where laborers worked in their own homes on individual looms. An early attempt at consolidating the process, a mill at Beverly, Massachusetts, had been a failure owing to the crudeness of its machinery. Arkwright's device, already proven across the Atlantic, was the answer, so Quaker financier Moses Brown engaged Slater to come to Providence and put

INDUSTRIAL CENTER

New England in the 19th century was the center of industrial America. The region boasted two-thirds of the nation's cotton mills, while tiny Rhode Island alone processed more than 20 percent of America's wool. In Connecticut, Sam Colt (of six-shooter fame) and Eli Whitney manufactured the first firearms to have interchangeable parts.

In the paper, shoe, and metal-working industries, New England also stood unchallenged. The Connecticut firm of Edward and William Pattison minted coins for South American governments, while Boston's Frederick Tudor made a fortune exporting ice to places as far away as India.

$10,000 of his own money, he collected another $90,000 from the so-called "Boston Associates" – the families of Lawrence, Cabot, Eliot, Higginson, and others – to establish a small mill (with a power loom and 1,700 spindles) at Waltham.

A "commercial utopia"

Lowell died in 1817, but his plans were realized by his associates under the aegis of the Merrimack Manufacturing Company. In 1820, the mill was moved to a tract on the Merrimack River, just above the village of Chelmsford.

Paying dividends as high as 28 percent, the operation was wildly profitable. Sales went from a respectable $3,000 in 1815 to an unprecedented $345,000 in 1822; 100,000 spindles wove more than 30 miles (48 km) of cloth daily. In 1826, the growing community was named after its founder.

The Merrimack Company took care of its people. Though grievously overworked by modern standards, "mill girls" enjoyed clean, safe dormitory housing and opportunities for cultural enrichment. New England's first company town was, in the words of the English novelist Anthony Trollope, "the realization of commercial utopia."

Life on the frontier

Not everybody shared in the boom. During the second half of the 18th century, the northern areas of New England had enjoyed a dramatic infusion of people, as land began to grow scarce in the densely populated coastal areas. More than 100 new towns were established in New Hampshire in the 15 years preceding the Revolution; between 1790 and 1800, the populations of Vermont and Maine nearly doubled.

On the craggy hillsides, the pioneers set up small farms, built their own houses and barns, and raised wheat, corn, pigs, and cattle to fill the dinner table. These rugged families prided themselves on being almost completely self-sufficient. This was a new frontier, New England's frontier.

But this frontier's potential was limited by nature. The climate was inhospitable: in 1816, for instance, a June snowfall resulted in total

crop failure. Agricultural machinery could not plough the irregular farmland. Property consolidation was difficult, as families jealously guarded original claims; small-scale production could not compete with more efficient new suppliers elsewhere in the United States and around the world. Save for a few scattered industrial concentrations such as Manchester, New Hampshire, northern New England had seen its zenith by 1850.

After that, a slow, sapping decline attacked upland vitality. By the turn of the century, population growth had leveled and agricultural production dived. More than half of New

Hampshire's farmland lay abandoned. Cheese production in Maine, New Hampshire, and Vermont fell by some 95 percent between 1849 and 1919. Young men went off on the more promising Western trails, girls to the Massachusetts mills.

Cultural laurels

Long before the wheels of industry started to turn, New England minds had been establishing a cultural life unparalleled in the New World. In education, the media, the arts, and letters, America looked to New England for guidance and inspiration. Boston led the way in the first flowering of American culture.

LEFT: new textile machinery made it possible to produce cheap cloth using low-skilled labor.
RIGHT: the State House, Boston, around 1801.

As one might expect, New England claimed the laurels of many cultural firsts. Ever mindful of the responsibilities of being God's chosen, the Puritans had hardly built their churches before they set about educating their future clergymen. The nation's first secondary school, Boston Latin, opened its doors in 1635, and Harvard College, destined to join Oxford and Cambridge among the world's finest academic institutions, was founded the next year. New Haven's Yale, established by young Harvard graduates, followed in 1701.

During the 18th century, New Englanders continued to establish colleges that today number among the finest in the country: Rhode Island College, founded in 1764 and later renamed Brown University; Dartmouth College (1769); and Bowdoin College in Maine, which counts among its alumni Nathaniel Hawthorne, Henry Wadsworth Longfellow, Admiral Robert Peary, and President Franklin Pierce.

Libraries, meanwhile, gave ordinary citizens the chance to investigate the issues of their day, and of other days, in greater depth. The Wadsworth Atheneum in Hartford, founded in 1842, and the Providence Atheneum, a haunt of Edgar Allen Poe, provided members with access to impressive collections and cultural events. And in 1854 the Boston Public Library became the world's first free municipal library.

Sophisticated tastes

"High culture," once a preserve of the privileged classes, was similarly opened up to broader audiences in the late 1800s. In 1871 came the Museum of Fine Arts. The Boston Symphony Orchestra, established a decade later by Henry Lee Higginson, took its place among the globe's foremost ensembles and soon gave rise to a less strictly classical offshoot, the Boston Pops, debuted in 1885; the BSO's summer festival at Tanglewood in the Berkshires, inaugurated in 1936, is a mecca for music lovers everywhere.

As a favored tryout spot, New Haven significantly influenced the development of Broadway theater; an experimental counterpart was spawned in a Cape Cod fishing shack by Eugene O'Neill and the Provincetown Players.

Such institutional achievements are impressive. But behind them lay great individual minds, the region's many intellectual and artistic giants. Among these were transcendentalist philosopher and essayist Henry David Thoreau (1817–62), famed for his celebration of nature in *Walden*; poet Emily Dickinson (1830–86); and painter Winslow Homer (1836–1910). The painting of John Singleton Copley, and the prose and poetry of Ralph Waldo Emerson, Henry Wadsworth Longfellow, John Greenleaf Whittier, Nathaniel Hawthorne, Herman Melville, Robert Lowell, and Robert Frost are known the world over. Their lives testify to the spirit of New England. ❑

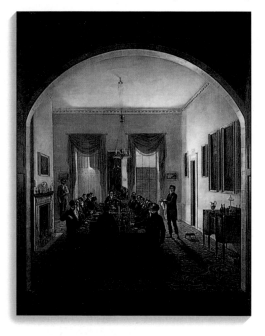

OFF THE PRESS

In 1639 a printing press was assembled in Cambridge. Its early releases included the *Bay Psalm Book*, the *New England Primer*, and the freeman's oath of loyalty to Massachusetts. In 1690, the colonies' first newspaper, *Publick Occurrences Both Foreign and Domestick*, appeared in Boston but was succeeded by the more popular *Boston News-Letter* in 1704. Other memorable tabloids, including the *Rehearsal*, the *Massachusetts Spy* and the *Independent Advertiser*, kept New England informed, if not always accurately, as the country roared to revolution. By the 1850s, the region hosted no fewer than 424 periodical publications.

LEFT: society life in late 19th-century Boston.
RIGHT: a composite of portraits of the leaders of 19th-century manufacturing and industry.

DECLINE AND REVIVAL

Following the industrial and cultural zenith of the 18th and 19th centuries,
New England faced political corruption and economic recession

By the beginning of the 20th century, New England had done all that it could. It had been America's leader in politics, in economics, in culture. In many ways, New England was America, epitomizing its ideals, drive, determination, and success. Considering the heights attained, however, New England

could not help but falter, as other regions competed for political and economic ascendancy.

The symptoms of political decay emerged both at the national level, where New England's influence diminished, and locally, where corruption and social divisions humbled once proud democracy. If only by virtue of America's physical expansion – the great westward surge of the 19th century – New England suffered in Washington. The region no longer represented a physical or psychological frontier; it was not here that battles had to be fought, decisions made, examples set. The White House was no longer the domain of Harvard and the Adamses.

New England turned to the task of managing itself after two last gasps of political preeminence: the abolitionist crusade led by William Lloyd Garrison; and the social-reform movements of the late 1800s, aimed at correcting conditions in the nation's prisons, mental institutions, and public hospitals.

Difficulties on the homefront were formidable indeed. Most important, ethnic and religious homogeneity, which had contributed to the political consensus, was diffused as migrating non-Anglo, non-Protestants hit the northern shores. Uprooted by the Potato Famine of 1845–50, the Irish sailed to the land of opportunity. They arrived in Boston at a rate of more than 1,000 a month. Others, primarily Catholic, followed from Italy, French Canada, Portugal, and Eastern Europe. The influx touched every corner of New England; even in backwater New Hampshire, one out of every five residents had adopted, not inherited, the American flag.

Electoral corruption

In the wake of this human shock wave, a predictable, if deplorable anti-immigrant backlash erupted among the established citizenry, whose forebears had fought so hard to achieve democracy and equal rights.

The doors of society were shut to even the most successful of the new arrivals, and their children and grandchildren. Politically, anti-immigration groups campaigned for tightened entry requirements. In the 1850s, the openly racist Know-Nothing Party controlled governorships in Massachusetts, Rhode Island, Connecticut, and New Hampshire. Later organizations such as the American Protective Association and the Immigrant Restriction League gathered substantial memberships in their efforts to contain the electoral power of their upstart neighbors.

Their efforts failed. No matter how unfamiliar the immigrants were with the workings of democracy, they soon learned the power of votes well orchestrated – particularly the Irish. In 1881, John Breen of Tipperary became the first Irish-born politician to take high office as mayor of Lawrence, Massachusetts. His triumph launched fellow Irishmen not only to political influence but also to political domination. Hugh O'Brien won the mayoral election in Boston three years later, and Patrick Andrew Collin represented Suffolk County with a congressional seat in Washington. By the turn of the century, all levels of government were being run by what was, after all, the majority of the population.

> ## STATE FOR SALE
>
> "The political condition of Rhode Island is notorious, acknowledged and it is shameful," deplored journalist Lincoln Steffens; "Rhode Island is a State for sale and cheap."

elected mayor of Boston five times in the first four decades of this century; and governor of the state for one term, 1934–38. The "Irish Mussolini," as his detractors tagged him, undoubtedly improved the economic welfare of his less privileged constituents. His imperious methods, however, left much to be desired. Inspired by New York's Tammany Hall, perhaps the most corrupt political machine of all American history, Curley doled out jobs and money to community leaders who in turn

But with newfound responsibility came insidious corruption. Rhode Island, once again, was the object of biting criticism as "Boss" Charles Brayton and the *Providence Journal* ring bought their way to office. Individual votes cost the political machine between $2 and $5 in normal elections, as much as $30 in hotly contested ones.

Many leaders, vividly embodied in the figure of James Michael Curley, abused the privileges of solid ethnic support. Curley displayed enormous political staying-power: he was

LEFT AND ABOVE: Boston's wharves at the end of the 19th century.

carefully steered their neighborhoods in the appropriate direction when election day rolled around. There was some justice to the critics' call, "This is a Republic and not a Kingdom." When the mayor went to a ball game at Fenway Park, howitzers trumpeted his arrival.

Cultural suppression

In Boston, cultural freedoms came under increasingly harsh attack. Led by Catholic leader William Cardinal O'Connell and the associated Watch and Ward Society, moralists lobbied successfully for prohibitions on such classics as Theodore Dreiser's *An American Tragedy* and Ernest Hemingway's *The Sun Also Rises*.

"Banned in Boston!" sang the crusaders, and the phrase survives in American idiom today.

Days of industrial glory passed. In much the same way that international competition now threatens America's economic might, other regions of the country challenged and overcame New England and its once-proud manufacturers. It was a question of costs, specifically labor costs, and the South underbid New England. Hourly wages in New England averaged 16 to 60 percent higher than those below the Mason-Dixon line. Owners gravitated to the cheaper

> ### BOSTON POVERTY
>
> In 1930, only 81 out of 5,030 apartments in the North End had refrigerators, and only one in two had bathrooms.

quarters. Here, wages plunged by half, and unemployment jumped to almost 40 percent after the Wall Street stock market crash.

Political revival

It took New England a long time to recover from this economic displacement. Employment in textiles bottomed out in the early 1970s and, virtually bereft of natural resources, including oils, the region was at that time hostage to Louisiana, Texas, and the Middle East during the energy crisis.

workforce, in an industrial exodus dramatically illustrated by statistical indices. Up from a mere 6 percent in 1880, the South wove almost half the nation's cotton goods by 1923. Industrial production in Massachusetts alone fell by $1 billion during the 1920s. Unemployment in factory towns left idle a quarter of the total labor pool. Gone, too, were the heady days of Lowell's 28 percent dividends: expenditures in New England mills now surpassed the factories' earnings.

New England felt the brunt of the Great Depression. In Boston it cramped even upper-class lifestyle; hardships were, of course, far more shocking in already squalid working-class

But New England bounced back. On the political front, the "new" New Englander had more than mastered the mechanisms of democracy and readily adopted its spirit. Irish leaders forged a partnership with the old establishment on equal terms; indeed, it was the "Green Brahmins" (Irish successors to Boston's self-appointed aristocracy) who produced one of the nation's mostly highly regarded chief executives, John Fitzgerald Kennedy.

Having more or less cleaned up its own political house, New England returned its attention to national politics with a thoughtful, progressive voice, and commenced playing a prominent role in a number of important grassroots campaigns

– from violence prevention to nature preservation – that it continues to adopt today.

The 1980s saw a resurgence in the region's industrial base. Precision products – computers, electronic and biomedical machinery, special papers and plastics, and photographic hardware – made New England a nexus of the high-tech revolution. Boston became (and still is) the heart of the nation's mutual-fund industry. Hartford's insurance companies, capitalized at billions of dollars, continued to protect much of American business against damage and risk.

ANTIWAR RULING

In 1970, the Massachusetts Supreme Court, heir to the nation's oldest democratic tradition, ruled that its citizens could not be forced to fight in an undeclared war: a clear condemnation of the Vietnam conflict.

At the millennium

The region's economy continues to be driven by the high-tech and financial services industries. The Boston-based mutual funds is a multi-trillion dollar industry. Fidelity (the largest mutual-fund company in the US), Putnam and MFS are here. Second only to Silicon Valley and perhaps a newly burgeoning Texan high-tech field, New England boasts a thriving technology quarter west of Boston. Graduates from MIT, Harvard

But the recession of the early 1990s deeply wounded the economic complacency that had so long sustained New England. White-collar jobs came under threat. As elsewhere in the world, service industries assumed a new importance as manufacturing industries retreated. In this respect, New England was fortunate. Graced with a unique scenic beauty, it turned to tourism as a major growth area.

LEFT: Bostonian legends: Irish mayor James Curley (left) and John F. Kennedy.
ABOVE: the Boston skyline seen from the harbor.

and other institutions of higher learning fall in love with the place, and don't want to leave. They set up fledgling companies and parlay them into the likes of Digital and Lotus (both of which are in the Boston area).

The so-called "Massachusetts miracle" of the 1990s, which Republicans say was fueled by fiscally irresponsible government spending, marshaled a Republican governor in office in 1990. Although Massachusetts has a higher percentage of Democratic voters than any other state in the country, it elected a Republican governor boasting socially liberal values. Stagnant in the early 1990s, New England's business climate is in a boom cycle again. ❑

THE PEOPLE OF NEW ENGLAND

New England's indomitable Puritan heritage is complemented by the pioneering spirit shared by the region's numerous immigrant ethnic groups

The product of centuries of "plain living and high thinking," New Englanders have long considered themselves the conscience of the nation. New England has contributed more distinguished legislators, writers, teachers, and thinkers to the United States than has any other region. It's true that it had a head start on the rest of America. But even after the other states had caught up in terms of population, the flow of outstanding people produced by this unpromising land never let up.

The Puritan heritage, and the region's harsh landscape and weather, have led New Englanders to view life a bit more seriously than do the residents of more forgiving cultures and climes. Although New Englanders have, as a rule, eschewed frivolity, they're quite in favor of individualism, provided that it enhances self-reliance and does not impinge on others' rights to pursue their own individual vision. This mindset pervades both the opulent enclaves of the ultra-rich and the plainest of rural villages; it even informs the day-to-day dealings of city life.

Most would consider this fierce independence to be a carryover from colonial days. However, the genius of the New England style is that it is an amalgam of all the disparate groups that have settled here and forged common bonds and goals: Native American, English, African-American, Irish, Italian, French Canadian, Latin American, Asian... The list continues to grow.

The Algonquins

New England has been inhabited since about 12,000–10,000 BC. When the first English settlers arrived in the early 17th century, most of the native inhabitants were concentrated in Rhode Island, Connecticut, and Massachusetts. They were divided into tribes with well-estab-

PRECEDING PAGES: Irish colleens; outdoor pursuits such as fishing are a major attraction in New England.
LEFT: William Garrett and his Brahmin ancestor.
RIGHT: a Micmac from Connecticut.

lished rivalries and territorial boundaries. All of Algonquin blood, they had two distinct but grammatically similiar languages, within which 13 different dialects have been identified.

These Algonquins were friendly to the first English settlers, who seemed far too few in numbers to represent any threat. The Mohegans

and Pequots of Connecticut, the Wampanoags of Massachusetts, and the Narragansetts of Rhode Island imparted their age-old hunting, fishing, farming, and canoe-making skills to the newcomers.

But this honeymoon was to last only about 15 years. In 1636, the English waged war against the Pequots in revenge for some real or imagined Indian outrage. The Narragansetts took the fatal step of allying themselves with the English, destroying the possibility of a united native front. When the war was over, the Pequots had been obliterated as a people. By 1670, there were 75,000 English settlers in New England and only about 10,000 Indians. The natives had sold much of their land, their settlements having been penetrated everywhere. Many had been converted to Christianity and lived in what were called "Praying Towns."

The wars of 1675–76 marked the last desperate gasp of native resistance. In 1675, an alliance to fight the English – formed by the Wampanoag *sachem* Philip with several smaller tribes – was crushed. Philip was caught in July the following year, and was beheaded, his body quartered, and the parts displayed in Plymouth for 24 years.

DEADLY DISEASE

In 1763, during one six-month period, 222 of the 358 natives living in Nantucket succumbed to an epidemic.

The English weren't content until the last threat of a native uprising had been eliminated. After the Pequots and the Wampanoags, it was the Narragansetts' turn. By the time the English were through with them at the end of 1676, fewer than 70 were left out of the original 4,000 to 5,000.

Beginning of the end

The Algonquin's cultural integrity was shattered. Many fled west. Some native groups, like the Narragansetts on Rhode Island, were granted reservations. Those who stayed on the reservations never adopted European farming methods (the notion of private property was entirely foreign to their way of life); instead, they rented out their land, while eking out a meager existence from the manufacture of craft items.

These native-held territories steadily dwindled over the following two centuries; great tracts of land were sold off by the tribes or simply appropriated. Although the reservations were allowed some degree of self-government (they had, for example, their own magistrates or justices of the peace), they were also appointed nontribal overseers, who often administered to the natives' detriment. In 1869 the Massachusetts legislature voted to end reservation status for those Indians still on reservations, and 11 years later the Rhode Island legislature abolished the Narragansett tribe as a legal entity. Their disenfranchised descendants became ordinary US citizens with no special rights – until recently, when activists began mobilizing for the restoration of tribal lands.

Most Indians did not live on reservations, however; they simply merged into the surrounding population at the lowest level of colonial society, assuming menial jobs as indentured servants or day laborers. Some signed on board whaling ships – a grueling and perilous, if colorful, livelihood. In Rhode Island, Indians gained renown for their skill in building stone walls.

For the most part, the 18th and 19th centuries saw a sad, slow decline of the old tribal associations. The colonists' diseases finished what their guns had begun, causing a continual attrition in population. The Algonquin dialects died out almost completely, and Indians in New

SAMSON OCCOM

Although Indians fought bravely in both the Revolutionary and Civil Wars, few outstanding figures emerged from their own ranks to guide and lead them.

An exception was Samson Occom, a Mohegan born in Connecticut in 1723. A brilliant student at Eleazar Wheelock's school for the "Youth of Indian Tribes" (which later became Dartmouth College), Occom became a vigorous Christian missionary. He was bitterly disappointed when his mentor Wheelock moved his school from Connecticut to its present location in rural New Hampshire, where, as Occom pointed out, few indigenous residents remained.

England became so marginal that they faded out of public consciousness.

Native Americans today

Today, there are only about 21,000 American Indians in New England; about a third live on the nine existing reservations. Many are not the descendants of the natives encountered by the Puritans in the 17th century – except in Maine, a great many have relocated from other parts of the country. For most of this century, Indians in New England lived an unobtrusive, unnoticed life. In recent years, however, there has been something of a renaissance.

councils moved into action. They brought suits against their respective New England towns contesting the 1869 law which, in effect, deprived Indians of their reservations. Denied their tribal status in two trials (in 1977 and 1982), the Mashpee Wampanoags, who now number approximately 600, have as yet had no success reclaiming any part of the 10,500 acres (4,250 hectares) which the Plymouth General Court accorded them in perpetuity in 1660. The Gay Head Wampanoags fared a bit better: in 1987, the federal government granted them $4.5 million for the repurchase of 475 acres (192 hectares).

A new consciousness of tribal identity has taken hold in the region. It has found expression in cultural events and in attempts to right some of the wrongs perpetrated by the colonists. Throughout the 1960s, the annual *powwow* of the Wampanoag Indians of Massachusetts, which previously had been a modest affair, grew to include more dances, rituals, performances of music, and meetings with other tribes. In 1972, the Wampanoag communities in Mashpee and Gay Head, Martha's Vineyard, elected tribal councils. Four years later the

The Narragansetts – 4,000 to 5,000 people of mixed American Indian, European, and African ancestry in southern Rhode Island – filed a similar suit in 1976; in an out-of-court settlement, they were awarded 1,900 acres (780 hectares). The 700 Penobscots of Maine, the only New England natives who still speak their original tongue, sued the state in 1975 for recovery of 10 million acres (4 million hectares), and reached a compromise settlement three years later. The most unusual case in recent years is of the Mashantucket Pequots in Connecticut, who in 1992 won a Supreme Court ruling to keep open their Foxwoods High Stakes and Bingo, the largest casino in the

LEFT: a park ranger, Ferry Beach State Park Maine.
ABOVE: education is one of the region's big industries.

western hemisphere. The legal battles are far from done, but for the first time in 300 years, New England's Native Americans have begun to recoup some small portion of the losses they suffered at the hands of high-minded colonists.

The proud Puritans

The world has rarely seen a group of immigrants quite like the New England Puritans of the 17th century. Fleeing religious persecution in England, they were fired by an extraordinary sense of mission. As the first immigrants to America, they would create a civilized society in the harsh, inhospitable New England

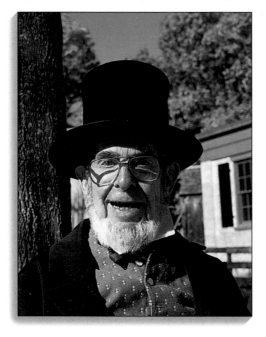

wilderness, and they would set an example of purpose and industry for the rest of the world.

Because their motive for coming to New England was primarily religious and not economic, the Puritans were a socially diverse lot. Although most of these early comers were peasants and artisans, an unusually large number of educated men – ministers, theologians and teachers – were among them. These learned men set a tone for the Puritan community of strict disciplined piety, with religion pervading every aspect of life.

The religious organization of the Puritan church was congregational: that is, members of the community elected the governors of the church. Leaders of church, community, and state were usually the same. From the earliest days of colonization, the Puritan leaders felt compelled to settle the rest of New England. There were two reasons: a high birth rate called for the rapid expansion of the Puritan community beyond the boundaries of Massachusetts; and the churchmen were eager to Christianize the Indians.

For 200 years, New England's settlers consisted of this tightly knit, homogeneous group. What Yale president Timothy Dwight said of Bostonians in 1796 could have been applied to *all* New Englanders: "They are all descendants of Englishmen and, of course, are united by all the great bonds of society – language, religion, government, manners and interest." Having grown from a strictly controlled religious state to a cradle of revolutionary democratic ideas, this community was thought of as a distinctive nation-within-a-nation by other Americans at the end of the 18th century. According to Dwight, New Englanders were distinguished by their "love of science and learning," their "love of liberty," their "morality," "piety" and "unusual spirit of enquiry." Dwight was a New Englander himself and he naturally idealized his origins. For him the typical New Englander was a combination of Ethan Allen, the Connecticut boy who led a daring guerrilla fight against the English in the hills of Vermont; fire-breathing Massachusetts preacher Cotton Mather; and learned statesman and patriot John Adams.

The rest of the country was more likely to characterize Yankees, as they became known, as speculators, entrepreneurs, inventors, or investors. They were men like early 19th-century Boston textile baron Francis Cabot Lowell, who established one of America's first modern factories; or members of a great Boston family that made its fortune in Far East trade.

The "exalted" Brahmins

New Englanders considered themselves the national elite. The self-proclaimed heads of this elite were the Boston Brahmins – rich Boston families such as the Lowells, Cabots, Welds, Lodges, and Saltonstalls, who secured their fortunes in the first half of the 20th century in the railroad, banking, shipping, and textile industries. The Welds, for example, forebears of Massachusetts governor William Weld, had been in 17th-century Governor John Winthrop's entourage and had fallen into obscurity for six generations before they prospered in shipping and railroads in the 19th century. This dynasty carefully nurtured itself at a group of socially select schools and colleges such as Harvard.

Despite this, and despite the fact that many of today's Brahmins hold exalted notions of the extent of their lineage, few descend from the *Mayflower* Pilgrims, from prominent Puritans of the 17th century, or even from rich merchants of the 18th century. For the Boston social system was

HARVARD MEN

Boston Brahmin Edmund Quincy once said of the Harvard Triennial Catalog, which contained a list of all Harvard University graduates: "If a man's in there, that's who he is. If he isn't, who is he?"

Indomitable Yankees

Other Yankees might contest this characterization. President Calvin Coolidge, a famous Vermonter, once declared at Vermont's Bennington College: "I love Vermont... most of all because of her indomitable people. They are a race of pioneers who have almost beggared themselves to serve others. If the spirit of liberty should vanish in other parts of the Union and support for our institutions should languish, it could all be replenished from the

not an aristocratic one; when Brahmins lost their money, as happened to a good many of them at various times in the 18th century, they ceased to be Brahmins.

The Brahmins may think of themselves as European-style aristocrats (some have even adopted family coats of arms), but James Michael Curley, the notorious Irish mayor of Boston, was not far wrong when he remarked acidly that Boston's prominent Yankee families "got rich selling opium to the Chinese, rum to the Indians, or trading in slaves."

LEFT: a Puritan lives again at Old Sturbridge Village.
RIGHT: soaking up the sun by a lake in Vermont.

generous store held by the people of this brave little state of Vermont."

The first inhabitants of the state were hardy trappers, not farmers; and this has contributed to the independent characteristics of the modern Vermonter. Freedom is a personal issue for the Vermonter, not just an abstract historical one, although Vermont has a long tradition of idealism. When neighboring states were laying claim to its territory during the Revolution, Vermont declared itself an independent republic. It maintained this status for 14 years, during which time it declared universal suffrage (excepting women, of course) and prohibited slavery. It was the first state to do so.

New Hampshire Yankees are much like their cousins to the west, but have the reputation of being somewhat less tolerant than Vermonters, and more frugal and stubborn. The Maine Yankee was historically the most isolated inhabitant of the three northern New England states. Roads connecting Maine to the outside were traditionally poor. "Downeasters," as they have come to be called, had to put up with bad weather and unyielding terrain. This may explain why they're commonly characterized as crusty and

quirky; they have a reputation for being down to earth and for saying little beyond what counts.

Rhode Island and Connecticut Yankees are perhaps less distinctive than other old New Englanders. The original populations of these states were the products of the first emigrations from Massachusetts, and today these states tend to be conservative. Unlike those in Massachusetts, the original Yankees here retained political control long after the waves of 19th- and 20th-century immigration greatly reduced their proportion of the areas' total populations.

After the Civil War, New Englanders knew their region was in decline and their numbers were dwindling. Nevertheless, they continue to

MOTHER TONGUE

Until recently, a form of Elizabethan English was spoken in Washington County's Beals Islands in Maine, as well as in parts of Appalachia and the Ozarks.

think of themselves as the essential representatives of the nation's most cherished values and today remain convinced that they symbolize all that is best about their country.

African-Americans

The first African-Americans in New England came to Boston from the West Indies in 1638 as "perpetual servants." Within a century, slavery was well implanted in the region: by 1752, Boston's 5,000 African-Americans constituted 10 percent of the population. That percentage declined dramatically during the Revolution, when Tory masters fled the region, removing their entire households. By the end of the 18th century, Massachusetts abolished slavery, and Connecticut soon followed.

In Boston, a thriving black community congregated on the northern slope of Beacon Hill. Though poor, it was organized and ambitious. About 2 percent of the population were doctors, ministers, teachers, or lawyers. Several fraternal organizations were founded to serve as a safety net for the indigent. The most famous, the African Society, founded in 1796 as a mutual-aid and charity organization, mirrored Puritan morality. Black-owned shops served as informal community centers, and black churches helped bring the community together. Ministers were looked up to as leaders, and towering above them were figures such as anti-slavery activist Jehial C. Bemon.

Although blacks in 19th-century Boston rarely lived outside their own quarter, they did mingle freely. Black and white laborers drank together in North End taverns, and after 1855, when schools were desegregated, children of both races studied together. Black students attended Harvard before the Civil War. Freemen laborers could be found in every New England industry, especially along the coast. Often half of crews of whaling vessels were African-American, and black labor contributed largely to the construction of Providence and New Haven.

As the vanguard of the Abolitionist movement, Massachusetts was unique in allowing blacks to stand for a political party (the Abolitionist Free-Soil Party in 1850) in elections to the state legislature. Their ability to excel was never in question, partly because of the accomplishments of such prominent figures as John Swett Rock, an abolitionist, doctor, and lawyer, and Charles Remond, the first black to argue a case before the Supreme Court. Over the past century, Massachusetts has produced an extraordinary number of Civil Rights activists.

Despite such efforts, the decline suffered by the region after the Civil War was particularly devastating to those struggling to subsist as porters, laborers, janitors and household domestics. Even well into the 1950s, few gains were made in improving the lot of this underclass. Although the number of blacks holding white-collar jobs in Boston nearly doubled between

and Charlestown. Adding to the tension is fierce competition for jobs in a local economy hit hard by the recession of the early 1990s. However, the era of equal opportunity, a long time in coming, is quickly becoming a reality, as evidenced by such African-American role models as newscaster Liz Walker and Cambridge mayor Kenneth Reeves.

Connecticut is the only other New England state with a large and long-standing black population. A small number arrived in the colonial days, and a great many relocated from the South in the 1870s to work on tobacco farms. Like Boston, Connecticut cities have had

1950 and 1970, the vast majority remained poor and resolutely working class. In recent decades, Boston's black community – now representing roughly a quarter of the population – has made considerable strides, but inequities persist.

To this day, Boston retains vivid memories of ugly race riots touched off by a federal judge's order in 1974 to desegregate schools through busing. Although the situation has calmed down considerably, inter-racial strife is still rampant in Boston's more clannish neighborhoods, such as "Southie" (the Irish stronghold of South Boston)

their share of racial tensions. Busing met with opposition in New Haven and Hartford, and in the summer of 1967 these and many other towns were shaken by riots. Despite enduring obstacles, blacks are at last making inroads in politics and other areas of influence.

Irish power

The Potato Famine of 1845–50 killed at least a million people in Ireland, and drove another million to seek better conditions elsewhere. Many came to Massachusetts. No precise figures are available, but one statistic claims that by 1860, 61 percent of Boston's population was foreign-born. Virtually all of these people

LEFT: father and son at a Connecticut apple festival.
RIGHT: Red Sox star John Valentin and coach Jim Rice.

would have been Irish, the only immigrant group to come in large numbers at that time.

The Irish did not receive a warm welcome. Not unlike the British oppressors back home, Yankees showed considerable contempt for Catholicism, and, in turn, the Irish felt little sympathy for the idealism of the reform-minded Yankees. During the Civil War, Irish immigrants in Boston rioted when faced with a draft for the freeing of slaves, a cause in which they had no specific interest.

POLITICAL FAMILY

The political life of the Kennedys began with John F. Fitzgerald, known as "Honey-Fitz," grandfather of John F. Kennedy. He became mayor of Boston in 1905.

The Irish community in Massachusetts grew at an extremely rapid rate. Before long, the Irish went into politics, with great success. The first Irish-born mayor of Boston was elected in 1884, and the first Irish governor took office in 1918. Between the world wars, the Irish controlled both Boston and state politics. Economic as well as political clout was assured once Joe Kennedy, the father of the late President John F. Kennedy, penetrated the Yankee stronghold of finance and banking on Boston's State Street.

Middle-class Irish have long been assimilated into the mainstream of Boston and Massachusetts life. Blue-collar Irish are a different story.

Especially in South Boston and Charlestown, the Irish have fiercely maintained the separateness both of their communities and of their ethnic identity. To this day, many residents identify more with their neighborhoods than with the city as a whole.

In South Boston pubs, Irish-Americans sing a song called "Southie Is My Home Town." This "tribalism," as it has been called, erupted in 1974 when "Southie" rioted over busing. The Irish felt that their neighborhoods were gravely threatened, and busing had been forced on them by upper-class Yankees, their traditional enemies.

Eighteen months after busing began, public schools had lost one-third of their white pupils. In 1980, Melvin King, a black who was then state representative, ascribed racial hatred in Boston to the historical relationship between Irish Catholics and "WASPs" (White Anglo-Saxon Protestants): "The Irish still view themselves as a persecuted minority and therefore don't play the positive role in race relations that one would expect from people who experienced bigotry."

French-Canadians

French-Canadians have been emigrating to New England since the middle of the last century. Although there are more French-Canadians in Massachusetts than in any other New England state, their influence is most evident in New Hampshire, where they make up as much as a quarter of the population; and in Maine, where 15 percent of the people are only one or two generations from Canadian birth.

The Canadians came to work in the textile mills, and (in Maine) as lumberjacks. More than any other group in New England, they have clung to their ethnic identity and maintained a remarkable degree of distinctiveness. They are strongly Catholic, and they still consider French their first language, although most children attend English-speaking schools.

French-Canadians in Maine live together in close-knit communities, have their own radio station, and frequently visit Quebec. Although French-Canadians have been slower than some other groups to move up the social and economic scale, they have a reputation for being hard-working and thrifty, and for keeping to their own.

The Italian and Jewish influx

Italians came to the United States in the first decades of the 20th century, most of them as poor peasants from southern Italy and Sicily. Many of them settled in Massachusetts and Rhode Island. Italians and Irish have traditionally been rivals in Massachusetts, the Italians tending to vote with the Yankee Republicans, the Irish with the Democrats. Despite the incursions of gentrification, Italians – representing a tenth of the city's population – have managed to preserve a distinctive village subculture in certain areas, such as Boston's North End and East Boston.

> **BRANDEIS UNIVERSITY**
>
> In 1948, Brandeis University was established in Waltham, near Boston. This was thanks largely to the fund-raising efforts of the Jewish business community.

The Italians are among the wealthiest ethnic groups in the state, having made their money in law, real estate, construction, and a variety of other businesses. The success of the Italian community in Rhode Island is reflected in the career of John O. Pastore, the first Italian-American governor, later a senator.

Jewish settlers were among the earliest colonists: a community was established in Newport, Rhode Island, in 1658, with the help of Puritan dissident Roger Williams. The first families, from Holland, were Sephardics, descendants of exiles expelled from Spain at the end of the 15th century. Nineteen years after arriving in Newport, they organized North America's second congregation (the first was in New York). Free of the restrictions imposed on them in the Old World, they prospered in Newport.

The Newport community began to dissolve around the beginning of the 19th century as members emigrated to other parts of the country. For 100 years, there was little Jewish presence in New England, mainly because of the intolerance and rigidity of the Protestant Yankees. But by the end of the century, Boston had become a much more ethnically and religiously diverse place, and so Jews from Eastern Europe began to settle there in large numbers.

By 1910, 42,000 East Europeans, mostly Jewish, lived in the Boston area. Ten years later 10 percent of Boston's population was Jewish. Jews have made their mark in Boston, notably in education.

LEFT: capitalism in action at a Grateful Dead concert in Foxboro, Massachusetts.
RIGHT: country cook and friend.

Other late arrivals

New England boasts pockets of small ethnic groups which contribute greatly to the region's diversity. Among the more unusual are the Arabic-speaking Syrian-Lebanese of Rhode Island, Christians who fled the religious persecution by the Turks at the beginning of the 20th century. Portuguese communities exist along the coast, in such fishing ports as New Bedford and Provincetown. These Portuguese arrived in the middle of the 19th century from the Azores, as

whaling hands picked up by American ships. When whaling foundered, they shifted to fishing and into the textile mills.

The 1988 presidential campaign of second-generation Greek Michael Dukakis, though unsuccessful, is just one example of New England's growing acceptance of "outsiders." In the 1990s, among the newcomers making inroads in New England are large numbers of Hispanics and Asians; in Boston, these groups represent 11 and 5 percent of the population.

The transition may not always be easy, but the presence of these groups signals how a region once regarded as inflexible has been enriched by an ever-expanding ethnic diversity. ❑

THE PURITAN TRADITION

The Puritans regarded discipline and hard work as spiritual values, and it was those characteristics which laid the firm foundations of New England

The Puritans did more than settle New England; they created it. Out of the Calvinistic doctrines regarding humanity's inherent evil and the predestination of the soul grew a society that was stern and uncompromising. At its best, the Puritans' was a hard creed, an ultimate faith that required everyone – from the most prominent minister to the humblest child – to strain toward an ineffable God. Puritans argued that humans, in their fallen state, could never know God and could thus never truly know the state of their own souls. Salvation came not through human action, but through God's mysterious grace. Abject though we human creatures may be, we must always examine our conscience, always repent our inevitable sin, always attempt to lead a just life.

Spiritual values

The Puritans' difficult faith stood them in good stead: regarding discipline and hard work as spiritual values, these early settlers labored long for the greater glory of God – and incidentally accumulated wealth and built prosperous communities. At their worst, the Puritans came to identify worldly success with godliness, nonconformity with devil-worship. Their faith found little room for gentleness or pleasure.

The many world-class schools and colleges found in New England stand as tangible reminders of that legacy. Education was essential to the Puritans' vision of what their new society in America was to be. Most of the settlers were well educated; four officers of the Massachusetts Bay Colony – John Winthrop, Sir Richard Saltonstall, Isaac Johnson, and John Humphrey – had attended Cambridge University. For them, the journey to the New World was more than an adventure to a new frontier; it was a chance to transport their old society in purified form to a new land. Discontented in a country where they were persecuted for their

religious practices, they came to America to build an ideal society, their "city on a hill." These men knew that unless they provided for the education of clergymen, they might quickly lose sight of the New (and perfect) England.

In America, as in England, class distinctions were important. But the Puritans, eschewing such worldly signs of status as expensive clothes and fancy carriages, had to devise other more subtle ways of indicating social class. Thus, the title "Master" was reserved exclusively for educated men.

A society in which education established one's credentials before God and the world was destined to develop an impressive school system. As early as 1635, Boston voted a declaration that "our brother, Mr Philemon Pormont shall be intreated to become scholemaster for teaching and noutering of children with us." He established Boston Latin School, the country's first secondary school and still one of Boston's finest high schools. In 1642, the General Court

---

LEFT: guns and God – early settlers go to worship.
RIGHT: John Winthrop, the Cambridge-educated Puritan leader.

of the Bay Colony required every town to see to the education of its youth. By 1671, all colonies but Rhode Island, ever the renegade, had instituted compulsory education.

Higher education

Still, the settlers had yet to provide their colony with an institution of higher learning. In 1636, the Bay Colony's General Court voted £40 toward a public "school or college." What was then the village of Newtowne, across the Charles River from Boston, was chosen as the site for the institution, which opened that same year as Newtowne College. In 1638, a

other Harvard graduates – all Congregational ministers – founded the Collegiate School in Saybrook, Connecticut, in 1701. The school was renamed Yale College in honor of its benefactor, Elihu Yale, when it moved to New Haven in 1716.

Nicholas Brown, who made his fortune in the molasses, rum, and slave trade, founded Rhode Island College as a Baptist school in 1764; it was renamed Brown University in 1804, upon its relocation to Providence. Reverend Eleazar Wheelock founded Dartmouth College in 1769 "for the education of Youth of the Indian Tribes" as well as for "English Youth and Others."

newly arrived young Charlestown minister named John Harvard, a graduate of Emmanuel College at Cambridge, died and left his 400-volume library and half of his estate to the college. In 1638 it was renamed Harvard in his honor, and Newtowne was renamed Cambridge to signify the community's new role.

For the rest of the 17th century, the college served primarily as a training ground for the Puritan clergy. At the outset of the 18th century, however, Harvard, feeling the effects of Enlightenment, liberalized its curriculum and added the teachings of Locke and Newton. Decrying the change in their alma mater's educational philosophy, James Pierpont and several

In 1778, Samuel Phillips and his uncle, Dr John Phillips, complaining of "a growing neglect of youth in our time," founded the Phillips Academy at Andover, Massachusetts. Several years later, Dr Phillips established a similar school, the Phillips Exeter Academy in Exeter, New Hampshire. Exeter's charter illuminates the Puritan mind: the school's purpose was "to promote piety and virtue" in its students and "to learn them the great and real business of living."

Proselytizing through persecution

A far less benign expression of Puritan didacticism emerged in the Salem witch trials of 1692.

Since its founding in 1626, the town (whose name derives, ironically, from *shalom*, the Hebrew word for peace) had never been a bastion of tolerance and good will: it was from Salem that Roger Williams, the founder of Rhode Island, had been exiled for preaching religious freedom.

The townspeople's rigid ways took a destructive turn when Tituba, a Barbados slave serving the household of Salem's minister, Samuel Parris, began regaling his daughter, Elizabeth, and niece, Abigail Williams, with vivid accounts of

THE CRUCIBLE

Arthur Miller's celebrated 1953 play, *The Crucible*, is based on the Salem witch trials.

examine the girls and, after medicine failed to cure them, he diagnosed them as victims of witchcraft.

The Rev. Mr Parris suggested that Tituba might be their tormentor, and the slave was charged with witchcraft. In confessing, under pain of torture, she gave a lurid account of how a tall man from Boston, accompanied by witches, had molested the girls. Satan himself, she claimed, had ordered her to murder the girls, and other witches had beaten her for her refusal to comply; she merely tormented them, trying to abate

voodoo. Fascinated, Elizabeth and Abigail invited a handful of their friends to listen to Tituba's tales. Meetings of such a nature, being strictly forbidden in Puritan Salem, held an illicit appeal that the girls must have found difficult to resist, but no doubt they also found their guilty pleasure difficult to live with, for all soon began to exhibit bizarre behavior: they would crawl on the floor, making choking sounds, and cry out that needles were piercing their flesh. The town doctor was called in to

FAR LEFT: a pillory, designed for public humiliation.
LEFT AND ABOVE: the trials of Mrs Hutchinson (left) and George Jacobs in Salem's era of Puritan hysteria.

her own pain. In her stories, she pointed a finger at two women unpopular in the village, Sarah Osborne and Sarah Good, who were charged with everything from bewitching cattle to using voodoo dolls. Enflamed by the oratory of such self-promoting preachers as Cotton Mather, subsequent accusations spread like wildfire. Ultimately, 400 people ended up accused – many of them marginal members of society, whose lack of prosperity the Puritans took to mean a lack of godliness.

Imprisoned in cold, damp cells, several of the accused women died while awaiting trial. Of those found guilty in Salem, 19 were hanged between June and September, and many more might have been sacrificed had Governor General Sir William Phips not returned from the north woods, where he had been fighting an alliance of French and Native Americans, and put a stop to the madness. In December 1692, he ordered all the suspects released – including his own wife.

Always ready to discover depravity in someone else, the Puritans sat in eager judgment on the accused. Unrelenting in their desire to purge their world of evil and in their arrogant belief in their own righteousness, they sent innocents to their death. Too late, the Salemites repented of their actions: in 1693, the Salem jurors wrote that they begged the forgiveness of everyone who had been harmed by their actions.

A transcendentalist manqué

The gradual liberalization of New England's colleges in the 18th century gave way to a true intellectual flowering in the 19th century. Flushed with the success of the Revolutionary War and the founding of the nation, growing prosperous from the lucrative China trade, the Puritan temperament was ready for a transformation. Casting off the dour, joyless outlook of their Puritan forebears, New England's intelligentsia readily embraced the sweet optimism

NATHANIEL HAWTHORNE

The descendant of Salem Puritans, Hawthorne grew up with a family legend of a Judge Hawthorne who, as a magistrate at the witchcraft trials, was cursed by a woman he convicted. Hawthorne would later use this story in *The House of the Seven Gables*. In fact, much of Hawthorne's work was drawn from real life. In the 1836 tale, *The Minister's Black Veil*, the protagonist explains: "If I hide my face for sorrow, there is cause enough, and if I cover it for secret sin, what mortal might not do the same." Hawthorne was no doubt familiar with the story of the Rev. Joseph Moody of York, Maine, who, after accidentally shooting and killing a friend on a hunting trip, became morbidly frightened of having his friend's family and fiancée look upon him, and therefore covered his face with a black handkerchief.

Young Goodman Brown, one of Hawthorne's greatest tales, also draws on his Salem heritage. In what may be a dream, Brown, wandering in the dark forest, comes upon the devil, who leads him to a clearing where villagers are engaged in devil-worship; among the congregation is Faith, Goodman's wife. In this tale, Hawthorne depicts a world sunk in evil: if Goodman Brown's vision is true, the devil rules; if not, and if Goodman has imagined innocent people in Satan's service, he reveals, like the Salem Puritans, the depth of his own corruption.

of transcendentalism, a mystical philosophy which argued the existence of an Oversoul unifying all creation, and which preached the primacy of insight over reason and the inherent goodness of humankind.

The movement spawned several experiments in living, the best known being Henry David Thoreau's solitary retreat on Walden Pond, and short-lived communal farms at Brook Farm in Concord and Fruitlands in Harvard. Led by Ralph Waldo Emerson, the transcendentalist movement attracted some of the brightest minds of the day – including, for a short while, Nathaniel Hawthorne, one of the founding members of Brook Farm. His disillusionment with this experiment reinforced his essentially somber cast of mind, however. Far from being sweetly optimistic, his writing broods on human sin.

Cradle of reformation

As if to live down the small-mindedness of their predecessors, the New England philosophers and legislators of the 19th century stood in the very vanguard of political reform. Having abolished slavery themselves by the end of the 18th century, high-minded New Englanders dedicated themselves to nationwide abolition. William Lloyd Garrison founded his weekly newspaper the *Liberator* in Boston in 1831 (not all shared his views at that time: he was nearly killed by a Boston mob in 1835) and persisted until 1865, when the 13th amendment was finally passed. Joining him in the struggle were writers such as Harriet Beecher Stowe, who delivered one of the Abolitionist movement's most effective tracts in the form of her best-selling 1852 novel, *Uncle Tom's Cabin*. After the Civil War, New England's reformists turned their attention to the labor abuses brought on by the Industrial Revolution and to the role of women in society. The first women's college to open in the US was Vassar Female College, founded in Poughkeepsie, New York, in 1861. By 1879, four outstanding colleges for women had been established in Massachusetts: Smith, Wellesley, Mount Holyoke, and Radcliffe.

Despite this growing willingness to entertain change – reinforced by decades of stability and

prosperity – remnants of the Puritan strain persisted. For the most part, New England remained a deeply moral, and occasionally moralistic, society. At their worst, New Englanders banned books they deemed offensive to public taste (a practice their descendants now deplore among less enlightened, fundamentalist backwaters). They considered theater – and worse yet, actors – a pernicious influence on impressionable minds. Blue laws, first introduced in Connecticut in 1781 to control public and private conduct, especially on the Sabbath, enjoyed regular revivals in the 19th and 20th centuries and linger to this day in

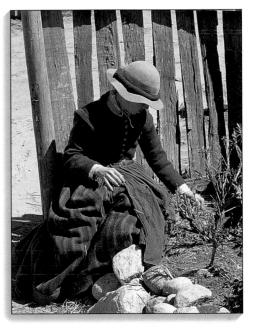

very watered-down form; in Massachusetts, for instance, on Sundays liquor stores are closed and would-be imbibers must wait till noon to be served at a bar.

This seems a relatively small inconvenience to pay as homage to the settlers who, with admirable fortitude if little sense of fun, established so firm a foundation for the New World. And just as the Puritans struggled mightily to maintain a spiritual purity, New Englanders today are in the forefront of the drive to preserve some degree of ecological integrity. The Puritans' conservative zeal lives on – in what has become, ironically enough, one of the country's most progressive regions. ❑

FAR LEFT: Ralph Waldo Emerson.
LEFT: Nathaniel Hawthorne. **RIGHT:** keeping crafts alive at Plimoth Plantation Pilgrims Settlement.

THE TRADITION OF FRESH FOOD

Seafood remains one of the New England classics, but the influence of immigrants and new traditions are making their mark

The Pilgrims would not have known what to make of our mania for lobster. They considered the crustaceans fit only for pig food, or bait; well into the late 19th century, boatloads of lobsters sold for pennies, and prisoners rioted at the prospect of yet another lobster dinner. New England's lobster harvest

New England's fabled clam chowder got its name from the French settlers of Breton in Canada, who simmered their soups in a *chaudière* (cauldron). Such long, slow cooking is needed to render large hard-shell quahogs (pronounced "co-hogs") palatable. The small and medium-size versions – cherrystones and

is today a $150 million-a-year enterprise. And while creative preparations abound, menus still feature traditional boiled lobsters and "lobster rolls" – toasted hot dog buns filled with chunks of lobster meat, tossed with celery and mayonnaise.

The settlers weren't quite so blind to the appeal of oysters, however. As early as 1601, Samuel de Champlain had singled out the area now known as Wellfleet, on Cape Cod, for its exceptional beds. He named the harbor "Porte aux huitres." And to this day, tiny Wellfleet, as well as the town of Cotuit, also on Cape Cod, is world-renowned for these home-grown delicacies.

littlenecks – are delectable served raw, on the half-shell. Soft-shell, longneck clams – commonly known as "steamers" – are a favored repast all along the coast, dipped first in brine (to wash off the grit), then melted butter. Clam shacks fire up their fry-o-lators to prepare another favorite: clams batter-coated and fried.

Clambakes were once a New England tradition, especially on Cape Cod. The customary procedure was to lay out a stone pit on the beach, build a driftwood fire, cover the hot stones with seaweed, add clams and their accompaniments (typically, lobsters, potatoes, corn on the cob), and then top it all off with more seaweed, a sailcloth tarp, and plenty of sand, leaving the whole to bake for about an hour. Most restaurants these days dispense with clambake *per se*, and just serve what's called a "shore dinner" – steamed.

It was the abundant cod, however, that initially lured English fishermen, and eventually settlers, to this land. Fillet of young cod, called scrod (from the Dutch *schrood*, for "a piece cut off"), still graces traditional menus.

Exposure to European traditions has introduced two relatively new seafood treats. Mussels, long ignored by New England restaurants, are now very nearly ubiquitous, usually served *marinière* or poached in white wine.

Another specialty is available only a few weeks each year. Enthusiasts await late spring to feast on shad roe, from the Connecticut River. As the poet Ogden Nash wrote, "I'm sure Europe never had/A fish as tasty as the shad."

Unlikely elixirs

Cranberries – so named by Dutch settlers who thought the flowers resembled cranes – are one of the few fruits native to North America (among the others are Concord grapes and blueberries, a cash crop in Maine). Native Americans used the sassamanesh – "bitter berries" – as a dye, a poultice, and as food,

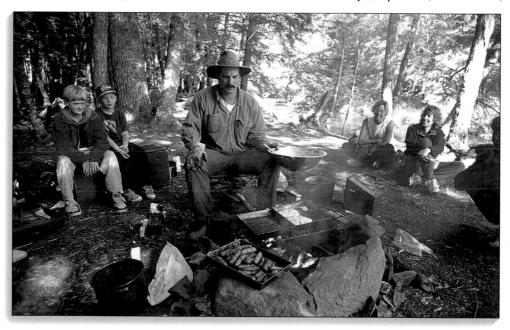

Seasonal bay scallops have always enjoyed greater gourmet cachet than the larger, tougher sea scallop but, until recently, restaurants invariably threw away the tastiest part, serving only the adductor muscle. Thanks to the efforts of scallop cultivator Rod Taylor of Fairhaven, Massachusetts, bay scallops are now available year-round, and the more adventurous fine restaurants have begun serving them whole, whether on the half-shell or cooked.

LEFT: interpreters at Plimoth Plantation prepare a meal the settlers would have eaten.
ABOVE: Randy Cross prepares breakfast during a canoe expedition.

pounded with venison to make "pemmican" (meat cakes) or sweetened with maple sap. Long before the need for Vitamin C was recognized, whalers would set off to sea with a barrel of cranberries to prevent scurvy. Today, visitors can tour Massachusetts cranberry bogs and celebrate fall festivals from Plymouth to Nantucket.

Maple syrup

New Englanders have also continued the Indian practice of boiling maple sap into syrup, and Vermont is America's leading producer of maple syrup. The trees of the "sugarbush" are tapped in early spring, when just the right combination of cold nights and warm days sets the thin sap rising. However modern the equipment, it still takes 40 gallons of sap to boil down to just one gallon of syrup. Visitors can watch the process at dozens of commercial sugar houses.

Beer, wine, and cider

With no access to safe drinking water, the Pilgrims – adults and children alike – had no choice but to drink beer (the alcohol content kept the microbes in check). Today they could travel around New England and never wander far from a microbrewery. Popular regional beer

makers include Vermont's Catamount, New Hampshire's Red Hook and Smuttynose, Maine's Gary's, and Massachusetts' Boston Beer Company (makers of Sam Adams), Ipswich, Harpoon, and Atlantic Coast (home of Tremont brews). Many of these producers open their doors to visitors. In Boston, visitors can join Brew Pub Tours.

It's even possible to find good locally produced wine: New England's notoriously rocky soil is at long last proving good for something. Many vineyards are still in the fledgling stage, but at least three have a proven track record: Stonington Vineyards in Stonington, Connecticut; Sakonnet Vineyards in Little Compton,

Rhode Island; and Chicama Vineyards on Martha's Vineyard, Massachusetts. Some New England vintners are turning other indigenous fruits into novelty wines: sample the Plymouth Bay Winery's cranberry wine or Nashoba Valley Winery's blueberry and apple creations.

Apple seeds, which came to New England with the Pilgrims in 1620, contributed another popular beverage – apple cider. This fresh-pressed apple juice was a favorite drink in colonial times and was also converted into "hard" or alcoholic cider. President John Adams claimed that a tankard of hard cider every morning calmed his stomach and alleviated gas. Hard cider has enjoyed a trendy revival in the 1990s, led by New England brands such as Wood-chuck from Cavendish, Vermont. Sweet cider, often served hot with cinnamon or spiked with rum, makes a warming treat after a long day of leaf peeping or traversing the ski slopes.

The classic diner

New England is home to one of the original fast food restaurants – the diner. First created in Providence in 1872 as a horse-drawn lunch wagon, diners grew into a major manufacturing business in Worcester, Massachusetts, in the early part of this century. Many traditional New England diners serve breakfast all day – eggs any style, hash browns, pancakes – while waitresses circle with bottomless coffee pots, asking "Warm it up, hon?" Yet even diners have not escaped gentrification into college hangouts or more upscale incarnations: some diner-style spots mix four types of cheese into the classic baked macaroni dish or spike their French toast batter with amaretto.

Specialty products

A new wave of "back-to-landers" has created a trendy land of plenty, raising deer for venison, goats for farmstead chèvre, trout and salmon for smoking. In Connecticut, the actor Paul Newman has claimed a third of the $3.3 billion salad dressing market with Newman's Own, profits from which go to charity. In Vermont, some 300 specialty food producers whip up everything from "Putney pasta" to salsa and tortilla chips from Stowe; the entrepreneurs behind Ben & Jerry's ice cream empire, in Waterbury, parlayed a $5 correspondence school diploma into a business grossing $500 million a year.

New traditions

Throughout New England, flavors that would previously have been considered "exotic" have entered the mainstream food vocabulary, in part due to the waves of immigration that have brought new culinary traditions to the area. The Italian immigrants who settled in the late 1800s and early 1900s left an indelible stamp on the region's food. Italian-American restaurants serving pizza, spaghetti and meatballs can be found in countless New England towns, while

> **A NEW ENGLAND THING**
>
> The United States currently leads the world in per capita ice cream consumption, and New Englanders are said to eat 14 pints more of the stuff every year than the average American.

Since 1960, almost 80 percent of immigrants to the US have come from Asia, Latin America, and the Caribbean. New England towns boast Chinese, Japanese, Thai, Vietnamese, Puerto Rican, Mexican, Haitian, and many other ethnic eateries, where clams in black bean sauce and lobster sautéed with ginger and scallions blend local ingredients into the classic cuisines of their home countries.

This melting pot of flavors has also turned into more upscale fusion cuisine, where

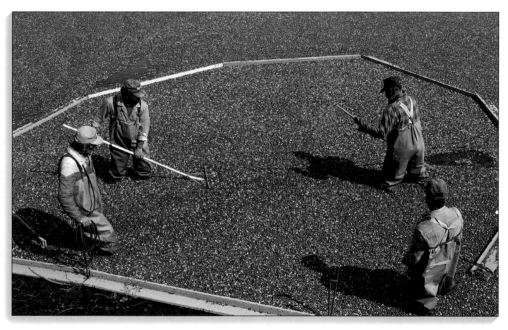

urban enclaves – including Boston's North End, Providence's Federal Hill, and Hartford's Franklin Avenue – add more contemporary Italian regional cooking.

In several Rhode Island and Massachusetts cities, home to large numbers of Portuguese-Americans, the land of the bean and the cod has been transformed into the home of the feijão and the bacalhau. Doughy sweet bread, spicy linguiça (pork sausage), and all manner of salt cod preparations are among the Portuguese contributions to New England tables.

LEFT: fresh lobster on offer in Rhode Island.
ABOVE: creating a stir with cranberries.

celebrity chefs are transforming traditional New England products into creative new preparations. Adventurous eaters can indulge in salad of Maine rock crab with lobster knuckles and fried taro, crispy squash risotto cakes, pumpkin ravioli with mussels *marinière*, lightly fried lobster with lemongrass and Thai basil, ginger barbecued skate wing served over spicy jalapeño slaw with Boston baked beans, or seared scallops in cider sauce.

But tradition endures. Those boiled lobsters, that baked cod, and that paper cup overflowing with fried clams, washed down with a cool frappé (that's Massachusetts-speak for milk shake), remain New England culinary favorites. ❑

THE MARITIME TRADITION

The sea has always been important to New Englanders – first for transport and trade and as a fishing ground, more recently for recreation

The little ship had been at sea for two months. It was November 1620, in the North Atlantic, not a kind season. The passengers and crew, more than 100 people, had squeezed into this one ship after its sister ship had proven unseaworthy. They were headed for the tiny English colonies in America.

At last, the call came: "Land ho!" The weary passengers who crowded the railings could barely make out the tops of several small islands on the horizon. As the ship drew closer, they discovered that the "islands" were actually hills arising above a long bar of sand. Weary from the months at sea and eager to set foot in the New World, the Pilgrims disembarked at the tip of Cape Cod to rest and reconnoiter. After five weeks on land, they set sail again for Virginia. But, battered by storms that seemed endless, the tiny yet sturdy barque *Mayflower* was driven across Cape Cod Bay and into the mainland at a place the Pilgrims named Plymouth.

A path to the New World

The sea had allowed early New Englanders to escape the spiritual confines of the old country. It had brought them to the New World. But it had not given them any choice about their landing place. Down through the centuries, the sea has written the history of New England and determined its people's destiny.

The sea could move people speedily between continents – or condemn them to a watery grave. It has toppled granite buildings, even torn away the land itself, and it has made men fabulously wealthy overnight. A rich merchant, pillar of his community, might come into his warehouse on Boston's Long Wharf one morning only to find that his entire fleet and all its cargo had been swept away and lost forever, and that he was no better than a beggar. Or a lonesome beachcomber slowly tracing the sinuous miles of Cape Cod's sandy shores might come upon 100 gold doubloons washed up only minutes before by a whim of the sea.

New Englanders have had no choice but to learn the sea's strict laws and abide by them. The sea brought them here, the sea nourished them and, if it did not destroy them, the sea even made them rich. Only one of the six New England states (Vermont) has no maritime coast. For the rest, the outlet to the sea is a source of continuing prosperity.

The first generation of Europeans in America all had the same "baptism by sea:" a two-month voyage across the stormy North Atlantic. Most of the settlers who came were landlubbers; many had never seen the ocean before. Shipbuilding was one of the first enterprises the early colonists undertook. Ships maintained the connection to the homeland and provided an income from trade. The vast virgin forests of the New World supplied ready-at-hand materials for their construction. One hundred years after the Pilgrims stepped on Plymouth Rock, New England's coastal shipyards were launching a ship a day. With labor and lumber costs so cheap compared to those in England, American-made ships dominated the market.

For the early colonists, the sea brought news from home, fresh legions of colonists to do battle with the wilderness, and ships involved in the Triangular Trade (the transport of slaves, molasses, and rum between ports in Africa, the Caribbean, and New England). The vast virgin forests of colonial Maine seemed an inexhaustible storehouse of straight, lofty white pines for the masts of the Royal Navy. The fishing grounds along the coasts teemed with marine wealth.

THE "SACRED COD"

The "Sacred Cod" – a wooden effigy presented to the legislature by a Boston merchant in 1784 – was kept in the Massachusetts Colony House, and now hangs at the State House on Beacon Hill.

The whaling boom

The lamps of colonial New England were fired by vegetable and animal oils; candles were made from animal tallow. The light was dim and the lamps were smoky until someone made the discovery that blubber from a beached whale could be rendered, and the oil thus extracted would provide a clearer, brighter light.

Whales beached themselves frequently on the New England shores during the early colonial days, and whaling got its start

One of the first important acts of the Great and General Court of Massachusetts was to set standards for the regulation and encouragement of the fishing industry. Early on, fishing was seen as a prime source of the region's prosperity. In fact, many settlers came not so much to enjoy religious freedom as to catch fish. Codfish, high in protein, iodine, and Vitamin A, nourished and strengthened not just New England's colonists, but those in Mid-Atlantic and Southern towns and even in many ports of Europe.

LEFT: the port of Boston in 1768, before areas of the harbor on either side of Long Wharf were infilled.
ABOVE: a 19th-century lobsterman.

as a shore activity. Teams of townsfolk gathered whenever they saw a whale, tethering the creature to a stake to prevent the tide from taking it out to sea. The blubber was cut away, rendered in the kettles of a "tryworks" set up on the beach and transformed into a high-quality oil which could be burned in the town's lamps or traded for other goods.

The demand for this excellent oil became so great that fishermen, hoping to get rich from the sale of oil, began actively to pursue whales along the shore, thus initiating New England's famous whaling industry. The trade took a great leap forward in 1712, when Captain Christopher Hussey of Nantucket was blown off course into deep water and accidentally bagged the first sperm whale. Although it had teeth in lieu of coveted baleen – bony upper jaw slats useful as stays for collars and corsets – the spermaceti oil proved far superior to that of the already endangered "right" whale (so called because it was the right one to pursue). Nantucket whalers came to specialize in the pursuit of this purer, lighter, and more profitable oil.

Whalers out of Nantucket and New Bedford pursued their mammoth quarry for months, even

SCRIMSHAW

Sailors on the whaling ships whiled away the hours making intricate carvings in whale-bone or teeth, etched in black, known as scrimshaw.

was the world's great proven oil reserve. For a closer look at this fascinating chapter in maritime history, see the last surviving whaler, the Charles W. Morgan, tied up at Mystic Seaport in Connecticut, or visit the whaling museums in Nantucket or New Bedford.

Watery highways

The sea formed the path from England to America, and served as the road system from one point in America to the next. In colonial times, roads were expensive to build and maintain, and the colonies did

years, as far as the Pacific, until their holds were filled with barrels of the oil that would fire the nation's lamps and illumine the capitals of Europe. The whaling ships served as complete processing plants. Once a whale was sighted, men pursued it in small dories, harpooned it, and then braced themselves for the "Nantucket sleighride" that followed. The hapless whale would drag the men in the dory many miles before exhausting itself. Tied up alongside the whaling ship, the whale carcass was stripped of blubber. Rendered in a tryworks right on deck, the oil was then stored in casks in the hold.

Until 1859, when petroleum-derived kerosene was discovered in Pennsylvania, the sea

not have the resources to establish a good system of roads. Nor did they have the need. Coastal freighters and passenger boats carried colonists and their wares from Boston to New York and Philadelphia. Every young American knows the story of Master Benjamin Franklin, a loaf of bread under each arm, arriving from Boston on the docks in Philadelphia, where he would make his fortune.

Dozens of boats out of Salem harbor headed for home with decks full of salt cod. But the enterprising captains headed south, where they unloaded their cod at Philadelphia or Annapolis and took on corn and flour, beans, and barrels of pork, which could be sold at a greater profit at home than could codfish. New England never produced such goods in sufficient quantities; cod it had in great abundance.

Though a boon to New England's maritime economy, the coastal trade, like fishing and whaling, was not an easy way to make a living. Every trip between Boston and ports to the south involved a voyage around Cape Cod, and the weather that had so discouraged the Pilgrims was a constant threat. Ships and men were regularly lost to the ravages of the sea.

Though fishing and the coastal trade helped New England employ its people and pay its bills, the region was not a rich one. Because New England always imported more goods than it exported, ways had to be found to balance the trade deficit. New endeavors were always welcomed, and Yankee ingenuity was always coming up with new ideas.

Merchants and sea captains from New England towns saw themselves as the world's transport agents: if they couldn't produce the goods from their rocky soil and primitive industries, they reasoned, at least they could carry across the oceans the goods produced by others. Like the whalers that roamed the world for years in search of their fortune, New England merchant vessels undertook long and arduous voyages to Europe, Africa, and the Orient. And it was not only the cargoes that were put up for sale: the ships themselves were frequently on the auctioning block, bringing added revenue to their builders back home in New England.

Trade was good to New England. While the pioneer towns of inland America were primitive and rough, New England seaports took on the polish of wealth and culture. Fortunes made at sea were translated into fine mansions and patronage of the arts. From the profits of their voyages, captains brought home art treasures, luxury goods, and curiosities from exotic destinations. The Peabody Essex Museum of Salem is filled with the incredible wealth that came to New England on returning merchant ships.

Clocks, shoes, and ice

As time went by, the new republic developed industries that produced goods for trade. Connecticut's household utensils, machines,

clocks, pistols, and rifles, plus shoes and cloth from Rhode Island and Massachusetts, ultimately made their way around the world.

Perhaps the most ingenious export of all was ice. Cut from ponds, rivers, and lakes, ice was packed in sawdust, loaded into fast clipper ships and sent off to Cuba, South America, and beyond. The rulers of the British Raj in India sipped drinks cooled by ice from New England. In exchange for a commodity that was free for the cutting, New Englanders brought back spices, fine porcelain, silks, and other items.

The volume of New England's trade soon fell behind that of the Southern ports along the

Atlantic and Gulf of Mexico coasts. But trade continued to be important in maintaining the region's economy and its cosmopolitan outlook.

The taming of the sea

The end of the 19th century saw profound changes in the way New Englanders put to sea. The speedy sloops, or clipper ships, with small holds, were economical only for high-profit items (such as ice). For a while, the profits shifted to larger, heavier craft such as the great schooners with four, five, and even six masts. But the magnificent six-masted schooners that could carry huge payloads of coal went nowhere when the wind died, and the

---

LEFT: mural of Mystic Seaport, Connecticut.
RIGHT: a ship is launched at Bath Iron Works, Maine.

newfangled steamships went anywhere on schedule. Steamships could sail around Cape Cod, ignoring the winds that had caused so much trouble since the time of the Pilgrims.

With the coming of steam came the railroads and the Atlantic and Pacific coasts were finally connected by steel rails. Where once the ships had sailed all the way around South America to reach California, rail transport steamed west in a straight line, undaunted by storms.

Yet transport by sea, for both goods and passengers, hung on in New England well into the 20th century. What finally laid it to rest was not the railroad but the highway.

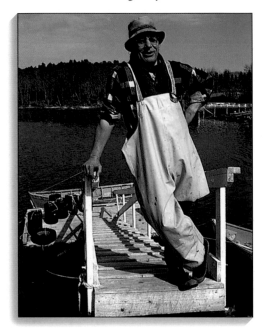

Safer waves

Today, the sea is still a major source of income – and at a much lower price in lives lost to storms. Although yachts, motorboats, and fishing fleets fill the harbors, disasters at sea are a relative rarity. A century ago whole families, even most of a town, might be lost to a single ferocious storm. There are still tragedies at sea – oil tankers breached, pleasure craft wrecked, swimmers drowned – but stricter safety precautions and radio beacons and radar that pierce the fog help prevent many accidents.

The taming of the sea has allowed New Englanders to put it to other uses. Dependable passenger service by steamship opened up the coasts to vacation travelers in the early part of this century. Newport, Block Island, and Bar Harbor turned into flourishing resorts as soon as they became accessible swiftly, comfortably, and safely by sea.

These newer settlements are not the only ones to have benefited from the taming of the sea. Although the whalers and clipper ships may be gone, excepting a few rare survivors, the beautiful port towns built by the wealth of maritime commerce survive. Tourists come in droves to stroll among the handsome sea captains' houses of Nantucket, Edgartown, Salem, and Newport. Having seen the houses, they then explore in museums the world of the seafaring men who built them.

A salty playground

In other times, a New Englander either went to sea or remained a landlubber. Now every New Englander is part mariner, taking a motorboat or yacht out for a Sunday cruise or climbing aboard a launch for a tour of Boston Harbor. There is a direct service by sea between Boston and Provincetown each summer, and Nantucket, Martha's Vineyard, Block Island, and other islands are all served by ship.

In fact, New England's seacoast has become a major playground, and the variety of maritime sports seems limitless. As in so many other realms, the world of work has become the world of play, and occupations once perilous or tedious are now pursued just for fun. A hundred years ago, for example, "wreckers" used to trudge the beaches of New England with a keen eye for the remains of lost ships. Today, the beaches serve a distinctly different purpose. Forty miles (64 km) of Cape Cod's sandy beaches have been set aside as the Cape Cod National Seashore, one of the great tourist attractions of New England. The beaches of Connecticut, Rhode Island, New Hampshire, and Maine continue to attract visitors from near and far.

The whalers that sailed out of New Bedford and Nantucket are long gone. Or are they? Boats from a dozen New England ports still head out each day in search of whales, but now it's the camera lens and not the harpoon that "captures" the whale for good. Whale-watching cruises are among the most popular summer activities at sea. It's ironic, and heartening, that the leviathans that once made New England "oil-rich" should still be helping its economy.

Cruising the coast

Perhaps the clearest indication of the taming of the sea is this: the perilous voyage undertaken by the Pilgrims in 1620 is now done for sport. Transatlantic yacht racing began in 1866 when the *Henrietta* raced the *Vesta* to England. In 1851, the schooner *America* won the Royal Yacht Squadron Cup, and the America's Cup became the great event of yachting with the first race held in Newport in 1870. The beauty and science of yacht design and racing is pursued passionately in Newport and in dozens of other ports along the coast.

New England's waters are particularly suited to yachting: Long Island, off the coast of Connecticut, protects spacious Long Island Sound; and Cape Cod Bay has provided calm sailing ever since the days of the Pilgrims. With the cutting of the Cape Cod Canal and the establishment of the Intra-coastal Waterway, coastal cruising has been made safer and more enjoyable than ever before.

The highpoint of coastal cruising in New England is undoubtedly the rocky shore of Maine. The jagged coast, cut with bays, inlets, coves, peninsulas, and islands, is some 3,500 miles (5,600 km) long, and blessed with exceptional beauty. One of the most thrilling ways to see it is aboard a windjammer out of Rockport or Camden. Since 1935, these sturdy sailing ships have taken amateur crews out into the cold waters to experience New England's maritime heritage at first hand.

By the late 1980s it had become clear to lawmakers that the New England fishing industry was on its way to over fishing itself into non-existence. Massachusetts fishermen of New Bedford, Provincetown and Gloucester were forced to go farther and farther out to the sea to catch fewer and fewer fish. And those they did find were smaller; mature stocks were dwindling. Although many fishermen – a fiercely independent lot – disagreed, laws were enacted to close and monitor the once fertile fishing banks. Some fishermen trained their sites on more abundant, less glamorous fish: formerly overlooked species began to show up on menus in fancy presentations. Others reluctantly took government subsidies for job

retraining and switched careers. Some sold their boats. Today, it looks as if the regulation is working. Mature stocks are starting to return and fishing banks have been reopened – with strict limits placed on the amount and size of fish that can be caught.

New England's relationship with the sea is changing. The codfish has yielded to the computer as the most important element in New England's economic life; the schooner and whaler have yielded to the yacht and, more recently, sailboard. Over the years ahead New Englanders will no doubt discover new ways to enjoy and profit from the sea. ❑

LEFT: the tide has turned and the future is beginning to look healthier for fishing once more.
RIGHT: a young yachtsman enjoying the ocean.

SCIENCE OF THE SEA

Scientists say we have barely begun to tap the wealth of the sea, and the potential is enormous. To explore that potential, New England has its own world-class research facilities at Woods Hole, Massachusetts, just south of Falmouth. Woods Hole attracts tens of thousands of tourists each summer, most passing through to board the ferryboats to Martha's Vineyard. However, a knowledgeable few come to see what's new at the National Marine Fisheries Service, established in 1871; at the Marine Biological Laboratory, founded in 1888; or the Woods Hole Oceanographic Institute, begun with a $2.5 million Rockefeller grant in 1930.

THE ARCHITECTURAL TRADITION

Shingles and clapboards, gables and steeples – the buildings are so graceful and sturdy that it's no wonder conservation is an important issue

Buildings capture the essence of New England's character; they sum up what was at once noble and humble about the ambitions of the region's settlers. And the charm of the old houses and churches is not lost on today's New Englanders, whose tireless efforts have preserved much of the architectural traditions of the previous centuries.

To learn New England, read its buildings, for they tell rich tales about the lives of their builders and inhabitants. Always aware of its heroic past, New England has retained enough of its architectural heritage to sketch a vivid picture of a distinguished history. Studying its buildings will not only stimulate the mind and seize the imagination; it will delight the eye.

17th-century practicality

Beauty is not a strong point of 17th-century New England homes, although there is something attractive about the stark simplicity of the early one-room dwellings built by the first several generations of settlers. Heavy and medieval though these houses may appear, they are a testament to the unaffected motivations of the Puritans. Stylistic vestiges of English country homes governed building design and construction, but none of these was applied solely for decorative effect: there is virtually no ornamental indulgence in the 1640 Whipple House in Ipswich or the *c.*1641 Wing Fort House in East Sandwich, both in Massachusetts. After all, when one was living for the glory of God and laboring for community good, there was little room for excess.

The Whipple and Wing Fort houses and the handful like them were nothing more than offspring of homes the Pilgrims had left behind in southeastern England. Simple oblong boxes, they were framed painstakingly and filled with the wattle-and-daub that on half-timbered Eng-

lish country homes was left visible. Clapboards, providing a blanket of protection against New England winters, created a stern look, relieved only by small, randomly placed windows. The steep roof and the massive central chimney, shared by the two lower and two upper rooms, crowned the house with an authoritative air.

In very early homes, the upper floor extended slightly beyond the lower. The 1683 Capen House in Topsfield, Massachusetts, offers a marvelous example. This overhang, recalling English townhouses where the lower floor stepped back in deference to the street, was a feature that was dropped as designs began to allow for expansion and reflect the colonists' growing sense of security. Diamond-paned windows were replaced by double-hung ones that brightened the interior and lightened the facade. Roofs were extended, giving additional space on the lower floor in the form of a lean-to addition. The *c.*1675 Hoxie House in Sandwich is a fine example of this "Cape Cod salt box."

PRECEEDING PAGES: Greek Revival Courthouse at Newfane, Vermont.
LEFT: white paint was introduced in the 19th century.
RIGHT: Hoxie House, Sandwich: a Cape Cod salt box.

Many 17th-century meetinghouses, also unadorned and otherwise simple, remain throughout New England. (The Old Ship Meetinghouse in Hingham is a fine example.) The large meetinghouses often served as the village's town hall and religious nucleus, reflecting early ties between church and state.

Coming of age

With a growing sense of confidence and prosperity, the colonists began adding flourishes to their humble homes. At the turn of the 18th century, commerce was growing beyond town borders, and with expanding horizons

England. London burned in 1666, and out of the ashes rose tributes to the ideas of the 16th-century Italian architect Andrea Palladio. Palladio's work recalled the classical architecture of antiquity, restating it in a refreshing, heroic way.

Christopher Wren, among others, championed this Renaissance spirit in London. In the United States, Palladian ideas spread through such design handbooks as Palladio's *Four Books of Architecture*. Guides in hand, the first tentative but unmistakable steps were taken toward the establishment of a conscious esthetic in this new country. Not insignificantly,

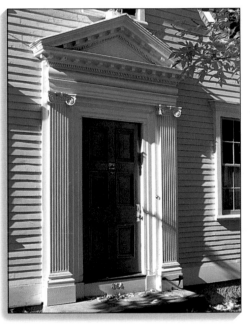

there came a more adventurous spirit and a weakening of the religious principles that had dampened individual expression.

The architectural symbols of this change vary according to place and time. Along the coast, where maritime trading and fishing were making their mark, money and exposure to influences from abroad combined to produce splendid mansions. Inland, changes in building style were more subtle and slower to peak.

The Georgian style

The inspiration for the new Georgian style, as the pre-Revolutionary period of 18th-century design is known, stemmed from misfortune in

a style was born that is as often termed Colonial as it is Georgian; the modern American landscape certainly attests to its staying power.

Symmetry, a sense of strength and a quality of ease characterize the Georgian style. (The term Georgian was derived from the three King Georges who succeeded each other in England from 1714 to 1820.) The Georgian house was a simple two-story rectangle, but classical elements gave it definition: scrolled, often broken pediments capped centered doorways and windows; fluted attached columns marked the entrances of houses; and, in the grander examples, bulging cornerstones bracketed the corners of the structures from the eaves to the foundations. Mostly in wood, but sometimes in brick, the elements were carried off with precision by skilled New England carpenters.

Georgian homes, with wood-paneled walls and broad stairways, had larger rooms and more privacy. Four full rooms both upstairs and down were the norm. Two separate chimneys serviced the two, now larger, halves of the house. A massive central chimney was replaced by two leaner towers, adding to exterior elegance and richness while leaving room for a deep hallway where the chimney had been.

As for changes in meetinghouses, Wren-style steeples were added. For two opposite

While the precise Georgian proportions and details exude a calm and assurance, their dark, unpainted clapboards suggest a ruggedness absent in later painted facades. Indians were regularly raiding Deerfield, but when one's eyes rest upon these buildings, there is no sense of trepidation, and the marvelous doorways welcome visitors warmly.

Equally gracious is the 1754 Dwight-Barnard House. This rambling residence is a lovely example not only of Georgian architecture but also of the New England practice of connecting the house, the barn and any outbuilding that had to be reached during the bitter winter.

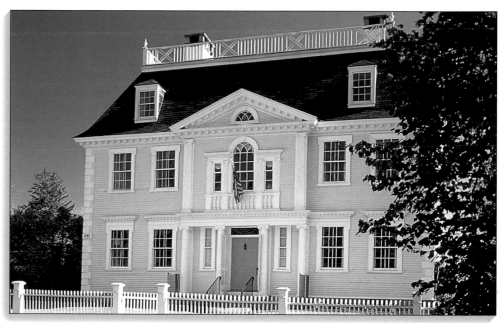

examples, from plain to elaborate, look to the Old South Meeting House in Boston and the Baptist Church in Providence.

Old Deerfield, Massachusetts, has several charming renderings of early Georgian ideals. At the north end of a marvelous mile of 18th-century historical structures stand the 1733 Ashley House and the 1743 Hawks House.

FAR LEFT: the early colonial (1646) West Parish Meeting House, near West Barnstaple on Cape Cod.
LEFT: 18th-century Georgian houses on Benefit Street, Providence, Rhode Island.
ABOVE: the impeccably Georgian Julius Deming House at Litchfield, Connecticut (1793).

By mid-century, coastal ports were very profitable, as sea captains' and merchants' houses attested. Many of these were later remodeled to keep up with architectural fashions, making it quite difficult to find the purely Georgian. Portsmouth, New Hampshire, is blessed with unsullied originals in its 1763 Moffatt-Ladd House – as handsome as any – and the delightfully understated 1760 Wentworth-Gardner House.

Aspects of Georgian architecture, particularly Palladian motifs, remained in the vernacular of New England design beyond the 18th century, but for the most part the style had run its course by the Revolutionary War. One lovely exception is the handsome town of Litchfield, Connecticut, where pristine homes lining the village green compose the perfect picture of idyllic New England.

Some of the finest homes were built or remodeled after 1780, when the Litchfield China Trading Company brought wealth to the town. The residence of one of the company's founders, a Mr Deming, and the remodeled Sheldon's Tavern are impeccably Georgian, down to the three-part Palladian window not commonly used before 1780. All other buildings in the borough of Litchfield are meticulously preserved, although not necessarily in

The Federal style

Following the revolution, optimism was palpable in the harbors of Salem and Boston. Even inland, whaling, shipbuilding and the expansion of trade brought the sea to many New Englanders as the coastal merchants commanded the goods and natural resources of the whole region. But no country carpenter could rival the skills of Salem's Samuel McIntire or Boston's Charles Bulfinch, whose combined work represents the finest of the period.

In Salem, success in the pepper trade and other undertakings made wealthy men of captains and cabin boys alike. It is fortuitous

their original state. The predominantly white exteriors date from a later 19th-century taste that conveys a feel quite different from that of the original yellow, blue or red hues that comprised a Georgian palette.

No style since the Georgian has lingered so long in New England. Deriving from familiar forms, but with more space and embellishments, New England builders adapted to it with ease. If the Georgian style took a long time to mature into its successor, the Federal, the lag was surely a result of the many preoccupations of a nation in adolescence, rather than an absence of active architectural acumen. The century that followed was to prove that.

that McIntire and Salem developed together, for the local carpenter may otherwise have had no outlet for his self-taught architectural proficiency.

McIntire's work shows the clearest Federal style notations. While New England's roofs had lost some of their cant during the Georgian period, their Federal counterparts virtually disappeared behind delicately carved balustrades. These "widow's walks" provided a vantage point from which a sea captain's wife could scan the harbor for her husband's incoming or departing ship. The effect was urbane, as evidenced by the 1804 Gardner-Pingree house in Salem, a rather neat summation of Federal motifs. Although primarily plain and boxy, its four-square facade is relieved by the semi-circular portico, its refined columns and the arching fanlight over the door – Federal era signatures. The front doorways of Federal houses are often distinguished by their narrow, leaded side windows, too.

McIntire performed his own carpentry with a skill that left him in constant demand up until his death in 1811. His inspiration was Robert Adam, the English architect who raised the art of interior decoration to exquisite heights with his dainty stucco reliefs. McIntire introduced these same embellishments to Salem, as can be

when the sea captains decided to move away a little from the noise and clutter of the port.

Elsewhere in Salem, a 1970s facelift not only turned around a declining city but, in doing so, reversed plans to topple many Federal-era buildings, which have been renovated and put to new use. A similar turnabout occurred in nearby Newburyport, where life and charm have been reintroduced to the dilapidated, deserted commercial buildings.

The brilliance of Bulfinch

The Federal era peaked with the work of Charles Bulfinch, who pursued architecture

seen inside the Gardner-Pingree house. Classical detailing, free-standing curved stairways and delicate fireplace mantels characterize Federal interior design.

The full impact of McIntire's work on the rest of Salem is best grasped on Chestnut Street, which in its entirety has been designated a National Historic Landmark. Up and down both sides of this majestic street are stunning Federal-style mansions, built in the early 1800s

LEFT: an example of a wooden Federal-style house with typical semi-circular portico and roof balustrade.
ABOVE: a typical Adam-style Federal interior.
ABOVE RIGHT: Charles Bulfinch's State House.

first as a leisure activity and then as a profession. Building – or his speculations in it – bankrupted him twice. One can only surmise, however, that misfortune fired rather than smothered his talents. Unfortunately, many of his more daring buildings have been destroyed, but the jewel among those standing, the Massachusetts State House, rests atop Beacon Hill. Here is as grand a composition as any Bulfinch realized, and to picture it surrounded by open land is to begin to appreciate what a dazzling paean to the promise of government it must have appeared to the Bostonian of 1798.

The classical State House, very Palladian in inspiration, has been extended twice in two contradictory styles. The 1890 addition to the back of the building is a lumpish but highly mannered baroque echo of its opposing side. The second addition of 1914 totally neutralized the first by blotting it out, at least from the front, behind two thoroughly impassive marble wings – dull perhaps, but a mute backdrop to the golden-domed Bulfinch original.

Bulfinch was in on the beginning of Beacon Hill speculation, and the three homes he built for the investor Harrison Gray Otis summarize not only his growth but the maturation of the Federal residential style. The 1796 house, now the headquarters for the Society for the

beautiful cluster of buildings and has protected a rare haven of tranquility in the heart of modern Boston.

Greek grandeur

New England is a peaceful place, and among the emblems of this serenity are scores of white steeples, visible on every horizon as landmarks for travelers. This ubiquitous New England image can be traced back to Asher Benjamin, one of the most influential forces in turn-of-the century New England architecture. It was Benjamin's first of seven widely read architectural handbooks, in which he rendered a

Preservation of New England Antiquities, is the least developed, a harmonious albeit basic expression of Federal-style concepts. In his 1802 house, Bulfinch took a few cautious steps to animate the street facade – the first-floor windows are recessed inside well-defined brick arches. By his third house, completed around 1805, Bulfinch's confidence was established. This Beacon Street residence, of noble proportions and refined detail, set a tone of sophistication for the entire neighborhood.

Bulfinch's contributions to Beacon Hill were recognized in 1955 when residents established the Beacon Hill Historic District. This organization has overseen the preservation of a

steepled church, that became the basis for decades of church design. The simple classicism changed little over time, but the detailing, particularly of the steeple, incorporated changing architectural fashions, giving a clue to the era in which a church was built.

It was Benjamin who, in his final 1830 volume, judged New England ready for the Greek Revival style, a style that elsewhere in America was already vying with the Gothic. The same sense of self-importance that had characterized the Federal era, along with the influence of learning and intellectualism, gave the imposing Greek style a certain snob appeal. New England allowed the style in without totally letting go of the integrity of its previous architectural traditions. Particularly in non-residential examples, the Greek Revival style produced buildings that were a logical extension of the refinements made during the Federal era. The tops of Greek Revival churches were squared-off or had multi-story steeples, but Greek Revival houses proved less successful.

The economy of Greek architecture gives it a superior air, and scale is the key to its grandeur. Civic buildings, institutions and halls of commerce lent themselves to the heroic Greek scale, usually constructed of either marble or granite; houses were dwarfed by it.

colonnaded and handsomely detailed facade. Inside, the two-story, sky-lit interior has been beautifully restored, its cast-iron balconies once again offering an elegant setting for shops.

The most celebrated New England project of its kind, Boston's Faneuil Hall Marketplace, as restored by Ben Thompson & Associates, is now a consumer's cornucopia, with food and specialty stores galore. The renovation was carried out with care and charisma; although the sober Greek references of Alexander Parris's 1826 domed building are generally overwhelmed by their surroundings, it seems fitting that this hive of activity be housed in such splendor.

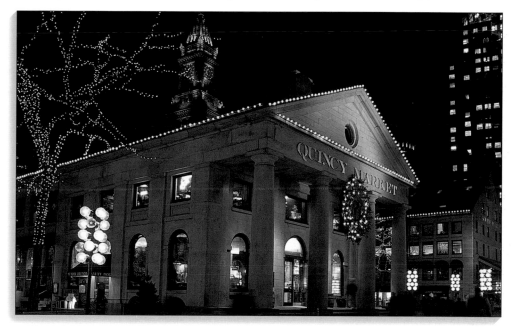

(There were two residential benefits, however: tall windows and high ceilings.) Although New England is not particularly rich in examples of the style, two exemplary Greek Revival buildings – both marketplaces, temples of commerce, if you will – are among the most clever and renowned examples of recently restored 19th-century buildings.

Providence's 1828 Arcade has been described as "something worthy of London or Paris," an apt compliment to its crisply

The addition of heavy columns and crushing pediments did little, however, for otherwise well-proportioned Federal and Georgian homes. Neither remodeled nor new, Greek Revival houses carry themselves with particular ease, but one of their fundamental features was effortlessly assimilated into the vocabulary of vernacular New England design – the passion for white paint (white being associated with Greek temples). Some unusually fine examples of this style can be found in Grafton, Vermont, a quiet town remarkable less for its architecture than for its rescue by the Windham Foundation, which since 1963 has restored the entire core of this idyllic New England village.

LEFT: Charles Bulfinch's first house for Harrison Gray Otis, 141 Cambridge Street, Boston.
ABOVE: Faneuil Hall, renovated by Bulfinch in 1806.

Enlightened industry

Harrisville, New Hampshire, survives as an unchanged emblem of how pervasive the textile industry was in New England after 1830. The town comprises handsome granite and brick mills, boarding houses and storehouses. Today, these buildings house a weaving school and offer an abridged version of the rapid rise and fall of New England's mill towns, a story that began with windmills and small-town enterprise and climaxed with the building of entire towns designed to support the textile industry. The effects on the social fabric were profound and lasting.

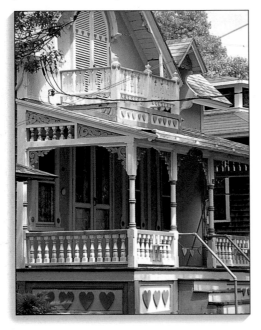

In Lowell, Massachusetts, aggressive efforts preserved an extensive industrial architectural legacy. The Lowell National Historic Park and the Lowell Historic Preservation District celebrate factory buildings designed in the boxy, brick, frugal industrial version of the Federal style. They line the city's intricate canal system, with rows of boarding houses nearby.

Lowell is once again a healthy and active city, a rich visual lesson in the architecture of a tumultuous historical chapter. The mills are among many saved from the wrecking ball and reused for housing, commercial and retail purposes. Towns such as Fall River, Manchester and Pawtucket are the richer for these efforts.

The loss of innocence

The opening of the industrial age marked the closing of an era of architectural innocence in New England. For its first 200 comparatively stable years, New England architecture had been governed by conservative principles that emphasized function first; form existed to serve the central purpose of shelter. While European ideas had clearly dictated design, they had been tempered by restraint. But by 1850, something had changed. Perhaps for no other reason than boredom with symmetry, scale and four-square plans, architecture took off in all directions, most in opposition to the language of the past.

Gothic, Italianate, Renaissance and Romanesque are among the eclectic labels attached to the late 19th-century architectural revivals. The Gothic Capitol building in Hartford is particularly asymmetrical, while the "gingerbread" carpenter Gothic style of Martha's Vineyard cottages represents a more quaint interpretation. Newport mansions exemplify a dizzying range of styles, from the shingled Hammersmith Farm "cottage" to the gilded Breakers (Italian Renaissance), the Victorian Chateau-sur-mer to the beaux-arts Marble House (*see pages 240–41*).

In the hands of architects such as Henry Hobson Richardson (who designed Boston's Trinity Church with Romanesque influences) and McKim, Mead and White (Boston Public Library), these styles could be expressed with uncommon panache. But the spiritual link to New England began growing remote, and these buildings – with massive stones and ornamentation – have only a distant kinship with the carefully proportioned, cautiously decorated creations of New England's early centuries.

Further European grafts have been attempted, with varying degrees of success. Harvard University boasts the only LeCorbusier building in the United States (the Carpenter Center), and Gropius built a model Bauhaus house in the Boston suburb of Lincoln. The future of New England architecture, however, clearly lies in the hands of native architects, such as Graham Gund of Cambridge, who acknowledge the contributions of their forebears even as they strive to break new ground. ❑

LEFT: well preserved Carpenters Gothic cottages can be found at Oak Bluffs on Martha's Vineyard.
RIGHT: Boston's "Richardson Romanesque" Trinity Church contrasts with the 1970s Hancock Tower.

PLACES

*A detailed guide to New England, with principal sites
clearly cross-referenced by number to the maps*

> *Meanwhile it occurs to me that by a remote New England fireside an
> unsophisticated young person of either sex is reading in an old volume
> of travels... The young person gazes in the firelight at the flickering
> chiaroscuro of the future, discerns at last the glowing phantasm of
> opportunity, and determines with a wild heart-beat to go and see it all –
> twenty years hence.* —HENRY JAMES

There's no need to wait 20 years to see New England, no need to
delay at all, for its rewards are well established. It is a region
bursting with 300 years of historical sights and influence – considerably more than any other place in America. But it is also a
remarkably vital place: attend a town meeting in one of the superfi-
cially sleepy rural communities and you'll find that the robust tradition of democracy bequeathed by the founding fathers lives on,
making many a town manager's life little easier than the president's.

It is precisely this juxtaposition of past influence and present pres-
tige that is so compelling. Comprising six politically defined states,
New England has a thousand states of mind – Maine for solitude
and contemplation, Massachusetts for bustle and culture, Vermont for
beauty and peace, Connecticut for its carefully kept white clapboard
homes, Rhode Island for its renowned sailing, and tranquil New
Hampshire, whose bellwether presidential primary every four years
suggests the political fortunes that are about to be won and lost.

A trip to New England can mean finding a priceless antique in an
out-of-the-way backwoods store, or dining in a sophisticated Boston
bistro. It can mean rafting down a Maine river and skiing down a
New Hampshire mountain, lounging on a Nantucket beach or picnicking on the harbor in Newport, Rhode Island.

State delineations serve as convenient although somewhat artifi-
cial labels for New England's varied regions. In the following pages,
each state is explored in depth and treated as a self-contained unit. But
Massachusetts, the most populous, has been divided into sub-sections:
Boston, Boston Day trips, Cape Cod and the islands of Martha's Vineyard and Nantucket, Central Massachusetts and the Berkshires.

States of mind – calm, contentment, excitement, pride, surprise,
intrigue, enjoyment, pleasure – are to be found throughout New
England. From the scrub pines on Martha's Vineyard to the granite
outcroppings of Vermont's Green Mountains, from the cobbled
streets of restored Newburyport to the sleek Boston skyline, from
Rhode Island's natural wonderland, Block Island, to the country's
history that began in Lexington and Concord, this is New England,
home of American dreams, both real and still to be actualized. ❑

PRECEDING PAGES: winter in the White Mountains, New Hampshire; summer in the
White Mountains; Back Cove, Maine.
LEFT: Brant Point Lighthouse and Children's Beach, Nantucket.

e St Paul
La Pocatiere
lawrence

Edmundston
Fort Kent
Madawaska

Mount Carleton
Provincial Park

17

St Leonard
Nictau

201
St-Pamphile
Dickey
Winterville
Grand Falls
Riley Brook
Caribou

C A N A D A

ntagny

Ashland
Presque
Isle
Plaster Rock

Perth-Andover
Stickney
Doaktown

Allagash
Wilderness
Waterway

Machias

SW Miramichi

Knowles
Corner
Juniper

Mt. Katahdin
5267
Patten
Island Falls
95
Houlton
Woodstock

N e w
B r u n s w i c k

North
East Carry
Baxter
State
Park

2

Fredericton
10
Minto

Moosehead
Lake
Rockwood
Kokadjo
Millinocket
East
Millinocket
2
2A
Danforth
Canterbury
2
Oromocto
102

Moosehead
Greenville
6
Mattawamkeag
1
Topsfield
Tracy
McAdam
102

Jackman

Bingham
Milo
Lincoln
Howland
3
Saint John

ustis
Stratton
201
Guilford
Dover-
Foxcroft
Princeton
Calais
St Stephen
Pennfield

a i n e
Kingfield
Dexter
Wesley
1
Eastport
1

Phillips
Farmington
2
Bangor
9
Aurora
Deblois
Machias
9
Grand Manan
Island

Weld
Pittsfield
202
Brooks
Whiting

ford
Waterville
202
3
Ellsworth
1
Steuben
Jonesport

urner
Augusta
Belfast
Blue Hill
Bar Harbour
Freeport

4
Lewiston
Waldoboro
Camden
Stonington
Acadia
National
Park

Auburn
493
Rockland
N o v a   S c o t i a

95
Brunswick
New
Harbor

Yarmouth

Portland
Saco
nebunk

G u l f   o f   M a i n e

Massachusetts
Bay

A T L A N T I C

incetown
6
ape Cod
Bay
Cape Cod

O C E A N

Chatham
ahnis
South
Yarmouth
Monomy Island

Nantucket
Island
Nantucket

N

New England

0   50 miles

0   50 km

Bunker Hill Monument 5

CHARLESTOWN

USS Constitution 4
(Old Ironsides)

Boston

Bunker Hill
Pavilion

Hoosac
Pier

Charlestown
Navy Yard

0   500 yds

0   500 m

Boston Inner Harbor

Gilmore Bridge

Charlestown Av.

Front Street

City
Square

Constitution

Washington Street

Charlestown Bridge

93

1

Charles River Dam

Nashua Street

Science Park

Museum of
Science 38

Hayden
Planetarium

North
Station

T

FleetCenter 37

North
Station

NORTH END
PLAYGROUND

COPP'S HILL
BURYING GROUND

Commercial Street

Snowhill St

Charter St

3

Old North Church 2
Paul Revere
Mall

St
Stephen

Battery
Wharf

Lincoln Wharf

Union
Wharf

Sargents
Wharf

Pilot
House

Lewis
Wharf

Commercial
Wharf

WATERFRONT

Aquarium

Long Wharf

Central
Wharf

New England
Aquarium 6

Commercial Street

Atlantic Av.

Keany
Square

Prince St

Hull

Snowhill St

Salem St

Sheafe
St

Bennet St

Prince St

Endicott

Thacher St

Cooper

Margin St

NORTH
END

Paul Revere
House 1

North
Square

Cross

Richmond
St

Hanover

North St

Fulton

Commercial

1A

WEST END

CHARLESBANK
PARK

Martha Rd

Lowell St

Blossom St

Cardinal
O'Connell
Way

Portland Street

Friend Street

Canal Street

Merrimac Street

State Service
Center

Haymarket

New Sudbury St

John F. Kennedy
Federal
Office Building

Blackstone Street

Congress Street

HOLOCAUST
MEMORIAL 11

COLUMBUS
PARK

Massachusetts
General Hospital

Fruit St

Parkman
St

Charles Street

Blossom St

Anderson

Cambridge

Street

Old West
Church

Harrison
Gray Otis House

Bowdoin

T

Saltonstall
Building

Suffolk University

Center
Plaza

City
Hall

Sears
Crescent
Building

Government Center 12

T

Quincy
Market 10

Faneuil
Hall

Chatham St

Custom House 9

Community
Boating

Charles/MGH

T

Phillips Street

Garden Street

Russell Street

Hancock

Derne St

Ashburton

Court St

Suffolk
County
Courthouse

Old State
House 13

Boston
Massacre Site

State

T

FINANCIAL

India Street

Broad St

Boston
Harbor
Hotel

BEACON HILL

Pinckney

Mt. Vernon Street

Joy

Bowdoin

Tremont

Nichols
House Museum 22

Mass.
State
House 20

Park Street T

Old City
Hall

Old Corner
Bookstore

King's
Chapel 16

Boston
Athenaeum 17

Old South
Meeting
House 14

Milk

DISTRICT

Post
Office
Square

Franklin St

Federal Street

Congress Street

Devonshire

Water

Federal
Courthouse

Charles Street
Meeting House 24

Louisburg
Square 23

Chestnut Street

Branch St

W. Cedar St

Grove

Mt. Vernon St

Walnut St

Beacon

Street

Spruce

Third Harrison
Gray Otis
House

Robert Gould
Shaw & 54th
Regiment
Memorial

Park
Street

Beacon

Winter

Bromfield

Orpheum
Theater 15

Province

School St

T

Hatch
Shell 30

Gibson
House
Museum 26

PUBLIC

Byron St

Chestnut Street

Arlington Street

Charles Street

28

19

Washington
Monument

GARDEN

Soldiers
& Sailors
Monument 18

Parkman
Bandstand

COMMON

Boylston

Street

Tremont

Park

West St

Washington St

Temple Pl

Avery St

Downtown
Crossing

T

Filene's
Basement

Macy's

Summer St

Otis St

Chauncy St

Arch St

Hawley St

Summer Street

Lincoln St

Purchase Street

Atlantic

Ritz-Carlton
Hotel

Newbury Street

Arlington

T

Plaza
Castle

Four Seasons
Hotel

Boylston
Street

Park
Square

Eliot St

Colonial Theater

Emerson
Majestic
Theater

Schubert Theater

Stuart St

Piedmont St

Chinatown

Essex Street

Beach

Bedford St

Kingston

Essex St

South Station

T

South Station

John Fitzgerald Expressway

Northern Av.
Bridge

Evelyn Moakley
Bridge

Beaver II 8
(Tea Party Ship)

Children's
Museum 7

Boston Fire
Museum

Federal
Reserve
Bank

Congress Street
Bridge

John Hancock
Tower 31

Clarendon

Berkeley

Stuart

Arlington Avenue

S. Charles St

Tremont St

Washington St

Harrison Avenue

Wilbur
Theater

Tyler Street

Hudson Street

Kneeland Street

CHINATOWN

Lincoln

South

Albany Avenue

Atlantic

Dorchester Avenue

Summer Street

Fort Point Channel

Summer St

A Street

Melcher St

Midway St

Granite St

Cortes St

NE Medical
Center

Oak

Washington
Street

Marginal
Road

Mass.
Turnpike

Herald

Street

Shawmut

Tremont

Troy

Dwight St

Milford St

E. Berkeley St

Warren Av.

SOUTH
END

Boston Center
for the Arts 32

Montgomery St

Appleton St

Chandler Street

Berkeley

Columbus

Mass.

93

1

Broadway
Bridge

Broadway

Kennedy Library 41

━━━ Freedom Trail

BOSTON

The city has always taken itself seriously. But it does, after all, all, have unequaled Revolutionary history, famed universities, vibrant arts, creative cuisine, and the Red Sox

Map on pages 102–3

T he poet and essayist Ralph Waldo Emerson, wrote "This town of Boston has a history… It is not an accident, not a windmill, or a railroad station, or a crossroads town, but a seat of humanity, of men of principle, obeying sentiment and marching to it…"

Oliver Wendell Holmes was even more extravagant: "All I claim for Boston is that it is the thinking center of the Continent, and therefore of the Planet." He went on to christen his city "The Hub of the Universe." New York may be more dynamic, Washington more imposing, Seattle more beautiful, but no city in America so nobly mingles its past with its present, tradition with innovation.

Short story of a long history

Founded in 1630 when a band of Puritans who had landed in Salem (north of Boston) went searching for drinking water, Boston early on felt that "the eies of all people are upon us," as their first leader, John Winthrop, said. Driven by this relentless self-consciousness and the certainty that God, too, was watching, the little "Bible Commonwealth" quickly made something of itself.

Prosperity came from the sea. By 1700, thanks to cod fishing and the maritime trade made possible by Boston's natural harbor, the colony was booming: its fleet was the third largest in the English-speaking world, its population the largest in North America.

Success, however, brought attention from home, and in the mid-18th century, the English Crown began to tighten its hold on its precocious offspring, imposing a series of tough new revenue measures which cooled relations between the colonies and the motherland. Tensions escalated; the Boston Massacre of 1770 and the Boston Tea Party (*see page 37*) three years later eventually flared into a brief but famous war – the American Revolution.

The Athens of America

During the high noon of the 19th century Boston took its present-day form. The merchant princes created a great city that would eventually become known not only as "The Hub," but also as "The Athens of America."

Boston's maritime industries surged again with the coming of peace. Piloting swift clipper ships, sea captains traded in ports farther abroad – Java, the West Coast and newly opened China. The Boston fishing fleet increased tenfold between 1789 and 1810, and created a "codfish aristocracy" of fortunes netted from the sea. A seemingly unending flow of gold made Bostonians with names such as Cabot, Lowell, Otis and Hancock incredibly rich. These wealthy mercantilists, adopting the name of the priestly class of the

PRECEDING PAGES: Boston seen from the Charles River. **LEFT:** Acorn Street, Beacon Hill. **BELOW:** George Washington's statue in the Public Garden.

Hindus who performed sacred rituals and set moral standards, emerged as the self-styled "Brahmins".

Growth accelerated as Yankee ingenuity triumphed, and helped Boston lead America into a prosperous Industrial Age. By the century's end, in one of the great testimonies to the American knack for making something from nothing, Boston had tripled its size with landfill.

Boston was also expanding its mind. With its legacy of Puritan high-mindedness, its publishing houses and its fashionable literary salons run by earnest first citizens, Boston suddenly found itself at the radiant center of intellectual America. Henry Wadsworth Longfellow, Robert Lowell, John Greenleaf Whittier, Ralph Waldo Emerson, Henry David Thoreau, Oliver Wendell Holmes, Bronson Alcott, Nathaniel Hawthorne: all were at one time or another citizens of the New England Parnassus; all could be found browsing at the Old Corner Book Store or dictating standards for civilization over seven-course meals at the Parker House, where Emerson convened his luminous Saturday Club.

A whole slew of cultural institutions celebrated and embodied it. Among these were the Boston Public Library, the Boston Symphony Orchestra, the Massachusetts Institute of Technology (MIT) and Boston University, the first American university to admit women on an equal basis with men. Harvard had already ascended to its place among the world's great universities.

The great immigration

When the Irish Potato Famine began in 1845, Boston was at the apogee of its gleaming social and cultural pre-eminence. Suddenly, thousands of impoverished Irish immigrants arrived, promptly constituting a new underclass.

It was the Boston-designed sewing machine, along with the loom, imported from England, that inaugurated an era of heavy textile and shoe manufacturing in New England.

BELOW: Boston Public Library.

Map on pages 102–3

As the population exploded – swelled further by additional waves of Italians, Poles and Russians in the 1880s – census figures multiplied thirtyfold during the 19th century to about 560,000 people in 1900. Newcomers and incumbents clashed, and Boston was divided into two distinct cultures. Established Bostonians withdrew into their own carefully defended elite of genealogy and crypto-Puritanism.

The new citizens became virtual slaves as they sweated in factories and did handwork; they remade Boston in their own image. Once dominated by English names, the Puritan "City upon a Hill" became a predominantly Catholic megalopolis of Irish and Italian names: numbers prevailed, most dramatically in the arena of city politics.

For all Boston's glory and growth during the 1800s, the century's end brought decline, a decline that would continue until the 1960s. New York superseded Boston as a port; the textile mills and shoe factories headed south for cheaper labor and lower taxes. By the 1940s and 1950s, Boston was shrinking.

But then the city woke up. For the first time, Boston's Protestant elite, representing wealth, and its Irish Catholics, representing political power, cooperated in the management of city affairs and began a success story of rejuvenation. The Prudential Center, including what was then the tallest skyscraper outside New York, materialized. Government Center supplanted Scollay Square. Faneuil Hall Marketplace was created from meat warehouses. The waterfront was revived. Suddenly, Boston was a different, altogether exciting place.

The city further benefited as the Baby Boom generation grew up, went to college, then looked for jobs and apartments. Millions of young people have attended one of the three score colleges in Boston. Many have set up shop and transformed the Boston area into one of the centers of the Technology Revolution. Together with Cambridge, its neighbor across the Charles River, it is at the fore as a seat of learning and as a center for scientific research. Boston of today is young in demographics as well as spirits.

Park Rangers have an educational role.

BELOW: festival time in "Little Italy," Boston's North End.

A walking city

Despite urban development, one of Boston's primary charms remains unchanged: its tangled streets and the art of walking them. Boston changes so abruptly in mood and nuance from one street to another that it cries out to be explored on foot. The city is charmingly, perversely bereft of a main drag, and its streets practice the old European vices of waywardness and digression. The visitor should, too. There's no telling what you'll find.

Every day hundreds of visitors walk the red line on the sidewalk that marks the **Freedom Trail**, a self-guided tour that takes in the major sites of the city's momentous Revolutionary history (*see pages 132–3*).

The North End

This picturesque old neighborhood is Boston's original heart, and to walk its streets is to walk among legends. The Freedom Trail threads its way through the North End on its way between Boston Common and the Bunker Hill Monument in Charlestown.

TIP

Look out for the feste, or saint's festivals, on weekends in July and August, when the streets of the North End are spanned by arcs of colored lights and jammed with people surrounding Madonnas bedecked with dollar bills.

BELOW: the Paul Revere House.

The North End is the ethnic heart of Boston: once Irish, then Jewish, and now Italian. Laundry hangs from lines stretched from building to building across the street, and freshly ground sausages are invitingly displayed in storefront windows.

A stroll through the North End can start at the **Paul Revere House ❶** (open daily) in North Square. Built around 1680, it is the oldest building standing in the city, and the period furnishings on display include some items owned by the Reveres. From here, head toward Hanover Street and the Old North Church, but walk at a leisurely pace and take in the sights – and smells – of Old World Italy. Here is a paradise of fresh-baked bread, dried squid, pastries, provolone and braided garlic. Within a few blocks of Hanover Street are dozens of first-class Italian restaurants.

At the end of Hanover Street stands the Revere Mall with its rather comic equestrian statue of Revere looking a tad drunk. At the end of the tranquil, tree-shaded mall, also occupied by a fountain and old Italian men playing checkers, stands Boston's oldest church, the **Old North Church ❷** (officially Christ Church, 193 Salem Street; open daily 8:30am–6pm; Sunday services at 9am, 11am and 5pm), where beneath the graceful spire the sexton Robert Newman famously hung two lanterns on April 18, 1775, on the orders of Paul Revere, to signify to the citizens the British troops' plan to cross by sea rather than by land. Inside, the stately pulpit and a bust of George Washington preside over the original box pews. The beauty of this space finds lovely accompaniment in the "royal peal" of its eight bells, considered the best and sweetest in America. One is inscribed, "We are the first ring of bells cast for the British Empire in North America, Anno 1774."

Behind Old North, between Hull and Charter streets, stand the weathered headstones of **Copps Hill Burying Ground ❸**, where many early Bostonians are buried – including Cotton Mather, the Puritan instrumental in inciting the persecution of the Salem "witches' – and where several gravestones bear evidence of British soldiers using them for musket practice.

Charlestown

Across Charlestown Bridge from the North End a famous bit of history lies at anchor: the **USS** *Constitution* ❹ (open daily), the venerable frigate known as "Old Ironsides," built in 1797 and the oldest commissioned vessel in the world (she makes one voyage a year, a ceremonial "turnabout" on the 4th of July); she fought over 40 battles in the War of 1812 and never lost one. The majestic masts soar above the Boston Naval Shipyard, which opened during the War of 1812 and functioned until 1974, up to the latter days of the Vietnam War.

The historic shipyard includes enough to fill a day's visit: the **USS** *Constitution* **Museum** (open daily) tells the ship's story, while the **Boston Marine Society** within the old octagonal Muster House contains an array of ship models and paintings, and the **Commandant's House** is preserved as it was when last occupied in 1876. Also in dock, the **USS** *Cassin Young* is a World War II destroyer, open for tours. The Bunker Hill Pavilion has a multimedia extravaganza depicting the Patriots' heroic loss to the Redcoats in the second battle of the Revolution.

The Freedom Trail's finale from the Charlestown Navy Yard is less appealing than the rest of the Trail, but it is worth persevering to the very end, to the outsized obelisk of the **Bunker Hill Monument ❺** (open daily), a granite needle 221 ft (67 meters) high, commemorating one of the first major battles of the Revolutionary War. Climb this be warned that there are 294 steps – and contemplate the complexity of the Harbor, speckled with dozens of islands. Many of these have odd histories, some linked with Native American legends, others – as in the case of Nix's Mate Island – with the visits of pirates such as Captain Kidd. Two islands have supported hospitals, another a prison, and others have been fortified. During the Civil War, hundreds of soldiers trained for the Union Army at Fort Warren on George's Island, and more than 1,000 Confederates were imprisoned there.

The Waterfront

The eastern boundary of the North End is the Waterfront District. If the tall ships – or rather, their modern copies – now appear only sporadically, the great wharves remain, many now recycled as apartments, shopping arcades and upscale restaurants. At the center of it all is the modest Columbus Park; with the completion of a huge project (due for completion 2006) to demolish the I-93 ramp and bury the traffic in tunnels, a much larger park will link the Waterfront with the downtown area.

By Aquarium subway station, Long Wharf is the starting point for harbor cruises, or you can get harbor views for free by walking along the walkway south-

Map on pages 102–3

TIP

In summer the MuSEAm Connection water shuttle links USS *Constitution*, the Aquarium, and Museum Wharf (for the Computer Museum, the Children's Museum and the Boston Tea Party Ship).

BELOW: "Old Ironsides".

Wind-blown sculpture outside the Aquarium.

wards to Rowes Wharf. The **New England Aquarium** ❻ (Central Wharf; open daily; entrance fee) has the largest seawater fish tank in the world, a gargantuan three-story, 200,000-gallon (900,000-liter) cylinder in which sharks, sea turtles, moray eels and other tropical species glide in never-ending circles. By its base African and rockhopper penguins play on the Ocean Tray, while other highlights include The Edge of the Sea exhibit, a fiberglass re-creation of a New England shore. You can watch through the window on to the Aquarium Medical Center, a laboratory caring for injured and sick animals. The Aquarium operates "Science at Sea" and whale-watch cruises, with researchers and naturalists on board, from Central Wharf.

Follow Harborwalk southwards past Rowes Wharf and cross Northern Avenue Bridge to find **Museum Wharf** ❼, home of the **Children's Museum** (open Tues–Sun; Fri till 9pm; entrance fee). Housed in a renovated warehouse, it is a hands-on adventure, where children can play shoppers at the Supermercado (based on a real Latino supermarket in Boston), climb a three-dimensional maze, and take their shoes off to enter an authentic Japanese house transplanted piece by piece from Boston's sister city, Kyoto. New England's maritime traditions are reflected in hands-on boating exhibits and an environmental exhibit, Under the Dock, which simulates the underwater landscape of Fort Point Channel and includes a 14-ft (4-meter) fiberglass lobster. Children accustomed to constant warnings of "Don't touch!" and "Be careful!" will find a paradise of things to squeeze, crank, push, pull and explore. On the wharf, an immense milk bottle (a vestige of 1930s advertising kitsch) dispenses ice cream and more substantial snacks.

Nearby, on Congress Bridge, is the **Boston Tea Party Ship** ❽ (Congress Street; open Mar–Nov daily; entrance fee), which offers a not-too-serious ican mythology for schoolchildren of all ages within the *Beaver II*, a full-size replica of one of the three tea ships whose cargo, on that chilly night in 1773, helped make the Harbor into a rather large pitcher of iced tea. You get the chance to participate in a town meeting based on the momentous one that took place in Old South Meeting House, and to hurl a tea chest into the Harbor from the deck.

Map on pages 102–3

Faneuil Hall, Government Center and Downtown

Just west of the New England Aquarium rises the **Custom House Tower ❾**, for many years Boston's tallest building, and today certainly the city's quaintest high-rise (now converted into time-share condominiums), with the 1915 clock tower placed somewhat incongruously on the Greek Revival-style Custom House of 1847. Close by is Faneuil Hall Marketplace, lodestone of the tourist trade and a famed experiment in urban redesign.

Street entertainment in Faneuil Hall Marketplace.

Faneuil Hall ❿, the fulcrum of the place, was donated to Boston by Peter Faneuil, a French Huguenot merchant who traded in slaves. This future "Cradle of Liberty," where Patriot orators would soon stir the embers of Revolution, was built in 1742 on a site that was at the time, remarkably enough, Boston's Town Dock. In 1976, after 250 sometimes glorious, sometimes scruffy years of service, Quincy Market and Faneuil Hall opened again, after a massive renovation that converted their boisterous, rugged markets into a chic, cleverly remodeled and wildly successful array of flower stalls, jewelry emporia and designer-clothing outfits. In addition, several dozen food stands line the long hall of the central building, tempting strollers with an endless array of classic American and international snacks, from freshly shucked oysters to Italian sausage subs and exquisite French pastry.

BELOW: reliving the past at the Boston Tea Party Ship (left) and Faneuil Hall.

The New England Holocaust Memorial.

The upper floor of Faneuil Hall itself, where the meetings were held, is open daily (tours every 30 minutes) and houses regimental memorabilia of the Ancient and Honorable Artillery Company.

For those who may wonder why all the shopping bags and restaurant menus bear an image of a cricket: when Faneuil gave Boston the hall, he had a large cricket weathervane placed atop its cupola. During the War of 1812, "cricket" became a password and patriot rallying cry of the Boston port. Strangers who could not identify the cricket as the image of the city of Boston met uncertain fates as spies.

Beside Union Street, six glass towers comprise the **New England Holocaust Memorial ⓫**, the "windows" etched with rows of numbers in memory of six million murdered Jews in World War II.

Looming just inland from Faneuil Hall, across Congress Street, is **Government Center ⓬**. Here, in the 1960s, Boston Redevelopment Authority director Edward Logue, Mayor Collins and architect I.M. Pei leveled the colorful tenements of the West End and constructed a city of their own, a radical "New Boston." This was urban renewal on a grand scale – either inspiring or forbidding, depending on your viewpoint. The designers razed buildings and removed streets to create a huge open space – some 56 acres (23 hectares). On this new plaza, they arranged several buildings of imposing scale and abstract design. A massive concrete City Hall designed by Kallmann, McKinnell and Knowles dominates, described as an "Aztec temple on a brick desert."

For a little comic relief, the quirky little Sears Crescent, built in 1816, has been allowed to remain from pre-Pei days. A 227-gallon (1,033-liter) teapot, steaming happily, hangs from a corner of the adjoining 1848 Sears Block building; a late 19th-century advertising gimmick, it lives on as a charming totem for a key government institution, the bureaucrat's breakfast.

To the southeast rises the tall confusion of pinstriped Boston, the banks and office towers along Franklin, Congress, Federal, State and Broad streets. Rising confidently from a primitive warren of jumbled byways, these well-tailored behemoths constitute the Hub of Business. They are evidence that in one way, at least, Boston has not changed much since the 17th century. Even today, it regards money as sacred, a sign of election.

To the southwest beats the throbbing heart of downtown, as well as some buildings illuminated brightly in history. At Washington Street's intersection with Court and State streets stands the **Old State House ⓭** (open daily; entrance fee) a glorious center of 18th-century public life that today exhibits its heritage of survival by the stubbornness with which it holds the city's predatory skyscrapers at bay; the Bostonian Society has a museum inside, charting aspects of the city's history with changing displays. It was here, in 1761, that James Otis first fulminated against the British Writs of Assistance in a spellbinding speech that prompted John Adams to write that "then and there the child Independence was born." In 1770, the infamous Boston Massacre took place just outside the State House. Some years later, after the Revolution,

BELOW:
Quincy Market, which attracts over 10 million visitors a year.

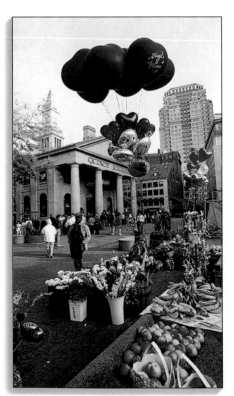

the building served as the meeting place for the Commonwealth Government until the present State House was built.

The **Old Corner Bookstore**, now called the Boston Globe Bookstore, at the corner of Washington and School streets, was once a sort of clubhouse for such writers and thinkers as Hawthorne, Emerson and Thoreau (*see page 148*). Later it was the home of the *Atlantic Monthly* when it was launched in 1857, and of the *Boston Globe*, Boston's journal of record.

Continue down Washington Street to the **Old South Meeting House ⓮** (open daily; entrance fee), from which on December 16, 1773, 60 whooping patriots dressed as Mohawk Indians set off for Griffin's Wharf and the Boston Tea Party. An audio historical display sets the scene. Around the corner at 1 Milk Steet, the house in which Benjamin Franklin was born, is **Dreams of Freedom**, a multimedia show tracing the history of Boston's immigration.

A little further on comes **Downtown Crossing ⓯**, where hordes of suburban shoppers stampede the city's major department stores. Probably the busiest intersection in Boston, it is the location of the phenomenal **Filene's Basement**, the world's most celebrated bargain store. Every day, thousands of sharp-eyed professionals, discerning matrons, and blown-dry teen angels can be seen shoving and elbowing each other as they rummage frantically through this cut-rate El Dorado in search of designer seconds, three-piece suits, and household essentials. Goods are progressively marked down until they sell.

Alternatively, at the Boston Globe Bookstore, turn into School Street, pass the Old City Hall, a grand affair that out-Second Empires the French Second Empire, and at Tremont Street turn right to look into **King's Chapel ⓰** (open mid-Oct–mid-Apr, Sat; mid-Apr–mid-June and Sep–Oct, Mon, Fri, Sat;

Map on pages 102–3

Free, ranger-led tours of the Freedom Trail start from the Boston National Historical Park office, opposite the Old State House.

LEFT: a bookstore with a history.
BELOW: the Old State House.

mid-June–Aug, Mon, Thur–Sat; Sun pm). Built in 1754 of Quincy granite, it retains its crisp white box pews as well as Paul Revere's largest bell; its burial ground is Boston's oldest.

Crossing over Tremont Street, head left to the **Old Granary Burial Ground**, a pleasant glade where are found the graves of Peter Faneuil, John Hancock, Samuel Adams, Paul Revere, six Massachusetts governors and the victims of the Boston Massacre. Overlooking the burial ground are the windows of the **Boston Athenaeum** , which in the 19th century became the preserve of wealthy intellectuals and, although anyone is free to walk in, it has retained that atmosphere virtually intact (10A Beacon Street; first two floors open Mon–Sat; tours of entire building 3pm Tues, Thur; reservation required; tel: 617-227 0270). There are reading rooms, marble busts, and prints and paintings, as well as books from George Washington's library. On the top floor there are seven pairs of recessed bays flanking a barrel-vaulted reading room; members can sit out on the balcony and lunch, overlooking the Old Granary Burial Ground.

A few more paces down Tremont lead to Peter Banner's elegant **Park Street Church** (1809) on the corner of Boston Common. Henry James decided it was "perfectly felicitous" and "the most interesting mass of brick and mortar in America." On July 4, 1829, William Lloyd Garrison made his first anti-slavery speech here, launching his far-reaching emancipation campaign.

The Boston Common and the Public Garden

Every metropolis has a great park somewhere in its outline, but only Boston can claim the oldest, the venerable **Boston Common** , a magical swath of lawn and trees and benches bounded by Tremont, Park, Beacon, Charles and Boylston

The song "America" was first sung in Park Street Church on July 4, 1831.

BELOW:
the Old Granary Burial Ground.

streets. Sitting in the sun-mottled shade, watching pigeons strut and children frolic around Frog Pond, the out-of-towner can understand how Bostonians might mistake this spot for the very center of the world.

The land that was to become the Common originally belonged to Boston's first English settler, one Reverend William Blaxton. Having fled first England and then an aborted colonial attempt farther south, Blaxton settled in 1625 on the western slope of what is now known as Beacon Hill. There, he tended his orchard and read in peaceful solitude until his serenity was somewhat rudely interrupted in 1631 by the arrival of a band of new settlers led by Governor John Winthrop of the Massachusetts Bay Company. The new Bostonians were nobly determined, as Winthrop had written on the ship, to "be a Citty upon a hill," and their presence did not please Blaxton. In 1634, he sold his land to the town for around $150 and fled farther into the wilderness.

The 45 acres (18 hectares) he left behind quickly became a versatile community utility. During the next 150 years, it was used as a cattle and sheep pasture and as a drilling ground. And although, as an account written in 1663 says, "the Common was the beauty and pride of the Town, ever suggesting the lighter side of life," it also proved useful as a place to hang people – for stealing, for piracy, for being a Quaker, or a Native American, or a woman who snatched a bonnet worth 75 cents. The whipping post and the pillory stood there, and many a duel took place at dawn. As a military post, the Common put up the Redcoats all through the Revolution, and during the Civil War it provided a backdrop for the tears of recruiting and departures.

Now the Common is an urban oasis, a park and nothing else. Climb the little knolls and walk the meandering paths past bronze statues and dignified

Map on pages 102–3

The Emerald Necklace is a 6-mile (9-km) corridor of forests, parks and ponds in and around Boston. Begun in 1881 by Frederick Law Olmsted, it links the Public Garden with Franklin Park in West Roxbury.

BELOW LEFT: the dome of the State House seen from the Common.
BELOW: cooling down in Frog Pond.

fountains. The Common is at its best all year – when the magnolias bloom, or when snow at sunset evokes the impressionist paintings of Childe Hassam.

West from the Common and across Charles Street, the elegant **Public Garden ⑲** beckons, and, though it continues the pleasant green of the Common, it has quite a different past. Indeed, these variegated trees, meandering paths, and ornate beds of flowers were mere marsh when the Common was well into its second century of tempestuous history. First deeded at the end of the 18th century as a riverside ropewalk – the Charles had not yet been filled here – these 24 acres (10 hectares) at the Common's foot were bought back by the city in 1825 for $55,000. In a series of disputes during the first half of the 19th century, some argued that the valuable land would be best sold. But the park soon began to be laid out, though the destruction by fire of an early conservatory for birds and camellias slowed development. By 1867, the Garden had taken its present graceful shape, complete with weeping willows, a bridge for daydreamers, and a shallow 4-acre (2-hectare) pond.

In summer, one can't overlook the swan boats, those fabled gondolas that carry happy tourists across the placid waters. At the Commonwealth Avenue entrance, an equestrian *George Washington* bronze by Thomas Ball presides, while a row of bronze ducks on the north side pays tribute to Robert McCloskey's children's story *Make Way for the Ducklings*.

Beacon Hill

Back up at the east end of the Common rises the gold dome of the **State House ⑳** (open weekdays) gleaming atop Beacon Hill. Completed in 1798 when the Old State House became too small, this design by Charles Bulfinch,

Statues in the park include tributes to Edward Everett Hale, author of "The Man Without a Country" (at the Charles Street entrance opposite the Boston Common) and Charles Sumner, who led abolitionist forces in the Senate before the Civil War (at the Boylston Street perimeter).

BELOW: a swan boat in the Public Garden.

with additions by several others, symbolizes the eminence of politics in Boston. The approach to the legislative chambers passes through a series of splendid halls, beginning with the Bulfinch era Doric Hall and leading to the Senate Staircase Hall and the Hall of Flags, both symphonies of fin de siècle marble opulence supplied plentifully with statues, busts, flags and patriotic mottos.

But none of this dulls the eye to the House Chamber in the Brigham extension, a paneled hall under a two-stage dome. Great moments of Massachusetts' freedom decorate the walls in a series of Albert Herter paintings, while above circles a frieze carved with a roll-call of the state's super-achievers. The portentous codfish known as the "Sacred Cod," a sleek, stiff carving in pine that commemorates Boston's great Federal-era fishing industry, was first hung in the Old State House. Without this old mascot, the house refuses to meet.

The State House, now hemmed in by Beacon Hill residences, seems about as centrally located as a building can be, but it wasn't always that way. In 1797, residents of Boston thought that the Wild West itself began on the far side of the Common, hardly a quarter-mile from the State House. Cows still grazed there, and much of the surrounding land had the bucolic air of pastures trailing off into forest. Even Beacon Hill rose, not as a polite demi-hill, but as a rugged mass of wilderness, then called the Trimount because of its triple-peaked summit. The westernmost peak was isolated enough from the Puritan stronghold that it could be put to the purposes suggested by the name Mount Whoredom.

Predictably enough, moving the State House into this setting focused the city's attention on this area and changed things for good. While the Common became a true park, the Trimount became the subject of land speculation. It was quite ingeniously leveled and quickly became the compressed but still

The Boston window in the State House.

BELOW: inside the State House.

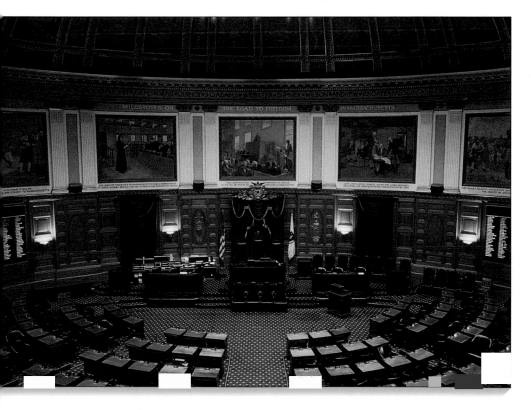

Beacon Hill has several sites that were of significance in the history of Boston's African-Americans. The focal point of the Black Heritage Trail that links them is the Museum of Afro-American History, in the African Meeting House, 46 Joy Street (open daily).

BELOW:
the gas lamps on Beacon Hill are permanently lit.
BELOW RIGHT:
Beacon Street.

idyllic gaslit neighborhood of bow-fronted townhouses now known as "The Hill." At first, everyone expected that the new residences of Beacon Hill would be urban estates along the lines of Bulfinch's No. 85 Mount Vernon Street, which is to this day one of Boston's most majestic houses. But the mansion plans were quickly scaled down to the smaller blocks one sees today. At No. 55 Mount Vernon, the **Nichols House ㉑** (open Tues–Sat pm; tours every half hour; entrance fee) offers a more typical example of Beacon Hill building. Also a Charles Bulfinch project, the house is now a small museum.

To get a sense of The Hill, walk west down Beacon Street from the State House. At numbers 39 and 40 Beacon stand twin 1818 Greek Revival mansions, one built for Daniel Parker, owner of the Parker House, Boston's oldest hotel. At numbers 42 and 43, the Somerset Club, built in 1819 as a mansion for David Sears, was acquired by the most exclusive of Boston social clubs in 1872. At number 45 Beacon stands the third of Harrison Gray Otis's houses, built in 1805. The **Harrison Gray Otis House ㉒** at 141 Cambridge Street, just outside Beacon Hill proper (open Wed–Sun 11am–4pm; tours every hour; entrance fee), gives a chance to see inside the first of the Otis houses. It has period furnishings,. and is decorated with with authentic, period paints and wallpapers,.

Louisburg Square ㉓, developed between Pinckney and Mount Vernon streets around 1840, epitomizes the Beacon Hill style and its urban delicacy. The Square has long stood at the summit of Boston society. William Dean Howells, the novelist and *Atlantic Monthly* editor; Louisa May Alcott, author of *Little Women*; and Jenny Lind, the "Swedish Nightingale," all lived at one time or another in the houses surrounding the Square's elegant green. Lind married her accompanist Otto Goldschmidt at No. 20 during an American tour in 1852.

Another charming example of Beacon Hill's spirit can be found at numbers 13, 15 and 17 Chestnut Street, where Bulfinch built for the daughters of his client Hepzibah Swan three exquisite townhouses in a prim little row. Chestnut Street vies for the title of prettiest street on the Hill, so fetching is the gently animated conversation of its porches and windows, flower-box geraniums and romantic gaslights.

On the west side of Beacon Hill, Charles Street is a prime spot to stroll, shop and snack. Here is Boston's leading concentration of antique stores and a diverse collection of coffee houses, bakeries, florists, cafes and boutiques. DeLuca's Market brims with the smells of ripe melons, fresh sausage and coffee beans. Nearby, Café Bella Vita serves coffee and pastries, but the real draw is people-watching.

The street's principal landmark is the **Charles Street Meeting House** ❷❹ at the corner of Charles and Mount Vernon streets. Built first for the Third Baptist Church in 1804, it served as the home of the African Methodist Episcopal Church and later the Unitarian-Universalist Church. At street level, this unpretentious building houses shops and a cafe-scale outpost of the popular New American restaurant, Rebecca's.

Wander off Charles on to the shady, peaceful streets that parallel it and lead back up the hill. Many of the houses here are noteworthy either for the talent of their architects or the luminous names of their former occupants. Polar explorer Admiral Richard E. Byrd lived in Nos. 7–9 Brimmer Street, while No. 44 in the same street was the lifelong home of the great historian Samuel Eliot Morison. The Victorian clergyman and philosopher William Ellery Channing lived at No. 83 Mount Vernon Street, next door to the Otis mansion.

Map on pages 102–3

Charles Street has dozens of antiques shops.

BELOW:
Louisburg Square.

Back Bay

From Beacon Hill, it's an easy transition both in distance and architectural feeling to the handsome streets of Back Bay, the area that has come in recent years to epitomize "Old Boston." Don't be fooled by its old-money airs, though. Back Bay literally crawled from the mud into prominence, with a massive program of filling in a festering swampland that, in 1849, was declared "offensive and injurious" by the Board of Health.

The heroic story begins in 1857 when the legislature adopted a grand plan for the Back Bay: there would be long vistas down dignified blocks, and a wide boulevard with a French-style park down the middle. In 1858 the first load of fill, which had been collected with an innovative new tool called the steam shovel, arrived by train from Needham, about 10 miles (16 km) to the southwest. During the next 20 years, some 600 acres (240 hectares) of dry land emerged from the muck that was Back Bay.

And sure enough, as houses began to appear, they were dignified. Despite the vagaries of individual taste and the piecemeal selling of lots, the new blocks went up with a harmoniousness that from the beginning gave Back Bay the stately unity it still possesses. One young man who planned to build his bride a house in Back Bay was icily informed by his prospective father-in-law that he would never allow a daughter of his to live on "made ground." But such qualms were rare, and the new streets quickly became fashionable.

Back Bay presents as great a showing of the Boston domestic architecture of the second half of the 19th century as Beacon Hill does of the first. The verdant mall of **Commonwealth Avenue** ㉕ centers things, and the houses along it, as well as those on Marlborough and Beacon, reveal choice architectural cameos.

In 1814 a developer, Uriah Cotting, built a dam across Back Bay, hoping to harness the tidal currents to power as many as 80 mills. But there was less tidal power than expected and only a handful of mills were built.

BELOW:
the rooftops of
Back Bay.

Starting at the Arlington Street entrance to the Public Gardens, the visitor may want to cross over to the Ritz-Carlton Hotel, on the corner of Newbury Street. The Ritz-Carlton is the perfect place to fortify oneself with a cocktail or a cup of tea and to observe Brahmin society in its element.

From here, head north to No. 137 Beacon Street, between Arlington and Berkeley (the cross-streets ascend in alphabetical order). Built in 1860 at the start of Back Bay construction, the **Gibson House** ❷❻ (open May–Oct: Wed–Sun, tours 1, 2 and 3pm; Nov–Apr: weekends, tours 1, 2 and 3pm; entrance fee) has been left substantially as it was; it now houses a museum that recreates the feel of Back Bay living in its heyday. Continue to the corner of Commonwealth and Clarendon for a look at the First Baptist Church, a handsome design by H.H. Richardson. Its tower is graced with figures modeled after celebrities of the day – Emerson, Hawthorne and Longfellow.

In the block between Clarendon and Dartmouth, Commonwealth Avenue (known as "Comm Ave" to most of the locals) displays its most memorable structures. The romantic houses that march down this stretch perfectly justify the avenue's reputation as America's Champs-Elysées.

Paralleling Commonwealth Avenue on the south are Newbury and Boylston streets, the Back Bay that has been taken over by commerce and the rarefied air of uptown chic. On **Newbury Street**, the hairstyles are elaborate and the clothes are designer. Pricey restaurants, sidewalk cafes and seductive storefronts abound, and a number of fine galleries operate in sleekly converted townhouses. The best of the contemporary galleries – Alpha and Barbara Krakow – are located at No. 14 and No. 10, respectively. Vose's Gallery, at No. 238, specializes in American painting, 1669 to 1940. A fixture since 1897, Vose's is the oldest private gallery in the United States. Five generations of the same family have faithfully maintained the tradition.

Back Bay has seen the most ambitious building sprees in the past few decades. A controversial project, **Copley Place**, a megaplex occupying over 9 acres (4 hectares) atop the Massachusetts Turnpike, has proved – despite a considerable degree of initial skepticism – an enjoyable addition to city life, with its 11-screen cinema, hotel, and dozens of inviting restaurants and upmarket shops. Although many of the latter are clones of those found in other upscale malls, a few are unique, such as the Artful Hand Gallery (exceptional crafts) and Treasured Legacy (African American literature and art).

Connected to this complex by a "skyway," is Boston's original skyscraper, the **Prudential Center** ❷❼ (800 Boylston Street), dating from the early 1960s. It has 52 stories and a **Skywalk** (open daily 10am–10pm; entrance fee) which provides an exhilarating, map-like, four-way view of the city. Envisioned as a bold new look for the city, "The Pru" turned out to be, in fact, a rather graceless development of the sort favored by the builders of the former Soviet Utopia. Developed out of an old railroad yard, the complex encompasses the John B. Hynes Veterans Memorial Convention Center (a striking 1988 design by Kallmann, McKinnell & Wood), a hotel, two department stores, and a lively mix of shops and restaurants spruced up in 1994.

Map on pages 102–3

One of several murals along Newbury Street.

BELOW: street café in Newbury Street.

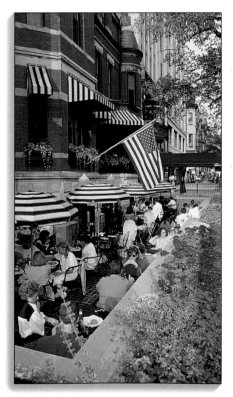

The story of Christian Science

The **Christian Science Church Center** ❷ (Sunday services at 10am and 7pm) occupies the 22 acres (9 hectares) immediately south of the Prudential Center on Huntington Avenue. The complex includes three older buildings – the Romanesque Mother Church (1894), the Italianate Mother Church Extension (1904) and the Publishing Society (1933) – as well as I.M. Pei's recent additions. The expanded center, a happy marriage of old and new architectural styles, makes an impressive Vatican for a religious denomination scarcely a century old.

In the publishing wing, the **Mapparium** (call 617-450 2000 for opening times) is an extraordinary stained-glass walk-in representation of the globe, constructed between 1932 and 1935 to symbolize the Christian Science Publishing Company's worldwide outlook. Illogical it may be – you stand inside the sphere surrounded by the map in concave form, but it is certainly one of the sights of Boston. The weird acoustics compound the hallucinogenic effect.

The founding of Christian Science dates to 1866 when a frail, impoverished 45-year-old woman named Mary Baker Patterson took a severe tumble on the ice as she was walking home from a temperance meeting in Lynn, north of Boston. Several days later, after turning to the New Testament for strength and inspiration, Mrs Patterson was suddenly healed, not only of the injuries she'd suffered in the fall, but of the chronic illness that had plagued much of her younger womanhood.

After several years of Bible study, she set out to heal others. In 1875, she posted a notice on her Lynn house designating it as a "Christian Science Home." She was on her way to establishing a major American religious movement at an age when she might have been expected, in her own ironic words, to be a little

The Christian Science Monitor, *a much respected daily newspaper that today claims hundreds of thousands of readers worldwide, was founded by Mary Baker Eddy in 1908, at the age of 87.*

BELOW: the Christian Science Church Center.

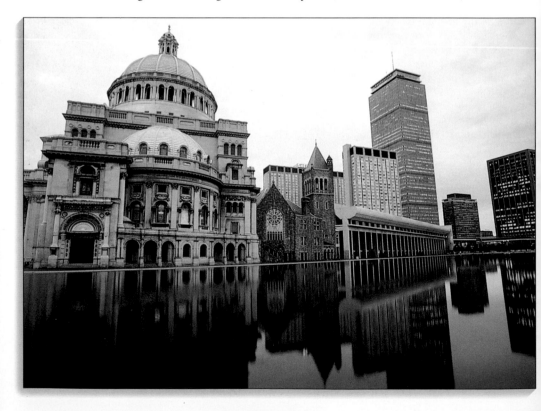

old lady in a lace cap. After marrying a follower named Asa Eddy, she moved to Boston, where she continued teaching, writing and guiding the establishment of her church. Since then more than 3,000 Christian Science societies have been established in some 50 countries.

Map on pages 102–3

Copley Square

Follow Dartmouth Street to Boylston for one of the city's most stimulating displays of architecture: Copley Square. First, Charles McKim's **Boston Public Library** ㉙ (1895). This simple, serene and high-minded Parnassus might well be the center of the Boston that claims to be the "Athens of America." What better monument to a literary legacy populated by the likes of Emerson, Hawthorne, Thoreau and Alcott? (Bret Hart once observed that in these parts it was impossible to fire a pistol without bringing down the author of a two-volume work.) With more than 5 million volumes, this is one of the great libraries in the world. But it's more than a building of books. There's art everywhere – murals by Sargent, statues by Saint-Gaudens and Daniel Chester French – and, at the center of a maze of stairs and passages, a peaceful inner courtyard. Philip Johnson's massive but compatible 1972 addition completes the complex.

A "Duck Tour", in a World War II amphibious vehicle, includes a ride on the River Charles. Tours start from the Prudential Center.

Across the square stands H. H. Richardson's wonderful **Trinity Church** ㉚ (1877), a tour de force in Romanesque inventiveness and a striking medievalist contrast to the Public Library's classicism. Inside, what impresses is the wealth of murals, mosaics, carvings and stained glass.

Above everything looms I. M. Pei & Partners' magnificent blue-green mirror, the **John Hancock Mutual Life Insurance Tower** ㉛, built in 1976. The Tower initially had a propensity in windy weather to lose the huge sheets of

BELOW: Copley Square Park.

glass covering it; miraculously, no one was hurt when the glass fell. That problem was solved soon after the tower was completed, when all 10,344 panes – some 13 acres (5 hectares) worth – were replaced at a cost of $8.5 million. One of Boston's top attractions used to be the magnificent view from the 60th-floor observatory, but it was closed for security reasons after the terrorist attacks on New York and the Pentagon in September 2001.

Every April, on Patriots' Day, Copley Square becomes the destination of the thousands who enter the famous Boston Marathon, perhaps the most celebrated running event on the planet.

The first Boston Marathon, staged in 1897, involved 15 runners. Today, about 8,000 line up for the starter's gun as 1½ million spectators look on.

South End and The Fenway

To the south and east of the Christian Science Center and Copley Square sprawls the South End, an ethnically diverse, up-and-coming expanse of Victorian bowfront townhouses. Particularly pleasing architecturally are the areas around Worcester Square, Rutland and leafy Union Park Square.

The **Boston Center for the Arts ㉜**, at Clarendon and Tremont streets (tel: 617-426 5000), is almost always hopping: this lively complex encompasses artists' studios and galleries, several small experimental theaters, the Cyclorama (an 1884 dome now used for antique markets and special exhibits and events), and one of the city's favorite bistros, Hamersley's.

From the South End, Huntington Avenue leads southwest past several of Boston's greatest institutions. At the northwest corner of Massachusetts Avenue ("Mass Ave") stands the majestic gable-roofed **Symphony Hall ㉝** (tel: 617-536 0944 or 800-274 8499; tours by appointment), the acoustically impeccable 1900 building that is home to the renowned Boston Symphony Orchestra and, in summer, its less formal offshoot, the Boston Pops Orchestra. Tickets can be hard to come by, but any amount of exertion will be well rewarded.

BELOW: the John Hancock Tower.

Continuing down Huntington Avenue, one arrives at the spectacular **Museum of Fine Arts ㉞** (open daily; Wed till 9:45pm; also West Wing Thur and Fri till 9:45pm; entrance fee; reduced admission Wed 4–9pm, Thur and Fri after 5pm). Built in 1909 to house holdings that were bursting the joints of an earlier building situated in Copley Square, Guy Lowell's imposing design affords space for plenty of Impressionists – including the largest number of Monets outside France. This impressive museum boasts the most complete assemblage of Asian art under one roof anywhere; the world's best collection of 19th-century American art; and the finest collection of Egyptian Old Kingdom objects outside Cairo. The latter includes what some consider one of the greatest portraits ever executed by the human hand – a limestone bust of Prince Ankh-haf (2520 BC) that is wholly unearthly in its magnificence.

In 1981, I. M. Pei added a stone-clad, glass-topped new wing that perfectly complements the original building and creates an inspiring, expansive space ideal for a changing array of exhibits. From spring through early fall, the **Japanese Garden**, beside the West Wing, is fragrant and restful. (*For more on the museum, see pages 134–5).*

Within sight of the Museum of Fine Arts stands the **Isabella Stewart Gardner Museum** ③ (280 The Fenway; open Tues–Sun; entrance fee) an exquisite 1903 neo-Venetian palazzo assembled by Boston's most flamboyant grande dame. The unstoppable "Mrs Jack" may have scandalized Brahmin Boston (she was known to parade two pet lions down Beacon Street), but she proved a generous and astute patron of the arts.

During the 1890s, she set her sights on such masterpieces as Titian's *Rape of Europa*, Rembrandt's *Storm on the Sea of Galilee*, and Vermeer's *The Concert*. In 1896, when her collection was bursting the seams of two adjoining Beacon Hill brownstones, she commissioned her fantasy palace at the very edge of town, alongside the marshes of the Fens.

The galleries that frame the four-story glass-roofed courtyard remained, by her posthumous order, unchanged until March 1990, when thieves, disguised as policemen, made off with works of art worth $300 million, including the Vermeer, three Rembrandts, five works by Degas and a Manet. To date, none has been recovered. There is still much to see, however, and this eclectic collection, displayed in a charmingly hodge-podge fashion, constitutes one of the great small museums in the world.

North of the museums broods another of Boston's great shrines, **Fenway Park** ⑥ (4 Yawkey Way; tours weekdays 10am–2pm on non-game days only; tel: 617-267 8661 or 617-267 1700) on whose brightly-lit green baseball diamond the Boston Red Sox do heroic, if usually tragic, battle for the pennant. Here, as the world turns slowly during a muggy twilight doubleheader, the out-of-towner can experience first-hand how Boston turns sport into religion. Indeed, such past stars as Ted Williams and Carl Yastrzemski are almost deified.

Map on pages 102–3

TIP

A delightful way to spend a Sunday afternoon in winter is to attend a concert in the Gardner Museum's Tapestry Room. Tickets at the door, or tel: 617-734 1359.

BELOW: the courtyard of the Isabella Stewart Gardner Museum.

Henry Moore's Three-piece reclining figure, draped, on the MIT campus.

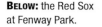

BELOW: the Red Sox at Fenway Park.

The home of the Boston Celtics, one of the success stories of the National Basketball Association, and the Bruins, Boston's major ice-hockey team is the state-of-the-art **FleetCenter** ❸, near North Station.

On the banks of the Charles River

Great cities embrace great rivers from which they are inseparable. This is true of Boston. Here, before the townhouses of Back Bay, the Charles River, having meandered 40 miles (64 km) from its source, widens into a large basin, like a giant mirror held up to the city's profile. It was designed to do just that, by the civic-minded citizens who created the Charles River Dam in 1908. The dam itself is home to Boston's **Museum of Science** ❸ (open daily; Fri till 9pm; entrance fee). Here, visitors can watch simulated lightning, climb into a model of the Apollo lunar module, cower under a plastic Tyrannosaurus Rex, and enjoy a wide variety of ever-changing hands-on exhibits.

In ensuing decades after the construction of the dam, the **Esplanade** was landscaped, a winding park of lagoons, trees and walks. Once a festering, polluted eyesore, the river's edge has become one of the city's favorite places to stretch its legs. Roller skaters wired for sound, joggers, bike riders and sunbathers all migrate here. So do the great crowds that turn out to hear the Boston Pops play under open summer skies at the **Hatch Memorial Shell** ❸.

In Cambridge, but separate from the other sights of Cambridge and across Harvard Bridge, is the **Massachusetts Institute of Technology (MIT)** ❹. Housed in solid, geometrical buildings, as impersonal and mysterious as natural laws, MIT produces Nobel laureates, new scientific advances and White House science advisors with absolute reliability. The Finnish architect Eero Saarinen

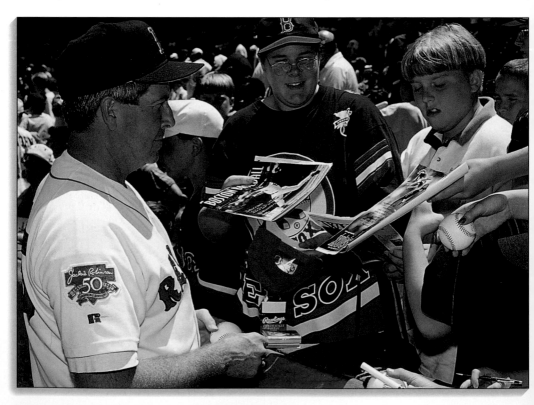

designed two of its highlights: the inward looking, cylindrical MIT Chapel, illuminated by light reflected from a moat, and the tent-like Kresge Auditorium which rises from a circular brick terrace, its roof apparently balanced by slender metal rods on three points.

Separate, too, from sights in central Boston but a point of pilgrimage for many, is the **John F. Kennedy Library and Museum** ❹ (Columbia Point; MBTA red line south to JFK/UMass and shuttle bus; or, in summer, boat from Long Wharf; open daily; entrance fee). Set dramatically beside the ocean, the museum makes excellent use of film, videos and recreated settings (including the Oval Office) to recall JFK's life, career, and legacy.

Cambridge and Harvard Square

Elizabeth Hardwick once described Boston and Cambridge as two ends of the same mustache. Indeed, across the Charles lies a separate city that is absolutely inseparable from its companion metropolis. Neither suburb nor next town down the pike, Cambridge is the brains of the act, the nerve center of the body.

At the heart of Cambridge is lively **Harvard Square** ❹, the playground of book stores, coffee houses, and shops to the west and north of the Yard, with a menagerie of horn-rimmed professors, "B School" overachievers and fresh-looking undergraduates in evidence. At its center, as a matrix for all wanderings, is the international **Out of Town News**, housed in a historic kiosk, and beside it, Dmitri Hadzi's gently humorous stone sculpture, *Omphalos*, suggesting that Harvard is, as its supporters have long held, the center (or navel) of the universe.

Opposite Out of Town News is the venerable **Harvard Cooperative Society** ("Coop" for short), a Harvard institution founded in 1882 as an alternative to

Maps:
102–3
& 127

The JFK Library is one of nine "presidential libraries," which hold the papers of nine of the presidents since Herbert Hoover. Presidents may establish a library in the location of their choice; this one was set up near the home of Rose Kennedy, JFK's mother.

BELOW: busking in Harvard Square.

overpriced local shops; today the prices are pretty much at a par (except for affiliated students and faculty, who enjoy a discount), but the full-scale department store is a favorite with tourists for Harvard-seal mementos.

Every block presents some window or door to investigate. Browse the fine bookstores such as WordsWorth and the Harvard Book Store, check the movie schedules at the area's local collegiate-oriented theaters. There's even a great old tobacco store, a dark cave called Leavitt and Peirce, that carries an interesting collection of ruminative games. In fair weather, chess masters invariably hold court – and court challengers – at the Au Bon Pain café within Holyoke Center, a Harvard administrative building that now hosts a corridor of inviting restaurants and shops.

Nearby, on Dunster Street, is a mecca for ice cream fans, Herrell's, and John Harvard's Brew House, an atmospheric brew pub based on the conceit that Harvard's pious benefactor was descended from brew masters.

Standing proudly above the red brick and green ivy, are the spires of **Harvard University**, America's oldest institution of higher learning. Self-confident and backed by enormous wealth, Harvard has been a world index of intellectual accomplishment almost since that day in 1638 when the first 12 freshmen convened in a single frame house bordered by cow pastures. The alma mater of six American presidents to date, Harvard remains a formidable force.

The heart of the place is **Harvard Yard ❽**, withdrawn tranquilly behind the walls that separate it from Harvard Square outside. Passing through the gate that proclaims "Enter to Grow in Wisdom," the visitor enters a hallowed world of grass and trees, ghosts and venerable brick – a living, eminently walkable museum of American architecture from colonial times to the present.

BELOW: Harvard Square and its historic news stand.

Map on page 127

Massachusetts Hall (1720), Harvard's oldest standing building, shows the beautiful simplicity of its period, but its history is complex. While it has always provided students with rooms, the Hall has also quartered Revolutionary troops, as well as housed a lecture hall, a famous drama workshop and, since 1939, the offices of the University president. Nearby stands little Holden Chapel (1744), once described as "a solitary English daisy in a field of Yankee dandelions."

At the Yard's center stands Charles Bulfinch's University Hall, built of white granite in 1815. In front is Daniel Chester French's 1814 statue of John Harvard, the young Puritan minister for whom the college was named after he left it half his estate and all his books. Since no likeness of John Harvard existed, French fashioned an idealized figure for his statue, using a student as his model.

East of University Hall, three massive buildings set off the central green on which commencement is celebrated each June. These are H. H. Richardson's 1880 masterwork Sever Hall, with its subtle brick decorations; Memorial Church (1932), with its Doric columns; and the monumental Widener Library, fronted by a broad flight of steps and 12 stone columns. Given by the mother of one Harry Elkins Widener, who died on the *Titanic*, the library is the center of Harvard's network of 92 libraries, which together house over 12 million volumes, America's third largest book collection.

Around this historic core, the university sprawls throughout central Cambridge. The Harvard Houses (1930), between the Yard and the Charles, represent a return to the Georgian traditions of the 19th century. These are the residences of sophomores, juniors and seniors. To the east of the Yard stands the **Carpenter Center for the Visual Arts ☉** (1963), a cubist, machine-like design that represents the only American work of the great French architect

Chess is traditionally played in Harvard Square.

BELOW: a regatta at Cambridge Boat Club, on the Charles River.

Map on page 127

TIP

Admission to the Harvard University Art Museums is free on Saturday mornings 10–12am.

BELOW: Longfellow House, Brattle Street. **RIGHT:** students with founding father John Harvard.

Le Corbusier. Harvard extends even beyond the banks of the Charles; the Business School is across the river, and the Medical School is near the Museum of Fine Arts.

Of special interest to visitors are the university's museums. Just outside the Yard to the east are the **Fogg and Busch-Reisinger Art Museums D** (32 Quincy Street; open Mon–Sat, Sun pm; entrance fee except on Sat am). The Fogg's massive holdings include such masterpieces as Van Gogh's *Self Portrait*, Renoir's *Seated Bather*, Fra Angelico's *Crucifixion* and several early Picassos. It also owns a world-class collection of Chinese cave paintings and archaic Chinese jade. Adjoining the Fogg, Werner Otto Hall houses central and northern European art. Housed in the same building, the Busch-Reisinger has outstanding examples of German expressionism and Bauhaus artifacts. Along the street, the **Arthur Sackler Museum E** (open Mon–Sat; Sun pm; entrance fee except on Sat am) houses the Ancient, Islamic and Oriental collections.

A few blocks north on Oxford Street stands a huge complex housing four science museums. The displays are old-fashioned – they are university collections, after all – but a major draw is the **Botanical Museum F** (open Mon–Sat; Sun pm; entrance fee), with its famous "Glass Flowers," a collection of true-to-life models of more than 700 plant species executed by Leopold Blaschka and his son Rudolph in 19th-century Dresden. In the same building, the **Museum of Comparative Zoology** includes George Washington's pheasants (inevitably in stuffed form) as well as the world's oldest reptile eggs. Also on the site are the **Mineralogical and Geological Museum**, and the **Peabody Museum of Archaeology and Ethnology**, which has an interesting shop reflecting its anthropological collections.

On July 4, 1775, George Washington assumed command of the Continental Army on **Cambridge Common G**. A trio of cannons abandoned by the British when they left Boston in 1776 stand close to a bronze relief of Washington on horseback under an elm tree; the elm enclosed by a fence is a token replacement of the original "Washington's elm." On the south side of the Common, just across Garden Street, Christ Church (1761) was used as a barracks by patriots, and its organ pipes were made into bullets. Close by is an entrance to **Radcliffe College H**, the women's college that merged with Harvard in 1975.

In the 18th century Brattle Street was home to so many British loyalists that it was known as Tory Row. There are numerous houses the visitor can admire from the street, including No. 90, designed by H. H. Richardson of Trinity Church fame, and No. 94, the 17th-century Henry Vassal House. The yellow clapboard **Longfellow House I** (105 Brattle Street; open May–Oct; tours Wed–Sun; entrance fee) was the idyllic wedding present given to the poet Henry Wadsworth Longfellow and his wife, Fanny, by her father in 1843. Little has changed inside; Longfellow's library and furniture are here, including a chair made from the "spreading chestnut-tree," which stood at No. 56 Brattle Street and was immortalized in Longfellow's poem *The Village Blacksmith*. Unhappily, Fanny was fatally burned in the house in 1861. ❏

Map on pages 102–3

THE FREEDOM TRAIL

Given the dense traffic, it's simpler to walk in Boston than to drive.
Taking advantage of that fact, this signed route provides an
easy way of absorbing the city's revolutionary history

BELOW: Paul Revere as portrayed by John Singleton Copley in 1768.

The shot heard round the world – the starting gun of the American Revolution – was fired in Lexington, just west of Boston, on April 18, 1775. In the months and years that followed, until the war for American independence from Britain ended in 1781, Boston would continue to play a leading role in the conflict. The "midnight ride of Paul Revere" (made famous in the poem by Henry Wadsworth Longfellow), the Boston Tea Party, the Battle of Bunker Hill – all are part of Boston's colorful Revolutionary past.

In Lexington and Concord, which today are suburbs of Boston, national parks preserve the legacy of the conflict's beginnings. And in the heart of Boston, a cleverly designed 2½-mile (4-km) footpath, the Freedom Trail, invites visitors to experience Boston as it was in the Revolutionary era, to visit historical sites associated with the war, and to walk where the founders of the country walked more than 200 years ago. It is estimated that some 3 million people visit the Freedom Trail each year.

Although most of the trail follows city streets, it is not advisable to drive it: Downtown Boston is famously hard to negotiate with a car, and parking spaces are hard to find and pricey. The Freedom Trail is easy to follow as a self-guided tour – just follow the red brick road (or more accurately in many places, the red painted line). At some sites, costumed interpreters and docents greet trail-walkers.

It takes an hour or so to walk the length of the trail at a brisk pace, but to appreciate the history of its 16 official sites, you should allow at least a half-day. Detailed brochures and guidebooks are available at the information booth (tel: 617-227 8800) at the start of the trail on Boston Common at Tremont Street.

Walkers may begin anywhere along the Trail, but the logical starting point is the Common, itself a mustering ground for Colonial militia before and during the Revolutionary War. Today, the Common is one of the most beloved public spaces in Boston – a 45-acre swath of green that is overlooked by the gold dome of the State House.

From Boston Common, the Freedom Trail leads to the Old Granary Burying Ground adjacent to the Park Street Church on Tremont Street. Revolutionary heroes such as Samuel Adams, John Hancock, Paul Revere, and James Otis are buried here.

Nearby is King's Chapel, built of granite in 1749 and containing the largest bell ever cast in Paul Revere's foundry. Revere, one of the best-known patriots of the Revolution, lived in the North End and was a silver- and metalsmith by trade. Among those buried in the King's Chapel Burying Ground (the city's oldest graveyard) is William Dawes, the lesser-known of the two Lexington messenger-riders who carried the warning that the British were on the march. (Dawes's name is less well known than Revere's in part because he took a longer route to reach Lexington and so arrived later than his compatriot did.)

At the 1729 Old South Meeting House, one of the most notable sites of the Revolutionary era, a small historical museum includes a scale-model diorama depicting Colonial-era Boston. A crowd of 5,000 rallied at Old South on December 16, 1773 to oppose the British tea tax. Following the meeting, the Sons of Liberty headed off to dump a shipload of British tea into Boston Harbor in a famous protest, an incident later known as the Boston Tea Party.

From here the trail leads to the Old State House. Boston's oldest public building was built in 1713 to serve as the center of political life in the emerging Massachusetts Bay Colony. The proclamation of the Declaration of Independence was read to Boston citizens on July 18, 1776. Afterward, in a gesture of elated defiance, two leftover symbols of British rule – a lion and a unicorn – were removed from the roof of the State House and burned. Today, the landmark Old State House is dwarfed by towering financial center buildings.

Wending its way through Faneuil Hall Marketplace (a key meeting point for Boston's revolutionaries), the Freedom Trail heads into the North End. The North End is the oldest section of Boston: its narrow, crooked streets were laid out over what were originally cow paths. Here, at 19 North Square, is the steep-roofed wooden house that belonged to Paul Revere. Already almost 100 years old when Revere bought it in 1770, the little peaked house where the patriot lived for some 30 years is the oldest structure in Boston.

Not far away, on Paul Revere Mall, a statue of Revere on horseback in front of the Old North Church is one of Boston's most-photographed sites. A pair of lanterns hung in the Old North (whose steeple has since been replaced) on the eve of the war signaled that the British forces were leaving Boston (then almost an island) by sea, rather than by land.

From the North End, the Freedom Trail crosses the Charlestown Bridge to Charlestown. (An inexpensive water shuttle runs between Charlestown and Long Wharf, near the trail, making it possible to go one way on foot and the other by ferry.) Here a 221-foot (66-meter) granite obelisk commemorates the June 17, 1775 Battle of Bunker Hill. Here, on what is actually Breed's Hill, the Colonials hastily built an earthwork fort in anticipation of a British attack. During the ensuing battle, which was ultimately a British victory, the revolutionaries managed to strike a resounding blow by wounding or killing about half the British force.

"The Whites of Their Eyes," a half-hour audio-visual presentation on the battle, is shown in the Bunker Hill Pavilion near the Charlestown Navy Yard. Berthed nearby is the frigate USS *Constitution* – not part of Boston's Revolutionary past, but famous as the oldest commissioned warship afloat in the world. Her first mission after being launched in Boston in 1797 was to guard the new country's commercial interests in the Caribbean against the French. During the War of 1812, she earned the nickname Old Ironsides, by which she has been known ever since. ❏

The Freedom Trail is self-guided and can be joined at any point.

BELOW: the Bunker Hill Monument, Charlestown.

THE MUSEUM OF FINE ARTS, BOSTON

Few museums in the world rival the MFA for the quality and scope of its decorative and fine art collections. Every one has something exceptional

One of the first museums in America, the MFA opened in 1870 and in 1909 moved into the present building. Cyrus Edwin Dallin's bronze equestrian statue *Appeal to the Great Spirit* (left) was placed in the forecourt in 1913.

The highly cultured citizens of 19th-century Boston were keen collectors. Many were passionate about things Asian, and their treasures in due course came to the MFA, forming the nucleus of an outstanding collection. Others travelled to Europe, and the museum acquired one of the foremost holdings outside Paris of Impressionist painting, in particular works by Monet, Pissaro, Sisley, Renoir and Manet. It has nearly 70 works by Jean-François Millet. The American art collection is one of the best in the US; the European and American decorative arts rooms display superb silver, porcelain, furniture and musical instruments. The Nubian and Egyptian collections are unrivalled in the world.

There is so much to see, the first-time visitor would be well advised either to pick out just one collection, or take a (free) tour that highlights the best from all the collections. *See also page 124.*

▽ **AMERICAN DECORATIVE ARTS**
The museum is strong in decorative arts from pre-Civil War New England. Below: a Paul Revere teapot, *c.*1760–5.

△ **THE JAPANESE GARDEN**
Tenshin-en, "The Garden of the Heart of Heaven," is one of three gardens in which visitors may draw breath (beside the West Wing; open spring through early fall).

▷ **THE IMPRESSIONISTS**
Renoir's *Dance at Bougival* (1883) shares wall space with equally important works by such European painters as van Gogh, Degas, and Gauguin.

◁ LANDSCAPE ART

The New England landscape is captured in works by such American artists as Winslow Homer and Edward Hopper. Left: Edward Hopper's watercolour *Lighthouse and Buildings, Portland Head, Cape Elizabeth* (1927)

△ AMERICAN ART

The Letter by Mary Cassatt (1890). More formal are the portraits by colonial painters Gilbert Stuart and John Singleton Copley, and society portraitist John Singer Sargent.

▽ THE ASIAN COLLECTION

A highlight of the excellent Asian collection is this little 12th-century AD (Jin Dynasty) Chinese buddha, made of lacquered wood with painting and gilding.

THE ANCIENT WORLD

For 40 years from 1905 Harvard University and the Museum of Fine Arts collaborated on an archeological excavation in Egypt, based at the Great Pyramids at Giza. From this, the museum acquired a world-famous collection of Egyptian treasures. Among many Old Kingdom sculptures is this beautiful statue of King Mycerinus, who built the Third Pyramid at Giza, and his queen, dated to *c.*2548–30BC.

Other treasures include gilded and painted mummy masks, and some amazingly well preserved hierglyphic inscriptions. The Giza expedition's director, Dr Reisner, also worked in the Sudan and brought home a dazzling collection of Nubian artifacts, the best in the world outside Khartoum. Particularly awe-inspiring is the exquisite gold jewelry, inlaid with enamel and precious stones, and the sculptures, varying in size from huge statues of Nubian kings to tiny shawabtis.

Boston Daytrips

0   10 miles
0   10 km

BOSTON DAYTRIPS

We've either read them or we've read about them: the witches of Salem, the Pilgrims of Plymouth, the Patriots of Lexington, and the writers – Alcott, Emerson and Thoreau – of Concord

Map on page 138

CANADA

Boston

E ven Boston's most committed devotees would concede that one of the city's strengths is its scope for daytrips, from the hugely popular cultural epicenters such as Plymouth to offbeat delights such as a Gropius house in suburban Lincoln. Public transportation from Boston makes many of the places described easy to reach; frequent commuter rail services from North Station serve Concord, Salem (for buses to Marblehead), Rockport, Manchester, Gloucester and Ipswich, and there are buses from South Station to Plymouth, New Bedford, Fall River and Newburyport; the T Red Line goes to Quincy Center. Providence (*see page 230*) is another easy daytrip by train from South Station, and buses from South Station serve Newport (*see page 233*).

The North Shore

Once home to a magnificent merchant fleet and a thriving shipbuilding industry and now busy with yachts, **Newburyport ❶**, 35 miles (56 km) north of Boston, has benefited from careful preservation to retain a period flavor. The town survived a devastating fire in 1811 – after which numerous handsome brick buildings were constructed. But by the early 20th century, the arrival of freighters had reduced the proud shipbuilding industry of "Clipper City" to an aging relic. The **Maritime Museum** (Derby Street; open daily; entrance fee) within the former Custom House tells the story.

However, an exemplary renewal program begun in the 1960s has restored Newburyport's beauty and popularity. The **Market Square** district is a symphony of brick and bustle, with fine shops and restaurants, plus live outdoor entertainment in good weather, when strolls along the boardwalk can be enjoyed. Whale-watching trips are big business.

On High Street successful sea captains built their Greek Revival and late Georgian palaces, some with the symbolic "widow's walks" atop the roofs, where anxious wives strained for a glimpse of their husbands' return to port. **The Cushing House**, (open May–Oct Tues–Sat; entrance fee) at No. 98 High Street, belonged to Caleb Cushing, a 19th-century lawyer (Newburyport's first mayor) and the first US Ambassador to China. Visitors to the house, now home to the Historical Society of Old Newbury, can view the exotic booty he brought back.

Just 3 miles (5 km) away via Water Street from Newburyport is the **Parker River National Wildlife Refuge ❷**, known simply as **Plum Island**. Depending on the season, the 6 miles (10 km) of sand dunes and ocean beach yield a riot of false heather, dune grass, scrub pine and delicious wild beach plums and cranberries. Geese, pheasants, rab-

PRECEDING PAGES: Annisquam, Cape Ann. **BELOW:** Newburyport.

bits, deer, woodchucks, turtles and toads roam freely over the preserve. In March and October the skies are black with migrating geese and ducks. Fishing, hiking and bird-watching are encouraged. Only a limited number of visitors (350 cars; parking fee) are allowed into the refuge at one time.

City and country meet about 4 miles (7 km) out of town in the **Spencer-Pierce-Little Farm** (Route 1A; tours June–mid-Oct Wed–Sun; entrance fee), a manor house built around 1675–1700 and now owned by the Society for the Preservation of New England Antiquities. A distinctively sturdy building for its day (built of stone and brick, instead of the customary wood), it is today, with its layers of structural alteration, a prime site for architectural archeology. Its farmland has been under three and a half centuries of continual cultivation.

The road to Ipswich

Route 1A leads out of Newburyport toward Ipswich along a lazy, tree-lined road, where hand-built stone walls (too low to keep people out but high enough to keep sheep in) give way to quaint roadside stands proffering eggs, apples, ice cream, fresh fish and lobsters-to-go. There are some fine antique bargains to be found along these roads, too.

The old streets of the town of **Ipswich ❸** are lined with restored 17th- and 18th-century houses. On Main Street, the 1640 **Whipple House** is a fine example of a Puritan homestead, furnished in period style and with a colonial herb garden. Out of town, adjacent to the Great House, a breathtakingly showy Stuart-style 59-room mansion (occasionally open for tours) is the **Crane Memorial Reservation**, with 4 miles (7 km) of glorious sandy barrier beach that can be explored by an interpretative trail.

TIP

In the fall, after Labor Day, visitors to Plum Island are allowed to pick beach plums and cranberries – three quarts per person, no rakes permitted.

BELOW: queueing for fried clams at Woodman's, Essex.

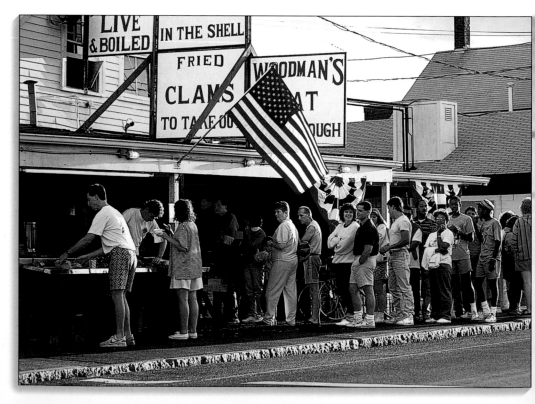

Despite local claims to grandeur, Ipswich is perhaps best known for its humble clams, an obsession it shares with the neighboring town of **Essex** ❹, 5 miles (8 km) southeast on Route 133, where, folk legend has it, the fried clam was born. Raw clams had been a staple of the New England diet since pre-Colonial days, and they're still a regional delicacy. It was at **Woodman's** restaurant (tel: 978-768 6451) that clams were first dipped in batter and fried.

Cape Ann

Named for the mother of England's King Charles I, Cape Ann is practically an island, compact enough to explore in a day. From Annisquam, at the mouth of Ipswich Bay, to Pigeon Cove, the landscape is quintessential New England – quaint fishing villages and a rockbound coast.

The area has witnessed some violent behavior. A gang of pirates led by one John Phillips terrorized Gloucester during the 1720s, until one day a fishing crew gained the upper hand and sailed into Lobster Cove, near Annisquam, with Phillips' head hanging from the mast. Today, life is more sedate and visitors enjoy the vistas of sea, shanty and rugged landscape that have lured such great American artists as Winslow Homer to this lovely peninsula.

An alluring nature reserve can be enjoyed at **Halibut Point State Park** ❺ in the quarries that once provided granite for Boston's buildings. Within the granite-strewn dwarf woods, the original quarry is now a huge pool edged by sheer cliffs; trees open out into heathland and scrub to reveal views over the rocky shore towards Plum Island.

The granite was shipped to ports around the world in the 19th century, from **Rockport** ❻, a bustling former fishing village-turned-artists' colony and tourist

Map on page 138

On a hot July day in 1915, restaurateur Lawrence Woodman was frying potato chips and complaining to a fisherman friend that business was slow. "Toss some clams in with those chips," suggested the friend. Woodman did, and thus created the first fried-clam.

BELOW: the much-painted harbor scene at Rockport.

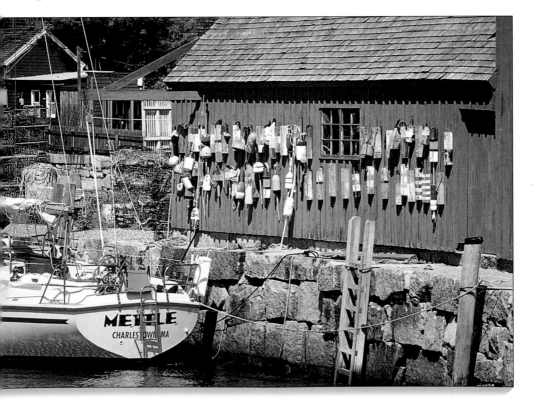

Gloucester was the setting for "The Perfect Storm", Sebastian Junger's 1997 best-seller recounting the loss of the "Andrea Gail" fishing boat in 120-mile-an-hour winds.

TIP

See page 183 for more information on whale-watching trips.

BELOW: Gloucester's most famous fisherman.

attraction. In the early 18th century, the Cape Ann fleet roamed as far south as Havana and as far east as London. The seagoers' cottages crowded on to Bearskin Neck have found a new use as tourist-oriented shops. The fishing shack on the harbor has become known as Motif No. 1 because it is said to be more frequently painted and sketched than any other building in America. Sign-posted off Curtis Street on the edge of the village, the **Paper House** (open July–Aug daily; entrance fee) is an endearing oddity, built entirely of rolled up newspaper reinforced with glue and varnish. Begun in 1924 by an inventor of office supplies (whose wife made the magazine-paper curtains), the project took some 20 years, and includes a desk made of copies of the *Christian Science Monitor*, of which the print is still legible.

Gloucester ❼ is one of the oldest seaports in the United States. Here, Leonard Craske's famous statue of the *Gloucester Fisherman* grips the wheel and peers oceanward, a moving tribute with the legend "they that go down to the sea in ships." The city still has an active fishing fleet, and the catch is processed in plants near the waterfront. Every year, the fishermen, who are predominantly of Portuguese and Italian ancestry, participate in the Blessing of the Fleet cere-mony. The town was the setting for Sebastian Junger's best-selling *The Perfect Storm*, which chronicled the climatic perils that lie in wait for fishermen.

Landlubbers get into the act, too, by taking one of the whale-watching cruises that leave daily from the Cape Ann Marina. To learn more about the heyday of whaling, visit the **Cape Ann Historical Association** (Pleasant Street; open Tues–Sat; entrance fee) for its small but select collection of furnishings and artwork, ranging from 19th-century painter Fitz Hugh Lane's rather sentimen-tal seascapes to semi-abstractions by modernist Milton Avery.

Facing Gloucester across the harbor are two intriguing examples of mono-maniacal nesting instincts. On Eastern Point Boulevard, the early 1900s **Sleeper-McCann House** also known as "Beauport" (open May–Sept daily; Oct weekdays; entrance fee), is a romantic labyrinth of cottagey rooms, using architectural fragments from other buildings. It served as a setting for the summer parties of collector and interior designer, Henry Davis Sleeper. The themes vary entertainingly: one bedroom is in chapel style, the belfry is rich in chinoiserie, and the book tower has wooden "damask" curtains that originated from a hearse.

Just south of Gloucester, off Route 127 on Hesperus Avenue, stands **Hammond Castle** (open Thurs, Fri, Sat; Sun am; entrance fee) the 1920s fantasy abode of organ inventor John Hays Hammond Jr, Hammond plundered Europe for elements to work into his dreamhouse, including a medieval village facade to overlook the indoor pool. The entire castle was built around the monumental 8,200-pipe organ (the largest such instrument in the US in a private home). Some of Hammond's other electronic creations are on show.

Westwards along Route 127 is **Manchester**, a lovely resort town that some still call Manchester-by-the-Sea. The town features stately mansions and Singing Beach, where a bare foot scraped across the hard-packed white sand produces an almost musical squeak.

Maps:
Area 138
City 143

Bewitching Salem.

Salem

Though the scandalous witch trials earned **Salem ❽** enduring notoriety (*see page 144*), the area has much else to recommend it. Salem (on Route 1A south of Route 128; 40 minutes' train journey from North Station) owes its grandeur, now carefully restored, to its former prominence as a seaport. A red line along

A ship's figurehead on display in the Peabody Essex Museum, Salem.

BELOW: Salem's Witch Museum.

the sidewalks marks the route linking the historic sites, which are also connected by trolley services.

On Turner Street is the forbidding-looking **House of the Seven Gables A** (open daily; entrance fee), which inspired Hawthorne's novel of that name; he lived in a smaller house in the grounds – his cousin owned the main house – and worked for a period at the Custom House, now part of the **Salem Maritime National Historic Site B** (open daily). Here visitors may tour the Derby Wharf and a replica of a 19th-century brigantine, the *Republic*, the Custom House, and Derby House, a merchant's mansion built in 1761.

No visit should omit the **Peabody Essex Museum C** (East India Square; open mid-May–mid-Nov, Mon–Sat; Sun pm; mid-Nov–mid-May, closed Mon; entrance fee), which features excellent displays related to the maritime trade – particularly memorable are the ships' figureheads, maritime paintings, views of old Salem and a superb collection of artifacts brought back from the Far East.

On Essex Street, the Essex Institute preserves six houses that span two centuries of New England architecture, from the Colonial/Georgian through to the Federal styles. On the institute's grounds is a museum displaying exhibits of period furniture and local memorabilia.

Salem's maritime glory notwithstanding, most visitors will want to tour the scenes of the infamous witchcraft trials of 1692, no mere instance of "hysteria," as it has so often been described, but essentially an act of political repression. The accusations and trials capped off an intense battle for power and property between the conservative, established gentry and an individualist faction. The gentry, personified by the convicting judges, fell back on the time-honored method of attacking political and social upstarts as moral deviants.

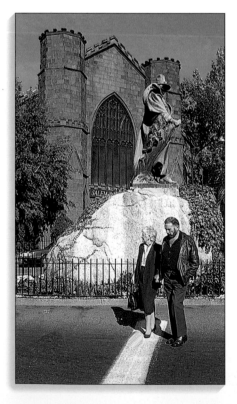

THE SALEM WITCHES

There's a certain grim irony that Salem now makes sweet economic hay out of its dark and witchy past. All year round – but particularly during October, leading up to Hallowe'en – the old seaport touts occult events. Salem's web site (www.haunted-happenings.com) fleshes out gory details on "Terror on the Wharf" and where to purchase a "Fright Pass," for admission to three haunted houses!

Although Salem has a self-proclaimed "resident witch" (Laurie – she's easy to spot), and although the civil rights of witch practitioners have been upheld in Massachusetts, witches weren't always so welcome. Three hundred years ago, when Puritans were self-appointed arbiters of both law and religion, hysteria swept through Salem. Fourteen women and five men were executed (by hanging or pressing with stones) and hundreds were imprisoned. Several more died in jail. The trials grew from the feverish imaginations of adolescent girls who, in January 1692, became swept up in tales of voodoo and mysticism as told to them by Tituba, a slavewoman from Barbados.

Jealousy and greed between townspeople stoked the fire, as one after another pointed an accusing finger at his or her neighbor. The frenzy didn't end until May 1693, when the Governor issued a pardon to those still in jail.

Most moving, for all its silent subtlety, is the **Salem Witch Trials Tercentenary Memorial** ⊙, a stark granite court adjoining Charter Street Burying Point, the final resting place of Witch Trials Court magistrate John Hawthorne. Incised along the paving stones and walls are passages from the accused women's pleas of innocence. The **Salem Witch Museum** ⊖ (Washington Square North; open daily; entrance fee) reenacts, in a rather sensationalist fashion, key scenes to a recorded commentary, while the **Witch Dungeon Museum** ⊖ (Lynde Street; open daily; entrance fee) is another live show evoking the persecutions, with a look at some reconstructed dungeons.

Chestnut Street ranks among America's finest shows of domestic architecture. Open to the public is the **Stephen Phillips Memorial Trust House** ⊙, furnished with the belongings of sea captains.

A short detour from Salem, **Marblehead** ⊙ makes for a refreshing day trip. A former port, it abounds in Federal captains' houses, including the **Jeremiah Lee Mansion** (Washington Street; open mid-May–mid-Oct, Mon–Sat; Sun pm; entrance fee); the pre-Revolutionary Old Town section invites strolling.

Echoes of the work ethic

At 244 Central Street, **Saugus** ⊙, the **Saugus Iron Works** have been reconstructed as they were, with furnace, forge, slitting mill, iron house, ironworks house and blacksmith's shop (open daily; tours at 9.45, 11.15, 2.15 and 3.45; entrance fee). The site was established in 1640 by John Winthrop Jr, who established a "Company of Undertakers of the Iron Works in New England," selling shares to English investors. However, the works were unprofitable owing to high costs and debts, and a shortage of skilled labor.

Maps:
Area 138
City 143

The word Salem derives from the Hebrew "shalom", meaning peace.

BELOW: Salem Harbor.

The one-time model mill town of **Lowell ⓫**, long an industrial dinosaur, is enjoying a renaissance as a major tourist attraction. Sightseeing ferries ply the old canals, trolleys clang through the streets, and looms pound again at the **Boott Cotton Mills Museum** (Market Street; open daily; entrance fee) operated with the Lowell National Historical Park Visitor Center. The many ethnic restaurants are reason enough to go. Added incentive is offered by the **New England Quilt Museum** (Shattuck Street; open Mon–Sat; Sun pm; closed Sun Nov–May; entrance fee) showcasing outstanding piecework, antique to contemporary, and by the **New England Sports Museum** (Shattuck Street; open Mon–Sat; Sun pm; entrance fee) with exciting hands-on displays of all things sporting.

Lexington and Concord

The Minutemen were armed civilians who were prepared to fight at a minute's notice .

The route of the British advance in 1775 through **Lexington ⓬** to **Concord ⓭**, where the opposing ranks met in battle, is designated the **Battle Road**, which although mostly a highway has a number of historical attractions along it, many part of the **Minute Man National Historical Park**. It is sometimes forgotten that the colonists' uprising was a truly conservative revolution, fought largely by well-to-do landowners concerned with a growing British bite out of their profit margins as well as with theories of liberty and participatory democracy.

In the 19th century the town of Concord was a seedbed of literary output. It is remarkable that so many of the cultural giants of America lived within a short stroll of each other. Route 126 out of Concord to **Lincoln ⓮** passes further points of literary and architectural interest.

BELOW: a Memorial Day procession, Concord.

Chronologically, a visit to the Battle Road sites should go east to west. South of Lexington, the **Museum of Our National Heritage ⓯** (Marrett Road; open

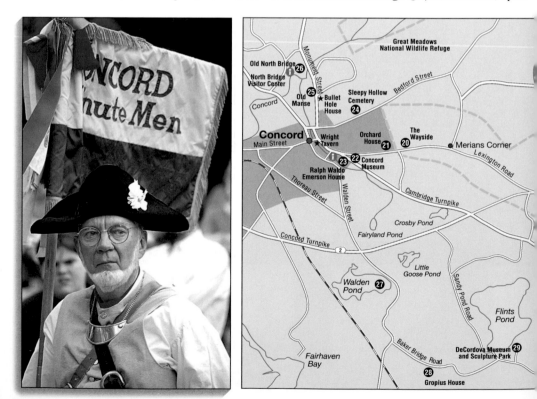

Mon–Sat; Sun pm) exhibits items of American history, with a section on Lexington. The **Munroe Tavern**, a russet-colored building of 1635 on the left side of the Battle Road, served as headquarters for the Redcoats and as a hospital on their retreat from Concord. At the heart of Lexington a statue of Captain John Parker stands on **Battle Green** ⑯, where on April 19, 1775, the first shot was fired (possibly by a nervous 14- or 15-year-old Minuteman whose gun went off accidentally); of the Minutemen, vastly outnumbered, eight were killed.

At the 1690 **Buckman Tavern** (Bedford Street; open Mon–Sat; Sun pm; entrance fee) now restored to its original appearance, Captain Parker and his 77 Minutemen sipped beer while awaiting Paul Revere's warning; a bullet hole is visible in one door. The **Hancock-Clarke House** ⑰ (Hancock Street; open May–Oct Mon–Sat; Sun pm; entrance fee) where John Hancock and Samuel Adams were woken by Paul Revere on the eve of the battle with news of the British advance, contains period furnishings as well as the drum on which William Diamond sounded a warning to his fellow patriots.

At the **Ebenezer Fiske House Site**, a historical trail explains the course of the fierce fighting that broke out there; a section of the Battle Road here is unpaved and closed to traffic, giving an idea of its original appearance.

The **Battle Road Visitor Center** ⑱, part of the National Park, has a movie showing the events of 1775, and there are talks and guided walks. Just to the west is the **Paul Revere Capture Site**, where Revere was taken but Prescott escaped to give the warning to those in Concord. Restored to its condition at the time of the battle, the **Hartwell Tavern** ⑲ hosts re-creations of colonial life.

As you enter Concord the theme digresses into literature. **The Wayside** ⑳ (455 Lexington Road, Route 2A; open May–Oct Thur–Tues; entrance fee) links

Maps: Pages 138 & below

The American flag still flies on the Buckman Tavern in Concord, where the Minutemen were warned that the British troops were on their way.

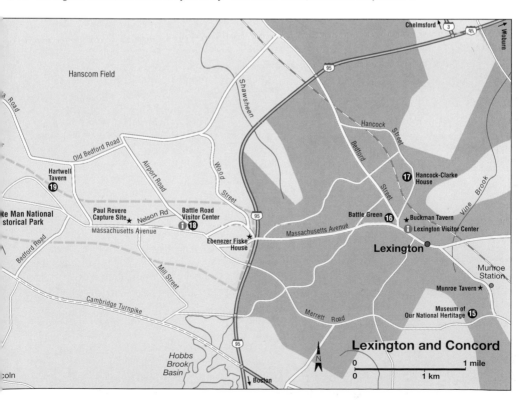

Lexington and Concord

0 ——————— 1 mile
0 ——————— 1 km

Transcendentalist thinker Henry David Thoreau.

the battle with the literary figures, for here Samuel Whitney, the muster master of the Concord Militia, lived during the Revolution. From 1845 to 1848 it was home to the Alcotts, and was purchased in 1852 by writer Nathaniel Hawthorne – he added the tower, but found it unsatisfactory for working in, and declared that he would happily see the house burn down.

Close by, the Alcott family lived from 1858 to 1877 at **Orchard House ㉑** (Lexington Road, Route 2A; open Mon–Sat; Sun pm; closed Jan 1–15; entrance fee) where Louisa May Alcott penned her first novel, *Moods*, as well as the hugely popular *Little Women* and *Little Men*, and hospital sketches of the Civil War, which became serialized. The Alcotts were initially a poor family, whose fortunes were reversed by the revenue from Louisa's writings. Her father, Bronson Alcott, founded the Concord School of Philosophy next door, which functioned from 1880 to 1888; the building still stands.

Near the junction of the Battle Road with Route 2, **Concord Museum ㉒** (200 Lexington Road, Route 2A; open Mon–Sat; Sun pm; entrance fee) has – in addition to samplers, period rooms and costumes – excellent displays relating to Revolutionary and literary Concord, including one of the two lanterns hung by Robert Newman in Old North Church in Boston. The gallery devoted to Thoreau has the largest collection of artifacts associated with the great author and naturalist, including furnishings from his cabin by Walden Pond. Ralph Waldo Emerson's study has been transferred here in its entirety for fear of fire, brought from the **Ralph Waldo Emerson House ㉓** (28 Cambridge Turnpike; open May–Oct Thur–Sat; Sun pm; entrance fee) just across Route 2, where Emerson resided from 1835 until his death in 1882 and wrote his transcendentalist works. Most of the furniture is Emerson's.

BELOW:
Walden Pond today.

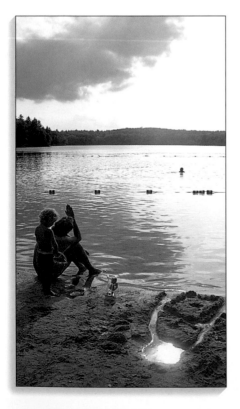

LITERARY CONCORD

If there were a Hall of Fame for 19th-century New England authors, it would have to be in Concord, Massachusetts. In this upper-middle class, rural town about 20 miles (32 km) northwest of Boston, some of the brightest lights of American fiction, poetry and philosophy during the transcendentalist years of the 1870s and 1880s lived and worked. Most are buried in Concord as well, on Author's Ridge in Sleepy Hollow Cemetery.

Ralph Waldo Emerson, Henry David Thoreau, Nathaniel Hawthorne and Louisa May Alcott all spent time in Concord, where they played host to a cavalcade of other literary luminaries that included Henry Wadsworth Longfellow, Henry James, Oliver Wendell Holmes, Walt Whitman and James Russell Lowell. Unlike some authors who work in relative obscurity and then become famous posthumously, the Concord writers were celebrities in their own time – so much so that Alcott (the popular author of *Little Women*) satirized the public's adulation and its fascination with Concord, suggesting (with tongue in cheek) that a hotel be built for the tourists and furnished with "Alcott's rustic furniture, the beds made of Thoreau's pine boughs, and the sacred fires fed from the Emersonian woodpile."

Sleepy Hollow Cemetery ㉔ is the resting place of most of the Concord big names, among them Hawthorne, the Alcotts, Emerson and Thoreau. **The Old Manse** ㉕ (Monument Street; open mid-Apr–Oct Mon–Sat; Sun pm; entrance fee) was built by minister William Emerson around 1770, and was used as a sanctuary for women and children in the battle. It became home to his grandson Ralph Waldo Emerson, who wrote *Nature* (1836) here, and was rented for three years to Nathaniel Hawthorne. Thus it preserves layers of history, with mementos of both these great men – a huge book collection and Hawthorne's desk.

At **Old North Bridge** ㉖ (a replica) where General Gage's British troops, crowded into the narrow pathway, were easily routed by the ragtag Americans, an obelisk marks where the first British soldier fell. Cross the bridge, pass Daniel Chester French's *Minute Man* statue, unveiled for the centennial of the famous fight, and walk up to the North Bridge Visitor Center.

South of Concord off Route 126, Thoreau spent 26 months in a one-room cabin (no longer in existence) by **Walden Pond** ㉗ living in experimental self-sufficiency and recording the progress of nature through the year, all of which he recounted in *Walden* (1854). The pond is now the focus of a state park.

At Lincoln, off Route 126, is the **Gropius House** ㉘ (68 Baker Bridge Road; open June–mid-Oct, Wed–Sun; mid-Oct–May, weekends; entrance fee), built in 1938 by the seminal Bauhaus architect; it is now the most modern of the historic homes preserved by the Society for the Preservation of New England Antiquities. The **DeCordova Museum and Sculpture Park** ㉙ (off Route 2 or Route 128; open Tues–Sun; entrance fee) shows contemporary work in a turreted 1880 mansion; the grounds house oversize sculpture (often playful in mood) and an outdoor theater ideal for a summertime series of jazz concerts.

The Minute Man *statue, by Daniel Chester French, on* Old North Bridge, *Concord.*

Below: Old North Bridge, Concord.

The South Shore and Plymouth

Within 8 miles (13 km) of Boston, the **Adams National Historical Site** (Adams Street; open daily; entrance fee) at **Quincy ㉚** includes the house built in 1731 and repeatedly enlarged, home to four generations of the illustrious Adams family, among them a unique father-and-son presidential pair, John Adams (second President of the US), and his son, John Quincy Adams (the sixth). High points of the tour are the stone library, packed with 14,000 volumes, and the formal garden, especially appealing when the daffodils are in bloom. The Adams birthplaces, 17th-century saltbox farmhouses, also form part of the National Historical Site.

Further down the coast is **Hingham ㉛**, beautified by Frederick Law Olmsted, creator of Boston's Emerald Necklace (*see page 115*) and Central Park, New York; his handiwork here is the **World's End Reservation**, a 250-acre harbor-side estate that is a protectorate of the Trustees of the Reservations. Also noteworthy, at the center of town, is the **Old Ship Meetinghouse**, the oldest wooden church in America in continuous use. Built by ship's carpenters in 1681, the interior resembles a giant hull turned upside down.

Enclosing Hingham Bay and curving toward Boston like a beckoning finger is the sandy spit of **Nantasket**, a long-time summer playground (note the 1928 Carousel under the Clock) grown tacky over the years but still offering, from the tiny town of Hull at the tip, an optimal view of Boston Light, said to be the oldest operating lighthouse in America. The **Hull Lifesaving Museum** (1117 Nantasket Avenue; open June–Sept, Wed–Sun; Oct–May, Fri–Sun; entrance fee) gives a good idea of the heroic measures required when the lighthouse warnings didn't succeed in staving off disaster.

Abigail Adams is remembered today not only as the wife and mother of a president (a unique distinction), but as the mother of American feminism; in 1776, she urged her husband to "Remember the Ladies" at the fateful Continental Congress where independence was declared.

BELOW: the Adams Homestead, Quincy.

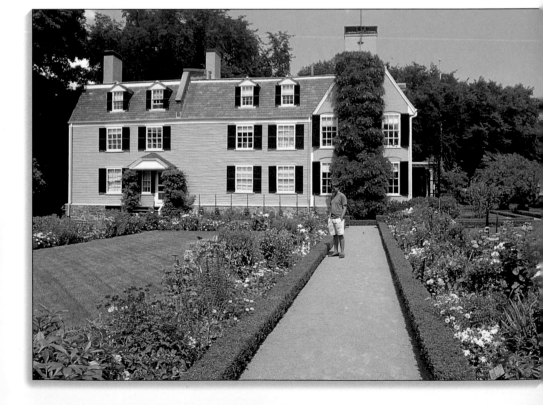

Directly southward lies **Plymouth** ㉜, which proudly claims the distinction of being "America's Home Town." Earlier attempts at colonization had been assayed, but, thanks to the Pilgrims' grit and determination, this was the first to make a go of it. The very rock they landed on (or so the story goes, passed down to the next generation) enjoys a place of honor under an elaborate portico overlooking the harbor.

The **Pilgrim Hall** (Court Street; open Feb–Dec daily; entrance fee), the first custom-built museum in the US, designed in 1824 by Alexander Parris, gathered the more outstanding relics of Pilgrim life early on (though they are rather unimaginatively displayed), and several houses from the period still survive in town, tucked in haphazardly among younger contenders. Actually, it's two fairly recent replicas that give the best sense of what early colonial life was really like.

Docked in the harbor, the *Mayflower II* (Water Street; open daily; entrance fee) is a full-scale replica that was built in England and sailed to Plymouth in 1957; actors on board portray the original passengers and field visitors' questions with accuracy and wit.

About 3 miles (5 km) south of town, on Route 3, **Plimoth Plantation** (open daily; entrance fee) is a painstaking reconstruction of the 17th-century Pilgrim village; its every detail has been meticulously researched. It is inhabited by actor/interpreters who so convincingly enact the quotidian rituals of the original village that visitors can easily lose themselves in the fantasy of those heady days full of hardship and dreams.

Plymouth town also possesses a number of historic houses to visit. The oldest is the **Richard Sparrow House** (42 Summer Street; donations) built in 1640,

Map on page 138

Playing the part at Plimoth Plantation.

LEFT: Plimoth Plantation.
BELOW: *Mayflower II.*

Map on page 138

and still retaining its diamond-shape leaded windows; the **Howland House** (No. 33 Sandwich Street; open late May–mid-Oct) originated in 1667 as a home for the son of one of the original Pilgrims. The **Mayflower Society Museum** (4 Winslow Street; entrance fee) a house built in 1754, has a graceful flying staircase and a variety of period rooms.

Moving on further south again, pause at **New Bedford** ㊸ to explore the narrow cobblestone streets of the old town – the busiest fishing port on the East Coast. Here the outstanding sight is the **Whaling Museum** (Johnny Cake Hill; open daily; late May–early Sept, Thur till 8pm; entrance fee), the best place to find out about this aspect of New England's maritime past. In addition to informative sections evoking the lifestyles of the whalers and fishermen, there is a huge show of ship models – most memorably the *Lagoda*, a half-size replica of a whaling bark – and some fine paintings on the theme, plus examples of scrimshaw, intricately carved out of whalebone by members of the ships' crews on their long voyages.

At the mouth of the Taunton estuary, 9 miles (6 km) east from New Bedford, **Fall River** ㊵ is dominated by the huge mills that act as reminders of the long-defunct cotton industry. Some of these Victorian relics now house the thriving factory outlet stores that have put the town on the map. Another reason for coming is for **Battleship Cove** (open daily 9am–sunset; entrance fee), a collection of World War II vessels berthed on the river – among them the submarine USSS *Lionfish* and the 46,000-ton battleship USS *Massachusetts*. Virtually adjacent, the **Marine Museum** (open weekdays; Sat and Sun pm; entrance fee) is packed with nautical paraphernalia, including a model of the doomed *Titanic* and more than 150 steamship models. ❑

BELOW:
going fishing.

BOSTON HARBOR ISLANDS

Until recently, few Bostonians even knew that their harbor had islands. But look on a map and there they are, some 30 of them, sprinkled within the embracing peninsular arms of Winthrop and Hull. They range from little more than piles of rock (The Graves) to 214-acre (85-hectare) Long, which stretches out into the middle of the harbor from the town of Quincy. For centuries, the islands served no more purpose than a dumping ground or shelter for Boston's sick or homeless. As for the harbor, it was little more than a cesspool for the city's waste. But thanks to a $3.5 billion clean-up, Boston Harbor is clean enough now on most days for swimming. And in 1996, Congress created the Boston Harbor Islands National Recreation Area to support ongoing local and state efforts to turn the islands into valuable recreational space for the city. Already, you can catch a ferry from downtown Boston or Hingham to Georges Island, which serves as a nucleus for the recreation area. Free water taxis travel to other islands, some of which feel as remote and unspoiled as those off the coast of Maine – except for that great view of the Boston skyline. For specific information about reaching the islands, or about camping, call 617-727 7676.

Outlet Shopping

Kittery and Freeport, ME, are both scenic coastal towns, but for many their names are more synonymous with outlet shopping than beaches. This was not always so. Factory outlets once referred to shops within factories that sold discounted wares to employees. The modern concept of New England factory outlets began in the mid-1970s in Fall River, MA, when the Anderson-Little clothing store opened a retail outlet.

Anderson-Little no longer exists, but outlets are here to stay. Fifty stores now occupy the original granite-faced Fall River mill buildings, and the popularity of outlet shopping has grown well beyond this industrial city. The outlet malls in Freeport and Kittery are now among Maine's most popular tourist destinations, and North Conway, NH, and Worcester, MA, also harbor large outlet malls advertising 20 to 70 percent discounts on products ranging from clothing to housewares to books. Many shoppers come armed with maps and strategies, and entire books have been written on the most productive way to shop.

There are three kinds of stores: national outlets for single brands selling in-season merchandise at a discount; regional value outlets carrying name-brand and designer merchandise; and manufacturer-owned clearance centers with discontinued and irregular merchandise at sharply reduced prices.

The Fall River Factory Outlet District (800-424 5519), also known as the Heart District, consists of three independently owned malls. Big draws are Bugle Boy, Levi's, the Burlington Coat Factory, and the L'eggs, Hanes, Bali, and Playtex Outlet. The district is at the junction of I-195 and Route 24 South, about one hour from Boston and 20 minutes from Newport and Providence, Rhode Island. Farther west in Massachusetts is Worcester, home to Worcester Common Outlets (508-798 2581), the only fully enclosed outlet center in New England. Anchors here are Filene's Basement, Off 5th–Sachs Fifth Avenue, Sports Authority, BB and Beyond, and Media Play.

One hour north of Boston, at Kittery, ME (888-KITTERY), 14 outlet centers with 120 stores line over a mile of Route 1 (Exit 3 from I-95). Farther north on I-95, at Exit 20, is Freeport, home to the never-closed headquarters of L.L. Bean. The outdoor outfitter's store is now flanked by 170 shops and outlets, and L.L. Bean draws over 2.5 million customers each year (800-865 1994).

L.L. Bean also has a store in North Conway, NH, two hours' drive north of Boston, along with 200 other outlet stores. Two large outlet malls, Settlers' Green OVP. (603-356 7031) and the Tanger Outlet Center (603–436 6277) are the anchors, with about 100 stores. Dozens of smaller outlet centers in stand-alone factory stores are also strung along Route 16, creating long traffic jams.

Vermont also chases tourists intent on parting with greenbacks. Goods in Manchester's high-end outlet shops are generally more expensive than factory stores but still less than retail. If the notion of a "perpetual sale" gets your heart fluttering, you'll be moved by such purveyors as Calvin Klein, Timberland, Baccarat, Giorgio Armani, Cole Haan, Dansk, and Brooks Brothers. ❑

RIGHT: L.L.Bean's "Maine Hunting Shoe."

CAPE COD AND THE ISLANDS

Map on pages 158–9

This is a sandy summer playground with fine clam shacks, historic B&Bs, undeveloped National Seashore beaches, and a lively arts scene – plus two sharply contrasting little isles

S haped like a bodybuilder's flexed arm, Cape Cod extends 31 miles (50 km) eastward into the Atlantic Ocean, then another 31 miles to the north. Well forested up to about the "elbow," then increasingly reduced to scrub oak and pitch pine, this sandy peninsula is lined with more than 310 miles (500 km) of beaches. The crook of the arm forms Cape Cod Bay, where the waters are placid and free of often treacherous ocean surf. Lighthouses guide mariners plying the cold Atlantic waters. Geologically the Cape is relatively new, a huge mass of debris dumped after the melting of a vast ice sheet.

Bostonians consider Cape Cod their own private playground, but its fame has spread so far that it attracts international travelers. In high season (July and August), lodgings are filled to capacity, traffic on the Cape's few highways is heavy, and local merchants work hard to make the profits that will carry them through the all-but-dormant winters. (The pleasures of the Cape off-season, however, are a well-guarded secret not likely to remain a secret much longer.) Even at the height of its summertime popularity, when the roads, restaurants, and beaches tend to be jammed, Cape Cod manages to preserve its wild charm and dramatic beauty.

Much of this quality is protected within the boundaries of the Cape Cod National Seashore, a vast 27,000-acre (11,000-hectare) nature reserve established by foresighted legislators in 1961. Precisely because it has not been commercially exploited, this huge expanse of untouched dunes – a natural phenomenon created by geological forces about a million years ago – survives as one of the Cape's most alluring features.

PRECEDING PAGES: old coastguard station at Eastham. **LEFT:** looking out to sea, at Douse's Beach. **BELOW:** waiting for the waves.

Getting your bearings

Note the nomenclature. "Upper Cape" refers to the portion nearest the mainland; "Mid-Cape" is roughly from Barnstable County eastward to Chatham and Orleans, where the "arm" bends; "Lower Cape" is the "forearm" jutting northward to Eastham, Truro and Provincetown.

Itineraries on the Upper and Mid-Cape offer a choice of speedy, featureless highways or scenic, meandering roads. Those intent on reaching the Outer Cape in a hurry generally opt for Route 6, the four-lane, limited-access Mid-Cape Highway; those headed for Falmouth and Woods Hole can take the equally speedy Route 28. Anyone wishing to get a true sense of the Cape, however, will be well rewarded by taking the prettier non-highway counterparts. Roughly parallel to the Mid-Cape Highway, two-lane Route 6A starts in Sagamore and runs eastward through old towns full of graceful historic houses, crafts and antique shops. The same can be said of Route 28A, hugging the shore en route to Falmouth. As Route 28 veers northeastward from Falmouth to Chatham it's marred by recurrent stretches of overdevelopment but, again, one has only to venture off the main road a bit to discover such towns as Osterville and Centerville, Harwich Port and Chatham itself. Once Route 28 and Route 6 merge in Orleans, Route 6 north is pleasant all the way to Provincetown, if traffic-clogged.

For those wishing to avoid the drive, there are ferries between Provincetown and Boston, Provincetown and Plymouth, and flights into Hyannis (*see page 169*).

Simple pleasures

The first hordes of tourists arrived in the late 19th century, brought by steamship, railroad and – eventually – automobile. Escaping the summer heat of Boston, Providence and New York for the cool sea breezes along the shore, they found low prices, inexpensive real estate and simple pleasures in abundance.

Before the advent of modern transport, Cape Cod was a hardscrabble area peopled by the Wampanoag tribes, hardy Yankees and industrious immigrants from the coasts and islands of Portugal. Since the land was too poor to farm for more than local consumption, most people earned their living from the sea. Fishing, saltmaking, whaling, ship-building and "wrecking" – scavenging the beaches for the flotsam and jetsam of ships lost at sea – provided the local people with a livelihood, however uncertain.

In 1602, Bartholomew Gosnold, a British mariner sailing by this long arm of sand, noted a great many codfish in the waters and added the name "Cape Cod" to his map. In 1620, the *Mayflower* pulled into the harbor of what is now Provincetown and, before debarking to explore, its passengers drew up the Mayflower Compact, whereby they constituted themselves

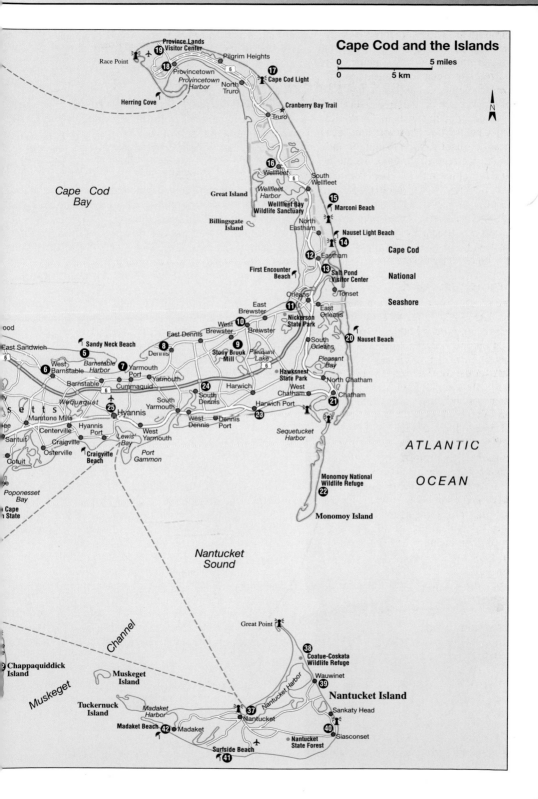

Cape Cod and the Islands

The Cape Cod National Seashore Trail, found at the northern tip of the Cape, is a spectacularly sculpted landscape of sweeping dunes descending into green hollows of scrub brush and stunted forest, with the sea all around to provide invigorating breezes.

as a "civil Body Politick" and vowed to work together under just laws for the good of all. This early "constitution" grew into the government of the Commonwealth of Massachusetts.

The Cape Cod Canal

Purists could actually call Cape Cod an island, for in 1914, after five years of work, the Cape was effectively severed from the mainland by the **Cape Cod Canal ❶**. Improved and widened in 1927, the canal is a boon to ships travelling north–south along the coast of New England, for they no longer have to venture into the stormy Atlantic to circumvent the Cape.

Expressways funnel traffic to the two access bridges over the Canal. To the east is the **Sagamore Bridge ❷**, a graceful arched structure with one foot in the Cape town of Sagamore. Route 3 comes south from Boston and crosses the Sagamore Bridge to join Route 6, the Mid-Cape Highway.

Just past the bridge on the north side are the **Pairpoint Glass Works**, where glassblowers give demonstrations daily. Near the southwestern end of the Canal is the Bourne Bridge, leading to Route 28, headed for Falmouth and Woods Hole. West of the bridge and by the canal, the **Aptucxet Trading Post ❸** (open July–Aug, daily; May–June and Sept–mid-Oct, Tues–Sat; Sun pm; entrance fee) is a replica of the first English-speaking trading post in North America, set up in 1627 to trade with the Wampanoag Indians, the Dutch in New York and the Plymouth settlement. There are views of the third great span over the canal, the 270 ft (82 meters) high and 540 ft (165 meters) long Buzzards Bay Vertical Railroad Bridge, which is left raised, and lowered to allow trains to cross.

BELOW:
going clamming.

CAPE COD RAIL TRAIL

In the Cape's early heyday, summertime visitors arrived by train – an option still available to a limited number of towns in July and August from New York City (Amtrak's Cape Codder, tel: 800-872 7245). Otherwise, with a singular lack of foresight, most of the train network has been dismantled. However, at least one lengthy section of roadbed has been put to an energy-saving, pleasure-making use: the Cape Cod Rail Trail is a 28-mile (45-km) paved recreational path ideal for bicycling, skating, walking and jogging. Along the way, it passes lakes and marshes, woods and a harbor. The most scenic or dramatic sections are the National Seashore spur trails in Eastham and Wellfleet that terminate at the Atlantic Ocean. The trail runs from just off Route 134 in South Dennis through Nickerson State Park and on to Wellfleet.

You can rent bicycles at a number of places along the way, including Barbara's Bike & Sport (tel: 508-760 4723) at the trailhead, Idle Times Bike Shop (tel: 508-896 9242) on the edge of Nickerson, and Little Capistrano Bike Shop (tel: 508-255 6515) across from the National Seashore headquarters in Eastham. If you forget to pack a lunch, there are a few places along the way where you can get a sandwich or fried seafood.

The Bayside: Sandwich to Brewster

This region gained world renown for its glass after Boston merchant Deming Jarvis founded a glass factory in **Sandwich ❹** in 1825.

By taking advantage of local resources (sand shipped in from the Outer Cape, local timber to stoke the furnaces, and salt marsh to pack the delicate product) and using mass-production techniques, Jarvis put glassware – formerly a rare and precious commodity – within the reach of ordinary people. His Boston and Sandwich Glass Company factory thrived until threatened by coal-powered plants in the Midwest; that, and a strike by exploited workers, shut the enterprise down in 1888. However, examples of their output, in an astounding range of styles, can still be found in the **Sandwich Glass Museum** (Main Street; open Feb–Dec, daily; entrance fee), and in the antique shops that line this historic old route.

Exhibits at Sandwich Glass Museum.

Sandwich was the first town to be founded on the Cape, in 1637, and today – with the factories long since razed and the groves of trees regrown – it's one of the prettiest, and best-preserved. At its center stands the restored **Dexter Mill and the Hoxie House**, dating from colonial times (Water Street; open mid-June–mid-Oct, Mon–Sat; Sun pm; entrance fee).

For more glimpses into the American past, follow the signs – past a lovely historic cemetery overlooking **Shawme Pond** – to **Heritage Plantation**, a spacious museum complex whose grounds, in spring, are awash in the vivid pinks and purples of flowering rhododendrons (Grove Street; open May-Oct, daily; entrance fee). Several buildings display extraordinary collections, from children's toys (including a working carousel) to military artifacts and artwork. A round stone barn (copied from the Shaker original in Hancock, Massachusetts)

BELOW:
the carousel at
Heritage Plantation,
Sandwich.

TIP

You'll find more fine old houses lining the section of Route 6A around Yarmouth Port – once called Captains' Row – than anywhere else on the Cape. South Yarmouth was settled by Quakers in the early 1800s and many of their lovely houses remain.

BELOW: the Town Hall and Dexter Mill, Sandwich.

houses an outstanding array of early cars, including one particular beauty, Gary Cooper's 1931 Deusenberg.

Motoring east, into the county of Barnstable, you'll pass a 6-mile (9-km) barrier beach, **Sandy Neck** ❺, which is a favored habitat of the endangered piping plover. Hikers and swimmers are welcome to explore this sandy spit, provided they don't disturb the birds' nesting sites. Whale-watching cruises depart from Barnstable Harbor (it's a shorter trip to Stellwagen Bank from Provincetown, but for those who don't mind some extra time out on the water, this departure point is just as good).

Just up the hill from the harbor is the **Trayser Memorial Museum** (3353 Route 6A; open mid-June–mid-Oct, Tues–Sun pm), the former Custom House, which now houses Native American artifacts, children's toys and other bygones. In **West Barnstable** ❻, West Parish Meetinghouse, built in 1646, is an outstanding example of early colonial architecture and has a Paul Revere bell cast in 1806.

East of Barnstable, **Yarmouth Port** ❼ is a delightful village with fine old houses to tour, including the **Captain Bangs Hallett House** (Strawberry Lane; open June–Oct, Sun pm; July–Aug, Thurs pm; tours on the hour; entrance fee), an 1840 Greek Revival showcase house now owned by The Historical Society of Old Yarmouth, and the **Winslow Crocker House** (250 Route 6A; open June–Oct, Sat and Sun; entrance fee), a Georgian manse from around 1780. For a pleasurable glimpse of more recent history, stop for an ice cream soda at **Hallett's**, a well-preserved 1889 drugstore.

In the town of **Dennis** ❽, follow signs for the Scargo Hill Tower, a stone turret from which it's possible to see, on a clear day, Cape Cod laid out like a map, with Provincetown easily visible at the northern tip. Dennis is home to America's oldest, and most outstanding, professional summer theater: aspiring thespians such as Bette Davis (an ambitious usher) and Henry Fonda began their careers at the Cape Playhouse (Route 6A; tel: 508-385 3838; performances late June–mid-Sep), founded in 1927 by Raymond Moore, a renegade from Provincetown's "little theater" movement. Productions here are skilled and lavish, and movies at the adjoining Cape Cinema are a sensory treat: the cinema features leather armchairs with antimacassars and Art Deco frescoes by Rockwell Kent.

The **Stony Brook Mill** ❾ (Stony Brook Road southwest off Route 6A) grinds cornmeal several days a week; there's a small museum upstairs. Each spring, from mid-April to early May, the mill hosts an eye-catching event: here, in a timeless ceremony similar to a salmon run, schools of alewives (a fish resembling herring) leap up a series of ladders to spawn in the freshwater pond behind the mill. Besides its fine old houses and inns, **Brewster** ❿ has a variety of attractions. The **Cape Cod Museum of Natural History** (Route 6A; open daily; entrance fee) explores the local habitat with hands-on exhibits and a small network of nature trails. The **New England Fire and History Museum** (1429 Route 6A) has large collections of vintage fire-fighting equipment and memorabilia.

Railroad magnate Roland Nickerson once owned 2,000 acres (800 hectares) of open land in Brewster and held them as his personal hunting and fishing preserve. In 1934 his widow donated most of this tract to the state; today **Nickerson State Park** ⓫ (Route 6A), is a popular spot for camping, swimming, picnicking, and walks.

Map on pages 158–9

Vintage exhibit at the New England Fire and History Museum.

BELOW:
the New England Fire and History Museum, Brewster.

Summer Activities

New England's summer season may be short, but locals savor every balmy day that July and August bring. And although May/June and September/October may not qualify as "summer," the fine if less predictable weather of these "shoulder" months makes for excellent outdoor adventuring without the mid-summer crowds.

With 400 miles (640 km) of coastline, Rhode Island looks to the sea for recreation. Newport, known as "The Sailing Capital of the World" for its years hosting the America's Cup, is a good base for harbor sailing or learn-to-sail vacations.

At America's oldest sailing school, Boston's Community Boating, skiffs cruise the Charles River against a backdrop of brick bowfronts and downtown office towers. For longer adventures, many head for the Maine coast, where several outfitters offer multi-day sailing expeditions.

Maine has also become a center for sea kayaking, wiith over 2,000 coastal islands and their protected waters, The Maine Island Kayak Company (*see Travel Tips*) offers sea kayaking lessons and tours. Rhode Island kayakers are rewarded with seaside views of Newport's grand Ocean Drive estates.

West of Boston, canoeists on the lazy Sudbury and Concord Rivers can visit Revolutionary-era sights, while on Cape Cod, naturalist guides lead canoe tours of salt marshes and tidal rivers. Along the Deerfield River in western Massachusetts, visitors can rent canoes and take whitewater rafting trips. Connecticut's Housatonic River is a favored destination for canoeing and rafting. North American Whitewater Expeditions (*see Travel Tips*) organizes trips on the Housatonic and on Maine's Kennebec and Penobscot Rivers.

Swimmers will find beaches on Cape Cod or Nantucket Sound warmer and calmer than those on the Atlantic. The Atlantic, however, sometimes offers reasonable surfing, especially after an offshore storm.

Fishermen head for the trout-filled Battenkill River, near Manchester in Vermont, where the Orvis Company runs a fly fishing school. Orvis also teaches saltwater fishing on Cape Cod. Near New Hampshire's Mount Washington, Great Glen Trials (*see Travel Tips*) offers introductory fishing classes and arranges guided fly fishing excursions.

There's hiking for all abilities, from leisurely strolls on conservation land – such as the 11 self-guided nature trails within Cape Cod's National Seashore – to rugged mountain climbs. The 2,000-mile (3,200-km) Appalachian Trail crosses Maine, New Hampshire, Vermont, Massachusetts and Connecticut on its way south to Georgia. Serious hikers also follow the Long Trail, 445 miles (712 km) across Vermont's highest peaks. The Appalachian Mountain Club has a network of overnight huts for walkers in New Hampshire's White Mountains.

Many ski resorts have become summer mountain biking centers, including Vermont's Mount Snow and Killington. The self-guided Franconia Notch Bike Tour in New Hampshire starts at Echo Lake, passes the Old Man of the Mountain, to end at Loon Mountain's ski area. ❑

LEFT: Cape Cod and Acadia are two areas that offer excellent, easy cycling.

The National Seashore and the Outer Cape

The Cape Cod National Seashore extends along the Atlantic coast of the Lower Cape all the way to Provincetown. Its glorious sandy beaches are backed by high dunes; by contrast the (western) bayside has calmer, warmer waters and marshy inlets.

The town green at **Eastham** ⓬ has a 1793 windmill. For a deeper side trip into Cape Cod's history, head west to **First Encounter Beach**. It's here that a Pilgrim scouting party out of Provincetown first encountered a band of Indians, who, wary after earlier encounters with kidnappers, attacked the Pilgrims and were rebuffed by gunfire. This uneasy meeting is among the reasons the Pilgrims pressed on to Plymouth. Today the historic site is a peaceful town beach (which, like most, charges a parking fee in summer).

Further up Route 6A is the **Salt Pond Visitor Center** ⓭ (open mid-Feb–Dec, daily; Jan–mid-Feb, weekends) of the Cape Cod National Seashore. Interpretive films and exhibits explain the ecology of the Cape, and a bicycle trail (bikes can be rented nearby) winds through pine forests and marshes to end at **Coast Guard Beach**, where, in the 1920s, Henry Beston wrote his classic *Outermost House*; further north is **Nauset Light Beach** ⓮, graced with a picturesque lighthouse.

At **Marconi Beach** ⓯, Guglielmo Marconi set up the first wireless station in the United States and transmitted the first trans-Atlantic wireless message to Europe in 1903. The **Atlantic White Cedar Swamp Trail**, starting from the Marconi site, is especially beautiful.

Famous for its oysters, **Wellfleet** ⓰ is one of Cape Cod's most appealing towns, full of fine galleries and fun restaurants, and surrounded by inviting

Map on pages 158–9

TIP

The best beaches in the area are Nauset Beach and Skaket Beach, both in Orleans (see page 168), and Nauset Light, Coast Guard and First Encounter Beaches, all in the vicinity of Eastham.

BELOW: Nauset Light Beach.

*Cranberries are a
Cape specialty.*

wildlife areas. Just south of town, off Route 6, the Audubon Society maintains the 700-acre (280-hectare) **Wellfleet Bay Wildlife Sanctuary** (off Route 6; open 8am–dusk, daily; entrance fee); to the west of town is Great Island (part of the Cape Cod National Seashore), which reattached itself to the mainland and became a barrier beach.

Farther north, the landscape becomes ever more wild and barren. Scrubby vegetation gives way to desert-like sand dunes. East of Truro, the **Cranberry Bog Trail** (within the Cape Cod National Seashore) offers a look at the natural habitat of the tiny red fruit that proved such a boon to Cape Cod agriculture. Another road east leads to **Highland Light**, towering over **Head of the Meadow Beach**.

Cape Cod Light ⓱, also known as Highland Light, is one of the much-photographed landmarks of the Cape; erected in 1857 it is the peninsula's oldest lighthouse.

Provincetown

BELOW: a trio of
transvestites in
Provincetown.

Contrast the subtle beauties and serenity of the National Seashore lands with the raucous and sometimes tawdry atmosphere along Commercial Street in **Provincetown** ⓲. Sidewalk artists will run off a pastel portrait, or perhaps a cartoon caricature. Shops emblazoned with advertisements sell fine works of art, bad works of art, kitsch souvenirs and an infinite variety of snacks. There are good restaurants and bad ones, delightful old inns and inexpensive guest houses, tacky shacks and beautiful landscaped captains' mansions. The artiness of "P-town" (a term *never* used by the locals) has coincided with its status of one of the most overtly gay capitals of the East Coast.

With its well-protected harbor, Provincetown started out as a natural fishing port – long before the Pilgrims came along. So it remains to this day. Portuguese fishermen, many from the Azores, came here in the heyday of the whaling trade and stayed on for the good fishing. Their descendants still make up a sizable proportion of the town's year-round residents. Led by painter Charles Hawthorne, who in 1899 founded the Cape Cod School of Art, hordes of artists and writers from New York's Greenwich Village flocked to Provincetown in the early decades of the 20th century, drawn partly by the area's stark beauty and largely by the cheap rents and food to be found here (thanks to the tourist boom they inspired, the latter are of course history).

Among the innumerable notables who passed through here, if only briefly, are dramatists Eugene O'Neill and Tennessee Williams, and writers Sinclair Lewis and John Dos Passos. Perhaps the best-known recent writer-in-summer-residence is Norman Mailer. A dozen or more illustrious painters, such as Robert Motherwell, have left their mark, with new contenders cropping up year after year in such cutting-edge galleries as the Long Point and Bertha Walker. A number of galleries now specialize in Provincetown art going back to the beginning of the century.

Other places to catch outstanding early work are the **Provincetown Art Association and Museum** founded in 1914 (460 Commercial Street; open Sun–Thurs, pm; Fri and Sat, 8am–10pm); the relatively new **Provincetown Heritage Museum** (356 Commercial Street; open daily; entrance fee), which also harbors a half-scale model of a fishing schooner; and the poorly-lit corridors of the 1878 Town Hall, where concerts and performances are held throughout the year.

Map on pages 158–9

TIP

A good way to see the principal sights is to take the Provincetown Trolley which runs along Commercial Street and continues on to the National Seashore. The main pick-up point is outside the Town Hall.

BELOW: Provincetown Heritage Museum.

PROVINCETOWN ART COLONY

Bay and ocean, sand and sky: the natural beauty of Provincetown at the tip of Cape Cod has attracted artists since the town was little more than a fishing pier at the end of a sand spit. Today, Provincetown boasts dozens of art galleries, many of which specialize in contemporary works by local painters, photographers, and sculptors such as Joel Meyerowitz, Paul Bowen, and Paul Resika.

The artists who live and work in Provincetown today are drawn to the area by its pure, Mediterranean-like light – the same light that nearly a century ago inspired a group collectively known as the "Provincetown Art Colony," as renowned as those in Taos in New Mexico, Carmel in California, and East Hampton in New York State.

The colony began in the late 1800s, when a new railroad bed made Provincetown more easily accessible to artists in search of inexpensive lodging and studio space. In 1899, impressionist painter Charles Webster Hawthorne opened the Cape Cod School of Art, which was soon followed by the Summer School of Painting.

By the summer of 1916, more than 300 artists and students – associated with six schools of art – were thriving in the tolerant town, leading the *Boston Globe* to dub it "the Biggest Art Colony in the World."

*Just keeping an
eye on things.*

The lofty Italianate tower looming above the town is the **Pilgrim Memorial** (off Winslow Street; open Apr–Nov, daily; entrance fee), built early in the century to ensure that Provincetown's place in colonial history would not be overlooked. The determined climber (there's also an elevator) will be rewarded with a panoramic view of the town and the entire Cape. At the monument's foot is the **Provincetown Museum** (off Winslow Street from Bradford Street; open July–Aug, daily till 7pm; entrance fee), with intriguing local history exhibits. Spoils from the *Whydah*, a pirate ship discovered off Wellfleet in 1984, are displayed at **Exhibition Whydah** on MacMillan Wharf (open Apr–mid-Oct, daily; June–Aug till 7pm; mid-Oct–Dec, weekends; entrance fee).

The very tip of Cape Cod – which is almost entirely within National Seashore boundaries – is unusual and fascinating. Two vast beaches, **Race Point** and **Herring Cove**, invite exploration: by bike, on horseback, on foot, and off-road vehicle tours. For information, call in at the **Province Lands Visitors' Center ⓳** (open mid-Apr–Nov, daily), which has a good viewing platform.

The Sound: Chatham to Falmouth

A popular base for touring the Cape, **Orleans** offers in the form of **Nauset Beach ⓴** one of the Cape's finest stretches of coast. The settlement was called by its Indian name of Nauset until it was incorporated in 1797 and renamed for the Duke of Orleans (the future king of France), a recent visitor. Orleans has another "French connection" – it was the stateside terminus for a transatlantic telegraph cable to Brest in France. Hooked up in 1879, the cable performed well for decades before it become obsolete, and is now commemorated in the **French Cable Museum** on Route 28 (South Orleans Road).

BELOW:
the Hyannis ferry to
the Nantucket and
Martha's Vineyard.

Cape Cod's southern shore, from Chatham to Falmouth, is a zone where the battle for – and against – commercialization has raged for the past few decades. Some pockets of subdued gentility still reign just off the honky-tonk stretches.

Chatham ㉑ numbers among the aristocratic enclaves. The handsome Chatham Bars Inn was built as a private hunting lodge early in the century. The nearby Fish Pier is a perfect spot to watch the fishing fleet bring in the daily catch. The **Chatham Railroad Museum** (153 Depot Road) is housed in the town's ornate Victorian railroad station, out of commission for several decades. **Chatham Light**, yet another picturesque Coast Guard lighthouse, overlooks South Beach.

Bird fanciers will want to make a visit to **Monomoy Island ㉒**, a stopping point for hundreds of species of birds traveling the Atlantic Flyway. Protected as the Monomoy National Wildlife Refuge, it is accessible only by boat; both the **Audubon Society** (tel: 508-349 2615) and the **Cape Cod Museum of Natural History** (tel: 508-896 3867) offer cruises.

Picturesque Harwich and **Harwich Port ㉓** are the last peaceful settlements before the Cape's commercial belt. From West Harwich to Hyannis, Route 28 is lined with motels, restaurants, businesses and amusements. It's a long, tawdry stretch, where traffic usually crawls all summer.

Map on pages 158–9

South Dennis ㉔, perversely north of West Dennis, has on Old Main Street a typical shingled Full Cape house (*see panel*) of 1801, known as **Jericho House** (open July–Aug, Wed and Fri pm only). Look behind the house for an 1810 barn filled with farming implements, plus a remarkable "driftwood zoo" of carved flotsam created by Sherman Woodward in the 1950s.

Hyannis ㉕, the Cape's year-round commercial center, boasts more than a score of worthwhile restaurants and nightclubs, the **Cape Cod Melody Tent** (for intimate concerts featuring top-name talent; West Main Street; tel: 508-775 9100), and, in the old Town Hall, the **John F. Kennedy Museum** (397 Main Street; open Mon–Sat, Sun pm; entrance fee) featuring photos and mementos of the President who summered in adjoining Hyannis Port. (Although the Kennedy Compound is the object of many a pilgrimage, it is not open to the public and very little of it can be seen from the road.) A small park dedicated to Kennedy's memory adjoins Veterans Beach, on Hyannis's harbor.

West of Hyannis, the tide of commercialism subsides occasionally to provide glimpses of Cape Cod's signature beauty. Make a southward detour for Centerville, where relatively warm-watered **Craigville Beach** (parking fee in summer) has drawn Christian "camp meetings" since the mid-19th century, and for affluent Osterville, a rarefied village surrounded by awe-inspiring seaside mansions.

Heading on toward Falmouth, take a side trip north to **Mashpee** ㉖, located amid Wampanoag tribal lands which in recent decades have been carved up by development. The **Old Indian Meetinghouse**, the oldest church building on the Cape, built in 1684, is well worth a look (Meeting House Road at Route 28; call for hours; tel: 508-477 208).

"Full Cape" denotes a shingle-hung house with two windows either side of the door. Three-quarters Cape means two windows on one side and one on the other, while a Half Cape has the door on the left and two windows to the right.

BELOW: Spohr's Garden, Falmouth.

*A bird box in
Trinity Park,
Martha's Vineyard.*

Below: Quissett
Harbor, worth a
detour off the road
from Falmouth to
Woods Hole.

Falmouth ㉗ is like a microcosm of Cape Cod life. The town green – a Revolutionary militia training ground – is among the prettiest on the Cape; it's ringed by fine old houses, including several delightful B&Bs, and the **Falmouth Historical Society Museums** (Palmer Avenue on the Village Green; open mid-June–mid-Sept: weekdays pm; mid-Sept–mid-Oct: Tues and Thurs am; entrance fee). Falmouth Harbor is filled with pleasure craft; swimmers and windsurfers favor the beaches and guest houses of Victorian-era Falmouth Heights, overlooking Nantucket Sound.

One of the most pleasant activities in Falmouth is to rent a bicycle and follow the old railroad bed, now a bike path, down to **Woods Hole ㉘**. This small town is devoted almost exclusively to maritime activities. Most travelers pass through here merely to board the ferry for Martha's Vineyard, a 45-minute voyage away. But Woods Hole itself warrants a stopover. The world-famous **Woods Hole Oceanographic Institute** (School Street; open Tues–Sat; Sun pm) maintains a visitor center to describe its fascinating research; visitors can also tour the **Marine Biological Laboratory** (MBL Street at Water Street; reservations must be made in advance; tel: 508-548 3705), and the small but intriguing **National Marine Fisheries Service Aquarium** (open weekdays). Though no larger than a couple of city blocks, this tiny town supports a number of superb casual restaurants, where the specialty, naturally, is seafood.

The island of Martha's Vineyard

Over the decades, Vineyard residents have grown blasé about the celebrities in their midst, and precisely because of that laissez-faire attitude, the roster just keeps growing. World-renowned actors, musicians, writers, and public figures (including the late Jacqueline Onassis) have felt comfortable here. It took a Presidential visit – the Clintons' during the mid-1990s – to shake things up a bit, but, despite the hordes lining the roadways, most people went about their business, and leisure, as usual.

Islanders have worked too hard to create and preserve a relaxed way of life to let a little glitz and glamour throw them. For many, the island represents a true escape from the pressures of city life and the stresses of high-powered careers. Though the price of admission may be high, once one has arrived, a kind of barefoot democracy prevails.

Like Cape Cod, Martha's Vineyard is a geological remnant from the last Ice Age. Two advancing lobes of a glacier molded the triangular northern shoreline, then retreated, leaving hilly moraines, low plains and many-fingered ponds. And Martha herself? She was the daughter of Thomas Mayhew, who in 1642 bought a large tract of land, including Nantucket Island, for the sum of £40. (Mayhew named Elizabeth Islands after another daughter.)

Vineyard Haven, Oak Bluffs and Edgartown, the three protected harbor towns of the northeastern portion of the island, were always active and prosperous, and to this day represent the commercial half of the island, although the main order of business is no longer shipping and whaling, but tourism and summer homes. By contrast, the sparsely populated "up-island" towns of West Tisbury, Chilmark, Menemsha, and Gay Head remain determinedly rural and non-ostentatious, despite a number of famous residents.

It may come as a disappointment to many visitors to find that, as a rule, Martha's Vineyard's extensive beaches are not accessible to outsiders but have been reserved for homeowners; the major exception, beyond the placid Joseph Sylvia State Beach on the bay side, is South Beach, fronting the rolling Atlantic south of Edgartown; other public beaches are Katama (good for surfing and for strong swimmers), Moshpu, Oak Bluffs and Menemsha.

Vineyard Haven, Oak Bluffs and Edgartown

Long before the Cape Cod Canal provided a shortcut between Boston and ports south, boats had to travel around Cape Cod to make a coastal journey. As traffic on this route and the routes striking out to the West Indies increased, the harbor at the tip of the Vineyard grew in importance as a shelter and a source of supplies.

Known until 1870 as Holmes Hole, **Vineyard Haven** ㉙ (the official name of the town is Tisbury, but everyone calls it by the name of its primary village) blossomed into a busy port during the 18th and 19th centuries, with both maritime businesses and farmers profiting from the constant movement of ships in and out of the port. Today, the homey **Black Dog Tavern** (open weekdays), with its offshoot bakery, store, and catalog business, enjoys a similar relationship with the legions of vacationers who arrive by ferry from Woods Hole.

Vineyard Haven has a no-nonsense, matter-of-fact quality about it, with little of the preciousness of Edgartown or the cuteness of Oak Bluffs. Handsome

Map on pages 158–9

Bikes and blades for rent.

BELOW: Oak Bluffs, Trinity Park.

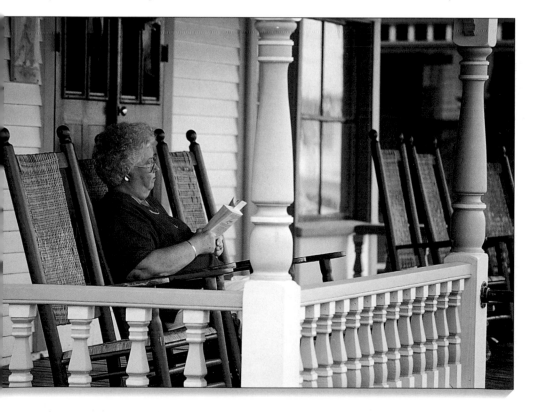

houses dating from the years before the great fire of 1883 can be found on Williams Street, a block off Main Street.

Nearby, the collection at the **Old Schoolhouse Museum** (Main Street; open July–Aug, weekdays, am only) includes ivory carvings, schooner models, and early island photographs. At the western end of Main Street (bicycle or take the car) stands the **West Chop Lighthouse**.

Religion tinged with tourism produced an unusual community in **Oak Bluffs ㉚**, a town renowned for its engaging cottages built in "carpenter gothic" style. In 1835, Methodists took to the backwoods out of Edgartown in search of a suitable site for a camp meeting, a place where the faithful could come for a short period of spiritual replenishment. They found a secluded circle of oak trees, named it Wesleyan Grove, and conducted the first summer camp meeting on the site. Twenty years later, there were more than 320 tents and many thousands of people. Small houses soon replaced the tents, laid out along circular drives that rimmed the large central "tabernacle" where the congregation assembled.

Today this camp meeting site is known as **Trinity Park**. Tiny gingerbread cottages are a riot of color and jigsaw carvery, with all manner of turrets, spires, gables and eaves. Yet the park remains remarkably serene and intimate. The huge cast iron-and-wood theater in the center of the campground, built in 1870, still hosts community gatherings. **Illumination Night**, held every August, recreates the camp's traditional closing-night ceremony, when colorful glowing lanterns were strung up throughout the park. Circuit and Lake Streets mark the hub of town and the site of the 1876 **Flying Horses**, one of the oldest merry-go-rounds in America (Circuit Avenue; open mid-Apr–mid-Oct, daily).

Oak Bluffs was one of the first resort communities where black visitors were welcomed openly. Film director Spike Lee bought a summer house here and one resident, Harlem Renaissance author Dorothy West, set her novel "The Wedding" in the town.

BELOW: Edgartown.

South of Oak Bluffs on Beach Road, **Edgartown** ❸ is the oldest settlement on Martha's Vineyard. In 1642, missionary Thomas Mayhew, Jr, son of the Watertown, Massachusetts, entrepreneur who bought the islands off the Cape for a pittance, arrived at Great Harbor, now Edgartown, and set about converting the island's native population. Relying on fishing or farming, the town grew at a slow pace until the 18th century, when it became a capital in the worldwide whaling trade, vying with Nantucket and, later, New Bedford. The captains who made their fortunes from the sea left behind a treasure: their elegant Federal and Greek Revival houses, especially those lining North and South Water streets.

The most dignified Edgartown residence is that built in 1840 by whale-oil magnate **Dr Daniel Fisher**, who once supplied all US lighthouses with Edgartown oil. His house (open late May–mid-Oct, 11am–2pm daily; tours available; entrance fee) sits on upper Main Street, next to the imposing Greek Revival **Old Whaling Church** of 1843, whose enormous pillars and soaring tower are a rare instance of monumental scale in Edgartown. Tucked behind the church is the **Vincent House** (1672), an example of the popular 17th-century Cape design (open late May–mid-Oct, pm, daily; entrance fee). At the corner of Cooke and School streets is **The Vineyard Museum** (open June–mid-Oct: Tues–Sat; Nov–May: Sat and Wed–Fri pm; closed last two weeks in October; entrance fee), whose collections include whaling items, artifacts from daily Vineyard life and the famous French-made Fresnel lens, which until 1952 cast the warning beam from Gay Head Lighthouse.

A stone's throw away from Edgartown, across a narrow neck of the harbor, is **Chappaquiddick Island** ❸, which hit the world's headlines as a result of the 1969 accident in which Senator Edward Kennedy drove his car over a bridge on the island, drowning his 28-year-old passenger, Mary Jo Kopechne. The island's native name means "The Separated Island," which it steadfastly remains, although the *On-Time III* regularly ferries cars (a few at a time) and clusters of pedestrians over the 200-yard (180-meter) crossing (tel: 508-627 9427). The main attraction on "Chappy," several miles from the ferry landing, is the **Wasque Reservation** and **Cape Poge Wildlife Refuge** at the island's eastern front.

Up-island escape

Should you tire of the enticing stores and restaurants to be found down-island, you need only retreat to the tranquility of up-island life (although the drive west from Edgartown, leading through forests of pine and oak, starts the transition to a vineyard where nature still decisively holds the upper hand).

The 4,000-acre (1,640-hectare) **Martha's Vineyard State Forest** ❸ – laced with walking and bridle paths and containing the island's only youth hostel – brings the scent of pines to the outskirts of **West Tisbury** ❸ center. This modest and unassuming village traditionally has been a center of small industry (including woolen and flour mills). Quirky attractions such as the Field Gallery (where Tom Maley's fanciful sculptures frolic in a field) and the Granary Gallery at the Red Barn Emporium (showcasing the historic

Map on pages 158–9

TIP

Christmas visitors to the Old Whaling Church can attend Handel's "Messiah". Films, lectures and concerts are presented in the 500-seater church as well as services.

BELOW: the ferry to Chappaquiddick.

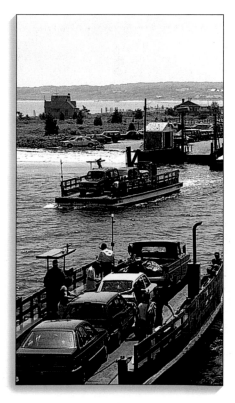

photos of the late Alfred Eisenstaedt, a summer regular) draw more attention these days, but the county fair is still a high point of the summer.

Of the three parallel roads traveling from West Tisbury to Chilmark, Middle Road traverses the most rugged, interesting glacial terrain. At **Chilmark Center** is Beetlebung Corner, a stand of tupelo trees from which "beetles" (mallets) and "bungs" (wooden stoppers) were once made.

Nearby **Menemsha ㉟** is a tiny fishing village on Vineyard Sound, famed for its appearance in *Jaws* and prized for its Technicolor sunsets.

The most spectacular natural sight on Martha's Vineyard is at its western-most tip, looking away from the commotion of the domesticated island and out to the untamed sea. From Chilmark, follow the single hilly road that at several points offers breathtaking views of Menemsha Pond northward and Squib-nocket Pond to the south. At the end, a lighthouse marks the western terminus of the island and the location of the stunning, ancient geologic strata that compose the cliffs at **Gay Head ㊱** (newly renamed Aquinnah). Clays of many colors – from gray to pink to green – represent eons of geological activity: fossils found amid the ever-changing contours of this 150-feet (46-meter) promontory have been dated back millions of years.

Gay Head is one of only two Native American communities in Massachusetts; it has been more successful than the Mashpee settlement in asserting its rights, and remains a cohesive social entity, over three centuries since the advent of colonizing forces.

On Indian Hill Road, heading back toward Vineyard Haven, is the site of Christiantown, settled by "praying Indians" in 1659; a plaque fixed to a boulder honors Thomas Mayhew's missionary efforts. At the end of the road, the

Playwright Lillian Hellman and actor John Belushi are buried in Chilmark Cemetery. Belushi's simple stone, which fans sometimes adorn with a beer can, is set up in front, but his body lies in an undisclosed plot.

BELOW:
Gay Head cliffs and lighthouse.

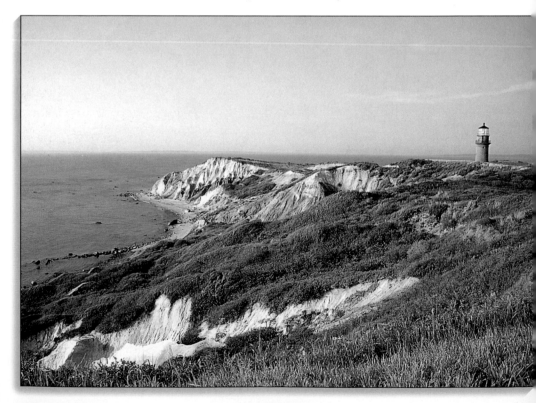

Cedar Tree Neck Wildlife Sanctuary provides a commanding view of the Vineyard Sound, across to the Elizabeth Islands, and a fine spot for strolling and contemplating nature.

The island of Nantucket

In 1830 the whaling ship *Sarah* returned home to Nantucket island, carrying 3,500 barrels of valuable whale oil after a voyage of nearly three years. On the island, stately mansions, decorated with silks and china from faraway lands, awaited the returning captains. Schools, hotels, a library and the commercial activity on Main Street were indications of a prosperous people.

These were the halcyon days of little Nantucket island, the shining moment in its turbulent past. Although its fortunes soon declined, time has stood still on Nantucket, and the intimate scale and refined taste of its heyday have survived to the present day to endow the island with its charm, beauty and magnetic appeal.

Nantucket may never again know the excitement and adventure of the whaling trade, but its new industry – tourism – has brought an equal amount of fame and fortune. Like the earliest settlers, who came to escape the Puritan lifestyle, people today come to Nantucket to leave behind the harsh realities of life on the mainland.

Chasing the whales

Since its earliest days, Nantucket has been populated by determined and spirited people. The first colonists, who arrived from Massachusetts in 1659, were taught "onshore" whaling by the native Algonquins; they traveled out in open boats to chase and harpoon whales sighted from land. By the beginning of the

Map
on pages
158–9

TIP

The ferry to Nantucket leaves from Hyannis and the trip takes around two and a half hours. Call (508) 540 2022 for schedules.

BELOW: cocktails by the harbor, Edgartown, Martha's Vineyard.

18th century, offshore whaling had begun and, with each generation of larger, more seaworthy craft, the whaling industry grew.

The natives, however, lost out. Although they sailed on whaling boats, their way of life on the island was irreversibly changed by the colonists. By 1855, disease (introduced to the country from Europe) and alcohol had taken the last of Nantucket's original residents.

By the time of the Revolutionary War, Nantucket had a fleet of 150 whaling ships. But Quaker pacifism and Nantucket's interest in London markets for whale oil divided islanders' loyalties, and their ships suffered greatly at the hands of the Tories and Revolutionaries alike. No sooner had they rebuilt their fleet than the War of 1812 erupted; by the conflict's end, their whaling empire had once again been left battered and exhausted.

Tenacity brought Nantucket back to life. Nantucket ships again sailed throughout the world and brought back record quantities of oil from their catches. It was during this period that the town acquired much of its urbanity, but the islanders' prosperity was destined to be short-lived: the Great Fire of 1846 razed the port, and in the 1850s kerosene replaced whale oil. Too heavily dependent on whaling, Nantucket was left high and dry.

BELOW LEFT: Great Point Lighthouse, Nantucket.
BELOW RIGHT: a former sea captain's house, Nantucket

From a peak of around 10,000, Nantucket's population dropped to 3,200 in 1875. Those who remained applied their ingenuity to a new venture, one that thrives today and continues to capitalize on the gifts of the sea. Tourism took off toward the end of the 19th century, as the arrival of the steamboat made the island more readily accessible. Land speculators built hotels and vacation homes. Quaint Siasconset, linked to the town by a narrow-gauge railroad built in 1884, was especially popular, drawing such luminaries as actress Lillian

Russell. The railroad is gone now (it was used for scrap metal during World War I), but tourism lives on.

An Indian word meaning "that faraway land," Nantucket isn't too far away for the thousands of people who visit each year by ferry and airplane. The winter population of 7,000 – lower than that recorded for the peak of the whaling era – increases sevenfold when the "summer people" take over the sidewalks of town and give it its cheery aspect.

In sharp contrast to Martha's Vineyard, Nantucket's mid-island moors and miles of beautiful, unspoiled beaches are open to visitors, most of whom use the preferred island mode of transportation: bikes (several shops stand ready to equip tourists near the ferry dock). Though smaller residential neighborhoods dot the island's coast, the harbor town of Nantucket, centrally located on the north shore, is unquestionably the focal point of the island.

The pleasures of Nantucket town

One can spend days walking through the town of **Nantucket ㉧** and always be sure of seeing something new. The community is a gem of 18th- and 19th-century architecture, from the dominant clapboard-and-shingle Quaker homes to the grandeur of the buildings lining **Upper Main Street**. And while the town may seem a maze of narrow streets, it is actually very ordered in its own cluttered way: early in the 18th century, its center was laid out in lots that ran roughly east–west from the harbor.

Nevertheless, it is best to tour with a street map (available from the bike shops, or in the free local newspapers distributed on the ferry), for the twists and turns can prove disorienting.

Map
on pages
158–9

Information point for visitors.

BELOW:
Nantucket Town.

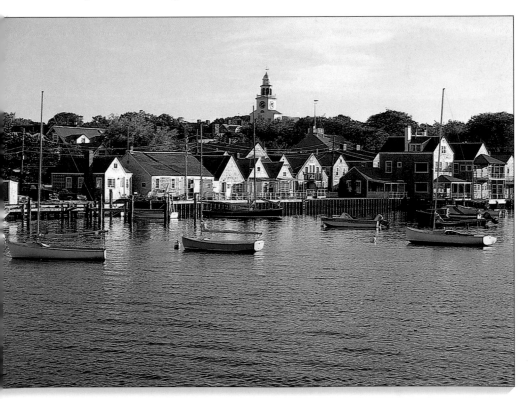

The waterfront is certainly the spiritual center of town. Several wharves extend into the harbor, the most central of which – **Straight Wharf** – is an extension of Main Street. First built in 1723, rebuilt after the 1846 fire, and renovated in the late 1950s to accommodate shops and restaurants, it's now like a small village unto itself, surrounded by luxury yachts and sailboats, some of which are available for charter. (The untouched barrier beach of Coatue is an ideal destination.)

Old South Wharf has also been spruced up and rendered tourist-friendly with boutiques and cafés; it's possible to rent tiny but picturesque wharfside cottages here.

Along Main Street up from Straight Wharf, a picturesque shopping district lines the gently rising cobblestone street. Although the square-mile (2.5 sq. km) National Landmark Historic District contains some 800 pre-1850 buildings, the red-brick facades lining Main Street are relatively "young," post-fire replacements. With its tree-lined, brick-paved sidewalks, Main Street is always a hub of activity in the summer months, offering every kind of distraction from collectibles to edibles. Among the more noteworthy emporia are the Main Street Gallery (actually, just off Main, on South Water Street) and Espresso Café, a lively place with the look of a classic ice-cream parlor.

Nantucket is justly proud of its history, especially its grand old homes and museums. The Nantucket Historical Association oversees more than a dozen properties (one ticket gains entry to all of them; tel: 508-228 1894).

A walk down South Water Street to Broad Street leads past three important institutions. Located at the corner of Lower India Street, the Greek Revival **Nantucket Atheneum** (constructed by local architect Frederick Brown Coleman

TIP

A good rainy-day stop in summer is the Dreamland Theatre, on South Water, which shows first-run films. It started life in the mid-1800s as a Quaker meeting house.

BELOW: the tools of a gardener's trade, Nantucket town.

Map
on pages
158–9

in 1847) represents the intellectual flowering that accompanied the island's era of prosperity: Ralph Waldo Emerson gave the inaugural address and was followed by the leading thinkers of the day. Now a public library, this temple of learning contains interesting exhibits relating to island history. Also on Broad Street, the **Whaling Museum** (housed in a former spermaceti candle factory) commemorates Nantucket's seafaring days in a highly dramatic manner, with impressive displays (open May–Dec, daily; entrance fee).

Nearby, the **Peter Foulger Museum**, also on Broad, mounts temporary exhibits deriving from the research conducted upstairs by the Nantucket Historical Association (open daily; entrance fee). There's also a small **Life Saving Museum**, paying tribute to the work of the United States Life Saving Service (Polpis Road; open daily; entrance fee).

A bracing walk out of town, to the corner of South Mill and Prospect streets, leads to the **Old Mill** (1746), where, on windy days, visitors can watch corn kernels being ground into fine powder.

A few blocks away, at the corner of Vestal and Milk streets, is the **Maria Mitchell Science Center** (call for opening hours; entrance fee; tel: 508-228 9198) honoring the local savant – and Atheneum librarian – who discovered a comet at the age of 29 in 1847, garnering international acclaim. She went on to become the first woman admitted to the American Academy of Arts and Sciences, as well as the first female college professor in the United States (she taught astronomy at Vassar).

The somewhat scattered complex comprises five facilities open to the public, including the Mitchell House, her childhood home; the Hinchman House, a natural history museum; the Science Library, located in a former school house;

TIP

One of the island's better kept secrets is the subterranean Brotherhood of Thieves, an old whaling bar on Broad Street. It has no listed telephone number and doesn't take credit cards, but serves good pub food and chowder by candle-light.

BELOW:
the Wauwinet inn,
Nantucket.

Doorknocker, Jared Coffin House.

the Loines Observatory, located farther along Milk Street; and, on Washington Street, a small harborside Aquarium geared to children.

Further out on Vestal is the **Old Gaol**, built in 1805 and in use until 1933 (open mid-June–Sept). It looks like a normal house on the outside but is shockingly crude within; especially dangerous prisoners were confined in an iron-walled cell. But the island has never had much of a crime problem, and in any case prisoners were allowed to spend their nights at home.

The oldest house on Nantucket is the **Jethro Coffin House** (1686) on the northwest edge of town on Sunset Hill Lane (open mid-June–Sept). This plain saltbox design reflects the austere lifestyle led by the island's earliest settlers. In contrast, the three-story red-brick Jared Coffin House, at the corner of Centre and Broad streets, made its 1845 debut as the showiest dwelling on the island; within two years it became a hotel, and to this day it remains one of the island's finest inns.

Two more Coffin residences (the family was so prolific, it accounted for half the island's population by the early 19th century) stand at No. 75 and No. 78 Main Street, examples of the brick Federal style of architecture.

Farther up Main Street are the "**Three Bricks**," architectural triplets built by wealthy whaler Joseph Starbuck for his three sons. Across the street, and worlds apart in style, stand the "**Two Greeks**," Greek Revival mansions built by Frederick Coleman for two Starbuck daughters. One, the **Hadwen House** (96 Main Street; open mid-June–mid-Sept, daily; entrance fee) is maintained as a museum by the Nantucket Historical Association.

No. 99 Main Street, with its detailed and finely proportioned facade, is one of the most handsome wooden Federal-style buildings on Nantucket; it was

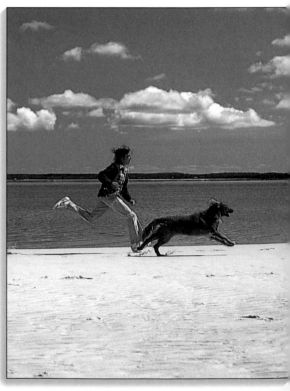

built by forebears of Roland Macy, who left the island to seek his fortune and founded a well-known namesake store.

Overlooking the harbor from **Brant Point** is one of America's oldest lighthouses. Visitors departing by sea often toss the traditional penny into the water off Brant Point to ensure that they'll return to the shores of Nantucket.

The rest of Nantucket island

"Nantucket! Take out your map and look at it," urged Herman Melville in his whaling adventure classic *Moby Dick*. An inspection of the map reveals an island with hamlets and hideaways sprinkled across its 14-mile (23-km) length. Despite some mid-island development in recent decades, about one-third of the island is under protective stewardship, thanks to the intercession of the Nantucket Conservation Foundation; although environmental restrictions limit activity on dunes, moors and other fragile areas, much of the land can be explored.

Stretching to the northeast from the town of Nantucket is a 6-mile (10-km) inner harbor, protected from Nantucket Sound by **Coatue**, a thin spit of land with flat white beaches accessible only by boat or four-wheel-drive vehicles (driven around the Head of the Harbor). This sweep of land, encompassing the **Coatue-Coskata Wildlife Refuge** ㉚, extends north to **Great Point**, where a lighthouse – a solar-powered 1986 replica of the 1818 original, swept away by a 1984 storm – warns boats away from the sandbars of Nantucket Sound.

Residential neighborhoods extend along the south side of the harbor. Monomoy, the nearest to town and the most populous settlement, affords spectacular views from its bluffs.

Map on pages 158–9

TIP

The Nantucket Trustees of the Reservations (tel: 228 6799) offer a three-hour over-sand tour of the Coatue-Coskata Wildlife Refuge. Pick it up in the Wauwinet Inn parking lot.

BELOW:
much of Nantucket is protected from development.

Map
on pages
158–9

A seaside treat.

BELOW: a
Siasconset cameo.

From here, the Polpis Road leads across the rolling and delicate **Nantucket Moors**, which are carpeted with bayberry, beach plum, heather and other lush vegetation – a lovely green and flowering pink in summer, brilliant red and gold in the fall.

Wauwinet ㊴, a tiny community of cottages tucked amid the beach grass at the head of the harbor, is home to the ultra-elegant (and ultra-expensive) Wauwinet, a finely refurbished 1850 hostelry within splashing distance of both ocean and harbor. (It's located on the "haulover" where fishing boats used to avoid the long trip around Great Point.)

Tourists discovered **Siasconset ㊵** (pronounced "Sconset"), the easternmost and second-largest town on Nantucket, in the 1880s. Theater people from the mainland mingled with local fishermen; the resulting architecture ranges from Lilliputian cottages to large rambling shingle-style houses along the bluffs.

Nantucket's most popular beaches are located on the flat, windswept south shore, open to the cold, spirited waters of the Atlantic Ocean. At **Surfside Beach ㊶**, a colorful Victorian lifesaving station serves nowadays as the island's only Youth Hostel. Surfers favor the beach at **Cisco**, a bit more remote, at the end of Hummock Pond Road, while **Madaket Beach ㊷**, at the southwestern tip of Nantucket, is popular for swimming, fishing, and, especially, sunset-gazing.

The northern coast east of Madaket Harbor, heading back toward town, offers the gentle surf of **Dionis** and **Jetties** beaches. The latter gets its name from its proximity to the West Jetty, which protects the channel leading into Nantucket Harbor. **Children's Beach**, tucked well inside the West Jetty, near Steamship Wharf, is especially placid and enhanced by a playground. ❑

Whale Watching

Destination: Stellwagen Bank, a shallow underwater deposit of sand and gravel off the coast of Massachusetts, to which pods of gentle humpbacked whales return yearly after spending the winters breeding in the West Indies. Sightseers are hot on their tails, for it's truly breathtaking to see these huge (often endangered) spectacles lunge, breach and flipper in the open ocean.

It's so rare for visitors not to see whales during a trip that most companies offer a "rain check," good for another trip. More often than not, the boats approach to within 50 ft (15 meters) of these magnificent mammals.

The world's largest concentration of whales (both in numbers and in species) are drawn to the fertile feeding grounds of Stellwagen Bank by huge quantities of plankton and an infinite number of small sand eels. The vast majority of the 500 or so whales who summer here are humpbacks, but their number also includes minkes, finbacks and a few endangered right whales (so called because, being slow swimmers, they were the "right" whales to hunt). Hundreds of frolicking dolphins and immense basking sharks will be close by, too.

The humpback is basically a bulk feeder, diving deep below schools of sand eels and lunging upward through the school with its mouth open. On the way up, it engulfs large quantities of fish and water, while its rorquals (folds of skin that begin at the chin and stretch to the navel) balloon to double its oral capacity. This allows the whale to catch hundreds, perhaps thousands, of fish with every lunge.

Whales also breach – that is, leap from the water, and flipper-roll on to their sides and lift their long white flipper out of the water before slamming it down hard on the surface.

Experts recognize individual humpbacks, which often reach lengths of 40–50 ft (12–15 meters) and weights of 30 tons, by their body markings, especially those on their tail flukes.

Whale watching was popularized in 1975 by Captain Al Avellar, a deep-sea fisherman from Provincetown, who invited Charles Mayo, a Provincetown-based marine biologist, to act as a guide on his first trips. Today, whale-watching excursions, all with experts on board, attract over 100,000 visitors annually.

Sightseeing boats generally depart two or three times daily in summer and on weekends in spring and fall. Trips last about three hours. Take jackets and seasickness pills, even on calm and seemingly warm days.

Many companies are based in Provincetown on Cape Cod: the Dolphin Fleet (tel: 508-349 1900, 800-826 9300) has an on-board biologist from the Center for Coastal Studies. In mid-Cape's Barnstable Harbor, call Hyannis Whalewatcher Cruises (tel: 508-362 6088).

From Boston, the New England Aquarium (tel: 617-973 5277) sponsors whalewatching trips, as does Boston Harbor Cruises (Rowes Wharf; tel: 617-723 7800).

On the North Shore in Gloucester, call Cape Ann Whale Watch (415 Main Street; tel: 978-283 5110, 800-877 5110) and Yankee Fleet Whale Watch (Route 133; tel: 978-283 0313, 800-942 5464). In Plymouth, Captain John Boats (tel: 508-746 2643, 800-242 2469) and Captain Tim Brady and Sons (tel: 508-746 4809) leave from Town Wharf. ❏

RIGHT: dolphins frolic alongside.

CENTRAL MASSACHUSETTS AND THE BERKSHIRES

Famed outdoor museums recall the past and students enliven the present. In the west, art, dance, music, literature, and crafts flourish like nowhere else in New England

New England's legacy of rural beauty and industry lives on in Central Massachusetts. Whereas Boston belongs to the modern world of cosmopolitan cities and the Berkshires to the Gilded Age tradition of opulent leisure, the Commonwealth's mid-section harkens back to an earlier, mostly agricultural era when the living was hard and plain, the rewards what ready hands and determined souls could create.

The vigor and sincerity of early Americans' social vision is on display from mid-May to mid-October at **Fruitlands Museums** in the little town of **Harvard ❶**, an hour or so west of Boston via Route 2 (Prospect Hill; open daily; entrance fee). In the mid-19th century, transcendentalist Amos Bronson Alcott, father of Louisa May Alcott (author of *Little Women*), left his Concord home with political activist Charles Lane and a group of followers to found an anti-materialist utopian community on the 18th-century Fruitlands farm.

Vegetarianism, asceticism and a philosophical return to nature were their mandates but, despite their inspiring view of the beautiful Nashua River Valley, the commune soon dispersed. Today, however, the farmhouse has been transformed into a transcendentalist museum with presentations on Alcott, Emerson, Thoreau and others; its tearoom offers the same view of the Nashua Valley, and is surrounded by several other small museums.

Some 19th-century utopian experiments enjoyed greater longevity than that of Fruitlands. The most notable was that of the chaste and fervent Shakers, who persisted in Harvard from the late 18th century until 1918 (other New England Shaker settlements are intact to this day, although the sect is now virtually extinct; *see pages 296–97*). Fruitlands' 1794 Shaker House contains their crafts and furnishings which bespeak a lifestyle of studied simplicity.

The Indian Museum has a fine collection of artifacts, and the Picture Gallery displays folk portraits by itinerant artists and landscapes by such Hudson River School artists as Asher Durand and Frederick Church.

Ski center

Farther west, off Route 62 between Westminster and North Rutland, **Wachusett Mountain State Park ❷** has chair lifts and trails leading up to one of the state's highest summits (2,006 ft/649 meters), with views of the Boston skyscrapers. It doubles as the nearest ski and snowboard center to Boston, particularly geared to beginners and families, and has 100 percent snow-making; booking on busy weekends (tel: 978-464 2300).

To the southeast is **Worcester ❸**, the state's

PRECEDING PAGES: fall in the west of the state. **LEFT:** at Old Sturbridge Village. **BELOW:** in the Indian Museum at Fruitlands Museums.

Central Massachusetts and the Berkshires

second-largest city. Where would America be without Worcester? This gritty industrial city spawned the country's first park, first wire-making company, first steam calliope, first carpet loom, first diner, first Valentine, and (suitably enough) first birth-control pill, not to mention the beginnings of liquid-fuel rocketry, female suffrage and the Free Soil Party, now known as the Republican Party. Notable residents have included abolitionist-composer Stephen Foster and socialist leader Emma Goldman; Sigmund Freud gave his only US lecture at Clark University.

The humorist Robert Benchley grew up in Worcester, as did the notorious 1960s radical Abbie Hoffman, and no doubt both owed their unfettered freedom of speech to publisher Isaiah Thomas, a Son of Liberty who fled Boston in advance of the British Army in 1770 and continued to publish his rabble-rousing revolutionary newspaper, the *Massachusetts Spy*, from Worcester. Thomas went on to become one of the wealthiest men in America, establishing the American Antiquarian Society on New York's Park Avenue in 1818; the original Worcester headquarters, on Salisbury Street, now serve as a research library.

The city, though left somewhat depressed in the wake of Masschusetts' industrial boom, is itself a trove of antiquarian delights. The **Worcester Historical Museum** (30 Elm Street; open Tues–Sat; Sun pm; entrance fee) is chockful of interesting memorabilia; the museum also maintains the splendid 1772 Georgian Salisbury Mansion. Awe-inspiring in its scope, the **Higgins Armory Museum** – the legacy of a local steel magnate – features a vast collection of medieval armor, as well as armaments dating back to 6th-century BC Greece (100 Barber Avenue; open Tues–Sat; Sun pm; entrance fee).

The **Worcester Art Museum** (55 Salisbury Street; open Wed–Sun, entrance fee) is the second largest in New England and perhaps the most adventurous: its sponsorship of excavations at Antioch, Syria, in the 1930s yielded a remarkable collection of 2nd-century AD Roman mosaics. The museum contains many other valuable antiquities along with fine collections of European and Eastern art. But perhaps most ppealing is the extensive gallery of 17th-, 18th- and 19th-century American art, including paintings by Winslow Homer, John Singer Sargent and John Singleton Copley. In their portraits and landscapes, one can trace the gradual emergence of a distinctly American culture.

Worcester Common (tel: 508-798 2581) is an all-in-one covered factory outlet mall in the heart of the city, with some 90 stores; there are direct buses from Boston South Station.

Reliving the past

Off Route 20, **Old Sturbridge Village** ➍ – a recreated community encompassing some 40 period buildings scattered over 200 acres (80 hectares) – offers a "you are there" take on early 19th-century rural life (Route 20; open May–Oct, daily; Nov–Apr, Tues–Sun; entrance fee; tel: 508-347 3362).

Visitors are given illuminating explanations, couched in modern parlance, as the interpreters go about the daily business of farm and town life: tending their animals, making tin lanterns, or leading prayers.

Map on page 188

Robert Benchley's bomb-proof quote: "The surest way to make a monkey of a man is to quote him."

BELOW: interpreting the past at Old Sturbridge Village.

Though a delight any time of year, Old Sturbridge is especially captivating in winter, when the crowds are sparser and the harshness of New England weather that so shaped the early settlers' moral and physical fiber can be experienced firsthand. Of special interest is the Pliny Freeman Farm, where, depending on the season, workers in period dress engage in making soap, shearing sheep, and laboriously building stone walls. Concepts of political freedom and discourse grew, in part, from the emergence of a free and vibrant press, and the activities of the Isaiah Thomas Printing Office are designed to show how printed communication became an integral part of the new nation's growth.

Continuing west, through rolling hills verdant in spring and summer, an explosion of color come fall, travelers reach the huge **Quabbin Reservoir ❺**, 128 sq. miles (331 sq. km) of flooded valley that holds 412 billion gallons and supplies the drinking water to Greater Boston. Four towns were flooded in 1939 to create this great body of water; the **Swift River Historical Society** in New Salem preserves mementos of these vanished communities. More than a water source, Quabbin is prized as a place to fish, hike and admire the rare bald eagles that breed by the reservoir.

The pioneer heritage

The well-preserved pioneer village of **Old Deerfield ❻** – where 14 museum houses are preserved as **Historic Deerfield**, off Route 5 (Main Street; open daily; entrance fee) – has a fascinating history that dates from its settlement by farmers in 1669. The Pocumtuck, who had been using the fertile valley to raise pumpkins, corn, and tobacco, were not pleased to see their land usurped, and massacred the entire population (by then 125 strong) in 1675. That

It is not excelled by anything I have ever seen, not excepting the Bay of Naples.

– JOHN QUINCY ADAMS, WRITING OF DEERFIELD'S MAIN STREET

BELOW: Old Sturbridge Village.

Map on page 188

deterred settlers for the next seven years, but the lure of the land was irresistible, and the interlopers eventually won out, despite another raid in 1704 in which half the village was burned, some 100 colonists were abducted into slavery, and another 50 slaughtered.

Tomahawk marks can still be seen on one sturdy wooden door, but the town's lurid history is not what attracts most visitors. The draw is an extraordinary architectural cache: the carefully restored Colonial and Federal structures along "The Street," Deerfield's mile-long main thoroughfare. The treasures inside the houses, representing decades of changing decorative styles, easily equal the exteriors. Among the more interesting of the buildings open to the public are the Ashley House (1730), a former parson's home with intricately carved woodwork and antique furnishings; the Asa Stebbins House (1810) with early paintings, Chinese porcelain and Federal and Chippendale furniture; the Dwight Barnard House (1725), immediately recognizable by its handsome carved door, behind which is an 18th-century doctor's office; and the Hall Tavern (1760), where Historic Deerfield maintains its information center.

The Pioneer Valley: a cultural nexus

About 10 miles (16 km) south of Old Deerfield, along the region designated as Pioneer Valley (the Massachusetts section of the Connecticut River Valley), is the town of **Amherst** ❼, long a hotbed of intellectual vigor and social independence. Noah Webster, creator of the American dictionary, lived here, as did a reclusive genius of the English language.

Visitors to the **Emily Dickinson Homestead** can experience the spartan environment that housed a sensitive, self-confined soul, who poured her

I never lost as much but twice,
And that was in the sod;
Twice I have stood a beggar
Before the door of God!

— EMILY DICKINSON, REFERRING TO THE DEATH OF TWO YOUNG MEN WHO INFLUENCED HER WRITING

BELOW:
Amherst Common.

Beinfield Flea Market, held three times a year, is the world's largest outdoor crafts show, with more than 5,000 dealers.

BELOW: canoeing on the Connecticut River.

emotions solely into her poetry (280 Main Street; tours by appointment; tel: 413-542 8161). Just off the spacious central green, **Amherst College's** stately fraternity houses flank a campus quadrangle that is a classic of early 19th-century institutional architecture; American and European works are exhibited at the college's **Mead Art Museum** (call for hours; tel: 413-542 2335).

Down Route 9 and across the Connecticut River is **Northampton** ➑, which can also boast a taciturn celebrity. Calvin Coolidge (1872–1933), the governor of Massachusetts who went on to serve as 30th US President, began his law practice in Northampton and eventually died there. His reputation as a man of exceptionally few words once prompted a determined matron at a society banquet to coax him: "Mr President, I have a wager with a friend that I can persuade you to say more than two words." Coolidge's reply: "You lose."

Surrounded by colleges (Amherst, Hampshire, and the University of Massachusetts – known to all as U-Mass – to the east, Mount Holyoke to the south, and Smith, right in town), Northampton has benefited from the youthful, energetic company it keeps. Once drab and dull, it now hosts a lively mix of fashionable stores and international restaurants, earning it the sobriquet of "Noho." With a sophistication level equal to that of New York's SoHo district, Northampton has attracted hundreds of artisans and artists, who showcase their wares at craft shops such as the Ferrin Gallery and Pinch Pottery and at the fine-art Hart Gallery.

The **Smith College Museum of Art**, one of the finest collections in the country, with a special focus on French impressionists, is on hand to lend inspiration (Route 9; tel: 413-585 2760); the college's Lyman Plant House, a delicate 1896 greenhouse, makes a lovely rainy-day retreat. In complete contrast is the **Words and Pictures Museum**, which pays homage to the art of comic books (140 Main Street; open pm only Tues–Fri; Fri till 8pm; Sat 10am–8pm; Sun pm; entrance fee).

Holyoke Range State Park ❾ has some of the best scenery in the Pioneer Valley. A road climbs up from Route 47 at Hadley to a viewpoint that was immortalized in Thomas Coles's 1830 painting, *The Oxbow*, with New Hampshire's Mount Monadnock is in sight. Just down the road in nearby South Hadley the **Mount Holyoke College** campus, designed by the famed landscape architect Frederick Law Olmsted, is the loveliest of the five colleges.

Bouncing back: Springfield

Springfield ❿ is one of those large American cities that just seem to lack pizzazz – or at least it did, until recently. The problem was an insensitive highway project, I-91, that chopped up neighborhoods and cut the city off from its most valuable natural asset, the Connecticut River. Now its banks have been reclaimed for the populace, in the form of a refreshing Riverfront Park, where summertime concerts are held.

Close by is the **Basketball Hall of Fame**, a lively, interactive museum dedicated to the game invented in 1891 by Springfield YMCA instructor Dr James Naismith (1150 West Columbus Avenue; open daily; entrance fee). Visitors have an opportunity to experience the fast-paced thrills in the "Shoot-Out," where a conveyor belt moves participants along a line of hoops.

Among the other "firsts," Springfield is known for its role as the nation's original arsenal (George Washington chose the site in 1779). The **Springfield Armory National Historic Site**, home of the first American musket, now

Map on page 188

YMCA instructor James Naismith nailed up a pair of peach baskets to keep his charges occupied; the game was more absorbing, they discovered, once the bottoms of the baskets were removed. And so basketball was invented.

BELOW LEFT: the Connecticut River Valley.
BELOW RIGHT: at the Basketball Hall of Fame.

houses a museum featuring one of the largest collections of firearms in the world (Armory Square; open Wed–Sun; entrance fee).

Springfield supports four more outstanding museums, all clustered around "the Quad" – the **Springfield Museum Quadrangle** on State Street.

The **George Walter Vincent Smith Art Museum** (open pm only Wed–Sun; entrance fee) features oriental decorative arts, from Persian rugs to Japanese netsuke and Chinese cloisonné (the largest collection of the latter in the Western world). The **Science Museum** contains the first American-built planetarium and plenty of intriguing, hands-on exhibits (open pm only Wed–Sun; entrance fee). The **Connecticut Valley Historical Museum** showcases artifacts – from folk paintings to fine furniture – chronicling several centuries of regional life (open pm only Wed–Sun; entrance fee). The **Museum of Fine Arts** (open pm only Wed–Sun; entrance fee) has an impressively broad collection, including portraits by the noted itinerant painter Rufus Porter; contemporary shows are also mounted.

Springfield's rich cultural life is reflected in the musical offerings, ranging from classical to popular, of the Springfield Symphony Orchestra, and in the sophisticated stagings of **StageWest** (tel: 413-781 2340). And no visit to the city would be complete without a pilgrimage to the **Student Prince and Fort Restaurant**, a colorful 1935 redoubt of German beer and sauerbraten (8 Fort Street; tel: 413-734 7475).

Across the river, in **West Springfield**, are the 175-acre (71-hectare) fairgrounds for the **Eastern States Exposition** (the "Big E"), New England's major agricultural fair and one of the nation's largest (tel: 413-732 2361). Every September, prize livestock and top-name talents entertain the crowds. Permanently ensconced on the grounds is the **Storrowton Village Museum**, seven trans-

Springfield's federal armory produced its first musket in 1795 and was still turning out rifles in World War II. It finally closed in 1968.

BELOW: small farms like this one in the Berkshires often offer bed and breakfast facilities.

Map on page 188

planted 18th- and early 19th-century buildings where traditional crafts are demonstrated (Route 147; open late June–Aug Mon–Sat; entrance fee).

The Berkshires

Making up western Massachusetts, Berkshire County – sometimes called the American Lake District – encompasses a landscape that provides almost every variety of beauty – valleys dotted with shimmering lakes, rolling farmlands punctuated by orchards and wheatfields, deep forests abundant with deer, powerful rivers that cascade into waterfalls under the bluest of New England skies.

Everywhere one turns in this corner of Massachusetts, the horizon is piled and terraced with mountains. Though less dramatic than the White Mountains of New Hampshire or the Green Mountains of Vermont, these gentle ranges have nonetheless provided the Berkshire Hills with an insularity that has historically set them apart from the rest of the state.

The Dutch, who settled New York in 1626 and moved north into the Hudson Valley, were prevented from further advancement by the stony resistance of the Taconic Range. Similar difficulties were met by the English, who found their progress west from the Connecticut River Valley blocked by the Hoosac Mountains – a wall of granite later dubbed the Berkshire Barrier.

Contained within this natural barricade, the Berkshires remained a wilderness until 1725, when Matthew Noble traveled through its dense forests to build a cabin in what is now the town of Sheffield. In the years that followed, farmland was cleared and towns were established along the Housatonic River and its tributaries. During the 19th century, the Industrial Revolution brought prosperity to the Berkshires: its iron foundries melted ore for the country's first railroads, while marble quarried from its hills graced the dome of the Capitol in Washington, DC.

As big business lured succeeding generations to the cities and better land beckoned farmers farther west, the Berkshires receded into a sleepy silence. But city dwellers seeking pretty scenery and respite from summer heat have periodically rediscovered the Berkshires. During the 1890s, for example, the county became a playground for such wealthy families as the Carnegies and Vanderbilts, who built their mansions in the hills surrounding Stockbridge and Lenox. More recently, visitors have come for the renowned summer music festivals, the splendor of fall foliage, or the challenge of winter skiing.

The first settlers reached the Berkshires through the Housatonic Valley from Connecticut. The modern traveler can do the same, following US Highway 7 north along the Housatonic. Many of Berkshire County's best-known attractions are located along Route 7 (or just a short distance from it).

The South Berkshires

Just inside the Connecticut border on Route 7A is **Ashley Falls** ⓫, a village surrounded by hayfields and dairy farms. The village was named for Colonel John Ashley, a prominent lawyer and major-general of the Massachusetts militia during the Revolutionary War. The **Colonel John Ashley House**, built in 1735,

BELOW: fall in the Berkshires.

is the oldest structure in Berkshire County. It has been restored as a colonial museum (off Route 7; open June–early Sept; pm only Wed–Sun; entrance fee).

Also located in Ashley Falls is **Bartholomew's Cobble** . This natural rock garden, with hiking trails that meander along the banks of the Housatonic, is a bird-watcher's paradise and an excellent place to search for the trilliums and trout lilies of early spring. It contains more species of fern than any other area in the continental United States.

Sheffield ⓭, established in 1733, is the oldest town in Berkshire County and boasts two of the best-preserved covered bridges in Massachusetts. Traffic still travels over the larger, a narrow, barn-red structure that spans the Housatonic just east of town, on the road to New Marlborough.

At the far corner of the county, 2,000 ft (600 meters) up and teetering on the edge of New York State, is the tiny hill hamlet of **Mount Washington**. The smallest town in the Berkshires, Mount Washington offers some of the finest fall-foliage viewing in New England.

Continuing along the Mount Washington road, the traveler arrives at **Bash Bish Falls** ⓮, a 275-ft (84-meter) natural waterfall where, legend has it, a Native American maiden jumped to her death after being spurned by her lover. When the moon is full, her ghost, it is said, may be seen walking through the mountain laurel to wade in the pool beneath the falls.

The Berkshires' true beauty lies in its backroads and small villages. **New Marlborough** and nearby **Mill River**, small communities that prospered in the heyday of the Industrial Revolution, are gems. At the Old Inn on the Green in New Marlborough, once a stagecoach stop en route from New York to Boston, visitors can dine on fresh lamb or breakfast on blueberry muffins.

TIP

There is excellent blueberry picking to be had on Mount Washington.

BELOW: capturing the Berkshires on canvas.

Great Barrington offers an excellent base from which to explore the towns and villages of the southern Berkshires. Although it does not have the architectural treasures of towns farther north such as Stockbridge and Lenox, Great Barrington does have a homey quality. The Housatonic River courses through the center of town, and it was here, at a natural ford in the river, that the Mohicans built their Great Wigwam. It was also here that William Stanley (later to found the General Electric Company) first successfully demonstrated the use of alternating current; in 1886, the town became one of the first communities in America to be lit by electricity.

Great Barrington has been home to a large African-American community since before the Civil War, when fugitive slaves traveled to Massachusetts on the Underground Railroad. Socialist and scholar W. E. B. DuBois was born here in 1868.

A literary and artistic heritage

North of Great Barrington is **Monument Mountain** ⓰, a craggy peak whose summit is a pleasant half-hour hike from the parking lot at its base. The mountain is a Berkshire literary landmark of considerable repute. The poet William Cullen Bryant sang its praises while practicing as a local attorney in the 1830s.

The tiny village of **Tyringham** ⓱, where a community of Shakers settled in the 19th century, is unspoiled. In the early years of this century, the beauty of the landscape transformed the Tyringham Valley into an artists' colony. Today, in summer, Tyringham Art Galleries, founded in 1953, continue to operate out of the fairy-tale Gingerbread House, a former sculpture studio.

Stockbridge ⓲ was incorporated as an Indian mission in 1739. Its first missionary was John Sargeant, a young tutor from Yale who lived among the

Many poets and writers have visited the Berkshires. Longfellow once hiked these trails, as did Emerson and Thoreau. Henry James visited often and, more recently, Berkshire County has been home to Thornton Wilder and Norman Mailer.

BELOW: the historic Sargeant House, Stockbridge.

Fall colours.

BELOW: Church on the Hill, Lenox.

natives for 16 years. He slept in their wigwams, shared their venison and spoke their language, while introducing them to the colonists' ways. Eventually, Sargeant helped them establish a town, build homes and cultivate the land. Some among the Mohican tribe held public office, serving alongside whites in the town government. The Stockbridge Mission was so successful that it became a model of cultural adaptation; but the experiment was not to last. As more colonists moved into the area, the tribes were slowly deprived of their land. By 1783, the mission was history, and surviving Indians were forced to settle on the Oneida reservation in New York State. All that remains is the **Mission House**, now a museum on Stockbridge's Main Street (open late May–mid-Oct; entrance fee).

If the stately mansions and quaint shops located along Route 102, the Main Street of Stockbridge, look familiar, it may be because their New England essence was captured on the canvases of that remarkable illustrator of American life, Norman Rockwell. Rockwell, who created more than 300 covers for the *Saturday Evening Post,* kept a studio in Stockbridge and made his home here for a quarter of a century, until his death in 1978. Located on Route 183, the stunning **Norman Rockwell Museum**, designed by Robert A.M. Stern, showcases his oeuvre and even recreates his Stockbridge studio. No visitor, however sophisticated, should miss this display: reflecting a time when American ideals were simpler, Rockwell's portraits capture an age of innocence with humor and modesty (open daily; entrance fee; tel: 413-298 4100).

The Red Lion Inn, located in the center of Stockbridge at the intersection of Routes 7 and 102, is one of the *grandes dames* of New England country inns. Its flower-laden front porch, complete with rocking chairs, is a place of pilgrimage for Berkshires travelers.

Map on page 188

Naumkeag, 2 miles (3 km) north of Stockbridge, is a Norman-style mansion designed by Stanford White for Joseph Choate, US ambassador to Great Britain in 1899; the furnishings and gardens are unusually lavish (Prospect Hill Road; open late May–early Sept daily; weekends until mid–Oct; entrance fee). **Chesterwood**, the summer home of sculptor Daniel Chester French, is 3 miles (5 km) west of Stockbridge (off Route 183; open May–Oct daily; entrance fee). It was here that he created his masterpiece, *The Seated Lincoln*, focal point of the Lincoln Memorial in Washington, DC. Casts are displayed in the house.

In **Lenox** ⓳ is **The Mount**, novelist Edith Wharton's grand Italianate 1890s mansion (Routes 7 and 7A; open late May–Oct Tues–Sun; entrance fee), now the headquarters of the theater troupe Shakespeare & Co (see below). Here she wrote *Ethan Frome*, set in the Berkshire town of West Stockbridge.

The sounds of music

Is it possible to vacation in the Berkshires without stopping at **Tanglewood** ⓴, summer home of the Boston Symphony Orchestra? This 200-acre (80-hectare) estate, located on Route 183, 1½ miles (2.5 km) west of Lenox, has been a haven for performers, students and music lovers since the orchestra first began its outdoor concert series in 1931. The 6,000-seat Music Shed, designed by architect Eero Saarinen, has excellent acoustics; but many visitors prefer to pack their dinners, come early and picnic on the lawn. They need blankets and plenty of warm clothes to counter the cool night air.

During the summer, near Tanglewood's lawn, a replica of the little red cottage where Nathaniel Hawthorne lived and wrote *The House of the Seven Gables* and *Tanglewood Tales* can be visited.

TIP

The BSO Tanglewood season begins in late June and runs through August, with concerts on Fridays, Saturdays and Sundays (tel: 413-637 1600).

BELOW: a Housatonic potter at work.

CULTURE IN THE BERKSHIRES

Tanglewood is the best-known of several summer festivals in the Berkshires. The South Mountain Concerts (tel: 413-442 2106), featuring chamber music on weekends, take place south of Pittsfield, on Route 7. For Renaissance and Baroque music head for the Aston Magna Festival (tel: 413-528 3595), in Great Barrington; performances on original instruments are given at St James Church on weekends in July.

When the Jacob's Pillow Dance Festival (tel: 413-243 0745) was launched in the early 1930s, modern dance was in its infancy and many viewed the likes of Martha Graham and Merce Cunningham as a passing fad. Today, Jacob's Pillow (in the hilltown of Becket, southeast of Pittsfield on State 8) is a national institution.

Also impressive is the Williamstown Theater Festival (tel: 413-597 3399), which stages some of the finest summer theater in the country. Running the gamut from Greek tragedy to Restoration comedy, and from Chekhov to Pirandello, the festival also has a fine company of actors.

At Berkshire Theater Festival (tel: 413-298 5536), in Stockbridge, the emphasis is on American classics. For fans of the Bard, there's Shakespeare & Co (tel: 413-637 3353), which performs outdoors at The Mount in Lenox.

Map on page 188

The simple Shakers

"'Tis a gift to be simple," says the old Shaker hymn. A visit to **Hancock Shaker Village ㉑**, on Route US 20, 3 miles (5 km) west of Pittsfield, is testimony to the virtues of simplicity (tel: 413-443 0188; open daily; entrance fee).

The Shakers (*see pages 296–97*) settled in Hancock during the late 1780s. The community prospered through farming, printing, selling garden seeds and herbs and manufacturing their distinctively designed furnishings. The elegance and functionalism of Shaker architecture is exemplified by Hancock's famous 1826 round stone barn. It enabled one farmhand, standing at its center, to feed an entire herd of cattle. Shakers lived in Hancock until the 1950s, when the community had dwindled to a few staunch survivors, celibacy and changing times having led to their decline.

Returning to Route 7, the northbound traveler passes through **Pittsfield ㉒**, the Berkshire County seat and largest city (population 52,000) and the town that General Electric built. Writer Herman Melville lived here and completed *Moby Dick* (1851) while at **Arrowhead** (Route 7; open May–mid-Sept daily; mid-Sept–Oct Fri–Mon; entrance fee); there is Melville memorabilia at the Berkshire Athenaeum.

Williamstown and the north Berkshires

North of Pittsfield, **Jiminy Peak ㉓** is a ski area with night skiing. It offers something to suit all levels of skill; in summer an alpine slide operates, making an exhilarating drop down the mountain, and fishing, tennis, putting and swimming are on offer (tel: 413-738 5500).

In the state's northwest corner **Williamstown ㉔** is among the most beautiful of New England villages. It is home to **Williams College**, founded in 1793. A major reason to come to Williamstown is for the exceptional **Sterling and Francine Clark Art Institute**, located on South Street just west of the town center (open Tues–Sun; entrance fee). Between World War I and 1956, the Clarks amassed a superb private collection of European and American paintings, including works by Botticelli, Goya, Gainsborough and Fragonard. But the museum is best known for its Impressionist collection, which includes many works by Monet, Degas and Renoir.

Rising to 3,491 ft (1,064 meters), east of Williamstown, **Mount Greylock ㉕** is the tallest peak in Massachusetts. Hardy travelers can ascend on foot, while those less energetic can drive to the summit via a steep and winding access road. From the top, writer Nathaniel Hawthorne looked down upon Williamstown – "a white village and a steeple set like a daydream among the high mountain waves."

The **Mohawk Trail ㉖** (Route 2) winds eastwards from Williamstown, across the top of Berkshire County. An old Indian path-turned-roadway – as recalled by a number of roadside stores selling "Indian" souvenirs – it offers some of the most rugged and romantic scenery in the Berkshires. It is a popular leaf-peeping route in the fall. The best of the views are around Hairpin Turn, east of North Adams. ❏

BELOW: on the Mohawk Trail: "Hail to the Sunrise" recalls the Mohawk Indians.

Sporting Traditions

E ver since football was introduced to the nation on Boston Common in 1862 and basketballs were first stuffed into baskets in Springfield, Mass., in 1881, New England has been a sports trailblazer. Long before expansion became the buzz word, Boston was one of the only cities to boast major league teams in baseball (Red Sox and Braves), basketball (Celtics), and ice-hockey (Bruins). The Braves decamped after 1952; football expansion led to the 1960 appearance of the Patriots; and in 1979 the Hartford Whalers entered the major ice-hockey arena.

Yet it seems the fate of New England fans nearly always to follow losers. Only the Celtics have bucked the trend by winning 16 National Basketball titles, more than any other team. But their last pennant was in 1986.

Admittedly, the Red Sox won the first World Series, in 1903, and clinched it four times between then and 1918, but never since then. In the 1986 World Series, they were within a heart-beat of winning, but they lost that game and the decisive seventh and, with it, the title. In 1988, 1990, 1995 and 1998 they made it to the playoffs but never got to compete in the World Series. The Bruins have won the coveted Stanley Cup five times, but the last time was in 1972. In 1990 they succumbed to the Edmonton Oilers in the third period of overtime in the seventh and last game of the Stanley Cup.

The formerly hapless Patriots, who made it to the 1986 Superbowl but were trounced by the Chicago Bears 46–10, turned a corner in 1993 with the arrival of quarterback Drew Bledsoe and coach Bill Parcels. In 1994 they won the AFC wildcard game but got no further; in 1996 they made it to the Superbowl, but were beaten by Green Bay 35–21. In 1997, under a new coach, they won the AFC wildcard game but lost the next AFC division game.

Patience should, but does not, grow thin: there are always demi-gods to worship: Ted Williams and Carl Yastrzemski in baseball; Bobby Orr in hockey and Bob Cousy and Larry Bird in basketball. Some, however, prefer to remember Rocky Marciano of Brockton, Mass., the heavyweight boxer who, when he retired in 1956, was the only world champion to have won every fight (49) of his professional career.

New England's sporting scene is enlivened by teams from its myriad colleges but mostly these have little impact nationally. Exceptions are Boston College (football and basketball) and the University of Connecticut (basketball). Boston University and Harvard often contribute players to the US Olympic ice-hockey squad. And in squash and sailing New England college teams are often in the fore. Since 1965 oarspeople from around the globe have come to Cambridge in October for the Head of the Charles, the world's biggest one-day regatta.

In spring, thousands of runners, again from all over the world, line up at Hopkinton, Mass., for the start of the celebrated Boston Marathon (tel: 617-236 1652). It's the world's oldest annual marathon, first run in 1896, and is the only marathon to offer equal prize-money, in all classes, to both men and women. The last time New Englanders came in first was 1983, when Gregory Meyer of Wellesley won the Men's and Joan Benoit of Watertown the Women's. ❏

RIGHT: little league baseball in Newton, Mass.

CONNECTICUT

Map on page 206

This historic state encompasses Yale University in New Haven, maritime traditions in Mystic Seaport, antiquing and art in the Litchfield Hills – and, unexpectedly, America's biggest casino

Driving admiringly through the neat-as-a-pin village of Guilford, a one-time resident once remarked: "Connecticut always looks as if the maid has just been in to clean." There, as in so many of Connecticut's picturesque colonial villages, the carefully kept, white clapboard homes and manicured lawns evoke an image of quiet wealth, propriety and old school ties.

Indeed, this state has always had something of a conservative mien. The Puritans who settled here were staunch Congregationalists, little given to the radical ideas of Roger Williams or the autocratic piety of John Winthrop. They may have been farmers and seafarers, but they were primarily involved in commerce; they understood the value of a dollar and the importance of its proper investment.

Though generations have come and gone, this aspect of the Connecticut character has not changed. It has, however, been tempered with pride for the place and a heartfelt sense of its history.

Many visitors make the mistake of traveling non-stop through Connecticut (pronounced *kuh-ned-eket*) en route to vacations elsewhere in New England. Perhaps because its riches are so accessible, people tend to take them too much for granted. For those who exit from the highways and take to the back roads and small towns of Connecticut, there is a wealth of colonial heritage waiting to be explored.

With Long Island Sound as its southern border, Connecticut roughly forms a rectangle measuring 90 miles (145 km) from east to west and 55 miles (89 km) north to south. The Connecticut River, New England's longest, bisects the state; along with the Connecticut River, the Thames and Housatonic rivers were vital in the settlement and later industrialization of the state.

The Constitution State

Adrian Block, a Dutch navigator, was probably the first to understand the possibilities of the region when he sailed along the coast and up the Connecticut River in 1614. Nineteen years later, the Dutch established a trading post near the future site of Hartford, naming their new colony Fort Good Hope.

Beaver and timber had attracted the Dutch first, but it was the British who, lured by fertile land and religious freedom, finally settled the region in 1635. By that time, the original colony of Massachusetts Bay was overcrowded, and newcomers arriving from England had to extend their search for arable land to the upper reaches of the Connecticut River. Added to economic causes were the personalities of strong-willed leaders such as the Reverend Thomas Hooker, who, unwilling to submit to the autocratic theocracy

PRECEDING PAGES: Southbury. **LEFT:** a Middlebury farmer. **BELOW:** Patriot John Wadsworth hides the royal charter in an oak tree.

of the Massachusetts colony, chose to lead his congregation to an area beyond the reach of any colonial authority.

By 1636, settlements had been established in Hartford, Windsor and Wethersfield. Calling themselves the Hartford Colony, the three towns adopted the Fundamental Orders of Connecticut on January 14, 1639. This document, sometimes called "the grandfather of the Constitution" is regarded by many historians as the world's first written constitution. From that historical first comes the legend on the license plates, "The Constitution State."

New settlements were organized along the shores of the Long Island Sound. Old Saybrook was first, followed by New Haven, Guilford, and Stamford. Later towns, cleaving to the staunch Congregationalism of their settlers, took such Biblical names as Goshen, Sharon, Canaan, and Bethlehem.

When the time came to fight in the American War for Independence, Connecticut soldiers were eager participants. No major battles were fought on Connecticut soil, but the state had its patriots. Among them were General Israel Putnam and Ethan Allen. Most famous was Nathan Hale, the Coventry, Connecticut, schoolteacher who, when hanged by the British as a spy, uttered the immortal words: "I regret that I have only one life to give for my country."

With the end of the Revolution, Americans returned home to set about building their new nation. But Connecticut citizens quickly realized that they could not make their fortunes in farming. The stony, glacial soil that covered most of the region was poorly suited to cultivation. With the exception of the upper Connecticut valley, where tobacco is still grown under wide, cheesecloth tents, the land could support only small dairy farms and family fruit orchards.

Undeterred, Connecticut citizens turned to commerce, and from the years

Map on page 206

Hallowe'en pumpkin.

BELOW:
after milking.

1780 to 1840, the Yankee peddler reigned supreme. His sturdy wagon, loaded with tinware, soap, matches, yard goods and tools, was a familiar sight up and down the Atlantic seaboard, over the Appalachians into Detroit and St Louis, and even down to New Orleans. Success brought with it the demand for more and more products, and it was here that the Connecticut Yankees made their major contributions to the pioneering American economy.

New products called for new systems of manufacture: Eli Whitney, inventor of the cotton gin, first introduced the use of standardized parts at his firearms factory in New Haven. With the introduction of interchangeable parts came the creation of the assembly line – and the rise of the Industrial Revolution. No longer would manufacturing rely on the talents of a few, skilled craftsmen. Mass production had entered the marketplace, and the American economy prospered accordingly.

Not surprisingly, industry made Connecticut's fortune. In Hartford, entrepreneur Samuel Colt gave his name to the Colt .45 revolver, the "gun that won the West." Winchester rifles were manufactured in New Haven, hats in Danbury, clocks in Bristol, and fine brass in Waterbury.

New industry meant new workers, and the late 19th and early 20th centuries saw waves of immigrants settle in such manufacturing centers as Bridgeport, New Haven, and Torrington. While Connecticut may present a colonial face to the casual traveler, those who remain long enough appreciate the contributions of Italians, Germans, Portuguese, and Eastern Europeans to the essential Connecticut character.

Connecticut's past is also its present, and today the state continues to rely on industry for its economic good fortune. Airplane engines are manufactured in

Since the US Patent Office opened in 1790, Connecticut inventors have filed more patents per capita than any other state. Hats, combs, cigars, seeds, clocks, kettles, furniture and firearms – all came out of the factory stamped "Made in Connecticut."

BELOW:
colonial piper in West Hartford.

East Hartford, helicopters in Stratford; nuclear submarines are designed and built in Groton.

Despite its industry, Connecticut has remained a largely rural enclave. With manufacturing concentrated along the South Shore and in Hartford, 75 percent of the state is given over to small towns and deeply forested woodlands. Narrow, winding roads lead the visitor from one charming village to another, to communities proud of their colonial heritage and seemingly untouched by modern times.

Maps:
Area 206
City 209

Capital of Connecticut: Hartford

In any game of free association, the name of **Hartford** ❶ immediately elicits the response, "insurance." And, indeed, the skyline of Connecticut's capital city is dominated by the steel-and-glass skyscrapers of the nation's largest insurance companies. Today several dozen are located in the greater Hartford area, together employing approximately 10 percent of the total work force.

The first insurance policy, covering a shipowner's losses in the event his ship didn't make it safely back to port, was written in the 18th century. The early industry served the maritime trade, but, as shipping declined during the 19th century, Hartford's canny insurance companies expanded their coverage to fire and casualty. Their reputation is well founded; from their earliest days, the insurance firms honored their commitments. In 1835, New York City suffered a disastrous fire that destroyed more than 600 buildings. Unable to pay the claims, many New York insurance companies folded. Not so the Hartford Insurance Company, however. Its president traveled to New York and personally guaranteed payment of every claim. Similar incidents in Boston and

The population of Hartford, the state capital, is around 124,000.

Chicago, as well as the 1906 San Francisco earthquake, bolstered the reputation of Hartford's ambitious insurance companies.

But Hartford means more than insurance companies. It is also Connecticut's oldest city, settled in 1635 by a group of Puritans from the Massachusetts Bay Colony. Its location on the navigable waterways of the Connecticut River has made Hartford a major force in the political, economic and social development of the region. In 1662, a royal charter was drawn up uniting the colonies of Hartford and New Haven, and guaranteeing their independence. Sir Edmund Andros, appointed governor of Connecticut in 1687, had the charter revoked. In defiance of this move, the Hartford patriot John Wadsworth stole the charter and hid it in the trunk of an oak tree at the center of the town. Two years later, on the accession of William III, Andros was recalled to England and the charter was reinstated. A plaque at Charter Oak Place, in the south end of the city, marks the spot where the magnificent oak stood until 1856, when a windstorm felled it. Hartford's museums are filled with items supposedly made from the wood.

As with many US cities, the downtown area was allowed to deteriorate as the middle classes moved to the suburbs; but efforts to control crime and encourage nightlife have been having some effect. Any tour should begin with a visit to the **Old State House Ⓐ**, located at the intersection of Main Street and Asylum Avenue (open Mon–Sat). The nation's oldest state house, it was the first public commission for architect Charles Bulfinch, who would later design the state capitols of Maine and Massachusetts. Neither quite compares to his Hartford creation, which stands as a supreme example of Federalist architecture.

Directly south of the State House, also on Main Street, is the **Wadsworth Atheneum Ⓑ**, the oldest continually operating public art museum in America

In the early days of maritime insurance, ratings were based on the type of wood, as well as the size and number of timbers, used in a ship's construction. Oaks were recommended for the ship's frame, hard pine for the keel, and hard pine, oak or mahogany for the planking.

BELOW:
Connecticut State
Capitol, Hartford.

Map on page 209

(open Tues–Sun; first Thur of month till 8pm; entrance fee). Built in the Gothic Revival style, the Atheneum was erected to house the library and art gallery of Daniel Wadsworth. Numerous additions have been made since, and the museum's collection – which includes paintings by Goya, Rubens, Rembrandt and van Dyck, in addition to works by American masters such as Thomas Cole and John Singer Sargent – remains a proud part of the city's cultural heritage.

The **Connecticut State Capitol** ❻, a Gothic wedding cake of turrets, gables, porches, and towers, was designed by Richard Upjohn in 1879 (tours Mon–Fri am; also Sat Apr–Oct). Though some might question its good taste, there is no doubt that its ornate interiors of hand-painted columns, marble floors and elaborate stained-glass windows were designed to reflect the wealth and prosperity of the community it served. Located on Capitol Avenue overlooking **Bushnell Park** ❼ (which contains an enchanting 1914 carousel; open in summer), the Capitol is flanked by the State Library, which maintains an excellent collection of Connecticut clocks and firearms; and the Bushnell Memorial Auditorium, a center for concerts, ballet, opera and theater.

Constitution Plaza ❽, a 12-acre complex completed in the 1960s, provides Hartford with an open mall, a vast array of shops, office buildings and the starkly modern, elliptically shaped Phoenix Mutual Life Insurance Building, so familiar to the Hartford skyline.

Travelers Tower ❾, the tallest building in the city, has an **Observation Deck**, which offers an excellent view of the Hartford area (tours by appointment mid-May–late Oct weekdays; tel: 860–277 0111). The Travelers Insurance Company was founded in 1683, when Colonel James Bolter insured his life for $5,000 to cover his lunchtime trip from home to the post office.

BELOW: Hartford's Constitution Plaza at Christmas.

Truth is stranger than fiction, but it is because fiction is obliged to stick to possibilities; truth isn't.

— MARK TWAIN,
PUDD'N'HEAD WILSON'S
NEW CALENDAR

Mark Twain (1835–1910) was Hartford's most famous resident. His mansion, now known as the **Mark Twain Memorial** , is at Nook Farm, just north of exit 46 on I-84, less than 2 miles (3.5 km) from downtown Hartford (open daily; entrance fee). Now a busy residential area, it retains little of its pastoral charm. The adjacent **Harriet Beecher Stowe House** is also open to visitors (open late May–mid-Oct Mon–Sat; pm only Sun; entrance fee).

Nook Farm was the intellectual center of Hartford, settled in the second half of the 19th century. Twain's home is easily the largest, a great Victorian mansion designed by Edward Tuckerman Potter in 1874. Exquisitely decorated by Louis Comfort Tiffany and his associates, the house very much reflects the character of its owner. Outdoor porches and balconies give the impression of a Mississippi riverboat, while the interiors are grand and whimsical. Of particular interest is the upstairs billiard room, where Twain did much of his writing.

The riverboat pilot-turned-author spent the happiest years of his life in Hartford. Twain, whose real name was Samuel Clemens, settled here soon after his marriage to Olivia Langdon, and it was in their home at 351 Farmington Avenue that they raised their three daughters, Clara, Jean and Susy. Although Twain originally moved here in 1874 merely to be close to his publisher, he frequently sang the praises of his adopted city. "Of all the beautiful towns it has been my fortune to see, this is the chief…You do not know what beauty is if you have not been here." It was also in Hartford that he penned his most successful novels, including *The Adventures of Tom Sawyer*, *The Adventures of Huckleberry Finn*, and *A Connecticut Yankee in King Arthur's Court*.

BELOW: Nook Farm, Mark Twain's Gilded Age mansion.

The author remained in Hartford until 1891, when poor investments forced him to move to Europe or face bankruptcy. The family always intended to return, but after the sudden death of his daughter Susy in 1896, Twain could not bear to go back to the site of their happiest memories. He sold the house in 1903.

Side trips from Hartford

Wethersfield ❷, on the Connecticut River just south of Hartford, is one of the oldest villages in the state. More than 150 of the 17th- and 18th-century homes in its downtown area have been preserved. Look at the 1760 Congregational Meetinghouse on Main Street, and the **Webb-Deane-Stevens Museum** (open May–Oct, Wed–Mon; Nov–Apr, weekends; entrance fee).

Farmington ❸, a village situated on the Farmington River just 10 miles (16 km) west of Hartford, is considered by many to be one of the loveliest towns in New England. Certainly, its elegant 18th- and 19th-century mansions display a clarity of architectural detail seldom equaled in the area. **Hillstead Museum** is a particular gem (Mountain Road; open Tues–Sun; entrance fee). Designed by architect Stanford White, the Hillstead was originally conceived as a retirement home for a wealthy industrialist, Alfred Atmore Pope. A self-made man, Pope was a personal friend of the artist Mary Cassatt and a great admirer of the French Impressionist school of painters. Pope's home, which remains as it was in the early 1900s, reflects his taste in art. Scattered throughout the mansion are a number of familiar canvases, including paintings from

Monet's *Haystack* series, Manet's *The Guitar Lady*, and Degas's *The Tub*. Whistler and Cassatt are also well represented.

Bristol ❹, 18 miles (29 km) west of Hartford, was the 19th-century clock-making capital of the country, producing more than 200,000 clocks in a single year. The neighboring towns of **Terryville** and **Thomaston** were named for Eli Terry and Seth Thomas, craftsmen who at one time put a clock on every mantel in America. The **American Clock and Watch Museum** is located on Maple Street in Bristol, and houses a superb collection of the region's finest and most valuable timepieces (open Apr–Nov daily; entrance fee).

Maps:
Area 206
City 209

The Litchfield Hills

Connecticut's northwestern corner constitutes its wildest forests and mountains, dotted with quintessential New England bridges and covered bridges – an area known as the Litchfield Hills. Through it runs the **Housatonic River**, crystal clear and freckled with trout, and excellent for canoeing. Hikers may want to follow the Appalachian Trail from Kent to Canaan.

Old stone walls recall the days when farmers tried to till the soil; the area was settled somewhat later than the southern reaches of the state. The mountains made access difficult, and many of those who came soon packed their wagons and headed west for the more fertile regions of Ohio and Illinois.

Litchfield ❺ is dominated by a spacious green, graced by the tall-steepled Congregational Church, at the meeting point of the village's four main streets. Lining North and South streets are handsome, white, clapboard houses, which can be toured only on Open House Day in mid-July. On South Street (Route 63) stands the **Tapping Reeve House**, behind which is a small building that housed

Litchfield, founded in 1719, owed its early properity to the stagecoaches which stopped there en route from Hartford to Albany.

BELOW: Dixieland comes to the Constitution State.

A barn window in the quiet northwest corner of the state.

the nation's first school of law (open Apr–Nov Tues–Sat; Sun pm; entrance fee). Visitors can see the desks where many a distinguished jurist learned his trade, among them Aaron Burr and John C. Calhoun, two vice presidents of the United States. This simple schoolroom also graduated six cabinet members, 28 senators and more than 100 Congressmen.

Litchfield merchants prospered during the early days of the China trade when their money backed the sailing ships of Mystic and New Haven, but industry faltered when a new railroad bypassed the town center. Commerce was relocated to the more industrialized communities of Waterbury and Naugatuck. Litchfield was left as a sleepy town nestled in the past.

To the north, **Norfolk** ❻ is another classic town focused on a green, a summering place for wealthy industrialists, and retaining numerous opulent-looking homes. In summer, the Hillside Gardens (free) on Litchfield Road (Route 272) display a choice range of perennials.

Follow Route 44 west to **Lakeville** ❼, which offers another grand display of traditional 19th-century mansions. The **Holley-Williams House** in downtown Lakeville (Millerton Road; open Memorial Day–Labor Day Tues–Sat) is an excellent example of a Classical Revival house built by one of the area's more prosperous "Iron Barons." To the south on Route 7, in **West Cornwall** ❽, look for the covered bridge, erected in 1836 across the Housatonic.

The Housatonic Valley has one of its most dramatic moments at **Kent Falls State Park** ❾, where water tumbles some 200 ft (65 meters) down a natural stone staircase. A short way south on Route 7, ruins of the Old Kent Furnace recall the discovery of iron ore in the Litchfield Hills during the 18th century. Forges such as this produced pig iron until the discovery of coal in Pennsylvania

BELOW: Litchfield.

made Connecticut's ironworks obsolete. Adjacent to the furnace, the **Sloane-Stanley Museum** is an extensive collection of early American wood and iron tools gathered by the writer and artist Eric Sloane (open mid-May–Oct, Wed–Sun; entrance fee).

To the east just outside New Preston, **Lake Waramaug ⑩** is a tranquil hideaway with boating and swimming potential, and ideal shores for picnicking.

Map
on page
206

The southwestern shore

From the harbors of New Haven, New London, Mystic and Stonington, China clippers and Yankee whalers sailed out to seek their fortunes. Such associations may be merely historical, but people along Connecticut's coast still retain a fondness for salt air and a genuine love of the sea. Most towns have at least one marina, and on a clear summer's day the horizon of the Long Island Sound is filled with billowing sails.

Greenwich, Cos Cob, Stamford, Darien and Rowayton – to the thousands of Connecticut residents who work in New York City, this is a railroad conductor's litany. About an hour away from Manhattan by train, the Connecticut suburbs are among the most luxurious bedroom communities in the nation. Many of New York's wealthiest business executives make their homes here, attracted by the pleasant, countrified locale.

This **"Gold Coast"** has an artistic streak, too, exemplified in the galleries and shops of newly trendy **South Norwalk ⑪**, dubbed "SoNo" for its emulation of New York's SoHo district. Once a gritty, run-down neighborhood, it's now a great place to while away a day pleasantly – especially if you spend part at the huge **Maritime Aquarium** (open daily; entrance fee), which has plenty

The Puritans founded a colony in New Haven as early as 1637 but admitted only believers.

BELOW: cooking planked shad in Old Saybrook.

Detail, Barnum Museum in Bridgeport.

BELOW:
Yale University buildings.

of hands-on displays relating to the marine life and maritime culture of Long Island Sound, including boat-building demonstrations and an aquarium stocked with marine species from Long Island Sound. There is a busy events program and an IMAX movie theater.

Bridgeport ⓬, a major industrial center producing everything from clothes to electrical appliances, is an exception to the coast's general aura of ease and affluence. One fun note is the **Barnum Museum**, a showcase for big-top memorabilia connected to Phineas Barnum, with a miniature circus, clown props and items relating to Barnum and General Tom Thumb (820 Main Street; open Tues–Sat; pm only Sun; entrance fee).

New Haven ⓭, settled by Puritans in 1638, was an independent colony until 1662, when it merged with the Hartford settlement. In the early 19th century, the port brought prosperity to the town, and more than 100 ships regularly sailed along the coast to the West Indies and the Orient.

However, it was not until the Industrial Revolution that the town made the big leap to becoming a major manufacturing center. Eli Whitney first instituted a system of mass production in his firearms factory. Since that time, New Haven has pioneered such inventions as the steel fish hook, the meat grinder, the corkscrew, and the steamboat.

New Haven is perhaps best known not as an industrial center, but as a center of learning. It is the home of **Yale University**, which dominates much of the city's cultural life. Founded in 1701 by a group of Puritan clergymen, Yale was originally located in nearby Saybrook. In 1716, the school was moved to New Haven, and two years later it took the name of the wealthy merchant Elihu Yale, its benefactor.

Alma mater to famous personalities such as Eli Whitney, Nathan Hale and Noah Webster, Yale has pursued a policy of commissioning leading architects to design its buildings. But the dominant style on the Yale campus is Gothic Revival – much of it evoking the British universities of Oxford and Cambridge.

Any visit to the university should include its excellent museums and libraries. Start from the **Beinecke Rare Book and Manuscript Library** on Wall Street (open Mon–Fri; Sat am), where an edition of the Gutenberg Bible is on display. Two blocks south is the **Yale University Art Gallery** (1111 Chapel Street; open Tues–Sat; Sun pm), which has well over 100 paintings by patriot artist Jonathan Trumbull, impressive collections of African and pre-Columbian art, as well as canvases by Manet, Van Gogh, Corot, Degas, and Matisse.

Across the street stands the **Yale Center of British Art**, with a vast collection of British paintings (including works by Constable and Turner), drawings and sculpture donated in 1966 by industrialist Paul Mellon (1080 Chapel Street; call for hours; tel: 203-432 2800).

Adjacent to the university, New Haven Green is surrounded by a trinity of churches constructed in Gothic Revival, Georgian, and Federal styles.

New Haven's cultural offerings include the Yale Repertory Theater on campus (Chapel and York streets; tel: 203-432 1234) and the Long Wharf Theater on the downtown waterfront (222 Sargent Drive; tel: 203-787 4282), which mount some of the most interesting productions in the country. The New Haven Symphony Orchestra (tel: 203-865 0831) frequently performs at Woolsey Hall on the Yale campus.

Out at East Haven, the **Shore Line Trolley Museum** has a collection meriting inclusion on the National Register of Historic Places, with some 100 trolleys,

Map on page 206

TIP

For a thorough tour of Yale University, inquire at the university's visitors' information office (149 Elm Street; tel: 203-432 2300). Tours start at 10:30 and 2 on weekdays, 1:30 on weekends.

BELOW: graduation day.

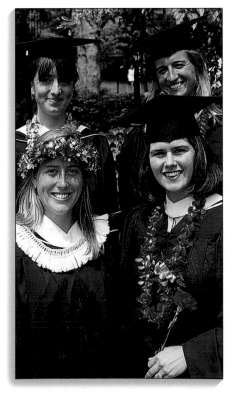

THE IVY LEAGUE

Home to most of the country's oldest and most highly regarded colleges and universities, New England is the region most closely associated with the "Ivy League." The phrase is now used somewhat loosely, referring to the top rank of American colleges, but it originated, with a core of eight prominent institutions, of which four are in New England: Harvard in Massachusetts, Yale in Connecticut, Brown in Rhode Island, and Dartmouth in New Hampshire. (The others are Columbia and Cornell in New York, the University of Pennsylvania, and Princeton in New Jersey.) Harvard, founded in 1636, is the country's oldest college. The eight make up an athletic league whose football games, especially, are among the most hallowed collegiate sporting events in the country

Ivy League schools began as all-male bastions, so the "Seven Sisters" developed as a consortium to provide women the same access. Four are located in Massachusetts: Mount Holyoke (the oldest, founded 1837), Smith, Wellesley and Radcliffe (affiliated with Harvard). It's likely that the "ivy" refers to the shiny-leaved climbing plant, introduced from Britain in colonial times (precisely when these schools were established), that widely covers the brick and brownstone buildings that dominate the campuses.

Guilford harvest.

the oldest rapid transit car and a rare parlor car (17 River Street; open late May–early Sept, daily; Apr–May, early Sept–Nov, weekends; entrance fee).

Up the coast from New Haven are two of the loveliest communities along this shore, the villages of Guilford and Madison. Of the two, **Guilford** ⓮ is the older, having been settled in 1639 by the Reverend Henry Whitfield. His home on Old Whitfield Street, the oldest stone dwelling in New England, is now called the **Henry Whitfield State Museum** (open Wed–Sun; entrance fee).

Guilford's town green, one of the purest in New England, is bordered by many of its original 17th- and 18th-century homes. Several are museums, including **Hyland House**, a typical colonial salt box of 1660, and the **Thomas Griswold House** of 1774 (open June–mid-Sept, Tues–Sun; mid-Sept–Oct, weekend; off season by appointment; entrance fee), both on Boston Street.

Nearby **Madison** has some of the most beautiful summer and year-round homes in Connecticut. **Hammonasset Beach State Park** ⓯, just 2 miles (3 km) east, is the state's longest public beach. At **Old Saybrook** ⓰, by the western mouth of the Connecticut River, **Fort Saybrook** has storyboards chronicling Saybrook Colony from 1635, and gives fine estuary views, with opportunities for bird-watching from the boardwalk.

Of all the towns on the Connecticut shore, **Old Lyme** ⓱ can boast the richest artistic heritage. There was a time when "a sea captain lived in every house," but later the community came to be known primarily as an artists' colony, thanks in large part to Florence Griswold, the daughter of a sea captain and a devoted, if impecunious, patron of the arts. Her Lyme Street house, now the **Florence Griswold Museum** (open June–Dec, Tues–Sat; Sun pm; Jan–May, pm only Wed–Sun; entrance fee) contains a stunning array of works by her illustrious

BELOW: the Connecticut River.

Map on page 206

American Impressionist boarders, including such notables as Childe Hassam. Some were so moved by her laissez-faire hospitality, they left painted mementos on the doors, mantels and paneled walls.

Cruising the Connecticut River

Beginning as a mountain stream tumbling from its source near the New Hampshire–Canada border, the Connecticut River travels 410 miles (660 km) through four states and ends its journey to the sea as a broad and majestic tidal estuary. The Native Americans named it "Quinnituckett," which means "the long, tidal river." Throughout history, the Connecticut has linked valley residents with the outside world. A fertile floodplain has made this area a center for agriculture, and water power has generated energy for a variety of small industries.

A tour of the Connecticut Valley can begin near the river's mouth with a visit to **Essex** ⑱, founded in 1645 and a long-time center of maritime activity. Essex developed as an important shipbuilding center during the 18th century. The *Oliver Cromwell*, America's first warship, was launched in 1776 from its docks. Yachts and cabin cruisers still make their berths at various Essex marinas, where tall masts and yards of tackle lend the town a distinctly nautical air. Contained in the dockside **Connecticut River Museum** (open Tues–Sun; entrance fee) is an exact replica of the *American Turtle*, the nation's first submarine. Invented by David Bushnell, a native of the nearby coastal town of Old Saybrook, it was employed in 1776 by Yankee forces to sink an English battleship during the blockade of New York Harbor. Though unsuccessful in its mission, the *Turtle* incorporated a number of engineering ideas that Robert Fulton later adopted in the design of the *Nautilus* (*see Groton, page 221*).

The Old Griswold Inn on Main Street has been in operation since 1776. The rare collection of maritime prints in its tap room warrants a special visit.

Those who want to get a firsthand glimpse of the Connecticut River may take an old-fashioned journey by steam locomotive and riverboat (round trip takes about 2½ hours). Board the 1920s coaches of the **Valley Railroad** at Essex Depot and ride along the river through the villages of **Chester** and **Deep River** (**Camelot Cruises**: cruises May–Dec; tel: 800-522 7463 or 860-345 8591 for departure times). At Deep River, transfer to a riverboat similar to the hundreds of passenger ships that ferried travelers between Old Saybrook and Hartford more than a century ago.

Those who continue their journey up the valley may cross the river by car ferry at Chester. It is a charming excursion that brings you to **Hadlyme**, home of the spectacularly eccentric **Gillette Castle** ⑲ (open late May–early Sept Fri–Sun; entrance fee). William Gillette (1853–1937) was a much admired American actor whose portrayal of Sherlock Holmes brought him fame and fortune. Gillette was one of the first actors who took to wearing the deer-stalker hat, the distinctive Holmes trademark; and it was he who uttered those memorable words onstage: "Elementary, my dear Watson."

Gillette was born and raised in Hartford and, when he decided to build the house of his dreams, the actor

BELOW: Goodspeed Opera House, on the banks of the Connecticut River at East Haddam.

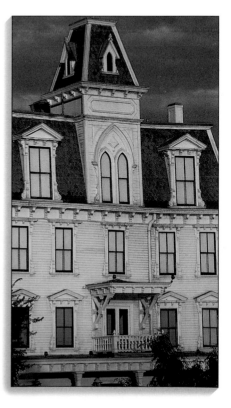

selected a hilltop aerie that commanded a breathtaking view of the Connecticut River and its surrounding countryside. Work began on the 122-acre (49-hectare) site in 1914, and it took five years and over $1 million before Gillette's architectural vision was completed. The results were whimsical and bizarre. The stone-and-concrete castle is filled with hand-hewn oak furnishings and specialized gadgetry. Javanese mats line the walls, and light fixtures are fashioned from numerous bits of colored glass. The estate grounds are now a state park with fine views and excellent picnicking facilities.

North of Gillette Castle, on Route 82, is the charming Victorian town of **East Haddam** ⑳. Still standing along the shoreline are the great rambling hotels (some now private homes) that served riverboat passengers in the 19th century. Before the railroad came, this was a point of embarkation for the many steamboat passengers crossing the Long Island Sound to New York City.

The **Goodspeed Opera House** (tel: 860-873 8668), which sits so majestically on the banks of the Connecticut River, is a reminder of the heyday of steamboat travel. Countless citizens paused here for a bit of entertainment before continuing their journey downriver. Beautifully restored, the Opera House presents musical revivals, as well as original productions, April–December.

The northeastern shore

New London ㉑, along with Nantucket and New Bedford, was one of the busiest whaling ports in the nation. In the early days of the 19th century, more than 80 ships sailed from its docks and many a vast fortune was accumulated by its merchants. Evidence of this wealth can be seen in Whale Oil Row on Huntington Street, where four Greek Revival mansions were built in the 1830s.

BELOW: approaching Groton on the New London ferry.

When oil was discovered in Pennsylvania in 1859, the whaling industry declined sharply, and manufacturing became New London's chief occupation. But the city maintained its ties to the sea and today is best known as the home of the **US Coast Guard Academy** (Route 32, off I–95; open May–Oct daily; entrance fee).

Across the Thames River from New London stands the city of **Groton ㉒**, known as the "Submarine Capital of the World" – the manufacture of nuclear submarines is the town's major industry. Non-claustrophobes who wish to view the interior of a submarine may visit the USS *Nautilus* Memorial at the **US Naval Submarine Base** (exit 86, off I–95; open Wed–Mon; Tues pm).

The delightful village of **Noank ㉓** has views to Fishers Island, New York. Lobstering is big; shingle-clad Abbott's serves lobsters straight off the boat.

The village of **Mystic ㉔**, an old maritime community of trim white houses, sits at the tidal outlet of the Mystic River. For generations, Mystic was the home of daring mariners and fishermen, and was feared by the British during the Revolution as a "cursed little hornets' nest" of patriots. The village teemed with activity during the Gold Rush days of 1849, when shipbuilders vied to see who could construct the fastest clipper ships to travel round Cape Horn to the boom town of San Francisco. It was the *Andrew Jackson*, a Mystic-built clipper launched in 1860, that claimed the world's record – making the journey in 89 days and 4 hours, 9 hours faster than the famous *Flying Cloud*.

Today, Mystic is best known as the home of **Mystic Seaport**, a living replica of a 19th-century waterfront community during the heyday of sailing ships (open daily; entrance fee; tel: 860-572 0711). Restoration of Mystic Seaport began in 1929 and, since then, the project has expanded to include a complex of over 60 buildings covering 17 acres (7 hectares). It's a big tourist draw, and

Map on page 206

Monument House, in Groton's Fort Griswold State Park, has a collection of Civil War memorabilia assembled by the Daughters of the American Revolution.

BELOW: mural painter, Mystic village.

Map on page 206

a full day and plenty of stamina are required to tour the entire seaport properly.

The restoration imparts a vivid sense of how life was lived by Mystic's residents in the 1860s. Visitors are encouraged to wander along the wharves and streets of the village, and taste the old seafaring way of life. Save time for a visit to the *Charles W. Morgan*, the last surviving vessel of America's 19th-century whaling fleet. Built in 1841, the *Morgan* plied the seas for more than 80 years and made 37 voyages, some of them lasting three or four years. Also board the *Joseph Conrad*, which was built in 1882 by the Danish as a training vessel, and now serves as a student dormitory; demonstrations of sail-handling and chanty singing are scheduled regularly aboard both ships. A major current project is the building of a faithful replica of the slave-trading ship *Amistad*, whose slaves seized control of the ship and eventually won their right to freedom, and returned to Africa from Connecticut; the work will be completed by 2000.

It's also worth stopping at the Stillman Building, a museum with an impressive collection of ship's figureheads, scrimshaw, ship models, logbooks, etc.

Just up the road, near I-95, visit the ambitious **Mystic Marinelife Aquarium**, with extensive indoor and outdoor exhibits spanning sea horses to sea lions, and pools containing Beluga whales (open daily; entrance fee). The Jason Project, to be completed in 2000, will allow visitors to watch a dive to the sea bed through kelp forests and reefs, and to see the resting place of such wrecks as the *Titanic*. The Aquarium operates seasonal seal, eagle and whale-watching cruises.

A few miles further east is the charming old whaling port of **Stonington** ㉕, huddled at the edge of the state near the Rhode Island border. Stonington was once the third-largest city in Connecticut and an important seaport. Although considerably reduced in circumstances, the village remains one of the prettiest coastal enclaves in New England. Its 1823 **lighthouse**, the first government-operated one in the entire state, is these days a museum with artifacts from the Oriental trade, whaling gear and a children's room (open May–Oct Tues–Sun; entrance fee).

BELOW:
Foxwoods Casino.

America's biggest casino

On the Mashantucket Pequot Reservation north of Mystic, the massive **Foxwoods Casino** ㉖ has grown within a few years to become the nation's largest casino (*see facing page*). Punters arrive by the busload.

On the same site is the **Mashantucket Pequot Museum and Research Center** (open daily till 7pm; entrance fee), by far New England's largest Native American exhibition. Visitors journey back in time through a simulated glacial crevasse, complete with the sounds of creaking ice and the blast of chill air. The World of Ice sets the glacial scene; then follows the arrival of the first peoples, and has a diorama depicting a caribou kill 11,000 years ago. There are further dioramas evoking Native life 6,000 years back, plus a re-created 16th-century Pequot village, showing daily life up to the first European contact, then a film of the Pequot war. You also see a computer recreation of a 17th-century Pequot fort excavated on the site. The exhibits lead right up to the present, with a 1970s mobile home and a film explaining how the tribe achieved Federal recognition in 1983. ❑

How the Pequots' gamble paid off

Not so long ago, the eastern Connecticut Mashantucket Pequot Indian tribe was regarded by most New Englanders as part of the area's quaint pre-Colonial past, remembered by tongue-twisting place names such as Wequetequock and Quanaduck that outsiders find all-but-impossible to pronounce.

Then, all of a sudden, the tribe emerged from centuries-long obscurity in the mid-1980s, and its name seemed to be on everyone's lips. The reason was that, taking advantage of new legislation exempting tribal reservation land from local laws against gambling, it began developing hundreds of acres of ancestral reservation land in sleepy Ledyard, Connecticut, into a vast casino-and-hotel complex called Foxwoods.

Incredibly, it now rivals some of the gaming palaces of Las Vegas or Atlantic City. In 1998, just six years after it opened, Foxwoods was the world's highest-grossing casino. In addition to high-stakes bingo, slot machines, and dozens of other gambling games, the resort offers a regular schedule of concerts and performances by Hollywood's entertainment elite, half a dozen restaurants ranging from casual to high-roller high-style, and an ultra-plush hotel.

Most recently, the tribe has added a Mashantucket Pequot Museum and Research Center to the resort complex. With a price-tag of some $135 million, the museum has already earned rave reviews for both its forward-looking architecture and its informative and engaging exhibits on tribal history, including a high-tech recreation of a 16th-century Pequot village that visitors may walk through, experiencing sights and sounds that would have surrounded them long before the era of jangling slot machines and smoky bingo halls.

The success of Foxwoods is unquestioned, but many local residents still decry its presence in the formerly rural area. Driving up the Old Stonington Road (Route 2) into the casino complex, you are confronted with a stunning contrast: rolling countryside, stone walls, and farms versus unabashed glitz. The shining towers of the resort complex, some nearly 200 feet (60 meters) high, appear like an alarming Oz materializing out of thin air.

Meanwhile, just up the road in Uncasville, the Mohegan tribe has opened its own casino, the Mohegan Sun. Smaller than Foxwoods, but similar in its glamorously seductive style, the Sun offers another winning hand: a slick combination of gambling, resort amenities, and Vegas-style concerts by big-name stars.

In the wake of the obvious success of both Foxwoods and the Mohegan Sun, it seemed for a while that every economically challenged small New England city was intent on rolling out a welcome mat for its own Indian-owned casino. Both Fall River in Massachusetts and Providence in Rhode Island flirted with Indian gaming promoters, but widespread local sentiment against more casinos (combined, perhaps, with a recognition that the existing venues might have cornered the market on regional gambling) has shelved such plans, at least for the time being. ❏

RIGHT: a statue inside Foxwoods.

RHODE ISLAND

Map on page 228

Between Providence's downtown, Newport's mansions, sailing in Narragansett Bay, and Block Island's rolling pastures and beaches, this tiny state packs a diverse punch

The smallest state in the nation, Rhode Island has nonetheless managed to hold on to a disproportionate share of wealth and clout. On the map, it may look more like an overgrown port than a genuine state, but that very sea-readiness accounts in large part for its long-term appeal.

Certainly, the millionaires who built their legendary summer "cottages" in Newport at the end of the 19th century recognized natural wealth when they saw it: the dramatic vistas of the Rhode Island Sound, the refreshing westerly breezes wafting in to relieve summer doldrums. The mansions they left behind still gleam atop the cliffs, jewels left over from the Gilded Age.

Centuries earlier, the reclusive Reverend William Blaxton found the area equally attractive. Blaxton, who had been living contentedly as a hermit in what would soon become Boston, fled to Rhode Island when the Puritans he'd invited to share his peninsula proved too proselytizing.

Rhode Island's official founder was a clergyman, Roger Williams. Driven out of Salem in 1635 for preaching religious tolerance, Williams headed south to establish a settlement where all were free to practice their own faith; traveling by canoe with a cadre of followers, he arrived in what is now Providence. Anne Hutchinson followed in 1637, to be joined by other dissidents. In 1663 Charles II granted a charter to the rather wordily named Colony of Rhode Island and Providence Plantations – a name it still officially retains as a state.

Soon people from even farther afield flocked to Rhode Island's shores. A large number of Quakers, fleeing Puritan persecution, made Newport their home, and as early as the 18th century, Jews from Portugal and Holland settled here as well. In the ensuing centuries came Italians, Irish, Russians, Poles, French, Swedes, Greeks, Armenians, Chinese and Cape Verdeans. By 1960 Rhode Island was the most densely populated state in America, with 859,000 inhabitants crowded into 1,214 sq. miles (3,144 sq. km). Today, with a population in excess of 1 million, Rhode Island is a bustling, multicultural cross-section of New England life.

The Ocean State

As Rhode Island's license plate attests, **Narragansett Bay** dominates the state. Taking a dinosaur bite out of the New England coast, it gives the state a shoreline out of all proportion to its land area. Rhode Island is only 48 miles (77 km) long and 37 miles (60 km) wide, yet it claims 400 miles (644 km) of coastline.

With such an abundance of water at their disposal, Rhode Islanders have long turned to the sea for their livelihood. Two of the nation's leading seaports in the early days of the republic were Providence and

PRECEDING PAGES: Rosecliff Manor, Newport. **LEFT:** sculpture in the Rosecliff gardens. **BELOW:** Villa Marina, Newport.

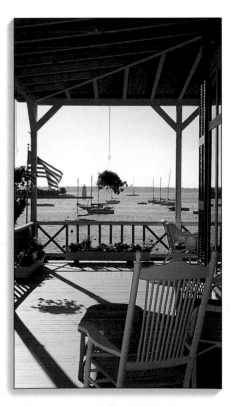

Newport. Using Rhode Island as a base, pirates raided merchant ships in the North Atlantic; the notorious Captain Kidd is rumored to have buried his cache of gold doubloons in Jamestown.

But Rhode Island is a land of contradictions. Despite the state's heritage as a sanctuary for pirates, Newport was the birthplace of the modern US Navy: President Chester Alan Arthur developed a new fleet – built of steel, rather than wood – there in the early 1880s, and enjoyed staging gun drills on the bay. (Though much of the navy pulled out in the mid-1970s, the Naval War College, founded in 1884, remains.) Founded as a haven of religious liberty, it became a world-class slave trade center.

Despite its considerable contributions to the success of the American Revolution, Rhode Island was the last holdout among states ratifying the US Constitution. Notorious for its exploitation of child labor, Rhode Island became a bastion of New Deal social ideals.

Until 1854, it couldn't even decide which city would be its capital. Each year

How the state got its name is uncertain. Some believe it was called after the Greek island of Rhodes. Others think the name derived from a Dutch word meaning "red."

Maps:
Area 228
City 230

the General Assembly packed up its belongings and moved lock, stock and barrel to one of the five locales contesting for the honor. Eventually, after a raucous battle in 1900, Providence won out over Newport. It remains the capital, but Newporters contend their city is truly the heart of the state.

If little Rhode Island is a land of contradictions, it is also a land of superlatives and firsts. Among the state's distinctions are: the world's widest bridge, in Providence, and the only operational water-powered snuff mill in the United States, in Saunderstown. The state boasts the country's first synagogue, its first department store, and its oldest enclosed shopping mall, built in the early 19th century. And lest it be forgotten, the first two-week paid vacation on record was spent in Rhode Island. In 1524, the Italian navigator Giovanni da Verrazano, on an exploratory mission for the King of France, was investigating the North American coast when he spotted Narragansett Bay. Verrazano was "so enthralled… he lingered for a fortnight."

Adamsville, Rhode Island, claims the world's only known monument to a chicken – the prolific Rhode Island Red.

Rhode Island, in the singular, is actually a misnomer. In fact, there are 35 islands within the state. Within and without Narragansett Bay are the four principal islands of Aquidneck, Block, Conanicut and Prudence; others include Hen, Hog, Rabbitt, Boat, Old Boy, Patience, Hope and Despair. In and about these islands, visitors enjoy boating, sailing, surfing and fishing.

Throughout the state – generously scattered through cities and towns such as Providence, Wickford, Bristol, Little Compton and Newport – are lovely old homes representing the decorative ideals of several centuries. Despite the concentrated population, park lands are plentiful, too. And precisely because the state is so small –it takes less than two hours to drive from one end to the other – it's possible to enjoy its variegated offerings within a short time span. A visitor can walk historic city streets in the morning, picnic in an idyllic grove at noon and savor the delights of the seashore by moonlight.

BELOW:
Narragansett Bay
offers good sailing.

Revitalized Providence

Rhode Island's capital has much in its favor: it has outstanding 18th and 19th-century architecture on Benefit Street, an excitingly rejuvenated downtown, and appealingly diverse neighborhoods – Italian, Portuguese, Ivy League university, and funky places such as Hope Street. It's also easily reached from Boston, a feasible day trip by car, train or bus.

In its early days, **Providence ❶** was the port of call for ships engaged in the lucrative Triangular Trade: New England rum for African slaves for West Indies molasses. In 1781, John Brown, one of four brothers whose family would dominate Providence for some years to come, sent the first of many ships to China. The maritime trade began to decline, however, following a series of international wars which resulted in embargoes and protectionism, and public interest and investment shifted toward industry.

As a major manufacturing center in the 19th century, Providence was dubbed "the cradle of American industry." Its huge plants were known worldwide – Brown & Sharpe (machinery and tools), Nicholson (files), Grinnel (sprinkler systems), Gorham (silverware), Davol (rubber goods), and so on.

The 20th century brought hard times. With the Great Depression and the textile industry's exodus to the south, Providence lost its pre-eminence as an industrial center. Although no longer the giant it once was, Providence has enjoyed a revitalization of business in recent decades, and has in turn lavished restorative attention on its variegated downtown. Artists have been given tax-free incentives to set up here; old warehouses and department stores have found new uses; I-195 is to be moved to free up more land for development close to the downtown area; and the ignored river has been beautified and made more accessible.

A city of hills: Providence

Providence is a city best seen on foot. Like Rome, Providence was built on seven hills. Most people remember three: College (officially, Prospect), Federal, and Constitution. The other four – Tockwotten, Smith and two now-leveled hills – seem to have melted in the metropolitan sprawl.

Constitution Hill is pretty much impossible to miss because of the **State Capitol A** that dominates its crest (Smith Street; open weekdays; tours am). This imposing 1891–92 McKim, Mead, and White structure is said to have the second largest self-support dome in the world, and contains an historic portrait of George Washington by Rhode Island native Gilbert Stuart. On opposite sides of the downtown area, College and Federal hills are favored haunts of tourists and natives alike.

To the south, **Waterplace Park B** is evidence of the city's waterside renaissance, where a new Italian-inspired piazza has been created. Once neglected, the riverside has been cleaned up, equipped with walkways and descriptive panels

BELOW: The Arcade, Providence, dating to 1828.

with photos of the old port days. In summer, Venetian-style gondolas offer trips and outdoor concerts take place.

Kennedy Plaza ⊙ is overlooked by the art deco skyscraper affectionately dubbed the Superman Building (not that *Superman* was ever filmed here); the Plaza is the arrival point for buses from Boston and elsewhere. To the east stands the restored Providence Station, worth a visit for a glimpse back to the times when train travel was a grand affair. Around the corner from Kennedy Plaza is the **Turk's Head Building**, a 1913 landmark with an ornate stone head over its entrance; and the **Customs House** (1856), with a dome and lantern that once welcomed ships returning from China.

For shopping or snacking and a bit of history, visit the **Arcade ⊙** on Weybosset Street. This Greek Revival "temple of trade" and the nation's first indoor shopping mall was built in 1828. Its three-story granite columns (said to be the second largest in America, after those at the Cathedral of St John the Divine in New York) were cut from single pieces of stone, which required 15 yokes of oxen to move.

In historic East Side, **Benefit Street**, the "Mile of History," deserves walking from one end to the other. There are more than 200 restored 18th- and 19th-century buildings (many are now private homes) originally built by sea captains and merchants; many houses, churches and schools bear bronze plaques identifying their original owners and dates of construction. In the late 1960s and early 1970s the street was run down, and nearly demolished as part of a renewal program; only the efforts of the Preservation Society saved the day.

Benefit Street was once a twisting dirt path informally known as Back Street because it led around the back side of homes to the family graveyards. When at

The dome of the State Capitol, Providence.

BELOW: Restored sea-captains' homes on Benefit Street, Providence.

Sculpture at Rhode Island School of Design.

last a communal burial ground was marked out and ancestral bones duly transferred to it, Back Street was straightened out and "improved for the benefit of the people of Providence."

The First Baptist Church (1775), designed by Joseph Brown, survives as a splendid example of the Colonial style. The same architect designed **John Brown House** , built in 1786 (for his brother) at Power and Benefit streets (2 Power Street; open Mar–Dec, Tues–Sat; Sun pm; Jan–Feb, weekdays by appointment only). John Quincy Adams described it as "the most magnificent and elegant private mansion that I have ever seen on this continent." It displays period furniture, paintings, pewter, silver, porcelain, and mementos of the China Trade; a later resident added an astonishingly showy bathroom. John Brown's chariot of 1782 is the earliest surviving American vehicle.

The **Old State House** (open weekdays) at 150 Benefit Street (between North and South Court streets) is worth a peep, if only to see the modest size of the former capitol, where the Rhode Island General Assembly renounced allegiance to King George III on May 4, 1776.

The bookstacks of **Providence Atheneum** (open Mon–Sat; Sun pm; closed summer weekends) reputedly witnessed the courtship of Edgar Allen Poe and a local resident, Sarah Whitman. She refused to marry him, however, because she claimed he couldn't stay sober. Such literary associations apart, the 1836 Greek Revival structure at 251 Benefit Street is well worth a visit for its collections of rare books, prints, and paintings.

Virtually opposite is the museum of the prestigious **Rhode Island School of Design (RISD) Museum of Art** with enough major works to fill a day's visit, including paintings by American masters and French Impressionists, a major oriental collection and some fine ancient artifacts (open Wed–Sun pm only; Fri 10am–8pm).

Brown University dominates this part of Providence (open weekdays). The Ivy League establishment was founded as Rhode Island College; the Brown family were Baptists and intended the college as a Baptist ministry school. The university still holds some commencement ceremonies in the First Baptist Church. University Hall dates from 1770 and was used as a barracks during the Revolutionary War.

Prospect Terrace, on Congdon Street north of the university, is a tiny park that gives a fine view of the city; a statue of Roger Williams, the city's founder (who is buried here), presides. The streets hereabouts are full of imposing 19th-century industrialists' mansions.

The heart of the **College Hill** shopping area is Thayer Street, four blocks east of Benefit, packed with interesting restaurants, bars, shops, and bookstores.

Continue south down Thayer Street to encounter one of Providence's best-kept secrets: **Fox Point**. Home to the city's Portuguese community, Fox Point speaks with an Old World accent. On holy days, celebrants parade with statues of the Virgin Mary while children dressed in their best suits and crinolines follow along. Early morning brings to Fox Point the tantalizing scent of Portuguese sweet bread wafting from small bakeries.

BELOW:
Brown University.

Perched on **Federal Hill** ❶ across the city is Providence's "Little Italy." Wander along Atwells Avenue and enjoy the aroma of crusty Italian breads, cheeses, pastas, herbs and spices. Some people come to stock up on traditional delicacies such as gorgonzola, Romano, homemade pork sausages and prosciutto, others for the restaurants, espresso shops and festive ambience. Without a doubt, Federal Hill is one of the friendliest parts of Providence.

Newport: domain of wealth

During World War II an anti-submarine net was strung across the entrance of the bay guarding **Newport** ❷. It was effective. But then, the elite of the city had long been expert at protecting their privacy. In the halcyon days of the Gilded Age, Newport was the domain of the very wealthy. Huge palaces built on expansive grounds were surrounded by mammoth fences and patrolled by guards and dogs. Now, however, a great many of these fiercely guarded fiefdoms are open to all comers, having become Newport's foremost tourist attractions.

Summering in Newport first became fashionable before the Revolution among Southern plantation owners intent on escaping the heat of Georgia and the Carolinas. After the Civil War, the nation's wealthiest families – Astors, Morgans, Fishers, Vanderbilts – discovered its charms. Arrivistes hoping to legitimize their newfound wealth with indisputable good taste tended to duplicate the palaces and chateaux that had so awed them on their grand tours of Europe. Edward Berwind, for instance, the son of poor German immigrants, managed to enter the ranks of this self-appointed aristocracy with The Elms (*see page 235*). Extravagance became obligatory. Harry Lehr hosted a formal dinner at which a monkey, complete with tuxedo and princely title, numbered

Maps:
Area 228
City 230

TIP

The East Bay Bicycle Path takes a level shoreline route from East Providence to Bristol, along a former railroad track, with good views for much of the way. The total distance is 14 miles (22 km).

BELOW: Newport marina.

For more on the Newport Mansions, see pages 240–41.

among the guests. James Gordon Bennett, the man who bought a Monte Carlo restaurant when it refused him a table, rode stark naked in his carriage through Newport's streets. The Coogans invited everyone who was anyone to a grand ball to celebrate the completion of their "summer cottage." When no one showed up, the Coogans simply walked out – leaving all the food, drink and furniture – never to return.

There is so much else to see and do in Newport, but a trip must include a tour of at least some of the mansions, the most impressive of which line **Bellevue Avenue** and **Ocean Drive**. Although literally hundreds of these establishments existed during Newport's Golden Age, only 70 remain. Many now house schools and charitable institutions.

The docks reveal a decidedly salty air. Watch boats being prepared and sails stitched in lofts along the wharves; admire the handsomely fitted craft tied up at yacht club slips. As night falls, brush off the sand and head for the waterfront. The parade of strollers on Bowen's Wharf resembles a prep-school reunion. Most action centers on the bars, cafés and restaurants along Thames Street, where the fresh seafood comes accompanied by sea breezes. The White Horse is the oldest tavern in the US.

Newport also has a remarkable legacy of colonial architecture, much of it badly neglected up to the 1960s, but Operation Clapboard encouraged people to buy up and rescue a historic house. Some 200 houses pre-date 1800 – the biggest concentration in the nation.

For a visual feast of Newport's great architectural wealth, tour The Point and the Historic Hill, the oldest colonial sections of the town. By the bayside, **Hunter House** (54 Washington Street; open May–Sept, daily; Apr and Oct, weekends; entrance fee) is a 1748 Georgian home considered an outstanding example of colonial American architecture, and the first building saved by the Preservation Society of Newport County back in 1945. Prominent in the heart of the town, the Brick Market contains the **Museum of Newport History** Ⓐ (Touro Street; in-season Wed–Mon; call 401-846 0813 for off-season hours; entrance fee), with an absorbing collection of local tidbits. **Touro Synagogue** Ⓑ (1763), America's first, in Georgian style, has an impressively lavish interior (85 Touro Street; summer tours Sun–Fri; spring and fall tours Sun pm). In nearby Touro Park stands the mysterious Old Stone Mill, an unexplained open-sided structure formerly said to have been left behind by the Phoenicians, Vikings, Portuguese, or Irish, but now known to be 16th- or 17th-century, and probably built by a Colonial farmer.

A landmark of Colonial Newport is the white clapboard **Trinity Church** Ⓒ (1725–26) on Queen Anne Square, said to be based on the designs of Christopher Wren (open June–Oct daily; Nov–May am only). By contrast the **Redwood Library and Atheneum** (1748–50) took its inspiration from Roman temple architecture; it is thought to be the oldest continuously used library building in the US and contains a noted collection of portraits (50 Bellevue Avenue; open Mon–Sat).

BELOW: Ocean Drive, Newport, facing the Atlantic.

Peruse the offerings of the **Newport Art Museum** ❶ on Bellevue Avenue, an 1862 Richard Morris Hunt mansion in the "Stick Style," which has changing exhibitions (open Mon, Tues, Thur–Sat; Sun pm; entrance fee).

The **International Tennis Hall of Fame** ❷ is housed in the Newport Casino (194 Bellevue Avenue; open daily; entrance fee) – casino only by name; this has never had anything to do with gambling – America's most exclusive country club when it was built in 1880; its grass courts hosted the first Men's US Lawn Tennis Association tournament, played in 1881. Today they're the only grass courts in America open to the public. Also in this complex is the Casino Theater, designed by Stanford White, where performing arts events are mounted.

Heading along Bellevue Avenue, the first mansion open to the public is **Kingscote** ❸ (open May–Sept daily; Apr and Oct weekends; entrance fee), the first of the summer cottages, built in Gothic Revival "Stick Style" – making playful use of asymmetry and varied textures, sprouting a wealth of pendants, lattices and gables. It has glass paneling by Tiffany and exquisite porcelain.

Touro Synagogue, Newport, the oldest in North America.

The coal-rich Edward Julius Berwind commissioned **The Elms** ❹ (open May–Oct daily; Nov–Apr weekends; entrance fee), built in French Renaissance style, based on Château d'Asnières near Paris. It borrows from a range of styles, including Chinese, Venetian and Louis XIV.

William S. Wetmore built **Château-sur-Mer** ❺ (open May–Sept daily; Oct–Apr weekends; entrance fee) in 1852, a confection of Victorian lavishness, and Newport's showiest mansion when it was built. Richard Morris Hunt enlarged it in the 1870s.

The Newport Preservation Society pays the grand sum of $1 a year to rent **The Breakers** ❻ (open Apr–Oct and Dec daily; entrance fee). Considered the most

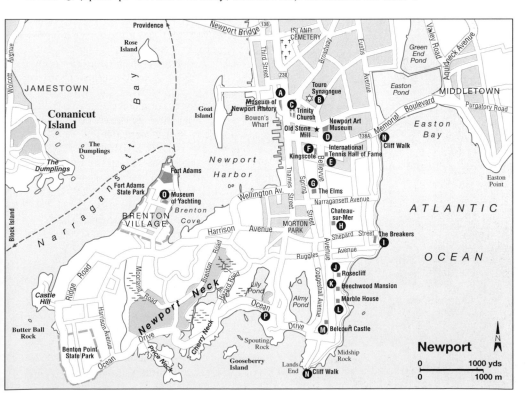

magnificent of the Newport cottages, this opulent Italian Renaissance palace, completed in 1895, took only two years to build. Cornelius Vanderbilt II commissioned American architect Richard Morris Hunt to design the mansion, whose 70 rooms are extravagantly adorned with marble, alabaster, gilt, mosaic, crystal, and stained glass. The kitchen alone is the size of a small house.

Mrs Hermann Oelrichs hired Stanford White to design **Rosecliff** ❶ (open Apr–Oct daily; entrance fee), an imitation of Versailles' Grand Trianon. It features a huge French-style ballroom and a heart-shaped staircase.

Caroline Schermerhorn Astor, the "Queen Victoria" of New York society, held court at the Astors' elegant **Beechwood Mansion** ❷ (open mid-May–Nov daily; Feb–mid-May Sun; entrance fee). Today, costumed actors show you round in your assumed role as a guest of the family.

Marble House ❸ (open Apr–Oct daily; Jan–Mar weekends; entrance fee), another of Hunt's designs, was built in 1892 for William K. Vanderbilt and styled after the Grand and Petit Trianons of Versailles. With scenes and figures from ancient mythology, it even manages to upstage The Breakers for ostentation, though it is not as large. A Chinese tea house stands in the grounds.

Belcourt Castle ❹ (open Feb–Dec daily; entrance fee), styled in 1894 on a Louis XIII hunting lodge at Versailles, has the largest collection of objets d'art of any of the mansions, including a full-size gold Coronation Coach.

Strollers can examine the backyards of the Bellevue Avenue mansions from the **Cliff Walk** ❺, a 3½-mile (5.5-km) path that overlooks Rhode Island Sound. Crusty local fishermen saved this path for public use by going to court when wealthy mansion owners tried to close it. Visitors who do not wish to walk the length of this path can start at the end of Narragansett Avenue and

Cornelius Vanderbilt II did not enjoy The Breakers for long. He died in 1899, aged 56, four years after its completion. Even though he had given vast amounts to charities during his life, his estate amounted to almost $73 million.

BELOW:
The Breakers.

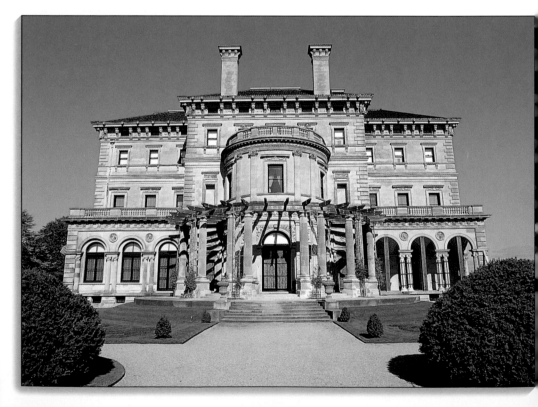

reach the water by way of the Forty Steps; or wander down to Brenton Point State Park on the island's southernmost tip, an ideal place to watch gulls, picnic or just enjoy a sunset.

During the summer, Newport hosts a number of major outdoor music events, such as the Ben and Jerry's Folk Festival and the JVC Jazz Festival, both of which take place in August at Fort Adams State Park. While there, take a look at the **Museum of Yachting ⊙** (Ocean Drive; open mid-May–Oct daily; entrance fee), which examines the pursuit through the centuries and across continents. Newport is the scene of many yachting events. The prestigious America's Cup was held in Newport waters 24 times from 1851 through 1983, when the Cup was lost (for the first time) to the Australians.

The 685-mile (1,102-km) Bermuda–Newport Race, held every other year, begins here, and the grueling Single-Handed Transatlantic Race, which starts in Plymouth, England, ends in Newport.

More mansions can be glimpsed from outside along **Ocean Drive ⊙**, which makes a pleasant cycle ride; cycle rental is available in the town.

The 28-room **Hammersmith Farm**, on Ocean Avenue, was built in 1887 for John Auchincloss and is much visited because one of his descendants, Jacqueline Bouvier, held her wedding reception there after marrying John Kennedy.

Block Island

When Rhode Islanders want to get away from it all, they head for **Block Island ❸**, a 3 by 7-mile (5 by 11-km) island some 12 miles (19 km) south of Narragansett Bay. Whereas Newport is packed to the gills with hotels, shops, restaurants, and tourists, Block Island remains a hideaway holding its own,

Maps:
Area 228
City 235

TIP

Newport is surrounded by fine beaches. The choice ranges from First, Second, and Third beaches in Middleton (north of Newport) to the more exclusive Bailey's, Hazard's, and Gooseberry.

BELOW: sea kayaking along Ocean Drive.

quite successfully, against developers and fast-food chains. There are ferry services from New London, Point Judith, and Providence via Newport.

Block Island is the least accessible of the state's islands: although regular or chartered planes fly out of Westerly, R.I., and points in Connecticut (a 10-minute hop), most people take the ferry, a 70-minute trip from Point Judith, R.I. (year-round ferry service; tel: 401-783 4613), or two hours from New London, Connecticut (service mid-June–mid-Sept). A good way to explore is by bicycle; rentals are available on the island.

Veranda detail, Block Island.

Greeting visitors to Block Island are fine beaches, popular fishing grounds, tranquility and the romantic allure of aging Victorian hotels with huge verandas and a sense of bygone splendor. A Dutch navigator, Adriaen Block, discovered the island in 1614; the landscape has changed so little, he would in all probability still recognize it today.

The island's claim to fame in maritime annals is the large number of shipwrecks off its coast. Thousands of luckless captains saw their vessels come to misery along the coast of New England, and a great many were wrecked on the submerged rocks and sandbars around "The Block." Scavenging goods from the holds of wrecked ships became such a lucrative trade that some islanders helped engineer more wrecks by setting up lanterns and flares to confuse the ships. Many island place names commemorate the wrecking trade; at Cow Cove, for instance, a cargo of cows from a wrecked ship waded ashore, and on Calico Hill, bolts of cloth collected from another disaster were hung out to dry in the sun.

BELOW: Mohegan Bluffs, Block Island.

Life in the early days was hard. In the turbulent years of the late 17th century, the island was constantly under siege from pirates. During the Revolution,

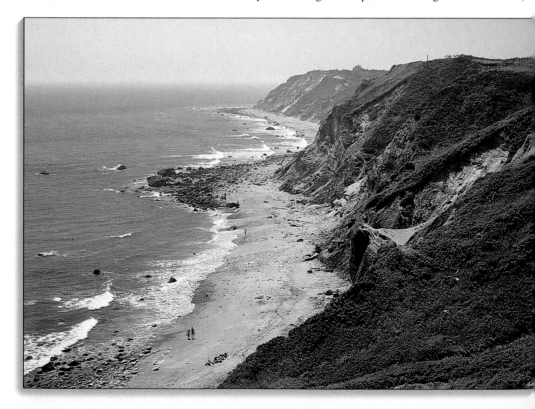

islanders – cut off from the mainland – nearly stripped Block Island of its trees building houses and ships.

Tourism arrived in 1842, when the first hotel was opened, and a party of 10 men checked in. The Spring House opened its doors 10 years later and is still accommodating visitors to this day. To spend time in this antique of a summer hotel, with its rambling corridors and simply furnished rooms, is to be caught in a time warp. From its perch high on a hill, one can gaze out over the Atlantic Ocean and breathe the beneficent sea air just as wealthy tourists from New York and Baltimore once did.

The island has several fine sand beaches. The waves are lively at Surfers Beach, as its name suggests; State Beach and others on the east are calmer and attract the most visitors. The westerly strands are windswept and, more often than not, deserted. One trek not to be missed is the hike to Mohegan Bluffs. Here, the entire Mohegan tribe met its doom at the hands of the Manasees, who either enslaved them or drove them over the 200-ft (60-meter) cliffs.

Fishing in New Harbor (formerly Great Salt Pond) can absorb an entire day, as can wandering along the roads and over the hills, looking for wildflowers and Indian relics. Shops in Old Harbor, the island's only town, sell local specialties, such as candles, jellies, and wool watch caps.

Map on page 228

Fishermen are attracted to Block Island for its abundant tuna, swordfish, bluefish, mackerel, cod and flounder.

The rest of Rhode Island

Techniques of factory production were pioneered and groundwork for the development of the region's textile industry was laid in 1789, with the construction of **Slater Mill** by Moses Brown at **Pawtucket ❹**, north of Providence. Now fully restored, the mill offers visitors a rare look into bygone industry; together with the Sylvanus Brown House and the Wilkinson Mill these form the **Slater Mill Historic Site** (727 Roosevelt Avenue; open June–Oct Tues–Sat; Sun pm; Mar–May and Nov–late Dec pm only weekends; entrance fee).

BELOW: Slater Mill.

At **Bristol ❺** is **Blithewold**, a 45-room mansion with landscaped grounds; a riot of colour in spring (grounds open daily; mansion open mid-Apr–Sept Tues–Sun; entrance fee). The "cottage" was built in a blend of Colonial, Dutch and English manor styles by a Pennsylvania coal magnate, Augustus van Wickle.

At **Portsmouth ❻** a worthwhile visit is **Green Animals Topiary Gardens**, a fanciful Victorian estate where 80 sculpted trees and shrubs represent everything from an ostrich to a camel (Cory Lane, off Route 114; open May–Oct daily; entrance fee).

Take a short detour to **Jamestown ❼** on Conanicut Island. The southern tip of the island offers New England scenery at its most picturesque. Among other notable sights, don't miss Mackerel Cove, the Beavertail Lighthouse, and the view from Fort Wetherhill.

From Jamestown, follow US 1A along the coast. From **Narragansett ❽**, an elegant resort town during the 19th century, proceed south to Scarborough State Beach, popular with Rhode Island's teenage crowd. The sheltered beach at **Galilee ❾**, Point Judith, is a perfect spot for passing a languid summer afternoon. ❏

NEWPORT'S "GILDED AGE" MANSIONS

Newport, a 19th-century summer playground for the rich and influential, became a showplace for America's greatest architects and designers

With the coming of the railways in the mid-19th century, vacationing became ever more popular, and the delights of Newport, set on an island with a fine summer climate, became readily accessible from New York and Philadelphia. Wealthy and influential families, began to spend their summers here. Many had made vast fortunes from industry and began to lavish unstinting funds on creating opulent summer homes, where they would entertain and impress all those who mattered.

The country's most innovative architects – names such as Stanford White and Richard Morris Hunt – were employed, creating designs that reflect the full range of styles in vogue at the time (*see also pages 235–6*). Building materials and furnishings were often imported from Europe (for Marble House, for instance, different coloured marbles were imported from Italy to be worked by Italian craftsmen in Newport). Interior decor frequently borrowed from European or Far Eastern styles; fine paintings, furnishings and objets d'art collected from around the world filled the rooms.

Eight of these mansions are now maintained by The Preservation Society of Newport County and are open to the public, as is the Astor family's Beechwood Mansion.

▷ **THE ELMS**
The splendid grounds are embellished with statues, fountains, and clipped and shaped trees – but, nowadays, no elms.

▷ **THE BREAKERS**
The grandest of grand dining rooms: all gold leaf, alabaster and marble – and two 12 ft (3.5 meters) chandeliers .

▽ **THE ELMS**
The Elms replicates a two-story château near Paris, with the servants' quarters behind the roof balustrade and the kitchens in a cellar.

THE LEGACY OF THE VANDERBILTS

The Breakers (above), was commissioned in 1893, to replace an earlier house destroyed by fire, by Cornelius Vanderbilt II, chairman of the New York Central railway, a director of 49 other railways, and the head of America's wealthiest family. His younger brother, William, had inherited equal shares in the family fortunes, some part of which he spent building Marble House, on nearby Bellevue Avenue. A serious, modest and gentle man, Cornelius II nevertheless gave free rein and an unlimited budget to Richard Morris Hunt, the architect of Marble House and of the grand Vanderbilt houses on Fifth Avenue in New York. Hunt followed the Italian Renaissance layout adopted for 16th-century palaces, where rooms were grouped symmetrically around a central courtyard. With 70 rooms, 33 of which were for resident staff and visitors' servants, The Breakers is indisputably Newport's largest "cottage".

▽ **CHATEAU-SUR-MER**
The solid granite 1850s Wetmore home was updated in the 1870s in the latest European fashions, including Arts and Crafts.

△ **ROSECLIFF**
The glittering ballroom, designed by Stanford White, witnessed many of Newport's most extravagant high-society summer balls.

◁ **MARBLE HOUSE**
The entrance hall of yellow Siena marble is dominated by a vast Venetian mirror over a bronze fountain custom-made for the house.

▷ **THE BREAKERS**
Magnificently sited on Ochre Point, The Breakers faces the Atlantic Ocean. Its grounds are skirted by Cliff Walk.

VERMONT

The Green Mountain State is alive with the sound of leaves crunching under foot; the sight of red barns and brick meeting-houses; the smell of country lanes and maple sugar boiling

Map on pages 246–7

Vermont is a great green slice of high ground, a measured wedge of American Pie left over, wrapped up and set aside as a souvenir of the homemade, agrarian utopia that America once aspired to be. Fatally vertical down-west and up-stream, "the land in-between" was a rocky byroad up and away from the parade route of national destiny.

Vermont had its brief, booming share of speculators, cash-croppers, side-wheelers, mother lodes and iron horses. But there was always something wildly tentative about the sweep and dash of its struggle to keep up with the American pageant, something mildly eccentric in its slapdash network of railways, turnpikes and fine rural academies.

Even before the hill towns could settle down properly, the westward exodus kicked in: the farmers' offspring were only too eager to abandon their flinty fields and frowzy home towns in search of more welcoming ground. For all its overlay of tradition, Vermont is a land of transience and experiment, a bottom land repeatedly reclaimed by nature, a country outstripped by the bigger wheels of progress, a land still imperfectly subjugated to human priorities.

PRECEDING PAGES: the Green Mountains. **LEFT:** downhill skiing. **BELOW:** Civil War monument, Newfane.

The Civil War

"Put the Vermonters ahead and keep the column well closed up," said General John Sedgewick at the Battle of Gettysburg. The price of such military strategy was high, for the Civil War decimated Vermont. No other state gave as large a share of its sons to the cause of Union. The year 1865 marked the beginning of its decline in population, which until 1960 grew gradually older and smaller.

The Civil War provided Vermont with one unexpected boon. Mrs Lincoln chose to spend the summer in Manchester in 1863, putting the area on the map (President Lincoln planned to join his family there in 1865, but fate had other plans). Other visitors soon discovered the subtler pleasures of what the 19th-century British historian Lord Bryce described as "the Switzerland of North America."

"Setting and viewing," fishing and strolling among the green hillsides became *de rigueur* during America's Gilded Age; Manchester, Burlington and Woodstock were simply the great places to summer and be seen summering.

At the height of the season, the population approached its pre-war numbers. By putting up city folk, boiling and peddling "sweet water" (maple syrup) and enclosing more of their land for pasturage, some Vermont farmers found a way to lead a somewhat softer life. Some of their neighbors, like marble baron Redfield Proctor and William Dean Howell's

Vermont and New Hampshire

fictive paint king, Silas Lapham, simply turned the fallow land over and made a mint out of bedrock mined by cheap foreign labor. But by the time the railways gave way to the automobile, tourism had become the state's unofficial No. 1 industry.

It is said that a 1763 picnicking party to Killington Peak gave the state of Vermont its name: instead of quaffing the champagne they brought for refreshment, Rev Samuel Peters broke it on a rock and christened the region "Verd Mont" ("Green Mountain" in French).

America's playground

"Vermont, Designed by the Creator for the Playground of the Continent," read a 1911 brochure published by Vermont's state publicity bureau, the first such in the nation. "Development" became the 20th-century battle cry, and roadside attractions outflanked each other from Brattleboro to Morses Line. Natives and visitors alike started grumbling in the 1930s, when rolling pastures and grassy meadows quietly gave way here and there to a lakeside resort, a new rambling "summer cottage," another country club or (finally) the slim interstate highway. Stories began to circulate, about the farmer and his 12-gauge shotgun versus a brigade of the Conservation Corps and their back-hoe. But the lawmakers in Montpelier didn't notice until, nearly overnight in the early 1950s, the ski industry blew land taxes through the rooftop. Suddenly the land of milk and honey was overflowing with New Yorkers from solstice to solstice. The real boom had finally begun.

In 1965, Vermont lost its distinction as the state with more cows than people. Today, few natives make a decent living off the land. But the new gentry – the second-homers with condos or splendid country estates, complete with Morgan horses and 30 head of sheep – are determined to reconstitute and preserve their township's special flavor, its fallow charm, its pastoral innocence, from latecomers. They have formed a shaky coalition with their neighbors – the

BELOW: cows built to survive the harsh Vermont winters.

disgruntled patricians, pillars of their community; refugees from the 1960s, back-to-land artisans of the post-industrial era; the seventh-generation Vermonters, whose trailer homes, pick-up trucks and snowmobiles are emblems of hardscrabble endurance. This is the backwoods elite – the holy alliance keeping the lobbyists and the developers at bay.

One of the toughest anti-pollution stances in the nation, a dizzying array of zoning ordinances, new wilderness designations, a "no off-premise billboards" mandate and even a touch of urban renewal have kept Vermont a superior place to live. Ironically, these factors, together with the protective attitude of its residents, have also made it one of the best places to visit.

The Lower Connecticut River Valley

The long, lazy Connecticut River forms the entire boundary between the states of Vermont and New Hampshire. Covered over by a hydroelectric dam at the southernmost end, Vermont's first permanent settlement – Fort Dummer, founded in 1752 – has been reduced to a mere marker on the shore. A few miles north, however, **Brattleboro ❶**, the town it was meant to protect, enjoyed resort status from 1846 to 1871, when a local physician parlayed its pure springs into a "water cure." In the 1960s and '70s, a new wave of adventurous folk washed upstream and settled right in. The back-to-the-land crowd, not just wandering hippies but dedicated communards, sunk their roots deep into the community, and though it's now their children who sport tie-dyes and flowing hair about town, the hippies managed to set up an economic infrastructure with surprising staying power. They – and a general populace whose tastes have come around – support natural foods markets, alternative shops, and a worker-owned restaurant, **The Common Ground**, which after several decades of broad-based success seems less a restaurant than a cultural touchstone (Eliot Street; open for lunch and dinner; tel: 802-257 0855).

Seek out the Art Deco **Latchis Building**, which houses a movie theater and hotel, and the **Brattleboro Museum and Art Center** (open Tues–Sun, 12–6pm) in the Union Railroad Station. This has a collection of Jacob Estey reed organs that were made in the town in the 19th century.

Naulahka, the ship-shaped manse where Rudyard Kipling wrote the first two *Jungle Books* and *Captain Courageous* in the 1890s, has been recently restored by Great Britain's Landmark Trust (not open to the public, but see Tip in margin). Kipling, an Englishman born in India, came here on his honeymoon in 1892 (his bride's parents had settled in Brattleboro after taking the cure) and he immediately warmed to the life of a country squire; he even enjoyed playing golf in the snow, with balls painted red. His grand airs, however, didn't endear him to the locals, and in 1896 when a property dispute with his roguish brother-in-law hit the headlines, destroying his rural idyll, he and his wife fled, never to return.

Follow US 9 to the west of Brattleboro to reach **Marlboro ❷** – hilltop home of experimental Marlboro College, which every summer hosts the world-renowned **Marlboro Music Festival**, founded

TIP

Kipling's house, Naulahka, is available for rent by the week from the UK's Landmark Trust. Telephone 802-254 6868 in the US or 0628 825925 in the UK for details.

BELOW: the Art-Deco Latchis Building, Brattleboro.

by the late Rudolf Serkin (book early for tickets; tel: 802-254 2394) – and the ski resort towns of Wilmington and West Dover. The latter two towns are somewhat overdeveloped in places (in the 1950s, the burgeoning Mount Snow ski resort, then the largest, turned these hamlets into veritable boom towns).

State 30 northwest out of Brattleboro follows the West River, past a picturesque covered bridge, to the postcard-perfect town of **Newfane ❸**. Its broad common is lined with shady elms and surrounded by stately Greek Revival public buildings – a white-columned courthouse with Congregational church to match, flanked by a grange, two outstanding inns famous for their culinary offerings, and some worthwhile antique stores. A flea market held summer weekends in a field north of town since the late 1960s has become something of an institution, and a draw for locals and visitors alike.

Further up Route 30 are two equally appealing, low-key villages to explore: **Townshend ❹** and **Jamaica**, with plenty of unspoiled parkland – including the beach at the West River reservoir behind the Townshend Dam.

A small town directly north of Brattleboro on US 5, **Putney ❺** predated the social experiments of the 1960s by a good 150 years: in the early 18th century, it was the site of a short-lived but sensational commune espousing free love. The countryside is still populated in part by '60s protesters, some clustered in communes of several decades' duration. Many artists and craftspeople ply their trades in Putney; look for hand-crafted signs announcing sculpture and woodworking studios and potteries.

Scenic backroads dotted with antique shops connect Bellows Falls with Grafton and Chester to the northwest. Purchased in its entirety and renovated by the Windham Foundation, **Grafton ❻** is a preserved-in-amber Greek Revival

BELOW:
near Putney.

town eerily close to its appearance in the early 1800s: visitors wander about in blissful disbelief, sampling a slice of cheddar at the **Grafton Village Cheese Company** (tel: 802-843 2221), and perhaps claiming a rocker on the porch of the 1801 Old Tavern, whose guests have included notables from Thoreau and Kipling to Ulysses S. Grant and Teddy Roosevelt. **Chester ❼** is a curious little strand of Victoriana on the Williams River. One especially ornate building houses the **National Survey Charthouse**. An 1850s stone village-within-a-village features 30 homes faced in gneiss ledgestone.

The Upper Connecticut Valley

A center of invention during the 19th century and today home of a thriving machine tool industry, the towns of Springfield and **Windsor ❽** form Precision Valley, a living testament to Yankee ingenuity. The **American Precision Museum** on Windsor's South Main Street (Route 12 East; open May–Oct, daily; entrance fee) is chock-full of all the gadgets, whatsits and thingamabobs that not only made the region famous, but helped the North win the Civil War.

Windsor is also famed as the birthplace of Vermont, because it was here in the **Old Constitution House** that delegates met in 1777 to establish the Free and Independent Republic of Vermont, draw up a constitution and create a Council of Safety to protect the new country as much from the other 12 states as from the Crown; the building is now a museum, with material relating to this event (open late May–mid-Oct, daily; entrance fee). On Route 5, the **Catamount Brewing Co**. offers tours and tastings (open Mon–Sat; Sun pm). The **Windsor-Cornish Covered Bridge**, spanning the Connecticut River to lovely Cornish, New Hampshire, is the longest covered bridge in the United States.

Cycling in the forest.

BELOW:
chicken farmer.

"I live in New Hampshire so I can get a better view of Vermont," explained artist Maxfield Parrish from his home in Cornish. He did sneak a considerable piece of that view into most of his paintings, notably Mount Ascutney, which looms south of Windsor. The largest monadnock in New England, **Ascutney** is home to a ski resort (tel: 802-484 7711) and conference center that mounts cultural events in the summer months.

The older money of **Woodstock** ❾ can, from time to time, be heard to lament inroads made by what one observer has called the "suburban gold-coast mink-and-manure set." Upscale shopping sprees along the refurbished downtown blocks of Cabot and French streets may have replaced placid strolls up Mount Tom as the fashionable summer pastime, but in general the enlightened despotism of philanthropist Laurance Rockefeller has preserved the tone of the town much as it must have been in the 1930s, when he met his future wife, Mary French, while summering here.

A passion for maintaining a graceful balance between society and nature has long been the keynote to Woodstock's renown. Mary's grandfather, Frederick Billings, returned from his lucrative law practice in San Francisco in the 1890s to become a pioneer in reforestation and a zealous model farmer. The slopes of Mount Tom and Mount Peg and the restored **Billings Farm Museum** (Route 12 East; open May–Oct, daily; entrance fee) are testaments to his love for rural Vermont. Growing up on the elder Billings' farm in the 1830s, George Perkins Marsh – later to become a noted linguist and diplomat – drafted a landmark treatise, *Man and Nature*, which, over a century after its publication, remains the ecologist's New Testament. In 1998 the Billings family mansion, most recently occupied by Laurance Rockefeller, was opened under the auspices of

BELOW: the Floating Bridge at Brookfield.

Marsh–Billings National Historic Park (Route 12 East; open mid-May–mid-Oct; entrance fee). Tours of the mansion and grounds are offered.

For further glimpses of Woodstock's past, visit the **Woodstock Historical Society** headquarters, nine rooms of period furnishings in an 1807 house – also known as the Dana House (Elm Street; open May–late Oct Mon–Sat; Sun pm; entrance fee).

The Rockefellers' Woodstock Inn and Resort on the green remains the place to stay – and the Robert Trent Jones golf course and **Suicide Six** ski area (tel: 802-457 6661) offer year-round amusements. On the other side of the green, a covered bridge leads to Mountain Avenue, a redoubt of old summer cottages, and a park at the base of Mount Tom. Trails to the summit overlook a guided floral walk through the Rockefeller estate, and the Vermont Institute of Natural Science maintains the fascinating **Vermont Raptor Center**, a habitat for 26 species of owls, hawks, and eagles unable to survive in the wild (Church Hill Road; open daily; entrance fee).

The hills surrounding Woodstock are horse country. At the fairgrounds in **Quechee ⑩** to the east, polo matches are played most Saturdays in July and August. In town, Irish artisan **Simon Pearce** has transformed The Mill at Quechee, an abandoned flannel factory, into a most inviting complex featuring his distinctive glasswork (glass-blowers can be observed at work on weekdays) and a delightful restaurant overlooking the mill pond.

To the east, **Quechee Gorge** is billed by local boosters as "Vermont's Little Grand Canyon."

Visionaries, religious and commercial

A major crossroads since the days when railroads ruled interstate traffic, **White River Junction** still serves as an Amtrak stop and marks the intersection of Interstates 91 and 89.

"A man can easily hear strange voices," said Kipling of the lonely Vermont winter, "the Word of God rolling between the dead hills; may see visions and dream dreams…" Joseph Smith, founder of the Church of Jesus Christ of the Latter-day Saints, was born in 1805 on **Dairy Mill Hill**, a mile from South Royalton on Route 14. Here Mormon followers maintain a 38½-ft (11.5-meter) obelisk and a museum.

Heading northward, seek out the unspoiled village of **Brookfield ⑪**, the geographical center of the state. In 1812, a 320-ft (98-meter) **Floating Bridge**, supported by 380 tarred barrels, was built across the pond at the center of town, and it survives to this day – as part of Route 65 – accommodating one car at a time; it's also popular for fishing. One of the last ice harvests in the east is now the occasion for an annual festival on the lake, held the last Saturday in January.

Between Brookfield and Barre is the town of **Graniteville ⑫**, site of the **Rock of Ages Quarry**, one of the largest granite quarries in the world. Mining began in the early 19th century, soon after the War of 1812, and boomed with the influx of skilled immigrant stoneworkers between 1880 and 1910. Fed up with poor wages and working conditions (many died

A participant in Woodstock's Wassail Parade.

BELOW: Brookfield's ice festival.

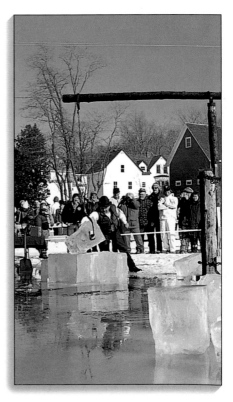

of silicosis), the granite workers managed to elect a Socialist mayor – many decades before liberal Burlington was ready to do the same. Today, the Rock of Ages firm owns nearly all of the quarries on and around Graniteville's Millstone Hill, which provide the nation with one-third of its memorial stones. The operation has long been a tourist-oriented showcase (Main Street; tours June–mid-Oct; entrance fee), with free access to the polishing and sculpting factory, and optional bus tours skirting the fully operational quarry a mile up the hill.

For a more evocative tour, however, visit Barre's **Hope Cemetery** (off Route 14), where the workers commemorated their own, with often touching artwork.

The smallest capital: Montpelier

Home to about 8,200 people, **Montpelier** ⓭ is the smallest state capital in the nation. The green ridge of Hubbard Park rises behind the gold-leaf dome of the **Vermont State House** (State Street; tours July–mid-Oct, Mon–Fri). Initially, Vermont's capital rotated through the state, but, with the completion of the original nine-sided building in 1808, the seat of power settled here. When an imposing stone successor, built in 1838, was gutted by fire in 1857, the Doric portico and native granite walls withstood the flames to form a shell for the - present structure. The Senate Chamber is rightfully considered the most beautiful room in the state.

The "Steamboat Gothic" Pavilion Hotel – "the Grand Old Lady of State Street," where so many lawmakers bedded down for the January–April session (following an agrarian calendar, legislators go about their ordinary lives the rest of the year) – was demolished in 1966. However, a skillful replica now occupies its place beside the State House Lawn and houses a collection of Vermont

Montpelier was the birthplace of Admiral George Dewey (1837–1917), who became a hero during the Spanish-American War when the US fleet under his command destroyed the Spanish fleet at Manila.

BELOW: Robert Burns stands guard in Barre.
RIGHT: State House, Montpelier.

icons which once decorated the capitol building. This, the **Vermont Historical Society Museum**, is a rewarding mishmash of Green Mountain artifacts (109 State Street; open Tues–Sat; Sun pm).

Map on pages 246–7

If you spot an unlikely number of chefs' hats about town, it's because Montpelier is also home to the **New England Culinary Institute**, a highly regarded training school that maintains two excellent public restaurants – the Main Street Grill and Bar (lunch, dinner; tel: 802-223 3188) and the Chef's Table (118 Main Street; lunch weekdays, dinner Mon–Sat; tel: 802-229 9202) – as well as an irresistible bakery.

The Green Mountains

Some 20 miles (32 km) west of Montpelier, the Green Mountain range attains heady heights highly tempting to skiers – as well as to mountain climbers and bikers. South of I-89, the towns of Waitsfield and Warren support two ski areas, the rustic, but challenging **Mad River Glen** and more developed and extensive **Sugarbush ⑭**. Both towns are full of the pleasures – inviting restaurants and cozy inns – that outdoors enthusiasts enjoy in their off-hours.

Waitsfield boasts an unusual cinema, Mad River Flicks, which offers café-style service and seating in overstuffed love seats. Spectators are also welcome at two summertime sporting venues, the **Sugarbush Polo Club** (the original players, in 1962, used ski poles and a volleyball) and the **Mad River Valley Cricket Club**. To get an unusual perspective on the countryside, consider a vintage airplane ride or soaring excursion out of the Warren-Sugarbush Airport (Route 100; flights May–Oct), or try horse-trekking at the Vermont Icelandic Horse Farm North (Basin Road off Route 100; rides year-round).

BELOW: a street vendor takes things easy.

CRAFTS IN VERMONT

With over 1,500 professional artisans, Vermont has more artists and craftspeople per capita than any other state. Thanks in part to a bucolic setting but also to state support – the Vermont Crafts Council in Montpelier has designated four "Vermont State Craft Centers" – you'll find outstanding creative work in every major town (and minor ones, too). Vermont's non-profit galleries exhibit and sell pottery, woodwork, jewelry, textiles, glassware, quilts and anything else you can think of.

The largest of these outlets, Frog Hollow, has shops in Burlington, Manchester and Middlebury (tel: 802-388 3177). Over 250 "juried" artisans (those whose work has been judged to be of the highest quality) show their work through this venue. The Vermont State Craft Center at Windsor House, Windsor, features works from 200 juried artisans (tel: 802-674 6729).

In summer and fall, large craft fairs are held throughout the state (*see Travel Tips*), and on Memorial Day weekend artists participate in a statewide "Open Studio" weekend. The Vermont Crafts Council (tel: 802-223 3380) publishes a free annual studio and gallery guide, and a calendar of fairs. This information, as well as links to member artists, is available on-line at www.vermontcrafts.com.

Ben & Jerry's.

In **Waterbury** ⓕ, midway between these peaks and Mount Mansfield to the north, a number of gourmet entrepreneurs have set up shop. Vermont Distillers, "the smallest (legal) distillery in the US," produces vodka, gin, and spicy Tamarack liqueur. And a pair of "flatlander" entrepreneurs have found a great use for Vermont's abundant ice and milk: the **Ben & Jerry's Homemade Ice Cream Factory** on Route 100 in Waterbury is now the largest tourist attraction in Vermont, offering tours (with tastings) daily (tours Mon–Sat; entrance fee; tel: 802-244 8687). Just up the road, you can watch cider being pressed in season, and sample some, at the Cold Hollow Cider Mill, and stop for a nibble at the Green Mountain Chocolate Co., a confiserie run by former White House pastry chef Albert Kumin.

Even before the advent of skiing in the 1930s, when the Civilian Conservation Corps cut the first of Mount Mansfield's precipitous trails, ensuring ascendancy of **Stowe** ⓖ as "the Ski Capital of the East," Stowe enjoyed a reputation as a stylish summer place. Three grand hotels were built in the mid-1800s, of which only the 1833 Green Mountain Inn, at the center of town, survives.

Summer or winter, sports opportunities abound, particularly along the **Stowe Recreation Path**, created in the 1980s through community donations and effort. Ideally suited for skiers, cyclists, skaters, wheelchair racers, runners, walkers and stroller-pushers, the 5.3-mile (8.5-km) paved path skirts the West Branch river from town all the way out to the Topnotch resort, passing a number of appealing inns, restaurants, and shops en route. Other notable Stowe inns, such as the Austrian-style Trapp Family Lodge (founded by the Baroness Maria Von Trapp of *Sound of Music* fame) are tucked away in the wooded hills; in summer, the meadows of the Trapp Family Lodge are alive with the sound of concerts and

BELOW:
Ben & Jerry's ice cream factory.
RIGHT: time to think.

equestrian shows. The Trapp Family Lodge has America's earliest cross-country ski area, which links with three other networks around Stowe to give one of the biggest trail systems in New England.

On **Mount Mansfield** Ralph Waldo Emerson had a bracing vacation at the Summit House, where, he recounts, his "whole party climbed to the top of the [mountain's] nose and watched the sun rise over the top of the White Mountains of New Hampshire." Hikers still favor this craggy human profile, and two short-cuts are popular: for a fee, the 4½-mile (7.5-km) **Auto Road**, a century-old toll road rising from the Inn at the Mountain on Route 108 (open late May–mid-Oct), offers an easy way to ascend to the "nose," and an eight-passenger **gondola**, the world's speediest (mid-June–mid-Oct; entrance fee), makes fast work of the 4,393-ft (1,338-meter) "chin," the state's highest point. The ski area has some long, challenging and intermediate runs. On adjoining Spruce Peak, the **Stowe Mountain Resort** (entrance fee; tel: 802-253 3000) also operates an alpine slide and the world's first alpine in-line skate park, opened in 1993.

Another big summertime draw is the early August classic car rally, and in mid-January, during the Stowe Winter Carnival, the whole town parties. As the Federal Writers' Project put it decades ago, "Stowe is a 'smart' place to be seen and many snowtime visitors are not skiers."

Wintertime visitors hoping to fit in a visit to the nearby ski area of **Smuggler's Notch** ⑱ (so named for its role during the War of 1812) are in for a rude surprise: the connecting road is closed in winter, and those who've traveled it in summer will understand why. Hundred-foot cliffs and giant boulders crowd the narrow, winding roadway – a popular staging point for mountaintop hikes. On the other side, the Smuggler's Notch ski resort (tel: 802-644 8851),

Map on pages 246–7

BELOW: Balloon Festival, Stowe.

encompassing three peaks (one offers ski access back to Stowe), is popular with families for its well-thought-out children's programs – giving among other things courses for adults on how to teach their children to ski, and courses for children on how to teach their parents to snowboard. The absence of winter through-traffic is a distinctive plus. In summer the attraction is an assortment of water slides – so far, the only such amusements in the state. The town closest to the resort, **Jeffersonville**, has a range of shops and restaurants.

About 8 miles (13 km) east, the sleepy town of Johnson has been all but taken over by the **Vermont Studio Center**, a working retreat for artists and writers that attracts many prominent instructors.

The Northeast Kingdom

North of State 15 is a remote and remarkable region. The Northeast Kingdom is a nearly 2,000-sq.-mile (over 5,000-sq.-km) swath of crystal lakes and climax forests, a region known for greater natural wealth and homegrown poverty than any other area in the state. The counties of Caledonia, Essex and Orleans are sparsely populated and make up Vermont's least industrialized area, except for a scattering of lake resort towns, paper company holdings in the far east corner, and various businesses in St Johnsbury, the Kingdom's unofficial capital. *Where the Rivers Run North* is the title Orleans writer Howard Frank Mosher gave his collection of short stories (it spawned an acclaimed locally produced movie in 1994) in honor of a region known for its backwater quirks.

Increasingly beset by competition from development and government regulation, Vermont's dairy industry has fallen on hard times of late. Not so the 500-odd farms involved with the Cabot Creamery Co-operative in **Cabot ⑲**;

BELOW:
Lake Willoughby.

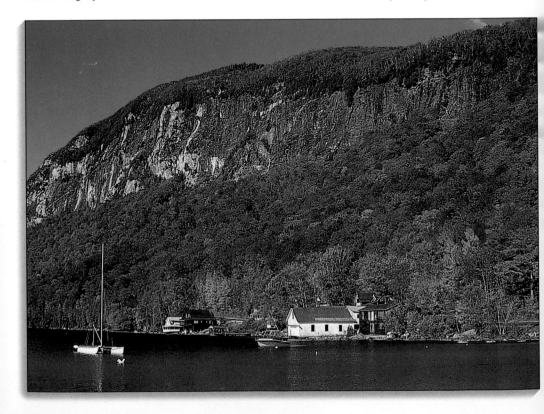

founded in 1919, the co-op thrives to this day, and offers factory tours, starting with a video recounting the history of farming in the region and ending with tastings of its outstanding Vermont cheddar (open June–Oct, daily; Nov–May, Mon–Sat; closed Jan; cheese is not made every day). Nearby Danville hosts another organization of unlikely survivors: the **American Society of Dowsers**, on Village Green, counts among its members hundreds of firm believers in the powers of the divining rod. Their headquarters, housed in a red clapboard hall, doubles as a store, and their annual fall gathering attracts curious observers.

The city of **St Johnsbury** ❷⓿ itself remains a vibrant pocket of Victorian charm. From the bank buildings downtown to the Fairbanks mansion on the Plains overlooking the valley, the stamp of architect Lambert Packard and his wealthy patrons is visible everywhere. Thaddeus Fairbanks started making the world's first platform scale here in the 1830s, and he and his sons reinvested the fruits of their precision instrument into the quality of civic life. The St Johnsbury **Athenaeum/Art Gallery** (Main Street; open Mon–Sat; Mon and Wed till 8pm) built in 1871–73, is a tastefully combined library, music chamber and exhibition space dominated by the huge skylit panorama *Domes of the Yosemite* by artist Albert Bierstadt. This is one of the oldest intact art collections in the country ("Welcome to the nineteenth century," reads a sign at the entrance) and one of the most inviting. With a collection of more than 3,000 stuffed fauna and its own vintage planetarium, the Romanesque **Fairbanks Museum and Planetarium** is a little bastion of natural history erected by the Fairbanks family in 1890 (Main and Prospect streets; Mon–Sat; Sun pm; entrance fee).

About 10 miles (6 km) north of St Johnsbury, the still relatively undiscovered ski area of **Burke** ❷❶ deserves its promotional billing as "Vermont's Northern

Map on pages 246–7

Bierstadt (1830–1902) belonged to the Hudson River School of painters, the country's first native school of painting. Its earliest leaders worked in the wilderness areas around the Hudson River north of New York, and in nearby New England.

LEFT: old postcard view of St Johnsbury Athenaeum.
RIGHT: a farmer at Norwich.

Vermont Athanaeum, St Johnsbury.

Star." With a challenging array of trails, and affordable lift tickets (tel: 802-626 3305), it's one of the best deals in the Northeast. It also serves as an outdoor campus for Burke Academy, which has consistently turned out Olympians.

Craftsbury Common ② and Greensboro are among the more moneyed summer communities hidden in these hills. The former has become a magnet for serious athletes – the Craftsbury Sports Center offers dormitory-style accommodation and year-round instruction in sports – and the latter remains a peaceful retreat favored by writers and other intelligentsia (the local general store stocks the *New York Times*).

Every summer, hordes of joyous pilgrims descend on the small town of Glover to partake in the Bread and Puppet Theater's "Domestic Resurrection Circus," a pageant and festival put on by the radical theater group founded by Peter Schumann in 1963 to illustrate the horrors of war and wonders of life. The **Bread and Puppet Museum** is an amazing barnful of fantastical creatures (Route 122; open May–Oct daily).

The **Old Stone House Museum** (off Route 58; open mid-May–June and Sept–mid-Oct, Fri–Tues; July and Aug, daily; entrance fee) at **Brownington** ㉓ is a collection of locally donated miscellenia, housed in the former county grammar school, built between 1827 and 1830 by "Uncle" Alexander Twilight. He was claimed by Middlebury College as the first black college graduate, Class of 1823, and said to be the first black legislator in the nation. Each of the building's 11 rooms is devoted to a particular township.

Once a fashionable watering hole on the Canadian frontier, the vast **Lake Memphrémagog** ㉔ lost most of its following in the 1920s with the retirement of the Mountain Maid and Lady of the Lake steam liners, but none of its inter-

TIP

The date of the Bread and Puppet Theater festival in Glover is not advertised, so as to minimize crowds, but details can be obtained from the Bread and Puppet Museum (tel: 802-525 3031).

BELOW: the Black River Valley near Craftsbury.

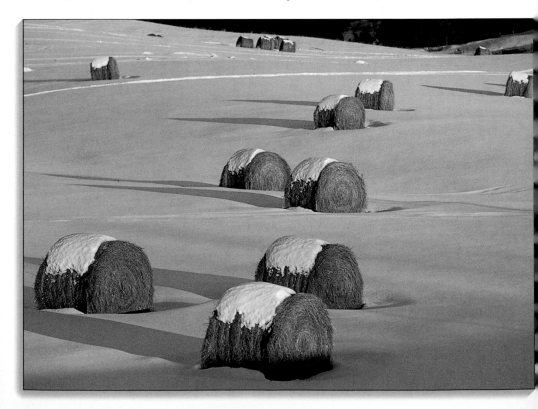

national charm. **Newport**, "the Border City," is a fair-sized town noted for its easy mingle of Canadian day-trippers, contented locals and southerly summer-ers strung along Cape Elizabeth Bluffs at the lake's eastern shore. Smelt, small-mouth bass and wall-eyed pike are all common catches over the Derby Line.

To the west, Route 242 climbs from Jay to the ski area of **Jay Peak** ㉕ (tel: 802-988 2611 or 800-451 4449), where an aerial tramway runs, transport-ing skiers, foliage peepers and summer sightseers to its 3,861-ft (1,177-meter) summit. The views into Canada are magnificent.

The northwestern corner

The northwest corner of Vermont's border with Canada, between Alburg and Morses Line, was a favorite route for smugglers in the steamboat era. But the notorious smuggling center of Highgate Spring was known chiefly for its springs (which supposedly had curative powers) until Prohibition, when bootleggers began running their nag brigades and motorcades right into Franklin County.

Over the years since 1609, when Samuel de Champlain discovered the body of water that now bears his name (and spotted a Loch Ness-like monster that has as yet eluded capture), the islands at its northern end have been compared to every place from the Isle of Man to the Louisiana bayou. Just fertile enough to support a few orchards and some grazing Jerseys, and just far enough out of the way to have withstood development, the Four Brothers Islands – Alburg, Isle La Motte, the Two Heroes and Grand Isle – stretch for 30 beautiful miles (48 km) south to the widest reach of **Lake Champlain** ㉖.

"Vermont's Cape Cod" is strewn with arcadian preserves, lakeshore drives and

Map on pages 246–7

BELOW: beach scene, Lake Champlain.

TIP

Lake Champlain offers great scope for cruises. From Burlington, a ferry plies from to Port Kent, NY, and there are scenic trips on the *Spirit of Ethan Allen* (College Street, Burlington Boathouse, tel: 802-862 8300).

sleepy little towns. **Isle La Motte** is perhaps the most satisfying of the islands, with its exquisite marble deposits, "the oldest coral reef in the world" (leftover from 10,000 years ago, when the Atlantic covered the Champlain Valley, it's littered with sunken steamboats and bobbing scuba buoys), and **St Anne's Shrine** (open mid-May–mid-Oct, daily; Sat till 8pm) honoring America's first French settlement (1664).

Franklin County was the center of Vermont's rise to eminence as a dairy state. Although the principal town, **St Albans** ㉗, lacks the vivacity it enjoyed as a major railyard on the way to Montreal, it does host a Vermont Maple Festival in mid-April which officially denotes the long-awaited end of winter. And it was also once the scene of the Civil War's most northerly skirmish: in 1864 a band of Confederates seized the town, robbed the banks and hightailed it to Canada. There they were caught and brought to trial; however, their exploits were excused as "legitimate" acts of war.

Burlington and environs

"The most miserable of one-horse towns," complained the young wife of an Army recruiting officer stationed here in the 1840s. "Startling incidents never occur in Burlington. None ever occurred there, and none probably ever will." Things have livened up along "New England's West Coast" since then. By the Civil War, fiercely competitive steamboat lines and a busy lumber trade were turning **Burlington** ㉘ into a plucky little inland port of entry. By 1900, the wharves were teeming with businessmen, seekers of pleasure and ships' crews.

Today, trendy restaurants and the lively Church Street Marketplace, a pedestrian mall lined with sidewalk cafés and gentrified shops, have further improved Burlington's outlook. But the view remains the same. From Battery Park or the Cliffs, the sunset over Lake Champlain and the Adirondacks is still – as novelist William Dean Howells maintained – "superior to the evening view over the Bay of Naples," and "parties of pleasures" are again threatening to outnumber the workaday commuters who board the evening ferry to Port Kent, New York. In fact, the dock itself has become a tourist attraction, with a lively bar and sailboards to rent, sailboats to charter.

A growing influx of industry – notably, IBM – and the new metropolitan tone mingle to make the core of Vermont's "Queen City" (population 40,000) a commercial and cultural nexus that keeps turning up on polls as being one of the US's "most livable cities." Thanks in part to the presence of the University of Vermont (called "UVM" for its Latin name, Universitas Viridis Montis), the city enjoys a year-round array of cultural events, including annual Mozart and Shakespeare festivals. The **Flynn Theater for the Performing Arts**, a 1930 Art Deco movie palace on Main Street, hosts an impressive line-up of dance, music and theater (tel: 802-863 5966).

There's a lot worth doing within Burlington's widening metropolis. When the city's famous woolen industry moved south, the nearby city of Winooski (straddling its namesake river) went completely bottom up. But in 1978, the huge mill was revamped

BELOW: the sun sets over Lake Champlain.

and refitted with an alluring bay of shops as the Champlain Mill Mall. Nearby, **St Michael's Playhouse**, on the campus of Saint Michael's College, has been mounting professional summer theater performances since 1951 (off Route 15; tel: 802-654 2281). Circling back into Burlington from the north, stop in at the **Ethan Allen Homestead Trust**, a restored 1787 farmhouse, for an insight into the exploits of this beloved native son as well as 5,000 years of local history (off Route 127; open mid-may–mid-Oct Mon–Sat; Sun pm; entrance fee).

About 7 miles (11 km) south of the city, at **Shelburne ㉙**, is the **Shelburne Museum**, which has to be seen to be believed (Route 7; tours mid-May–late Oct, daily; entrance fee). Neither a "living museum" nor a fusty historical collection, it's a 45-acre (18-hectare) complex reflecting the tastes of one very passionate and well-funded collector. Electra Havemeyer Webb developed an eye for Americana and folk art long before anyone else was paying attention, and managed to amass some 80,000 exemplary objects – 37 buildings full in all, with some train cars, a carousel and a Lake Champlain side-wheeler, the *Ticonderoga*, thrown in for good measure. It takes more than a casual stroll to do the collection justice; hence admission, though pricy, is good for two days.

Shelburne's other landmark is the Webbs' 100-room Queen Anne-style cottage on the lake. Carved from 22 lakeside farms by Frederick Law Olmsted, designer of New York City's Central Park, this 1,000-acre (400-hectare) estate is now a model ecological farmstead, **Shelburne Farms**, with a farm trail and guided tours (off Route 7; tours mid-May–mid-Oct, daily; entrance fee).

Charlotte, a few miles south of Shelburne, is home to the unusual **Vermont Wildflower Farm**, a 6-acre (2.5-hectare) preserve and learning center that offers delightful strolling (Route 7; open May–Oct daily; entrance fee).

Map on pages 246–7

Maple syrup – one of Vermont's specialties.

BELOW: a country store – for maple syrup and much, much more.

When I see birches bend to left and right/Across the lines of straighter darker trees,/I like to think some boy's been swinging on them./But swinging doesn't bend them down to stay./Ice storms do that.

— ROBERT FROST

BIRCHES

BELOW:
Vermont Marble
Exhibit, Proctor.

Middlebury and marble

Vermont spawned the world-famous Morgan horse, a barrel-chested steed, which, as one celebrant boasted, "can outrun, outpull, and outlast any other breed, just as you would expect a Vermont horse to do." The **UVM Morgan Horse Farm**, in the village of Weybridge, is a working farm with training demonstrations and tours (off Route 23; tours May–Oct daily; entrance fee).

Middlebury ㉚, a few miles southeast, is the ideal college town, a verdant campus of grand, well-spaced 19th-century buildings, accompanied by a lively community of shops and restaurants. The **Vermont State Craft Center** at Frog Hollow showcases the traditional and contemporary work of more than 300 of the state's most talented artisans.

The poet Robert Frost spent his summers writing in a log cabin in **Ripton** ㉛, not far from Bread Loaf, home of the prestigious **Bread Loaf Writers' Conference**. The mile-long **Robert Frost Interpretive Trail**, beginning at his home, the Homer Noble Farm, leads to the Bread Loaf campus by way of the cabin, which has been left untouched. For magnificent scenery, continue on State 125, through steep Lincoln Gap, and south through the unspoiled towns on this stretch of Route 100, which bisects the state vertically, and not always prettily.

The town of **Proctor** ㉜ is the home of the **Vermont Marble Exhibit** (off Route 3; open mid-May–mid-Oct daily; entrance fee), offering a glimpse of the Vermont Marble Company factory, a sculptor at work, and marble samples from around the world, including the local product – some of which can be seen lining the sidewalks of the more prosperous towns in the region. The abandoned quarries make tempting swimming holes, too, if you can wrest the location from a local source.

Map on pages 246–7

The region west of Vermont's second-biggest city, **Rutland ㉝**, was a popular summer spot in the Victorian era, but faded after World War II, when the trains stopped coming. Rediscovered in recent decades by starry-eyed innkeepers and their guests, pretty towns such as Middletown Springs (a one-time spa) and Fair Haven are making a comeback, offering little more than old-fashioned B&B hospitality and plenty of unspoiled countryside to roam. Though they're minuscule in comparison to Lake Champlain, Lake St Catherine and Lake Bomoseen are flanked by state parks and offer sandy beaches.

Rutland itself is rather drab, but it does harbor a hidden gem: **Wilson Castle** (West Road; tours mid-May–mid-Oct, daily; entrance fee), an improbably opulent mid-1800s mansion with 32 rooms, 12 fireplaces and such elegant appointments as a Louis XVI crown jewel case, with manicured walkways covering 115 acres (46 hectares).

New England's largest ski area is **Killington ㉞** (tel: 802-422 3333 or 800-621 6867) in Sherburne Center, which quickly eclipsed **Mount Snow**, expanding to cover seven peaks, and in 1999 was linked up by trail to the adjacent resort of **Pico** as well – the whole complex being owned by the American Skiing Company. It ranks top among the Northeast ski resorts for nightlife. With a 4,241-ft (1,296-meter) peak reached by gondola, for sightseers as well as skiers, the resort is active year-round – the skiing often lasts from October through June and then in summer mountain bikes take over.

Nearby **Plymouth** spawned the US's most taciturn president. The **President Coolidge Birthplace and Homestead ㉟** (Route 100A; open late May–mid-Oct, daily; entrance fee) serves as a hilltop shrine to silent Cal – that self-styled "Puritan in Babylon," and the only President born on the Fourth of July. When

BELOW: spring colors in Rutland.

President Warren Harding died on August 3, 1923, and Vice-President Calvin Coolidge needed to be sworn in as the 30th president, the news had to be conveyed to the Coolidges by hand; true to form, the family did not have a phone.

The picturesque, marble-paved village of **Dorset** ㊱ is home to the **Dorset Playhouse**, a rustic barn that served as Vermont's first summer playhouse (tel: 802-867 5777), and to a writers' colony .

Manchester and south: a pre-eminent summer place

Franklin Orvis gave the local tourist industry a boost in 1849 when he began taking in summer guests at his father's house, located next to the famed 1769 Marsh Tavern in **Manchester** ㊲, where Ethan Allen and his "Green Mountain Boys" had plotted the Tories' overthrow. The hotel kept expanding bit by bit until it became the grand Equinox, named for the mountain that presides over the town, and which can be reached 4 miles (6.5 km) south of town via the **Skyline Drive** toll road (open May–Oct, daily 8am–10pm). For all the former farmhands drawn to the metropolis, city-dwellers began to catch on to the attractions of open spaces and fresh air.

Meanwhile, Frank's younger brother, Charles, had a clever idea, too – why not teach the leisured class to catch their supper along the banks of the abundant Battenkill River? Less than 10 years after he sold his first bamboo flyrod, Manchester had become the place to get away from it all.

By the mid-20th century, the Equinox had deteriorated into white elephanthood, but in the early 1980s it was restored to showplace luster, along with its 18-hole golf course. And the Orvis Company has prospered all the while: today it operates a thriving mail-order business, and the store – with its history-of-the-

BELOW: the Dorset Inn.

Map on pages 246–7

art **American Museum of Fly Fishing** (Route 7A; open daily) next door – draws visitors from around the world, as do the company's three-day fly-fishing courses. Orvis's success inspired other upscale companies (Ralph Lauren, Esprit, et al) to open their own outlets here, so the shopping opportunities are unsurpassed in the state.

All this brisk commerce notwithstanding, Manchester Village remains as tranquil and elegant as ever, with its marble-slab sidewalks and showy summer homes, many of them creatively converted into inns and restaurants.

Although Abraham Lincoln never made it to the Equinox (several other presidents did), Mary Lincoln and son Robert cherished fond memories of the mountains; they later returned to build an estate, **Hildene**, which now opens its richly appointed Georgian Revival rooms to antiquity-lovers and its 412-acre (167-hectare) grounds to cross-country skiers and summer strollers (Route 7A; tours mid-May–Oct, daily; entrance fee). Another pleasant place to visit in town is the **Southern Vermont Art Center** (West Road; open mid-May–Oct, Tues–Sat; Sun pm; donations), with contemporary indoor exhibits, outdoor sculptures, and a well-marked botany trail.

On Route 11, 6 miles (9.5 km) east of Manchester, **Bromley Mountain** ski area (tel: 802-824 5522) has a 1,334-ft (407-meter) vertical; in summer you can sled down the Alpine slide.

South of Manchester on Route 7A, **Arlington** ㊳ is a former Revolutionary capital and one-time home to five *Saturday Evening Post* artists. The **Norman Rockwell Exhibition** (Route 7A; open daily, except closed January) displays a large number of *Post* covers and lesser-known prints, in which local uncles and grandmas figure largely; some former subjects actually serve as museum guides.

BELOW: a fall gathering at Peacham.

Map
on pages
246–7

Bennington Monument,
erected in 1887–91.

BELOW LEFT:
mountain biking,
Putney.
BELOW LEFT: pre-
Revolutionary
gravestone, Old
First Church.

Local author Dorothy Canfield Fisher needs no introduction to Vermonters: in a series of down-home novels and her glorious *Vermont Tradition: The Biography of an Outlook on Life*, Fisher celebrated the spirit of fairness and community that imbues the state. The Martha Canfield Library, named after Dorothy's grandmother, holds a rich store of the author's memorabilia.

The 1777 skirmish commemorated at **Bennington** ㊴ by the Battle Monument (open mid-Apr–Oct, daily; entrance fee) actually took place a few miles west, where General John Stark and 1,800 ragtag troops forced the Redcoats back across the Walloomsac River in Hoosick Falls. However, it was a colonial supply dump on this site that General John Burgoyne was after, and his failure to attain it proved a turning point in the entire British campaign.

For an interesting trove of local artifacts, from Revolutionary War mementos to vintage toys, visit the **Bennington Museum and Grandma Moses Gallery** (Route 9; open May–Oct, daily; entrance fee). The self-taught painter's endearing primitives of rural life are exhibited in the schoolhouse she attended as a child in Eagle Bridge, New York.

Old Bennington sprawls east toward Bennington proper, home of Bennington College, among the country's most progressive – and expensive – schools. The older part of town, free of commerce but for the occasional inn, is like an immaculate open-air museum along Monument Avenue. Wander about the green and visit the Old First Church, with its unusual three-tiered steeple. Beside it, in the Old Burying Ground, lie the founders of Bennington, five Vermont governors, and Robert Frost, whose epitaph epitomizes the feisty loyalty endemic to true Vermonters, whether native-born or transplanted: "I had a lover's quarrel with the world." ❑

Ski Fever

Scandinavian immigrants introduced skiing in New Hampshire's logging camps in the 1870s. The Norwegian-speaking Nansen Ski Club was founded in Norway Village near Berlin about 1872; with six other clubs it founded the US Eastern Amateur Ski Association in 1922, and survives to this day.

Ski fever spread to the college circuit after Dartmouth's Outing Club was founded in 1909. Just five years later, Dartmouth college librarian Nathaniel Goodrich was the first to descend Vermont's highest peak, Mount Mansfield in Stowe. This was all without trails, of course, much less the "up-ski" devices – rope tows, J-bars, and ultimately aerial trams, gondolas, and high-speed quads – that came decades later. The sport was essentially confined to "touring" (comparable to today's cross-country), jumping off wooden chutes and the odd foray into the woods. In 1926 Appalachian Mountain Club hutmaster Joe Dodge was the first to hurtle down Mount Washington's Tuckerman Ravine.

By then, skiing was well on its way to popularity. In 1929, fresh from a Switzerland ski trip, Katharine Peckett opened the country's first organized ski school at her family's resort in Sugar Hill, New Hampshire. Soon, the Boston and Maine Railroad began running ski trains to New Hampshire. Then, in 1934, New England's first rope tow was constructed at Gilbert's Hill, in Woodstock, Vermont.

The sport was dormant during the gasrationing of the early 1940s, but area after area sprouted up in the late '40s and '50s, among them Vermont's Mount Snow (tel: 800-451 4211), Smuggler's Notch (tel: 802-644-8851), Stratton (tel: 802-297 2200), Sugarbush (tel: 802-583 2381) and Killington (tel: 800-621 6867). For current slope conditions, call for an around-the-clock snow report (tel: 802-229 0531).

It was at Killington, in the mid-'60s, that the Graduated Length Method was introduced, easing the way for the general public to approach this often intimidating sport: tyros could start on short skis, gradually increasing the length as their prowess improved.

RIGHT: there are resorts to suit all abilities.

Just to keep the challenge fresh, though, a Stratton bartender came up with an innovation in the mid '60s that has changed the landscape of skiing. Jake Carpenter started experimenting with "snurfing" (as the underground sport of snowboarding was then called) secretly at night. It would take years, but his Burton snowboard company would become a leader in the field and, in the process, create a "rad" new skiing subculture. Stratton is still the most partial to snowboarders.

Today, Maine's big downhill resorts are Sugarloaf/USA (tel: 207-237 2000) in the Carrabassett Valley and Sunday River (tel: 207-824 3000) in Bethel. Sugarloaf has 43 miles (69 km) of trails and a vertical drop of 2,820 ft (860 meters); Sunday River has 121 trails. Snowmaking is excellent at both. There are almost 20 mountains developed for skiing in New Hampshire, but the two biggies are Loon Mountain, Lincoln (tel: 603-745 8111) and Waterville Valley (tel: 603-236-8311). "Skiophiles" will want to check out the New England Ski Museum, Franconia, NH (tel: 603-823 7177), for a full regional history. ❑

NEW HAMPSHIRE

This solidly conservative state serves outdoor pleasures on a platter – by way of the dramatic and rugged White Mountains and dozens of deep lakes

Map
on pages
246–7

lthough New Hampshire's primary appeal is its quiet country life and serene beauty, there are a number of special spots that warrant hitting the road. There are particularly elegant flourishes of nature, such as the Old Man of the Mountain, the Flume, the notches, and Mount Washington; there are examples of human ingenuity and history, like the Cog Railway, Canterbury Shaker Village, and Mystery Hill. More than half of the covered bridges in New England are in New Hampshire, including the nation's longest – the 460-ft (140-meter) span crossing the Connecticut River from Cornish.

Isolated until relatively recently, with few links to international industry, New Hampshire was slow to receive and absorb developments originating elsewhere. This cultural sluggishness has now paid off: while so much of the country has progressed into a wasteland of "miracle miles" and economic frenzy, many parts of New Hampshire have retained a calm, dignified pace and quality.

Here, there are still long, slow days to sit idle on a shaded porch or by the fire; evenings with the stars clear overhead and the startling silence of the countryside; old farms with pastureland arching down to a barn with a pond beside it; small towns where everybody is on a first-name basis with everybody else; and forests where the only signs of the modern age are the visitors themselves.

PRECEDING PAGES: Franconia Notch, in the White Mountains. **LEFT:** antique tractor rally **BELOW:** snowgiant in Hanover.

New Hampshire's town fairs feature ox-pulls and taffy-pulls, exhibits of handmade quilts, the rapid-fire patter of auctioneers hawking antiques, beans baked in a pit in the ground, homespun games involving baseballs and milk bottles and a prize for the best pig.

Once every four years, New Hampshire trundles out of general obscurity to perform one of the classic song-and-dance acts of American politics. The New Hampshire presidential primary is the first in the nation, the supposed diviner of political fortunes and, for many, a make-or-break event.

Though typically disdainful of such ephemeral trivia as fame and public attention, the people of New Hampshire jealously guard their self-appointed right to keep the nation's elections reasonably honest. Vermont (New Hampshire's perennial competitor for glories about which no one else much cares) once hinted it might steal the primary limelight by sneaking its elections in before New Hampshire's. Retaliation was swift and decisive: New Hampshire passed a law stipulating that its primaries be held on "the Tuesday preceding the date on which any other New England state shall hold a similar election." So there.

Crafty Massachusetts made its move in 1975, waiting until only a few months before the 1976 primaries began, to announce that it would vote on the same day as New Hampshire, the second Tuesday of March. New Hampshire promptly pushed its date up to the last Tuesday in February, even though this resulted in the inconvenience of voting in the primaries one week and then getting back together for Town Meeting Day the next (the two events had formerly been something of a political double-header). Though it's highly unlikely that many New Hampshirites lie awake nights worrying over the fact that the rest of the nation is reminded of their existence only once every four years, the Presidential primary is their moment center stage and they intend to keep it.

Politics in New Hampshire is definitely a participatory (and contact) sport. New Hampshire's state legislature, the General Court, is the third-largest governing body in the English-speaking world. The United Kingdom's House of Commons has 630 members; legislators in both houses of the US Congress total 485; New Hampshire manages to get by with 24 senators and 400 representatives (roughly, one for every 3,000 residents).

Much of the state's business, however, is conducted by that venerable, fundamentally American institution, the Town Meeting. Each Town Meeting Day, every eligible voter with an opinion on any part of that year's agenda has the opportunity to speak his or her piece and cast a vote. This is politics in the revolutionary vein that first shaped the nation. Without the camouflage of cloak-room deals, press-conference equivocation or media hype, the Town Meeting is pure, simple democracy, out in the open and accessible to immediate response, whether praise or scorn. The signatures of only 10 voters are needed to place an issue on the agenda. It's not a very efficient system, but it is difficult to corrupt.

It's no surprise, then, that New Hampshire is something of an acid test for Presidential hopefuls. Most of the voters are amateur politicians themselves, and they are not easily fooled. They're also pretty accurate in anticipating the

BELOW:
an old-fashioned
toboggan ride.

nation's mood. Since its first primary in 1952, New Hampshire has picked the candidates nominated by both parties nine out of 10 times. In the great majority of the contested elections in the nation's history (George Washington ran unopposed), New Hampshire has voted for the winner.

All this hands-on governmental process both reflects and, no doubt, fosters the feistiness that is deeply ingrained in the state's collective temperament. New Hampshire has yet to institute a general sales tax or state income tax. Instead, it rather deviously allows outsiders to make sizable donations by deriving over half of its general-fund revenue from tax-free liquor sales, state-run gambling and other "sin taxes." New Hampshire's constitution retains (in its Bill of Rights) the right of revolution when "all other means of redress are ineffectual."

This is not to suggest that New Hampshire is a haven for rampant radicals. In fact, the state is decidedly right-of-center on most issues, yet fervently independent. Though predominantly Republican, New Hampshire has voted for Democratic presidential candidates about one-third of the time in recent decades. The Republican predominance is kept in check by a nearly equal (if not entirely opposite) force of registered Independents. Public opinion falls mostly between the two poles represented, on the one hand, by the arch-conservative viewpoint of the *Manchester Union-Leader*, which is distributed statewide and, on the other, by the more liberal *Concord Monitor*, which is not.

Yankee ingenuity

The rugged individualism which typifies the people of New Hampshire is intricately bound up in both their land and their history. The first settlers came not to escape religious or political pressures, as was the case in many of the other

Map on pages 246–7

BELOW: riding low.

"Our liberty is protected by four boxes: the ballot box, the jury box, the soap box and the cartridge box."

BELOW: shopping the old way.

original colonies, but simply to have a little space in which to apply their Yankee ingenuity productively. They encountered and eventually subdued a land that was obstinate and rugged – with thin, "cold" soil, fresh crops of rock pushing through the surface each year, a forested wilderness that had to be cleared before settlements and farming were possible, and long, hard winters. The Indians, if initially welcoming, soon learned that the arrival of these foreigners was no blessing and began to retaliate.

The main assets of the region at the beginning of the colonial period were the deepwater port and surrounding shores of what is now Portsmouth; and the tall, straight pines, which became highly prized in the construction of ships. Fisheries established along the coast prospered from the sale of salt cod and other catches, hauled from the Atlantic as far north as the Grand Banks off Newfoundland.

The impetus behind these first forays was provided by Sir Ferdinando Gorges, head of the council established by King James to govern all of New England, and Captain John Mason, an early governor of Newfoundland. They obtained grants to an ill-defined territory lining the coast from the Naumkeag to the Sagadahock rivers and extending roughly 60 miles (100 km) inland. Gorges and Mason proposed a variety of commercial enterprises and promised healthy dividends to investors. The venture never really paid off. Lack of supplies limited the scheme's progress, the company eventually collapsed and the settlers simply divided the land up among themselves and proceeded to amass their own fortunes, without giving much thought to the niceties of property laws.

At first, relations with the Indians, primarily Abenakis and Pennacooks, were harmonious and mutually rewarding. In exchange for coats, shirts, kettles, and other goods, and in anticipation of assistance in repelling assaults by other tribes

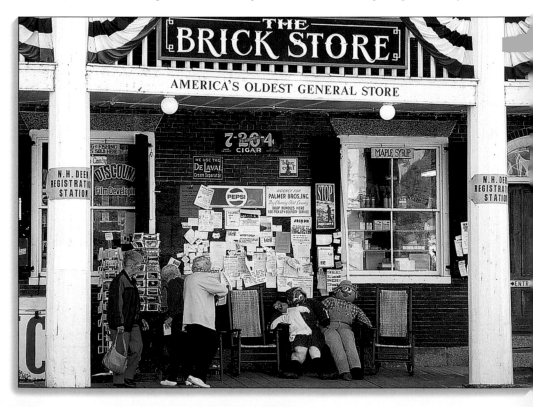

and of a market for their furs, the Indians granted the settlers access to the land between the Piscataqua and Merrimack rivers, including the rich fishing bases of the Isles of Shoals. In principle, the Indians were to retain the right to hunt, fish, and farm in the area.

The original deal was reasonably fair to both parties. Soon, however, the settlers became more ambitious. They built dams that obstructed the migration of salmon along the rivers, introduced livestock that wandered into and consumed the Indians' crops, conducted lumbering operations that frightened off game, and clogged the waterways with sawdust from mills. Realizing they had been taken, the tribes of New England banded together in 1675 and unleashed "King Philip's War," named for Philip, chief of the Wampanoags. For one year, they raided settlements and garrisons, and the turmoil continued, on a lesser scale, for nearly a century.

Throughout this period, New Hampshire's commercial reputation and prosperity rested primarily on its supplies of mast pines. They were invaluable to the expanding fleets of England's merchant marine. The best of them were reserved solely for the use of the King, providing in due course one of many motives leading to the Revolution.

Settlement and Revolution

Strong-willed settlers, gradually pushing their way inland from Portsmouth and up the Connecticut River from the south, laid claim first to the lush valleys, then to the harsher hillsides and finally to the forbidding mountains in the north. The first man to lend the colony some cohesion was John Wentworth, a prosperous merchant appointed by the King in 1717 to govern the province of New

Map on pages 246–7

Soaring 150–200 ft (46–61 meters), and as much as 6 ft (2 meters) in diameter, the massive shafts of wood used for masts – up to 1,000 years old – required as many as 100 oxen to haul them from the forest.

BELOW: logging.

Hampshire. Though hardly an altruist (his land grants always reserved a portion for himself, a token 500 acres/250 hectares), he did begin the process – later carried on by his son and nephew – of stabilizing the province, encouraging settlement and promoting commerce. Largely through their enthusiasm for gracious living, the Wentworths helped transform Portsmouth into a genteel oasis, traces of which are still evident.

For most of the settlers, however, life was anything but genteel. When not warring with the Indians, they cleared land, produced crops without much help from either climate or terrain and, by sheer obstinance, endured. Matters were not improved by the unresponsiveness of their government, and when the Revolution came, New Hampshire joined early in the fight, moved not so much by political fervor as by a general acknowledgment that change could hardly be for the worse. Savvy in the ways of guerrilla warfare after a century of skirmishes with the Indians, New Hampshire's militia was particularly skilled at battle tactics, which the orderly British were ill-equipped to combat.

Despite its active involvement in all the major campaigns of the war, New Hampshire, alone of the 13 original colonies, was spared the task of fighting the British within its own boundaries.

Among its Revolutionary credits, New Hampshire was the first colony to assert its independence from England (establishing its own government on January 5, 1776) and the first to suggest the idea to the Continental Congress in Philadelphia (in 1775). Late in 1774, alarmed by an edict from the King forbidding the shipment of gunpowder to the colonies, and informed that a British ship was on the way to fortify Fort William and Mary near Portsmouth, 400 New Hampshire rebels invaded the garrison, locked up the British guard and stole 100 barrels of gunpowder, later used at Bunker Hill.

BELOW: many rural farms remain in the southern part of the state.

Following the Revolution, the people of New Hampshire went back to the task of coming to terms with their land. The push inland was by now extending up into the White Mountains, already rich with Native American myth and soon to generate new legends of the courageous settlers. Revolutionary fervor gave way to the more tiresome task of transferring high ideals to workable practice. Given the combination of a terrain ill-suited to plantation farming and an innate resistance to the idea of constraint, New Hampshire resolved the issue of slavery for itself by effectively abolishing it early in the 19th century. An unfortunate pragmatism, however, kept the only New Hampshire-born US president, Franklin Pierce, from advocating Abolition throughout the country. He argued that slavery was morally wrong, but that the issue should be decided by the states practicing it.

By the middle of that century, it was becoming evident that New Hampshire's weak soil and short summers could not support competitive agriculture. Farmland was abandoned as people moved West in hopes of greater success. Textile mills were established and logging operations continued, but the most notable shift in New Hampshire's economy resulted from the discovery that it possessed one asset that promised a good return for relatively little investment or labor: scenery.

The summer people

By the 1850s, "summer people" were a well-established industry. Executives on holiday, retired librarians with a nest-egg set aside, and an assortment of temporary bohemians came to sit on farmhouse porches in rocking chairs, dine in the lavish resort hotels newly built in splendid surroundings, or hike the expanding network of trails through the hills and mountains. Others, professedly more serious in intent, came to paint, sculpt, or write. Among them were essayist Ralph Waldo Emerson, novelists Nathaniel Hawthorne and Willa Cather, sculptor Augustus Saint-Gaudens, and playwright Thornton Wilder.

Over the decades, the ranks of summer people have steadily swelled and spilled over into other seasons as well. Autumn draws connoisseurs of vibrant foliage which reaches its peak in early October to the north, then proceeds south. And New Hampshire's heavy snowfalls provide for superb skiing. The state boasts over a dozen ski areas; Cannon, Loon, Wildcat and Waterville Valley are among the largest, each with a vertical rise in excess of 2,000 ft (600 meters). Wildcat boasts cozy gondolas-for-two, and Cannon a roomy aerial tram; both run through the summer for sightseers.

New Hampshire's river, streams and lakes are kept well stocked with game fish: brook trout, smallmouth and largemouth bass, salmon, pickerel, perch, whitefish and shad, among others. Hunters – and, more often these days, photographers – track deer, hare and rabbit, porcupines, raccoons, gray squirrel, ruffed grouse, pheasant, and migratory birds. The lucky few might spot a lynx or wildcat.

In addition to the White Mountain National Forest (of which nearly 700,000 acres/283,000 hectares are situated in New Hampshire, roughly 40,000

Map on pages 246–7

BELOW: covered bridges are found in most New England states.

COVERED BRIDGES

It is surmised that the covered bridges across waterways and railroads throughout New England were designed not to protect travelers from the region's brutal winters, but to insulate the bridges' wooden supports. Other theories hypothesize that horses were more comfortable crossing covered spans than open ones where they could see the water. Although the bridges were covered, people were employed to shovel snow on to the surface since most winter travel was by sled.

Covered bridges were originally made of wood, with sides supported by triangular trestles; hardwood "tree nails" held it together. Today's renovated bridges often have metal roofs. The nation's longest covered bridge connects Cornish, NH., and Windsor, VT., and is a National Historic Civil Engineering Landmark. New Hampshire's oldest bridge, built 1829, connects Bath and Haverhill on Route 135 over the Ammonoosuc River.

New Hampshire's bridges have been more fortunate than Maine's in that 54 have survived fire, floods, ice, and modern traffic. (In Maine, only nine of 120 remain.) Most have been patiently repaired. Although many are open to traffic, most cannot take trucks and are only one-lane. For the official state highway map, tel: 1-(800) 386 4664.

TIP

Portmouth's finest historic houses are linked by a popular 2½-mile (4-km) walking tour. A "Portsmouth Passport" gives reduced admission if you are visiting more than one.

acres/16,000 hectares in Maine), there are 32 state parks in New Hampshire, with some 1,000 campgrounds in the 11 largest. Depending on location, these parks offer swimming, boating, fishing, cross-country and downhill skiing, snowmobiling, hiking, camping, and picnic facilities.

Local enterprise has also resulted in an impressive crop of roadside attractions – compact amusement parks, miniature golf courses, water slides and just about anything else that might possibly be termed "entertainment." Although not always in the best taste, and rarely sophisticated, they do at least ensure that no one can complain of a lack of activities, and most are fun.

A sliver of seacoast: Portsmouth

Portsmouth ➍ – the state's major seaport, is the jewel at the northernmost edge of its narrow and otherwise predominantly drably developed 18-mile (28-km) coast. Standing at the mouth of the Piscataqua River, a superb natural harbour, the town is the nation's third oldest settlement (after Plymouth and Jamestown). The **Strawbery Banke Museum** (the English settlers named their 1623 colony for the profusion of wild strawberries that greeted them) is an ongoing restoration project that recaptures the look and feel, and some of the activities, of this old seaport neighborhood, encompassing over 40 buildings and covering 10 acres (4 hectares) (Marcy Street; open May–Oct and weekend after Thanksgiving daily; first two weekends in December 3:30–8:30pm; entrance fee; tel: 603-433 1100). A handful of restored and refurnished homes, ranging from humble to grand, illustrate changes in architectural style; the Drisco House has even retained 1950s features. Some feature displays of construction and restoration techniques; others await restoration.

BELOW: tugboats in Portsmouth harbor.

Several of the lesser abodes serve as workshops for artisans whose work harks back to the past: open on a revolving schedule, there are studios for a cabinet-maker, cooper, potter, and weaver. Here, also, one of the oldest boat shops in America continues to produce dories, skiffs, and other vessels, employing archaic copper clench nails. Strawbery Banke is literally an open-air museum: tours are self-guided and open-ended, permitting visitors to proceed at their own pace.

Several other worthy historic manses are scattered about this enchanting, compact town. Among these is the 1763 **Moffatt-Ladd House** (Market Street; mid-May–mid-Oct, Mon–Sat; Sun pm; entrance fee), an imposing three-story mansion topped with a captain's walk and graced with terraced English-style gardens, a splendid carved staircase, a Gilbert Stuart portrait and some choice examples of Portsmouth-made furniture – a flourishing craft in the 18th century. Seek out, too, the 1716 **Warner House** (Daniel Street; open mid-May–mid-Oct, Mon–Sat; Sun pm; entrance fee). America's first house to be registered as a National Historic Landmark back in 1962, it was the first of Portsmouth's many brick houses, and the stair hall is endowed with an intriguing array of early 18th-century murals. Rediscovered in 1852, they include depictions of Mohawk Indians and a British soldier on horseback.

Also well worth a visit is the Port of Portsmouth **Maritime Museum and Albacore Park** (Market Street; open daily; entrance fee). The *Albacore* is a grounded 1952 submarine, 205 feet (62 meters) long, which for two decades carried a crew of 55 in sardine-like quarters.

For a more pleasant experience on the water, consider a cruise to the **Isles of Shoals ㊶** 6 miles (9.5 km) offshore; "barren piles of rock" charted in 1614 by

Map on pages 246–7

Backroad scene.

BELOW: Strawbery Banke, Portsmouth.

Captain John Smith and long haunted by pirates and other nefarious outcasts. Improbably enough, an arts colony blossomed here at the turn of the century, after poet Celia Thaxter, the daughter of an innkeeper, created a miraculous garden on Appledore which inspired no fewer than 400 paintings by the noted American Impressionist Childe Hassam. Whale-watching trips are also on offer from Portsmouth.

The best of the rest of the coast comprises Great (or New Castle) Island, with its old forts and lighthouses, and **Odiorne Point State Park**, where a World War II fort stands amid extensive dunes.

The industrious Merrimack Valley

Driving north from Boston, the first site worth a detour off Interstate 93 (after it crosses the border into New Hampshire) may also be the oldest. **America's Stonehenge** in **North Salem** ❷ (Haverhill Road; open Mar–Nov, daily; July and Aug, till 7pm; call for Dec–Feb hours; entrance fee; tel: 603-893 8300), long known as "Mystery Hill," has purportedly been carbon-dated to about 2000 BC. Though considerably scaled down from its British namesake – its circle of standing stones measure only 3 ft (1 meter) tall – the site is thought to have served much the same purpose as Stonehenge: as a giant calendar tracing celestial movements.

Within the circle are a series of stone buildings and passageways, altars, walls, chambers, and carvings, which have been attributed, variously, to ancient Greeks, Phoenicians, Celts, and Native Americans, or more recent settlers of a mystical or perhaps mischievous bent – take your pick. The identity of the builders and the purpose the site served remain matters of pure speculation. Indeed, much of its charm derives from the fact that questions outnumber answers: your guess is as good as anyone's.

Further north on I-93 is **Manchester** ❸, which together with Nashua and several other New Hampshire cities, served as centers of textile manufacturing, attracting large numbers of French-Canadian immigrants to work in the mills. Manchester retains the vast red-brick buildings of Amoskeag Mills and much of its French-Canadian legacy, including a large bilingual population and the nation's most comprehensive archives of material on French-speaking Canadians, L'Association Canado-Américaine, founded by a Manchester grocer in 1918. For a précis of local history, visit the Manchester Historical Association, three floors of old-fashioned exhibits spanning Indian relics to a Victorian parlor.

The **Currier Gallery of Art** (201 Myrtle Way; open Mon, Wed–Sun; Fri till 9pm; entrance fee; tel: 603-669 6144) features fine collections of European and American paintings, New England decorative arts, and contemporary crafts; it also offers modern architecture buffs access to the **Zimmerman House**, a 1950 design by Frank Lloyd Wright.

Some 15 miles (24 km) north of Manchester is **Concord** ❹, where the gold-domed 1819 **State House** (the granite centerpiece was built by prisoners) is fronted by statues of New Hampshire's political

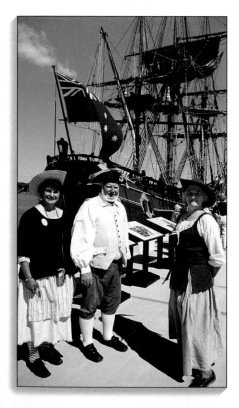

BELOW: a replica of the *Endeavour*, in Portsmouth, with an interpreter in period costume.

Map on pages 246–7

luminaries – Daniel Webster, Franklin Pierce, General John Stark and others – striking imperial poses in bronze. Its Hall of Flags contains 88 Civil War standards carried into battle (North Main Street; open Mon–Fri).

Its entrance topped by a Daniel Chester French sculpture, the grand **Museum of New Hampshire History** houses the collections of the New Hampshire Historical Society, from furniture and folk art to tools and toys (Eagle Square off Main Street; open Tues–Sat; Tues till 8:30pm). Among the highlights is an original Concord Coach, the 19th-century vehicle known as "the coach that won the West." Also worth a visit is the **League of New Hampshire Craftsmen** gallery in North Main Street (New Hampshire was the first state officially to support its artisans, with the establishment of the New Hampshire Commission of Arts and Crafts in 1931), and the **Christa McAuliffe Planetarium**, dedicated to the New Hampshire teacher/astronaut who perished in 1986 in an explosion aboard the US's first civilian space shuttle (3 Institute Drive, New Hampshire Technical Institute; open Tues–Thurs; pm only Sat and Sun; entrance fee). A fitting tribute to her dream, this highly interactive museum claims to be the most advanced digital planetarium projection system in the world, capable of simulating space travel in three dimensions.

Located in its namesake town, about 17 miles (27 km) north of Concord, **Canterbury Shaker Village** ㊺ (Shaker Road off I–93; open May–Oct, daily; Apr, Nov, Dec, Fri–Sun; entrance fee; tel: 603-783 9511) is an eloquent testament to the ingenuity and gentle faith of the Shakers, one of the religious sects that sought asylum in the New World (*see pages 296–97*). The Shakers believed all should be made welcome, a commitment that continues today as docents, rather than family members, greet each visitor.

BELOW: Canterbury Shaker Village.

The 1½-hour tours of the Village provide a glimpse of the skill and faith of this remarkable community. Crafts on display (some reproductions of which are available for purchase) include basketry, tin-smithing, wood-working and "the sewing arts." In addition, there is the simple grandeur of Shaker architecture, a host of intriguing inventions and a restaurant offering Shaker specialties.

The Mount Monadnock region

More than one local booster is not keen on the marketing monicker "The Quiet Corner", often used for the southwestern corner of the state ("Might as well come right out and call it boring," grouses one). Crowned by **Mount Monadnock** ⓰, a rocky 3,165-ft (968-meter) peak whose 360° views attract record numbers of climbers (the ascent is surpassed in popularity only by Mount Fuji), this is a region of meandering back roads past prim white churches, innumerable antique stores, and historic inns.

In the former mill town of **New Ipswich** ⓱, **Forest Hall (the Barrett House)** of 1800 (Main Street; tours June–mid-Oct, weekends; entrance fee), maintained by the Society for the Preservation of New England Antiquities, is an elegant Federal-style building, erected as a wedding present for Charles Barrett and his bride by his father, and contains many original items, including portraits and musical instruments. It will be instantly familiar to some as the setting of the Merchant-Ivory film adaptation of Henry James's *The Europeans*. The terraced grounds rise to a Gothic Revival summerhouse.

The small town of Rindge hosts the 2,000-seat **Cathedral of the Pines** ⓳, an open-air war memorial chapel with a set of Norman Rockwell bas-reliefs. It began when the Sloane family planned a small chapel to their son, a bomber pilot who was killed in action in Germany in 1944, and later became an interdenominational place of worship and a national memorial. Every President since Truman sent a stone to built the altar, which is backed by a view of Mount Monadnock.

Peterborough, home to the McDowell Colony, the country's most prestigious artists' retreat, inspired Thornton Wilder's famous play, *Our Town*. The **Peterborough Historical Society and Museum** contains intriguing relics and photographs, as well as two mill houses and an early general store (Grove Street; open pm only weekdays; entrance fee).

Bucolic **Harrisville** ⓴ has perfectly preserved its 19th-century mill-town mien; a self-guided tour of its beautifully proportioned brick buildings (one is now a renowned weaving center) is a lovely way to travel back in time. The region's largest town is **Keene** ⓾, where manufacturing companies flourished at the turn of the 19th century. It is said to have the widest street in America.

Along the Connecticut River valley

In **Charlestown** ⓿, about 22 miles (35 km) northwest of Keene, the **Fort at Number 4** recreates a 1746 settlement which, in its day, was the northernmost frontier of colonization (Route 11 West; open late May–mid-Oct, Wed–Mon; weekends only first two weeks of Sept; entrance fee). Within its stockade,

BELOW:
on the summit of
Mount Monadnock.

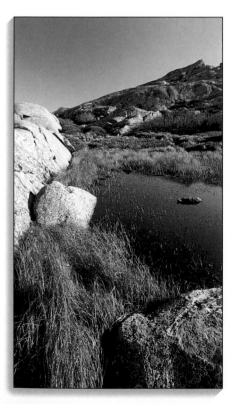

interpreters demonstrate such crafts as candle-dipping, weaving and the molding of musket balls and, at certain dates, re-enact skirmishes.

Some 10 miles (16 km) farther north, in Cornish, is the **Saint-Gaudens National Historic Site** ❷ – the summer residence, garden and studios of Augustus Saint-Gaudens, one of America's most celebrated classical sculptors (off Route 12A; open May–Oct, daily; entrance fee; tel: 603-675 2175).

Another 15 miles (24 km) north is **Hanover** ❸, home of Dartmouth College. One of the bastions of Ivy League tradition (*see page 217*), Dartmouth was founded in 1769, primarily for "the education and instruction of youth of the Indian tribes in this land." The college retains much of its colonial appearance while accommodating such modern touches as the **Hood Museum of Art**, with galleries spanning many cultures over the centuries, and the Hopkins Center, with an impressive performing arts roster (Wheelock Street; open Tues–Sat; Wed till 9pm; Sun pm). Hanover is very much a college town, and for that very reason full of interesting shops and restaurants.

Across the river in Norwich (Vermont), the wonderful **Montshire Museum of Science** – a hit with children – addresses the whys of natural processes to all ages (Montshire Road; open daily; entrance fee). For the extraordinary sight of a row of magnificent Charles Bulfinch mansions, it's worth pressing on to Orford.

The Lakes Region

At the center of the state, north of Concord, is New Hampshire's "Lakes Region," where **Lake Winnipesaukee** ❺ sprawls in convoluted splendor with 183 miles (294 km) of shoreline and 274 islands, the centerpiece of a cluster of

Map on pages 246–7

The schools of Dartmouth College include the under-graduate college, the medical school (1797), the Thayer School of Civil Engineering (1867), and the Amos Tuck School of Business Administration (1900).

BELOW: a Dartmouth College, Hanover.

Flights over Lake Winnipesaukee.

BELOW: the Baptist Meeting House Cemetery, Center Sandwich.

lakes and ponds scattered among rolling hills. According to legend, Winnipesaukee means "the smile of the Great Spirit," the name given to it by Chief Wonotan on the occasion of his daughter's marriage to a young chief from a hostile tribe. Wonotan regarded the overcast sky on their wedding day as a bad omen but, just as the two lovers were departing, the sun broke through the clouds and sparkled over the lake.

Weirs Beach 55 (named for the weirs, or fishnets, which Indians once stretched across a narrow channel there) brings a touch of Atlantic City to Winnipesaukee's western shore, with its boardwalk, arcade, marina, and elaborate miniature-golf links. Other attractions include two water-slide parks and cruises on the MS *Mount Washington*.

Wolfeboro 56, on the eastern side, can lay claim to being the oldest summer colony in the nation. In 1769, John Wentworth, the last of New Hampshire's colonial governors, built a summer home here, and comfortable old money has been following his example ever since; a stroll around reveals a wealth of architectural styles, including Georgian, Federal, Greek Revival, and Second Empire.

On South Main Street the **Wolfeboro Historical Society** maintains the 1778 **Clark House**, a 19th-century firehouse and an 1820 schoolhouse (open July–Aug Mon–Sat). In nearby Wakefield, two sisters who are inveterate doll collectors have opened an appealing **Museum of Childhood**, complete with an 1890s schoolroom (off Route 16; open May–Oct, Mon, Wed–Sat; Sun pm; entrance fee).

Looking down over the lake from the north, the **Castle in the Clouds 57**, near Moultonboro, stands as an imposing monument to one man's rather megalomaniacal vision of a tranquil idyll. Built in an inventive amalgam of styles by eccentric millionaire Thomas Gustave Plant, this 1910 mansion is set in a 5,200-acre (2,100-hectare) estate with waterfalls, ponds, streams, miles of forest trails, and magnificent views out over the surrounding countryside.

Moultonboro, and other towns north of the lake, offer a refreshing respite from the commercialism that has claimed the western shore. Particularly pretty is the predominantly early 19th-century village of **Center Sandwich 58**, with several appealing crafts and antique shops.

About 8 miles (13 km) southwest, a visit to the **Science Center of New Hampshire 59** is sure to intrigue: exhibits include a nature preserve for injured animals unable to survive in the wild (Routes 113 and 25; open May–Oct daily; entrance fee). Here's a rare opportunity to observe bears, owls, perhaps even a bobcat; there is a ¾-mile (1-km) trail with wheelchair access, and live animal demonstrations with a naturalist. Squam Lake, where *On Golden Pond* was filmed, is famed for its loons.

Lake Sunapee 60, finely set beneath the hills, has a small sandy beach by shallow water, and is popular for canoeing, windsurfing and picnicking. Mount Sunapee State Park includes the ski area, with a chairlift open year round taking you up to the summit, from where a short trail makes the most of the views across to Mount Washington and other points some 75 miles

(135 km) distance. The League of New Hampshire Craftsmen holds its August fair at the base of the lift.

Map on pages 246–7

The White Mountains

Continuing north, travelers now begin their ascent into the **White Mountain National Forest**, a vast tract encompassing the Franconia Range, clustered along an east-to-west axis, and the Presidentials, running northeast and culminating in New England's tallest peak, Mount Washington. Long a forbidding wilderness, the White Mountains have evolved into an enormously popular region, with an ambience as distinct as the landscape.

Here, hikers can enjoy the serenity of seemingly endless stretches of untrammeled (though no longer quite so forbidding) nature. The region also supports a thriving tourist industry, contained – by law and convenience – in pockets along the major highways. All the rest is reserved (and preserved) for backwoods purists.

A typical trail will lead from a parking lot along the highway directly into the forest, over gradually inclining terrain, maybe taking in a viewpoint or waterfall. Trails are well marked, with color-coded blazes cut into tree trunks at regular intervals, so there's little risk of taking a wrong turn. Eventually, towering trees give way to twisted dwarf pines and lichen-encrusted boulders. Above the tree line are the summits, from which adventurers may gaze down over the world spread at their feet, savoring that peculiar sense of accomplishment that comes from finding oneself on top of the world.

Most of these peaks are not, for all their massive beauty, too demanding. Many summits can be reached with an hour or so of fairly leisurely walking.

Boat tours can be taken on Squam Lake, the setting for the movie On Golden Pond.

BELOW: tranquil scene in the White Mountains.

One of the most rewarding excursions (in terms of view obtained relative to energy expended) is the short (45-minute) romp up Mount Willard, along an old bridle path. Those reaching the summit are rewarded with a magnificent panorama of **Crawford Notch** – particularly splendid at sunrise.

There are too many trails – some 1,200 miles (1,900 km) all told – to attempt even a partial description here; the White Mountain National Forest offices (various locations in the area) and the Appalachian Mountain Club at Pinkham Notch can provide further information. The AMC also maintains a network of "huts" (some are fairly large) offering bunk lodgings and hearty meals; they're often booked up months in advance, so reserve well ahead (tel: 603-466 2727). The AMC's White Mountain Guide is the "walker's bible."

For enjoying the scenery from the car, however, the **Kancamagus Highway** ⓺ (Route 112), is hard to beat, and passes numerous trailheads offering anything from short strolls through the forest to major upland hikes. Seek out especially the signed overlooks at the western end (notably Kancamagus, Pemi and Hancock); views are at their best when the fall foliage reaches its most brilliant phase, but then you may find the traffic nose to bumper. Worthwhile short walks include the Champney Falls Trail and the Boulder Loop Trail, while pleasant roadside stopping picnic areas are at Rocky Gorge and Sabbaday Falls.

Continue through **North Woodstock** on Route 12 for the pay booth for **Lost River** ⓺, where a river disappears through a labyrinth of boulder caves and re-emerges. A slow-going trail leads through this remarkable place, discovered by two brothers out fishing when one of them fell into a cave.

Just off I-93 north of **Lincoln** and somewhat easier on the feet, **The**

BELOW: in the White Mountains.

Flume , an 800-ft (243-meter) gorge with granite walls attaining 90 ft (27 meters) and ending at a waterfall, was reportedly discovered in 1803 by 93-year-old Aunt Jess Guernsey, who happened upon it while out fishing. Unfortunately, it's no longer quite as she found it – viewing platforms have been added to accommodate the busloads of sightseers – but some hint of the awe this natural wonder must have inspired remains (open May–Oct, daily; entrance fee). Off the main path is the Pool, another fine waterfall. In winter the wooden walkways are dismantled as the ice forms a massive layer.

Northward, pull into the parking lot at Profile Lake for a glimpse of the **Old Man of the Mountains**. Noteworthy not so much for its size – it measures 40 ft (12 meters) from top to bottom – as for the fine detailing of its features, the Old Man has generated a sense of reverence over the years. The jutting brow, regal nose, lips slightly pursed as if in meditation and sharp line of the bearded chin all conspire to produce not merely a likeness, but a real sense of character. As Nathaniel Hawthorne described it in his story *The Great Stone Face*: "all the features were noble, and the expression was at once grand and sweet, as if it were the glow of a vast, warm heart, that embraced all mankind in its affection, and had room for more."

Though credit for its discovery has been ascribed, rather presumptuously, to a road-survey team in 1805, no doubt the region's Indians were acquainted with the Old Man long before then. According to some sources, they saw in it the features of Manitou, the Great Spirit, and reserved for their chiefs the right to view it – and, even for them, only in times of crisis. Legend has it that the face was not always as stern as it now appears, but became so through sorrow over the conflicts and cruelty of the human race.

Directly to the north is **Cannon Mountain** ski area (named for a cannon-shaped rock perched on its ridge; tel: 603-823 5563). An easy year-round means of ascent is offered by the **Aerial Tramway** (a 1980 replacement for the 1938 original) at its base (fee), rising above the timberline and offering a short trail at the summit. Also located here is the **New England Ski Museum**, with historical paraphernalia (such as hand-crafted wooden skis from the 19th century) and various audio-visual exhibits (open Dec–Apr, Thurs–Tues; May–Oct, daily pm only).

Two classic villages await the visitor just past Franconia Notch. **Franconia** was home to poet Robert Frost in 1915–20, where he "farmed a little, taught a little and wrote a lot." Looking out towards his favorite three New Hampshire mountains, the modest **Robert Frost Place** ("R. Frost" still marks the mailbox on Route 116) preserves manuscripts and other assorted memorabilia and hosts a changing roster of worthy successor poets who are amenable to giving readings (Ridge Road, May–Oct Wed–Mon pm; entrance fee).

The small town of **Sugar Hill**, once a magnet for summer manses, is a mecca for maple-lovers. **The Sugar Hill Historical Museum** (Route 117; open July–mid-Oct pm only Thurs, Sat, Sun; entrance fee) contains relics of 19th-century resort life, but most of those who flock here come to feast on

Map on pages 246–7

The Robert Frost mailbox.

BELOW: the Old Man of the Mountains.

unlimited "seconds" at **Polly's Pancake Parlor**, which produces its own maple syrup (Route 117).

A few miles north of Franconia, US 302 veers eastward, through another handsome town, **Bethlehem** ❻ (full of dazzling summer homes, some turned B&B), and southeast toward Bretton Woods, nestled on the western flank of magnificent Mount Washington.

An "awful" peak

Nathaniel Hawthorne (who played an important role in promoting and preserving the region) accurately pointed out that the White Mountains, and particularly the Presidential Range, are "majestic, and even awful, when contemplated in a proper mood, yet their breadth of base and the long ridges which support them, give the idea of immense bulk rather than of towering height." **Mount Washington** ❻, at 6,288 ft (1,197 meters), is high enough to qualify as the tallest summit north of the Carolinas and east of the Rockies, and its sheer bulk is impressive, at least from the bottom, but to really appreciate its height, one must tackle the peak.

There are three ways to "climb" Mount Washington: on foot, by car (from Gorham, on the eastern side), or by train. The first option is, of course, the preference of outdoors enthusiasts, but the ascent is not easy and, even in summer, can be extremely dangerous, even deadly. A spectacular and very popular approach is from Pinkham Notch, taking in Tuckerman's Ravine; be sure to ask at the Appalachian Mountain Club headquarters (tel: 603-466 2727) at Pinkham Notch about conditions before setting out. The summit bears several chilling markers commemorating those who, like 23-year-old Lizzie Bourne in

BELOW: Polly's Pancake Parlor.

Map
on pages
246–7

September 1855, died of exposure only a few hundred yards from the top. The destination she sought, a rustic hotel called the Tip Top House, survives as a small museum; visitors can marvel at the cramped dormitories, where travelers bunked down on crude beds cushioned with moss.

Climatically, the summit is classified as arctic. Its topographic isolation results in alarmingly abrupt changes in weather, including blizzards even in summer. The highest-velocity winds ever recorded – 231 miles (372 km) an hour – were measured here in 1934, and some of the buildings that are part of a weather observatory (founded in 1932) are tethered to keep them from blowing away.

Visitors have access to the Sherman Adams Summit Building, surrounded by a deck with 70-mile (112-km) views, and within it the small but fascinating **Mount Washington Observatory Museum**, which focuses on mountaineering history and on the summit's unusual ecology.

On the east side of Mount Washington it's possible to drive up – provided your car's in fighting trim. The 8-mile (13-km) climb up the **Mount Washington Auto Road**, via endless switchbacks, can be hell on radiators, the return journey tough on the best of brakes (off Route 16; open mid-May–mid-Oct, weather permitting; daily in summer 7:30am–6pm; shorter hours in spring and fall; entrance fee; tel: 603-466 2222). For those who'd rather spare their vehicles the ordeal (and forgo the campy "This Car Climbed Mount Washington" bumpersticker), there's also a van shuttle service from the base.

Alternatively you can reach the summit by the remarkable 1869 **Cog Railway** ⑲, a testament to American ingenuity in the pursuit of diversion (Route 302; June–Oct, daily; tel: 603-846 5404). The train serves no more noble purpose than that of carting tourists 3½ miles (5.5 km) up and down the

BELOW: Mount Washington Cog Railway.

The Fall

One of the most revered rituals of New England life is "leaf-peeping" – driving to see the green leaves of summer turn to vivid shades of orange, yellow and red each fall. Droves of dedicated leaf-peepers come by the car and busload from all over the US and the world (advance reservations at inns and even restaurants are essential during October). In the far northern parts of the region, the leaves usually start turning mid-September, farther south a little later; by the end of October, the show is pretty much over.

New Hampshire and Vermont are most often linked with great foliage, but all six states have favored routes for colorful fall vistas. The advantage the northern states have is their mountains: From certain routes through the Green or White Mountains (a misnomer in fall!), the views across valleys to neighboring peaks can be breathtaking.

Each New England state has a toll-free foliage hotline telephone number. There's

even a Maine "leaf lady" whose Web page contains frequently updated photos of the show (access the page through the state's website at www.visitmaine.com).

By trying too hard to pinpoint the absolute peak of foliage, however, you risk missing the majesty of the leaf-changing phenomenon: If you're lucky enough to be in New England in October, you're sure to see peak foliage somewhere, because each tree changes its color according to an inner timetable that's affected by moisture, temperature, and the shorter days of fall. Botanists call the color change "leaf senescence" – the process by which the green pigment chlorophyll is drawn back into the tree to nourish it, permitting other, brighter pigments in the leaves to shine through. Brightest of all are red swamp maples and sumac. Aspen and birch turn yellow, sugar maples a peachy orange.

While it can be fun to drive back roads in search of great fall color, interstates often have the best foliage. Designed to cut through swaths of forest bypassing populated areas, I-95, for example, offers some of Maine's best leaf-peeping in the 75-mile (120-km) stretch from Augusta to Bangor. Similarly, in Connecticut, I-95, from Danielson to Waterford, always puts on a fine leaf show.

Almost any highway route designated as "scenic" on a state map will yield bountiful leaf color. In Massachusetts, one of the best foliage drives is westward along the Mohawk Trail (Route 2, Greenfield to Williamstown) in the northwestern corner of the state. Turn north on Route 7 into Vermont, then east on Route 9 and south on I-91 for an exceptionally pretty loop tour.

New Hampshire's mountains and lakes make it particularly appealing. A 340-mile (550-km) mid-state tour that takes in a little bit of mountain and lake begins at the Massachusetts border on I-93. Take Exit 24 to reach Route 3 south to Route 113 east to Route 16 north. At the Kancamagus Highway (Route 112), go west through the White Mountains National Forest back to I-93.

Foliage hot-line numbers – New Hampshire: 1-800-258 3608; Vermont: 1-800-837 6668; Massachusetts: 1-800-227 6277; Maine: 1-888-624 6345. ❑

LEFT: tupelo leaves and white pine needles.

mountain, but it does so with an admirable inventiveness. The average grade is 25 percent, the steepest 37.4. Relying on a failsafe rack-and-pinion system, the railroad was devised by Sylvester March, a local inventor who hoped to capitalize on the tourist trade attracted to the mountain. He obtained a charter to build the railroad from skeptical Concord legislators (they offered him the right to extend it all the way to the moon) and completed it in three years. It was the first railroad of its kind and has since been emulated, though outdone only once by an even steeper version in the Swiss Alps.

Just beyond the access road to the Cog Railway stands one of the few remaining symbols of New Hampshire's heyday as the home of numerous luxury resorts. Its genteel grandeur still intact, the colossal **Mount Washington Hotel**, which opened in 1902, continues to welcome well-heeled visitors in a manner to which most people could all too easily become accustomed.

Circled by a 900-ft (274-meter) veranda set with white-wicker chairs, and topped with red-tiled turrets, this elongated white-stucco wedding-cake contains some 174 rooms (many marked with plaques commemorating famous former residents) and a voluminous lobby with 23-ft (7-meter) ceilings supported by nine sets of columns and illumined with crystal chandeliers. Without leaving the hotel grounds, guests can enjoy golf (on an 18-hole PGA course), swimming (indoor or out), tennis (12 clay courts), and horseback riding. Though the lovely formal dining room has yet to catch up with an admittedly trend-crazy age, diners can at least console themselves with the thought that, because of the room's intentionally octagonal design, they'll never be relegated to a corner table. And with a band playing throughout the dinner hour, they can work in some dancing as well.

Map on pages 246–7

In the glorious age of the grand hotel, resorts such as the Mount Washington Hotel and the Balsams (see page 295) often had private rail lines. Their wealthy guests would arrive for the season, complete with entourage of servants, in their own rail carriages.

BELOW: Mount Washington Hotel.

Cradle of tourism

From Bretton Woods, US 302 cuts south through **Crawford Notch** , a narrow pass named for two notable early entrepreneurs. The notch was "discovered" in 1771 (more or less accidentally) by Timothy Nash, who was tracking a moose at the time. When Nash informed Governor Wentworth of his discovery, the disbelieving governor offered to grant him a tract of land including the notch if Nash could bring a horse through it and present the animal, intact, at Portsmouth; he was even willing to provide the horse. Nash met the challenge – incidentally opening up the White Hills (as the mountains were then called) to a steady influx of settlers, and eventually tourists.

Among the first to anticipate and capitalize on the area's potential were Abel Crawford and his son, Ethan Allen Crawford. They blazed the first path to the summit of Mount Washington (in 1819), advertised both it and their services as tour guides and established inns to accommodate their clients and other travelers – thereby masterminding the White Mountains' debut as a tourist attraction. Both men were as rugged as the mountains. In his 80s, Abel is said to have hiked five mountainous miles each morning to his son's house for breakfast. He was 75 when he made the first ascent of Mount Washington on horseback. Known as the "Giant of the Hills" – he was nearly 7 feet (2.1 meters) tall – Ethan was fond of wrestling bears and lynx and could carry a live buck home on his shoulders.

Just up the road from Jackson is **Pinkham Notch** , home to the pristine Wildcat ski area, set amid national forest (the gondola welcomes sightseers), and opposite it, the Appalachian Mountain Club's **Pinkham Notch Visitor Center**, which offers lodgings, workshops, and trail information (tel: 603-466 2727).

BELOW:
winter scene.

Every spring, skilled skiers make the arduous pilgrimage to shoot the headwall at Tuckerman's Ravine, a natural snow bowl affording a precipitous descent; others climb up just to watch.

On Route 16 is the "cross-country capital" of **Jackson** , which communally maintains a 90-mile (150-km) network of trails. Its many delightful restaurants are just as appealing in summer, and **Jackson Falls**, a series of cascades trickling toward town past glacial "potholes," decidedly more so. Young children might enjoy a stopover at **Story Land** in **Glen** ❼❸, a small-scale amusement park guaranteed to delight the 10-and-under set (Route 16; open mid-June–Labor Day, daily; Labor Day–Columbus Day weekends; entrance fee).

Reached off West Side Road (itself a useful way of avoiding the jams in North Conway, leaving the Kancamagus Highway as Dugway Road, and joining Route 302 just east of Attitash Bear Peak), by a road climbing up west of North Conway, **Cathedral Ledge** ❼❹ is a vertigo-inducing rock-climbers' cliff high above Echo Lake (not to be confused with the other Echo Lake by Franconia Notch). **Attitash Bear Peak** ❼❺ has extensive snow-making in winter, but in summer you can mountain bike or take the Alpine slide (summer, daily; late May–mid-June, early Sept–early Oct, weekends; entrance fee).

The bustling town of **North Conway** ❼❻ is doing its best to steal some of the mountains' thunder – an odd amalgam of historic structures, rather tacky modern "resorts," and discount outlets. One reason to venture into town is to take a 1-hour, 11-mile (18-km) journey on the vintage **Conway Scenic Railway**, based at an 1874 Victorian railroad station in the center of town (Routes 16 and 302; open May–Oct, daily; Apr, Nov–Dec, weekends; entrance fee; tel: 603-356 5251 or 800 232 5251).

The North Country

This isolated, sparsely populated region is one of New Hampshire's better-kept secrets. The landscape is as stunning as any in the state, if less than inviting during the long months of winter. Vast stretches of forest cover most of the region and provide its primary industry – logging. A lacework of lakes, rivers, ponds, and streams offers a delicate counterpoint to the craggy hills and mountains. It is up here that the Connecticut River has its source, in a string of lakes just a few miles from the northern tip of the state, in a corner so out of the way that its allegiance was not decided, nor its boundary with Canada fixed (and then, by force), until 1840.

There is one grand old resort up here: **The Balsams** at **Dixville Notch** ❼❼, a sprawling 1866 establishment with some 233 rooms and recreational facilities (golf, tennis, skiing, trout-fishing, canoeing, riding) spread over an area the size of Manhattan Island; it even has its own small ski area. Not the least among its appeals are the groaning buffets set out three times a day.

From here northward to Canada, it's a world of forest, water, scattered hunting camps and occasional towns hugging quiet highways, a world well suited to an exploring spirit. Those prepared to explore an environment such as this one don't need a guide to tell them how to go about it. ❑

Map on pages 246–7

TIP

North Conway's outlet shops are especially attractive because New Hampshire has no sales tax. Be warned that this commercial strip is prone to bottlenecks.

BELOW: cutting strawberries in Franconia.

THE SHAKERS

These disciplined people were famous for their unique way of life, their manner of worship, and a craftsmanship that permanently influenced design

The Shakers aimed for perfection in life. Devoted to orderliness and simplicity, they were also dedicated to such progressive notions as sexual equality (facilities for men and women were identical and jobs were shared on a rota), and they welcomed technological advances that might improve the quality of their work. They were inventors (of, for instance, the circular saw and clothes pegs). They ran model farms and, as keen gardeners, were the first to packet and sell seeds; they also marketed medicinal herbs. They sold their meticulously crafted baskets, boxes, chairs and textiles. By blending discipline, business acumen, ingenuity and superb craftsmanship, they achieved prosperity, both spiritual and financial.

Celibacy was a key principle, but the ranks were swelled by converts, and orphans were adopted, Numbers dwindled after the mid-1800s, however, and today just a handful of "Believers" remain, in Sabbathday Lake, Maine. The Shaker ideals of simplicity and practicality live on, however, in a legacy of architecture, furniture and crafts. The villages at Canterbury, NH, and Hancock, Mass., are preserved as museums, where visitors watch craftsmen make baskets, boxes and chairs in the Shaker manner. In the Dwelling Houses (above, at Hancock) they can see the efficient kitchens, the wall pegs on which chairs and utensils were hung, and the built-in cupboards (so no dust could accumulate on top or underneath).

▷ **THE LADDERBACK**
These light but sturdy chairs were made for Believers by the thousand. The woven-tape seat was a Shaker innovation.

▽ **THE ROUND BARN**
Envied by many, the round barn at Hancock, Mass., was a large one, built not only for its efficiency, but as a status symbol.

▷ **THE SHAKER BOX**
Shakers did not make anything unless it served a purpose. Oval boxes of every size, with distinctive "swallowtail" joints, stored household goods.

THE VISION OF MOTHER ANN LEE

The founder of the Shakers was Ann Lee, born in 1736 in Manchester, England. An illiterate factory-worker, she was a woman of deep convictions at a time of religious persecution. She became the spritual leader of a group of dissidents from the Anglican Church called the "Shaking Quakers" because of the movements they made as the holy spirit took hold of them. Persecuted and sent to jail, she had a vision that she had a mission to teach a new way of life, one where men and women were equal, free from lust, greed and violence, with their lives governed by material and spiritual simplicity. She was convinced that only through celibacy could men and women further Christ's kingdom on Earth. After a second vision, she and eight followers set sail for New York in 1770. It was not until the 1780s, however, that converts were attracted in great numbers. Mother Ann died in 1783, soon after a prosetylizing tour of New England and before the full flowering of Shakerism. At its peak in the 1840s, 6,000 members lived in 19 communities.

△ SONG AND DANCE
The Shaker dance was an integral part of worship, instituted as an ordered alternative to the whirlings and tremblings of the early

Believers (above). Brothers and sisters danced in perfect unison to the sound of song. In time, thousands of songs were composed, many under divine inspiration.

▷ COMMUNAL DINING
The Hancock dining room: believers ate at fixed times, in silence, with men and women at separate tables.

MAINE

Map on page 302

Maine is a land of jagged coastlines and vast pine woods, of remote peninsulas, fresh lobster and famed outlet shops – a state inimitably evoked in the soft canvases of Winslow Homer

CANADA
Boston

Even by New England standards, Maine – beyond its heavily trafficked southern coast – remains a mysterious wilderness. Larger in area than the other five New England states combined, but less populous than any one of them, the "Pine Tree State" (nine-tenths of it are covered with forest) bears little resemblance to its comfortably settled neighbors. Winters here can be an endurance test: some joke that Maine has only two seasons, winter and July.

It's little wonder, then, that residents pride themselves on their rugged independence and turn a bemused eye on the strange habits of "summer people" – or "rusticators," as they're sometimes still called. The term dates back to the late 19th century, when the first brave tourists came to reconnoiter this uncharted territory.

Henry David Thoreau explored the Mount Katahdin region in 1846 and came back raving about its savage beauty. "What is most striking in the Maine wilderness is the continuousness of the forest," he mused in Katahdin. "It is even more grim and wild than you had anticipated, a damp and intricate wilderness." Despite the inroads of civilization, vast stretches still fit the description, offering nature-lovers of a Thoreauvian bent the opportunity truly to get away from it all.

For those who prefer to encounter nature on their own terms, with a certain modicum of creature comforts, old-fashioned "camps" are still scattered along remote lakes interspersed among rugged mountains. Long prized by skilled canoeists and kayakers, Maine's wild waterways have been harnessed for the sport of whitewater river rafting. The ocean waters may prove too chilly for all but the most stalwart of swimmers, but sailboats, including majestic restored windjammers, ply the crenulated coastline – only 400 miles (640 km) as the gull flies, but 3,500 miles (5,600 km) if all the coves, inlets, and peninsulas were magically ironed out.

Drowned valleys and Red Paint

Traditionally, the Maine coastline has been the focus of the state's commercial and cultural activity. Geologists refer to it as a "drowned" coastline: the original coast sank thousands of years ago, its valleys becoming Maine's harbors, its mountains the hundreds of islands that cling to the shoreline from the New Hampshire border to New Brunswick, Canada. While the coastline was sinking, receding glaciers exposed vast expanses of granite, which not only gave Maine's mountains their peculiar pink coloration, but provided settlers with a valuable source of building material.

The first known residents, 11,000 years ago, were paleolithic hunters and fishers who lived along the

PRECEDING PAGES: Portland Head Light.
LEFT AND BELOW: lobstering.

Maine

coast. Other tribes followed, including a race known as the Red Paint People because lumps of red ocher (powdered hematite), thought to have been part of a religious sacrament, have been found in their grave sites. The earliest European explorers, in the 15th and 16th centuries, were greeted by the Abenaki tribe, whose name means "easterners" or "dawnlanders."

John Cabot visited Maine in 1497–99 (his explorations established all future British claims to the land), but it wasn't until after Captain John Smith sounded "about 25 excellent harbors" in 1614 that the "Father of Maine," Sir Ferdinando Gorges, was granted a charter to establish British colonies. Rival French explorers also claimed parts of Maine and Canada, and territorial disputes eventually led to the French and Indian Wars of the 18th century. Maine became a part of the Commonwealth of Massachusetts and remained so until 1820, when it became, as residents still like to call it, the State of Maine.

The South Coast

The best way to see Maine is to start at the southern tip and head northeast along the old coastal highway, US 1. (I-95 is bigger and faster, for those who have a specific destination in mind, but utterly lacking in scenery.) Although, geographically, the coast represents only a tiny fraction of the state, 45 percent of Maine residents call it home, and the overwhelming majority of visitors to "Vacationland" (Maine's license plate slogan) are also headed for the shore.

The southernmost segment, extending from Kittery to Freeport, attracted the earliest settlers and to this day is the most heavily traveled, blending historic enclaves with built-up beaches and discount shopping malls. Just across the New Hampshire border from Portsmouth, is **Kittery ❶**, where **Portsmouth**

Map on page 302

Maine's coast has been much battered by the sea. On the map it extends only 228 miles (367 km) as the seagull flies, but it has been calculated than anyone walking the length of its indented shore would have to tramp nearly 3,500 miles (5,600 km).

BELOW: Long Sands Beach, York, on the South Coast.

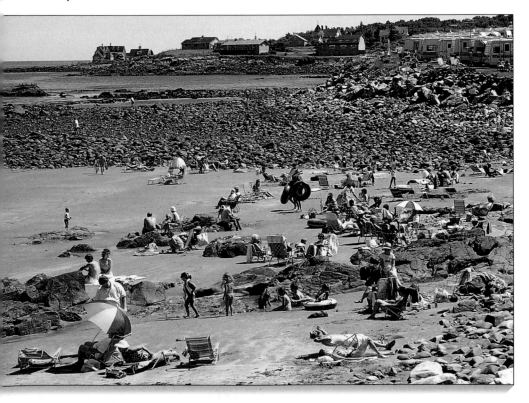

Navy Yard – the nation's first, founded in 1806 – is still active; the **Kittery Historical and Naval Museum** (Routes 1 and 26; open June–mid-Oct, Tues–Sat; entrance fee) documents the shipyard's history, from the construction of *Ranger* (the first ship ever to fly the Stars and Stripes, under the command of John Paul Jones) to a more recent focus on submarines. Nearby **Fort McClary** was first fortified in 1715 and rebuilt repeatedly right up until the 1898 Spanish-American War. All that remains is the 1844 hexagonal wooden blockhouse, and the granite seawall – a scenic vantage point from which to view racing yachts in Portsmouth Harbor.

York ❷ was a center of dissent during the Revolutionary era. The local chapter of the Sons of Liberty decided to hold their own tea party when a British ship carrying tea anchored in **York Harbor**. Being Mainers, however, they were much too practical to waste all that good tea by dumping it in the harbor – they hijacked it instead.

The Yorks epitomize that odd blend of historical preservation and beach-oriented tourism typical of the lower Maine coast. The **Old York Historical Society** (York Street; open mid-June–mid-Oct, Tues–Sat; Sun, pm; off–season by appointment; entrance fee) maintains seven historic buildings, including the **John Hancock Warehouse** (a contemporary wrote that the signer of the Declaration of Independence was "more successful in politics than in business"), the 1759 **Jefferds Tavern** and the **Old Gaol**, built in 1719, thought to be the oldest public building in the US. With its 2-ft (60-cm) thick fieldstone walls and tiny windows bordered with sawteeth, the jail served its purpose right up until 1860. It has now been restored to its 1790s appearance, complete with dungeon. The **Elizabeth Perkins House** is a prime example of Colonial revivalism,

BELOW: John Hancock Warehouse and wharf, York.

Map on page 302

an 18th-century farmhouse lovingly adapted by the Perkins, a family that was proud of its New England roots, in the early 20th century.

The other side of York, physically and philosophically, is **York Beach**, a narrow mile-long strip of fine sand, lined with every imaginable type of fast-seafood shack and family-entertainment facility. The Cliff Walk off York Harbor's boardwalk affords beautiful views of the coastline, and of Cape Neddick's 1879 **Nubble Light**.

To the north is Perkins Cove, a quaint fishing village that is now part of **Ogunquit** ❸ (whose Indian name meant "beautiful place by the sea"); its 3-mile (5-km) beach is a big draw. Boston painter Charles Woodbury "discovered" the area in the late 19th century, and the word soon spread to other artists, including Edward Hopper and Maurice Prendergast. Where the artists wandered, the gentry soon followed. Today, tourists crowd the countless small galleries and eateries that have taken over the fishing shacks. The **Ogunquit Museum of American Art** (Shore Road; open July–Sept, Mon–Sat; Sun, pm; entrance fee) displays locally produced work, including a sampling by such renowned summer residents as Reginald Marsh. **Marginal Way**, a 1-mile (1.6-km) seaside walk along the cliff is still quite scenic, in spite of its popularity.

Ogunquit itself is a bustling summer colony so thronged with visitors that a quartet of reproduction trolleys offer the easiest way to get around (parking is tight). On fine summer days, the magnet is the 2½-mile (4-km) beach. Night spots abound, and a perennial pleaser is the **Ogunquit Playhouse**, a highly regarded straw-hat theater founded in 1933; Tallulah Bankhead, Bette Davis, and Helen Hayes all trod these boards (Route 1; late June–Aug; tel: 207-646 5511).

Once the shipbuilding center of York County, the town of Kennebunkport

TIP

To escape the bustle of town, try a contemplative – and educational – walk amid the 3,100-acre (1,252-hectare) Rachel Carson Wildlife Refuge (off Route 9). The pioneering ecologist spent many summers exploring these fertile wetlands.

BELOW: Perkins Cove, Ogunquit.

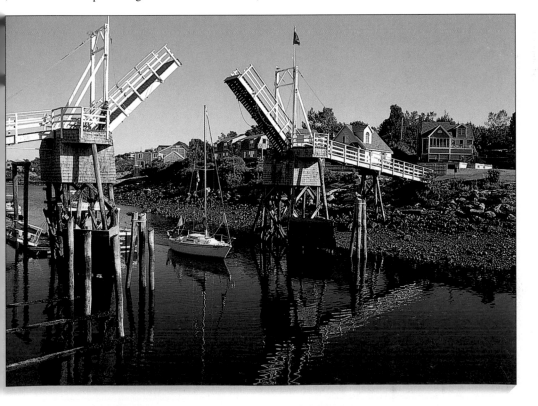

has long since turned its attention to tourism: the commercial center of **Kennebunkport ❹**, Dock Square, is practically impenetrable in summer, but worth pressing through for a visit to the **Kennebunkport Book Port**, specializing in Maine and maritime titles and housed in a 1775 brick warehouse that served, variously, as a boarding house, post office, harness shop, fish market, and artist's studio. The town's legacy shines on in its stately elms and handsome white houses. To get a closer look at these buildings (a few of which are open to the public), take the architectural walking tour conducted by the **Brick Store Museum**, an old general store now devoted to exhibits about local history (Main Street; open Tues–Sat; entrance fee).

Among the sights not to be missed is the unmistakable 1826 **Wedding Cake House** (Route 53), festooned with elaborate carved wooden scrollwork. Legend has it that a sea-bound captain who married in haste had it built to compensate his wife for the lack of a cake at their rushed ceremony. For intimations of a slower-paced age, visit the **Seashore Trolley Museum**, which showcases streetcars, vintage buses and public transit memorabilia, with rides along a 2-mile (3-km) track through the woods (Log Cabin Road off Route 1; tours late May–mid-Oct, daily; entrance fee).

Further up the coast is **Old Orchard Beach ❺**, a turn-of-the-century seaside resort popular among French Canadians. The 7-mile (11-km) beach is flanked with motels and condos and, at the Ocean Pier, an amusement park and waterslide complex. Eastward, just south of Portland on **Cape Elizabeth ❻**, is the oldest lighthouse on the eastern seaboard, the Portland Head Light, commissioned by President George Washington in 1791. The **Museum at Portland Head Light** (Shore Road, Fort Williams Park; open June–Oct, daily; Nov, Dec, April, May, weekends; entrance fee) documents the history of lighthouses from early Egypt up to the present, when satellites have led to the decommissioning of towers such as this one. With its sweeping views of the bays, it's still immensely scenic – much as it was in Henry Wadsworth Longfellow's day. The Portland-born poet often walked here from town to chat with the keeper and draw inspiration from the surroundings. His *Wreck of the Hesperus* was inspired by an actual shipwreck off Peak's Island in 1869.

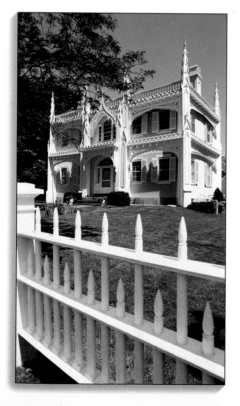

BELOW: Wedding Cake House, Kennebunkport.

The phoenix of Maine: Portland

The state's most populous city (with only about 65,000 residents, or 125,000 in the metropolitan area), **Portland ❼** presides over Casco Bay. Founded as Casco in the middle of the 17th century, the city soon became a center of international commerce. Located more than 100 miles (160 km) closer to Europe than any other major US seaport, and blessed with a sheltered, deep-water harbor, it presented itself as a natural port for trade.

Yet Portland's success has often been choppy and beset by sudden storms. Three times the city was burned completely to the ground – by Indians in 1675, by the British in 1775, and by accident in 1866. Three times the city rose quickly from its ashes, improved and rejuvenated. After the last fire, it was reconfigured. Streets were widened, and an elaborate network of municipal parks instituted. The city stands today as a shining example of urban planning – all the more so with the revitalization, in recent decades, of the atmospheric **Old Port Exchange ⓐ** district, a salty warren of old brick buildings and cobbled streets, packed with sophisticated shops and restaurants.

Portland remains a thriving cultural crossroads, known for its innovative dance and theater troupes. (Theater stood a better chance here after the repeal of a Puritan statute holding that plays "have a pernicious influence on the minds of young people and greatly endanger their morals by giving them a taste for intrigue, amusement and pleasure.") The city is also home to the outstanding **Portland Museum of Art ⓑ**, designed by I.M. Pei and strong on such locally inspired artists as Winslow Homer, Edward Hopper and Andrew Wyeth, as well as the internationally renowned Van Gogh, Degas and Picasso (7 Congress Square; open July–mid-Oct, daily; Thurs and Fri till 9pm; off–season: same except Sun, pm only and closed Mon; entrance fee; free Fri 5–9pm; tel: 207-775 6148). Next door, the **Children's Museum of Maine ⓒ** is imaginatively set up (142 Free Street; open Wed–Fri; Fri till 8pm; Sun pm only; entrance fee).

Several Portland neighborhoods warrant strolling – especially the Western Promenade, a parade of 19th-century architectural styles. The 1859–63 brownstone Italianate villa **Victoria Mansion ⓓ** (109 Danforth Street; tours May–Oct, Tues–Sat; Sun pm; entrance fee), is by far the most elaborate dwelling in town – with showpiece interiors, featuring painted ceilings and carved walls in the Rococo manner, every square inch seemingly subject to intense ornamentation. By contrast is the somewhat restrained 1785–86 **Wadsworth-Longfellow House ⓔ** (485 Congress Street; tours June–Oct, daily; entrance fee), built by the Longfellows' grandfather, a Revolutionary War officer, and

Maps:
Area 302
City 307

Which way?

BELOW: decoy carver's stand at a blueberry festival.

Portland

0   400 yds
0   400 m

home to three generations of the family. Inside are the parlor where the poet's parents were married and the room where he wrote *The Rainy Day*.

Spread out below are the Calendar Islands – so named because John Smith reported that there were 365 of them, when in fact they number only 136. Cruises to the various islands leave from Portland's State Pier Wharf. The islands range in size from a few square yards of exposed rock to fully functional suburbs like Peaks Island; they tend to get wilder and more beautiful, the farther out to sea. Though rumors of pirate booty have been bruited about for centuries, none – at least on record – has been found so far. Portland's residents and visitors find treasure enough in these peaceful retreats, ideal for biking and picknicking.

Following in L.L. Bean's boots

The little town of **Freeport** ❽ on the Bay, attracts customers from around the world – all because, in 1912, a young man named Leon Leonwood Bean decided to build a better hunting boot. In his initial circular, he offered the new, improved waterproof boot with a money-back guarantee. Legend has it that 90 out of the first 100 pairs fell apart: the soles separated from the leather uppers. True to his word, Bean replaced the defective boots with pairs of a newer, improved design and – after absorbing the loss – began building the legendary **L.L. Bean** empire that he controlled until his death in 1967 at the age of 94.

Bean lived long enough to see his store, built in 1951, grow from a humble hunting and outdoors outfitter to a purveyor of casual fashion and recreational sporting goods. The back-to-the-land movement of the 1960s and '70s, along with a boom in mail-order sales, soon prompted expansion into a three-story

Morethan 3½ million visitors a year turn up at L.L. Bean's store in Freeport. World-wide mail order sales exceed $1 billion a year.

BELOW: sign of a seagoing heritage.

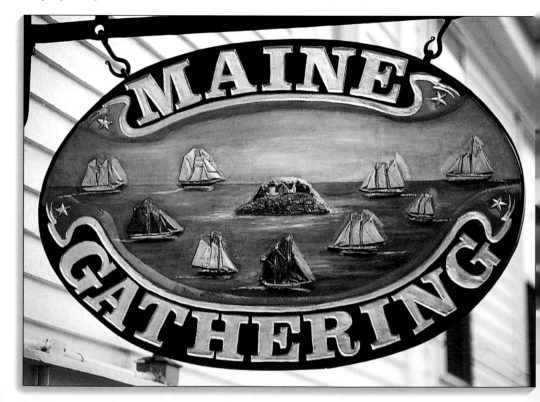

department store (95 Main Street; tel: 800-221 4221), open 24 hours, 365 days a year since 1951 (Bean announced he had "thrown away the keys."). Though a boon to the local economy, Bean's has inspired imitators, so that the entire village is now overrun with discount outlets – tasteful, for the most part, but nonetheless intrusive. In the final irony, Bean's original customer base, the liberally inclined baby boomers, have begun to shun the enterprise because of his daughter's ultra-conservative stance. All the same, ardent shoppers continue to throng here; doing the outlets has become one of Maine's more popular sports.

A rather peculiar attraction in this area is the **Desert of Maine 9**, a former farm that was overcultivated, then logged, eventually losing all its topsoil. Sand took over, eventually engulfing entire trees... Amateur mineralogists and children alike will enjoy this overgrown sandbox.

The Mid-coast

Brunswick **10** is best known as the home of Bowdoin College. Founded in 1794, Bowdoin was originally slated to be built in Portland, but the college's benefactors found that that city offered too many "temptations to dissipation, extravagance, vanity and various vices of seaport towns" for impressionable young minds. Nathaniel Hawthorne and Henry Wadsworth Longfellow were college classmates in 1825.

The **Pejepscot Historical Society Museums** (the Indian name for the Androscoggin River meant "crooked like a snake") provides a good overview of 19th-century life in this region (Joshua Chamberlain Museum; Maine Street; open May–mid-Oct, Tues–Sat; entrance fee; and the Pejepscot Museum, Park Row; open weekdays; plus June–Oct, Sat pm). The campus harbors two worthwhile museums. Bowdoin College's **Museum of Art** houses a small but astute sampling of paintings by such notables as Start, Copley, Homer, Eakins, and Wyeth (Walker Art Building; open Tues–Sat; Sun pm; tel: 207-725 3275).

The **Peary-MacMillan Arctic Museum** (Hubbard Hall; open Tues–Sat; Sun pm) heralds the accomplishments of Polar explorers Robert E. Peary and Donald MacMillan, who achieved their objective in 1909. Etched over the doorway is the Latin inscription Peary carved over his shipboard bunk after frostbite claimed most of his toes on a failed 1899 mission: *Inveniam viam aut faciam* ("I shall find a way or make one"). It's also possible to visit the house Peary built on Eagle Island, via cruises out to Bailey Island; inquire at the museum.

East of Brunswick on US 1 sits **Bath 11**, once the state's shipbuilding center, and the nation's fifth-largest seaport. For a time during the 19th century, Maine's shipyards were responsible for one-third to one-half of all ships on the high seas. Timber cut north of Augusta was floated down the Kennebec River to Bath, where the riverbank slopes perfectly for laying keels into the water. The era of the wooden ships ended, however, on the day the iron hull was invented. Not ready to give up a lucrative business, Bath constructed the **Bath Iron Works**, today one of the country's busiest producers of Navy ships. The

Map on page 302

It was in Brunswick that Harriet Beecher Stowe wrote her 1852 masterpiece Uncle Tom's Cabin, *after having a vision while listening to her husband preach at the town church.*

BELOW: launching the *Arleigh Burke* at Bath Iron Works.

Sardines to go at Prospect Harbor.

BELOW: the trail to Popham Beach.

shipyard is off-limits to civilians (except for occasional open houses), but a good view of the towering cranes and other equipment can be obtained from the Carleton Bridge over the Kennebec.

The history of shipbuilding in Bath and other coastal towns is preserved in a beautiful riverside complex, the **Maine Maritime Museum and Shipyard** (Washington Street; open daily; entrance fee; tel: 207-443 1316). Exhibits on nautical tools and gadgets capture the flavor of seafaring days, while a working boatyard demonstrates techniques of different stages of shipbuilding. For a small additional fee, visitors can cruise up the Kennebec to view the Iron Works. The museum also maintains an authentic 142-ft (43-meter) Grand Banks schooner, the *Sherman Zwicker*, which can be boarded, when in port, for a glimpse of the seafaring life.

The town of Bath has restaurants lined up along Front Street and Elm Street.

Directly south of Bath is **Popham Beach State Park** (entrance fee), featuring an unfinished 1861 fort and a 4½-mile (7-km) stretch of sand, one of the prettiest in the state. This was also the site of a failed 1607 colony, of which no trace remains.

Wiscasset ⑫ claims, with some justification, to be the "prettiest village in Maine." It's certainly a contender, with its many grand houses, several of them built by prosperous sea captains. Two are open to visitors: the Federal-era **Nickels-Sortwell House** (Main and Federal Streets; open June–Sept Wed–Sun pm; entrance fee), maintained by the Society for the Preservation of New England Antiquities, and **Castle Tucker** (overlooking the Sheepscot River; open June–mid-Oct, tours Wed–Sun; entrance fee), a prim 1807 Federal building aggrandized in 1860 by Captain Richard H. Tucker and with Victorian furnishings. The 1852 **Musical Wonder House** is an aptly named mansion full of vintage music boxes, player pianos, and other automata from around the world – often playing against one another in improbable euphony (High Street; open late May–Oct, daily; entrance fee).

One of the most picturesque sights in town, oddly enough, is a pair of scuttled World War I schooners, the *Hesper* and the *Luther Little*, mouldering in the mudflats near the town landing. Another offbeat tourist attraction is the **Old Lincoln County Jail and Museum**, an 1811 hoosegow with granite walls up to 41 inches (over 1 meter) thick (Route 218; open July, Aug Tues–Sun; entrance fee). Considered a model of humanity in its day, because prisoners were afforded individual cells, this grim repository was used right up until 1913, and has the graffiti to prove it. On the southeast side of the village **Fort Edgecoomb**, an octagonal fort of 1808–9, is empty inside, but has a great view over the estuary.

Although certainly subdued compared to the commercial excesses of the south coast, **Boothbay Harbor** ⑬ is decidedly touristy. In summer, tens of thousands of visitors throng the streets of this former fishing village to inspect the shops, sample seafood delicacies, and charter boats to explore offshore islands with names such as the Cuckolds and the Hypocrites. There are yacht and golf clubs, flower shows, auctions, and clambakes to pass the time. **Boothbay Railway Village** (Route 27; open late May–mid-Oct daily; entrance fee) features a narrow-gauge railroad, encircling a range of reconstructed buildings of yesteryear, including a barber-shop, bank and country store.

South of Damariscotta on Route 130 is **Pemaquid Point** , a rocky penin-sula whose Indian name meant "long finger." Early explorers couldn't miss it, and in fact there's some evidence to support a claim – unsubstantiated as yet – that a settlement here may have predated Plymouth. It's known that Pemaquid's settlers provided the Pilgrims with supplies to survive their first harsh winter in the New World; lacking a chronicler like Governor William Bradford, however, Pemaquid's history was never recorded, so details remain hazy.

Its cellar holes filled in by 19th-century farmers, this "Lost City" was entirely unknown until the early 1960s, when Helen Camp, a Rutgers University professor, noticed clay pipes and other detritus in a freshly plowed field. She alerted the Smithsonian Institution; the state bought the land and began excavations. Some 40,000 artifacts have been unearthed so far. The more remarkable ones – such as a 16th-century German jug – are displayed in the state-run museum, **Colonial Pemaquid Restoration**, alongside a diorama recreating the settlement (off Route 130; open late May–early Sept, daily; early Sept–mid-Oct, weekends; entrance fee).

Admission to the museum also includes **Fort William Henry**, a 1907 replica on the site of several unsuccessful stockades. The 1630 original was burned by pirates, and a 1677 replacement, thought impregnable, was destroyed in 1689 by the French Baron de Castin (for whom the town of Castine was named) and his Indian cohorts. A Fort Frederick was built here in 1729, but during the Revolution locals leveled it, lest it fall into the hands of the British.

Map on page 302

BELOW: Pemaquid Point Lighthouse.

Lobsters and Lobstering

The colorful lobster buoys dotting the coast of Maine are one of the state's hallmarks. And rightly so – more lobster is fished in Maine than in any other state. Lobstering is a $130 million business in Maine, and in 1997 alone, over 40 million pounds of Maine lobster were consumed throughout the US and shipped all over the world. Yet despite all this, most lobsters in Maine are still caught by independent fishermen in small boats.

A lobsterman's day starts early and goes on late: many head out before dawn, when waters are calmer, and return in the late afternoon. Traps need to be checked at least once a week, and many professional lobstermen – "high-liners" – have 1,000 to 1,500 traps or more, and may need to check several hundred a day. Although proximity to shore makes lobstering safer than other commercial fish-

ing, it is still a dangerous profession, a year-round activity that in the bitter Maine winter can be particularly grueling. Slipping on an icy deck and going over would mean the end, so most high-liners take a helper with them in the form of a "sternman."

On the southern coast of Maine, guided lobstering trips give visitors a gentler taste of a lobsterman's work. In York Harbor, tourists can join Tom Farnum, a retired middle-school science teacher, as he checks traps from his fiberglass skiff. Farnum has been lobstering for 25 years, and, as he leads groups through York River to the mouth of York Harbor, he shares his knowledge of the history of lobstering and the lobster life cycle.

Lobsters are crustaceans whose external skeletons do not grow. Every year they molt, shedding their old shells and growing larger ones. This process happens when the water is warmer, in late June or early July. Conveniently for tourists, molting brings the lobsters closer to shore, making them easier to catch during the peak summer months.

Without shells, the soft lobsters are vulnerable to predators – cod fish and sharks among others – so they migrate to shallow waters for safety. Here, they hide, absorbing sea water and expanding 15 to 20 percent in size. Over four to six weeks, the lobsters produce new shells, then return to deep water, where they shrink again. The lobsters are now known in the trade as "new-shell," or in restaurants as "soft-shell," as opposed to "hard-shell" before molting. A hard-shell lobster's meat can be up to 33 percent of its body weight, while a soft-shell's is only 25 percent; accordingly, hard-shell lobster tends to be more expensive. The taste is slightly different, and each Maine connoisseur has a preference. Some say new-shell is sweeter, some prefer hard-shell for its stronger taste. Visitors have ample opportunity to decide for themselves at the hundreds of lobster pounds along the coast, where lobsters are cooked in seawater in wood-fired barrels.

Farnum's tours leave from Town Dock 2 in York Harbor, Maine; mid-June–mid-Sept weekdays, on the hour 10am–2pm and by reservation at 3 and 4pm; $7.50 per person; (tel: 207-363 3234 5–6pm). ❑

LEFT: at work in Corea Harbor, Down East coast.

At the tip of this peninsula on Route 130 stands the **Pemaquid Point Lighthouse**, built in 1824. With powerful surf constantly breaking on the rocks, the point is a favorite spot for painters and photographers, as well as families who enjoy poking around the tide pools.

An island in time: Monhegan

An early European explorer, David Ingram, astounded Europe with tales – most rather tall – of the marvelous peoples and cities he encountered on a journey from the Gulf of Mexico to Canada. Lured by such promising reports, a group of Germans settled Waldoboro in 1748, with, as a plaque at the center of town attests, "the promise and expectation of finding a prosperous city, instead of which they found nothing but wilderness." Another Ingram allusion, to "a great island that was backed like a whale," was naturally dismissed as fantasy.

However, the cliffs of **Monhegan Island ⓯**, 12 miles (19 km) south of Port Clyde, do indeed lend the island the appearance of a whale. And yet an otherworldly air still pervades this 700-acre (283-hectare) isle, little changed in the past century. Cars have made no inroads, and virtually all of the cottages – including two out of the three hotels – not only lack electricity, but like it that way. A magnet first for fishing fleets (the abundantly stocked waters attracted European fleets as early as 1605, and possibly the Vikings six centuries earlier) and later artists (the most famous summer resident is painter Jamie Wyeth), most of the island remains undeveloped.

Visitors are free to explore the Cliff Trail circling the island, and the Cathedral Woods Trail, where the island children are in the habit of constructing tiny "fairy houses" out of twigs and moss. Monhegan is served by ferries from both

TIP

For information on Maine's 61 surviving lighthouses, visit the Fishermen's Museum, in the old keeper's residence, next to the Pemaquid Point Lighthouse (open mid-May–mid-Oct daily). *See also page 320.*

BELOW: Monhegan Island meadow.

The weathered house featured in Andrew Wyeth's signature painting Christina's World *still stands in Cushing, and is the site of many a reverential pilgrimage. The house – and the painting – belong to the Farnsworth Art Museum.*

Boothbay Harbor (Balmy Days Cruises, tel: 207-633 2284; June–late Sept, daily) and Port Clyde (tel: 207-372 8848; May–Oct, daily; rest of the year: Mon, Wed, Fri; the vessel is a rugged mailboat named the *Laura B.*), and though it's possible to make the round-trip in one day, an overnight is advised for those who wish to ease back into a less stressful age. Traditionally, departing visitors are given bouquets of some of the 600 species of wildflowers scattered throughout the island meadows.

Penobscot Bay

On the west end of Penobscot Bay is the town of **Rockland ⑯**, once a great limestone producer and now the world's largest distributor of lobsters. Thanks to the 1935 bequest of "Aunt" Lucy Farnsworth, a frugal spinster who lived in but three rooms of her family mansion and left the town $1,300,000 to start a museum, Rockland has a world-class collection of art. The **Farnsworth Art Museum** (Main Street; open late May–mid-Oct, daily; mid-Oct–late May, Tues–Sat; Sun, pm; entrance fee; tel: 207-596 6457) counts among its holdings many noted 19th- and 20th-century works, including sculpture by Louise Nevelson, who grew up in a Bath lumberyard, and paintings by all three Wyeths – N.C., Andrew, and Jamie. Andrew Wyeth still summers in nearby Cushing. Another pleasant way to pass the afternoon is to peruse the **Shore Village Museum** (Limerock Street; open June–mid-Oct, daily), not big but crammed with a collection of lighthouse artifacts unrivalled elsewhere in the nation, together with other maritime bits and pieces such as ship models and navigational instruments, and straying into Civil War items and costume dolls.

To view an interesting assortment of vehicles, airborne and otherwise, visit

BELOW: artist Jamie Wyeth's house on Monhegan Island.

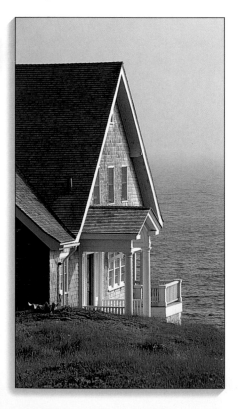

the **Owl's Head Transportation Museum**, housed in a spiffed-up hangar at the Owl's Head airport south of Rockland (off Route 73; open daily; entrance fee). The collections range from vintage bicycles to a 1910 Harley, a Model T Ford and a Model F plane (a Wright Brothers prototype). On summer weekends, some of the displays are taken off their blocks and sent for a spin.

A ferry out of Rockland (Maine State Ferry Service, tel: 207-596 2202) serves the large, mostly old-money island of **Vinalhaven ⑰**, where old granite quarries (the stone went into Boston's Museum of Fine Arts, among other edifices) make fine swimming holes and the paved roads are ideal for day-tripping bicyclists.

Up the coast, **Rockport ⑱** is home base to a fleet of windjammers (sailings late May–mid-Oct; tel: 207-374 5400 or 800-807 9463). These two- or three-masted schooners, sails billowing in the wind, are a throwback to an earlier era, and a wonderful way to discover the coast as the earliest explorers encountered it. Weekend and weeklong excursions may be booked aboard more than a dozen venerable vessels, including the *Stephen Taber*, believed to be the oldest sailboat in continuous use.

Rockport is also a summer mecca for shutterbugs attending the **Maine Photographic Workshops** (tel: 207-236 8581); they can be spotted prowling the town, snapping up picturesque tableaux. A gallery with changing exhibits (often by nationally known professionals and teachers) is open to the public.

Camden ⑲ ("Where the Mountains Meet the Sea") has enjoyed a long reign as the ultimate in genteel summering spots. It was here, as a chambermaid at the gracious Whitehall Inn, an 1834 home turned hotel in 1901, that Rockland native Edna St Vincent Millay first began to polish her poetry, and even recite some aloud (one of the guests, noting her talent, arranged for a scholarship to Vassar). One of her verses (*see panel*) was penned after climbing to the summit of 800-ft (244-meter) Mount Battie in the **Camden Hills State Park** (off Route 1), now accessible on foot or via a toll road.

A modern statue of the poet stands watch in a waterfront park overlooking the Megunticook River falls which once powered a half-dozen woolen mills; it's a pleasant place to catch one's breath amid the hubbub of town. Camden is once again in full flower as a summer destination, and the port is packed with restaurants and shops. Many of the grander "cottages" gracing the hilltops have become luxurious B&Bs.

Much quieter than Camden, **Belfast** is starting to attract some fun shops to its Victorian brick storefronts, and its fine houses, too, are turning B&B. **Searsport** ⑳, lined with dazzling white sea captains' homes (nearly 300 lived here in the 19th century), calls itself "the antiques capital of Maine," and the pickings are indeed unusually good. Between 1770 and 1920, this one town produced more than 3,000 vessels, and evidence of its rich history, along with China Trade treasures, can be found at the **Penobscot Marine Museum** (Route 1; open late May–mid-Oct, Mon–Sat; Sun, pm; entrance fee)

Farther along the coastal road and near the mouth of the Penobscot,

Map on page 302

All I could see from where I stood
Was three long mountains and a wood
I turned and looked another way
And saw three islands in a bay

— EDNA ST VINCENT MILLAY, ON THE VIEW FROM MOUNT BATTIE

BELOW: looking down on Camden.

Bucksport is dominated by the vast and crumbling Fort Knox, built 1844–69 but never completed.

Detours "down east"

Intent on getting to the justly famed Mount Desert Island, many tourists never veer from US 1 and thus miss one of the most scenic areas in Maine. The peninsulas along the eastern side of Penobscot Bay well warrant some poking around.

Established as a trading post by the Plymouth Pilgrims, **Castine ㉑** became one of the most hotly contested chunks of property in New England: changing hands nine times, it was owned by the French, Dutch, British, and, eventually, Americans (it was a Tory outpost during the Revolution, and the British managed to take it over again after the War of 1812). Plaques around town, as well as a free walking-tour brochure distributed by the Castine Merchants' Association, fill in the details, but it's enough to wander around, beneath a canopy of elms, taking in the array of fine white houses. Some belong to the **Maine Maritime Academy** (one of five such schools nationwide that train merchant marines). Their 1952 troop ship, the decommissioned *State of Maine*, is a floating classroom (hourly tours, mid-July–Aug, daily; Sept–Dec, weekends).

Take a detour off this detour to make a circuit of **Deer Isle**, where the principal occupations are lobstering and fishing, and tourists, though welcome, won't find themselves catered to unduly. On the eastern side of the isle is the prestigious **Haystack Mountain School of Crafts**, whose 1960 "campus" is a cluster of small modern buildings perched precipitously on a piny bank overlooking Jericho Bay (sessions mid-June–early Sept; visitors may be admitted some afternoons and for evening lectures and concerts; tel: 207-348 2306).

BELOW: conductors check their watches on the Belfast to Moosehead railroad.

Map on page 302

For a true getaway, take the mailboat from the picturesque port of **Stonington** ❷ to the sparsely inhabited 2,800-acre (1,130-hectare) **Isle au Haut** ❷. Half is privately owned, the other half part of the Acadia National Park (most of which is situated on Mount Desert Island).

Heading northeast to hook up with US 1 again, one passes through **Blue Hill** ❷, long the choice of blueblood summerers who didn't care for the showy social season in Bar Harbor. This lovely town attracts craftspeople (especially potters), musicians, and restaurateurs, so the pleasures are varied. One early citizen was the cleric Jonathan Fisher, who served here from 1796 to the mid-19th century and was a man of many enthusiasms. One of his primitive landscapes hangs at the Farnsworth Museum in Rockland, and the 1814 **Jonathan Fisher House** (Routes 15 and 176; open July–mid-Sept, Mon–Sat, pm; entrance fee), which he built himself, is full of his handiwork, from furniture and maps to the wooden clock he made while at Harvard.

Souvenirs of Down East.

Mount Desert Island

The reason there's so much territory to explore in Mount Desert Island is that 35,000 acres (1,414 hectares) of the16 by 13-mile (26 by 34-km) island belong to Acadia National Park, which draws over 5 million visitors a year. "Society" discovered this remote spot in the mid-19th century, inspired in part by Hudson River School painter Thomas Coles. By the time the stock market crashed in 1928, millionaires arriving by steamboat and yachts had constructed more than 200 extravagant "cottages." (Only a few survive, some as institutions or inns: many were destroyed in 1947's devastating fire.) Fortunately, Harvard University president Charles W. Eliot had the foresight to initiate the park in 1916, and

BELOW: Stonington, Deer Isle.

many of his peers contributed parcels. John D. Rockefeller threw in 11,000 acres (4,400 hectares) crisscrossed with 50 miles (80 km) of bridle paths he built to protest against the admission of horseless carriages on to the island in 1905. The trail network makes for great mountain-biking, cross-country skiing, and just plain walking.

Bar Harbor's heyday as a fashionable summer resort was in the 19th century, when a railroad from Boston and a steamboat service lured the wealthy. A forest fire in 1947 destroyed 60 of the grand summer cottages and finally ended the resort's gilded age.

Bar Harbor ㉕ is Mount Desert Island's main town – a bit overcommercialized, but with a pretty town green, a marvelous Art Deco cinema, and some exceptional crafts stores, along with appealing restaurants, and a good choice of accommodations.

Spotting the 17 exposed pink granite peaks of **Mount Desert Island** ㉖, now the main part of Acadia National Park, in 1604, Samuel de Champlain described the place as "*l'île des monts deserts*" – and the French pronunciation still holds, more or less, so be sure to accentuate the final syllable, as in "dessert."

Exploring Acadia

Off Route 3 in Hulls Cove is the National Park's **Visitor Center** (open mid-Apr–Oct, daily; tel: 207-288 3338). Here you can pick up a park map and a schedule of naturalist activities; there are excellent hiking maps on sale. Most visitors will want to experience the view from Cadillac Mountain, whose form dominates the whole park, and to drive or cycle the Park Loop Road, but there are many other possibilities, including horse and carriage tours from Wildwood Riding Stables, kayaking, sailing, and hiking in the less frequented areas. Even the shorter trails tend to be over uneven rock, so suitable footwear is essential.

Car traffic is kept under control by a permit system covering the mostly one-way 22-mile (35-km) Park Loop Road, which makes a clockwise circuit of

BELOW: Bar Harbor.

all the more scenic spots along the eastern coast; the reasonably priced permits are good for a week. Close to the Visitor Center, the **Acadia Wild Garden** shows a range of flora that can be found in a variety of sites within the national park, such as mountain heath and bog; adjacent are the Nature Center, with exhibits on the cultural and natural history of Acadia, and the **Robert Abbe Museum** (off Route 3 and Park Loop Road; open May–Oct, daily; entrance fee). Sweeping views follow, from the Champlain Mountain Overlook across Frenchman Bay to the distant Gouldsboro Hills. The road passes the start of the Precipice Trail, which features iron rungs and ladders for the steep sections, and further on are Sand Beach – edged by low cliffs, and Acadia's one sandy beach – and the Beehive Trail, which gets superb panoramas but involves some potentially dizzying sections. Thunder Hole needs a wind to stir things up; in the right conditions, the spray blasts up through this chink on the coastline. Otter Point provides another memorable coastal outlook before the road heads inland, past Jordan Pond, with walks along the lakeside or on the short trail past Bubble Rock, a huge boulder transported and dumped by glacier, to South Bubble Summit.

Reached by road or on foot, the tallest peak, 1,530-ft (466-meter) Cadillac Mountain, is the highest point along the Atlantic coast north of Rio de Janeiro, and affords glorious 360° views stretching inland as far as Mount Katahdin, Maine's highest summit, and seaward to encompass myriad smaller islands – a particularly lovely vista when bathed in the orange glow of sunset.

On the other side of Somes Sound, the only fjord on the East Coast, the landscape is just as lovely and a bit less traveled. Visit the spectacular seaview **Thuya Gardens**, and stop in Southwest Harbor to try your hand at the "touch

Map on page 302

Wild lupins.

BELOW: biking on one of Acadia's carriage roads.

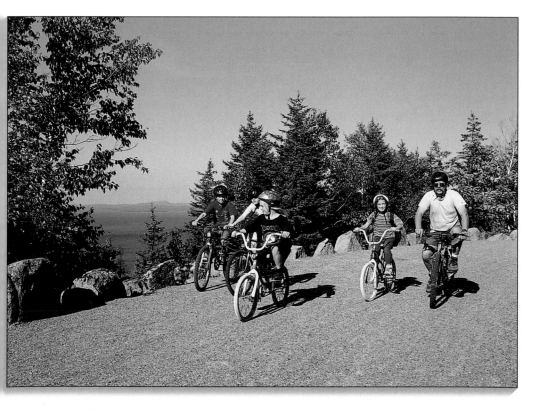

tanks" and "mystery barrels" in the ramshackle **Oceanarium** (open mid-May–mid-Oct, Mon–Sat; entrance fee). At the most southerly point of the island, Bass Harbor Head Lighthouse is a classic Maine cameo.

To the Canadian Border

In Washington County – also known as "Sunrise County" for its easterly location – tourism takes a back seat to lobstering and growing blueberries and Christmas trees. The patient will be rewarded with a vision of the true Maine, much as it looked 50 years ago. It's worth a detour to the small, unspoiled fishing town of Winter Harbor, and, to the south, **Schoodic Peninsula ㉗**, a little-visited portion of Acadia National Park with fine views of Cadillac Mountain across the bay.

Machias ㉘, about 35 miles (60 km) farther east on US 1, was once a haven for pirates and smugglers. It was also the site of the first naval battle of the Revolutionary War. In June 1775, a month after the Battle of Lexington, the *Margaretta* set anchor off Machias to stand guard over a freight ship collecting wood with which to build British barracks in Boston. After debating their course of action at **Burnham Tavern** (now restored and open as a museum; open early June–Sept weekdays), the townspeople rounded up two smaller ships and successfully attacked. *Margaretta*'s captain died of his wounds when brought back to the tavern, but the crew, nursed back to health there, vowed revenge – and followed through, with subsequent attacks and conflagrations.

Lubec is the easternmost town in the United States, and the easternmost American soil is **West Quoddy Head ㉙**, graced with a candycane-striped 1858 lighthouse surrounded, in summer, by wild roses and day lilies. A walking trail leads along a 50-ft (15-meter) cliff, to Quoddy Head State Park. Having come

BELOW: West Quoddy Head Lighthouse, sited where the rising sun first strikes the United States.

MAINE'S LIGHTHOUSES

With thousands of miles of deep craggy coastline and treacherously rocky shores, it isn't surprising that Maine has 63 lighthouses. What's really surprising is that there aren't three times as many! These sentinels guard the entire coast – from East Quoddy Head Lighthouse on Campobello Island at the Canadian border (accessible only at low tide) to the southern Nubble Light on York Beach. You could easily structure a coastal drive with them acting as a focal point. These picturesque outposts, where sea meets shore, have long represented hope, strength, security and romance in the American imagination. Although several are privately owned, many are open to the public. Portland Head Light, Maine's oldest – built in 1791 under President George Washington's authorization – houses a charming museum in the lighthouse keepers' quarters. Pemaquid Point Light, at the tip of the eponymous peninsula, rises 79 ft (24 meters) above the water from a dramatic rock ledge. (You're guaranteed to spot painters at their easels here.) In 1934 it became the first automated lighthouse. Like others, however, it still relies on a Fresnel lens – a technology designed in 1822 that bends the light into a narrow beam by means of a magnifying lens and concentric rings of glass prisms.

this far, don't miss **Campobello Island** ⑳, only a bridge away from Lubec but officially in Canada. Franklin Delano Roosevelt summered here from the age of one (in 1883) to 1921, when he was crippled by polio. After a self-guided tour of the house, which remains as the family left it, visitors can enjoy 8 miles (13 km) of walking trails, including a 2-mile (3-km) stroll along the ocean.

Map on page 302

The North Woods

Much of the northernmost part of Maine consists of millions of acres of soft-wood forest, owned by a couple of dozen corporations who sometimes admit visitors onto their gravel logging roads for a fee. For an overview of the logging boom that swept the area in the mid-19th century, when papermakers turned to timber in lieu of rags, visit the **Lumberman's Museum** (Route 159; open late May–Sept, Tues–Sun; entrance fee) in **Patten** ㉛, whose 10 buildings of exhibits include a reconstructed 1860s cabin.

Potatoes are a staple crop in Maine.

   To the west, via State 159, is **Baxter State Park** ㉜, the legacy of Percival Baxter, governor from 1920 to 1925. Unsuccessful in his efforts to get the state legislature to purchase and protect this land, he bought and donated a total of 201,018 acres (81,211 hectares), and deeded them to the state, requiring only that the tract remain "forever wild." The park contains 45 peaks over 3,000 ft high, including 5,267-ft (1,605-meter) Baxter Peak, the tallest of Mount Katahdin's three peaks and the second highest point in New England. Baxter is connected to nearby Pamola Peak by a narrow, mile-long strip of rock known as the Knife Edge. Only a few feet wide in spots, the Knife Edge is an acrophobe's nightmare – 3,000 ft (915 meters) straight down on one side, 4,000 ft (1,200 meters) on the other. Would a person fall straight down to the bottom? No, a park ranger

BELOW:
a frequent sight in northern Maine.

reassures: they'd bounce a couple of times. Don't try to cross in high winds.

Pamola Peak is named for the Native American god Pamola, said to have the wings and talons of an eagle but the arms and torso of a man. In *The Maine Woods*, Thoreau warned of Pamola's legendary ire for mortals who reach the top of Katahdin, thus entering the territory of the gods. Those who attempt to scale Katahdin – particularly up the most difficult trails, Cathedral and Dudley, which present the most rugged rock-climbing possible without benefit of ropes and pitons – might well wonder whether Thoreau was right.

Here immigration is a tide which may ebb when it has swept away the pines.
– HENRY DAVID THOREAU
ON CHESUNCOOK

Running northward from the northwest corner of Baxter State Park, the **Allagash Wilderness Waterway** provides 92 miles (150 km) of the most scenic canoeing available in the United States; the trip takes a week to 10 days. South of the park, the Penobscot River's West Branch offers some of the state's most hair-raising whitewater rafting, through granite-walled Ripogenus Gorge. And to the west of the park, accessible only by boat or float plane, is the preserved-in-amber 19th-century logging town of **Chesuncook**. Logged out and left to recover, this lovely little village welcomes outdoors-oriented guests eager to leave the 20th century behind.

BELOW: a successful cast on Maine's St. Croix River.
BELOW RIGHT: rafting on the Kennebec River.

Several dozen such "camps," unchanged for decades, are tucked away in this region pocked with lakes and ponds, where the fish are plentiful and moose and black bear still roam. Many are clustered around **Moosehead Lake ㉝**, the largest body of freshwater in New England, with 320 miles (512 km) of shoreline. The SS *Katahdin*, a restored 1914 steamship, tours the lake out of Greenville on the southern shore (cruises: July and Aug, daily except Mon and Fri; early Sept, weekends; mid-Sept–mid-Oct, Tues, Thurs, and weekends), and the **Moosehead Marine Museum**, which operates the ship, contains fascinat-

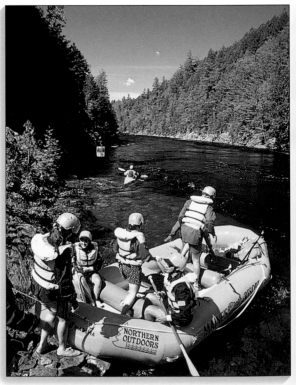

ing displays on Greenville's history, from frontier town to logging capital to turn-of-the-century tourist destination. Another great way to get a full grasp of this mammoth lake is to take a float-plane tour; several operators offer "fly-and-canoe" packages (Folsom's Air Service, Greenville; tel: 207-695 2821).

About 20 miles (32 km) southwest of Greenville as the crow flies (or thrice that distance by car), **The Forks** has turned into a major tourist attraction in recent decades, attracting thousands of amateurs eager to try whitewater rafting along the Kennebec and Dead rivers. Suitable for anyone over the age of 10 and in reasonably good health, these thrilling descents take only a day and alternate roiling rapids with placid floats.

The western lakes and mountains

The ski area at **Sugarloaf** ㉞, Maine's second highest peak, has a treeless top offering superb views (including Mounts Katahdin and Washington), and gets more vertical descent (2,820 ft/860 meters) than any other winter resort in New England (tel: 207-237 2000). Snowboarders can try the largest halfpipe in the country. All the runs filter into the one resort village at the base. The 18-hole golf course and abundant wilderness trails for hiking and mountain-biking make Sugarloaf a year-round destination.

A useful base for Sugarloaf is **Kingfield** ㉟, which has been a magnet for sporting types since the mid-18th century. It also fostered a family of home-grown geniuses, whose accomplishments are showcased in the **Stanley Museum** (School Street; open Tues–Sun pm; closed Apr, Nov; entrance fee). The twins, F.O. and F.E., invented the Stanley Steamer, which wowed enthusiasts at the first New England auto show in 1898 and set a land-speed

Map on page 302

BELOW: winter scene: Sugarloaf and the Carrabassett Valley.

MOOSE CROSSING

NEXT 9 MILES

Woody Allen built one of his early stand-up sketches around the not uncommon experience of hitting a moose.

BELOW:
a lake camp.

record of 127 miles (203 km) an hour in 1906. Three restored, working samples are garaged in this Georgian-style schoolhouse, which the family built for the town in 1903. Also on display are the photographs of their younger sister, Chansonetta, who had an eye for rural customs now all but forgotten.

About 30 miles (42 km) west is **Rangeley** ❸, also popular with outdoors enthusiasts for more than a century, and the unlikely home of one-time Freud protégé Wilhelm Reich. His renegade theories on sexual energy ended in his ignominious death in jail – the victim, many believe, of an overzealous Food and Drug Administration. Some of the "orgone energy accumulators" he built stand at his remote home and laboratory, **Orgonon** (Wilhelm Reich Museum; off Routes 4 and 16; open July, Aug, Tues–Sun pm; Sept, Sun pm; entrance fee). The tour is fascinating, the view of Rangeley Lake inspiring.

The **Norlands Living History Center** (open July–early Sept, daily; early Sept–mid-Oct: weekends; entrance fee) in **Livermore** offers a rare opportunity to time-travel back to 19th-century farm life. Most visitors content themselves with a two-hour tour, but true aficionados can sign up for a weekend "live-in" program, in which they'll enact historic characters associated with the farm – and carry out all their chores. **West Paris**, about 12 miles (19 km) west, might prove more attractive to those with "get rich quick" inclinations: Perham's of West Paris, founded in 1919, is a rockhound's mecca, not just for its store, but for the chance to poke around in the five quarries it owns within 10 miles (16 km). Gem-quality tourmaline – striated in a watermelon-like color scheme – is fairly common in these hills, and even gold is not unheard of.

Bethel ❸ gained prominence as a spa town when Dr John Gehring attracted to his clinic many Harvard academicians suffering from nervous disorders. The hotel he built in 1913 on the pretty town green, the Bethel Inn, is still a restorative treat. Also in town, the **Moses Mason House** (Mason Street; open July–early Sept, Tues–Sun pm; early Sept–June, Tues–Fri pm; entrance fee), an 1813 Federal manse maintained by the Bethel Historical Society, is a treasure house of American primitive painting: the itinerant muralist Rufus Porter decorated the entryway and second-floor landing with, respectively, a seascape and forest tableau.

North of town, the **Sunday River ski resort** ❸ (tel: 207-824 3000) covers seven mountains, with plenty for intermediates and beginners, and scope for some more challenging black runs, together with the largest snow-making system in New England – virtually guaranteeing good snow conditions. There are also ski programs for the disabled. It is also excellent for views, looking across the highlands of western Maine. There is mountain biking in summer. Nearby is Sunday River Cross-Country Ski Center (tel: 207-824 2410, at the Sunday River Inn), where trails get fine views, and there are some easy ups and downs for novices, as well as more challenging routes.

To the south, lovely **Kezar Lake** is ringed by opulent summer houses, some of them transformed into inns, and the various villages of Waterford, scattered amid the Oxford Hills, present an unspoiled reminder of the era when vacation "amenities" consisted largely of cool water, lots of trees, and plenty of fresh air.

Augusta ❸❾, Maine's modest-sized capital (population 22,000), stands on the Kennebec River and began its days in 1628 as a trading post. Its gold-domed **State House** (open weekdays) was designed by Charles Bulfinch in 1832, but substantially altered and enlarged in 1909–10. Close by is the **Maine State Museum** (State Street; open Mon–Sat; Sun pm), with displays on "12,000 years of Maine," plus the "Made in Maine" exhibition, which includes a waterpowered woodworking mill and hundreds of Maine-made items. The city's other major sight is **Fort Western**, built close to the river in 1754 and America's oldest wooden fort (City Center Plaza; open late May–early July, daily pm only; early July–early Sept, weekdays and weekends pm; early Sept–mid-Oct, weekends pm; entrance fee). It became a trading post – like the original Pilgrim settlement which preceded it on the same site – and later became the home of its commander, William Harvard. The stockade and block-houses have been evocatively re-created, complete with replica cannons.

With its easy access from Portland, **Sebago Lake** ❹⓿ is one of the most popular of the Western Lakes, offering swimming, boating, camping, and fishing in the state park at its northern end.

Willowbrook at Newfield ❹❶ (off Route 11; open mid-May–Sept, daily; entrance fee) is a reconstituted late 19th-century museum village, between the southern end of Sebago Lake and the New Hampshire border, which captures many of the pleasures of this slower, gentler time, from horse-drawn sleighs to bicycles built for two, from a classic ice-cream parlor to a musty general store. In Maine, none of these pleasures is necessarily confined to the past tense. ❏

Map on page 302

Augusta was incorporated in 1797 but was soon renamed after Pamela Augusta, the daughter of the Revolutionary War general Harry Dearborn.

BELOW: canoe expeditions on local lakes are popular.

FOREST, LAKE AND MOUNTAIN WILDLIFE

New England's wilderness areas are one of its big draws. Locals hunt there; visitors have a more benign interest in the animals, birds and plants

It's obvious from the air and just as clear from the freeways: trees cover more than three-quarters of New England, cloaking the mountains of New Hampshire, Maine, and Vermont. These woods and mountains ring with birdsong and are carpeted with wild flowers; particularly enthralling are the alpine flowers on Mount Washington (above and far right).

The most exciting animal to see in the forests is moose. Desperately ungainly, and sporting hairy dewlaps beneath large snouts, they can often be spotted in New Hampshire's White Mountains and in inland Maine, especially in and around lakes and marshes – or licking the salt that runs off the roads in winter. A bull can grow to well over 6 feet (2 meters) tall, with huge antlers on top, and can weigh half a ton (give him a wide berth). You may see moose as you drive around, particularly at dawn or dusk; if not, join one of many moose-waching trips organised locally.

Black bears are also often seen in the forests. They don't normally attack humans, but don't feed them or leave food scraps on the ground. Keep food in sealed containers. Look out, too, for porcupine, chipmunk and stripey-tailed raccoon.

In the lakes and streams that lace the forests, especially in northern Maine, beavers fell trees with their teeth, busily building lodges and dams and creating deep ponds. The lodges, or houses, built of mud and sticks, may be up to 6 feet (2 meters) tall.

△ **BEAVERS AT WORK**
A beaver dam (above) is an amazingly effective construction of mud and sticks. Sticks stripped of their bark are a give-away sign of a beaver colony.

▽ **THE LOON**
The loon is the state bird of New Hampshire and, some say, the oldest bird on Earth. The diver is often to be seen on Squam Lake, New Hampshire (above).

◁ **WHITE-TAIL DEER**
White-tailed deer are common in forested areas, and hunting them is a popular pastime in the fall. This faun wears its white-spotted, spring-time coat.

▽ BIRDLIFE
Waders include American egret (below) and black-crowned night heron. Forest birds include pine siskin, blue jay, golden-crowned kinglet and chickadee.

▽ FOREST FLOOR
In the cool, moist forests, pine seedlings grow up through a silver-gray carpet of mosses and lichens, some of which are native to Arctic tundra regions.

ALPINE FAUNA AND FLORA

Mount Washington in New Hampshire, subjected to three continental storm systems, has some of the worst weather in the world, and the treeline occurs as low as 1,400 feet (420 meters). This arctic zone supports a few mammals – voles and shrews, for instance, living in deep crevices – and some 100 species of alpine plants, many of which grow only here, on Mount Katahdin in Maine's Baxter State Park, and in Labrador and the Arctic. These plants have successfully adapted to dessication caused by biting winds, poor soil, minimal sunlight, and a short growing season. For some, it is 25 years before they flower. It's a fragile ecology. These exquisite plants, growing in and around the lichen-covered rocks with sedges and dwarfed balsam firs, include gold thread, fireweed, alpine bearberry, starflower, arnica, mountain cranberry, wren's egg cranberry, skunk currant and the dwarf cinquefoil *Potentilla robbinsiana*, unique to Mount Washington. Their vibrant colors are best seen mid-June to August.

△ DAWN OUTING
A sunrise canoe trip on a lake or river (look out for advertisements locally in Maine and New Hampshire) is often the time to see beavers and moose.

▷ DRIVERS BEWARE!
A collision with a moose could cause serious damage not only to your car, but also quite possibly to you and your passengers. Go slowly if you see one by the road.

BRAKE FOR MOOSE
IT COULD SAVE YOUR LIFE
HUNDREDS OF COLLISIONS

INSIGHT GUIDES
Travel Tips

Insight FlexiMaps

Maps in Insight Guides are tailored to complement the text. But when you're on the road you sometimes need the big picture that only a large-scale map can provide. This new range of durable Insight Fleximaps has been designed to meet just that need.

Detailed, clear cartography
makes the comprehensive route and city maps easy to follow, highlights all the major tourist sites and provides valuable motoring information plus a full index.

Informative and easy to use
with additional text and photographs covering a destination's top 10 essential sites, plus useful addresses, facts about the destination and handy tips on getting around.

Laminated finish
allows you to mark your route on the map using a non-permanent marker pen, and wipe it off. It makes the maps more durable and easier to fold than traditional maps.

The world's most popular destinations
are covered by the 125 titles in the series – and new destinations are being added all the time. They include Alaska, Amsterdam, Bangkok, Barbados, Beijing, Brussels, Dallas/Fort Worth, Florence, Hong Kong, Ireland, Madrid, New York, Orlando, Peru, Prague, Rio, Rome, San Francisco, Sydney, Thailand, Turkey, Venice, and Vienna.

INSIGHT GUIDES
The world's largest collection of visual travel guides

CONTENTS

Getting Acquainted

The Place

Situation: New England's six states form the northeastern tip of the Us, bordering Canada to the north and the Atlantic Ocean to the East.
Language: Though English is the national language, some communities speak other tongues, including French (northern Maine), Portuguese (Gloucester, New Bedford and coastal towns), and Italian (Boston's North End). Many notices in the Boston area are printed in English, Portuguese, Spanish, Vietnamese and Cambodian.
Time Zone: New England is within the Eastern Time Zone, which is 1 hour ahead of Chicago and 3 hours ahead of California. On the last Sunday in April the clock is moved ahead 1 hour for Daylight Saving Time, and on the last Sunday in October it is moved back 1 hour to return to Standard Time.
Currency: US dollar.
Weights and Measures: US metric.
Electricity: most wall outlets have 110-volt, 60-cycle, alternating current. If you plan to use European-made electrical appliances, be sure to step down the voltage with a transformer and bring a plug adaptor as many sockets are two-pin.
International Dialing Code: 001 (*see page 333* for the codes for each of the six states)

Government

New England's six states are all politically separate, with their own senators and representatives in Congress. Each has an elected governor as well, however, and the New England Governors' Council meets regularly to deal with shared interests and conflicts. There are also twice-yearly town meetings, attended by the whole adult population, at which anyone can air their views, and the town's business and finances are decided.

Doing Business

Most offices are open Monday to Friday 9am–5pm. Many businesses have free 800 numbers (some in operation 24 hours a day), and virtually all use voice-mail or answering machines. Fax machines are also ubiquitous.

Climate

New England's climate is as varied as its landscape, with large variations from state to state and from season to season:
Massachusetts Pittsfield in the west has an average annual temperature of around 7.2°C (about 45°F), while Boston in the east is about 10.8°C (about 51.5°C) and Nantucket about 9.7°C (49.5°F).
Connecticut Winters are just below freezing, and summers are warm and humid. The average yearly temperature along the coast is 10.6°F (51°F), while in the northwest it is 7.2°C (45°F); for most of the rest of the state the yearly mean is 8.3–9.4°C (47–49°F).
Rhode Island Summer temperatures are moderated by proximity to the ocean, but winters are quite cold. Providence has an average January temperature of about -2°C (about 28°F) and an average July temperature of about 22°C (about 72°F); Block Island has a mean January temperature of about -1°C (about 31°F) and a mean July temperature of about 21°C (about 70°F).
Vermont There are considerable variations in temperature depending on proximity to the mountains (which have heavy snows).Saint Johnsbury, in the northeast, has an average January temperature of about -8.1°C (about 17.5°F) and an average July temperature of about 20.8°C (about 69.5°F); Rutland, in the central part of the state, has a mean January temperature of around -5.8°C (about 21.5°F) and a mean July temperature of around 20.8°C (about 69.5°F).
New Hampshire Concord has an average July temperature of about 21°C (around 70°F) and a mean January temperature of about -6°C (about 21°F); atop Mount Washington, on the other hand, the average July temperature is around 10°C (about 50°F) and the mean January temperature about -14°C (about 6°F). In April 1934, winds of 231 mph (372 kph) were recorded on the summit of Mount Washington.
Maine As it is on the coast, the state enjoys a maritime climate. Winter temperatures are much milder than those inland, and summer temperatures are cooler. In the north, however, it is extremely cold with a high snowfall. In 1925, Maine's lowest recorded temperature of -44.4°C (-48°F) was observed. The south is the warmest part of the state.

Public Holidays

During the holidays listed below, some or all state, local and federal agencies may be closed. Local banks and businesses may also close on the following days.
● **January 1:** New Year's Day
● **Third Monday in January:** Martin Luther King Jr. Day
● **Third Monday in February:** Presidents' Day, celebrating Lincoln's and Washington's birthdays
● **Third Monday in April:** Patriots' Day (Massachusetts only)
● **Last Monday in May:** Memorial Day
● **July 4:** Independence Day
● **First Monday in September:** Labor Day
● **Second Monday in October:** Columbus Day
● **November 11:** Veteran's Day
● **Fourth Thursday in November:** Thanksgiving
● **December 25:** Christmas Day

Planning the Trip

Passports and Visas

To enter the United States most foreign visitors need a passport (which should be valid for at least six months longer than their intended stay). You should also be able to provide evidence that you intend to leave the United States after your visit is over (usually in the form of a return or onward ticket).

Visa requirements

Most foreign nationals (except Canadians and Mexicans) also require a visa to visit the US.

Citizens of the UK, New Zealand, Japan and European Union nations do not need a visa, however, as long as they are staying for less than 90 days and have a round-trip or onward ticket. Before entering the US, they must sign a Non-Immigrant Visa Waiver form, declaring, among other things, that they are not seeking to work during their stay.

Anyone wishing to stay longer than 90 days must apply for a visa. This can be done by mail or by personal application to the US Embassy or Consulate nearest their home. Visa extensions can be obtained in the US from the United States Immigration and Naturalization Service offices.

HIV

Anyone who is HIV positive or has Aids must also obtain a visa (unless they are the spouse, partner or child of a US citizen or have a green card). Although being HIV-positive is not grounds for exclusion from the States, the US Immigration and Naturalization Service requires proof of your current state of health, medication and so on. Failure to provide correct information on the visa application is grounds for deportation.

Immunization requirements

Visitors from some countries need to supply proof of immunization against yellow fever and cholera.

Money Matters

Travelers' checks

Despite the small fee (generally one percent of the cash value), travelers' checks are the best way to bring money into New England, as they can be replaced if lost or stolen. These should be in US dollars, as other currencies may be difficult to exchange. Most hotels, restaurants and stores will cash them for you or accept them as payment without charging commission. Make sure you have plenty of small-denomination checks, though, as stores may not cash $100 checks.

Foreign currency

Visitors may encounter problems exchanging foreign currency. A large number of banks throughout New England offer a foreign-exchange service (don't forget to take your passport), but this is not universal.

Banks

Many banks have only one branch in each town. Most banks open around 10am and close between 3pm and 5pm on weekdays, and operate from 10am to 1pm on Saturday.

Banks generally have ATMs that dispense cash and accept most credit cards.

Credit cards

These are widely accepted. If you rent a car, you may have to leave your card as a deposit.

Health

INSURANCE

Most visitors to New England have no health problems during their stay: sunburn in summer is the main nuisance for the majority. Even so, you should never leave home without travel insurance to cover both yourself and your belongings. It's not cheap to get sick in the United States. Your own insurance company or travel agent can advise you on policies, but shop around as rates vary. Make sure you are covered for accidental death, emergency medical care, trip cancellation and baggage or document loss.

HAZARDS

Lyme disease (borne by deer ticks hiding in high grass) is a potentially

Tourist Information Abroad

There is no American Tourist Office in the UK, US or Australia. If you have a business or visa enquiry, information can be obtained from the US Embassies in each country:
Australia: 21 Moonah Place, Yarralumla, ACT 2600.
Tel: 6 270 5900.
UK: 5 Upper Grosvenor Street, London W1.
Tel: 020 7499 9000,
www.usembassy.org.uk

For holiday information, the tourist organisation Discover New England supplies a color brochure with sights, useful telephone numbers and accommodation, plus maps of each state.

UK: 133a St. Margaret's Road, Twickenham, Middlesex TW1 1RG.
Tel: 0906 558 8555
(calls cost £1 per minute, maximum £2)
Other countries:
P.O. Box 3809
Stowe, Vermont 05672, US
Tel: 802-253 2500
Fax: 802-253 9064
e-mail: DNE@together.net
www.discovernewengland.org

There is also a Massachusetts Office of Travel and Tourism in the UK at: Molasses House, Clove Hitch Quay, Plantation Wharf, York Place, London SW11 3TN.
Tel: 020 7978 7429.

life-threatening condition. Starting with a rash, it develops into flu-like symptoms and joint inflammation, and possible longterm complications like meningitis and heart failure. Even though it is statistically rare, precautions are in order. When hiking in grass or brush, wear light-colored pants tucked into socks, and spray the clothing with an insecticide. Inspect your skin afterwards: if a tick has attached itself, disinfect the area with alcohol and visit a doctor or clinic immediately. An undetected bite may result in a red-ringed rash; again, see a doctor. If you suffer any of the symptoms described after exposure to ticks, a doctor can prescribe antibiotics.

Poison ivy causes only temporary discomfort, but this can be avoided by keeping an eye out for the shiny three-leaf clusters and washing immediately upon accidental contact. Camomile lotion is good for soothing the skin.

Tapwater is perfectly safe to drink, but avoid stream water as it can cause serious intestinal problems.

What to Wear/Bring

Clothing styles in New England vary from state to state, as well as from region to region. In New Hampshire, Maine, Vermont and the Berkshires in Massachusetts people tend to dress in casual clothes geared towards outdoor life, whereas attire in most other New England cities in Massachusetts, Connecticut and Rhode Island is more traditional.

To cover all occasions, bring a

Customs

Visitors aged 21 or over may bring the following to the US:
● 1 liter of duty-free alcohol
● 200 duty-free cigarettes, or 2kg tobacco or 50 cigars
● Gifts worth $100 if non-US citizens or $400 if US citizens
● up to $10,000 in US or foreign cash, travelers' checks or so on; any more must be declared. Import of meat, seeds, plants, and fruit is forbidden.

variety of clothing from sportswear to formal attire. For men, a jacket and tie, although not necessarily a suit, is standard dress for more formal restaurants and may in fact be required; women have more latitude, in terms of pants versus dresses, but be warned that even youth-oriented bars and nightclubs may ban jeans.

Some warm clothing, such as sweaters, jackets, and windbreakers, should be packed even during the summer, when evening temperatures tend to dip, especially in the mountains and on the coast. Winters necessitate heavy outerwear, including hats, scarves, gloves, and boots.

Getting There

Flying is by far the easiest way to get to New England from abroad. If you come overland from elsewhere in the US, cars are the preferred mode of travel. Trains are less frequent than flights, and although buses connect most cities and several major towns, they are not much cheaper than a discount airfare – and substantially longer and less comfortable.

BY AIR

Most major US carriers service the New England states. A variety of discount fares and special deals are offered, so shop around.

Logan International Airport in Boston is the 15th-busiest airport in the world, and smaller airports – many of them served by Delta – are scattered throughout New England, near larger cities such as Hartford, Bangor, and Burlington.

Some 15 international airlines fly direct to New England. Alternatively, you can fly into New York and catch one of the many connecting flights to the New England area, or the hourly shuttle to Boston (no reservations required, tickets can be bought just before boarding). Boston's Airport has a bureau de change and hotel reservation desk (which charges no commission), plus car hire outlets.

During holidays *(see page 330)* it may be difficult to find a flight,

Tour Operators

The following companies specialise in tailormade New England itineraries:
In the UK
North America Travel Service
7 Albion Street
Leeds LS1 5ER
Tel: 0113 243 1606
Fax: 0113 243 0919
www.americatravelservice.com
In the US
CST **International**
22 Moon Penny Lane
Centerville, MA 02632
Tel: 508-771 1423/
800-966 9445
www.newenglandtours.com
Tourco
29 Bassett Lane
Hyannis, MA 02601
Tel: 800-537 5378
www.tourco.com

especially at Thanskgiving, when most of the US seems to be on the move and discount tickets are virtually non-existent.

BY LAND

Train
Amtrak (tel: 800-872 7245) offers efficient rail services to New England from Washington, DC, and New York, routing through Connecticut and Rhode Island and terminating in Boston; another route extends from New Haven, Connecticut, to Springfield, Massachusetts, to St Albans, Vermont. Various commuter trains serve smaller towns, and seasonal trains – such as the Vermonter from Boston to Brattleboro and on up to Burlington – cater for tourists.

Bus
Large air-conditioned buses connect New England to most other US tourist destinations *(see page 335)*.

Car
Driving is by far the best way of exploring and experiencing New England *(see page 335)*.

Practical Tips

Media

Newspapers

As well as the US nationals such as *USA Today*, the tabloid *National Enquirer*, and the financial *Wall Street Journal*, New England has three local newspapers. The *Boston Globe* is a highly regarded daily, the *Boston Herald* a tabloid daily, with listings on Thursday and Friday respectively, and *The Boston Phoenix* is Saturday-only paper. Foreign magazines and papers are sold on newsstands in the larger cities.

Television and radio

Flick through the channels on both TV and radio, and you'll experience the gamut of American life, from game show to in-depth news. Most hotels receive the three major national networks (ABC, CBS and NBC), several dozen channels, plus many cable networks. The Public Broadcasting System (PBS) has some of the better-quality imported programs. National Public Radio (NPR), at the low end of the FM scale, is a good all-round station.

Postal Services

There are post offices in most New England villages and towns. Opening hours vary between central big city branches and those in smaller places, but hotel personnel will be able to tell you when the nearest post office is open.

If you do not know where you will be staying in a particular town, you can receive mail simply by having it addressed to you, care of General Delivery, at the main office in that town – but you must pick up such mail personally (within 10 days). Check with postal officials about charges and the variety of mail-delivery services available.

Stamps may be purchased from vending machines installed in hotel lobbies, in shops and airports, and at bus and train stations.

To facilitate quick delivery within the States, include the five-digit zip code when addressing communications. Zip code information may be obtained from any post office.

Telecommunications

Telephone

Public telephones are to be found in hotel lobbies, restaurants, drugstores, street corners, garages, convenience stores, and other general locations. Long-distance call rates decrease after 5pm, going down still further after 11pm, and are lowest on weekends. Several countries can be dialed directly

Telephone Codes

Dial the following codes, preceded by 1, when phoning from a different state or area:
Connecticut (southwest) 203
Connecticut (elsewhere) 860
Maine 207
Massachussets (west/central) 413
Massachussets (east) 508
Massachussets (Boston area) 617
New Hampshire 603
Island 401
Vermont 802

from many areas in New England, without operator assistance. For all specific information concerning telephone rates and conveniences, simply call the local operator (0) and inquire.

All 800 and 888 numbers are toll free. For numbers to dial in an emergency, *see over the page.*

Email

Although email is used extensively within the US, there are still few public places within New England from where you can use it. You are far better off faxing messages.

Fax

All but the smallest of hotels and B&Bs offer access to a fax machine; there's generally a fee for outgoing faxes (often exorbitant), but incoming are usually free.

Tourist Information in New England

The following state tourist agencies provide ample information on attractions, restaurants, lodgings, recreational options, and events. They can also refer you to local chambers of commerce, if required.

Connecticut
505 Hudson Street
Hartford, CT 06106
Tel: 860-270 8080/
800-282 6863.
www.ctbound.org

Maine
State House Station 59
Augusta, ME 04333
Tel: 207-287 5711/888-624 6345
www.mainetourism.com

Massachusetts
10 Park Plaza, Suite 4510
Boston, MA 02116
Tel: 800-227 6277
www.mass.vacation.com

New Hampshire
Box 1856
Concord, NH 03302

Tel: 603-271 2666
www.visitnh.gov

Rhode Island
1 West Exchange Street
Providence
RI 02903
Tel: 401-222 2601
www.visitrhodeisland.com

Vermont
6 Baldwin Street
Montpelier, VT 05633
Tel: 802-828 3237
www.800-vermont.com

Alcohol

The legal age for both the purchase and consumption of alcoholic beverages is 21 throughout New England. Alcoholic beverages are sold by package in state liquor stores and by the drink or the bottle at licensed establishments in all the six states. On Sundays, however, no package sales are allowed and drinks are sold only at specified hours.

Often a restaurant without a liquor license will permit customers to bring their own beer or wine; then again, some communities have elected to remain "dry," and if they do, you must, too. If you are driving, keep bottles of alcohol unopened and out of sight in the car.

Medical Treatment

Pharmacies stock most standard medication (though some painkillers that are available over the counter in other countries may be prescriptions only in the US), and staff are trained to help with most minor ailments.
Hospitals are to be found in most New England cities, signposted on highways with a white H on a blue background. Major hospitals have 24-hour emergency rooms – you may have a long wait before you get to see the doctor, but the care and treatment are thorough and professional. Boston's hospitals are particularly highly regarded. **Walk-in clinics** are also commonplace in cities, where you can consult a nurse or doctor for a minor ailment without an appointment. If cost is a concern,

Taxes

Most of the states levy taxes on meals and accommodation, and some on all sales. When restaurants and hotels quote prices, these taxes are not normally included – so ask, as they can bump up the cost by 11 percent. Ticket prices for transport have the tax included.

Emergency Numbers

911 Most of New England is connected to the national emergency number (no money required). Operators hook you up to police, firefighters or medical services.
0 If 911 does not work, call the operator, who will connect you to the appropriate local emergency services.
Yellow Pages Another option, time permitting, is to turn to the inside front cover of a local telephone directory, which lists emergency numbers.

turn first to clinics offering free or pro-rated care (look under "Clinics" in the *Yellow Pages*).

Security and Crime

Most of New England is relaxed and crime free – and it is generally safe to walk the streets. Despite the picture presented in the movies, violence is not endemic. But it still pays to exercise caution.
● Keep a firm grip on bags. Don't sling them over the back of a chair.
● Whenever possible, travel with another person, especially at night.
● When not driving, lock your car and never leave valuables in view. At night, park in lighted areas. When returning to your car, have your keys ready before you reach it.
● Never leave your luggage unattended or out of view. Lock your hotel door when out, and never leave valuables in your room.
● Do not carry more cash than you need. Whenever possible, use credit cards and travelers' checks; be discreet when paying cash.

Gay Travelers

Boston has a very active and proactive gay presence, as do, to a lesser extent, other large cities and even rural towns in New England. Northampton, for instance, emerged as a lively enclave for lesbians in the late 20th century, and Provincetown has long been a

preferred gay summer vacation spot; the town even has a gay counterpart to the Chamber of Commerce: the Provincetown Business Guild (tel: 508-487 2313, 800-637 8696, www.ptown.org).

Information concerning gay-oriented activities and businesses (including gay-owned and operated inns throughout the region) can be found in the Boston-based newspaper *Bay Windows*, and in *One in Ten*, a supplement produced by the alternative weekly, the *Boston Phoenix*.

A good in-town networking source, for those visiting Boston, is the We Think the World of You bookstore at 540 Tremont Street (tel: 617-267 3010, books@wethinktheworldofyou.com).

Travelers with Disabilities

Federal regulations regarding handicapped accessibility have made some inroads, but the work is by no means complete. Larger facilities, especially those of recent vintage, should pose no problem. Many B&Bs, mindful of their elderly clientele, have also done adaptive retrofitting. If in doubt, call ahead.

Tipping

Tip generously or it will be interpreted as an insult – or tourist ignorance. For meals, hairdressers, bartenders, and taxi drivers, around 15 percent is the norm (or 20 percent for exceptional waiter service). Give a few dollars to the doorman, bellhop, and housekeeper.

Dates

The convention for writing dates in the US is to put the month first, so 2/12/2002 is 12 February 2002.

Smoking

Smoking is banned in most public places and on transport. Most restaurants have a no-smoking zone, some are non-smoking. Some hotels have non-smoking rooms.

Getting Around

Information

The best source of information for travelling around New England is the tourist board of each specific state, which may also be able to book tickets for you *(see page 333)*.

By Air

Internal flights are expensive, but if you want to hop from place to place by air, airlines serve the following New England towns and cities:
Massachusetts Boston, Hyannis, Martha's Vineyard, Nantucket, New Bedford, Worcester
Maine Bangor, Portland
Connecticut Bradley Airport (near Hartford), Bridgeport, Groton, New Haven
Vermont Burlington
New Hampshire Lebanon-Hanover, Manchester
Rhode Island Providence

AIRLINES

Major domestic airlines include:
Cape Air Tel: 800-352 0714)
Delta Tel: 800-221 1212
Northwest Airlines Tel: 800-225 2525
USAir Tel: 800-428 4322

By Bus

Most New England cities and tourist sights can be reached by bus. Greyhound has the most comprehensive coverage of the US, and the following companies operate local services:
Bonanza Tel: 800-556 3815. Based in Providence, RI, with connections to New York and Massachusetts, and several routes within Rhode Island.

C&J Trailways Tel: 800 258 7111. Services mainly Maine.
Concord Trailways Tel: 603-228 3300/800-639 3317. Services mainly New Hampshire and based in Concord.
Greyhound Tel: 617-526 1800/ 800-231 2222. The most extensive bus network, with offices in Boston, MA, and elsewhere, and long-distance routes throughout the US.
Peter Pan Tel: 800-237 8747. Based in Springfield MA.
Plymouth & Brockton Tel: 617-773 9401. Based in Boston, with routes mainly within Massachusetts and Connecticut.
Vermont Transit Lines Tel: 802-864 6811/800-451 3292. The main Vermont service, based in Burlington.

Some bus terminals are in "problem areas," so take care when traveling to and from stations.

By Train

The most extensive train service throughout New England is offered by Amtrak.
Amtrak Tel: 800-872 7245, www.amtrak.com.

Connecticut is served by Metro North, with trains between New York and New Haven.
Metro North Tel: 800-638 7646/ 212-532 4900.

Boston has a commuter line (MBTA) from North Station traveling north and west, with stops at Concord, Rockport, Gloucester, and Manchester.
MBTA Tel: 617-222 3200, www.mbta.com.

By Car

A car offers the most popular and convenient means of getting around New England. Although the network of airplanes, buses, trains, ferries, and taxis is reliable, having your own car is the easiest way to get around (except, perhaps, in the congested heart of Boston), and it also offers the greatest leeway for getting off the beaten path.
Highways A number of well-maintained interstate highways (ranging from four to eight or more

lanes) make covering New England's distances easy. To get an idea of the range, picture a radius from Boston to Burlington, in northwestern Vermont – a trip which, on Routes 93 and 89, would take only about five hours. That radius, extended across New England, would cover all but the northernmost regions of Maine (beyond Bangor).
Secondary roads Travel on secondary roads is time-consuming, but all the more scenic. However, beware of dirt roads – usually represented by a broken line – in mud season (typically, March into May). And note that mountain roads may be closed in winter.

CAR HIRE

Visitors wishing to rent or lease a car after arriving in New England will find offices of all the major US firms at airports (usually more expensive than elsewhere) and other locations convenient to tourists. Toll-free arrangements can be made in advance. The most reputable firms are:
Hertz Tel: 800-654 3131
Avis Tel: 800-331 1212
Budget Tel: 800-527 0700

It's also worth calling around, referring to the *Yellow Pages* (under "Automobile Renting & Leasing"), for the best rates. Sometimes local rental firms may offer low rates, especially for lower-quality cars (several franchise chains, such as Rent A Wreck, have sprung up to cater for just this market). But be sure to check insurance coverage provisions before signing anything.

The cheapest rates for hire tend to be from Thursday noon until Monday noon.

Legal requirements

Most car-rental agencies require drivers to be at least 21 years old (sometimes 25), to hold a major credit card and a driver's license that is current and has been valid for at least a year; some will accept a cash deposit, sometimes as high as $500, in lieu of a credit card.

Drink Driving

Regulations are very strict. If you fail a breath test after drinking, your license will be removed on the spot. Avoid drinking and driving and keep alcohol out of sight and unopened in the car.

Foreign travelers may need to produce an international driver's license or a license from their own country.

Insurance

Liability is not included in the terms of your lease, so advertised rates usually do not include additional fees for insurance. Collision Damage Waiver (CDW) is strongly recommended, as it covers you if someone else causes damage to your car.

RULES OF THE ROAD

In general, state laws apply to the New England driver. Each state has specific laws and regulations regarding parking, speed limits and the like; most are clearly posted.

Seatbelts

These are obligatory for all front-seat occupants. Children under six must be buckled into safety belts, safety seats, or a proper child restraint. Many rental firms supply child seats for a small extra cost.

Fuel

Petrol, or gas, is lead-free and stations are plentiful, with many open 24 hours a day. British travelers should note, however, that the US gallon is 17 percent smaller than the English equivalent.

Special considerations

Rotaries (roundabouts), especially in Boston, pose a particular challenge. The official rule is that the cars already in the circle have the right of way in exiting, but this rule is rarely observed in practice. It's best to proceed cautiously, whether entering or exiting. Unless

otherwise posted, a right-hand turn at a red light is permitted throughout New England. On sighting a school bus that has stopped to load or unload children, the driver must stop completely before reaching the bus and may not proceed until the warning signals on the school bus have been switched off, or until directed to do so.

Hitching and car-jacking

Hitchhiking is discouraged; so is picking up hitchhikers. Car-jackings are rare, but a growing threat. If you are planning to drive, learn what areas of cities to avoid before starting out. Ask your rental clerk when you arrive, or check with tourist offices before taking a drive.

Breakdown

Some highways have emergency phones every few miles. Otherwise, park up with your bonnet raised and a police patrol will soon arrive. The American Automobile Association (tel: 800-222 4357) offers reciprocal breakdown services for some affiliated firms in other countries.

Parking

You must park in the direction of traffic, and never by a fire hydrant. A yellow line or yellow curb means no parking is allowed. In some towns a white line along the curb shows where you can park.

Speed Limits

New England states maintain their interstate highway system in fine condition. Highway speed is generally limited to 55 mph (89 kph), although along some stretches in certain states – check the roadside signs – a maximum of 65 mph (105 kph) is permitted.

On interstates, you may find your fellow drivers will be cruising along at about 10 miles more per hour than the posted limit, on the presumption that such an offense is likely to get them no more than a warning. Join them at your own risk. Enforcement, if sporadic, can be strict, with high penalties.

Where to Stay

New England has an especially diverse set of accommodation alternatives. The options vary in terms of location, price, amenities, atmosphere, and orientation, and can be anything from low-budget B&Bs and youth hostels, through roadside motels, to full-service grand hotels such as Boston's Ritz Carlton. For details in each state, see *Where to Stay* sections below.

COUNTRY INNS

Perhaps the most uniquely New England lodging is the famed country inn. If you are tired of motels and hotels, and willing to forego certain conveniences (such as an in-room phone or TV) for more simple pleasures, country inns are a wonderful option. They range from weathered farmhouses, with huge fireplaces and relaxing music, to grand elegance. In the UK, New England Inns & Resorts specialises in country inns. Tel: 01923 821469; fax: 01923 827157.

B&BS

B&B accommodation is widespread. Companies specialising in B&Bs include: **Bed & Breakfast Agency of Boston** Tel: 0800 895 128.

HOLIDAY HOMES

UK firms specialising in renting out New England houses include: **Bridgewater's Holiday Homes** 217 Monton Road, Monton Manchester M30 9PN Tel: 0161 707 8547 Massachusetts, all year round.

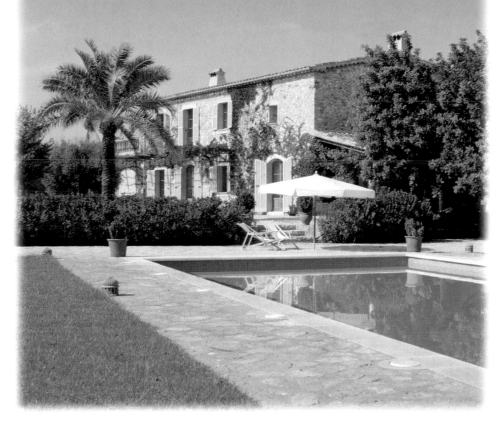

Holiday villas beyond indulgence.

BALEARICS ~ CARIBBEAN ~ FRANCE ~ GREECE ~ ITALY ~ MAURITIUS
MOROCCO ~ PORTUGAL ~ SCOTLAND ~ SPAIN

If you enjoy the really good things in life, we offer the highest quality holiday villas with the utmost privacy, style and true luxury. You'll find each with maid service and most have swimming pools.

For 18 years, we've gone to great lengths to select the very best villas at all of our locations around the world.

Contact us for a brochure on the destination of your choice and experience what most only dream of.

INTERNATIONAL
CHAPTERS

✕ INSIGHT GUIDES

The world's largest collection of visual travel guides

A range of guides and maps to meet every travel need

Insight Guides

This classic series gives you the complete picture of a destination through expert, well written and informative text and stunning photography. Each book is an ideal background information and travel planner, serves as an on-the-spot companion – and is a superb visual souvenir of a trip. Nearly 200 titles.

Insight Pocket Guides

focus on the best choices for places to see and things to do, picked by our local correspondents. They are ideal for visitors new to a destination. To help readers follow the routes easily, the books contain full-size pull-out maps. 120 titles.

Insight Maps

are designed to complement the guides. They provide full mapping of major cities, regions and countries, and their laminated finish makes them easy to fold and gives them durability. 60 titles.

Insight Compact Guides

are convenient, comprehensive reference books, modestly priced. The text, photographs and maps are all carefully cross-referenced, making the books ideal for on-the-spot use when in a destination. 120 titles.

Different travellers have different needs. Since 1970, Insight Guides has been meeting these needs with a range of practical and stimulating guidebooks and maps

Four Seasons in New England
Truendle Crockenell
Exeter EX6 6NB
Tel: 01647 24726
Houses and inns in all states.
New England Connection
PO Box 218, Dorking RH5 6YZ
Tel: 01306 877600
Vermont, New Hampshire and
Massachusetts. All year round.
New England Country Homes
Bignor , Pulborough RH20 1QD
Tel: 01798 869461
All states all year round.
North American Vacation Homes
86 Turners Mill Road
Haywards Heath RH16 1NJ
Tel: 01444 450034
Houses in Massachusetts, New
Hampshire, Maine and Vermont.
From April to October only.

Hotel Chains

Among the large chains that have
hotels throughout the New
England states are:
Best Western Tel: 800-528 1234;
www.bestwestern.com
Comfort Inn Tel: 800-424 6423;
www.comforthotels.com
Days Inn Tel: 800-325 2525;
www.daysinn.com
Choice Hotels Tel: 800-424 4777
Hilton Tel: 800-445 8667;
www.hilton.com
Holiday Inn Tel: 800-465 4329;
www.basshotels.com
Howard Johnson
Tel: 800-654 2000;
www.hojo.com
Hyatt Regency Tel: 800-233 1234;
www.hyatt.com
Marriott Tel: 800-872 9563;
www.marriott.com
Quality Inn Tel: 800-228 5151;
www.qualityinn.com
Radisson Tel: 800 333–3333
www.radisson.com
Ramada Tel: 800 272–6232
www.ramada.com
Red Roof Inn Tel: 800 843–7663
www.redroof.com
Sheraton Tel: 800 325–3535
www.sheraton.com
Super 8 Tel: 800-800-8000;
www.super8.com
Susse Chalet Tel: 800-524 2538

Where to Eat

"Land of the bean and the cod"
New England's culinary standing
made a stratospheric leap during
the late 1980s and 1990s. Once
bemoaned as the land of "the bean
and the cod", Boston started the
region's culinary renaissance rolling
with a group of world-class chefs
who trained their sous-chefs so well
that their ranks kept expanding.
Where once the highest quality you
could expect was provincial and
stodgy, now the offerings are fresh,
flavorful and sophisticated.

New England's chefs have not
only come up with brilliant new uses
and combinations for the area's
renowned bounty (especially
seafood), they've developed their
own network for securing new native
delicacies, from farmstead cheeses
to locally raised game birds.

Traditional fare revisited

If you've never tried the classics,
by all means try them. These range
from thick, wholesome soups, to
seafood specialties including lobster
bisque and shad roe, to old-timers
such as boiled dinner (a hotpot of
boiled beef, cabbage, carrots and
potatoes), to wicked desserts
including Indian pudding (a cornmeal
bake flavoured with milk, molasses,
ginger, cinammon and raisins), and
Boston cream pie (custard-filled
sponge cake covered in chocolate).
For regional traditions see the
Where to Eat section for each state.

But be prepared for some
surprises. New England's ingenious
cooks – from executive chefs at the
four-star hotels to the hardworking
chef/owners at country inns – are
having a year-round field day with
seasonal specialties, and lucky
customers are in for an ever-
changing array of treats.

Entertainment

New England offers a wide range of
entertainment. Rural areas tend to
be more slow-paced and relaxed
during the evening, while Boston
supports a varied, exciting nightlife.
Boston outgrew its staid image long
ago. At night, the city sparkles with
lively and sophisticated activity.
The Boston Symphony Orchestra
has earned an international
reputation; its less formal offshoot,
the Boston Pops, also commands a
great following.
Music permeates the region,
ranging from rural chamber groups
to big-city rock and jazz. Comedy
clubs are also increasingly popular.
Theater thrives not only in Boston
and New Haven (proving grounds for
Broadway) but in myriad regional
repertory companies and "straw-
hat" summer theaters.
Dance Professional modern dance
and ballet can be seen in bucolic
settings, as well as in towns. The
larger cities have dance clubs
where it's easy to meet and mingle.
Listings For more specific
information, check the listings in
local papers – especially alternative
ones, such as *Phoenix* (various
editions cover Boston, Providence,
and Worcester), *Advocate* (Pioneer
Valley), and *Vanguard* (Burlington,
Vermont). See also *Nightlife* and
Culture for each state, below.

Special Events

State tourist boards will gladly
provide detailed lists of seasonal
festivals, fairs, and other annual
events large and small – from
teddy-bears' picnics to antique car
rallies. Many are so appealing it
makes sense to plan a trip around
them – or at the very least commit
yourself to a detour.

Shopping

New England provides as great range of shopping as can be found anywhere in the country: large department stores, local country auctions, antique shows, craft stores and bargain factory outlets. Whether you want bargains or works of art, the six states have much to offer.

ANTIQUES

Antiques stores abound and antiquing in these shops can be fun and, depending on the level of the stock, relatively inexpensive.

HANDICRAFTS

US handicrafts are experiencing a renaissance. There are more quality craft items being produced now than at any time since the Industrial Revolution. Crafts, whether pottery, weaving, or woodworking, are less expensive and higher quality when bought directly from the artisans, at their studios or juried crafts fair.

FACTORY OUTLETS

Discount and "factory outlet" stores are increasingly popular in this area.

Filene's Basement The world-famous store in Boston (with dozens of branches throughout the country) initiated off-price retailing in 1908. The original store, at the corner of Winter and Summer Streets, is still a wild, lucrative place to shop: you might find a designer original reduced to a fraction of its original price.

L.L. Bean The famous store in Freeport, Maine, specializes in outdoor wear and gear.

Children

New England is a veritable paradise for children. They can be kept entertained with amusements as simple as observing a tide pool, or take in history at such "hands-on" and accesible living museums as Plimoth Plantation or Old Sturbridge Village. Staff members at these sites are skilled at engaging children's interests.

Boston

Boston's Children's Museum is one of the most appealing museums in the country, and smaller facilities with similar agendas are scattered through the surrounding countryside. Other Boston attractions sure to thrill little ones include the Computer Museum (next-door to the Children's Museum, on Museum Wharf) and the nearby New England Aquarium, the Swan Boats in the Public Garden.

Bernice Chesler's excellent book, *In and Out of Boston with (or without) Children* can provide leads on lesser-known but equally rewarding attractions.

Outdoor Activities

Whatever your age and whatever the season, New England offers plenty of active outdoor adventures. From urban walking to thrill-a-minute rafting, from downhill skiing to mountain biking, from fly fishing to gliding a canoe through the salt marshes, New England is an outdoor playground. Within each state are recommendations for outfitters who will help you enjoy the outdoors more fully.

Seaside attractions

Cape Cod might as well be a giant sandbox, and the calm, shallow waters on the bay side offer optimal swimming and splashing for those still acquiring their sea legs.

Children's reaction to the many whalewatching excursions offered on the Cape and along the coast up into Maine is invariably "Awesome!"

Resorts

A number of resorts – most notably Smuggler's Notch in northern Vermont – have made a specialty of catering for kids and the parents they hold in thrall. In summer, this ski area basically becomes a camp for all ages, with waterslides, special outdoors events, and a real sense of camaraderie.

Some of New England's family-oriented resorts, such as The Balsams, in remote northern New Hampshire, date back to around 1900 or earlier, and are attracting a fifth generation for mannered meals and unstructured enjoyment of the great outdoors.

Accommodations

Regrettably, many of New England's fussier B&Bs shun the company of children (though such discrimination is arguably illegal). If you're blessed with particularly well behaved youngsters, you might try pushing the envelope, but then again, it's no fun to go where you're not welcome. Fortunately, there are plenty of inns where their presence is not only tolerated but actively courted.

If in doubt, call ahead or check the detailed listings in *Best Places to Stay in New England*, by Kimberly Grant and Christina Tree.

Restaurants

The fancier restaurants may also exercise their own unpublished strictures regarding children – claiming, for instance, that the place is booked solid when you can see plainly that it's half-empty. Here, the best solution is a reservation. On the other hand, you may enjoy an equally pleasant and educational repast at a ramshackle lobster pound or a nostalgic diner.

Massachusetts

The Place

Known as: The Bay State.
Motto: *Ense Petit Placidam Sub Libertate Quietem* (By the sword we seek peace, but peace only under liberty).
Origin of name: May derive from an Algonquian Indian village meaning "place of big hills".
Entered Union: 6 February 1788, the sixth of the 13 original states.
Capital: Boston.
Area: 10,555 sq. miles (27,337 sq. km).
Highest point: Mount Greylock.
Population: 6 million.
Population density: 570 people per sq. mile (220 per sq. km).
Economy: Financial services; high technology; healthcare; academe.
Annual visitors: 33 million.
National representation: 2 senators and 10 representatives to Congress.
Famous citizens: Samuel Adams, Louisa May Alcott, Emily Dickinson, Ralph Waldo Emerson, John Hancock, Nathaniel Hawthorne, Oliver Wendell Holmes, Edgar Allen Poe, Henry David Thoreau.

Getting Around Boston

Boston is the only New England city with a subway system (the MBTA, or "T" for short); the cost is low (especially compared to other cities), the transit rapid, and the experience is on the whole fairly pleasant.

The Boston Passport, offering one, three or seven days of unlimited rides, can be purchased at the Boston Common Visitor Information Center at 147 Tremont St, tel: 617-426 3115. Alternatively, contact the MBTA on 617-222 5568 (www.mbta.com), for further information.

The Association for Public Transportation advocacy group publishes an excellent and comprehensive low-cost guide called *Car-Free in Boston*, available at newsstands and bookstores; it actually covers, in lesser detail, all of New England.

Where to Stay

BOSTON

Boston Harbor Hotel
70 Rowes Wharf, 02110
Tel: 617-439 7000/
800-752 7077
Fax: 617-330 9450
www.bhh.com
With 230 rooms, this is a modern beauty with old-world charm, perched on the harbor. **$$$$**

Bostonian Hotel
Faneuil Hall Marketplace, 02109
Tel: 617-523 3600/
800-343 0922
www.millennium-hotels.com
A mix of modern and historic, overlooking Quincy Market with 201 rooms. **$$$$**

Copley Square Hotel
47 Huntington Avenue, 02116
Tel: 617-536 9000/
800-225 7062
Fax: 617-267 3547
www.copleysquarehotel.com
Older, centrally located, European-style hotel with 143 rooms; often more affordable than neighboring hotels. **$$$$**

Eliot Hotel
370 Commonwealth Avenue, 02215
Tel: 617 267 1607/800-443 5468
Fax: 617-536 9114
www.eliothotel.com
Well-appointed hotel whose 95 rooms are all suites with a popular first-class restaurant. Convenient for both Back Bay and the Fenway. **$$$$**

Fairmont Copley Plaza Hotel
138 James Avenue, 02116
Tel: 617-267 5300/
800-795 3906
Fax: 617-247 6681
www.fairmont.com
A 1912 grand hotel with 379 rooms, 54 suites, and plenty of romance. **$$$$**

Four Seasons
200 Boylston Street, 02116
Tel: 617-338 4400/
800-332 3442
Fax: 617-423 0154
www.fourseasons.com
The standard-setter for luxury and service. The hotel has 274 rooms and overlooks the Public Garden. **$$$$**

Price Categories

A very approximate guide to current room rates for a standard double per night is:
$$$$ = over $200
$$$ = $150–200
$$ = $100–150
$ = under $100

Hotel Meridien
250 Franklin Street, 02110
Tel: 617-451 1900/
800-543 4300
Fax: 617-423 2844
www.lemeridien-hotels.com
A modern hotel with 314 rooms built atop a Renaissance Revival 1922 bank. Fabulous French service. **$$$$**

Lenox Hotel
710 Boylston Street, 02116
Tel: 617-536 5300/
800-225 7676
Fax: 617-236 0351
www.lenoxhotel.com
A 212-room hotel well situated for shopping, with Copley Place and Newbury Street on either side. **$$$$**

Omni Parker House
60 School Street, 02108
Tel: 617-227 8600
800-843 6664
Fax: 617-742 5729
www.omni.hotels.com
Hawthorne, Whittier, Emerson and Longfellow conducted literary salons at this grand 551-room hotel soon after it opened in 1854. **$$$$**

Boston B&Bs

B&B Agency of Boston
47 Commercial Wharf, 02110
Tel: 617-720 3540/
800-248 9262.
From UK free on 0800-895 128
Fax: 617-523 5761
www.boston-bnbagency.com
This is the largest B&B agency in
Boston, with rooms and self-
catering apartments in Beacon
Hill, Back Bay, North End, and
near the waterfront.

Ritz-Carlton Hotel
15 Arlington Street, 02117
Tel: 617-536 5700/
800-241 3333
Fax: 617-536 1335
www.ritzcarlton.com
Classic Bostonian white-glove
elegance, with the lovely Public
Garden at its doorstep and a total
of 275 rooms. **$$$$**
Boston Park Plaza Hotel
64 Arlington Street, 02116
Tel: 617-426 2000/
800 225-2008
Fax: 617-423 1708
A huge hotel with 950 rooms at the
hub of the Hub. **$$$–$$$$**
Gryphon House
9 Bay State Road, 02215
Tel: 617-375 9003/
877-375 9003
Fax: 617-425 0716
www.gryphonhouseboston.com
Near Kenmore Square and Boston
University, this bowfront brownstone
has been converted to a small
luxury hotel with just eight rooms.
Voice mail, fax machines, two
phone lines, CD players, and other
high-tech amenities draw business
travelers and technology junkies.
$$$–$$$$
Swissôtel Boston
1 Avenue de Lafayette, 02111
Tel: 617-451 2600/
800-621 9200
Fax: 617-451 2198
www.swissotel.com
Around 500 rooms offering modern
luxury in a convenient location for
the financial and theater districts.
Also good for the Common.
$$$–$$$$

Tremont House
275 Tremont Street, 02116
Tel: 617-426 1400/800-331 9998
www.wyndham.com
Offers 322 nicely refurbished rooms
in the thick of the theater district.
$$$–$$$$
Harborside Inn
185 State Street, 02109
Tel: 617-723 7500
Fax: 617-670 6015
www.hagopianhotels.com
A renovated mercantile warehouse
near Faneuil Hall, the financial
district, and the waterfront. All 54
modern rooms have exposed brick
and Victorian-style furnishings.
$$–$$$$
Mid-Town Hotel
220 Huntington Avenue, 02115
Tel: 617-262 1000/
800-343 1177
Fax: 617-262 8739
www.midtownhotel.com
One of Boston's better deals, a
motel-style building with 159 rooms
and an outdoor pool, near the
Prudential building and the
Christian Science Center. **$$–$$$$**
82 Chandler Street
82 Chandler Street, 02116
Tel: 617-482 0408/888-482 0408
Fax: 617-482 0659
www.channel1.com/82chandler
A five-room B&B in a 19th-century
brownstone with bay windows and
fireplaces in the revitalized South
End neighborhood. Credit cards not
accepted. **$$–$$$**
John Jeffries House
14 David G. Mugar Way, 02114
Tel: 617-367 1866
Fax 617-742 0313
Red-brick inn at the foot of Beacon
Hill. The 46 rooms are small and
simply appointed, but many have
kitchens or sitting areas. **$$–$$$**

Sightseeing in Boston

Guided Tours
You can hop on and off a tram-
style wooden bus for a sightseeing
tour of the historic parts of the
city and most of the Freedom Trail.
Start your tour at any stop, buy
tickets on the bus and get on and
off wherever you wish.

Newbury Guest House
261 Newbury Street, 02116
Tel: 617-437 7666/800-437 7668
Fax: 617-670 6100
www.newburyguesthouse.com
A trio of 1882 townhouses
converted into a well-appointed
Victorian-style inn right on the
"street of dreams". With a total of
32 rooms, this guest house offers
excellent value for the location, so
book far in advance. **$$–$$$**

Brookline
Bertram Inn
92 Sewall Avenue, 02446
Tel: 617-566 2234/
800-295 3822
www.bertraminn.com
Comfortably elegant Victorian
mansion with a grand staircase and
14 rooms. Situated on a quiet
street, it is convenient for the
Green Line MBTA trolleys that go to
downtown Boston. **$$$–$$$$**

Cambridge
The Charles Hotel
1 Bennett Street, 02138
Tel: 617-864 1200
800-882 1818
Fax: 617-864 5715
www.charleshotel.com
A modern hotel with 293 rooms
right in Harvard Square, with airy,
traditional-style rooms, some
overlooking the river. Home to the
popular Regattabar jazz club, which
draws nationally known jazz
performers. **$$$$**
The Inn at Harvard
1201 Massachusetts Avenue,
02138
Tel: 617-491-2222/
800-458 5886
Fax: 617-491 6520
www.innatharvard.com

Boat Cruises
Without doubt the most colorful
way of doing Boston is onboard a
Duck, or renovated World War II
amphibious landing vehicle. The
tours (with commentary) start in
the back bay area and include a
mini-cruise on the Charles River.

Price Categories

A very approximate guide to current room rates for a standard double per night is:
$$$$ = over $200
$$$ = $150–200
$$ = $100–150
$ = under $100

Graham Gund designed this intimate four-story inn encircling a peaceful atrium (113 rooms). $$$$
University Park Hotel at MIT
20 Sidney Street (off Massachusetts Avenue), 02139
Tel: 617-577-0200
Fax: 617-494-8366
www.univparkhotel.com
Business-class hotel (opened in 1998) between Central and Kendall Squares. Occasional quirky decorating touches in the 210 rooms, such as armoires with circuit-board inlays, play up the hotel's location near the Massachusetts Institute of Technology campus. $$$$
A Cambridge House B&B
2218 Massachusetts Ave, 02140
Tel: 617-491 6300/800-232-9989
Fax: 617-868 2848
www.acambridgehouse.com
B&B with 16 rooms in a quiet, lavishly restored 1892 Victorian house with carved cherry paneling and immense fireplaces in the common areas. Located about one mile (1½ km) north of Harvard Square, but only four blocks from a subway stop. $$–$$$$
Mary Prentiss Inn
6 Prentiss Street, 02140
Tel: 617-661 2929
Fax: 617-661 5989
www.maryprentissinn.com
Tastefully appointed Greek Revival B&B with a spacious deck. Some of the 20 rooms have antique armoires and four-poster beds. Situated between Harvard and Porter Squares. $$–$$$$
Irving House
24 Irving Street (off Cambridge Street), 02138
Tel: 617-547 4600/
800-854 8249
Fax: 617-576 2814

www.irvinghouse.com
Basic but comfortable 44-room B&B. Just a short walk from Harvard Square. $$$

BOSTON DAY TRIPS

Concord
Colonial Inn
48 Monument Square, 01742
Tel: 978-369 9200/800-370 9200
Fax: 978-369 2170
www.concordscolonialinn.com
A 1716 inn on Concord's town common with 56 rooms. $$
Hawthorne Inn
462 Lexington Road, 01742
Tel: 978 369–5610
www.concordmass.com
B&B with seven rooms in the historic district, opposite Hawthorne's Wayside. $$
Longfellow's Wayside Inn
Wayside Inn Road
South Sudbury, 01776
Tel: 978-443 1776/
800-339 1776
Fax: 978-443 8041
www.wayside.org
A mid-18th-century tavern with 10 rooms, close to Lexington and Concord. $$

Fall River
Lizzie Borden Bed and Breakfast
92 2nd Street, 02721
Tel: 508-675 7333
Fax: 508-673 1545
www.lizzie-borden.com
This B&B is the house where the infamous Lizzie Borden allegedly hacked her father and stepmother to death in 1892. The eight rooms in the 1845 Greek Revival-style home are small but feature Borden family memorabilia. $$$

Gloucester
Bass Rocks Ocean Inn
107 Atlantic Road, 01930
Tel: 978-283 7600/
800-528 1234
Fax: 978-281 6489
www.bestwestern.com/
bassrocksoceaninn
A 48-room motel looking straight out to sea. $$

Harborview Inn
71 Western Avenue, 01930
Tel: 978-283 2277/
800-299 6696
Fax: 978-282 7397
harborviewinn@amcp.net
A comfortable house-turned-B&B near the Fishermen Memorial statue. Some of the six rooms have ocean views. $–$$

Marblehead
Spray Cliff on the Ocean
25 Spray Avenue, 01945
Tel: 781-631 6789/
800-626 1530
Fax: 781-639 4563
www.spraycliff.com
A 1919 Tudor-style mansion turned B&B with seven rooms. Lovely situation near the beach. $$$$
Harbor Light Inn
58 Washington Street, 01945
Tel: 781-631 2186
Fax: 781-631 2216
www.harborlightinn.com
A formally decorated inn, built around an 18th-century house with a 19th-century addition. Decor in the 21 rooms ranges from traditional to contemporary. $$–$$$$

New Bedford
Days Inn
500 Hathaway Road, 02740
Tel: 509-997 1231/
800-329 7466
Fax: 508-991 5095
www.daysinn.com
A full-service chain hotel with 153 rooms. $$–$$$

Newburyport
Clark Currier Inn
45 Green Street, 01950
Tel: 978-465-8363

Hotel Meal Guide

B&Bs supply a complimentary full breakfast and are often quite sophisticated
MAP (Modified American Plan) rates include both breakfast and dinner
FAP (Full American Plan) supply all three meals

www.clarkcurrierinn.com
A dignified, three-story 1803
shipbuilder's home in the Federal
mode. Many of the eight rooms
feature wide-board floors, pencil-
post beds and other antique
furnishings. **$$$$**
Windsor House
38 Federal Street, 01950
Tel: 978-462-3778/
888-873 5296
Fax: 978-465 3443
www.bbhost.com/windsorhouse
B&B in a 1786 house with a British
bent (four rooms). **$$$**
Morrill Place Inn
209 High Street, 01950
Tel: 978-462 2808/
888-594 4667
Fax: 978-462 9966
A Federalist mansion, converted
into a lavishly decorated B&B with
nine rooms. **$–$$**

Plymouth
John Carver Inn
25 Summer Street, 02360
Tel: 508-746 7100/
800-274 1620
Fax: 508-746 8299
www.johncarverinn.com
An immaculate modern hotel, with
85 rooms near the sights. **$$–$$$$**
Whitfield House
26 North Street, 02360
Tel: 508-746 5289/
800-884 2889
www.whitfieldhouse.com
B&B in a charming 1782 home with
antique furnishings in the three
rooms. **$–$$$**
Governor Bradford Motor Inn
98 Water Street, 02360
Tel: 508-746 6200/800-332 1620
Fax: 508-747 3032
www.governorbradford.com
A motel with 94 rooms right on the
historic (and heavily trafficked)
harbor. **$–$$**

Rockport
Seaward Inn
44 Marmion Way, 01966
Tel: 978-546-3471/
800-648-7733
Fax: 978-546 7661
www.seawardinn.com
A welcoming summer house-turned-
B&B on a beautifully landscaped

seaside ledge. There are 38 rooms
available in the main inn building,
two nearby houses, and adjacent
cottages. **$$$–$$$$**
Yankee Clipper Inn
127 Granite Street, 01966
Tel: 978-546 3407/800-545 3699
Fax: 978-546 9730
www.yankeeclipperinn.com
A total of 16 rooms in three
buildings: a Georgian mansion
(where John and Jackie Kennedy
once stayed) on an ocean
promontory, an 1840 neo-classical-
style house across the street
designed by Charles Bulfinch, plus
a modern waterside building with
large picture windows. Facilities
include a heated saltwater pool.
$$$–$$$$
Eden Pines Inn
48 Eden Road, 01966
Tel: 978-546-2505
www.rockportusa.com/edenpinesinn
A cliffside mansion with dramatic
ocean views. Seven large bedrooms,
many with private balconies.
Continental breakfast. **$$$**
Addison Choate Inn
49 Broadway, 01966
Tel: 978-546 7543/
800-245 7543
Fax: 978-546 7638
www.cape-ann.com/addison-choate
Lovely summery decor and a quiet
in-town setting for an inn with six
rooms and two apartments.
$$–$$$
Seacrest Manor
99 Marmion Way, 01966
Tel: 978-546 2211
www.seacrestmanor.com
A 1911 clapboard mansion that is
now a quiet, comfortable B&B with
seven rooms, well-tended gardens,
sea views, some private decks. **$$**

Massachusetts Trivia

● Commercial electricity was
pioneered in the US in Great
Barrington, Massachusetts,
when inventor William Stanley
installed street lights in 1886.
● US currency is printed on paper
manufactured by the Crane
company at Waconah Mill
in Dalton.

Linden Tree Inn
26 King Street, 01966
Tel: 978-546-2494/800-865-2122
www.linden-tree.com
A captain's home with 18 well-
priced B&B rooms and an innkeeper
who loves to bake. **$–$$**
Sally Webster Inn
34 Mount Pleasant Street, 01966
Tel: 978-546 9251/
877-546 9251
www.sallywebster.com
Small antiques-filled town inn.
Several of the seven rooms have
wide-board pine floors, (non-
working) brick fireplaces, or canopy
beds. **$–$$**

Salem
Hawthorne Hotel
18 Washington Square West
01970
Tel: 978-744-4080/
800-729 7829
Fax: 978-745 9842
www.hawthornehotel.com
A 1920s hotel with 89 rooms and
harbor views from the top floors.
$$–$$$$
Amelia Payson Guest House
16 Winter Street, 01970
Tel: 978-744 8304
www.ameliapaysonhouse.com
1845 Greek Revival B&B with four
bright, airy rooms. Convenient for
the museums and sites. **$$**

CAPE COD AND THE ISLANDS

Barnstable
Charles Hinckley House
8 Scudder Lane, 02630
Tel: 508-362 9924
Fax: 508-362 8861
A B&B with four period rooms in
an 1809 Federal house. Lavish
breakfasts. **$$**
Crocker Tavern Bed and Breakfast
3095 Main Street (Route 6A)
02630
Tel: 800-773 5359
Fax: 508-362 5562
A tastefully renovated 1754 B&B.
The five rooms are furnished with
canopy or four-poster beds and also
have quilts, claw-foot tubs, and
antique sinks. **$–$$**

Brewster

Captain Freeman Inn
15 Breakwater Road, 02631
Tel: 508-896 7481/
800-843 4664.
Fax: 508-896-5618
www.captainfreemaninn.com
A luxurious 1866 Victorian B&B with
14 spacious rooms (some with
whirlpool tubs) and an outdoor pool.
Healthy yet decadent breakfasts.
$$–$$$$

Bramble Inn
2019 Route 6A, 02631
Tel: 508-896 7644
Fax: 508-896 9332
www.brambleinn.com
Two houses (1792–1861) offering
seven rooms with distinctive decor.
$$–$$$

Old Sea Pines Inn
2553 Route 6A, 02631
Tel: 508-896 6114
Fax: 508-896 7387
www.oldseapinesinn.com
A 1907 Shingle-style mansion that
once served as a girls' boarding
school. There are 24 rooms, and
the modern annex is wheelchair
accessible. **$–$$**

Chatham

Captain's House Inn of Chatham
371 Old Harbor Road, 02633
Tel: 508-945 0127/
800-315 0728
Fax: 508-945 0866
www.captainshouseinn.com
The 16 B&B rooms have luxurious
traditional decor; silver-service tea
is served in the garden room, as
are full breakfasts. **$$$$**

Chatham Bars Inn
297 Shore Road, 02633
Tel: 508-945 0096/800-527 4884
Fax: 508 945-5491
www.chathambarsinn.com
A 1914 private hunting lodge-turned-
grand hotel. The private Atlantic
beach has resort activities. **$$$$**

Wequassett Inn
Pleasant Bay, 02663
Tel: 508-432 5400/800-352 7169
Fax: 508-432 1915
www.wequassett.com
This inn has 104 rooms, in a
country club-style setting. There are
facilities for tennis, a pool and a bay
beach. **$$$$**

Pleasant Bay Village Resort Motel
1191 Route 28, 02633
Tel: 508-945 1133/
800-547 1011
Fax: 508-945 9701
www.pleasantbayvillage.com
A complex of 58 rooms with
elaborate gardens. Not your
average motel. **$$$–$$$$**

Dennis area

Lighthouse Inn
1 Lighthouse Road
West Dennis, 02670
Tel: 508-398 2244
Fax: 508-398 5658
www.lighthouseinn.com
An old-fashioned seaside resort
B&B with 68 rooms on a private
beach comprising cottages and a
1855 lighthouse-turned-inn. There
are supervised activities for
children during July and August.
$$$–$$$$

Isaiah Hall B&B Inn
152 Whig Street, Dennis, 02638
Tel: 508-385 9928/
800-736 0160
Tax: 508-385 5879
www.isaiahhallinn.com
Stars from the Cape Playhouse
favor this lovely 1857 farmhouse,
with its 10 rooms furnished with
country antiques, on a residential
street. **$$–$$$**

Beach House Inn
61 Uncle Stephen's Way
West Dennis, 02670
Tel: 508-398 4575
www.innsandlodging.com/
beachhouseinn
This gray shingled house right on
the beach is simply furnished with
practical oak and wicker pieces.
There are 7 bright and airy rooms.
No credit cards. **$–$$$**

Eastham

Whalewalk Inn
220 Bridge Road, 02642
Tel: 508-225 0617
This B&B in an 1830s Greek
Revival captain's house has 10
luxurious rooms decorated with
breezy panache. Gourmet
breakfasts are served, and there
are cottages, too. **$$–$$$**

Over Look Inn
3085 Route 6, 02642

Price Categories

A very approximate guide to
current room rates for a standard
double per night is:
$$$$ = over $200
$$$ = $150–200
$$ = $100–150
$ = under $100

Tel: 508-225 1886
Scottish hospitality in a colorful
1869 Victorian 11-room B&B near
the Salt Pond Visitors Center. **$$**

East Orleans

Nauset House Inn
143 Beach Road, 02643
Tel: 508-255 2195
Fax: 508-240 6276
www.nausethouseinn.com
A convivial 1810 farmhouse B&B
with 14 rooms and stylish 1900s
conservatory. Good situation near
the magnificent Nauset Beach. **$$**

Edgartown

Charlotte Inn
27 S Summer Street, 02539
Tel: 508-627 4751
Fax: 508-627 4652
An exquisite country inn
encompassing five buildings (from
18th century to new) and a total of
25 rooms, all romantically
decorated in various styles. **$$$$**

Harbor View Hotel
131 N Water Street, 02539
Tel: 508-627 4333/
800-225 6005
A lavishly renovated 1891 shingled
grand hotel, with 124 rooms and a
heated pool, near Lighthouse
Beach. **$$$$**

Colonial Inn
38 N Water Street, 02539
Tel: 508-627 4711/
800-627 4701
Fax: 508 627 5904
www.colonialinnmvy.com
Nicely updated and centrally
located, this shingled 1911 hotel
has 43 rooms. **$$$–$$$$**

Point Way Inn
104 Main Street, 02539
Tel: 508-627 8633/
888-711 6633
Fax: 508-627 3338

www.pointway.com
B&B with 15 rooms in a renovated, now-contemporary, 1840 Federal sea captain's house. **$$$–$$$$**

Falmouth Area
Inn at West Falmouth
Off Blacksmith Shop Road
West Falmouth 02574
Tel: 508-540 6503
Fax: 508-540 9977
www.innatwestfalmouth.com
Six rooms in a luxuriously renovated 1898 Shingle-style summer house with tennis court, small heated pool, and views of Buzzards Bay.
$$$–$$$$
Mostly Hall
27 Main Street
Falmouth, 02540
Tel: 508-548 3786/
800-682 0565
Fax: 508-457 5778
www.mostlyhall.com
This six-room B&B is an 1849 plantation-style mansion. It was built by a seafarer to please a homesick wife, and has large, handsome, high-ceilinged rooms, and friendly, knowledgeable hosts.
$$$–$$$$
Inn on the Sound
313 Grand Avenue South
Falmouth Heights 02540
Tel: 508-457 9666/
800-564 9668
Fax: 508-457 9631
www.innonthesound.com
A B&B in an 1880 shingled cottage on a bluff overlooking Vineyard Sound. A large porch offers great water views, as do four of the 10 rooms with private decks. **$$**

Harwichport area
Augustus Snow House
528 Main Street
Harwichport, 02646
Tel: 508-430 0528/

800-320 0528
Fax: 508-432 6638
www.augustussnow.com
Victorian splendor in a five-room B&B in a 1901 Queen Anne mansion near the Sound.
$$$–$$$$
Beach House Inn
4 Braddock Lane, 02646
Tel: 508-432-4444/
800-870 4405
Fax: 508-432 9152
www.winsteadinn.com
Four rooms with all the comforts of home including air-conditioning, color TV and much more. Great location, right on the beach.
$$$–$$$$
Commodore Inn
30 Earle Road, West Harwich, 02671
Tel: 508-432 1180/
800-368 1180
Fax: 508-432 3263
www.commodoreinn.com
A seaside motel with 27 rooms, only yards from the sandy beaches and warm waters of Nantucket Sound. Pretty country decor. **$$**

Hyannis
Inn on Sea Street
358 Sea Street, 02601
Tel: 508-775 8030
Fax: 508-771 0878
www.innonseastreet.com
A B&B with nine rooms in a cheerful inn, made up of two 19th-century houses. It's great value and is only a short stroll from downtown Hyannis and the beach. **$–$$**

Menemsha
Menemsha Inn and Cottages
off North Rd, 02552
Tel: 508-645 2521
Fax: 508-645 9500
www.menemshainn.com
Peaceful simplicity in 27 rooms and

National Parks

An extensive selection of accommodation is available in and around America's National Parks. For details of where to stay in the Freedom Trail area in Boston and Maine's National Park, contact:
The National Park Service
Public Inquiry
Department of the Interior
18th and C Streets NW
Washington, DC 20013
Tel: 800-365 2267

cottages, on 10 green acres with water views. **$$$**

Nantucket
The Wauwinet
120 Wauwinet Road
Wauwinet, 02584
Tel: 508-228 0145/508-228 6712/800-426 8718
www.wauwinet.com
A fabulously refurbished 1850 hotel with 30 rooms. Luxurious, secluded, and expensive. **$$$$**
Jared Coffin House
29 Broad Street, 02554
Tel: 508-228 2400/
800-248 2405
Fax: 508-325 7752
www.jaredcoffinhouse.com
Grand 1845 mansion with 60 rooms and several adjoining buildings make up this popular island inn. **$$$**
Martin House Inn
61 Centre Street, 02554
Tel: 508-228 0678
www.nantucket.net/lodging/martinn
Reasonably priced, this 13-room 1803 mariner's home is one of the prettiest and most congenial of the many historic B&Bs in town. **$–$$**

Oak Bluffs
The Oak House
Seaview Avenue, 02557
Tel: 508-693 4187/
800-245 5979
Fax: 508-696 7385
www.vineyardinns.com
A lavish, oak-filled Queen Anne B&B with 10 rooms overlooking Nantucket Sound. **$$$–$$$$**

Stay in a Lighthouse

Lighthouses are dotted along the whole New England coast, a memorial to the area's maritime past. A few of these are now B&Bs, and at some of them you can get a taste of how life was as a lighthouse keeper – complete with record-keeping jobs. For details contact:
New England Lighthouse Foundation, PO Box 1690, Wells, Maine 04090. Tel: 800-758 1444.

Provincetown

Beachfront White Sands Motel
Shore Road, PO Box 611 02657
Tel: 508-487 0244
www.provincetownlodging.com
Beachfront and poolside rooms with kitchen units, private beach, heated indoor and outdoor pool, spa, and sauna. **$$$**

Best Inn
698 Commercial Street, 02657
Tel: 508-487 1711
www.capeinn.com
Motel in the East End a mile from town center with comfortable rooms and ample parking. Some rooms have harbor views. **$$–$$$**

White Horse Inn
500 Commercial Street, 02657
Tel: 508-487 1790
Twelve rooms and six apartments in an 18th-century captain's house inn shaped by Provincetown's 20th-century artistic history. **$–$$**

Captain Lysander Inn (B&B)
96 Commercial Street, 02657.
Tel: 508-487 2253
An 1850s captain's house in the sedate West End (13 rooms). **$**

Sandwich

Dan'l Webster Inn
149 Main Street, 02563.
Tel: 508-888 s3622/
800-444 3566
Fax: 508-888 5156
A large 53-room luxury hotel on the site of a historic tavern. **$$–$$$**

Inn at Sandwich Center
118 Tupper Road, 02563
Tel: 508-888 6958/800-249 6949
Fax: 508-888 2746
www.innatsandwich.com
A 1750s saltbox, with five bright bedrooms decorated with Laura Ashley bedding. **$$**

Wingscorton Farm (B&B)
11 Wing Boulevard, 02537
Tel: 508-888 0534
Fax: 508-888 0545
A working farm with four rooms for B&B located about five minute's walk from the beach. The 1763 main house with original paneled bedrooms was once a stop on the Underground Railroad. **$$**

Summer House
158 Main Street, 02563.
Tel: 508-888 4991/

800-241 3609
An 1835 Greek Revival house with large, airy bedrooms. Most of the five rooms in this B&B have working fireplaces. **$**

Village Inn at Sandwich
4 Jarves Street, 02563
Tel: 508-833 0363/
800-922 9989
Fax: 508-833 2063
www.capecodinn.com
An 1837 Federal home converted into a B&B with eight rooms decorated in a spare, fresh style. **$**

Vineyard Haven

Martha's Place
114 Main Street
Tel: 508-693 0253
www.marthasplace.com
Handsome 1840 Greek Revival B&B with six immaculately designed and spacious bedrooms. **$$$–$$$$**

West Tisbury

Lambert's Cove Country Inn
Lambert's Cove Road, 02575
Tel: 508-693 2298
Fax: 508-693 7890
www.lambertscoveinn.com
A 15-room 1790s farmhouse on seven pastoral acres with an English garden. **$$$–$$$$**

Woods Hole

Woods Hole Passage
186 Woods Hole Road, 02540
Tel: 508-548 9575/
800-790 8976
Fax: 508-540 4771
A 1890s carriage house and barn converted into a romantic B&B with five room. "Breakfast in a bag" for early risers. **$$**

Yarmouth Port

Wedgewood Inn
Route 6A, 02675
Tel: 508-362 5157
An imposing 1812 Federal home, with six bedrooms that are at once formal and romantic. **$$**

Lane's End Cottage
268 Route 6A, 02675
Tel: 508-362 5298
A 300-year-old full Cape in a quiet wooded setting with three bedrooms for B&B. **$**

CENTRAL MASSACHUSETTS

Amherst

The Lord Jeffery Inn
30 Boltwood Avenue, 01002
Tel: 413-253 2576/
800-742-0358
Fax: 413-256 6152
www.lordjefferyinn.com
A traditionalist Colonial Revival-style inn with 48 rooms. Situated on the town green, near the Amherst College campus. **$–$$$**

The Allen House
599 Main Street, 01002
Tel: 413-253 5000
www.allenhouse.com
Meticulously restored inn of the Aesthetic period, blending Victoriana with Japanese influences. Seven B&B bedrooms. **$–$$**

Deerfield

Deerfield Inn
81 Old Main Street, 01342
Tel: 413-774 5587/
800-926 3865
Fax: 413-775 7221
www.deerfieldinn.com
A traditional inn surrounded by historic houses. The 23 large rooms are furnished with antiques and period reproductions. **$$$–$$$$**

Greenfield

Brandt House
29 Highland Avenue, 01301
Tel: 413-774 3329/
800-235 3329
Fax: 413 772 2908
www.brandt-house.com
An 1890s Victorian B&B with nine comfortable, simply decorated rooms and huge porches. Facilities include a tennis court. **$$–$$$**

Price Categories

A very approximate guide to current room rates for a standard double per night is:
$$$$ = over $200
$$$ = $150–200
$$ = $100–150
$ = under $100

Hadley
Clark Tavern Inn
98 Bay Road, 01035
Tel: 413-586 1900
Colonial tavern, originally built in
the 1740s and later transformed
into a romantically appointed B&B.
Amenities in the three bedrooms
include canopy beds, working
fireplaces, and guest refrigerators
in the sitting room stocked with
complementary snacks. The tavern
has spacious gardens and a
swimming pool. **$$**

Northampton
The Inn at Northampton
One Atwood Drive, 01060
Tel: 413-586 1211/
800-582 2929
Fax: 413-586 0630
www.thhg.com
On the edge of town, this place has
124 well-appointed motel rooms.
There are indoor and outdoor pools,
tennis courts, a restaurant, and a
whirlpool spa. **$$–$$$**

Youth Hostels

American Youth Hostels
733 15th Street, Suite 840,
Washington, DC 20005
Tel: 202-783 6161
Fax: 202-783 6171
This organisation can supply a
list of youth hostels in New
England. The group's publication
Hostelling North America is
available in bookstores.

Northfield
Centennial House
Main Street, 01360
Tel: 413-498 5921
www.thecentennialhouse.com
Handsome 1811 Colonial home in
the center of town with five
antiques-filled guest rooms (three
with private bath) and a third floor
suite that sleeps up to four people.
Extensive landscaped grounds. **$$**

Sturbridge
Publick House Historic Resort
The Common, 01566
Tel: 508-347 3313/
800-782 5425

Fax: 508-347 5073
A cluster of historic houses, plus a
modern motel-style annex offering
125 rooms in all. Good situation
near Old Sturbridge Village. **$$–$$$**

Worcester
The Beechwood Hotel
363 Plantation Street, 01605
Tel: 508-754 5789
Fax: 508-754 0731
www.beechwoodhotel.com
A handsome new 73-room hotel
overlooking the lake. **$$**

THE BERKSHIRES

Great Barrrington
Windflower Inn
684 S. Egremont Road, 01230
Tel: 413-528 2720/
800-992-1993
Fax: 413-528 5147
www.windflowerinn.com.
A B&B in an early 20th-century
country estate with gardens and a
pool. The 13 rooms have four-
poster beds and are decorated with
antiques; some have fireplaces.
$$–$$$$

Lenox
Apple Tree Inn
10 Richmond Mountain Road
01240
Tel: 413-637 1477
Fax: 413-637 2528
www.apple-tree.com
A 22-acre hilltop estate with heated
pool, within earshot of Tanglewood;
some 32 motel units **$$$$**
Blantyre
16 Blantyre Road (off Route 20)
01240
Tel: 413-637 3556
Fax: 413-637 4282
www.blantyre.com
An opulent mock-Tudor castle on
100 manicured acres with a heated
pool, sauna, tennis courts, and
croquet lawns. The sky-high prices
help ensure luxury and impeccable
service in this 23-room hotel. **$$$$**
Canyon Ranch
Bellefontaine
165 Kemble Street, 01240
Tel: 413-637 4100/
800-742 9000

Camping

New England has many
campsites. Government-run sites
(open mid-May to October) are
fairly spartan with flush toilets
and hot showers (at extra cost).
Private campsites (mainly for
RVs) have shops and snack bars
and offer extensive recreation
facilities, incuding playgrounds,
swimming pools and even mini-
golf courses. Book well in
advance in July and August, and
weekends.

Fax: 413-637 3659
www.canyonranch.com
New England's most elaborate
spa occupies an 1890s buildings
modeled on Versailles's Petit
Trianon. 120 rooms. **$$$$**
Cliffwood Inn
25 Cliffwood Street, 01240
Tel: 413-637 3330/
800-789 3331
Fax: 413-637 0221
www.cliffwood.com
An antiques-filled 1890 colonial
mansion with seven bedrooms and
an outdoor swimming pool on a
quiet residential street. **$$$–$$$$**
Rookwood Inn
11 Old Stockbridge Road, 01240
Tel: 413-637-9750/
800-223-9750
Fax: 413-637 1352
www.rookwoodinn.com
An 1885 "painted lady" B&B at the
center of town. Comfortably elegant
Victorian furnishings in the 20
rooms, creative modern breakfasts.
$$$–$$$$
Gables Inn
81 Walker Street, 01240
Tel: 413-637 3416/
800-382 9401

Price Categories

A very approximate guide to
current room rates for a standard
double per night is:
$$$$ = over $200
$$$ = $150–200
$$ = $100–150
$ = under $100

Fax: 413-637 3416
www.gableslenox.com
Edith Wharton stayed at this lavish Victorian mansion while her own home was built, and the 19th-century antiques evoke Wharton's time. The 18-room B&B now has modern amenities including an indoor pool and tennis court. **$$–$$$$**
The Village Inn
16 Church Street, 01240
Tel: 413-637 0020/
800-253 0917
Fax: 413-637 2196
A 1771 inn, with 31 comfortably furnished rooms. **$$–$$$$**
Garden Gables
135 Main Street, 01240
Tel: 413-637 0193
www.lenoxinn.com
Country charm in this 18-room B&B in a 1780s house. One of Lenox's better deals. **$–$$$$**
Walker House
64 Walker Street, 01240
Tel: 413-637 1271/
800-235 3098
Fax: 413-637 2387
www.walkerhouse.com
This B&B with eight rooms is a cultural mecca. Private recitals. **$$$**

New Marlbourough
Old Inn on the Green & Gedney Farm
Village Green (Route 57)
01230
Tel: 413-229 3131/
800-286 3139
www.oldinn.com
Fifteen antique-furnished rooms in a c.1760 stagecoach inn, plus luxury suites in a former Normandy-style cow barn. **$$$–$$$$**

Sheffield
Birch Hill B&B
254 S Undermountain Road
(Route 41), 01257
Tel: 413-229 2143/
800-359 3969
www.birchhillbb.com
Casual, sprawling, simply furnished country inn with pool, set in 20 acres. Seven rooms with fireplaces. Full breakfast. **$$$**
Staveleigh House
59 Main Street, 01257

Tel: 413-229 2129
A B&B with seven rooms in an 1821 parson's home. Spacious grounds beside the Housatonic. **$$**

Stockbridge area
Red Lion Inn
30 Main Street
Stockbridge, 01262
Tel: 413-298 5545/
Fax: 413-298 5130
www.redlioninn.com
A classic old inn (est. 1773) at the center of a Norman Rockwell town. Many guest rooms in the main inn are quite small; accommodations in the adjacent buildings offer a little more space. A total of 111 rooms. **$$–$$$$**
Merrell Tavern Inn
1565 Pleasant Street (Route 102)
South Lee/Stockbridge, 01260
Tel: 413-243 1794/
800-243 1794
Fax: 413-243 2669
www.Merrell-Inn.com
A ten-room B&B in an authentically restored 1794 stagecoach tavern, in a rural riverside setting. **$$–$$$**
Williamsville Inn
Route 41
West Stockbridge, 01266
Tel: 413-274 6118/
800-457 3971
Fax: 413-274 3539
www.williamsvilleinn.com.
A 16-room B&B in a restored 1790s farmhouse and barn on landscaped grounds. Summer sculpture garden. **$$–$$$**

Williamstown
The Orchards
222 Adams Road (Route 2)
01267

Tel: 413-458 9611/
800-225 1517
Fax: 413-458 3273
www.orchardshotel.com
A modern hotel with antique appointments in its 49 rooms. This is a peaceful, elegant oasis despite its location on an unappealing commercial strip of Route 2. **$$$–$$$$**
Field Farm Guest House
554 Sloan Road (off Route 43), 01267
Tel/fax: 413-458 3135
www.thetrustees.org
This 1948 American Modern mansion B&B set in over 250 acres of conservation land has five large rooms with modern furnishings and views of the grounds or the hills. Outdoor amenities include a pool, tennis courts, pond (with fishing poles available), and trails for hiking or cross-country skiing. **$$–$$$**
River Bend Farm
643 Simonds Road, 01267
Tel: 413-458 3121
A painstakingly restored 1770 colonial house. Furnishings are simple, even rustic, as befits the colonial period in this four-room B&B. No credit cards. **$**
Steep Acres Farm
520 White Oaks Road, 01267
Tel: 413-458 3774
A four-room B&B on a 50-acre hilltop, with orchards and animals. **$**

Where to Eat

BOSTON

Ambrosia on Huntington
116 Huntington Avenue
Tel: 617-247 2400

Restaurant Guidelines

Prices are approximate, but for a three-course meal for one (excluding beverages, tax, and tip), the following guidelines may prove helpful:
$$$$ = over $40
$$$ = $28–40
$$ = $15–28
$ = under $15
Meal tax varies from state to

state, but it is customary to tip 15 to 20 percent on the pre-tax total.
Credit cards The more expensive establishments generally accept credit cards, but call ahead to check just in case.
Reservations Most restaurants, except for the clearly casual, appreciate reservations (some require them).

Bold new American cuisine in a dramatic windowed dining room. Decide whether the patrons or plates are dressed more fancifully? Near the Prudential Center. **$$$$**

Aujourd'hui
Four Seasons Hotel
200 Boylston Street
Tel: 617-451 1392
The decor is corporate-opulent, the cuisine invariably artful. The best power tables overlook the Public Garden. **$$$$**

La Bettola
480A Columbus Avenue
Tel: 617-236 5252
Rene Michelena creates Italian-inspired wonders with Asian sensibilities in an unpretentious South End storefront. **$$$$**

Biba
272 Boylston Street
Tel: 617-426 7878
Even after more than a decade, there's no place trendier; owner-chef Lydia Shire is Boston's most resplendent culinary diva. The food may sometimes cross into weirdness, but it's always exciting, and it's served in one of Boston's most intriguingly decorated dining rooms. **$$$$**

Clio
Eliot Hotel
370A Commonwealth Avenue
Tel: 617-536 7200
Creative food but not excessively trendy in a polished spot for business or a night out. **$$$$**

L'Espalier
30 Gloucester Street
Tel: 617-262 3023
This ultra-elegant, ultra-romantic, ultra-expensive Victorian townhouse stays two steps ahead of the

culinary cutting edge with its *prix-fixe* French-inspired menu. One of Boston's most popular spots for marriage proposals. **$$$$**

Julien
Hotel Meridien
250 Franklin Street
Tel: 617-451 1900
First-class French cuisine, amid the marble grandeur of the former Federal Reserve Building. **$$$$**

Mistral
223 Columbus Avenue
Tel: 617-867 9300
One of Boston's hippest dining spots. The New American food, while stylish, is not always as creatively turned out as the dining room and the crowd. Dress up and have fun, nonetheless. **$$$$**

Rowes Wharf Restaurant
Boston Harbor Hotel
70 Rowes Wharf
Tel: 617-439 3995
Superb harbor views and superior regional cuisine. **$$$$**

Galleria Italiana
177 Tremont Street
Tel: 617-423 2092
Sublime modern Italian, including innovative seafood preparations and fresh pastas with inspired sauces, opposite Boston Common. The small, almost spare room, is jammed pre-theater. **$$$–$$$$**

Hamersley's Bistro
553 Tremont Street
Tel: 617-423 2700
This pioneer on the now-hopping South End restaurant row remains the standard for other eateries to match. Deft and imaginative touches dress up this excellent, sophisticated comfort food. **$$$–$$$$**

Pignoli
79 Park Plaza
Tel: 617-338 7500
A stylish Back Bay haunt for imaginative Italian/Mediterranean creations. Owned by Lydia Shire of Biba fame. **$$$–$$$$**

Sonsie
327 Newbury Street
Tel: 617-351 2500
A trendsetter's cafe, with exotic fare. Also a good spot for a light breakfast. **$$$–$$$$**

Aquitaine
569 Tremont Street
Tel: 617-424 8577
A happening French bistro and wine bar (although the "bar" is the size of a postage stamp) in the trendy South End restaurant district. **$$$**

Hampshire House
84 Beacon Street
Tel: 617-227 9600
Unparalleled jazz brunch with a view of the Public Garden. Above the bar made famous in TV's *Cheers*. **$$$**

Lala Rokh
97 Mount Vernon Street
Tel: 617-720 5511
Refined Persian cuisine in an intimate, romantically appointed Beacon Hill townhouse. The staff are happy to explain the intriguing, comforting dishes. **$$$**

Legal Sea Foods
Boston Park Plaza Hotel
64 Arlington Street
Tel: 617-426 4444
The freshest of fish, served the moment it's done. Other Legal branches are located in the Prudential Center, Copley Place, and across the river in Cambridge's Kendall Square. **$$$**

Locke-Ober
3 Winter Place
Tel: 617-542 1340
Brahmin (in other words, somewhat boring) cuisine in an atmospheric 1894 landmark. **$$$**

Ristorante Toscano
41 Charles Street
Tel: 617-723 4090.
True Tuscan delicacies in a handsome upscale trattoria on Beacon Hill. **$$$**

The Ritz Dining Room
Ritz-Carlton Hotel, 15 Arlington St
Tel: 617-536 5700

Restaurant Guidelines

Prices are approximate, but for a three-course meal for one (excluding beverages, tax, and tip), the following guidelines may prove helpful:
$$$$ = over $40
$$$ = $28–40
$$ = $15–28
$ = under $15
Meal tax varies from state to

state, but it is customary to tip 15 to 20 percent on the pre-tax total.
Credit cards The more expensive establishments generally accept credit cards, but call ahead to check just in case.
Reservations Most restaurants, except for the clearly casual, appreciate reservations (some require them).

The menu choices may be stuffy, but this is still the spot for Brahmin-watching. **$$$**

Sage
69 Prince Street
Tel: 617-248 8814
Hidden away on a North End side street, this tiny storefront, where there is barely any room to walk, blends warm service and New Italian cuisine. **$$$**

Skipjack's
199 Clarendon St
Tel: 617-536 3500
Native seafood with a modernist bent in the shadow of the massive John Hancock tower. **$$$**

Tremont 647
647 Tremont Street
Tel: 617-266 4600
Adventurous American "melting pot" cuisine in a hip South End dining spot. Wear black. **$$$**

29 Newbury St
29 Newbury St
Tel: 617-536 0290
A perennially popular bistro, with a strategic sidewalk cafe for assessing the passing fashion parade. **$$$**

Cottonwood Café
222 Berkeley Street
Tel: 617-247 2225
Upscale Tex-Max fare served in a trendy setting, with dishes such as deep-fried jalapenos with shrimp and cheese. Note that you can request "not too *caliente*" if you prefer. **$$–$$$**

Artu
6 Prince Street
Tel: 617-742 4336
Friendly, bustling trattoria in the North End. Offers very good value for fresh pastas, roasted vegetables, and updated Italian classics. **$$**

The Daily Catch
323 Hanover Street
Tel: 617-523 8567
Superb calamari and other seafood in the North End. The room is tiny and always jammed, so be prepared to wait. **$$**

Durgin Park
Faneuil Hall Marketplace
Tel: 617-227 2038
Cheap New England classics (chowder, pot roast, baked beans),

A Meal with a View

Look out over Boston's night lights when you dine on the 52nd floor at the Top of the Hub restaurant. You could also try the the 33rd floor at 30 State Street.

Top of the Hub
Prudential Center, Back Bay
Tel: 617-536-1775
Great seafood and delicious Sunday brunches.

with good-natured insults thrown in free. **$$**

East Ocean Seafood
25 Beach Street
Tel: 617-542 2504
Fresh-from-the-tanks Hong Kong-style seafood served in a low-key Chinatown eatery. **$$**

Ginza Japanese Restaurant
16 Hudson Street
Tel: 617-338 2261
One of Boston's best sushi spots, tucked away in Chinatown. The unusual *maki* rolls are particularly tasty. **$$**

Sakura-bana
57 Broad Street
Tel: 617-542 4311
Unparalleled sushi in the financial district. **$$**

Barking Crab
88 Sleeper Street, at Northern Avenue
Tel: 617-426 2722
Seaside clam shack transported to the city. Fried clams and other simple seafood with great harbor and city vistas. **$**

Commonwealth Brewing Co
138 Portland Street
Tel: 617-523 8383
The pub grub is hearty, the home brew alluring. **$**

Golden Palace
14 Tyler Street
Tel: 617-423 4565
Skip ordinary dinners here and come for dim sum on weekend mornings. Watch what others are eating in this loud, jam-packed room and point at the passing food carts. **$**

Sultan's Kitchen
72 Broad Street
Tel: 617-728 2828

A popular downtown take-out shop (with a few upstairs tables) serving fresh Turkish/Middle Eastern shish kebabs, salads, and the Greek sweet *baklava*. **$**

Cambridge

Chez Henri
1 Shepard Street (off Mass Avenue)
Tel: 617-354 8980
Modern French fare with a Cuban accent in a snug bistro north of Harvard Square. The spinach salad fired up with spicy duck *tamale* is destined to become a classic. **$$$–$$$$**

Rialto
Charles Hotel
I Bennett Street
Tel: 617-864 1200
Restaurateur Michela Larson and chef Jody Adams have earned international accolades for their flavorful Mediterranean cuisine. Cool, elegant dining room. **$$$–$$$$**

East Coast Grill
1271 Cambridge Street
(Inman Square)
Tel: 617-491 6568
A stylish, wildly popular spot – and deservedly so – for innovative grilled seafood (often topped with exotic spice rubs or fruit salsas), creative salads, barbecue and fiery "pasta from hell". Margaritas help ease the often long waits for a table. **$$$**

Harvest
44 Brattle Street
Tel: 617-492 1115
Recently refurbished, it remains one of Harvard Square's most reliably innovative bistros, with a civilized bar. **$$$**

Salamander
1 Athenaeum Street (off First Street)
Tel: 617-225 2121
Chef Stan Frankenthaler is a rising star in Boston's culinary firmament for his bold, sure hand and international inspiration. His inventive fusion cuisine lights up East Cambridge. **$$$**

Atasca
279A Broadway at Columbia Street
Tel: 617-354 4355
Way off the beaten path (between Central and Inman Squares), this

tiny storefront brings a satisfying taste of Portugal to Cambridge. **$$–$$$**

Casablanca
40 Brattle Street
Tel: 617-876 0999
Turkish/Moroccan menu within reach of student budgets. Go just for David Omar White's murals of the movie, but the comfortable bar is a fine spot for appetizers and drinks, too. **$$**

Green Street Grill
280 Green Street
Tel: 617-876 1655
A drab bar in a marginal neighborhood serves hyper-spicy Islands food (especially grilled fish), often with lively jazz accompaniment. **$$**

House of Blues
96 Winthrop Street
Tel: 617-491 2583
Southern to international fare, with musical accompaniment. In Harvard Square. **$$**

John Harvard's Brew House
33 Dunster Street
Tel: 617-868 3585
Surprisingly refined pub grub, and made-on-the-premises beers. In Harvard Square. **$$**

Rhythm and Spice
315 Massachusetts Avenue
Tel: 617-497 0977
A taste of the Caribbean near MIT. Jerk chicken, curried goat, and reggae music. **$$**

Fraser's
1680 Massachusetts Avenue
Tel: 617-441 5566
A comfortable neighborhood café between Harvard and Porter Squares serving interesting salads, sandwiches, and pastas. Good selection of microbrews. **$–$$**

Algiers Cafe
40 Brattle Street
Tel: 617-492 1557
Serves Turkish coffee and tabbouleh to the intelligentsia in Harvard Square. **$**

Charlestown
Olives
10 City Square
Tel: 617-242 1999
Avid patrons put up with long lines and often-deafening hubbub to

savor Todd English's first-class Tuscan country cuisine. **$$$$**

Figs
67 Main Street
Tel: 617-242-2229
Olives' pizza-parlor cousin, still upscale and only slightly less mobbed. **$–$$**

Somerville
Dali
415 Washington Street (at Beacon Street)
Tel: 617-6613254
Robust Spanish specialties (try the signature fish baked in salt) and particularly fine tapas in a lively atmosphere worthy of Hemingway. On the Cambridge/Somerville line. **$$–$$$**

eat
253 Washington Street
Tel: 617-776 2889
Creative comfort food – roast chicken, grilled fish with intriguing sauces – in a homey Union Square storefront. **$$**

Redbone's
55 Chester Street (off Elm Street)
Tel: 617-628 2200
The place to go when you're hungry for massive plates of barbecued ribs. A loud and rowdy Davis Square dive with an extensive beer list and valet parking for bicycles! **$–$$**

The Burren
247 Elm Street
Tel: 617-776 6896
Comfortable Davis Square Irish pub draws locals, yuppies and students. Stop in for a Guiness or some fish and chips. **$**

BOSTON DAY TRIPS

Concord
Aigo Bistro
84 Thoreau Street
Tel: 978-371 1333
Sophisticated if suburban Provencale. **$$$**

Colonial Inn
48 Monument Square
Tel: 978-369 2000
A 1716 inn serving traditional New England fare as well as afternoon tea. **$$–$$$**

Boston Ice Cream

Toscanini's Ice Cream
899 Main Street
Tel: 617-491 5877
In ice cream-crazy Boston, this is the Mecca. As well as excellent versions of the basics, it serves many more unusual flavors such as mango, green tea and ginger. The flagship store (which often hosts small art exhibits) is just off Massachusetts Avenue between Central and Kendall Squares. Another (smaller) location is on Mass Ave in Harvard Square. **$**

Walden Grille
24 Walden Street
Tel: 978-371 2233
Contemporary cuisine in an old brick firehouse. **$$–$$$**

Essex
Woodman's
The Causeway
Tel: 978-768 6451
Home of the original fried clam, invented in 1915. **$**

Fall River
Estoril
1577 Pleasant Street
Tel: 508-677 1200
A white-tablecloth introduction to classic Portuguese fare. **$$**

Tabacaria Açoriana Restaurant
408 S Main Street
Tel: 508-673 5890
A casual Portuguese cafe downtown. **$**

Gloucester
White Rainbow
65 Main Street
Tel: 978-281 0017
Rich, evolved Continental-style food served in a dramatic granite-walled hideaway. **$$$**

Passports
110 Main Street
Tel: 978-281 3680
Foods from around the world are on offer here, including fresh fish dishes from the Adriatic, sushi from Japan, and creative pastas from across Italy. Closed Sunday. **$$–$$$**

Evie's Rudder
73 Rocky Neck
Tel: 978-283 7967
A rollicking tavern in the Rocky Neck artists' colony. **$$**

Lexington
Dabin
10 Muzzey Street
(Off Mass Avenue)
Tel: 781-860 0171
Traditional Japanese and Korean fare in a peaceful shelter from the bustle of Lexington Center. A small patio for outdoor dining in warm weather. **$$**
Lemon Grass
1710 Massachusetts Avenue
Tel: 781-862 3530
A low-key Thai storefront café where the food is tempered for American palates. **$–$$**

Lowell
La Boniche
143 Merrimack Street
Tel: 978-458 9473
An intimate restaurant in a landmark Art Noveau building serving creative French fare. **$$–$$$**
The Olympia
453 Market Street
Tel: 978-452 8092
A friendly, family-run Greek restaurant. **$–$$**

Marblehead
The Landing
81 Front Street
Tel: 781-631 1878
The food – New England seafood standards – may not be terribly exciting, but the view of Marblehead Harbor is quite lovely. **$$–$$$**

Maddie's Sail Loft
15 State Street
Tel: 781-631 9824
Standard fried or broiled seafood in a lively, often-crowded casual room. Located between Front and Washington streets. **$$**

New Bedford
Antonio's
Coggeshalle and N Front streets
Tel: 508-992 7359
Enormous portions of Portuguese classics that draw crowds to this nondescript dining room. Situated near the intersection of Routes 95 and 18. **$$**
Davy's Locker
1480 E Rodney French Boulevard.
Tel: 508-992 7359
Traditional seafood preparations, since 1962, right on the harbor near the Martha's Vineyard ferry docks. **$$**

Newburyport
David's
Garrison Inn
11 Brown Square
Tel: 978-462 8077
Formal dining room emphasizing seafood in classic and updated preparations, with a more casual tavern downstairs. Offers childcare and dinner for kids while parents dine. **$$$**
Scandia
25 State Street
Tel: 978-462 6271
This is a small and intimate, candlelit dining room serving fine New American cuisine with the emphasis on seafood. **$$$**
Glenn's Restaurant
Merrimack Street

Tel: 978-465 3811
Glenn's offers creative cuisine in a former shoe factory. **$$**

Plymouth
Cafe Nanina
14 Union Street
Tel: 508-747 4503
Italian country cuisine. The deck looks out on the *Mayflower II*. **$$$**
Lobster Hut
on the Town Wharf
Tel: 508-746 2270
Basic fried seafood on the waterfront. **$**

Rockport
Note that although Rockport is a "dry" town, you are welcome to bring your own wine to the majority of restaurants.

The Glass Verandah
Yankee Clipper Inn
96 Granite Street
Tel: 978-546 3407
Studied and satisfying New American cuisine in a formal setting with ocean views. **$$$–$$$$**
Portside Chowder House
Bearskin Neck
Tel: 978-546 7045
A basic seafood hole-in-the-wall located in the heart of Rockport's tourist bustle. Specializes in chowder, but serves up sandwiches, burgers, and seafood plates, too. **$**

Salem
Grapevine
26 Congress Street
Tel: 978-745 9335
A peaceful, elegant spot for northern Italian fare sparked with an occasional fusion influence. **$$–$$$**
Lyceum Bar & Grill
43 Church Street
Tel: 978-745 7665
Seafood, chowder and grilled meats are on offer at this converted, 19th-century theater overlooking the Green. **$$–$$$**
Red Raven's Love Noodle
75 Congress Street
Tel: 978-745 8558
A more casual sister restaurant to Red Raven's Havana. **$$$**

Restaurant Guidelines

Prices are approximate, but for a three-course meal for one (excluding beverages, tax, and tip), the following guidelines may prove helpful:
$$$$ = over $40
$$$ = $28–40
$$ = $15–28
$ = under $15
Meal tax varies from state to state, but it is customary to tip 15 to 20 percent on the pre-tax total.
Credit cards The more expensive establishments generally accept credit cards, but call ahead to check just in case.
Reservations Most restaurants, except for the clearly casual, appreciate reservations (some require them).

Salem Beer Works
278 Derby Street
Tel: 978-745 2337
This is Salem's contribution to the microbrewery fad. Upscale bar food and fresh-brewed beers are served in a renovated warehouse building. **$–$$**

CAPE COD AND THE ISLANDS

Barnstable
Mattakeese Wharf
271 Mill Way
Tel: 508-362 4511
A classic wharfside seafood haven. **$$$**

Brewster
Chillingsworth
2449 Route 6A
Tel: 508-896 3640
Chillingsworth's splendid seven-course *prix-fixe* menu, a feast of classic French food, is among the ultimate dining experiences that the Cape has to offer. **$$$$**
Bramble Inn
2019 Route 6A
Tel: 508-896 7644
Intimate rooms with interesting decor and fascinating food. **$$$**
Old Manse Inn
1861 Main Street
Tel: 508-896 3149
This place has mediterranean panache. Try to sit in the flower-filled sunporch. **$$$**
Brewster Fish House
2208 Route 6A
Tel: 508-896 7867
"Nonconformist" seafood, snazzy desserts, and long waits. **$$**

Chatham
Chatham Bars Inn
Shore Road
Tel: 508-945 0096/
800-527 4884
A grand old dining room with French and regional cuisine. **$$$$**
Christian's Restaurant
443 Main Street
Tel: 508-945 3362
A lively New American bistro downstairs and an inviting, library-like piano bar upstairs. **$$$$**
Vining's Bistro
595 Main Street
Tel: 508-945 5033
A wood grill with a taste for exotic spices. **$$$**
Impudent Oyster
15 Chatham Bars Avenue
Tel: 508-945 3545
International takes on local seafood. Popular and packed. **$$**

Chilmark
The Feast of Chilmark
State Road
Tel: 508-645 3553
New York-sophisticate cuisine in a loft carved out of a plain clapboard house. **$$$$**

Dennis
Gina's by the Sea
134 Taunton Avenue
Tel: 508-385 3213
Hearty classics characterize this lively cafe set amid the Cape's "Little Italy". **$$$**
The Red Pheasant
905 Route 6A
Tel: 508-385 2133
Daring New American cuisine served in an 18th-century ship's chandlery. **$$$**

Scargo Cafe
799 Route 6A
Tel: 508-385 8200
Traditional favorites, plus a few wildcards, in a retro-fitted captain's house. **$$**
Captain Frosty's
219 Route 6A
Tel: 508-385 8548
A casual clam shack with exceptional lobster rolls. **$**

Eastham
Eastham Lobster Pool
4360 Route 6
Tel: 508-255 9706
No frills, just unbeatable fresh fish. **$$$**

Edgartown
L'Etoile,
Charlotte Inn
27 S Summer Street
Tel: 508-627 5187
Superlative nouvelle cuisine served in a candlelit conservatory. **$$$$**
Among the Flowers Cafe
Mayhew Lane
Tel: 508-627 3233
Omelets, quiches, pasta, and other filling, inexpensive fare. **$**
The Newes from America
23 Kelley Street
Tel: 508-627 4397
Pub grub in a recently unearthed 1742 tavern. A vast range of beers is available in sampler "racks". **$**

Falmouth
Coonamessett Inn Cahoon
Dining Room
311 Gifford Street
Tel: 508-548 2300
Classic country inn serves elegant fare, with an accent on fresh seafood and prime meats. Dress is semi-formal, and Sunday brunch is superb. **$$$–$$$$**
The Regatta of Falmouth-by-the-Sea
217 Clinton Avenue
Tel: 508-548 5400
One of the Cape's most sophisticated restaurants, with elegant appointments and celestial nouvelle cuisine, surrounded by the Sound. **$$$–$$$$**
Chapoquoit Grill
Route 28A
Tel: 508-540 7794

Restaurant Guidelines

Prices are approximate, but for a three-course meal for one (excluding beverages, tax, and tip), the following guidelines may prove helpful:
$$$$ = over $40
$$$ = $28–40
$$ = $15–28
$ = under $15
Meal tax varies from state to state, but it is customary to tip 15 to 20 percent on the pre-tax total.
Credit cards The more expensive establishments generally accept credit cards, but call ahead to check just in case.
Reservations Most restaurants, except for the clearly casual, appreciate reservations (some require them).

New American cuisine, grilled seafood, and wood-fired, brick oven pizza served in a casual environment. The desserts are all homemade. **$$–$$$**
Clam Shack
227 Scranton Avenue
Tel: 508-540 7758
A shack (albeit very picturesque), right on the water. **$**

Hyannis
Baxter's Boat House
177 Pleasant Street
Tel: 508-775 4490
Perched over the harbor, a 1950s clam shack with a very lively blues bar. **$$**
Starbuck's
950 Route 132
Tel: 508-778 6767
Eccentric decor and Mexican-American fare, by the airport. Unrelated to the coffee chain. **$$**
Steamers
235 Ocean Street
Tel: 508-778 0818
Mesquite-grilled seafood; live music, and a place-to-be deck. **$$**
Tugboats
21 Arlington Street
Tel: 508-775 6433
Fun food and great harbor views, especially at sunset. **$$**
Up the Creek
36 Old Colony Boulevard
tel: 508-771 7866
Boathouse decor and an international menu. **$$**

Menemsha
Home Port
North Road
Tel: 508-645 2679
Fresh-off-the-boat seafood in a picturesque harbor. **$$$$**

Nantucket
American Seasons
80 Centre Street
Tel: 508-228 7111
Adventurous dining amid colorful murals. **$$$$**
Boarding House
12 Federal Street
Tel: 508-228-9622.
Bold New American cuisine, and the island's most sophisticated sidewalk café. **$$$$**

Chanticleer Inn
9 New Street, Siasconset,
Tel: 508-257 6231
High-class traditional French cuisine served in an opulent auberge-like setting. **$$$$**
Rope Walk
Straight Wharf
Tel: 508-228 8886
Seafood with *nouvelle* splashes, on the harbor. **$$$$**
Straight Wharf Restaurant
Straight Wharf
Tel: 508-228 4499
Elegant regional fare in a handsome loft space. **$$$$**
21 Federal
21 Federal Street
Tel: 508-228 2121
Sensational regional cuisine in a tastefully spare 1847 Greek Revival house. **$$$$**
Brotherhood of Thieves
23 Broad Street
No phone
Great burgers, live music, and a nice crowd in an 1840 whaling bar. **$$**
Espresso Cafe
40 Main Street
Tel: 508-228-6930
Cheap, scrumptious international grazing at a vintage ice-cream parlor turned café. **$**

North Truro
Adrian's
Route 6
Tel: 508-487 4360
Irresistible neo-Italian treats plus spectacular views. **$$**

Oak Bluffs
Papa's Pizza
158 Circuit Avenue
Tel: 508-693 1400
An old-fashioned storefront serving traditional pies at long wooden tables. **$**

Orleans
Captain Linnell House,
137 Skaket Beach Road
Tel: 508-255 3400
Evolved Continental cuisine in a neoclassic 1854 villa. **$$$$**
Mahoney's
28 Main Street
Tel: 508-255 5505
Classy, contemporary US cuisine.

Shaker Meals

Hancock is Massachusett's best-kept Shaker village, now a living museum. You can watch craftspeople at work and cooks preparing meals using herbs from the original-style herb garden. In summer visitors can enjoy candlelit dinners, featuring dishes from Shaker cookbooks. But guests should take heed: the expression "shaker your plate" derives from the fact that leftovers were frowned upon by the Shakers. Tel: 413-443-0188

Live jazz is played on Thursday nights. **$$$$**
Land Ho!
38 Main Street
Tel: 508-255 5165
A pub known mostly to locals, who keep it packed. **$$**
Capt. Cass Rock Harbor Seafood
117 Rock Harbor Road
No phone
No-frills seafood shanty. **$**

Provincetown
Cafe Edwige
333 Commercial Street
Tel: 508-487 2008
Here you will find natural-foods breakfasts that are delicious enough to seem sinful. The candlelit New American dinners are among the best in town. **$$$**
Front Street
230 Commercial Street
Tel: 508-487 9715
The cuisine at Front Street is cutting-edge, and the ambiance is intimate and intense. **$$$**
Gallerani's Cafe
133 Commercial Street
Tel: 508-487 4433
An appealing bistro with cozy booths and eclectic cuisine. **$$$**
Martin House
157 Commercial Street
Tel: 508-487 1327
A c.1750 shingled house with intimate, rustic dining rooms and a skilled regional-cuisine chef. **$$$**
Napi's
7 Freeman Street
Tel: 508-487 1145

A colorful institution built of architectural salvage. The menu spans the world. **$$$**

Sal's Place
99 Commercial Street
Tel: 508-487 1279
Romantic classic Italian. **$$$**

Mews and Cafe Mews
429 Commercial Street
Tel: 508-487 1500
Beach-side elegance and creative cuisine. **$$–$$$**

Cafe Blase
328 Commercial Street
Tel: 508-487 9465
A sidewalk café that is perfect for people-gazing. **$**

Cafe Heaven
199 Commercial Street
Tel: 508-487 9639
The best burgers in town. Good breakfasts, too. **$**

Spiritus,
190 Commercial Street
Tel: 508-487 2808
A pizza mecca, and a magnet for the late-night crowd. **$**

Sandwich
Dan'l Webster Inn
149 Main Street
Tel: 508-888 3622
Offers surprisingly sophisticated cuisine for a restaurant on so large a scale. **$$**

Dunbar Tea Shop
1 Water Street (Route 130)
Tel: 508-833 2485
English tearoom serving pastries, light lunches and, of course, tea. **$**

Vineyard Haven
Black Dog Tavern
Beach Street Extension
Tel: 508-693 9223

Inventive American-style fare in a wharfside tavern. The signature T-shirts are everywhere. **$$$$**

Wellfleet
Aesop's Tables
Main Street
Tel: 508-349 6450
Festive and celestial regional cuisine and a really delightful attic bar. **$$$**

Bayside Lobster Hut
Commercial Street
Tel: 508-349 6333
Shore dinners in an 1857 oyster shack. **$**

Painter's
50 Main Street
Tel: 508-349 3003
A skilled young culinary artist whips up fine New American dishes. **$**

Woods Hole
Fishmonger Cafe
56 Water Street
Tel: 508-548 9148
Lively wharfside café with inventive natural foods and fresh seafood. **$$**

Landfall
Luscombe Avenue.
Tel: 508-548 1758
Seafood in a loft-like space festooned with nautical salvage. **$$**

Shuckers World Famous Raw Bar & Cafe
91A Water Street
Tel: 508-540 3850
The freshest of seafood, to be slurped dockside. **$$**

Yarmouthport
Abbici
43 Route 6A
Tel: 508-362 3501
This 1775 house sports drop-dead

modern decor and serves knockout Northern Italian cuisine. **$$$$**

Inaho
157 Route 6A
Tel: 508-362 5522
A superb Japanese restaurant, with the freshest sushi imaginable. **$$$**

Jack's Outback
161 Main Street
Tel: 508-362 6690
Looking for local color? You'll find it here in spades, along with tasty, affordable old-favorites food. **$**

CENTRAL MASSACHUSETTS

Amherst
Amherst Chinese
62 Main Street
Tel: 413-253-7835
A casual restaurant known for hearty portions at low prices. **$**

Deerfield
Deerfield Inn
81 Old Main Street
Tel: 413-774-5587
The setting is appropriately sedate, the menu is surprisingly forward thinking. **$$$**

Sienna
28 Elm Street
South Deerfield
Tel: 413-665 0215
Distinguished regional cuisine. **$$$**

Northhampton
Spoleto
50 Main Street
Tel: 413-586 6313
Italian classics in a lively contemporary cafe. **$$$**

East Side Grill
19 Strong Street
Tel: 413-586 3347
Wildly popular Cajun-influenced grill. The food may not convince you that New Orleans has come north, but the room is always bustling. **$$**

Springfield
Student Prince and Fort Restaurant
8 Fort Street
Tel: 413-734 7475
Established in the 1940s, this spot offers stout German cuisine and an authentic beer-hall ambience. **$$**

Restaurant Guidelines

Prices are approximate, but for a three-course meal for one (excluding beverages, tax, and tip), the following guidelines may prove helpful:
$$$$ = over $40
$$$ = $28–40
$$ = $15–28
$ = under $15
Meal tax varies from state to

state, but it is customary to tip 15 to 20 percent on the pre-tax total.
Credit cards The more expensive establishments generally accept credit cards, but call ahead to check just in case.
Reservations Most restaurants, except for the clearly casual, appreciate reservations (some require them).

Pioneer Valley Brew Pub
Taylor Street
Tel: 413-732 2739
Locally made microbrews paired
with surprisingly creative eats. **$–$$**

Sturbridge
Whistling Swan
502 Main Street
Tel: 508-347 2321
New American cuisine in a formal
dining room; more casual fare is
available in the converted barn. **$$**

Worcester
**Restaurant at Tatnuck Bookseller
Marketplace**
335 Chandler Street (Route 122)
Tel: 508-756 7644
Located on the West Side in the
city's largest bookstore, this
comfortable café serves interesting
New American fare. **$$**
Shorah's Ristorante
Foster and Commercial Streets
Tel: 508-797 0007
A casual downtown storefront, near
the Centrum, serving Italian dishes
ranging from basic pizza and
calzones to more creative chicken
or veal dishes. **$–$$**
Charlie's Diner
344 Plantation Street
Tel: 508-752 9318
A classic diner, manufactured in
1941 by the Worcester Lunch
Company, located on the East Side
near the Beechwood Hotel. **$**

THE BERKSHIRES

Great Barrington
Boiler Room Cafe
405 Stockbridge Road (Route 7)
Tel: 413-528 4280
Contemporary American/
Mediterranean food. **$$–$$$**
Castle Street Cafe
10 Castle Street
Tel: 413-528 5244
An American/Continental bistro with
big-city flair. **$$–$$$**

Lenox
Blantyre
off Route 20
Tel: 413-637 3556
Contemporary French cuisine in the

formal dining rooms of a Tudor
mansion. Summer only. **$$$$**
Village Inn
16 Church Street
Tel: 413-637 0020
New American artistry in a
venerable 1771 inn. **$$$**
Church Street Cafe
65 Church Street
Tel: 413-637 2745
American bistro fare and whimsical
decor. **$$**
Sweet Basil Grille
306 Pittsfield-Lenox Rd at
Brushwood Farms
Tel: 413-637 1270
Updated Italian in a comfortable
restored house. **$$**

New Marlborough
Old Inn on the Green & Gedney Farm
Village Green (Route 7)
01230
Tel: 413-229 3131
French auberge-style cuisine in a
c.1760 stagecoach inn. **$$$$**

West Stockbridge
Williamsville Inn
Route 41
Tel: 413 274 6118
Gourmet country cuisine with
produce from the garden. **$$$**
La Bruscetta Ristorante
1 Harris Street
Tel: 413-232 7141
Dinner only. Traditional, contem-
porary, and cutting-edge Italian. **$$**

Williamstown
The Orchards
222 Adams Road
Tel: 413-458 9611
Accomplished New American
cuisine in a setting of studied
elegance. **$$$**

Culture

DANCE

Boston Ballet (tel: 617-695 6950)
are world renowned and perform
regularly at the Wang Center for the
Performing Arts.
Dance Umbrella (tel: 617-482
7570) produce modern dance
presentations at theaters around
the city.

Buying Tickets

BosTix (tel: 617-723 5181),
with booths in Copley Square and
Faneuil Hall Marketplace, is a
major entertainment information
center. Half-price tickets can be
bought at 11am on the day of
the event. Cash and travelers'
checks only.

CLASSICAL MUSIC

Boston Symphony Orchestra and
Boston Pops are heard at the
acoustic and aesthetic **Symphony
Hall** (tel: 617-266 1492; 301
Massachusetts Avenue).
**New England Conservatory's
Jordan Hall** (tel: 617-585 1100; 30
Gainsborough Street) hosts its own
classical concerts.
**Berklee College of Music
Performance Center** (tel: 617-266
7455; 136 Massachusetts Avenue,
Boston) excels in jazz performances
by faculty and students, many
international.

OPERA

Boston Lyric Opera Company (tel:
617-542 4912; 114 State Street)
produces three operas per season.

ROCK AND POP

Boston Big-name national rock and
alternative talent can be heard at

Information Sources

Boston
The Phoenix (published weekly)
contains a large Arts and
Entertainment section.
The Boston Globe's pull-out
Calendar section (published
every Thursday) is devoted to
cultural events around the city.
Western Massachusetts
For cultural events, consult the
Five College Calendar of Events,
published monthly, or *The Valley
Advocate*, a free weekly paper.

Massachusetts Festivals

Spring

Spring officially arrives with the **Boston Marathon** (tel: 617-236-1652), held on **Patriot's Day** (the third Monday in April).

Meanwhile, modern-day Minutemen stage **Revolutionary War Reenactments** in Boston at the Paul Revere House (tel: 617-536 4100) and in Lexington and Concord (tel: 781-861 0928).

In late April, a colorful **Daffodil Festival** on Nantucket (tel: 508-228 1700) marks the first stirrings of summer.

In mid-May (and again in July and September), flea-market fever sweeps tiny Brimfield for the three **Brimfield Outdoor Antiques Shows** (tel: 413-283 6149/800-628 8379), mega-swap meets that attract over 1,000 dealers and some serious antiquaries.

Summer

Summer is music time, beginning in mid-June with the **Boston Globe Jazz Festival** (tel: 617-929 2649).

From mid-June to late August, the Boston Symphony Orchestra presides over the world-famous **Tanglewood Music Festival** (tel: 413-637 5165/800-274 8499) in Lenox.

Following roughly the same schedule are two fellow Berkshires institutions: the **Jacob's Pillow Dance Festival** (tel: 413-243 0745) in nearby Becket, and the outstanding **Williamstown Theatre Festival** (tel: 413-597 3400) in Williamstown.

While the BSO is off to the country, the Boston Pops wow the masses with a free **Fourth of July Concert** (with fireworks) at the Hatch Shell on the Charles River Esplanade (tel: 617-266 1492).

Later in July, the Lowell National Historical Park holds the **Lowell Folk Festival** (tel: 978-970 5000), a melange of traditional music and ethnic foods.

Summer is also a good time to catch up with local artisans. Five hundred of the country's very best (including a sizable New England contingent) exhibit in West Springfield at the **ACC Crafts Fair** (tel: 800-836 3470) in mid-June.

A smaller sampling show at the **Old Deerfield Craft Fair** (tel: 413-774 7476) in mid-June and late September.

Fall

Harvest festivals mark the foliage season, including large-scale extravaganzas such as Springfield's **Big E** (tel: 413-737 2443), and one of the nation's oldest county fairs, the **Topsfield Fair** (tel: 978-887 5000).

Also in October, college crew teams and spectators come to Cambridge for the **Head of the Charles Regatta** (tel: 617-864 8415), while in Salem, the annual **Haunted Happenings** week climaxes on Halloween (tel: 978-744 0013).

Winter

Communities across Massachusetts ring in the New Year with **First Night** festivities. Started by Boston artists in 1977, First Night has spread to more than 70 communities nationwide and offers a moveable feast of music, theatre, ice sculptures, parades and fireworks.

Towns in which First Night celebrations are held include the following:

Boston (tel: 617-542 1399)
Salem (tel: 978-744 0004)
several Cape Cod towns (tel: 508-709 2787)
and Northampton (tel: 413-584 7327).

For further information about venues and timings of the events listed above, consult the local tourist offices or newspapers with listings.

Mama Kin (tel: 617-536 2100; 36 Lansdowne Street) books a variety of rock bands on three stages. **Beverly** North Shore Music Theater (tel: 978-922 8500; 62 Dunham Road, off Route 128) hosts acts from April through December. **Cambridge** Try the incomparable Johnny D's (tel: 617-776 2004; 17 Holland Street near Davis Square) for everything from blues jams to Cajun music. **Hyannis** Cape Cod Melody Tent (tel: 508-775 9100) hosts national comics and musicians throughout the summer on the Cape.

JAZZ

Sculler's Jazz Club (tel: 617-783 0811; 400 Soldiers Field Road, Guest Quarters Suites Hotel, Cambridge) features blues, Latin, and jazz in a cozy setting. **Regatta Bar** (tel: 617-864 1200, 617-876 7777 for tickets; Bennett and Eliot Streets, Charles Hotel, Harvard Square, Cambridge) presents traditional, big-name jazz personalities. **Ryles Jazz Club** (tel: 617-876 9330; 212 Hampshire Street, Inman Square, Cambridge) features local jazz talent and a jazz brunch on weekends. **Berkshire Performing Arts Theater** (tel: 413-637 1800; 70 Kemple Street, Lenox) presents jazz at the National Music Center.

THEATER

Boston's theater district, at the intersection of Tremont and Stuart streets has many first-rate and historic theaters, including the **Wang Center, Schubert, Colonial,** and **Wilbur**. High-quality drama is found across the city, however, with performances on show at the **Boston Center for the Arts** (tel: 617-426 5000; 539 Tremont Street) and Boston University's **Huntington Theater** (tel: 617-266 0800; 264 Huntington Avenue), with Boston's largest professional company in residence.

American Repertory Theater Company (tel: 617-495 2668; 64 Brattle Street, Harvard Square, Cambridge), a highly acclaimed award winner, has two stages at the Loeb Drama Center.

On the north shore, the **Firehouse Center for the Performing Arts** (tel: 978-462 7336; Market Square, Newburyport) produces year-round plays, and specializes in children's theater. **Merrimack Repertory Theater** (tel: 978-454 3926; 50 East Merrimack St, Lowell) has professional productions.

Cape Playhouse (tel: 508-385 3838; off Route 6A, Dennis) offers some of the best summer stock on the Cape; check local listings for other current shows.

CINEMA

Brattle Theater (tel: 617-876 6837; 40 Brattle Street) and the **Harvard Film Archive** (tel: 617-495 4700; 24 Quincy Street), both in Cambridge, show classic, foreign, nostalgia, and art films. The Art Deco **Kendall Square Cinema** (tel: 617-494 9800; Kendall Square, Cambridge) offers frothy cappuccino with its foreign and art movies. **Pleasant Street Theater** (tel: 413-586 0935; 27 Pleasant Street, Northampton) runs independent, foreign, and art films. **Cape Cinema** (tel: 508-385 2503; off Route 6A, Dennis) was built in 1930 as a movie theater and is still true to its mission. A trip to the **Wellfleet Drive-In** (tel: 508-349 7176; Route 6, Wellfleet) is one of the best remembrances of a sultry, relaxing summer holiday.

COMEDY

Boston's Faneuil Hall Market Place has several comedy clubs, including **Comedy Connection** (tel: 617-248 9700). Also of note is **Nick's Comedy Stop** (tel: 617-482 0930; 100 Warrenton Street), in the theater district.

ART GALLERIES

Most of Boston's largest art galleries can be found on Back Bay's Newbury Street, while a number of upstarts have moved to the Fort Point Channel area near South Station. Also try Tremont Street in the South End.

The north shore town of Rockport has more than two dozen art galleries, as does Northampton in western Massachusetts.

In Lowell, **Brush Art Gallery and Studios** (tel: 978-459 7819; 246 Market Street) showcases the studios of 12 working artists.

On Cape Cod, head to the towns of Wellfleet and Provincetown and simply wander the streets from gallery to gallery.

Nightlife

NIGHTCLUBS/DISCOS

Boston's Lansdowne Street, behind Fenway Park in Kenmore Square, is the city's largest conglomeration of nightclubs. **Axis** (tel: 617-262 2437, 13 Lansdowne Street), one of the city's largest clubs with a capacity of 1,000 people, has music on several floors.

LIVE MUSIC

In Cambridge, head to **The Middle East** (tel: 617-354 8238; 472 Massachusetts Avenue, Central Square), an eclectic club with nightly jazz, rock and world music on two floors, and **The House of Blues** (tel: 617-491 2583; 96 Winthrop Street, Harvard Square), featuring blues performers and various "all-ages" shows. The venerable **Iron Horse** (tel: 413-584 0610; 20 Center Street, Northampton) puts on both live folk and jazz music.

GAY & LESBIAN VENUES

At **Avalon** (tel: 617-262 2424; 15 Lansdowne Street, Boston), Sunday is gay night.

Provincetown is the East Coast's Mecca (perhaps tied with Key West) for gays and lesbians. Although it's best to ask around for the current "in" club, you can always count on tea dances at **The Boatslip** (tel: 508-487 1669; Commercial Street), held every summer afternoon on the waterfront deck.

CABARET

Zeiterion Theater (tel: 508-997 5664; 684 Purchase Street, New Bedford), an all-vaudeville theater, stages theme performances.

LATE-NIGHT VENUES

Although Boston is notorious for shutting down early, its large student population usually keeps things rolling, at least on Friday and Saturday. Most nightclubs on Lansdowne Street are open until 2:30am, but don't forget: the "T" stops running at 12.30am.

DANCING

Bay Tower Room (tel: 617-723 1666; 60 State Street, Boston) is a beautiful spot for swing-dancing while taking in a twinkling cityscape.

MUSIC

During the summer, Boston has several free outdoor concert series at the **Hatch Shell** on the Charles River Esplanade. Check the *Boston Globe* for listings.

Spectator Sports

Generally, the New England states are represented by Boston's teams: basketball's **Boston Celtics** (tel: 617-523 6050; Fleet Center, Sept–May), baseball's Boston **Red Sox** (tel: 617-267 1700; Fenway Park, April–Oct) and hockey's **Boston Bruins** (tel: 617-624 1900, 617-931 2222 for tickets; Fleet Center, Oct–Mar).

The major exception is football, which the **New England Patriots** (tel: 508-543 8200/800-543 1776 for tickets, Foxboro Stadium, Aug–Dec) play in the southern suburb of Foxboro.

For up-to-date information on schedules and locations, check the sports section of any local daily.

Outdoor Activities

BIKING

In Eastern Massachusetts, mountain bikers can explore the trails of **Blue Hills Reservation** (tel: 617-698 1802) in Milton, just south of Boston, or in **Maudslay State Park** in Newburyport on the North Shore. In the western part of the state, **Mount Greylock State Reservation** (tel: 413-499 4262) near Williamstown has a number of mountain biking trails.

Bikers also flock to the **Cape Cod Rail Trail**, a scenic 30-mile (48-km) paved path along the former Penn Central Railway route from South Dennis to South Wellfleet *(see page 160)*.

A classic urban bike path is Boston's **Dr. Paul Dudley White Bikeway**, an 18-mile (29-km) loop that follows both sides of the Charles River.

CANOEING/KAYAKING AND RAFTING

In Boston and the nearby suburb of Newton, **Charles River Canoe and Kayak Center** (tel: 617-965 5110) rents canoes and kayaks on the Charles River for an hour or more.

South Bridge Boat House in historic Concord (tel: 978-369 9438) has canoes for rent on the lazy Sudbury and Concord Rivers.

Cape Cod Coastal Canoe & Kayak (tel: 207-326 9022), naturalists lead canoe and kayak tours of the Cape's salt marshes, tidal rivers, bays, and islands.

In western Massachusetts, **Zoar Outdoor** (tel: 800-532 7483), based along the Mohawk Trail in Charlemont, organizes whitewater

rafting expeditions for all levels on the Deerfield River. They also run two- or three-day learn-to-kayak or canoe clinics.

FISHING

For salt-water fly-fishing, check with **Orvis Saltwater School** (tel: 800-235 9763, Chatham) on Cape Cod. They run a 2½-day course that teaches basic saltwater techniques. Also on the Cape, **Patriot Party Boats** (tel: 508-548 2626), operating out of Falmouth Harbor, offers deep-sea fishing trips.

The Orleans-based **Rock Harbor Charter Fleet** (tel: 508-255 9757) also run fishing excursions.

HIKING

Close to Boston, hikers can explore the 150 miles of trails at **Blue Hills Reservation** (see *Biking* above). More ambitious hikers head west to **Mount Tom State Reservation** in Holyoke or **Mount Greylock State Reservation** (see *Biking, left)*, which includes a stretch of the Appalachian Trail.

SAILING

Boston's **Community Boating** (tel: 617-523 1038), America's oldest public sailing program, sells two-day (and longer) memberships for sailing along the Charles River.

Cape Cod Museum of Natural History (tel: 508-896 3867; Brewster) offers nature explorations in Orleans' Nauset Marsh on a motorized catamaran.

The schooner **Bay Lady II** (tel: 508-487 9308) makes two-hour sails from Provincetown into Cape Cod Bay.

SKIING

Massachusetts' best downhill skiing is in the Berkshires. Two of the major areas are **Jiminy Peak** in Hancock (tel: 413-738 5500) and

Brodie Mountain in New Ashford (tel: 413-443 4752).

However, weather permitting, there are options for skiing in the eastern part of the state; the largest area is **Wachusett Mountain** in Princeton, about an hour west of Boston (tel: 978-464 2300/800-754 1234).

The Berkshires are the most reliable for cross-country skiing. **Northfield Mt. XC Center** (tel: 413-659 3715) has around 25 miles (40 km) of trails.

Closer to Boston, two smaller but still popular areas are **Weston Ski Track** (tel: 781-891 6575) and in Carlisle, **Great Brook Farm** (tel: 978-369 7486).

Shopping

WHERE TO SHOP

Boston Downtown Crossing, a pedestrian-only zone, is Boston's largest shopping area, complete with outdoor kiosks and street-venders. The popular Faneuil Hall Marketplace has many small shops and foodstands. Boston's version of Fifth Avenue is Newbury Street, eight-block stretch of expensive clothing stores, salons, and art galleries.

Cambridge Harvard Square has more than 150 stores within a small radius.

Nantucket Good for shopping if you have money to burn; an excellent and dense concentration of shops.

MALLS

Boston's **Copley Place** (tel: 617-369 5000; Copley Square) has

Department Stores

Two mammoth retailers worth checking out on Washington Street, Boston are:
Filene's (tel: 617-357 2100; basement: 617-542 2011) and **Macy's** (tel: 617-357 3000). The floor below Filene's is the place to go for bargains.

almost 100 upscale stores and restaurants, while **Cambridgeside Galleria** (tel: 617-621 8666; 100 Cambridgeside Place, Cambridge) is a three-story mall with over 100 shops and three department stores. **Cape Cod Mall** (tel: 508-771 0200; Routes 132 and 28, Hyannis) isn't particularly distinctive, but it does have a very wide range of stock on offer.

MARKETS

Boston's historic **Haymarket,** selling inexpensive fruits and vegetables, meat, and seafood, is open every Friday and Saturday near Faneuil Hall Marketplace.

FASHION & ACCESSORIES

Chic Newbury Street in Boston is the place for high fashion, with stores such as **Brooks Brothers** at no. 46 (tel: 617-267 2600), **Alan Bilzerian** at no. 34 (tel: 617-536 1001), and **Ann Taylor** at no. 18 (tel: 617-262 0763).

One of Boston's oldest men's store, **Louis Boston** (tel: 617-262 6100; 234 Berkeley Street) also sells women's apparel now.

BOOKS

Boston and Cambridge are havens for buyers and browsers of new and used books. Check out **Waterstones** (tel: 617-859 7300; 26 Exeter Street; and tel: 617-589 0930, Faneuil Hall Market Place) and **Wordsworth** (tel: 617-354 5201; three stores in Harvard Square, Cambridge).

For travel, nothing beats **Globe Corner Bookstore** (tel: 617-859 8008; 500 Boylston Street, Boston and tel: 617-497 6277; 49 Palmer Street, Harvard Square, Cambridge.)

As for used bookstores, **Avenue Victor Hugo** (tel: 617-266 7746; 339 Newbury Street) and **Trident Booksellers and Cafe** (tel: 617-267 8688; 338 Newbury Street) are both great.

Schoenhof's (tel: 617-547 8855; 76A Mount Auburn Street, Cambridge) sells foreign-language materials, as well as fiction and dictionaries in almost any language.

Tatnuck Bookseller Marketplace in Worcester (tel: 508-756 7644; 335 Chandler Street) is the largest independent bookseller in the state, carrying over 500,000 volumes. Northampton has a particularly dense concentration of shops.

ANTIQUES

Boston's Charles Street has a large number of antique dealers, including the **Boston Antique Co-op** (tel: 617-227 9810; 119 Charles Street). Also try the **Boston Antique Center** (tel: 617-742 1400; 54 Canal Street, near North Station).

On the north shore, Gloucester's Main Street has lots of interesting antiques shops; in Essex there is the excellent **White Elephant** (tel: 978-768 6901; 32 Main St), one of the town's 40 antique dealers.

Antique Center of Sturbridge, 462 Main Street, Sturbridge (tel: 508-347 5150) has dealers on two floors.

On Cape Cod, the whole stretch of Route 6A from Sandwich to Orleans is lined with antique shops. Brewster has the most and generally the best.

CHINA AND GLASS

Fellerman & Raabe Glassworks Main Street, Sheffield Tel: 413-229 8533 Sells glassware of every shape, size, and color.
October Mountain Stained Glass 343 Main Street, Great Barrington Tel: 413-528 6681 Features stained glass. Both are in the Berkshires.
Martha's Vineyard Glass Works State Road, West Tisbury Tel: 508-693 6026 Carries an exceptional selection of glassware; you can also watch the master craftspeople at work.
Pairpoint Crystal Route 6A, Sagamore Tel: 508-888 2344/800-899 0953

Glassmakers use a variety of techniques developed in nearby Sandwich, which was world-renowned in the 1800s for its innovative glassmaking.

JEWELRY

Shreve, Crump & Low 330 Boylston Street, Boston Tel: 617-267 9100 One of Boston's oldest and most venerated shops, the store sells a dazzling array of fine jewelry, as well as exceptional china, crystal, and silverware.
Tiffany & Co Copley Place, Boston Tel: 617-353 0222 World famous and exceptional.

ARTS AND CRAFTS

Society for Arts and Crafts 175 Newbury Street, Boston Tel: 617-266 1810 A prestigious, non-profit institution with high-quality handmade items.
Worcester Center for Crafts 25 Sagamore Road, Worcester Tel: 508-753 8183 One of America's oldest crafts complexes.
Great Barrington Pottery Route 41 Tel: 413-274 6259 Sells pieces glazed in Japanese wood-burning kilns.

TOYS

F.A.O. Schwarz 440 Boylston Street, Boston Tel: 617-262 5900 Sells an astonishing variety of toys, both old-fashioned and high-tech, many of them at equally unbelievably high prices.

Children
THEME PARKS

Whalom Park Route 13, Lunenburg Tel: 978-342 3707

A waterslide, 50 carnival-style rides and a beach on Whalom Lake.

ZOOS

Franklin Park Zoo
Blue Hill Ave at Columbia Rd
Boston
Tel: 617-442 2002
Has a free-flight aviary and African Tropical Rain Forest exhibit.
Steam Train Journeys
Berkshire Scenic Railway
10 Willow Creek Road
Lenox
Tel: 413-637 2210
Train rides May through October.

THEATER

Priscilla Beach Theater
Rocky Hill Road
Plymouth
Tel: 508-224 4888
Presents children's shows on Friday and Saturday. Performing arts camp throughout the summer.

MUSEUMS

Children's Museum
Museum Wharf
300 Congress Street
Boston
Tel: 617-426 8855
A delight. Fun with learning.
Museum of Science
Science Park at the Charles River Dam, Boston
Tel: 617-723 2500
Hundreds of hands-on exhibits to spark the excitement of children aged three and up.
New England Aquarium
Central Wharf
Boston
Tel: 617-973 5200
A world-class facility that supports serious marine research.
Thornton W Burgess Museum
4 Water Street
Sandwich
Tel: 508-888 4668
This museum is dedicated to the creator of Peter Rabbit and many other children's books.

Connecticut

The Place

Known as: The Constitution State, because its delegates played a crucial role in drawing up the US Constitution in 1787
Motto: *Qui Transtulit Sustinet* (He who transplanted still sustains)
Origin of name: probably derived from Algonquian Indian term thought to mean "place of the long river"
Entered Union: 9 January 1788, the fifth of the original 13 states.
Capital: Hartford.
Area: 5,544 sq. miles (14,358 sq. km).
Highest point: Mount Frissell, 2,380 ft (725m).
Population: 3.29 million.
Population density: 593 people per sq. mile (229 per sq. km).
Economy: Hartford is a a major insurance centre. Also aircraft engines, helicopters, submarines, and firearms.
National representation: 2 senators and 6 representatives to Congress
Famous citizens: Phineas T. Barnum, Samuel Colt, Katharine Hepburn, J. Pierpoint Morgan, Harriet Beecher Stowe, Mark Twain, Noah Webster, Eli Whitney.

Where To Stay

AVON

Avon Old Farms Inn
Routes 44 and 10, 06001
Tel: 860-677 1651/
800-836 4000
Fax: 860-677 0364
Almost 165 modern rooms with traditional furnishings in several red-brick buildings spread across 20 acres. Swimming pool. **$$**

BRISTOL

Chimney Crest Manor
5 Founders Drive, 06010
Tel: 860-582 4219
Fax: 860-584 5903
Five-room B&B in an elegantly appointed 1930s Tudor-style mansion with views of the Farmington Valley, 20 minutes west of Hartford. **$$–$$$**

CHESTER

Inn at Chester
318 West Main Street, 06412
Tel: 860-526 9541/
800-949 7829
Fax: 860-526 4387
www.innatchester.com.
Modern amenities in a 42-room inn built around an original 1776 farmhouse. Located between Essex and East Haddam. **$$–$$$$**

EAST HADDAM

Gelston House
Main Street, 06423
Tel: 860-873 1411
Fax: 860-873 9300
Small elegantly appointed inn, built in 1853, located next to the Goodspeed Opera House. Some of the four rooms overlook the river, others have village views. **$$–$$$$**
Bishopsgate Inn
7 Norwich Road, 06423
Tel: 860-873 1677
Fax: 860-873 3898
www.bishopsgate.com
Six-room B&B in an 1818 shipwright's home with four fireplaces. **$$–$$$**

Connecticut Trivia

The following were all invented in Connecticut:
● Colt revolver
● portable typewriter
● can opener
● tape measure
● vacuum cleaner
● Polaroid camera
● Frisbee

ESSEX

Griswold Inn
36 Main Street, 06426
Tel: 860-767 1776
Fax: 860-767 0481
www.griswoldinn.com
A haven for wayfarers since 1776.
Historical appointments in the 31
rooms include ancient firearms,
Currier & Ives prints, and an old
popcorn cart. **$–$$$**

FARMINGTON

Barney House
11 Mountain Spring Road, 06032
Tel: 860-674 2796
Fax: 860-677 7259
www.lib.uconn.edu/barneyhouse
Imposing 1832 mansion with formal
gardens and Victorian greenhouse.
B&B with 7 rooms. **$–$$**
Farmington Inn
827 Farmington Avenue, 06032
Tel: 860-677 2821/
800-648 9804 (toll-free)
Fax: 860-677 8332
A handsomely renovated motel
with 72 traditionally decorated
rooms. **$$**

GLASTONBURY

Butternut Farm
1654 Main Street, 06033
Tel: 860-633 7197
Fax: 860-659 1758
www.butternutfarmbandb.com
B&B with five rooms in a 1720
colonial house with period antiques,
herb gardens, and a barn housing
goats, chickens (for fresh eggs),
ducks, pigs, and a llama. Full
breakfast served in the original
dining room or an intimate
breakfast room. **$**

HARTFORD

Goodwin Hotel
1 Haynes Street, 06103
Tel: 860-246 7500/888-212 8320
www.goodwinhotel.com
A luxury urban inn with 124 rooms
in the heart of town. There's a 24-

hour fitness center, and good
discounts are often available at
weekends. **$–$$$$**
The 1895 House B&B
97 Girard Avenue, 06105
Tel: 860-232 0014
A bay-windowed Victorian home with
three bedrooms in a residential
neighborhood. **$**

IVORYTON

Copper Beech Inn
46 Main Street, 06442
Tel: 860-767 0330/
888-809 2056
www.copperbeachinn.com
Luxuriously appointed 1890 home
and carriage house. Most of the 13
rooms have whirlpool tubs. **$$–$$$**

LAKEVILLE

Wake Robin Inn
Sharon Road (Route 41), 06039
Tel: 860-435 2515
Fax: 860-435 2000
www.wakerobininn.com
A Georgian colonial inn and motel
with 38 rooms set in more than 12
acres. **$$–$$$**

LITCHFIELD

Litchfield Inn
432 Bantam Road (Route 202),
06759
Tel: 860-567 4503/
800-499 3444
Fax: 860-567 5358
Central location is a plus at this
new inn, with its 32 rooms
traditionally decorated in the
Colonial style. The parlor has a baby
grand piano and fireplace. **$$–$$$**
Tollgate Hill Inn
Tollgate Road and Route 202,
06759
Tel: 860-567 4545/
800-445 3903
Fax: 860-567 4545
A romantically appointed 1745
Federal inn supplemented by a
renovated schoolhouse. Many of
the 20 rooms have canopy beds.
$$–$$$

Price Categories

A very approximate guide to
current room rates for a standard
double per night is:
$$$$ = over $200
$$$ = $150–200
$$ = $100–150
$ = under $100

MADISON

Tidewater Inn
949 Boston Post Road (Route 1)
06443
Tel: 203-245 8457
Fax: 203 318 0265
A former stage coach stop turned
cozy, antiques-filled B&B with nine
rooms. Walking distance to
Madison village. **$$–$$$**
Madison Beach Hotel
94 West Wharf Road, 06443
Tel: 203-245 1404
Fax: 203-245 0410
www.madisonbeachhotel.com
An old-fashioned wooden hotel with
a wraparound porch, right on the
Sound. 35 rooms. **$$**

MYSTIC AREA

Steamboat Inn
73 Steamboat Wharf
Mystic, 06355.
Tel: 860-536 8300
Fax: 860-536 9528
www.visitmystic.com/steamboat
Dramatic spaces right on the water.
10 rooms. **$$$–$$$$**
House of 1833 B&B
72 N Stonington Road, Mystic,
06355
Tel: 860-536 6325/
800-367 1833
www.houseof1833.com
Five-room romantic, elegant Greek-
revival mansion, built in 1833, with
a swimming pool and tennis court.
$$–$$$$
Inn at Mystic
Routes 1 and 27
Mystic, 06355.
Tel: 860-536 9604/
800-237 2415
www.innatmystic.com
Choose from motel units or 67

elegant rooms in the Colonial
Revival mansion. **$$–$$$$**
Red Brook Inn
2750 Gold Star Highway
Old Mystic, 06372
Tel: 860-572 0349/
800-290 5619
www.redbrookinnmystic.com
B&B in a pair of classic colonials on
seven acres. Rooms furnished with
American period antiques. Seven of
the ten rooms have working
fireplaces. **$$–$$$**
Whaler's Inn
20 E Main Street (Route 1)
Mystic, 06355
Tel: 860-536 1506/
800-243 2588
Fax: 860-572 1250
www.whalersinnmystic.com
Several 19th-century homes
transformed into a homey inn with
41 rooms, clustered near the
docks. **$$–$$$**
Harbour Inne & Cottage
15 Edgemont Street
Mystic, 06355
Tel: 860-572 9253
www.visitmystic.com/harbourinne.
A family-friendly pine-paneled 1950s
bungalow on the Mystic River, with
nautical-themed rooms. Walking
distance to the seaport. **$–$$**

NEW HAVEN

Three Chimneys Inn
1201 Chapel Street, 06511
Tel: 203-789 1201
Fax: 203-776 7363
A 10-room B&B in a luxurious
restored 19th-century urban inn
near Yale University. **$$$**
Colony Inn
1157 Chapel Street, 06511
Tel: 203-776 1234/
800-458 8810
Fax: 203-772 3929
www.colonyatyale.com
Located near the Yale campus, this
inn features a lobby with a grand
chandelier and 86 comfortable
guest rooms furnished with Colonial
reproductions. **$$**
New Haven Hotel
229 George Street, 06510
Tel: 203-498 3100/
800-644 6835

Price Categories

A very approximate guide to
current room rates for a standard
double per night is:
$$$$ = over $200
$$$ = $150–200
$$ = $100–150
$ = under $100

Fax: 203-498 3190
www.newhavenhotel.com
A 92-room city-center hotel with the
feel of an exclusive inn for business
or leisure travelers. Amenities
include an indoor swimming pool
and hot tub. **$$**

NEW LONDON

Lighthouse Inn
6 Guthrie Place, 06320
Tel: 860-443 8411/888-443 8411
Fax: 860-437 7027
www.lighthouseinn-ct.com
Restored 1902 mansion with
private beach and 51 rooms.
Located a few blocks from Ocean
Beach Park. **$$–$$$**
Queen Anne Inn
265 Williams Street, 06320
Tel: 860-447 2600/
800-347 8818
Fax: 860-443 0857
www.queen-anne.com
Eight-room B&B in a fanciful
Victorian inn. **$$–$$$**

NEW PRESTON

Boulders Inn
Route 45, 06777
Tel: 860-868-0541/
800-552-6853
Fax: 860-868-1925
www.bouldersinn.com
An 1895 stone mansion, now a 17-
room B&B or MAP, overlooking Lake
Waramaug. **$$$$**
Hopkins Inn
22 Hopkins Road, 06777
Tel: 860-868 7295
www.thehopkinsinn.com
11 rooms, 2 apartments. An 1847
Federal house with rustic Alpine
touches and lake views. **$**

NOANK

Palmer Inn
25 Church Street, 06340
Tel: 860-572 9000
www.visitmystic.com/palmerinn.
Grand Art Nouveau seaside
mansion with just six rooms. Noank
is a small fishing village, southwest
of Mystic. **$$–$$$$**

NORTH STONINGTON

Antiques & Accommodations
32 Main Street, 06359
Tel: 860-535 1736/
800-554 7829
Fax: 860-535 2613
www.visitmystic.com/antiques
Eleven-room B&B in an elegant
1861 Victorian country house
furnished with antiques, many of
which are for sale. **$$$–$$$$**
Randall's Ordinary
Route 2, 06359
Tel: 860-599 4540/
877 599-4540
Fax: 860-599 3308
www.randallsordinary.com
Colonial inn with 15 rooms on the
National Register of Historic Places.
$$–$$$$

NORFOLK

Greenwoods Gate
105 Greenwoods Road East
(Route 44), 06058
Tel: 860-542 5439
Fax: 860-542 5897
www.greenwoodsgate.com
A romantic country hideaway with
four sumptuous suites for B&B.
Fresh flowers and champagne on
request. **$$$–$$$$**

Hotel Meal Guide

B&Bs supply a complimentary
full breakfast and are often
quite sophisticated
MAP (Modified American Plan)
rates include both breakfast
and dinner
FAP (Full American Plan) supply
all three meals

Manor House
69 Maple Avenue, 06058
Tel/fax: 860-542 5690
www.manorhouse-norfolk.com
An opulent 1898 Tudor summer
home B&B with 20 Tiffany stained-
glass windows. Some of the 10
rooms have whirlpool tubs,
fireplaces. **$$–$$$$**

NORWALK

Silvermine Tavern
194 Perry Avenue, 06850
Tel: 203-847 4558
Fax: 203-847 9171
www.silverminetavern.com
A 1785 country inn with 11
bedrooms set by a waterfall. **$$**

OLD LYME

Bee & Thistle Inn
100 Lyme Street, 06371
Tel: 860-434 1667/
800-622 4946
Fax: 860-434 3402
www.beeandthistleinn.com
A 1756 Colonial home with 12
rooms, set peacefully beside a
river. **$–$$$$**

OLD SAYBROOK

Saybrook Point Inn
2 Bridge Street, 05475
Tel: 860-395-2000/
800-243-0212
Fax: 860-388 1504
www.saybrook.com
Well-appointed 81-room nautical
luxury hotel, with water views,
indoor and outdoor pools, and a
spa, offering luxury services from
exercise programs to massages
and facials. **$$**

SALISBURY

Under Mountain Inn
482 Undermountain Road
06068
Tel: 860-435 0242
Fax: 860-435 2379
www.innbook.com

MAP with seven rooms offering
British hospitality in an 18th-century
farmhouse. **$$$–$$$$**
White Hart Inn
Village Green (Routes 44 and 41)
06068
Tel: 860-435 0030/
800-832 0041
Fax: 860-435 0040
www.whitehartinn.com
A century-old landmark offering 26
rooms at the center of a timeless
town. **$$$$**

WASHINGTON

Mayflower Inn
118 Woodbury Road (Route 47)
06793
Tel: 860-868 9466
Fax: 860-868 1497
www.mayflowerinn.com
The ultimate in romantic country
luxury. A new building with 25
rooms built on the site of an old
country inn on 28 secluded acres
with gardens, woods, and ponds.
Facilities include a pool, tennis
courts, health club, and a highly
regarded restaurant. **$$$$**

WEST CORNWALL

Hilltop Haven
175 Dibble Hill Road, 06796
Tel: 860-672 6871
www.hilltopbb.com
A stone house on a 64-acre hilltop
estate, perched over the village,
with lovely views of the Housatonic
Valley and Taconic Mountains. Two
rooms only. **$$**

WESTPORT

Inn at National Hall
2 Post Road West, 06880
Tel: 203-221 1351/800-628 4255
www.innatnationalhall.com
An elegant new inn, styled like an
English manor house and fashioned
from a 19th-century Historic District
building on the banks of the
Saugatuck. There are 16 lavishly
decorated rooms and a first-class
restaurant. **$$$$**

Inn at Longshore
260 Compo Road South, 06880
Tel: 203-226 3316
Fax: 203-227 5344
This is an old-fashioned 12-room
inn on the Sound with a trendy
restaurant. **$$–$$$**

WETHERSFIELD

Chester Bulkley House
184 Main Street, 06109
Tel: 860-563-4236
Five-room B&B in an elegant 1830
Greek Revival home located in an
historic town 5 miles (8 km) from
Hartford. **$**

WOODBURY

Longwood
1204 Main Street South
06798
Tel: 203-266 0800
Fax: 203-263 3474
www.longwoodcountryinn.com
A simple rambling 1789 B&B,
decorated in an English country
style, in Connecticut's "antiques
capital". Located on four wooded
acres near the Pomperaug River.
$$–$$$$

Where to Eat

AVON

Avon Old Farms Hotel
Routes 44 and 10
Tel: 860-677 1651
This is one of the country's oldest
inns, having been founded in 1757.
Offers Yankee/Continental fare in a
suite of atmospheric rooms. **$$$**

Restaurant Prices

Prices are approximate, but for a
three-course meal for one
(excluding beverages, tax and
tip), the following guidelines may
prove helpful:
$$$$ = over $40
$$$ = $28–40
$$ = $15–28
$ = under $15

Restaurant Guidelines

Prices are approximate, but for a three-course meal for one (excluding beverages, tax, and tip), the following guidelines may prove helpful:

$$$$ = over $40
$$$ = $28–40
$$ = $15–28
$ = under $15
Meal tax varies from state to state, but it is customary to tip 15 to 20 percent on the pre-tax total.

Credit cards The more expensive establishments generally accept credit cards, but call ahead to check just in case.

Reservations Most restaurants, except for the clearly casual, appreciate reservations (some require them).

Fat Cat Cafe
Riverdale Farms
(Route 10)
Tel: 860-674 1310
This cafe serves upscale comfort food, and the house motto is "Fine Dining, No Whining". **$$**

Max A Mia
70 East Main Street
(Route 44)
Tel: 860-677 6299
A lively northern Italian spot; good for pizza, risotto, and seafood. **$$**

CANAAN

Cannery Cafe
85 Main Street
(Routes 44 and 7)
Tel: 860-824 7333
"American bistro" innovations. **$$–$$$**

CHESTER

Restaurant du Village
59 Main Street
Tel: 860-526-5301
Superb formal French cuisine is served in this country auberge, situated between Essex and East Haddam. **$$$$**

EAST LYME

Flanders Fish Market
22 Chesterfield Road
(Route 161)
Tel: 860-739 8866
This humble roadside restaurant does ultra-fresh, very good-value fish. **$**

ESSEX

Griswold Inn
36 Main Street
Tel: 860-767 1776
Good traditional fare offered in a traditional inn. **$$–$$$**

The Black Seal
15 Main Street
Tel: 860-767 0233
The Black Seal does contemporary grazing, with nautical touches thrown in for good measure. **$$**

FARMINGTON

Apricots
1593 Farmington Avenue
Tel: 860-673 5405
Creative Continental dishes in a formal room with river views. More casual pub fare is available downstairs. **$$–$$$$**

GLASTONBURY

J. Gilbert's
185 Glastonbury Boulevard
Tel: 860-659 0409
Steakhouse with southwestern and Mediterranean influences. Club-like dining room done in dark woods. **$$–$$$**

Max Amore
Somerset Square Shopping Arcade
Tel: 860-659 2819
A marriage of well-prepared Northern Italian dishes, oak-grilled meats, and seafood, and a handsome yet casual dining room make Max Amore a perenially popular spot for both lunch and dinner. **$$–$$$**

Bamboo Grill
875 Main Street
Tel: 860-633-3446
Fragrant Vietnamese fare in an ascetic and relaxing coffee-shop ambiance. **$–$$**

GROTON

Fun 'n' Food Clam Bar
283 Route 12
Tel: 860-445 6186
Tasty chili dogs, clams, chowder, and milkshakes. All at a very fair price. **$**

Norm's Diner
171 Bridge Street
Tel: 860-445 5026
A 1950s diner serving breakfast all day. The house cheesecake enjoys local acclaim. **$**

GUILFORD

Guilford Tavern
2455 Boston Post Road
Tel: 203-453 2216
The ambience in this one-time foundry is rustic, and the focus of the food is fresh seafood and prime beef. Pub fare also available. **$$–$$$**

Quattro's
1300 Boston Post Road
Tel: 203-453 6575
Ecuadoran chefs prepare traditional Italian dishes, with surprising good results. The pasta is homemade, the daily specials are creative. Reservations advised. **$$–$$$**

HARTFORD AREA

Max Downtown
185 Asylum Street, Hartford
Tel: 860-522 2530
Upscale power dining. Menu emphasizes fish and pasta. Cigar bar draws a business crowd. **$$$$**

Savannah
391 Main Street, Hartford
Tel: 860-278 2020
New England ingredients, Southern influences, white tablecloths and African art make for an intriguing dining adventure. **$$$–$$$$**

Arugula
953 Farmington Avenue
West Hartford
Tel: 860-561 4888
Contemporary Italian cuisine –
from roasted eggplant Napoleon
to grilled polenta with portobello
mushrooms, and asparagus-filled
sun-dried tomato ravioli to wild
mushroom lasagna – served in a
small, intimate dining room. **$$$**

Back Porch Bistro
971 Farmington Avenue
West Hartford
Tel: 860-231 1922
Popular, stylish bistro serving
creative American fare: crab cakes,
veal with porcini mushrooms, and
upscale pastas. **$$–$$$**

Carbone's
588 Franklin Avenue, Hartford
Tel: 860-296 9646
An old standard that has been
serving Italian classics since its
establishment in 1938. **$$**

Costa Del Sol Restaurant
901 Wethersfield Road
Tel: 860-296 1714
Spanish cuisine, with specialties
such as paella, garlic soup, and the
house special flan, in a pleasant
spot near the airport. **$$–$$$**

Quaker Diner
319 Park Road, West Hartford
Tel: 860-232 5523
Restored 1931 diner cooking up
"made from scratch" breakfasts
and homestyle food. **$**

Trout Brook Brewhouse
45 Bartholomew Avenue, Hartford
Tel: 860-951 1680
An historic rubber factory
transformed into a smokehouse
and brewery. **$**

Home of the Burger

Louis' Lunch
261 Crown Street
Tel: 203-562 5507
This homely, family-run burger
joint in New Haven holds the
dubious distinction of being
birthplace of the original 1900
hamburger. Today's burgers are
still served in time-honored style
on toast, *sans* frills), amid period
decor and Tiffany lamps. **$**

IVORYTON

Copper Beech Inn
46 Main Street
Tel: 860-767 0330
Classic French cuisine in a setting
of studied elegance. **$$$$**

LITCHFIELD

Village Restaurant
25 West Street
Tel: 860-567 8307
Reasonably priced New England
fare, including burgers, pot roast,
and homemade desserts, served
up in ample portions in this popular
local eatery. **$$–$$$**

West Street Grill
43 West Street (Route 202)
Tel: 860-567 3885
Trendy in black and white, this
citified bistro serves brilliant
regional fare. **$$–$$$**

MADISON

Cafe Lafayette
725 Boston Post Road (Route 1)
Tel: 203-245 7773
Once a church meeting house, now
an elegant spot for great, updated,
continental and regional cuisine. **$$$**

MYSTIC

Flood Tide Restaurant
The Inn at Mystic
Routes 1 and 27
Tel: 860-536 8140
Fax: 860-536 9604
Contemporary continental food
served with water views. **$$$**

Seamen's Inne
105 Greenmanville Road
Tel: 860-536 9649
American seafood. Convenient to
Mystic Seaport. **$$**

NEW HAVEN

Barkies
220 College Street
Tel: 203-776 0795
Casual American grill and rotisserie

serving up seared chops, chicken,
fish, and vegetarian sausages. **$$$**

LPika Tapas Cafe
39 High Street
Tel: 203-865 1933
Authentic Spanish tapas elevate
group-grazing to a high art. **$$**

Polo Grille and Wine Bar
7 Elm Street
Tel: 203-787 9000
Modern Italian-inspired fare with an
extensive wine list. Sophisticated
but not stuffy. **$$**

Sally's Pizza
237 Wooster Street
Tel: 203-624 5271
The hands-down local favorite. **$**

NEW LONDON

Lighthouse Inn
6 Guthrie Place
Tel: 860-443 8411
Traditional American fare with a
seafood emphasis in a restored
Victorian mansion. **$$–$$$**

NEW MILFORD

Adrienne
218 Kent Road (Route 7)
Tel: 860-354 6001
Chef-owned restaurant featuring
New American fine dining in a pretty
white country house. **$$$**

The Bistro
31 Bank Street
Tel: 860-355 3266
Classic French and contemporary
American fare. **$$$**

NEW PRESTON

Boulders Inn
Route 45
Tel: 860-868 0541
Tasty extrapolations of hearty
Continental fare, with a view of
Lake Waramaug. **$$$**

Hopkins Inn
22 Hopkins Road
Tel: 860-868 7295
Austrian and Swiss dishes are the
house speciality here. The inn has
delightful vistas of the lake.
$$–$$$

NOANK

The Fisherman
937 Groton Long Point Road
Tel: 860-536 1717
Seafood is the order of the day
here. Good steaks and a water
view, too. **$–$$**

Abbott's Lobster in the Rough
117 Pearl Street
Tel: 860-536 7719
A classic lobster shack on the
water. Summer only. **$**

OLD LYME

Old Lyme Inn
85 Old Lyme Street
Tel: 860-434 2600
Dazzling seasonal dishes served
with aplomb. **$$$$**

OLD SAYBROOK

Saybrook Point Inn
2 Bridge Street
Tel: 860-388 1111
Traditionalist decor, contemporary
fare, and lovely water views. **$$$**

Cafe Routier
1080 Boston Post Road (Route 1)
Tel: 860-388 6270
Tiny café serving decent French
bistro fare. **$$**

SALISBURY

White Hart Inn
Routes 44 and 41
Tel: 860-435 0030
Contemporary American fare in a
historic inn. **$$$**

SOUTH NORWALK AREA

Silvermine Tavern
194 Perry Avenue
Norwalk
Tel: 203-847 4558
American classics in an old inn
beside a mill pond. **$$$**

Côte d'Azur
86 Washington Street
South Norwalk
Tel: 203-855 8900
A casual, comfortable room offering
up quality French bistro classics.
$$–$$$

**Barcelona Restaurant and
Wine Bar**
63 N Main Street
South Norwalk
Tel: 203-899 0088
Savory Spanish tapas are on offer
at this stylish dining room and
sidewalk cafe. **$$**

Pasta Nostra Trattoria
116 Washington Street
South Norwalk
Tel: 203-854 9700
Pasta Nostra is a convivial
contemporary Italian café. **$$**

STONINGTON

Randall's Ordinary
Route 2
North Stonington
Tel: 860-599 4540
Authentic 17th-century open-hearth
cooking and serving staff in period
dress. Best to reserve. **$$$**

Boatyard Cafe
194 Water Street
Tel: 860-535 1381
A waterside café with priceless
sunsets. **$$**

Mystic Pizza

Connecticut cuisine hit the map
in curious way when the movie
Mystic Pizza was named after a
fast-food parlor in downtown
Mystic. Filming took place in a
nearby lobster warehouse.

VERNON

Rein's New York-Style Delicatessen
Route 30
(I-84, Exit 65)
Tel: 860-875 1344
The most authentic – and tasty –
deli fare available north of
Manhattan. Rein's is located just
east of Hartford. **$**

WASHINGTON

Mayflower Inn
Route 47
Washington
Tel: 860-868 9466
The "country American" cuisine is
far, far from being rustic – it is
every bit as rarefied, in fact, as this
fine country inn. **$$$**

G.W. Tavern
20 Bee Brook Road
Washington Depot
Tel: 860-868 6633
A restored colonial tavern honoring
the first president with updated
New England classics: clam
chowder, slow-roasted duck, and
homemade cherry pie. **$$**

The Pantry
Titus Square
Tel: 860-868 0258
A gourmet shop cum café, in a
charming town. **$–$$**

WESTPORT

Splash
The Inn at Longshore
260 Compo Road South
Tel: 203-454 7798
An elegant traditional inn serving
elegant, distinctly non-traditional
fare: eclectic Pacific Rim cuisine
with all courses designed for
sharing. **$$$–$$$$**

Restaurant Guidelines

Prices are approximate, but for a
three-course meal for one
(excluding beverages, tax, and
tip), the following guidelines may
prove helpful:
$$$$ = over $40
$$$ = $28–40
$$ = $15–28
$ = under $15
Meal tax varies from state to

state, but it is customary to tip 15
to 20 percent on the pre-tax total.
Credit cards The more expensive
establishments generally accept
credit cards, but call ahead to
check just in case.
Reservations Most restaurants,
except for the clearly casual,
appreciate reservations (some
require them).

Acqua
43 Main Street
Tel: 203-222 8899
Italian/Mediterranean fare is
offered in this wildly popular,
sometimes clamorous, two-story
riverside villa. **$$$**
Sakura
680 Post Road East
Tel: 203-222 0802
One of Connecticut's favorite sushi
spots. **$$–$$$**

WOODBURY

Good News Cafe
694 Main Street
Tel: 203-266 4663
A cheerful spot focused on local
bounty and extremely luscious
desserts. **$$**

WOODVILLE

Le Bon Coin
Route 202
Tel: 860-868-7763
Good for French classics. **$$–$$$**

Culture

DANCE

Hartford Ballet (tel: 860-525-9396;
166 Capitol Avenue, Hartford)

stages both classical and modern
dance productions.

CLASSICAL MUSIC

Hartford Symphony performs at
The Bushnell (tel: 860-246-6807;
166 Capitol Avenue).
New Haven Symphony Orchestra,
the fourth oldest in the States,
holds a concert series at Yale
University's Woolsey Hall (tel: 203-
865-0831; 33 Whitney Avenue).

CHAMBER MUSIC

The **Norfolk Chamber Music Festival**
(tel: 860-542-3000; Route 44 and
272, Norfolk) includes chamber
music and an annual choral concert.

OPERA

The renowned **Goodspeed Opera
House** (tel: 860-873-8668;
Goodspeed Landing, East Haddam)
showcases operas, musicals and
revivals from April to December.

ROCK AND POP

Concerts are held year-round at
the huge **Hartford Civic Center** (tel:

860-727 8010; 1 Civic Center Plaza).
Hartford clubs **Voodoo** (tel: 860-
525 3003; 191 Ann Street) and
Arch Street Tavern (tel: 860-246
7610) both feature live acts.

THEATER

Hartford Stage Company (tel: 860-
527 5151; 50 Church Street), an
award-winning ensemble, produces
new plays, as well as classics.
Theaterworks (tel: 860-527 7838;
233 Pearl Street, Hartford) features
more experimental theater.
The Little Theater (tel: 860-645
6743; 177 Hartford Road,
Manchester), Connecticut's oldest
theater, presents local talent.
   Two Tony-award-winning theater
companies reside in New Haven: The
Long Wharf Theater (tel: 203-787
4282; 222 Sargent Dr) premiered
Arthur Miller's *The Crucible* and still
produces many prize-winning shows.
Yale Repertory Theater (tel: 203-
432 1234; 222 York Street) shows
experimental work by Yale students.

CINEMA

Cinestudio (tel: 860-297 2463;
300 Summit Street, Trinity College,
Hartford) shows both first-run and
art films.

Connecticut Festivals

Spring
Meriden's annual **Daffodil Festival**
(tel: 203-630 4259) in April is one
sign that spring is on the way. In
May, the **Mystic Lobsterfest** (tel:
860-572 5312, (888) 973 2767)
draws lobster lovers to the seaport
for an old-fashioned outdoor
lobster bake.

Summer
Summer is arts festival time,
beginning in June with New
Haven's **International Festival of
Arts & Ideas** (tel: 888-278 3325),
which showcases world-renowned
groups and premieres of
commissioned works.

In July, the **Hartford Riverfest**
(tel: 860-293 0131) celebrates
Independence Day with
entertainment for everyone,
culminating in spectacular
fireworks over the Connecticut
River. The **SoNo Arts Celebration**
(tel: 203-866 7916) in August, a
two-day outdoor festival of the
performing and visual arts, draws
visitors to historic South Norwalk.

Fall
Connecticut's harvest festivals
begin in August with the **Brooklyn
Fair** (tel: 860-779 0012), the
oldest continuously active
agricultural fair in the US, followed

in September by the **Woodstock
Fair** (tel: 860-928 3246), the
nation's second oldest. In October,
Southington hosts the annual
Apple Harvest Festival (tel: 860-
628 8036).

Winter
First Night Hartford (tel: 860-728
3089) is the New Year's Eve
festival of the arts. In February,
skiers head for the Litchfield Hills
for the **Salisbury Invitational Ski
Jump** and the **US Eastern Ski
Jump Championships**, an Olympic-
level competition on the site of the
nation's oldest ski jumping
program (tel: 860-435 9729).

COMEDY

City Steam (tel: 860-525 1600; Hartford), a brew pub, features comedians from both Boston and New York on Friday and Saturday nights.

ART GALLERIES

"SoNo" (short for South Norwalk and a take-off of SoHo in New York City) has revitalized itself with art galleries, chichi cafés, and shops. Kent also has more than a dozen galleries.

Nightlife

NIGHTCLUBS AND DISCOS

Hartford's popular **Bourbon Street North** (tel: 860-525 1014; 70 Union Place) features a large dance floor and encompasses a variety of music styles.

The **"SoNo"** area of downtown South Norfolk contains a variety of tavernlike nightclubs.

LIVE MUSIC

Blue Star Cafe (tel: 860-527 4557; 26 Trumbell Street, Hartford) organises live blues, jazz, and swing gigs.
Toad's Place (tel: 203-624 8623; 300 York Street, New Haven) is a popular club that books a variety of major acts.

CASINOS

Foxwoods High Stakes Bingo & Casino (tel: 800-752 9244; Route 2 in Ledyard between I-395 and I-95), which is housed on what was formerly a small Native American reservation, is now the largest gambling casino in the US. **Mohegan Sun Resort Casino** (tel: 888-226 7711; Route 2A, Montville), situated 10 miles south of Foxwoods, has a massive 2,500 slot machines.

Outdoor Activities

BIKING

Winding Trails Recreation Area off Route 4 in Farmington (tel: 860-677 8458) and **Woodbury Ski & Racquet Area** (tel: 203-263 2203) are big with Connecticut mountain bikers.

For a free Connecticut Bicycle Map, write to the Connecticut Department of Transportation, 2800-Berlin Turnpike, P.O. Box 317546, Newington, CT 06131-7546.

CANOEING, KAYAKING, AND RAFTING

For whitewater rafting or canoeing, head for the Housatonic River. **North American Whitewater Expeditions** (tel: 800-727 4379) organizes Housatonic rafting trips.

Canoe rentals are available at several state parks; call the **Connecticut State Bureau of Parks and Recreation** (tel: 860-424 3200) for details.

FISHING

All along the Connecticut coast, charter boats run half-day or full-day fishing expeditions. The best thing to do is get a list of operators from the Connecticut State Tourism Office (tel: 800-282 6863) or head to the harbor where you want to go out and talk to the captains directly.

Catch-and-release flyfishing is popular on the Housantanic River. As for the Farmington River, home to trout, bass, and pickerel, call the **Farmington River Anglers' Association** (tel: 860-738 7327; Winstead) for details.

HIKING

The **Appalachian Trail**, a 2,000-mile (3,200-km) trail linking Maine and Georgia, traverses about 50 miles (80km) of western Connecticut and the Appalachian Mountain Club (tel: 617-523 0636; Boston) provides detailed trail information.

At **Talcott Mountain State Park** in Simsbury, hikers who reach the peak of the one-and-a-half mile (2.5 km) walk are rewarded with panoramic vistas of the Farmington River Valley. On clear days, visibility can be up to 50 miles (80 km).

Macedonia Brook State Park in Kent and **Sleeping Giant State Park** in Hamden run scenic day hikes. Contact **The Connecticut State Bureau of Parks and Recreation** (tel: 860-424 3200) for details.

SAILING

Mystic is a center for sailing activity in Connecticut. The **Offshore Sailing School** (tel: 800-221 4326) conducts five-day learn-to-sail courses in the town.

SKIING

While downhill skiing is not a major sport in Connecticut, the state does have several small downhill areas in the Litchfield Hills region: **Mohawk Mountain** in Cornwall (tel: 860-672 6100), **Mount Southington** in Southington (tel: 860-628 0954), and **Powder Ridge Ski Area** in Middlefield (tel: 860-349 3454).

For cross-country skiing, try the **Woodbury Ski & Racquet Area** (tel: 203-263 2203), **Blackberry River Ski Touring Center** in Norfolk (tel: 860-542 5100), or Farmington's **Winding Trails Cross Country Ski Center** (tel: 860-678 9582).

Connecticut Cruises

Voyager Cruises' Argia (tel: 860-536 0416), a replica of a 19th-century schooner, offers half-day excursions from Mystic to Fisher's Island
The Mystic Whaler (tel: 800-697 8420), a classic schooner, sails for one- to five-day trips along the New England coast.
Mystic Seaport (tel: 888-973 27678) offers cruises from Mystic on the last coal-fired passenger steamer to sail in the US.

Shopping

MALLS

Hartford Civic Center (tel: 860-275 6100; 1 Civic Center Plaza) hosts over 60 shops.

New England's largest shopping mall is the **Danbury Fair Mall** (tel: 203-743 3247; Backus Ave, off I-84, Danbury), which has 240 shops, including five department stores. The **Olde Mistick Village** (tel: 860-536 4941; Exit 90 off I-95, Mystic), has 60 Colonial-style shops.

MARKETS

For fresh farm produce, flowers and crafts in Hartford, head to **Main St Market** (Main and Asylum Streets).

BOOKS

In Hartford, try the **Gallows Hill Bookstore** (tel: 860-297-5231; 300 Summit Street) and in West Hartford, **Bookworm** (tel: 860-233-2653; 968 Farmington Avenue). **Hartford's Reader's Feast** (tel: 860-232-3710; 529 Farmington Avenue) sells feminist, gay, and children's literature.

Yale University Bookstore (tel: 888-730 9253; 77 Broadway) sells academic text and trade books.

ANTIQUES

New Haven sports over 30 antique dealers, among them **Antique Corner** (tel: 203-387 7200; 859 Whalley Avenue).

The Litchfield Hills are often referred to as the "antique capital" of the country (slight hyperbole, but there are an impressive number), with almost every village having multiple shops. Try **The Bittersweet Shop** (tel: 860-354 1727; Route 7, New Milford) and **Old Carriage Shop Antiques** (tel: 860-567 3234; 920 Bantam Road, Bantam). Both feature over 15 dealers.

Dealers in Mystic and Stonington are on Main and Water Streets.

The large **Old Saybrook Antiques Dealers** (tel: 860-388 1600; 756 Middlesex Turnpike, Route 154, in Old Saybrook) houses more than 100 dealers of 18th- and 19th-century pieces.

ARTS AND CRAFTS

Dozens of pottery and crafts shops are located in the Litchfield Hills; try either of these on Route 128 in West Cornwall: **Cornwall Bridge Pottery & Store** (tel: 860-672 6545) and **Ingersoll Cabinetmakers** (tel: 860-672 6334).

Farmington Crafts Common (tel: 860-674 9295; 248 Main Street, Farmington) features over 200 craftspeople.

Children

THEME PARKS

Lake Compounce (tel: 860-583 3631; 822 Lake Avenue, Bristol), America's oldest amusement park.

CAROUSELS

The Carousel (tel: 860-246 7739; Bushnell Park, Hartford) is a 1914 merry-go-round with hand-carved horses.

ZOOS

Beardsley Zoological Gardens (tel: 203-394 6565; Noble Avenue, Beardsley Park, Bridgeport), the state's largest zoo, features over 120 species, a carousel, and a New England farmyard petting zoo.

JOURNEYS BY STEAM TRAIN

New England Railroad Museum (tel: 203-575 1931; 83 Bank Street, Waterbury) offers a historic ride through Black Rock State Park. **Valley Railroad** (tel: 860-767 0103; Railroad Avenue, Essex) runs an old-fashioned service.

Rhode Island

The Place

Known as: The Ocean State.
Motto: Hope.
Origin of name: unknown. Perhaps reminded an early explorer of Rhodes in Greece. Or maybe derived from the Dutch for "red" after the color of its soil.
Entered Union: May 29, 1790, the last of the 13 original states.
Capital: Providence.
Area: 1,545 sq. miles (4,002 sq. km).
Highest point: Jerimoth Hill, 812 ft (247 meters).
Population: 1 million.
Population density: 649 people per sq. km (251 per sq. km).
Economy: manufacturing (fabricated metals, precision instruments, apparel and textiles, printed materials, rubber and plastic items, industrial machinery, primary metals, electronic goods, transportation equipment, chemicals, and processed foods.
Annual visitors: 29 million
National representation: 2 senators and 2 representatives to Congress.
Famous citizens: George M. Cohan, Nelson Eddy, Christopher and Oliver La Farge.

Where to Stay

BLOCK ISLAND

Atlantic Inn
High Street, Old Harbor, 02807
Tel: 401-466 5883/
800-224 7422
Fax: 401-466 5678
www.atlanticinn.com
An 1879 white-clapboard hotel, Block Island's *grande dame*, with a

spacious porch on a hill overlooking the sea. 21 pleasant Victorian-style rooms and two tennis courts. **$$$–$$$$**
Spring House Hotel
Spring Street, Old Harbor, 02807
Tel: 401-466 5844/
800-234 9263
Fax: 401-466 2633
www.springhousehotel.com
A classic 49-room hotel (built in 1852) with Victorian furnishings, a cupola-topped mansard roof and a wraparound porch. Set on 15 acres above the ocean. **$$$–$$$$**
Hotel Manisses and The 1661 Inn
Spring Street, Old Harbor, 02807
Tel: 401-466 2063/
800-626 4773
Fax: 401-466 3162
www.blockisland.com/biresorts
Victorian inns with ocean views; there are 53 old-fashioned rooms in the main inns and cottages. An animal farm on the property is home to llamas and emus. **$–$$$$**

BRISTOL

Chimney Crest Manor
5 Founders Drive, 06010
Tel: 860-582 4219
Fax: 860-584 5903
This 1930 English Tudor mansion overlooking the Farmington Valley and on the National Register of Historic Places has two rooms and three suites (some with fireplace and spa). Facilities include air-conditioning and a jacuzzi. **$$–$$$**
Joseph Reynolds House Inn
956 Hope Street, 02809
Tel: 401-254 0230/
800-754 0230
Fax: 401 254–2610
Built in 1693 and considered to be the oldest three-story building in

New England; now a B&B with suites and cozy guest rooms on a busy Street **$$**

JAMESTOWN

Bay Voyage Inn
150 Conanicus Avenue, 02835
Tel: 401-423 2100/
800-225 3522
Fax: 401-423 3209
www.equivest.com
Formerly a country house in Newport, this 32-room inn was transported across the bay in 1899. It's now an all-suite inn overlooking the harbor. **$$$–$$$$**

LITTLE COMPTON

Stone House Club
122 Sakonnet Point Road, 02837
Tel: 401-635 2222
A stone farmhouse overlooking the ocean, now a private club, that rents 15 simply furnished rooms. **$–$$**

NARRAGANSETT

Stone Lea
40 Newton Avenue (off Ocean Road), 02882
Tel: 401-783 9546
A Victorian summer "cottage" designed in 1884 by McKim, Meade & White, located on a cliff over-looking the ocean. This formal inn B&B – many of the nine rooms have ocean views – is set on a broad lawn that extends to the sea. **$$–$$$**
The Richards
144 Gibson Avenue, 02882
Tel: 401-789 7746
Fax: 401-783 7168

Hotel Meal Guide

B&Bs supply a complimentary full breakfast and are often quite sophisticated
MAP (Modified American Plan) rates include both breakfast and dinner
FAP (Full American Plan) supply all three meals

An 1884 stone English manor B&B surrounded by gardens. All four antique-furnished rooms have working fireplaces. Private access to the rocky coast. No credit cards. **$–$$**

NEWPORT

Cliffside Inn
2 Seaview Avenue, 02840
Tel: 401-847 1811/
800-845 1811
Fax: 401 848 5850
www.cliffsideinn.com
Near the Cliff Walk, an 1880 Victorian villa, carved into grand, dramatic quarters. The 15 rooms in this B&B are light, airy rooms, and some have working fireplaces and whirlpool tubs. **$$$$**
Elm Tree Cottage
336 Gibbs Avenue, 02840
Tel: 401-849 1610/
800-882 3356.
Fax: 401849 2084
www.elm-tree.com
A six-room "cottage" B&B only in the Newport sense, one block from the water, overlooking First Beach and Easton Pond. **$$$$**
Francis Malbone House
392 Thames Street, 02840
Tel: 401-846 0392/
800-846 0392
Fax: 401-848 5956
www.malbone.com
A 1760 Colonial brick mansion B&B on the harborfront. Twenty lavishly appointed rooms with period reproduction furnishings.
$$$–$$$$
Victorian Ladies
63 Memorial Boulevard, 02840
Tel/fax: 401-849 9960
www.victorianladies.com
A pair of vintage lovelies, in period style, offering 11 B&B rooms. Near First Beach and the Cliff Walk. **$$$–$$$$**
Ivy Lodge
12 Clay Street, 02840
Tel: 401-849 6865
Seven-room B&B in a Victorian home in the mansion district, designed by Stanford White. Dramatic old-English entryway, wraparound porch, and 11 fireplaces. **$$–$$$**

Melville House
39 Clarke Street, 02840
Tel: 401-847 0640
Fax: 401-847 0956
www.melvillehouse.com
A 1750 Colonial B&B on a gas
lamp-lit street on Historic Hill.
Eight small, but comfortably
appointed guest rooms, plus a
fireplace suite. **$$**

PROVIDENCE

Omni Biltmore Hotel
Kennedy Plaza, 02903
Tel: 401-421 0700/
800-843 6664
Fax: 401 455 3040
www.omnihotels.com
A 1922 Art Deco-style grand hotel
downtown, with 238 rooms nicely
restored. **$$–$$$$**
Old Court
144 Benefit Street, 02903
Tel: 401-751 2002
Fax: 401-272 4830
www.oldcourt.com
Near the Rhode Island School of
Design, an 1863 rectory retrofitted
as an elegant Victorian-style inn.
Ten spacious rooms with high
ceilings, chandeliers, and (non-
working) marble fireplaces. **$$–$$$**
State House Inn
43 Jewett Street, 02908
Tel: 401-785 1235
Fax: 401-351 4261
www.providence-inn.com.
An 1880s Colonial Revival home
located near the State House. The
10 B&B rooms are done in basic
Early American style; some have
canopy beds and working
fireplaces. **$$–$$$**

WEEKAPAUG

Weekapaug Inn
25 Spray Rock Road, 02891
Tel: 401-322 0301
Fax: 401-322 1016
www.weekapauginn.com
A classic FAP inn (65 rooms) with
a wraparound porch sheltering well-
heeled families since 1938. On
a peninsula surrounded on three
sides by Quanochontaug Pond in a

coastal village 6 miles (9.6 km)
from Westerly. Credit cards are
not accepted. **$$$$**

WESTERLY

Shelter Harbor Inn
10 Wagner Road (Route 1), 02891
Tel: 401-322 8883/
800-468 8883
Fax: 401-322 7907
www.shelterharborinn.com
Once a working farm, now a luxury
24-room getaway for B&B in a rural
setting near the beach. The roof
deck has a barbecue grill and a
hot tub. **$$**
Grandview Bed and Breakfast
212 Shore Road, 02891
Tel: 401-596 6384/800-447 6384
Fax: 401-596 3036
www.grandviewbandb.com
A comfortable turn-of-the-20th-
century house with 9 cozy guest
rooms (some with ocean views),
gardens, and a stone wraparound
porch. **$**

Where to Eat

BLOCK ISLAND

Atlantic Inn Restaurant
High Street, Old Harbor
Tel: 401-466 5883
Prix-fixe seafood and continental
dinners. Dress is more casual than
the food. **$$$$**
Spring House Hotel
Spring Street, Old Harbor
Tel: 401-466 5844
Seafood, pastas, and all-you-can-eat
barbecues overlooking Block Island
Sound. **$$–$$$**

Restaurant Guidelines

Prices are approximate, but for
a three-course meal for one
(excluding beverages, tax, and
tip), the following guidelines may
prove helpful:
$$$$ = over $40
$$$ = $28–40
$$ = $15–28
$ = under $15
Meal tax varies from state to

Juice 'n Java
235 Dodge Street, Old Harbor
Funky coffee house serving
sandwiches and pastries. Large
supply of magazines and board
games. **$**

BRISTOL

Quito's
411 Thames Street
Tel: 401-253 4500
Well-established spot for casual
seafood, overlooking the bay. **$–$$**
Aidan's Pub
5 John Street.
Tel: 401-254 1940.
Irish pub serving fish and chips,
bangers and mash and other simple
but tasty fare. **$**

JAMESTOWN

Bay Voyage Inn
150 Conanicus Avenue
Tel: 401-423 2100
American standbys – lobster
thermidor, rack of lamb, filet
mignon – and bountiful Sunday
brunch with harbor views. **$$$**
Jamestown Oyster Bar
22 Narragansett Avenue
Tel: 401-423 3380
Fresh fish, burgers, and quahogs
in a popular local spot. Lunch
Wed–Sun, dinner nightly. **$**

LITTLE COMPTON

Stone House Club
122 Sakonnet Point Road
Tel: 401-635 2222

state, but it is customary to tip 15
to 20 percent on the pre-tax total.
Credit cards The more expensive
establishments generally accept
credit cards, but call ahead to
check just in case.
Reservations Most restaurants,
except for the clearly casual,
appreciate reservations (some
require them).

A private club in an old farmhouse that is open to non-members for dinner. Traditional American and French-style fare. **$$–$$$**
The Commons Lunch
Tel: 401-635 4388
A downhome diner fit for gentleman (and lady) farmers. **$**
Olga's Cup and Saucer
261 West Main Road
Tel: 401-635 8650
A tiny take-away stand at Walker's Roadside selling creative, delectable baked goods: vegetable tarts, intriguing pizzas, and delicious fruit pies. Although the little shop is only open seasonally, you can find their goodies year-round at 103 Point Street, Providence, tel: 401-831 6666. **$**

NARRAGANSETT

Basil's
22 Kingstown Road
Tel: 401-789 3743
Continental fare, with an accent on French, in an intimate and elegant Victorian restaurant near the pier. **$$–$$$**
Woody's
21 Pier Marketplace
Tel: 401-789 9500
This place does savory tapas-style appetizers and substantial contemporary entrées. **$$**
Aunt Carrie's
1240 Ocean Road, Point Judith
Tel: 401-783 7930
A classic seaside clam shack. **$**

NEWPORT

Le Bistro
Banister's Wharf
Tel: 401-849 7778
A charming French café in a loft above the bustling harbor. **$$$$**
Clarke Cooke House
Bannister's Wharf.
Tel: 401-849 2900
A 1790 Colonial house with formal, waterview dining. **$$$$**
The Black Pearl
Bannister's Wharf
Tel: 401-846 5264
A classic harborside tavern. **$$$**

Price Guide

Prices ranges are approximate, but for a three-course meal for one (excluding beverages, tax, and tip), the following guidelines may prove helpful:
$$$$ = over $40
$$$ = $28–40
$$ = $15–28
$ = under $15

Le Petite Auberge
19 Charles Street
Tel: 401-849 6669
French fare served in an historic home. **$$$**
The Mooring
Sayer's Wharf
Tel: 401-846 2260
Former HQ of New York Yacht Club. Good on seafood staples. **$$–$$$**
Puerini's
24 Memorial Boulevard West
Tel: 401-847 5506
Traditional fresh Italian staples. **$$**
White Horse Tavern
Marlborough and Farewell Streets
Tel: 401-849 3600
Reputedly the oldest continually operating tavern in the US (est. 1673), this atmospheric place serves classics such as grilled lobster and Chateaubriand. **$$**

PROVIDENCE

Al Forno
577 S Main Street
Tel: 401-273 9760
Arguably New England's pre-eminent temple of *nuova cucina*. **$$$$**
Capital Grille
1 Cookson Place
Tel: 401-521 560
Premium dry-aged beef, in the renovated railroad station. **$$$**
Hemenway Sea Food
1 Washington Square
Tel: 401-351 8570
Superb seafood, with views of the Providence River. **$$$**
La Locanda del Coccio
265 Atwells Ave (DiPasquale Plaza)
Tel: 401-273 2652
Italian regional cuisine using ancient clay cookery techniques in

a comfortably upscale Federal Hill location. **$$–$$$**
Rue de L'Espoir
99 Hope Street
Tel: 401-751–8890
Chic, modern bistro fare in a pretty room near Brown University. **$$–$$$**
Big Alice's Ice Cream
100 Hope Street
Tel: 401-273 5812
Providence's premier ice cream vendor since 1980. Homemade and delicious. Near Brown University. **$**

WATCH HILL

Olympia Tea Room
Bay Street
Tel: 401-348 8211
A classic 1916 luncheonette. **$$**

WESTERLY

Shelter Harbor Inn
Route 1
Tel: 401-322 8883
Well-priced regional specialties. **$$$**
Three Fish
37 Main Street
Tel: 401-348 9700
Seafood and top desserts in a former mill by the Pawcatuck River. **$$–$$$**

Culture

CLASSICAL MUSIC

Rhode Island Philharmonic (tel: 401-831 3123; 222 Richmond Street, Providence) gives 10 concerts throughout the year.

ROCK AND POP

Providence Civic Center (tel: 401-331 6700; 1 LaSallle Square) hosts big-name touring rock bands.

Useful Listings

The daily *Providence Journal* and glossy *Rhode Island Monthly* have all the up-to-date information on what's happening culturally in and around Rhode Island.

THEATER

Trinity Repertory Company (tel: 401-351 4242; 201 Washington Street, Providence). This Tony-award-winning group always puts on among the country's finest and most innovative productions.
Brown University (tel: 401-863 2838; Leeds Theater, 77 Waterman Street, Providence) stages contemporary to classical and everything In between.
Providence Performing Arts Center (tel: 401-421 2787; 220 Weybosset Street) sets the stage for pre- and post-Broadway shows.
Astors' Beechwood (tel: 401-846 3772; 580 Bellevue Avenue, Newport) stages murder-mystery plays once a week in-season.

CINEMA

Cable Car Cinema (tel: 401-272 3970; 204 S Main Street, Providence) has seen better days, but perhaps that's the point.
Art films, old couches from which to watch the flicks, and cheap popcorn continue to survive in college towns.

ART GALLERIES

Providence's Wickenden Street has a number of galleries, including **Alaimao Gallery** (tel: 401-421 5360; 301 Wickenden Street) which has an unusual number of prints, playbills, and posters.

ALL-IN-ONE

AS220 (tel: 401-831 9327; 111 Empire Street, Providence) caters for so many interests: at various times it is a performance art space, gallery, theater, and musical venue for tastes as diverse as techno and folk.

Nightlife

The free *Providence Phoenix* can be found around town in shops and restaurants, and is slanted towards a younger, hip crowd.
Thames Street is where it's happening in Newport.

LIVE MUSIC

Thames Street Station (and Great American Pub) (tel: 401-849 9480; 337 America's Cup Avenue, Newport) puts on regular dance-music nights.
On Block Island, both **The National Hotel** (tel: 401-466 2901; Water Street) and **Govern's Yellow Kittens Tavern** (tel: 401-466 5855; Corn Neck Road) have music every night in summer. Govern's agenda is the more diverse of the two, with reggae and R&B included.

GAY & LESBIAN VENUES

Gerardo's (tel: 401-274 5560; Atwells Avenue at Franklin Square, Providence) is a popular gay and lesbian dance place.
David's (28 Prospect Hill Street, Newport) is primarily a men's bar with a DJ.

LATE NIGHT VENUES

The Hot Club (tel: 401-861 9007; 575 S Water Street, Providence), aptly named, is a popular waterfront hang-out.

Outdoor Activities

BIKING

The 14½-mile (23-km) **East Bay Bicycle Path** follows Narragansett Bay and winds through several towns between Providence and Bristol.
On Block Island and in Tiverton and Little Compton, the relatively quiet roads are popular destinations for bikers.
Bikers can also follow Newport's **Bellevue Avenue** and **Ocean Drive** for about 15 miles (24 km) past the mansions and along the shore.
For a free *Guide to Cycling in the Ocean State*, call 401-222 4203, extension 4042.

Rhode Island Festivals

Spring
In Bristol, the Blithewood Gardens & Arboretum sponsors the **Annual Spring Bulb Display** (tel: 401-253 2707) in April and May; it's one of New England's largest daffodil exhibitions.

Summer
In mid-July, Newport's gilded mansions scintillate to classical strains of the **Newport Music Festival** (tel: 401-846 1133).
The season is capped off by two extremely popular harborview events in mid-August: **Ben & Jerry's Newport Folk Festival** (tel: 401-847 3700) – the long-standing folkie Olympus, now sponsored by the ice cream company – and the **JVC Jazz Festival** (tel: 401-847 3700).
Bristol claims the nation's oldest **4th of July Parade** (tel: 401-245 0750). Then, in August, the **Charlestown Chamber Seafood Festival** (tel: 401-364 3878) spreads out a "roll-up-your-sleeves" gastronomic *smorgasbord*, including chowder, clam cakes, lobster, and more.

Fall
The capital city ushers in the autumn with the five-day **Providence Waterfront Festival** (tel: 401-785 9490) in September, where music, children's programs, an international food court and water activities celebrate the city's maritime heritage and the revitalization of downtown.

Winter
The 10-day **Newport Winter Festival** (tel: 401-849 8048) in January and February lures visitors with food, music, ice carving, and snow sculptures.

CANOEING, KAYAKING, AND RAFTING

Coastal sea kayaking is popular and the **Kayak Centre** (tel: 401-295 4400 in Wickford or 401 848 2920 in Newport) leads a variety of excursions, including a Newport tour with ocean glimpses of mansions; the company also runs a multi-day trip to Block Island.

In Providence, **Baer's River Workshop** (tel: 401-453 1633) rents canoes and kayaks and leads guided tours of local rivers. For information about canoeing the 45-mile (72-km) long Blackstone River, request a free copy of the *Blackstone River Canoe Guide* (tel: 800-454 2882).

SAILING

Newport, known as The Sailing Capital of the World, is a good base for short harbor excursions and learn-to-sail vacations.

Sightsailing of Newport (tel: 401-849 3333) offers harbor sails, rentals and instruction.

America's Cup Charters (tel: 401-846 9886) runs evening sails and half- or full-day sailboat charters. Other charters include **Flyer** (tel: 401-848 2100), a 57-ft catamaran; **Spirit of Newport** (tel: 401-849 3575); and the 72-ft schooner **Madeline** (tel: 401-847 0298).

Newport Sailing School (tel: 401-848 2266) runs narrated one- and two-hour sailing tours plus classes.

Offshore Sailing School (tel: 800-221 4326; Newport) conducts

Snow Tours

The following places offer cross-country ski tours led by ski instructors, or guided snowmobile tours:
● Killington, Wells and Post Mills in Vermont
● Bartlett, Colebrook, East Conway Littleton, and Tamworth in New Hampshire
● Rangeley in Maine

a learn-to-sail vacation program. **Block Island Club** (tel: 401-466 5939) offers comprehensive sailing instruction and one-week family memberships.

FISHING

Saltwater Edge (tel: 401-842 0062; Newport) offers fly-fishing lessons as well as guided saltwater fishing outings. Several charter fishing boats are based in Narragansett, including **Persuader** (tel: 401-783 5644).

HIKING

Rhode Island Audubon Society (tel: 401-949 5454) leads various nature hikes.

Shopping

WHERE TO SHOP

The Arcade (tel: 401-598 1199; 65 Weybosset Street, Providence) was the country's first indoor mall, built in 1828. Architecturally, it's a beauty to behold. It's still a bastion of consumerism, although styles have changed over the years.

Armory (tel: 401-848 2398; 365 Thames Street) in a sprawling 19th-century complex, sells the wares of more than 125 antiques, jewelry, and art dealers.

MARKETS

Route 77 to Little Compton is blessed with many roadside farm stands offering extra-fresh produce.

BOOKS

Map Center (tel: 401-421 2184; 671 N Main Street, Providence) sells every kind of imaginable map. **Armchair Sailor Books** (tel: 401-847 4252; 543 Thames Street, Newport), purveyors of maritime titles, is appropriately located in this sailing center.

ANTIQUES

In Providence head straight to Wickenden Street. In Newport, you'll find clusters of antiques shops on Thames, Franklin, and Spring streets. **Armory** (tel: 401-848 2398), 365 Thames Street, situated in a sprawling 19th-century complex, sells the wares of more than 125 antiques, jewelry, and art dealers.

CHINA AND GLASS

Thames Glass (tel: 401-846 0576; 688 Thames Street, Newport) blows glass in a neighboring studio and sells firsts and seconds from the shop.

SOUVENIRS & GIFTS

Jewelry
Coppacetic Rudely Elegant Jewelry (tel: 401-273 0470; The Arcade, 65 Weybosset Street, Providence) is a determinedly eclectic place, thanks to the diverse work of a very distinct group of artisans.

Arts and Crafts
MacDowell Pottery (tel: 401-846 6313; 220 Spring Street, Newport) displays the work of many state- and New England-wide potters.

Children

THEME PARKS

Flying Horse Carousel (no phone; Bay Street, Watch Hill), with beautiful hand-carved horses, lays claim as the oldest merry-go-round in the country.

ZOOS

Roger Williams Park Zoo (tel: 401-785 3510; Elmwood Avenue, Providence), a 400-plus-acre park with an antique carousel, tiny train, and lots of animals to keep the children entertained, and a quiet Japanese garden for adults.

Vermont

The Place

Known as: The Green Mountain State.
Motto: Freedom and unity.
Origin of name: from the French *vert* (= green) and *mont* (= mountain).
Entered Union: March 4, 1791, the 14th state.
Capital: Montpelier
Area: 9,615 sq. miles (24,903 sq km).
Highest point: Mount Mansfield, 4,393 ft (1,339 meters).
Population: 562,800.
Population density: 59 per sq. mile (23 per sq. km).
Economy: once agricultural, now relies increasingly on tourism.
Annual visitors: 7.9 million.
National representation: 2 senators and 1 representative to Congress.
Famous citizens: Ethan Allen, Calvin Coolidge and Admiral George Deweys.

Where to Stay

Many Vermont inns take a break between foliage and the holidays, and again during "mud season", so check first if you plan to visit in the late fall or early spring.

ARLINGTON

West Mountain Inn
River Road (off Route 313), 05250
Tel: 802-375-6516
Fax: 802-375 6553
www.westmountaininn.com
A family-friendly 1840s farmhouse turned 22-room MAP with mountain views on 150 country acres. Trails for hiking or cross-country skiing, children's game room, and the resident llama ranch amuse all ages. **$$$–$$$$**

Arlington Inn
Route 7A, 05250
Tel: 802-375 6532/
800-443 9442
Fax: 802-375 6543
www.arlingtoninn.com
An elegant Greek Revival mansion with comfortable Victorian-style interior furnishings in the 19 B&B bedrooms. Located between Bennington and Manchester. **$–$$$**

BENNINGTON

Four Chimneys Inn
21 West Road (Route 9), 05201
Tel: 802-447 3500/
800-649 3503
Fax: 802-447 3692
www.fourchimneys.com
French Provincial decor in a grand old manse with 11 rooms for B&B. **$$–$$$**

Molly Stark Inn
1067 E. Main Street, 05201.
Tel: 802-442 9631/
800-356 3076
Fax: 802-442 5224
www.mollystarkinn.com
A friendly, homey B&B. The nine cozy guest rooms have New England country-style furnishings, antique quilts and clawfoot tubs. **$**

BOLTON VALLEY

Bolton Valley Holiday Resort
Bolton Access Road, 05477
Tel: 802-434 3444/
877-926 5866
Fax: 802-434-2131
www.boltonvalleyvt.com
After a multimillion-dollar renovation, this family-friendly ski resort is better than ever. There's now a complex of condos and inn rooms at the base of the mountain, a sports center, six lifts, night skiing, and an excellent complex of cross-country and snowshoe trails. **$$–$$$**

The Black Bear
Bolton Access Road, 05477
Tel: 802-434 2126/
800-395 6335
Fax: 802-434 576
www.blkbearinn.com
Cozy countrified decor (with bear-adorned quilts) in a lodge located amid the Bolton Valley Resort. 24 rooms. **$**

BRATTLEBORO

Latchis Hotel
50 Main Street, 05301
Tel: 802-254 6300
Fax: 802-254 6304
www.brattleboro.com/latchis
A 1938 Art Deco hotel, right in the heart of downtown. Some of the 30 rooms have refrigerators, some have views of Main Street or the Connecticut River. **$–$$**

BRIDGEWATER CORNERS

October Country Inn
Upper Road, 05035
Tel/fax: 802-672 3412/
800-648 8421
www.octobercountryinn.com
A cozy MAP farmhouse with 10 rooms on a back road, about 5 miles (8 km) from the Killington ski area. **$$**

BROOKFIELD

Green Trails Inn
Main Street, 05036
Tel: 802-276 3412/
800-243 3412
www.greentrailsinn.com
A sprawling 13-room inn and lodge B&B, built around 1790 and 1830 farmhouses, on 17 acres overlooking Sunset Lake. The

Price Categories

A very approximate guide to current room rates for a standard double per night is:
$$$$ = over $200
$$$ = $150–200
$$ = $100–150
$ = under $100

owners maintain 19 miles (30 km) of trails for cross-country skiing and hiking. **$–$$**

BURLINGTON

Willard Street Inn
349 S. Willard Street, 05401
Tel: 802-651 8710/
800-577 8712
Fax: 802-651 8714
www.willardstreetinn.com
Built for a state senator in the 1880s, this stately, formally appointed house in Burlington's historic hill area has views of Lake Champlain. This is now a B&B with 14 rooms furnished with antiques and down comforters. **$$–$$$$**

CHITTENDEN

Mountain Top Inn
Mountain Top Road, 05737
Tel: 802-483 2311/
800-445 2100
Fax: 802-483 6373
www.mountaintopinn.com
This 52-room MAP is a large, comfortable family resort deep in the countryside north of Rutland. Outstanding Nordic skiing. **$$$$**

Tulip Tree Inn
Chittenden Dam Road, 05737
Tel: 802-483 6213/
800-707 0017
www.tuliptreeinn.com
An electricity magnate's 1920s' retreat 10 miles (16 km) north of Rutland. Five of the eight rooms in the MAP feature whirlpool tubs. **$$–$$$$**

CRAFTSBURY COMMON AND ENVIRONS

Inn on the Common
Main Street (Route 14)
Craftsbury Common, 05827
Tel: 802-586 9619
Fax: 802-586 2249
www.innonthecommon.com
A 17-room MAP with luxurious decor, including plush carpets, quilts, historic wallpaper reproductions, as well as a swimming pool, tennis

court, and mountain views. Ambitious cuisine served dinner party-style. **$$$$**

Craftsbury Outdoor Center
Craftsbury Common, 05827
Tel: 802-586 7767/
800-729 7751
Fax: 802-586 7768
www.craftsbury.com
A 47-room MAP offering dormitory-style accommodation, with skilled training available in various outdoor sports. There are more than 100 miles (160 km) of cross-country ski trails, plus sculling, running camps, mountain biking, and canoeing on offer. **$–$$$**

Craftsbury Inn
Main Street (Route 14)
Craftsbury, 05826
Tel: 802-586 2848/
800-336 2848
Fax: 802-586 2848
Country comfort in an 1850 Greek Revival inn. Ten rooms with wraparound verandahs overlooking lavish gardens. Just down the road from Craftsbury Common.
$** (B&B); **$$ (MAP)

DORSET

Barrows House,
Route 30, 05251
Tel: 802-867 4455/
800-639 1620
Fax: 802-867 0132
www.barrowshouse.com
An 18th-century Federal-style MAP inn and carriage house with homey touches in the 28 rooms and a well-regarded restaurant. Pool and tennis courts. Located 6 miles (10 km) north of Manchester. **$$$$**

Dorset Inn
Church & Main Streets, 05251
Tel: 802-867 5500

Price Categories

A very approximate guide to current room rates for a standard double per night is:
$$$$ = over $200
$$$ = $150–200
$$ = $100–150
$ = under $100

Fax: 802-867 5542
www.dorsetinn.com
One of the state's oldest – and reliably commendable – inns (MAP), opened in 1796, with 31 rooms.
$$$–$$$$

Cornucopia of Dorset
Route 30, 05251
Tel: 802-867 5751/
800-566 5751
Fax: 802-867 5753
www.cornucopiaofdorset.com
Five prettily appointed rooms; pampering services include champagne welcome, marvelous breakfasts (served by candlelight), cozy down comforters or quilts, and terry-cloth robes. **$$–$$$$**

Marble West Inn
Dorset West Road, 05251
Tel: 802-867 4155
An eight-room B&B in a marble-columned 1840s Greek Revival manse, elegantly decorated. **$–$$**

EAST BURKE

Inn at Mountain View Farm
Darling Hill Road, 05832
Tel: 802-629 9924/800-572 4509
Twelve lovely guest rooms with private baths and antiques in an 1890 Georgian inn on the grounds of a one-time creamery. With 440 acres of grounds, there are miles of cross-country, hiking, and mountain biking trails. Excellent restaurant on the premises. **$$–$$$**

Old Cutter Inn
143 Pinkham Road, 05832
Tel/fax: 802-626 5152/
800-295 1943
www.pbpub.com/cutter.htm
A small farmhouse converted into a quaint nine-room inn. The restaurant serves Swiss fare. **$**

ESSEX JUNCTION

Inn at Essex
70 Essex Way (off Route 15), 05452
Tel: 802-878 1100/800-288 7613
Fax: 802-878 0063
www.innatessex.com
A Georgian-style hotel with 97 rooms, a swimming pool and

outstanding cuisine (provided by the New England Culinary Institute); convenient to Burlington. **$$–$$$**

FAIR HAVEN

Maplewood Inn
1108 Route 22A South, 05473
Tel: 802-265 8039/
800-253 7729
Fax: 802-265 8210
www.maplewoodinn.net
A five-room B&B in a former dairy farm with fanciful decor and hearty breakfasts. Located west of Rutland near the New York border. **$–$$**

GRAFTON

Old Tavern at Grafton
Route 121, 05146
Tel: 802-843 2231/800-843 1801
Fax: 802-843 2245
www.old-tavern.com
An 18th-century stagecoach inn (plus several nearby buildings) with 59 bedrooms furnished with country antiques in a lovingly restored town. Swimming pond, tennis courts, ice skating, and cross-country ski trails. **$$–$$$$**

HIGHGATE SPRINGS

Tyler Place on Lake Champlain
Route 7, 05460
Tel: 802-868 3301
Fax: 802-868 5621
www.tylerplace.com
A family FAP "camp" with 60 rooms. Situated since the 1930s on 165 acres of lakefront property. Accommodations include cottages, an 1820 farmhouse, a Victorian guest house, and a modern inn. Many activities for children. **$$$$**

JAY

Hotel Jay & Jay Peak Condominiums
Route 242, 05859
Tel: 802-988 2611/800-451 4449
Fax: 802-988 4049
This place has 48 simple, ski lodge-style hotel rooms and 140 modern

Hotel Meal Guide

B&Bs supply a complimentary full breakfast and are often quite sophisticated
MAP (Modified American Plan) includes breakfast and dinner
FAP (Full American Plan) supply all three meals

one- to three-bedroom condos, most right on the slopes. **$$$**

KILLINGTON

Cortina Inn
Route 4, 05751
Tel: 802-773 3331/
800-451 6108
Fax: 802-775 6948
www.cortinainn.com
Some 97 surprisingly lush and spacious rooms. Facilities include an indoor pool, tennis courts, a health club, ice skating, and horseback riding. **$$–$$$$**

Inn of the Six Mountains
Killington Road, 05751
Tel: 802-422 4302/
800-228 4676
Fax: 802-422 4321
www.sixmountains.com
A 103-room modern hotel with a Rockies feel. Everything, including the central fieldstone hearth, is lavishly overscale. **$$–$$$$**

Inn at Long Trail
Route 4, 05751
Tel: 802-775 7181/
800-325 2540
Fax: 802-747 7034
www.innatlongtrail.com
A 1938 rustic 19-room ski inn/B&B constructed around an enormous boulder, which intrudes picturesquely into the dining room and Irish Pub. (The pub has Guinness on tap and, often, Irish music.) It's in a good location near the Pico ski area and the Appalachian Trail. **$$**

Mountain Meadows Lodge
Thundering Brook Road, 05751
Tel: 802-775 1010/
800-370 4567
Fax: 802-773 4459
www.mtmeadowslodge.com

A large lakeside farmhouse offering 20 rooms (MAP), with extensive cross-country trails. There's a child care center with a playground, and farm animals. **$$**

LOWER WATERFORD

Rabbit Hill Inn
Route 18, 05848
Tel: 802-748 5168/
800-762 8669
Fax: 802-748 8342
www.rabbithillinn.com
A Greek Revival stagecoach inn (MAP) on 15 wooded acres near Street. Johnsbury. There are 20 ultra-romantic rooms, a superb and elegant restaurant, and lots of pampering personal touches. Trails for walking or cross-country skiing; canoes can also be arranged. **$$$$**

LUDLOW

Governor's Inn
86 Main Street, 05149
Tel: 802-228 8830/
800-468 3766
www.thegovernorsinn.com
This nine-rooms MAP inn has formal Victorian decor, a romantic ambiance, and solicitous hospitality, and is located just 10 minutes from the Okemo Mountain ski area. French-influenced cuisine is served in the well-regarded dining room on antique china and sterling silver. **$$–$$$$**

LYNDONVILLE

Wildflower Inn
Darling Hill Road, 05851
Tel: 802-626 8310/
800-627 8310
Fax: 802-626 3039
www.wildflowerinn.com
This 21-room, cheerfully renovated 1796 B&B farmhouse (with modern carriage house annex) is great for families. There's a petting zoo, pool, and panoramic views to boot. It's also just a short drive from the Wildflower to the Burke Mountain ski area. **$$–$$$$**

Price Categories

A very approximate guide to current room rates for a standard double per night is:

$$$$ = over $200
$$$ = $150–200
$$ = $100–150
$ = under $100

MANCHESTER

The Equinox
Route 7A, 05254
Tel: 802-362 4700/
800-362 4747
Fax: 802-362 1595
www.equinoxresort.com
A grand old hotel with 172 finely refurbished rooms. A sister property to Scotland's Gleneagles. **$$$$**

Village Country Inn
Route 7A, 05254
Tel: 802-362 1792/
800-370 0300
Fax: 802-362 7238
www.villagecountryinn.com
A rambling 32-room old MAP inn with romantic French country decor. **$$–$$$$**

Wilburton Inn
River Road (off Route 7A)
05254
Tel: 802-362 2500/
800-648 4944
Fax: 802-362 1107
www.wilburton.com
A railroad baron's 100-year-old brick mansion set on 20 acres of lawn, with contemporary outdoor sculpture. The 34 elegantly appointed guest rooms for B&B feature canopy beds, fireplaces, and whirlpool tubs. Cottages are also available. **$$–$$$$**

1811 House
Route 7A, 05254
Tel: 802-362 1811/
800-432 1811
Fax: 802-362 2443
A Federal manse (former minister's home) at the north end of Manchester Village. The building has been an inn/B&B for most of its history and currently has 14 spacious, antiques-filled guest rooms, plus additional rooms in a separate cottage. **$$–$$$**

MARLBORO

Whetstone Inn
550 South Road, 05344
Tel: 802-254 2500
A 200-year-old farmhouse with 12 bedrooms decorated with a mix of Colonial appointments and contemporary Scandinavian furnishings. Pond for swimming or skating. No credit cards. **$**

MIDDLEBURY

Middlebury Inn
14 Court House Square, 05753
Tel: 802-388 4961/
800-842 4666
Fax: 802-388 4563
www.middleburyinn.com
An 1825 inn (plus 1827 annex and modern motel extension, offering a total of 80 rooms) overlooking the village green. Dining room serves traditional New England fare.
$–$$$$

Swift House Inn
25 Stewart Lane, 05753
Tel: 802-388 9925
Fax: 802-388 9927
www.swifthouseinn.com
An elegantly detailed 1815 Federal house with 21 luxurious guest rooms. The Carriage House has spacious suites with whirlpool baths. **$$–$$$**

MIDDLETOWN SPRINGS

Priscilla's Victorian Inn
South Street, 05757
Tel: 802-235 2299
A six-room Victorian home B&B with impressive porches and parlors. Located south of Rutland. **$**

MONTGOMERY

Black Lantern
Route 118, 05470
Tel: 802-326 4507/
800-255 8661
Fax: 802-326 2024
www.blacklantern.com
Built in 1803 to house mill workers, now a country-style inn with 15 rooms for B&B near Jay Peak. Several suites have whirlpool baths and fireplaces. **$$**

Inn on Trout River
Main Street, 05471
Tel: (802) 326 4391/
800-338 7049
Fax: 802-326 3194
A late 1800s inn with 10 B&B rooms that are furnished in English and Victorian country styles with down quilts and flannel sheets (in winter). The living/dining room has a large wood-burning stove; the downstairs recreation room has a pool table. Near Jay Peak. **$$**

MONTPELIER

Inn at Montpelier
147 Main Street, 05602
Tel: 802-223 2727
Fax: 802-223 0722
www.innatmontpelier.com
A pair of adjoining Federal mansions make a restful in-town retreat (19 rooms) for both business travelers and vacationers. The main inn has a wide wraparound porch and a formal sitting room. Both buildings have small guest pantries with coffee makers and snacks. **$$–$$$**

NEWFANE AREA

Inn at South Newfane
369 Dover Road
South Newfane, 05351
Tel: 802-348 7191
www.innatsouthnewfane.com
Six-room MAP. Pretty country decor, a pool and pond, and over 100 acres in which to roam. **$$$**

Four Columns Inn
230 West Street, Newfane, 05345
Tel: 802-365 7713/
800-787 6633
Fax: 802-365 0022/
www.fourcolumnsinn.com
A majestic white-columned Greek Revival inn beside one of New England's most photogenic greens. The 16 Colonial-style guest rooms have been updated with cassette players, and there is a pool and trout ponds. **$$–$$$**

NORTH HERO ISLAND

Shore Acres Inn and Restaurant
237 Shoreacres Drive, 05474
Tel: 802-372 8722
www.shoreacres.com
A sedate 23-room lakeside hotel with a vast verandah affording a 40 mile (64 km) view. **$–$$**

PUTNEY

Hickory Ridge House
Hickory Ridge Road, 05346
Tel: 802-387 5709/
800-380 9218
Fax: 802-387 5387
www.hickoryridgehouse.com
An 1808 brick Federal manor with six country-style rooms on 12 pastoral acres. Vegetarian breakfasts, with soufflés and homemade breads, are a specialty of this B&B. **$$–$$$**

QUECHEE

Quality Inn at Quechee Gorge
US Route 4, 05059
Tel: 802-295 7600/
800-732 4376
Fax: 802-295 1492
www.qualityinnquechee.com
Pleasant chain motel accommodations just a minute from the highway. Facilities include an indoor pool, fitness center, and restaurant. **$$–$$$**

Quechee Inn at Marshland Farm
Clubhouse Road, 05059
Tel: 802-295 3133/
800-235 3133
Fax: 802-295 6587
www.quecheeinn.com
A 1793 farmstead with 24 rooms (MAP) in a bucolic riverside setting. Cross-country skiing, hiking, canoeing. **$$$–$$$$**

RUTLAND

Inn at Rutland
70 N Main Street, 05701
Tel: 802-773 0575/
800-808 0575
Fax: 802-775 3506

A 10-room B&B in a renovated Victorian mansion with views of the surrounding mountains and valleys. Traditional appointments include an ornate oak staircase, carved ceiling moldings, and botanical prints. **$$**

SHELBURNE

Inn at Shelburne Farms
Harbor Road, 05482
Tel: 802-985 8498
Fax: 802-985 1233
www.shelburnefarms.org
Lila Vanderbilt's turn-of-the-20th-century Tudor-style mansion (24 rooms, MAP) set amid a grandiose working farm beside Lake Champlain. Tennis, boating, and fishing available. A gem. Open mid-May– mid-Oct. **$$$$**

SHOREHAM

Shoreham Inn
51 Inn Street, 05770
Tel: 802-897 5861/
800-255 5081
Ten-room B&B in a personable village farmhouse, with sophisticated hosts. Near Larabees Point on the southern end of Lake Champlain. **$**

STOWE

Topnotch at Stowe Resort and Spa
Mountain Road, 05672
Tel: 802-253 8585/
800-451 8686
Fax: 802-253 9263
www.topnotch-resort.com
A luxury 105-room establishment with a world-class spa, plus tennis and stables. **$$$$**

Trapp Family Lodge
700 Trapp Hill Road
05672
Tel: 802-253 8511/
800-826 7000
Fax: 802-253 5740
www.trappfamily.com
A modern 123-room replacement for the original lodge, which was lost to fire. There are 2,000 acres with skiing and walking paths. **$$$$**

Green Mountain Inn
Route 100, 05672
Tel: 802-253 7301/
800-455 6629
A rambling 1833 inn with 64 rooms, nicely restored. **$–$$$$**

Inn at the Mountain
Route 108, 05672
Tel: 802-253 3000/
800-253 4754
Fax: 802-253 3659
www.stowe.com
A tastefully decorated motel-and-condo complex with 40 rooms at the foot of Mount Mansfield, surrounded by state forest. **$$$**

Stowehof Inn
Edson Hill Road, 05672
Tel: 802-253 9722/
800-932 7136
Fax: 802-253 7513
www.stowehofinn.com
A hilltop hotel with intentionally eccentric decor in the 45 rooms and an outdoor pool with the best view in town. **$$–$$$**

Fiddler's Green Inn
Mountain Road, 05672.
Tel: 802-253 8124/
800-882 5346
www.fiddlersgreeninn.com
A homey seven-room 1820 lodge with a congenial host. **$–$$**

Alpenrose Motel
2619 Mountain Road, 05672
Tel: 802-253 7277/
800-962 7002
Fax: 802-253 4707
www.gostowe.com/members/
alpenrose
Charming, small motel halfway between the village and Mount Mansfield. Standard rooms and efficiencies, plus an outdoor pool. German spoken. **$**

VERGENNES

Basin Harbor Club
Basin Harbor Road, 05491
Tel: 802-475 2311/
800-622 4000
Fax: 802-475 6545
www.basinharbor.com
A classic lakeside summer colony, built around an old farmhouse, full of timeless pleasures. Most accommodations (138 FAP) are now

in newer cottages, many with fireplaces and refrigerators. Located on a 700-acre property that includes a beach, swimming pool, golf course, tennis courts, and a playground. Extensive children's activities. **$$$$**

WAITSFIELD

Inn at Round Barn
E Warren Road, 05673
Tel: 802-496 2276/
800-721 8029
Fax: 802-496 2276
www.roundbarninn.com
A luxuriously retrofitted farmhouse B&B with 12 plush guest rooms, some with whirlpool baths. The unusual 12-sided Shaker-style barn is used for summer concerts and parties. **$$–$$$$**
Lareau Farm Country Inn
Route 100, 05673
Tel: 802-496 4949/
800-833 0766
Fax: 802-496 7979
www.lareaufarminn.com
This 13-room B&B has an authentic farmhouse atmosphere, with country-style rooms and a dining room with many windows. On 67 acres of woods and pasture, near the Mad River. **$–$$$**
Knoll Farm Inn
Bragg Hill Road, 05673
Tel: 802-496 3939
A functioning farmhouse with four rooms on 150 acres; home-grown meals, and a pond for swimming or skating. **$$**
Mad River Barn
Route 17, 05673
Tel: 802-496 3310
www.madriverbarn.com
A 1948 ski lodge with 15 MAP rooms with a vintage game room. **$$**

WATERBURY

Inn at Blush Hill
Blush Hill Road, 05676
Tel: 802-244 7529/800-736 7522
Fax: 802-244 7314
www.blushhill.com
An exemplary B&B high on a hill with sweeping mountain vistas. Five

Price Categories

A very approximate guide to current room rates for a standard double per night is:
$$$$ = over $200
$$$ = $150–200
$$ = $100–150
$ = under $100

cheerful rooms and gourmet breakfasts in a 1790s room with its original open hearth fireplace. **$–$$**

WEATHERSFIELD

Inn at Weathersfield
Route 106, 05151
Tel: 802-263 9217/
800-477 4828
Fax: 802-263 9219
A 12-room MAP in a magical 18th-century country inn, where Early American style blends with modern amenities, with the promise of romance at every turn. Located south of Windsor. **$$$–$$$$**

WEST DOVER

Inn at Sawmill Farm
Route 100, 05356
Tel: 802-464 8131/
800-493 1133
Fax: 802-464 1130
www.vermontdirect.com/sawmill
AN MAP with 21 rooms in an old farmstead jazzed up with bold decorative touches. This is country elegance at its best, plus superb regional cuisine. Convenient to Mount Snow and Haystack Mountain ski areas. **$$$$**

WEST TOWNSHEND

Windham Hill Inn
Windham Hill Road, 05359
Tel: 802-874 4080/
800-944 4080
Fax: 802-874 4702
www.windhamhill.com
An elegantly appointed 1825 farmhouse-cum-cross-country-ski-center. 21 MAP rooms, set right in

the heart of the country. An extensive CD collection entertains music-loving guests. Facilities include a pool, tennis courts, and a skating pond. Located 10 miles (16 km) north of Newfane and 10 miles (16 km) east of the Stratton Mountain ski area. **$$$$**

WILMINGTON

Trail's End
Smith Road, 05363
Tel: 802-464 2727/
800-859 2585
www.trailsendvt.com
The 15 lovely rooms and suites at this B&B branch off from a cathedral-ceiling living room with fieldstone hearth. Convenient for Mount Snow and Haystack Mountain ski areas. **$–$$$**

WINDSOR

Juniper Hill Inn
153 Pembroke Road, 05089
Tel: 802-674 5273/
800-359 2541
Fax: 802-674 2041
www.juniperhillinn.com
An 100-year-old Greek Revival-style mansion B&B set on a broad lawn near Ascutney Mountain. There are 16 elegant rooms furnished with Queen Anne and Edwardian pieces. **$$–$$$**

WOODSTOCK AREA

Jackson House
37 Route 4 West
Woodstock, 05091
Tel: 802-457 2065/
800-448 1890

Hotel Meal Guide

B&Bs supply a complimentary full breakfast, often quite sophisticated
MAP (Modified American Plan) includes breakfast and dinner
FAP (Full American Plan) supply all three meals

www.jacksonhouseinn.com
A lovingly restored 1890s clapboard house, now a 15-room B&B. Has an award-winning restaurant, serving five-course breakfasts, and *hors d'oeuvres* with champagne.
$$$–$$$$
Woodstock Inn & Resort
14 The Green (Route 4)
Woodstock, 05091
Tel: 802-457 1100/
800-448 7900
Fax: 802-457 6699
www.woodstockinn.com
The Rockefellers' homage to country inns past, full of Americana. The decor is corporate/country with modern furniture and patchwork quilts. The impressive facilities include 144 rooms, indoor and outdoor pools, tennis courts, golf, a health club, and racquet ball and squash courts. **$$$–$$$$**
Kedron Valley Inn
Route 106
South Woodstock, 05071
Tel: 802-457 1473/
800-836 1193
Fax: 802-457 4469
www.kedronvalleyinn.com
Heirloom quilts line the walls and dress up the 28 prettily decorated rooms of this B&B, and the restaurant is exceptional. The ski lodge-style building situated just behind the main inn attracts families, with a swimming pool as an extra attraction. **$$–$$$$**
Applebutter Inn
Happy Valley Road
Woodstock, 05091
Tel: 802-457 4158/
800 486 1734
Fax: 802-457 4158
www.bbonline.com/vt/applebutterinn
Six-room B&B in a Federal house full of fluffy comforters; delicious breakfasts. **$–$$**
Three Church Street
3 Church Street
Woodstock, 05091
Tel: 802-457 1925
Fax: 802-457 9181
www.scenesofvermont.com/3church
An 11-room B&B in a gracious early 19th-century house near the common, with a tennis court and pool; well priced for this level of elegance. **$–$$**

Where to Eat

ARLINGTON

West Mountain Inn
River Road (off Route 313)
Tel: 802-375 6516
New American fare in a low-beamed paneled dining room at a romantic and family-friendly inn. **$$$–$$$$**
Arlington Inn
Route 7A
Tel: 802-375 6532
A formal candlelit restaurant with French Continental dishes – rack of lamb, roast duck – all prepared with local meats and produce. **$$$**

BENNINGTON

Four Chimneys
21 West Road (Route 9)
Tel: 802-447 3500
Polished continental cuisine in a showpiece mansion. **$$$$**
Blue Benn Diner
Route 7
Tel: 802-442 5140
A classic 140s diner serving unconventional as well as traditional fare. **$**

BRATTLEBORO

Latchis Grill
Latchis Hotel
50 Main Street
Tel: 802-254 6300
International fare and brews from the on-site Windham Brewery. **$$**
Mole's Eye Cafe
High Street
Tel: 802-257 0771

Restaurant Guidelines

Prices are approximate, but for a three-course meal for one (excluding beverages, tax, and tip), the following guidelines may prove helpful:
$$$$ = over $40
$$$ = $28–40
$$ = $15–28
$ = under $15
Meal tax varies from state to

A local institution since the 1930s. A neighborly basement spot serving hearty homestyle fare. **$$**
Peter Havens
32 Elliot Street
Tel: 802-257 3333
The locals' favorite New American bistro. **$$**

BURLINGTON

The Ice House
171 Battery Street
Tel: 802-864 1800
Fresh seafood and refreshing views of Lake Champlain. **$$$**
Pauline's
1834 Shelburne Road
(Route 7 S)
South Burlington
Tel: 802-862 1081
Deft New American cuisine, improbably located in a strip mall. **$$$**
NECI Commons
25 Church Street
Tel: 802-862 6324
New England Culinary Institute's students create a numerous lunch and dinner treats in this attractive and noisy two-level restaurant. There's a take-out section and outdoor tables. **$–$$$**
Daily Planet
15 Center Street
Tel: 802-862 9647
World-beat cuisine: Mediterranean with Asian influences in the pulse center of town. **$$**
Sweet Tomatoes
83 Church Street
Tel: 802-660 9533
A boisterous trattoria with a wood-fired oven that turns out

state, but it is customary to tip 15 to 20 percent on the pre-tax total.
Credit cards The more expensive establishments generally accept credit cards, but call ahead to check just in case.
Reservations Most restaurants, except for the clearly casual, appreciate reservations (some require them).

scrumptious pizzas and other Tuscan-inspired fare. **$$**

Trattoria Delia
152 Street Paul Street
Tel: 802-864 5253
Rustic Italian dishes. **$$**

Mirabelle's
198 Main Street
Tel: 802-658 3074
An inviting cafe/patisserie. **$**

CHESTER

Country Girl Diner
Route 11
Tel: 802-875 2650
A traditional 1950s diner on the western end of town. **$**

CRAFTSBURY

Craftsbury Inn
Main Street
Tel: 802-586 2848
Intriguing modern *prix-fixe* dinners are the order of the day from the talented chef-owner. **$$$**

DORSET

Barrows House
Route 30
Tel: 802-867 4455
New American in an intimate setting; the tavern serves lighter fare. **$$$**

Chantecleer
Route 7A, East Dorset
Tel: 802-362 1616
Swiss and French provincial cuisine in an former dairy barn. **$$$**

Dorset Inn
Route 30
Tel: 802-867 5500
The Dorset Inn does "Honest American cooking": a choice of formal dining or tavern feasting in a 1796 hostelry. **$$$**

EAST BURKE

Old Cutter Inn
Tel: 802-626 5152
Chef-owner Fritz Walther's native Swiss specialties, including irresistible *rosti*. **$$**

Restaurant Guidelines

Prices are approximate, but for a three-course meal for one (excluding beverages, tax, and tip), the following guidelines may prove helpful:
$$$$ = over $40
$$$ = $28–40
$$ = $15–28
$ = under $15
Meal tax varies from state to state, but it is customary to tip 15 to 20 percent on the pre-tax total.
Credit cards The more expensive establishments generally accept credit cards, but call ahead to check just in case.
Reservations Most restaurants, except for the clearly casual, appreciate reservations (some require them).

River Garden Cafe
Route 114
Tel: 802-626 3514
Bruschetta and *tiramisu* come to the Northeast Kingdom, along with rack of lamb and local smoked trout. **$$**

GRAFTON

Old Tavern at Grafton
Route 121
Tel: 802-843 2231
Hearty New England dishes, perhaps venison stew, or grilled quail, served in two dining rooms: one more formal, the other rustic tavern-style. **$$–$$$**

KILLINGTON

Hemingway's
Route 4
Tel: 802-422 3886
Truly inspired local cuisine, which is regularly hailed as among the nation's best. **$$$$**

Cortina Inn
Route 4
Tel: 802-773 3333
Chefs from the New England Culinary Institute ensure deft and innovative fare at this Killington institution. **$$$**

LOWER WATERFORD

Rabbit Hill Inn
Route 18
Tel: 802-748 5168
Dazzling New American cuisine served amid rural understated elegance. **$$$**

LUDLOW

Nikki's
Route 103
Okemo Mountain
Tel: 802-228 7797
The New American cuisine is delightful, and the hippie Deco decor is delightful. **$$**

MANCHESTER

The Equinox
Route 7A
Tel: 802-362 4700
Spectacular regional cuisine in a formal barrel-vaulted dining room looking out on Mount Equinox. **$$$–$$$$**

Bistro Henry's
Route 11/30
Tel: 802-362 4982
A spacious dining room on the edge of town preparing authentic Mediterranean cuisine. Extensive wine list. **$$$**

Mother Myrick's Confectionery and Ice Cream Parlor
Route 7A
Tel: 802-362 1560
The place to indulge your sweet tooth with a slice of freshly baked pie, homemade fudge, or an ice-cream treat. **$**

MIDDLEBURY

Woody's
5 Bakery Lane
Tel: 802-388 4182
Unfussy regional American fare and a congenial crowd. Looks out onto Otter Creek. **$$$**

Fire and Ice
26 Seymore Street
Tel: 802-388 7166/800-367 7166
Prime rib and fresh fish, a 55-item salad bar (with peel-and-eat shrimp), and an intimate atmosphere attract couples as well as families with small children, who opt for the "Children's Corner", complete with a VCR and cartoons. **$$**

MONTGOMERY

Black Lantern
Route 118
Tel: 802-326 4507
Contemporary American fare at this inn restaurant near Jay Peak. **$$**

MONTPELIER

The Chef's Table
118 Main Street
Tel: 802-223 9240
This New England Culinary Institute enterprise is thoroughly elegant, and culinarily eloquent. **$$$**
Main Street Grill
118 Main Street
Tel: 802-223 3188
Adventurous grazing courtesy of the highly skilled students of the New England Culinary Institute. **$$**

NEWFANE

Four Columns Inn
230 West Street
Tel: 802-365 7713
Creative European/American cuisine, auberge-style. **$$$$**

PUTNEY

Curtis' Barbecue
Route 5 (no phone)
Good ol' barbecue, slow-cooked next to an old school bus. Divine. **$**

QUECHEE

Parker House Inn
16 Main Street
Tel: 802-295 6077

Tasteful continental cuisine in a brick Victorian mansion with great views. **$$$**
Quechee Inn at Marshland Farm
Clubhouse Road
Tel: 802-295 3133
Seasonal specialties in a tastefully restored tavern. **$$$**
Simon Pearce Restaurant
The Mill, Main Street
Tel: 802-295 1470
Fine country cuisine, with some Irish touches, in a modern café in an old riverside mill. Extensive wine list. **$$$**

RUTLAND

Royal's 121 Hearthside
37 N Main Street
Tel: 802-775 0856
A Rutland institution. Traditional fare – rack of lamb, prime rib, pan-roasted salmon – prepared behind an open hearth. **$$–$$$**

ST JOHNSBURY

Anthony's Diner
Railroad Street
Tel: 802-748 3613
Traditional diner meals. A St Johnsbury institution. **$$–$$$**

SHELBURNE

Inn at Shelburne Farms
Harbor Road
Tel: 802-985 8498
Reservations required. Gourmet dining (and breakfasting) in a Queen Anne-style manor overlooking Lake Champlain. **$$$**

STOWE

Ten Acres Lodge
Luce Hill at Barrows Road
Tel: 802-253 7638
Skilled regional cuisine, in handsome old farmhouse set amid a meadow. **$$$–$$$$**
Cliff House
Mount Mansfield
Tel: 802-253 3000
Board the world's fastest gondola

for a culinary "peak" experience. Lunch only. **$$$**
Stowehof Inn
Edson Hill Road
Tel: 802-253 9722
Elegant and astute New American cuisine, with a dramatic view. **$$$**
Topnotch at Stowe
Mountain Road
Tel: 802-253 8585
A formal dining room and casual grill offer skilled contemporary cuisine, some calibrated for the health-conscious. **$$$**
Blue Moon Cafe
35 School Street
Tel: 802-253 7006
A contemporary bistro doing vivid cuisine at great prices. **$$**
Trapp Family Lodge
Luce Hill Road.
Tel: 802-253 8511.
Gemutlich treats with fine valley views from the Tea Room. Formal dining too. **$$**
Trattoria La Festa
Mountain Road
Tel: 802-253 8480
Authentic Italian cuisine in an 1859 farmhouse. **$$**
Miguel's Stowe Away
Mountain Road
Tel: 802-253 7574
A decent Mexican, for ski country. **$**

WAITSFIELD

Tucker Hill Lodge
65 Marble Hill Road

Amber Nectar

One of Vermont's specialties is maple syrup, which comes in three grades:
A (Light Amber) Light gold colour.
A (Dark Amber) Stronger and darker than Light Amber.
B Stronger still and a deep amber shade, best for cooking. During the maple season, from March to April, visitors are welcome at farms listed in *Maple Sugarhouses Open to Visitors*, published by the Vermont Department of Agriculture, tel: 802-828-2416.

Restaurant Guidelines

Prices are approximate, but for a three-course meal for one (excluding beverages, tax, and tip), the following guidelines may prove helpful:

$$$$ = over $40
$$$ = $28–40
$$ = $15–28
$ = under $15
Meal tax varies from state to state, but it is customary to tip 15 to 20 percent on the pre-tax total.
Credit cards The more expensive establishments generally accept credit cards, but call ahead to check just in case.
Reservations Most restaurants, except for the clearly casual, appreciate reservations (some require them).

Tel: 802-496 3983
Tucker Hill Lodge offers steakhouse fare in its restaurant and lighter food in its pub. **$$**

WARREN

Chez Henri
Sugarbush Village
Tel: 802-583 2600
An authentic romantic French bistro in the middle of a bustling ski resort. **$$$**
The Common Man
German Flats Road
Tel: 802-583 2800
Country-sophisticate fare is served in this delightful, atmospheric old barn. **$$$**
Sam Rupert's
Sugarbush Access Road
Tel: 802-583 2421
Superb New American cuisine in a cozy, romantic setting. **$$$**

WATERBURY

Cold Hollow Cider Mill
Route 100
Tel: 802-244 8771
Fresh apple cider and baked goods. Don't miss the exceptional cider donuts. **$**

WEATHERSFIELD

Inn at Weathersfield
Route 106
Tel: 802-263 9217
Fine regional fare in a library illuminated by candlelight. Piano accompaniment. **$$$**

WEST DOVER

Inn at Sawmill Farm
Off Route 100
Tel: 802-464 8131
Superb, seemingly simple, cuisine is served here amid elegant rusticity. **$$$$**

WEST TOWNSHEND

Windham Hill Inn
Windham Hill Road
Tel: 802-874 4080
Prix-fixe classic French cuisine in a romantically appointed inn. **$$$$**

WILMINGTON

The Hermitage
Coldbrook Road
Tel: 802-464 3511
Game birds raised on the grounds, and a legendary wine cellar. **$$$$**
Le Petit Chef
Route 100
Tel: 802-464 8437
Classic French cuisine in a refined farmhouse. **$$$**

WINDSOR

Juniper Hill Inn
Juniper Hill Road
Tel: 802-674 5273
Updated classics are served by candlelight in the traditional-style dining room of this equally traditional inn. **$$$**
Windsor Station
Depot Avenue
Tel: 802-674 2052
Traditional Continental fare in a converted railroad station, where the booths were constructed from the depot's railroad benches. **$$**

WOODSTOCK AREA

The Prince & the Pauper
24 Elm Street, Woodstock
Tel: 802-457 1818
This place, which offers a romantic Colonial setting, is known for its fine regional, seasonal fare, and exquisite desserts. **$$$$**
Woodstock Inn & Resort
Route 4 on The Green, Woodstock
Tel: 802-457 1100
Regional and New American cuisine in an ultra-formal setting. **$$$**
Kedron Valley Inn
Route 106, South Woodstock
Tel: 802-457 1473
Chef Tom Hopewell is not just an artist but a magician with regional ingredients. **$$$**
Bentley's Restaurant
3 Elm Street, Woodstock
Tel: (802) 457 3232
Eclectic, antique-ish decor and international dishes; a popular spot. Live music (jazz or blues) on the weekends. **$$**

Culture

Call **Burlington City Arts** (tel: 802-865 7166, 802 865 9163) for up-to-the-minute information on what's happening in this hip and lively city.

CLASSICAL MUSIC

Marlboro Music Festival (tel: 802-254 2394, Marlboro Music Center) has one of the most renowned line-ups in New England. Concerts are given in the summer.
Vermont Symphony Orchestra (tel: 802-864 5741) performs in Manchester, Woodstock, and Brattleboro in the summer and Bennington, Arlington, and Rutland during the winter.
Stowe Performing Arts (tel: 802-253 7792) puts on summertime jazz and classical performances at the Trapp Family Lodge.

OPERA

Opera North (tel: 603-643 1946; Hanover, NH) fords the Connecticut River to perform a few operas yearly in Vermont's Upper Valley region.

FOLK

Vermont Pub and Brewery (tel: 802- 865 0500; College and Street Paul Sts, Burlington) is one of the more popular places in this young college town, and hosts a range of folk musicians.

THEATER

St Michael's Playhouse (tel: 802-654 2281; Burlington) is Vermont's oldest equity playhouse, and you can always count on them for quality productions.
Flynn Theater for the Performing Arts (tel: 802-863 8778; 153 Main Street, Burlington) is the big venue for big-name and big-audience productions.
Weston Playhouse Theater Company (tel: 802-824 5288; Weston) is home to Vermont's oldest summer theater.
Dorset Playhouse (tel: 802-867 5777; Dorset) stages professional performances in the summer, but in the winter a fine consortium of community folks takes to the stage.

CINEMA

Catamount Arts (tel: 802-748 2600; 60 Eastern Avenue, St Johnsbury) brings a little bit of everything to this remote corner of Vermont: art films, dance, classical music. Stop by if you're in the area and something's on tap.

Nightlife
LIVE MUSIC

Club Metronome (tel: 802-865 4563; 188 Main Street, Burlington) has a beat all its own: reggae, blues, or whatever the newest

musical beat just happens to be. **Mulligan's** (tel: 802-297 9293) on Stratton has year-round music. **Common Ground** (tel: 802-257 0855; 25 Eliot Street, Brattleboro) has jam dance bands on most weekends, while more mellow guitarists play during brunch.

LATE-NIGHT VENUES

All of the big ski mountains have a phalanx of nightly live music from which to choose. You're bound to find something to your liking. **Bentley's** (tel: 802-457 3232; 3 Elm Street, Woodstock) has DJs on the weekends.

Outdoor Activities
BIKING

Quite a number of the downhill ski areas are converted into mountain-biking centers after the winter season ends.
Mount Snow (tel: 802-464 3333), home to the first American mountain bike school, has 45 miles (72 km) of bike terrain and runs one-day coaching programs, leads mountain tours, and hosts family bike weekends.
At **Killington** (tel: 802-422 6232), mountain bikers can cruise 50 miles (80 km) of trails. Vermont is a popular destination for upscale inn-to-inn tours.
The Berkeley, California-based **Backroads** (tel: 800-462 2848)

Leaf Peeping

For up-to-date information on where you can catch foliage is at its most magnificent in the fall during September and October, call the states' Autumn Foliage Hotlines on the following numbers:
Connecticut 800-282-6863
Maine 800-533-9595
Massachusetts 800-227-6277
New Hampshire 800-258-3608
Rhode Island 800-556-2484
Vermont 800-828-3239

offers several tours, as does **Bike Vermont** (tel: 800-257 2226).

CANOEING, KAYAKING, AND RAFTING

Vermont Canoe (tel: 802-257 5008; Brattleboro) rents canoes and kayaks and conducts guided paddling tours. Burlington-based **Paddleways** (tel: 802-660 8606) teaches kayaking fundamentals and runs kayaking trips, as does **True North Kayak Tours** (tel: 802-860 1910).

FISHING

Anglers flock to the trout-laded Battenkill River near Manchester, where **Orvis** (tel: 802-362 3622, 800-235 9763) runs a program of popular two-and-a-half day fly-fishing classes.
Battenkill Anglers (tel: 802-362 3184) organize fly-fishing vacations and schools.
Fishing guides at **Strictly Trout** (tel: 802-869 3116) work all Vermont rivers but specialize in the Connecticut River.

HIKING

Vermont's topography offers everything from easy day hikes to multi-day mountain jaunts. Long-distance hikers gravitate to the **Appalachian Trail**, which cuts across southern Vermont, and to the **Long Trail**, a 270-mile (435-km) traverse across Vermont's highest peaks between the Massachusetts state line and the Canadian border.
Green Mountain Club (tel: 802-244 7037) has specific trail information and publishes the *Day Hiker's Guide to Vermont*.
To mix serious hiking with country-inn comforts, contact **Country Inns Along the Trail** (tel: 802-247 3300), which organizes inn-to-inn tours. **Hiking Holidays of Bristol** (tel: 802-453 4816, 800-537 3850) also packages Green Mountain inn-to-inn tours.

Skiing Tour Operators to Vermont

Companies offering tailormade skiing package holidays to Vermont from the UK include the following:

American Dream
243 Euston Road
London NW1Y 4BS
Tel: 020-7388 2000

Crystal Holidays
Cyrstal House
The Courtyard
Arlington Road
Surbiton KT6 6BW
Tel: 020-8399 5144

Inghams
10–18 Putney Hill
London SW15 6AZX
Tel: 020-8780 4400

North America Travel Service
Suite 2000, 11 Albion Street
Leeds LS1 5ER
Tel: 0113-246 1466

Thomas Cook
PO Box 5, 12 Coningsby Road
Peterborough PE3 8XZP
Tel: 01733-563200

United Vacations
United House
Southern Perimeter Road
Heathrow Airport
Middlesex TW6 3LP
Tel: 020-8750 9674

Virgin Holidays
The Galleria, Station Road
Crawley RH10 1WW
Tel: 01293-617181

SAILING

Lake Champlain and **Lake Memphremagog** are Vermont's principal sailing lakes.

Burlington Community Boathouse (tel: 802-865 3377) both rents sailboats and runs charters and "bareboats" on Lake Champlain.

Winds of Ireland (tel: 802-863 5090; Burlington Boathouse) runs day and sunset sailing cruises. On Lake Memphremagog, you can rent sailboats at **Newport Marine** (tel: 802-334 5911) and **East Side Landing** (tel: 802-334 2340).

SKIING

For many, Vermont is synonymous with New England skiing. In the south, the largest downhill mountains are: **Stratton** (tel: 802-297 4000, 800-787 2886; Jamaica), **Okemo** (tel: 802-228 4041, 800-786 5366; Ludlow), and **Mount Snow** (tel: 800-245 7669). **Killington** (tel: 802-422 3261, 800-621 6867; Rutland) is monumental

In the north, check out: **Stowe** (tel: 802-253 3600), **Sugarbush** (tel: 802-583 2381, 800-537 8427; Warren), and **Jay Peak** (tel: 802-988 2611, 800-451 4449; Jay).

One of Vermont's largest cross-country skiing areas is **Craftsbury Nordic Center** (tel: 800-729 7751), but Stowe also boasts several excellent centers, including **Edson Hill** (tel: 802-253 8954), **Topnotch** (tel: 802-253 8585), and **Trapp Family Lodge** (tel: 802-253 8511).

Serious Nordic skiers may ski the 280-mile (450-km) **Catamount Trail**, which runs nearly the entire length of the state; contact the Catamount Trail Association (tel: 802-864 5794; Burlington).

Shopping

WHERE TO SHOP

Vermont's largest city, Burlington, has its most diverse and sophisticated offerings. The **Burlington Square Mall** on Church Street, **The Champlain Mill** (tel: 802-655 9477, Routes 2 and 7, north of the city), and the **Wing Building** on the waterfront have the greatest concentration of shops.

COUNTRY STORES

Vermont Country Store (tel: 802-824 3184; Route 100, Weston), the venerated institution that country stores all over the country

aspire toward, might as well be a department store, for the impressive range of merchandise you can get here. From Vermont-made food stuffs to folk remedies to flannel shirts.

Shelburne Country Store (tel: 802-985 3657; on the green, Shelburne) is a scaled-down version of the above, but still a very fine one at that.

MARKETS & FOODSTUFFS

Equinox Valley Nursery (tel: 802-362 2610; Route 7A south of Manchester) sells homegrown products; they always have a scarecrow display and other seasonal displays that make you want to take out your camera.

Harlow's Sugar House (tel: 802-387 5852; Route 5, Putney) takes kids and adults on horse-drawn sugaring rides. In the fall you can pick apples here, and in the summer, berries.

Cold Hollow Cider Mill (tel: 802-244 8771; Route 100, Waterbury Center) offers up glasses and cartons of fresh-pressed cider and other goodies grown in Vermont.

Green Mountain Chocolate Co. (tel: 802-244 1139; Route 100, Waterbury) sells the stuff of children's dreams and dentists' nightmares.

Cabot Creamery Annex (tel: 802-244 6334; Route 100, north of Waterbury), Vermont's largest cheese producer, offers free samples of smoked, aged, and sharp cheddar cheese. You can also tour of the state-of-the-art facility.

MARKETPLACES

Church Street Marketplace (tel: 802-863 1648; Main and Pearl Sts, Burlington) encompasses a pedestrian-only section of downtown lined with lively cafés and interesting shops.

Historic Marble Works (tel: 802-388 3701; Middlebury) is a warren of individual shops in a renovated marble factory.

FASHION & ACCESSORIES

Manchester is a Mecca for name-brand outlet shops, including Anne Klein, Giorgio Armani, and Orvis. **Manchester Commons** (tel: 802-362 3736; Routes 7 and 30) has the most outlets under one roof. **Johnson Woolen Mills** (tel: 802-635 7185; Main Street, Johnson), an old-fashioned factory store, has old-fashioned discounted prices to match.

BOOKS

Chain stores are well represented in Burlington by **Borders** (tel: 802-865 2711; 29 Church Street) and **Barnes & Noble** (tel: 802-864 801; 102 Dorset Street). For used books, **North Country Books** (tel: 802-862 6413; 2 Church St) has a fine selection. **Tuttle Antiquarian Books** (tel: 802-773 8229; 28 S Main Street, Rutland) publishes its own fine booklist pertaining to Asia and things spiritual, but they also have a great selection of rare and out-of-print titles.

Northshire Bookstore (tel: 802-362 2200; Main Street, Manchester) is one of the better shops in the state.

ANTIQUES

Danby Antiques Center (tel: 802-293 9984; off Route 7, situated north of Manchester) has a dozen rooms full of folk art and furniture. *(See also page 255 for information on crafts in Vermont.)*

GLASS

Simon Pearce (tel: 802-295 2711; Main Street, Quechee), perhaps the most famous glass emporium-owner in New England, employs a number of highly talented mastercraftsmen to carry out his vision, and you can watch them work here. The shop sells first- and second-quality glassware and other fragile items.
Luminosity Studios (tel: 802-496 2231; Route 100, Waitsfield) sells stained glass from former church.

Ben & Jerry's

As well as producing over 30 "euphoric flavors" of ice cream, Ben Cohen and Jerry Greenfield plough back 7½ percent of their profits into social causes and half the proceeds of their factory tours go to Vermont charities. **Ben & Jerry's Ice Cream Factory**, Route 100, north of 1–89, near Waterbury.

GIFTS

Scotland by the Yard (tel: 802-295 5351; Route 4, Quechee) sells everything Scottish, and although you came to Vermont not the Highlands, you might just find a warm sweater for an unusually early fall day.

ARTS AND CRAFTS

Vermont Artisan Design (tel: 802-257 7044; 115 Main Street, Brattleboro) is one of the state's best shops for handmade goods.

Vermont's Festivals

Spring
Over 90 varieties of lilacs offer a fragrant setting for family activities and musical entertainment at the **Shelburne Museum's Lilac Festival** (tel: 802-985 3346) in May.
Also in May, artists across the state open their studios to visitors during the annual **Open Studio Weekend** (tel: 802-223 3380).

Summer
The hills come alive with the sound of music as soon as summer arrives, starting with Burlington's **Discover Jazz Festival** (tel: 802-863 7992) in early June.
In July, Marlboro College, on a bucolic hilltop, welcomes the month-long, internationally renowned **Marlboro Music Festival** (tel: 802-254 2394).

Meanwhile, Burlington-area towns host the **Vermont Mozart Festival** (tel: 802-862 7352, 800-639-9097).
Circus Smirkus (tel: 802-744 6122) – the world's only international youth circus, with participants recruited from as far afield as Russia and China – raises its one-ring big top throughout Vermont mid-July to mid-August.
Early in August, the quirky **Bread and Puppet Theatre** (tel: 802-525 3031) in West Glover mounts its annual Domestic Resurrection Circus, a mix of radical agitprop and simple celebration.

Fall
The state's wide variety of autumn fairs and festivals includes the huge **Champlain Valley Fair** in Essex Junction (tel: 802-878 5545), the **Stratton Arts**

Festival – the state's oldest and largest juried exhibition of contemporary crafts (tel: 802-297 3265), and **Killington's Vermont Sheep and Wool Festival** (tel: 802-828 2416).

Winter
Vermonters celebrate New Year's Eve with **Burlington's First Night** festivities (tel: 802-863 6005). Then in mid-January, the ski town of Stowe, which views the frigid weather as one more excuse to party, hosts the **Stowe Winter Carnival**, a week-long bash featuring dog-sled races, ice sculptures, and fireworks.
Other ski areas also sponsor various special events to spice up the season.

For further details about events, contact the local tourist office.

Children's Museums

Lake Champlain Basin Science Center
One College Street
Burlington
Tel: 802-864 1848
Teaches youngsters and "oldsters" about the lake's history and ecology.
Montshire Museum of Science
Montshire Road
Norwich
Tel: 802-649 2200
Arguably second only to the Boston's Museum of Science, is a fine place to explore and discover both the natural and man-made world.

Bennington Potters (tel: 802-447 7531; 324 County Street, Bennington) sells seconds (as well as the best, of course) from the well-known (and expensive) Bennington Potters.
Newfane Country Store (tel: 802-365 7916; Route 30, Newfane) is the place to go for quilts.
Green Mountain Spinnery (tel: 802-387 4528; Exit 4 off I-91, Putney) offers home-grown, home-spun wool and mohair.
North Wind Artisans' Gallery (tel: 802-457 4587; 81 Central Street, Woodstock) carries a variety of excellent work.
Bennington Potters North (tel: 802-863 2221; 127 College Street, Burlington), purveyors of their own very popular pottery, also offers a selective line of complementary housewares.

TOYS

Vermont Teddy Bear Company (tel: 802-985 3001; 2236 Shelburne Road, Shelburne), which sells furry handmade creatures for significant sums of money, turned a small cottage industry into a multi-million dollar enterprise.

New Hampshire

The Place

Known as: The Granite State.
Motto: Live free or die.
Origin of name: Named in 1629 by Captain John Mason of Plymough Council for his home county in England.
Entered Union: June 21, 1788, the ninth of the 13 original states.
Capital: Concord.
Area: 9,351 sq. miles/24,219 sq. km.
Highest point: Mount Washington, 6,288 ft (1,917 m).
Population: 1.1 million.
Population density: 119 people per sq. mile (46 per sq. km).
Economy: Manufacturing (industrial machinery, precision instruments, and electronic equipment) and services (including tourism).
National representation: two senators and two representatives to Congress.
Famous citizens: Mary Baker Eddy, Robert Frost, Horace Greeley, and Daniel Webster

Where to Stay

BEDFORD

Bedford Village Inn
2 Village Inn Lane, 03110
Tel: 603-472 2001/800-852 1166
Fax: 603-472 2379

New Hampshire Trivia

The longest wooden bridge in the United States and longest two-span covered bridge in the world links Cornish, New Hampshire with Windsor, Vermont. It was built in 1866 and cost the princely sum of $9,000.

www.bedfordvillageinn.com
Some 14 luxury suites, with four-poster beds and marble bathrooms, carved out of a three-story barn, south of Manchester. $$$–$$$$

BETHLEHEM

Adair
80 Guider Ln (at Route 302), 03574
Tel: 603-444 2600/888-444 2600
Fax: 603-444 4823
www.adairinn.com
A 1927 mansion with 200 acres encompassing gardens and tennis courts, now a 9-room B&B. The common areas include a tap room with an honor bar, fireplace, and vintage pool table. The guest rooms are furnished with elegant antiques or reproductions. All rooms have either garden or mountain views.
$$$–$$$$
Mulburn Inn
2370 Main Street, 03574
Tel: 603-869 3389/
800-457 9440
Fax: 603-869 5633
www.mulburninn.com
A Tudor mansion constructed for the retail magnate Woolworths in 1913, with stained glass windows, ornately carved mantles, and imported fireplace tiles. This B&B has spacious and individually decorated guest rooms. $–$$

BRETTON WOODS

Mount Washington Hotel and Resort
Route 302, 03575
Tel: 603-278 1000/
800-258 0330
A grand hotel (195 rooms, MAP), preserved in all its glory since 1902. There's a formal atmosphere (jackets are required in the dining room in the evenings), but the hotel is still family friendly. There are kids' camps and other children's programs, plus swimming pools, tennis courts, horseback riding, movies, and a fitness center. A 900-foot-long verandah looks out across the Presidential Range. $$$$

CENTER HARBOR

Kona Mansion
P.O. Box 458, 03226
Tel: 603-253 4900
This Tudor-style, 1900s mansion on 100 acres has 10 guest rooms, four one-and two-bedroom housekeeping cottages, and two three-bedroom chalets. Breakfast and dinner are served in the ornate, Victorian dining room. Nine-hole golf course, tennis courts, private beach. MAP available. **$$–$$$**

Red Hill Inn
Route 25B, 03226
Tel: 603-279 7001/
800-573 3445
Fax: 603-279 7003
www.redhillinn.com
This early 20th-century red-brick summer home, plus a farmhouse and a stone cottage, once belonged to the inventor of the soda fountain. The majority of the 21 B&B rooms are equipped witgh either fireplaces or woodstoves. **$$–$$$**

CONCORD

Wyman Farm
Wyman Road
Loudon, 03307
Tel/fax: 603-783 4467
An 18th-century Cape on a 60-acre hilltop, about a 10-minute drive from Canterbury Shaker Village. There are just three bedrooms, with B&B offered. **$**

DIXVILLE NOTCH

Balsams Grand Resort Hotel
Route 26, 03576
Tel: 603-255 3400/
800-255 0600
Fax: 603-255 4221
www.thebalsams.com
A fabulous 19th-century resort hotel, set in its own natural preserve. Activities include dancing and entertainment nightly, pool, tennis courts, skiing, fishing, and children's programs. Opulent lunch buffets, creative dinners. 215 rooms. FAP. Open mid-May–mid-October. **$$$$**

EATON CENTER

Inn at Crystal Lake
Route 153, 03832
Tel: 603-447 2120/
800-343 7336
Fax: 603-447 3599
www.innatcrystallake.com
An 1884 Victorian in a sleepy lakeside village. Comfortable and relaxing B&B with 11 rooms, just minutes from Conway in a tranquil village on Crystal Lake. Walk to the beach. Complimentary bar for guests' use. **$–$$**

Rockhouse Mountain Farm Inn
off Route 153, 03832
Tel: 603-447 2880
An established family resort offering 15 MAP rooms on a 450-acre farm. There are resident horses, llamas, cows, chickens, and pigs, to keep the kids happy. **$**

ETNA

Moose Mountain Lodge
Moose Mountain Highway, 03570
Tel: 603-643 3529
www.moosemountainlodge.com
A classic 1938 ski lodge, with stone hearth and dizzying mountain views. Located right off the Appalachian Trail, only 7 miles (11 km) from the Dartmouth College green. 12 rooms. FAP. **$$$**

FITZWILLIAM

Amos A. Parker House
Route 119, 03447
Tel: 603-585 6540
www.amosparkerhouse.com
Four-room B&B in a formal 18th-century home with superb gardens.

Hotel Meal Guide

B&Bs supply a complimentary full breakfast and are often quite sophisticated
MAP (Modified American Plan) rates include both breakfast and dinner
FAP (Full American Plan) supply all three meals

Hallways and some rooms are decorated with elaborate flower murals. A short walk to Fitzwilliam Green, a short drive to Cathedral of the Pines. **$**

FRANCONIA

Bungay Jar Bed & Breakfast
Easton Valley Road, 03580
Tel: 603-823 7775
www.bungayjar.com
An imaginatively retrofitted 18th-century barn on 8 private acres with great views. 6 rooms. B&B. **$–$$$$**

Franconia Inn
1300 Easton Valley Road, 03583
Tel: 603-823 5542/
800-473 5299
Fax: 603-823 8078
www.franconiainn.com
A 19th-century inn-turned-resort with 107 acres to explore on foot, by ski, or on horseback. Other amusements include a pool, hot tub, tennis courts, and ice skating. 34 rooms. MAP. **$$**

Sugar Hill Inn
Route 117, 03580
Tel: 603 823 5621/
800-548 4748
Fax: 603-823 5639
www.sugarhillinn.com
An 18th-century country inn on the side of Sugar Hill. Comfortably appointed, country-style rooms In maln house and cottages. 16 rooms. B&B. **$–$$**

GLEN

The Bernerhof
Route 302, 03838
Tel: 603-383 9131/
800-548 8007
www.bernerhofinn.com
A Victorian inn with nine B&B rooms. Modern additions include double whirlpools. The restaurant serves Continental "Middle European" fare. **$$**

Covered Bridge House
Route 302, 03838
Tel: 603-383 9109/
800-232 9109
www.coveredbridgehouse.com
A basic Colonial with six B&B

rooms on the banks of the Saco River, near North Conway. Rooms are country-style with quilts, braided rugs, and rocking chairs. Guests can use the beach on the river for swimming. **$**

GORHAM

Appalachian Mountain Club
Tel: 603-466 2727
The AMC operates two roadside dorms and six high-mountain "huts" in the White Mountain National forest; reservations required. 10 dorms. MAP. **$–$$**

HANOVER

Hanover Inn
Main Street, 03755
Tel: 603-643 4300/
800-443 7024
Fax: 603-646 3744/643 4433
www.hanoverinn.com
An integral part of the Dartmouth campus, a four-story, traditionally decorated Georgian brick house with 92 rooms and rockers on a long porch overlooking the common. **$$$$**

HARRISVILLE

The Harrisville Squires' Inn
Keene Road, 03450
Tel: 603-827 3925
www.nhweb.com/squires_inn
An 1840s farmhouse with five rooms on 50 acres (with cross-country ski trails), near the historic mill town. East of Keene. **$**

HENNIKER

Colby Hill Inn
3 The Oaks, 03242
Tel: 603-428 3281/
800-531 0330
Fax: 603-428 9218
www.colbyhillinn.com
A rambling late 18th-century inn with a perennial garden and swimming pool. The 16 rooms. are furnished with antiques and

Colonial reproductions; four rooms have fireplaces. Located west of Concord, near the Pat's Peak ski area. B&B. **$–$$$**

HOLDERNESS

The Manor on Golden Pond
Route 3 and Shepard Hill Road
03245
Tel: 603-968 3348/
800-545 2141
Fax: 603-968 2116
www.manorongoldenpond.com
A 1903 English manor-style stone mansion with a clay tennis court, swimming pool, and private beach. 21 rooms. MAP. **$$$$**

JACKSON

Inn at Thorn Hill
Thorn Hill Road, 03846
Tel: 603-383 4242/
800-289 8990
Fax: 603-383 8062
www.innatthornhill.com
Stanford White designed this gambrel-roofed summer house, on a secluded slope with views of Mount Washington. Romantically decorated rooms. Adjacent to Jackson cross-country trail network. 19 rooms. MAP. **$$$–$$$$**

Wentworth Resort Hotel
Route 16A, 03846
Tel: 603-383 9700/
800-637 0013
Fax: 603-383 4265
www.thewentworth.com
An 1869 grand hotel and rental houses adjoining an 18-hole golf course and cross-country ski center. 54 rooms. MAP. **$$$**

Whitney's Inn at Jackson
Route 16B, 03846
Tel: 603-383 8916/
800-677 5737
Fax: 603-383 6886
www.whitneysinn.com
A simply furnished comfy inn (with three cottages and 30 rooms for B&B), geared towards families. The inn is situated at the foot of Black Mountain, in a small-scale ski area. Extras include a pub and game room. **$–$$**

Wildcat Inn & Tavern
Route 16A, 03846
Tel: 603-383 4245/
800-228 4245
A 12-room B&B with delightful, albeit tiny, suites in the social center of town. **$**

JAFFREY

Benjamin Prescott Inn
Route 124, 03452
Tel/fax: 603 532 6637
A sprawling 1820 house, decorated with handmade quilts and ship models, set amid a working dairy farm. Near Mount Monadnock. 9 rooms. B&B. **$–$$**

KEENE

Carriage Barn
358 Main Street, 03431
Tel: 603-357 3812
www.nhweb.com/carriagebarn
A Civil War-era barn that is simply furnished with antiques and handmade quilts in the four rooms. Situated just across the street from Keene State College. **$**

LINCOLN

Mill House Inn
Route 112, 03251
Tel: 603-745 6261/
800-654 6183
Fax: 603-745 6896
www.millatloon.com
A modern country-style inn complex built around three old paper mill buildings, adjacent to the Millfront Marketplace shopping center. Free transportation to Loon Mountain in winter. 95 rooms. **$$**

LITTLETON

Beal House Inn
2 West Main Street, 03561
Tel: 603-444-2661/
888 616 2325
Fax: 603-444 6224
www.bealhouseinn.com
An eight-roomed 1833 Federal-style

Price Categories

A very approximate guide to current room rates for a standard double per night is:
$$$$ = over $200
$$$ = $150–200
$$ = $100–150
$ = under $100

farmhouse B&B full of antiques.
$$–$$$$

NEW LONDON

New London Inn
140 Main Street, 03257
Tel: 603-526 2791/
800-526 2791
www.newlondoninn.com
A 28-room 1792 B&B inn with eclectic decor, a well regarded restaurant, and an inventive chef/innkeeper. **$–$$**

Pleasant Lake Inn
Pleasant Street, 03257
Tel: 603-526 6271/
800-626 4907
Fax: 603-526 4111
www.innatpleasantlake.com
A 1790 inn on 5 pastoral lakeside acres. 10 rooms. **$–$$**

Maple Hill Farm
200 Newport Road, 03257
Tel: 603-526 2248/
800-231 8637
A family-friendly, comfortably furnished 1824 farmhouse/B&B near Little Lake Sunapee (canoes and rowboats available). Owners raise chickens, sheep and rabbits; younger guests may help gather eggs or watch yarn being spun. **$**

NORTH CONWAY

The 1785 Inn
Route 16, 03860
Tel: 603-356 9025/
800-421 1785
Fax: 603-356 6081
www.the1785inn.com
One of the oldest buildings in the Mount Washington valley, this colonial inn with spectacular mountain views is comfortably furnished with colonial, Victorian, and country-style pieces. 17 rooms.
B&B. **$$–$$$**

Farm By The River
2555 West Side Road, 03860
Tel/fax: 603-356 2694/
888 414 8353
www.farmbytheriver.com
A 1785 classic country farmhouse set on 65 acres, with gardens, a sugar maple orchard, and a beach on the Saco River. Jacuzzis and year round horseriding. Located on a back road parallel to Route 16/302, one mile (1.6 km) from Echo Lake State Park. 10 rooms.
B&B. **$–$$**

Stonehurst Manor
Route 16, 03860
Tel: 603-356 3113/
800-525 9100
Fax: 603-356 3217
www.stonehurstmanor.com
A 100-year-old mansion with 25 rooms, an outdoor pool, hot tub, and tennis court. **$$**

NORTH SUTTON

Follansbee Inn
Route 114, 03260
Tel: 603-927 4221/
800-626-4221
Fax: 603-927 6301
www.follansbeeinn.com
A cozy lakeside inn with 2½ acres of land on the beach. There are 20 rooms for B&B. **$–$$$**

NORTH WOODSTOCK

Woodstock Inn
Main Street (Route 3), 03262
Tel: 603-745 3951/
800-321 3985
Fax: 603-745 3701
www.woodstockinnnh.com
Three Victorian inns in a bustling tourist town. The 21 rooms vary from romantic to family-friendly.
Outdoor hot tub. **$–$$**

PORTSMOUTH

Sise Inn
40 Court Street, 03801

Tel: 603-443 1200/
800-267 0525
Fax: 603-433 1200
An 1881 Queen Anne inn with 34 rooms in the center of town. Amenities include antique furnishings, fireplaces, whirlpool baths, and stereos in some rooms.
$$–$$$

Inn at Strawberry Banke
314 Court Street, 03801
Tel: 603-436 7242/
800-428 3933
An 1800-captain's house adjoining the historic preserve. 7 rooms.
B&B. **$–$$**

Martin Hill Inn
404 Islington Street, 03801
Tel: 603-436 2287
www.portsmouthnh.com/martinhillinn
An 1812 Colonial main house and a country-style 1850 guest house across the perennial gardens. Solicitous hosts and lavish breakfasts. 7 rooms. B&B. **$$**

Inn at Christian Shore
335 Maplewood Avenue, 03801
Tel: 603-431 6770
An antique appointed 1800-Federal house, near the historic district.
6 rooms. B&B. **$**

SNOWVILLE

Snowvillage Inn
Off Route 153, 03832
Tel: 603-447 2818/
800-447 4345
Fax: 603-447 5268
www.snowvillageinn.com
Austrian motifs pervade this high-perched eyrie. The 18 rooms are in the New England farmhouse-style main house, an old carriage barn, and a new lodge. Located south of Conway, near Crystal Lake. Tennis courts, hiking trails, sauna, cross-country skiing (including lessons), snowshoeing. **$$–$$$$**

SUGAR HILL

Sunset Hill House
Sunset Hill Road, 03585
Tel: 603-823 5522/
800-786 4455

Price Categories

A very approximate guide to current room rates for a standard double per night is:

$$$$ = over $200
$$$ = $150–200
$$ = $100–150
$ = under $100

Fax: 603-823 5738
www.sunsethillhouse.com
Built in 1880, this inn (with a 30-ft deck and 30 B&B rooms) sits on a 1,700-foot ridge with sweeping views of the Presidential Range. The homey rooms all have mountain views, and some have bay windowed reading nooks. Facilities include pool, a golf course, and cross-country ski trails. **$–$$$**
Hilltop Inn
Route 117, 03585
Tel: 603-823 5695/
800-770 5695
Fax: 603-823 5518
www.hilltopinn.com
A homey 1895 Victorian inn serving large country-style breakfasts. Located 10 minutes from Franconia Notch. Six rooms. B&B. **$–$$**

SUNAPEE

Dexter's Inn and Tennis Club
Stage Coach Road, 03782
Tel: 603-763 5571/
800-232 5571
A secluded yellow clapboard 1801 house with three all-weather courts and an outdoor pool. 17 rooms. MAP. **$$–$$$**
The Burkehaven
179 Burkehaven Road, 03782
Tel: 800-567 2788
Fax: 603-763 9065
www.burkehavenatsunapee.com
Ten pleasant motel units overlooking Sunapee Harbor; outdoor pool. Pets welcome. **$**

TEMPLE

Birchwood Inn
Route 45, 03084
Tel: 603-878 3285

Fax: 603-878 2159
www.virtualcities.com
An 1800-brick inn with Rufus Porter murals. Guest rooms each have a theme: the Editorial Room is decorated with newspapers (with noteworthy headlines), and the Train Room has photos and models of trains (of course). Convenient to Cathedral of the Pines. 7 rooms. B&B. **$**

TROY

The Inn at East Hill Farm
460 Monadnock Street
03465
Tel: 603-242 6495/
800-242 6495
www.east-hill-farm.com
This 150-acre resort/working farm has cottages and inn rooms with mountain views. There are indoor and outdoor pools, a sauna, and facilities for tennis and horse-riding. Special programs for children are also on offer. **$$–$$$**

WATERVILLE VALLEY

Waterville Valley Resort
Waterville Valley, 03223.
Tel: 800-468-2553
Fax: 603-236 4174
A resort complex with more than 700 rooms. cupped in a high valley, with skiing in winter, hiking, tennis, and other sports the rest of the year. **$–$$$$**

WEST CHESTERFIELD

Chesterfield Inn
Route 9, 03466

Hotel Meal Guide

B&Bs supply a complimentary full breakfast and are often quite sophisticated
MAP (Modified American Plan) rates include both breakfast and dinner
FAP (Full American Plan) supply all three meals

Tel: 603-256 3211/
800-365 5515
Fax: 603-256 6131
www.chesterfieldinn.com
A 1798 house, originally a tavern, converted to a luxurious 15-roomed B&B. Attractions include wet bars, whirlpool tubs, and antique fireplaces. **$$–$$$$**

WHITEFIELD

Spalding Inn
Mountainview Road, 03598
Tel: 603-837 2572/
800-368 8439
A quiet but full-scale country resort, operating since 1926, with golf course, tennis courts, and heated pool. Famous for lawn bowling. Accommodations in the main inn, a lodge, and separate cottages. 45 rooms. B&B. **$$–$$$**

WOLFEBORO

Wolfeboro Inn
90 North Main Street, 03894
Tel: 603-569 3016/
800-451 2389
Fax: 603-569 5375
A luxury lakeside inn since 1812. Located a short walk from the village, the inn has a private beach, excursion boat, and fishing. 49 rooms. **$$–$$$$**

Where to Eat
BEDFORD

Bedford Village Inn
2 Old Bedford Road
Tel: 603-472 2001
Country club atmosphere in an updated 18th-century inn south of Manchester. Traditional New England menu often features lobster and Atlantic salmon. **$$$**

BETHLEHEM

Tim-Bir Alley
Adair Country Inn
80 Guider Lane (at Route 302)
Tel: 603-444 6142

Restaurant Guidelines

Prices are approximate, but for a three-course meal for one (excluding beverages, tax, and tip), the following guidelines may prove helpful:

$$$$ = over $40
$$$ = $28–40
$$ = $15–28
$ = under $15
Meal tax varies from state to state, but it is customary to tip 15 to 20 percent on the pre-tax total.

Credit cards The more expensive establishments generally accept credit cards, but call ahead to check just in case.

Reservations Most restaurants, except for the clearly casual, appreciate reservations (some require them).

Extraordinary sophistication for a small-scale restaurant. **$$$**

BRETTON WOODS

Mount Washington Hotel
Route 302
Tel: 603-278 1000
Old-fashioned fare in a formal dining room, but a fascinating glimpse of luxury past. **$$$**

CENTER HARBOR

Red Hill Inn
Route 25B
Tel: 603-279 7001
New American creativity in a red-brick summer estate. Ask about the signature vinegar pie. **$$–$$$**

CENTER SANDWICH

Corner House Inn
Main Street
(Routes 109 and 113)
Tel: 603-284 6219
Continental fare in a delightful 1849 house. **$$**

DIXVILLE NOTCH

Balsams Grand Resort Hotel
Route 26
Tel: 603-255 3400/
800-255 3400
Lavish buffet spreads are on offer at this impressive resort hotel/ Reservations are required and the place is only open from mid-May–mid-October. **$$$**

FRANCONIA

Franconia Inn
1300 Easton Valley Road
Tel: 603-823 5542
Ambitious Continental cuisine served in a formal dining room with mountain views. **$$$**
Lovett's Inn
Profile Road
Tel: 603-823 7761
A mix of traditional favorites and more adventurous fare. **$$**

GLEN

The Bernerhof
Route 302
Tel: 603-383 4414
Alpine delights, including *spaetzle* and Provimi veal, are on offer at the ski-country Bernerhof. **$$$**

HANOVER

The Hanover Inn
Main Street
Tel: 603-643 4300
Come here to experience a successful New American eating experiment. Numerous appetizers and wines by the glass, set in a bastion of traditionalism. **$$$**

HENNIKER

Colby Hill Inn
3 The Oaks, Henniker
Tel: 603-428 3281
A late 18th-century inn with country views and Continental cuisine with New England accents. **$$$**

HOLDERNESS

The Manor on Golden Pond
Route 3 and Shepard Hill Road
Tel: 603-968 3348
Rich continental cuisine in a baronial setting. **$$$**

JACKSON

Inn at Thorn Hill
Thorn Hill Road
Tel: 603-383 4242
A four-course *prix-fixe* menu of country-sophisticate cuisine in a handsome country house. Reservations required. **$$$**
**Wentworth Resort Hotel
Dining Room**
Route 16A
Tel: 603-383 9700
Exceptional Continental cuisine with New England ingredients in a fancy French provincial dining room. The more casual lounge serves mountain specialties including fondues and raclette. **$$$**
Thompson House Eatery
Routes 16A and 16
Tel: 603 383 9341
Closed in winter. Innovative salads and sandwiches, and luscious entrées, in an 1800s barn with flowery patio. **$$**
Wildcat Inn & Tavern
Route 16A
Tel: 603-383 4245
The owner/chef Marty Sweeney caters for gourmets and gourmands alike. **$$**

KEENE

One Seventy Six Main
176 Main Street
Tel: 603-357 3100
Upscale pub grub (burgers, pasta, and seafood) and good beer list. **$$**

LITTLETON

Beal House Inn
2 West Main St (Routes 302 and 28)
Tel: 603-444 2661.
European cuisine in a handsome carriage house. **$$–$$$**

Restaurant Guidelines

Prices are approximate, but for a three-course meal for one (excluding beverages, tax, and tip), the following guidelines may prove helpful:

$$$$ = over $40
$$$ = $28–40
$$ = $15–28
$ = under $15

MANCHESTER

Red Arrow Diner
61 Lowell Avenue
Tel: 603-626 1118
A 1903 luncheonette, open 24 hours. **$**

MOULTONBORO

The Woodshed
Lee's Mill Road
Tel: 603-476 2311
New England classics – clam chowder, scrod, and Indian pudding – plus a raw bar in an 1860s barn. **$$–$$$**

NEW LONDON

New London Inn
140 Main Street
Tel: 603-526 2791
Good for inventive nouvelle regional cuisine. **$$–$$$**

NORTH CONWAY

Stonehurst Manor
Route 16
Tel: 603-356 3113
Continental cuisine, plus stone-hearth pizzas. **$$$**

NORTH WOODSTOCK

Woodstock Inn
Main Street (Route 3)
Tel: 603-745 3951
A variety of appealing options, at a range of prices. Continental cuisine is served in the Victorian parlor, casual fare from meatloaf to fajitas

is on offer at the Woodstock Station cafe, and microbrews are served in the Woodstock Inn Brewery. **$–$$$**

PINKHAM NOTCH

Appalachian Mountain Club
Pinkham Notch Camp
Route 16
Tel: 603-466 2727
Hearty dinner only for hikers. **$**

PORTSMOUTH

Library Restaurant at the Rockingham House
401 State Street
Tel: 603-431 5202
International cuisine (rack of lamb, filet mignon) served amid carved mahogany paneling and masses of books in a former luxury hotel (now converted to condominiums). **$$$**
Muddy River Smokehouse
21 Congress Street
Tel: 603-430 9582
Great BBQ, homemade chili, and a large selection of beers. Blues club downstairs. **$$**
Porto Bello
67 Bow Street
Tel: 603-431 2989
Italian restaurant with harbor views. **$$–$$$**
Dolphin Striker
15 Bow Street
Tel: 603-431 5222
A riverfront tavern specializing in New American seafood. **$$**
Portsmouth Brewery
56 Market Street
Tel: 603-431 1115
A microbrewery with international munchies. **$$**
Cafe Brioche
14 Market Square
Tel: 603-430 9225
Tasty French pastries including croissants, brioches, and quiches are served at this friendly sidewalk cafe. **$**

SNOWVILLE

Snowvillage Inn
92 Stuart Road (Off Route 153)

Tel: 603-447 2818
Austrian specialties and inspiring, unparalleled views. **$$**

SUGAR HILL

Polly's Pancake Parlor
Route 117
Tel: 603-823 5575.
The place to go for pancakes. **$**

WOLFEBORO

The Bittersweet
Route 28
Tel: 603-569 3636
An artifact-packed barn featuring local specialties, ranging from seafood to Chateaubriand. **$$**

Culture

CLASSICAL MUSIC

The Music Hall (tel: 603-436 2400; 28 Chestnut Street) features international classical musicians, while **Music in Market Square** is a classical summer series (tel: 603-436 9109, North Church); both are located in Portsmouth.

ROCK AND POP

Gaslight Co (tel: 603-430 8582; 64 Market Street, Portsmouth)

Live Music

Press Room
77 Daniel Street, Portsmouth
Tel: 603-431 5186
Has live folk, Irish and blues music, with a country-western jam session every Friday.
The Music Hall
28 Chestnut Street, Portsmouth
Tel: 603-436 2400
Offers a variety of musical performances all year.
Hopkins Center for the Arts
Dartmouth College, Hanover
Tel: 603-646 2422
Arts venue with live music all year round.

New Hampshire Festivals

Spring

The town of Lisbon, near Cannon Mountain, bids farewell to winter in May with the annual **Lilac Festival** (tel:603-828-6336).

The Sheep and Wool Festival (tel: 603-763 5859) in New Boston (near Manchester) readies in a different way – with shearing, spinning and weaving, as well as border collie demonstrations.

Summer

Portsmouth's **Market Square Days** (tel:603-431 5388) in June draw over 100,000 people to an outdoor street fair with concerts, a 10km road race, and other festivities.

Later in June, the **Portsmouth Jazz Festival** (tel:603-436 7678) showcases local performers.

Motorcycle fans may want to visit the **Laconia Motorcycle Rally and Race Week** (tel:603-466 3988) for eight days in June.

For a different sort of excitement, the annual **Mount Washington Road Race** (tel:603-466 3988) takes runners up the 6,288-foot (2,000-meter) peak along the historic Auto Road.

With about 200 artists exhibiting at Mount Sunapee State Park, the **League of New Hampshire Craftsmen's Fair** (tel:603-244 3375) in August draws thousands of visitors interested in traditional New England crafts.

Fall

In September, Loon Mountain looks like Scotland when the **New Hampshire Highland Games** (tel: 800-227 4191), with Scottish music, dances and other cultural events, come to Lincoln.

During the annual **Hampton Seafood Festival** (tel:603-926 8718), also in September, local restaurants take their seafood creations to the streets for a two-day food fair.

Winter

Both Concord and Manchester host **First Night** (tel:603-746 9555) celebrations on New Year's Eve.

In March, more than 50 sugarhouses statewide open their doors for syrup-making demonstrations (and free samples) during the **Maple Weekend** (tel:603-267 7070).

features local rock acts from mid-May to mid-October.

OPERA

Opera North (tel: 603-643 1946; Hanover, NH) performs operas in the area.

THEATER

Seacoast Repertory Theater (tel: 603-433 4472; 125 Bow Street, Portsmouth) features adult and children's productions from September to June.
Colonial Theater (tel: 603-352 2033; 95 Main Street, Keene) showcases live performances and films.
Palace Theater (tel: 603-668 5588; 80 Hanover Street, Manchester) puts on six productions a year, including dinner theater by its resident company **Stage One Productions**.
Hopkins Center for the Arts (tel: 603-646 2422; Dartmouth College, Hanover) stages multiple musicals and various other theater productions.

CINEMA

Hopkins Center for the Arts (tel: 603-646 2422, Dartmouth College, Hanover) shows classic and experimental films, while **Nugget Theater** (tel: 603-643 2769; S Main Street, Hanover) shows current films.

ART GALLERIES

Your best bets are in Portsmouth: **New Hampshire Art Association-Robert Lincoln Levy Gallery** (tel: 603-431 4230; 136 State Street) exhibits paintings, photographs, and prints, while **Pierce Gallery** (tel: 603-436 1988; 105 Market Street) offers New Hampshire and Maine coastal scenics.

Outdoor Activities

BIKING

Several ski areas offer summer and fall mountain biking. **Loon Mountain** attracts novice through advanced riders to 21 miles (34 km) of trails, where lifts serve the steepest biking routes. Nearby, the self-guided **Franconia Notch Bike Tour** starts at Echo Lake, passes the Old Man of the Mountain, and ends at the Loon Mountain ski area.

Near Mount Washington, **Great Glen Trails** (tel: 603-466 2333) offers learn-to-mountain-bike courses, ranging from a short introductory class to more in-depth skill-building. If inn-to-inn touring is more your speed, contact Harrisville-based **Monadnock Bicycling Touring** (tel: 603-827 3925).

CANOEING, KAYAKING, AND RAFTING

Saco Bound (tel: 800-677 7238) runs a river kayaking school, and leads canoeing expeditions, guided kayak trips, and white-water rafting excursions at several New Hampshire and Maine locations.

North Star Canoe Rentals (tel: 603-542 5802), based in Cornish, conducts canoe trips on the Connecticut River. Appalachian Mountain Club's New Hampshire chapter (tel: 603-466 2725; www.amc-nh.org) offers a **Spring Whitewater Canoe School** one weekend each April.

Whale Watching

Whale watching and cruises to the nine Isles of Shoals are some of New Hampshire's big attractions. Firms offering these include:

The Isles of Shoals
Tel: 800-441-4620/
603 431-5500
New Hampshire Seacoast Cruises
Tel: 603-964-5545
Portsmouth Harbor Cruises
Tel: 800-776-0915/
603 436-8084

FISHING

Great Glen Trails *(see Biking, page 395)* offers introductory fishing classes and arranges guided fly fishing excursions. **North Country Angler** (tel: 603-356 6000), also based in the White Mountains, runs guided fly-fishing weekends.

For ocean fishing, several charter companies operate on the seacoast, including **Atlantic Fishing Fleet** (tel: 603-964 5220; Rye) and **Al Gauron Deep Sea Fishing** (tel: 603-926 2469; Hampton Beach).

HIKING

The 86 major peaks of the White Mountains provide plenty of hiking challenges. The **US Forest Service** (tel: 603-528 8721; Laconia) provides specific trail information.

The **Appalachian Mountain Club** (tel: 603-466 2725) has detailed hiking trail information; this group maintains a network of huts in the White Mountains providing overnight accommodations. For hut reservations, tel: 603-466 2727.

For inn-to-inn hiking tours, contact **New England Hiking Holidays** (tel: 603-356 9696, 800-869 0949) in North Conway or **Great Outdoors Hiking & Biking Tours** (tel: 603-356 3113, 800-525 9100).

SAILING

Marinas abound on Lake Winnipesaukee, the state's largest

lake. Although it's a popular power boating spot, some marinas rent sailboats, including **Fay's Boat Yard** (tel: 603-293 8000; Guilford).

SKIING

Major areas include:**Waterville Valley** (tel: 800-468 2553), **Loon Mountain** (tel: 603-745 8111; Lincoln), and **Cannon Mountain** (tel: 603-823 5563; Franconia).

Smaller areas include: **Attitash** (tel: 800-223 7669; Bartlett), **Bretton Woods** (tel: 603-278 5000) and **Wildcat** (tel: 603-466 3326, 800-255 6439), both in Jackson.

The state's largest cross-country ski centers are **Jackson Ski Touring Foundation** (tel: 800-927 6697) and **Mt Washington Valley Ski Touring** (tel: 603-356 9920; off Route 16, Intervale).

South of the White Mountains you'll find the **Nordic Center** (tel: 603-236 4666; Waterville Valley) and **Franconia Village Cross Country Center** at the Franconia Inn (tel: 603-823 5542, 800-473 5299).

Shopping

WHERE TO SHOP

Shops fill Portsmouth's revitalized waterfront area near Market, Bow and Ceres Streets. Route 16 in North Conway – a mecca of more than 200 outlet stores – is also good for shopping.

MALLS

The 19th-century **Colony Mill Marketplace** (tel: 603-357 1240; 222 West Street, Keene) houses 33 stores.
Mall of New Hampshire (tel: 603-669 0433; 1500 S Willow Street, Manchester) has 88 shops and three department stores.

BOOKS

Book Guild of Portsmouth (tel: 603-436 1758; 58 State Street), which

sells maritime and local books, and **Portsmouth Book Shop** (tel: 603-433 4406; 1 Islington Street), which sells local history, travel guides, and maps, are two of this hip city's specialized bookstores.

Eagle Books (tel: 603-357 8721; 19 West Street, Central Square, Keene) specializes in writer's projects books, and **Toadstool Bookshop** (tel: 603-352 8815; Colony Mill, Keene) carries general titles and also has a large café. **Dartmouth Bookstore** (tel: 643 3616; 33 S Main Street, Hanover) stocks upwards of 130,000 titles.

ANTIQUES

Antique stores, including **Antiques at Colony Mill** (tel: 603-358 6343; West Street, Keene), which represents more than 100 dealers, abound in the Monadnock region.

ARTS AND CRAFTS

League of New Hampshire Craftsmen (tel: 603-224 1471; 205 North Main Street, Concord, and other locations throughout the state) has a gallery of handmade crafts.

Children

JOURNEYS BY STEAM TRAIN

Winnipesaukee Railroad (tel: 603-279 5253; S Main Street, Meredith) runs historic coaches around the eponymous lake.
Conway Scenic Railroad (tel: 603-356 5251; North Conway) offers excursions from the 1874 station.
Mount Washington Cog Railway (tel: 603-846 5404, 800-922 8825) has the second-steepest railway track in the world.

THEATER

Hampton Playhouse (tel: 603-926 3073; Route 101E, Hampton) showcases children's productions on summer Saturdays.

Maine

The Place

Known as: The Pine Tree State.
Motto: *Dirigo* (I direct).
Origin of name: called after ancient French province.
Entered Union: March 15, 1820, when it was separated from Massachusetts to form the 23rd state.
Capital: Augusta.
Area: 35,387 sq. miles (91,653 sq. km).
Highest point: Mount Katahdin, 5,268 ft (1,606 meters).
Population: 1.23 million.
Population density: 35 people per sq. mile (13 per sq. meter).
Economy: services (including tourism) and manufacturing (paper and paper products, footwear and other leather goods, lumber), plus fishing, agriculture, and forestry.
Annual visitors: 8 million.
National representation: two senators and two representatives to Congress.
Famous citizens: Longfellow, Sir Hiram and Hudson Maxim, and Edna Street Vincent Millay.

Where to Stay

Note that many of Maine's hotels and inns are open only in summer.

BAR HARBOR

The Tides
119 West Street, 04609
Tel: 207-288 4968
barharbortides.com
An 1887 Greek Revival manor B&B with views of Frenchman's Bay. Three elegant suites with working fireplaces and ocean vistas. **$$$$**

Bar Harbor Inn
Newport Drive, 04609
Tel: 207-288 3351/
800-248 3351
Fax: 207-288 5296
For more than 125 years, a Bar Harbor institution; 153 rooms in three buildings close to town. Most rooms have fireplaces and views; some have private decks. **$$$–$$$$**
Manor House Inn
106 West Street, 04609
Tel: 207-288 3759/
800-437 0088
Fax: 207-288 2974
www.barharbormanorhouse.com
An 1887 Victorian inn with 14 bedrooms surrounded by gardens. **$$–$$$**
Nannau-Seaside Bed & Breakfast
396 Main Street, 04609
Tel: 207-288 5575
Fax: 207 288 5421
www.nannau.com
A 1904 Shingle-style summer "cottage" (read "estate") with four B&B rooms near to the water, 1 mile (1.5 km) from downtown. **$$**

BATH

Inn at Bath
969 Washington Street, 04530
Tel: 207-443 4294/
800-423 0964
Fax: 207-443 4295
www.innatbath.com
An elegant, comfortable antiques-filled 1810 inn/B&B with nine guest rooms with wood-burning fireplaces and whirlpool baths. **$$–$$$**
Fairhaven Inn
North Bath Road, 04530
Tel: 207-443 4391/
888-443 4391
www.maincoast.com/fairhaveninn
A 1790 Colonial inn B&B set in

Price Categories

A very approximate guide to current room rates for a standard double per night is:
$$$$ = over $200
$$$ = $150–200
$$ = $100–150
$ = under $100

Maine Trivia

● At 33,215 sq miles, Maine is almost as big as the other five states of New England combined. One county, Aroostook, covers an area greater than Connecticut and Rhode Island together.
● Maine has 6,000 lakes and ponds, 32,000 miles (51,000 km) of river and stream, 17 million acres of forest, 3,478 miles (5,565 km) of coastline, and 2,000 islands.
● Nearly 550,000 acres of Maine, an area roughly the size of Rhode Island, consists of national and state parks.
● More than 80 percent of the state is forested.
● Maine is the only state in the US to be bordered by only one other state (New Hampshire).

20 acres overlooking the Kennebec river. The eight guest rooms furnished with four-poster beds and handmade quilts. Trails for hiking and cross-country skiing. **$–$$**

BETHEL

Bethel Inn & Country Club
Village Common, 04217
Tel: 207-824 2175/
800-654 0125
Fax: 207-824 2233
www.bethelinn.com
A rambling yellow clapboard 1913 country inn, with tennis, golf, and a lake for water sports. MAP with 57 rooms. **$$$–$$$$**
Telemark Inn
RFD 2, Box 800, 04217
Tel: 207 836 2703
www.maineguide.com/bethel/telemark
A secluded 1900 Adirondack-style lodge with six B&B rooms. The lodge is located 10 miles (16 km) west of Bethel, and outdoor activities offered include llama treks and "skijouring", cross-country skiing pulled by dogs. **$–$$**
The Ames Place
46 Broad Street, 04217
Tel: 207-824 3170

Price Categories

A very approximate guide to current room rates for a standard double per night is:

$$$$ = over $200
$$$ = $150–200
$$ = $100–150
$ = under $100

Two-room B&B in a lovely 1850 home with personable hosts. **$**
Holidae House,
Main Street, 04217
Tel: 207-824 3400
A bargain seven-room B&B, considering the in-town location. **$**
Sunday River Inn
23 Skiway Road, 04217
Tel: 207-824 2410/
866-232 4354
Fax: 207-824 3181
www.sundayriverinn.com
A handsome ski dorm with its own cross-country center. 23-room MAP. **$**

BLUE HILL

Blue Hill Inn
Union Street, 04614
Tel: 207-374 2844/
800-826 7415
Fax: 207-374 2829
www.bluehillinn.com
A 12-room MAP in an 1830s Federal-style inn with six fireplaces one block from Blue Hill bay in a lovely village. **$$$**
Blue Hill Farm Country Inn
Route 15, 04614
Tel: 207-374 5126
Fax: 207-374 5126
www.bluehillfarminn.com
A 14-room B&B in a rural retreat on 48 acres 5 miles (8 km) from Blue Hill village. **$**

BOOTHBAY HARBOR AREA

Spruce Point Inn and Lodges
Grandview Avenue, Boothbay Harbor, 04538
Tel: 207-633 4152/
800-553 0289
Fax: 207-433 7138

www.sprucepointinn.com
An 100-year-old MAP inn and resort (including cottages and condominiums, totalling 67 rooms) on a 100-acre peninsula. Activities include swimming pool, tennis court, fitness room, croquet, badminton, and a putting green. Shuttle bus into town. **$$$$**
Five Gables Inn
Murray Hill Road
East Boothbay, 04544
Tel: 207-633 4551/
800-451 5048
fivegablesinn.com
This 16-room B&B in a spiffed-up 1865 summer hotel has views of Lineken Bay and the ocean from the broad verandah (complete with hammock). **$$–$$$**
Linekin Bay Resort
Wall Point Road
Boothbay Harbor, 04538
Tel: 207-633 2494/
866-847 2103
Fax: 207-633 0580
www.linekinbayresort.com
An old-fashioned seaside resort with complimentary sailing instruction. 70 rooms FAP. **$$–$$$**
Green Shutters Cottages
76 Bay Street,
Boothbay Harbor, 04538
Tel: 207-633 2646
A comfortable family resort; weekly rentals (MAP) in five cottages. **$**

BROOKSVILLE

Oakland House
Herrick Road, 0461
Tel: 207-359 8521/
800-359 7352
Fax: 207-359 9865
www.oaklandhouse.com
A casual 1889 complex with waterside cottages offering 33 MAP rooms set in 50 acres near Blue Hill. **$$–$$$$**

BRUNSWICK

Captain Daniel Stone Inn
10 Water Street, 04011
Tel/fax: 207-725 9898/
877-573 5151
www.captaindanielstoneinn.com

An upscale Federal inn overlooking the Adroscoggin River. Quite a number of the 34 rooms have whirlpool baths. **$$$**
Bethel Point Bed and Breakfast
Bethel Point Road, 04011
Tel: 207-725 1115
888-238 8262
Fax: 207-725 2901
www.bethelpoint.com
Three-room B&B in an 1830s farmhouse on Hen Cove, overlooking the sea. **$$**
Brunswick Bed and Breakfast
165 Park Row, 04011
Tel: 207-729 4914/
800-299 4914
Fax: 207-725 1759
www.brunswickbnb.com
An historic house decorated with handmade quilts, within walking distance to the Bowdoin College campus. Five simply furnished guest rooms. **$–$$**

CAMDEN

Camden Harbor Inn
83 Bayview Street, 04843
Tel: 207-236 4200/
800-236 4266
Fax: 207-236 7063
www.camdenharborinn.com
A porch-encircled 1874 B&B. The 22 rooms are furnished with period antiques; some have fireplaces and decks, balconies, or patios. **$$$$**
Norumbega
63 High Street (Route 1), 04843
Tel: 207-236 4646/
877-363 4646
Fax: 207-236 0824
www.norumegainn.com
13 rooms. B&B. A grand 1880s Victorian stone castle overlooking the bay. Furnished like an English country house, the inn has a three-story turret and seven fireplaces. Much photographed. **$$$–$$$$**
Windward House
6 High Street, 04843
Tel: 207-236 9656
Antiques, an English garden and all-out breakfasts in this eight-room B&B. **$$–$$$**
Lodge at Camden Hills
P.O. Box 794, Camden
04843, (Route 1)

Tel: 207-236-847/
8800-832 7058
Twenty units, including suites and
jacuzzi cottages, in park-like setting
with views of woods. **$$**
Maine Stay Inn
22 High Street (Route 1), 04853
Tel: 207-236 9636
Fax: 207-236 0621
www.camdenmainestay.com
An 1802 house with period
furnishings, a five-minute walk from
the town center. Two parlors have
wood-burning fireplaces; a glass-
enclosed porch overlooks the
gardens. 8 rooms. B&B. **$–$$**
Whitehall Inn
52 High Street (Route 1), 04843
Tel: 207-236 3391/
800-789 6565
Fax: 207-236 4427
www.whitehall-inn.com
A venerable 1834 home, converted
into an inn/B&B in 1901. The 50
rooms are small and simple, but
have a literary charm. **$–$$**

CAPE ELIZABETH

Inn by the Sea
40 Bowery Beach Road
(Route 77)
04107
Tel: 207-799 3134/
800-888 4287
Fax: 207-799 4779
www.innbythesea.com
A superb inn and resort connected
by boardwalk to Crescent Beach.
Rooms, suites and cottage
condominiums with Chippendale-
style pieces, plus wicker and white
pine. Facilities include a pool and
tennis courts. **$$$$**

CASTINE

Pentagoet Inn
Main Street at Perkins Street
04421
Tel: 207-326 8616/
800-845 1701
A turreted Victorian beauty with 16
rooms for B&B. **$$**
Castine Inn
Main Street, 04421
Tel: 207-326 4365

Fax: 207-326 4570
www.castineinn.com
A simply furnished 1898 clapboard
inn with 20 rooms for B&B.
The comfortable living room has
a fireplace and there's also a
distinguished restaurant here. **$–$$**
Village Inn
6 Water Street, 04421
Tel: 207-326 9510
The four rooms at this B&B are very
simple but there's a wonderful in-
house bakery. **$**

CHEBEAGUE ISLAND

Chebeague Island Inn
Box 492, 04017
Tel: 207-846 5155
Fax: 207-846 4265
www.chebeagueinn.com
Constructed in 1925 after the
original structure was destroyed in
a fire, this three-story clapboard inn
with 21 rooms for B&B is a classic
summer hotel, accessible only by
ferry, just north of Portland. **$$**

DEER ISLE

Pilgrim's Inn
Main Street (Route 15A)
04622
Tel: 207-348 6615
A four-story 1793 inn with antique-
filled guest rooms and seaside
cottages. Nice views over the
harbor and a mill pond. 15 rooms.
MAP. **$$–$$$**

EASTPORT

Weston House
26 Boynton Street, 04631
Tel: 207-853 2907/

Hotel Meal Guide

B&Bs supply a complimentary
full breakfast and are often
quite sophisticated
MAP (Modified American Plan)
includes breakfast and dinner
FAP (Full American Plan) supply
all three meals

800-853 2907
Fax: 207-853 0981
www.westonhouse-maine.com
This 1802 Federal manse (former
minister's house), at the
easternmost town in Maine near
Campobello Island, is now a four-
room B&B. It once hosted the
naturalist John James Audubon
(1785–1851). **$**

FREEPORT

Harraseeket Inn
162 Main Street, 04032
Tel: 207-865 9377/
800-342 6423
Fax: 207-865 1684
www.harraseeketinn.com
Luxury in a town of bargains. An
1850 Greek Revival home with
modern appointments. 84 rooms.
B&B. **$$$–$$$$**
Isaac Randall House
10 Independence Drive
Tel: 207-865 9295/
800-865 9295
Fax: 207-865 9003
www.isaacrandall.com
A 12-room B&B in an 1823 Federal-
style farmhouse, Freeport's first bed
and breakfast. Rooms mix country-
style and Victorian furnishings. The
"Caboose" room, in a railroad car
next to a playground, is designed for
families. **$$**
Bagley House
1290 Royalsborough Road
(Route 136), 04222
Tel: 207-865 6566/
800-765 1772
Fax: 207-353 5878
www.bagleyhouse.com
A 1772 Colonial B&B with eight
rooms in the country, 10 minutes
from town. Breakfasts are served in
the kitchen with its massive brick
fireplace and beehive oven. **$–$$**

GEORGETOWN

Grey Havens Inn
Reid Park Road, 04548
Tel: 207-371 2616
Fax: 207-371 227
www.greyhavens.com
A Shingle-style 1904 inn with a

wraparound verandah on an oceanfront hillside near Bath. 14 rooms. B&B. **$$–$$$**

GREENVILLE

Lodge at Moosehead Lake
Lily Bay Road, 04441
Tel: 207-695 4400
Fax: 207-695 2281
lodgeatmooseheadlake.com
An eminently civilized wilderness retreat in a 1917 summer estate. Rooms have four-poster beds and whirlpool baths, some have private decks and spectacular lake views. 8 rooms. B&B. **$$$$**

Greenville Inn
Norris Street, 04441
Tel: 207-695 2206/
888 695 6000
Fax: 207-695 0335
www.greenvilleinn.com
A lumber baron's opulent 1895 mansion, plus several simpler cottages, overlooking Moosehead Lake. Ornate woodwork and stained glass set a formal tone in the inn's common rooms. 12 rooms. **$$–$$$**

HULLS COVE

Inn at Canoe Point
Eden Street (Route 3)
04609
Tel: 207-288 9511
Fax: 207-288 2870
www.innatcanoepoint.com
A secluded 1889 Tudor mansion perched on a rocky point at Frenchmen's Bay near Bar Harbor. 5 rooms. B&B. **$$$–$$$$**

ISLE AU HAUT

The Keeper's House
Stonington 04681
Tel: 207-367 2261
A 100-year-old lighthouse keeper's house, on an island off Stonington, accessible only by mailboat. No electricity – light comes from gas lamps – but indoor plumbing and hot water are part of the package. The house has 6 rooms and offers FAP. **$$$$**

ISLESBORO

Dark Harbor House
Jetty Road, 04848
Tel: 207-734 6669
Fax: 207-734 6938
www.darkharborhouse.com
A waterside 1890s mansion with an elegant double staircase and spacious guest rooms. Set up on a hill on an island accessible by ferry from Lincolnville Beach, on Route 1 north of Camden. 11 rooms. B&B. **$$–$$$$**

KENNEBUNKPORT

Captain Lord Mansion
Pleasant and Green Streets, 04046
Tel: 207-967 3141
Fax: 207-967 3172
www.captainlord.com
In Kennebunkport's historic district, an elegant formally decorated 1812 inn topped by an octagonal cupola. 16 rooms. B&B. **$$$$**

Inn at Harbor Head
Pier Road, 04046
Tel: 207-967 5564
Luxury lodgings and gourmet breakfasts, alongside quaint Cape Porpoise harbor. 5 rooms. B&B. **$$$–$$$$**

Old Fort Inn
Old Fort Avenue, 04046
Tel: 207-967 5353/
800-828 3678
Country decor in a converted barn and brick carriage house. 16 rooms. B&B. **$$$–$$$$**

The Colony
Ocean Avenue and Kings Road, 04046
Tel: 207-967 3331/
800-552 2363
Fax: 207-967 8738
www.thecolonyhotel/maine.com
A coastal grand hotel built in 1914. 124 rooms. FAP. **$$–$$$$**

White Barn Inn
Beach Street, 04046.
Tel: 207-967 2321.
Relais et Château-level luxury. 25 rooms. R**$$–$$$$**

Bufflehead Cove
Bufflehead Cove Road, 04046
Tel/fax: 207-967 3879

www.buffleheadcove.com
A comfortably appointed early 20th-century summer home overlooking the Kennebunk River. Private dock with rowboats available for guests. 5 rooms. B&B. **$$–$$$**

Green Heron Inn
Ocean Avenue, 04046
Tel: 207-967 3315
www.greenheroninn.com
Plain and pleasant lodgings; excellent breakfasts. 11 rooms. B&B. **$$**

Captain Jefferds Inn
Pearl Street, 04046
Tel: 207-967 2311
An antique-filled 1804 Federal home, with three carriage-house suites. 15 rooms. B&B. **$–$$**

KINGFIELD

Sugarloaf/USA
RR 1, Box 5000, 04947
Tel: 207-237 2000/
800-843 5623
www.sugarloaf.com
New England's largest ski village with two hotels and hundreds of condominiums (with over 400 rooms) attracts hikers, mountain-bikers, and golfers when the snow subsides. **$$–$$$**

Herbert Hotel
P.O. Box 67, 04947
Tel: 207-265 2000/
800-843 4372
Fax: 207-265 4594
www.mainemountaininn.com
This columned hotel, which was heralded upon its 1918 debut as "A Palace in the Wilderness", is now the unofficial heart of town. 27 rooms. **$–$$**

Inn on Winter's Hill
33 Winterhill Street, 04947
Tel: 207-265 5421/

800-233 9687
Fax: 207-265 5424
www.wintershill.com
An 1895 Georgian Revival mansion with a total of 20 rooms in the main house and the simply furnished former barn. Amenities include pool, tennis, hot tub, and cross-country skiing. **$–$$**

Three Stanley Avenue
3 Stanley Avenue, 04947
Tel: 207-265 5541
Comfy, country-style rooms and a fine regional restaurant. Open only in the winter. 6 rooms. B&B. **$**

KITTERY

Inn at Portsmouth Harbor
6 Water Street
Tel: 207-439 4040
www.innatportsmouth.com
An 1889 brick Victorian B&B overlooking Portsmouth Harbor and the Piscataqua River. Named for "gundalows", the sailing barges that worked the river for 250 years. **$$**

MONHEGAN ISLAND

The Island Inn
Ocean View Terrace, 04852
Tel: 207-596 0371
Fax: 207-594 5517
www.islandinnmonhegan.com
Hundred-year-old simplicity on a painter's dream of an island. 34 rooms. MAP. **$–$$$$**

Tribler Cottage
Monhegan 04852
Tel: 207-594 2445
Plain but appealing accommodations, including apartments with kitchens and private decks. **$**

NEWAGEN

Newagen Seaside Inn
Route 27, 04552
Tel: 207-633 5242/
800-654 5242
Fax: 207-633 5340
www.newagenseasideinn.com
An old-fashioned inn, with saltwater

and freshwater pools, at the tip of Southport Island, south of Boothbay Harbor. 26 rooms. B&B. **$$**

NEW HARBOR

Gosnold Arms
Northside Road, 04554
Tel: 207-677 3727
Fax: 207-677 2662
www.gosnold.com
Shoreside rusticity at Pemaquid Point since 1925. The inn's glassed-in dining room overlooks the water. Rooms are available in the main inn and in 14 cottages. 26 rooms. B&B. **$–$$**

NORTHEAST HARBOR

Asticou Inn
Route 3, 04662
Tel: 207-276 3344
Fax: 207-276 3373
www.asticou.com
A cultured carryover from Bar Harbor's heyday as Society's summer playground. Elegant Victorian-style accommodations, views of Great Harbor. 47 rooms. MAP. **$$$$**

Harbourside Inn
Northeast Harbor 04662
Tel: 207-276 3272
www.harboursideinn.com
A Shingle-style 1889 inn with 14 guest rooms beside Acadia National Park. **$$–$$$$**

OGUNQUIT

The Anchorage
133 Shore Road, 03907
Tel: 207-646 9384
Fax: 207-646 6256
www.anchoragebythesea.com
A modern waterside resort offering 242 rooms with classic detailing. **$$$–$$$$**

Sparhawk Resort
Shore Road, 03907
Tel: 207-646 5562
Fax: 207-646 9143
A luxury motel with beach views and private decks. 82 rooms. **$$$–$$$$**

Cliff House
Shore Road (off Route 1), 03907
Tel: 207-361 1000
Fax: 207-361 2122
www.cliffhousemaine.com
A classic New England summer resort since 1872. Several buildings, 164 rooms. swimming pools, and tennis courts, set on 70 acres with gorgeous ocean views. **$–$$$**

Gorges Grant Hotel
239 Route 1, 03907
Tel: 207-646 7003/
800-646 5001
www.ogunquit.com/gorgesgrant/
A sleek contemporary hotel with traditionalist furnishings, just north of the town center. 81 rooms. **$$**

The Dunes on the Waterfront
Route 1, 03907
Tel: 207-646 2612
www.dunesmotel.com
A 1930s cottage complex with 36 rooms on the tidal Ogunquit River, 200 yards from Ogunquit Beach and situated on the trolley line to the town center. Swimming dock, with rowboats. **$–$$**

Morning Dove
13 Bourne Lane, 03907
Tel: 207-646 3891
www.themorningdove.com
A lovingly decorated 1860s farmhouse. 7 rooms. B&B. **$–$$**

PORTLAND

The Danforth
163 Danforth Street, 0410
Tel: 207-879 8755/
800-991 6557
Fax: 207-879 8754
www.danforthmaine.com
Three-story brick mansion restored to a first-class hotel three blocks from the Old Port. The 11-roomed inn has 12 fireplaces, a library, and a restored billiards room, as well as antiques-adorned guest rooms with two-line phones and other modern conveniences. **$$–$$$$**

Portland Regency in the Old Port
20 Milk Street, 04101
Tel: 207-774 4200/
800-727 3436
Fax: 207-775 2150
www.theregency.com

A snazzily refurbished, centrally located 19th-century armory. 95 rooms. **$$–$$$$**

Pomegranate Inn
49 Neal Street, 04102
Tel: 207-772 1006/
800-356 0408
Fax: 207-773 4426
www.pomegranateinn.com
An elegant art- and antiques-filled home with eight bedrooms for B&B in Portland's upscale residential West End. **$$–$$$**

Eastland Park
157 High Street, 04101
Tel: 207-775 5411/
888-671 8008
Fax: 207-775 2872
A 1927 hotel with modern amenities and harbor views. The rooftop lounge is a fine spot to watch the sunset. 215 rooms. **$$**

PROUTS NECK

Black Point Inn
510 Black Point Road
Tel: 207-883 2500/
800-258 0003
Fax: 207-883 9976
www.blackpointinn.com
An 1870s resort, on a peninsula favored by Winslow Homer. Located between Old Orchard Beach and Cape Elizabeth, 10 miles (16 km) south of the Portland airport. Facilities include an 18-hole golf course, 14 tennis courts, two beaches, indoor/ outdoor pools, boating, nature trails, and a health club. 84 rooms. FAP. **$$$$**

RANGELEY

Country Club Inn
Mingo Loop Road, 04970
Tel/fax: 207-864 3831
www.countryclubinnrangeley.com
A 1920s inn, plus 1950s-era motel units. The inn's grand living room has two fireplaces, a cathedral ceiling, and game trophies, and there are lovely views of the lake. Amenities include a swimming pool and golf course. B&B. **$$**

Rangeley Inn and Motor Lodge
Main Street, 04970

Tel: 207-864 3341/
800-666 3687
Fax: 207-864 3634
www.rangeleyinn.com
An old-fashioned three-story lakeside inn with 50 guest rooms (built around 1907), with some modern motel units. **$–$$**

ROCKLAND

Captain Lindsey House Inn
5 Lindsey Street, 04841
Tel: 207-596 7950/
800-523 2145
Fax: 207-596 2758
www.lindseyhouse.com
An 1885 building that used to house the Camden Rockland Water company. Now transformed into an antiques-filled inn with nine spacious guest rooms. **$$–$$$**

Limerock Inn
96 Limerock Avenue, 04841
Tel: 207-594 2257/
800-546 3762
Fax: 207-594 1846
www.limerockinn.com
Elegantly decorated Queen Anne Victorian B&B on a residential street near the Shore Village and Farnsworth Museums. Some of the rooms have whirlpool tubs and private decks. **$$–$$$**

ROCKPORT

Samoset Resort
220 Warrenton Street, 04856
Tel: 207-594 2511/
800-341 1650
Fax: 207-594 0722
A full-scale, seaside golf resort with 178 rooms. Sports facilities include a swimming pool and tennis courts. **$$$$**

Price Categories

A very approximate guide to current room rates for a standard double per night is:
$$$$ = over $200
$$$ = $150–200
$$ = $100–150
$ = under $100

ROCKWOOD
(MOOSEHEAD LAKE)

The Birches
off Route 15, 04478
Tel: 207-534 7588
Fax: 207-538 8835
www.birches.com
A rustic 1940s lakeside lodge with log cabins and wood-burning stoves or fireplaces. Amenities include boating on the lake, saunas, and hot tubs. 33 rooms. B&B. **$**

Maynard-in-Maine
Rockwood 04478
Tel: 207-534 7703
www.maynardinmaine.com
A classic hunting camp, founded in 1919. 13 rooms. FAP. **$**

Rockwood Cottages
Route 15, 04478
Tel/fax: 207-534 7725
www.mooseheadlodging.com
Eight lakeside cottages with screened porches and fully equipped kitchens. Sauna and boating facilities. **$**

SEARSPORT

The Homeport Inn
121 E. Main Street (Route 1), 04974
Tel/fax: 207-548 2259/
800-742 5814
www.bnb.com/inns/20015
10 rooms, two cottages. B&B. A cupola-topped 1860s captain's house filled with Victorian appointments in the "antiques capital" of Maine. Some rooms have private decks and views of the bay. **$**

SOUTH CASCO

Migis Lodge on Sebago Lake
P. O Box 40, 04077
Tel: 207-655 4524
Fax: 207-655 2054
www.migis.com
A rustic, elegant, and old-fashioned 100-acre resort with 32 rooms for FAP. There are rooms in the main lodge and in cottages, all overlooking the lake. Sports facilities include sailing, canoeing, waterskiing, and tennis courts. In

the dining room, you can enjoy traditional New England fare, including steamers, clam chowder, and lobster. **$$$–$$$$**

SOUTHWEST HARBOR

The Claremont Hotel
P. O. Box 137, 04679
Tel: 207-244 5036/
800-244 5036
Fax: 207-244 3512
www.theclaremonthotel.com
Mount Desert Island's oldest grand hotel, built in 1884. Rooms in the main inn, two guest houses, and a dozen cottages. Waterfront location for swimming, boating. Also tennis and croquet. 41 rooms. MAP.
$$–$$$
Inn at Southwest
371 Main Street
Tel: 207-244 3835
Fax: 207-244 9879
www.innatsouthwest.com
Seven elegant, romantic rooms with antique furnishings in an 1884 Victorian home overlooking the harbor. B&B. **$$**

SPRUCE HEAD

Craignair Inn at Clark Island
St George, 04859
Tel: 207-594 7644/
800-320 9997
Fax: 207-596 7124
www.craignair.com
A basic, cheerful shorefront B&B inn near a nature preserve between Rockland and Tenants Harbor. Originally built in 1928 to house workers from the nearby quarries. The 20 rooms in the main inn share baths, the somewhat more upscale rooms in the annex have private baths. **$–$$**

STOCKTON SPRINGS

The Hichborn Inn
Church Street, 04981
Tel: 207-567 4183/
800-346 1522
www.hichborninn.com
An Italianate mansion in an old

Hotel Meal Guide

B&Bs supply a complimentary full breakfast and are often quite sophisticated
MAP (Modified American Plan) rates include both breakfast and dinner
FAP (Full American Plan) supply all three meals

ship-building village north of Searsport. 4 rooms. B&B. **$**

STONINGTON

Inn on the Harbor
Main Street, 04681
Tel: 207-367 2420/
800-942 2420
Fax: 207-367 5165
Waterside lodgings with a spacious deck in a scarcely touristed harbor town. 13 rooms. **$$**

SUNSET

Goose Cove Lodge
Deer Isle, 04683
Tel: 207-348 2508/
800-728 1963
Fax: 207-348 2624
www.goosecovelodge.com
An informal family resort with a rustic, simply furnished lodge and cottages in a remote natural setting. The lodge overlooks Penobscot Bay, adjacent to nature conservatory land. There are 22 rooms, offering MAP. **$$$–$$$$**

TENANTS HARBOR

East Wind Inn and Meeting House
Mechanic Street (Route 131)
04860
Tel: 207-372 6366/
800-241 8439
Fax: 207-372 6320
www.eastwindinn.com
This is a simply decorated, harborside inn with a wraparound porch in an unspoiled fishing village south of Rockland. There are 26 rooms, available for B&B. **$$–$$$**

VINALHAVEN

Tidewater Motel
Main Street, 04863
Tel: 207-863 4618
A simple harborside motel, right on the water, on a moneyed island ideal for biking. 11 rooms. **$**

WISCASSET

Squire Tarbox Inn
Route 144 (RR 2, Box 620)
04578
Tel: 207-882 7693
Fax: 207-882 7107
A colonial country farmhouse on a working farm where the owners raise goats. Delicious home-grown dinners feature the farm's goat cheese. 11 rooms. B&B. **$$–$$$**
Marston House
Main Street, 04578
Tel: 207-882 6010/
800-852 4137
Fax: 207-882 6965
A small private carriage house with just two rooms, simply appointed with Shaker- and Colonial-style furnishings and fireplaces. No public spaces so breakfast (continental) is delivered to your room. **$**

YORK AREA

View Point Inn
229 Nubble Road
York Beach, 03910
Tel: 207-363 2661
Fax: 207-363 6788
www.viewpoint-maine.com
Nine rooms at this inn on the rocky shore. Views of Nubble Light. **$$$$**
Stage Neck Inn
off Route 1A, York Harbor, 03911
Tel: 207-363 3850/
800-222 3238
Fax: 207-363 2221
www.stageneck.com
A contemporary seaside resort known for its 60 low-key luxury. Queen Anne-style rooms with refrigerators, many with ocean views. Indoor pool with whirlpool spa. **$$$–$$$$**

Price Categories

A very approximate guide to current room rates for a standard double per night is:

$$$$ = over $200
$$$ = $150–200
$$ = $100–150
$ = under $100

York Harbor Inn
Route 1A
York Harbor, 03911
Tel: 207-363-5119
800-343 3869
Fax: 207-363 7151
www.yorkharborinn.com
A fresh seaside inn, which accrued around a 1637 sail loft. There are 33 Colonial-style rooms, some with fireplaces or whirlpools. $–$$$$
Dockside Guest Quarters
Harris Island Road
(Off Route 103)
York, 03909
Tel: 207-363 2868/
888 (860) 7428
Fax: 207-363 1977
www.docksidegq.com
Classic 19th-century seacoast home flanked by cottages.
27 rooms. $–$$

Where to Eat

BAR HARBOR

Porcupine Grill
123 Cottage Street
Tel: 207-288 3884
The Porcupine Grill is Yacht-club spiffy, and culinarily up-to-date. Offerings include fish with citrus relish, cornbread-stuffed pork chops, and fresh pastas. The wine bar has a lighter menu. $$$
Jordan Pond House
Park Loop Road
Tel: 207-276 3316
A classic spot for popovers and tea (and other meals, too), with an expansive mountain view within Acadia National Park. $$
Lompoc Cafe
36 Rodick Street
Tel: 207-288 9392
A brew pub with international accompaniments. $$

BATH

Beale Street Barbecue & Grill
215 Water Street
Tel: 207-442 9514
A comfortable, affordable barbecue joint, with choices ranging from a basic pulled pork plate to a New York sirloin. $–$$
Kristina's
160 Center Street (Route 209)
Tel: 207-442 8577
A popular cafe housed in a pair of 19th-century homes. Don't miss the sticky buns. $

BETHEL

Bethel Inn & Country Club
Village Common. 04217
Tel: 207-824 2175
Yankee classics and impressive mountain views. $$
Mother's
Upper Main Street
Tel: 207-824 2589
A cozy house serving homemade soups and sandwiches, as well as substantial dinners, including steaks, pastas, and crab cakes. $$

BLUE HILL

Blue Hill Inn
Union Street
Tel: 207-374 2844
Creative preparations of Maine seafood and local produce in a Federal-style inn. $$$
Jonathan's
Main Street
Tel: 207-374 5226.
A contemporary café serving robust international dishes. $$–$$$

BOOTHBAY HARBOR

Black Orchid
5 Byway
Tel: 207-633 6659
Mediterranean influences pervade this harborside summer house with roof deck. $$–$$$
Ebb Tide
67 Commercial Street
Tel: 207-633 5692

A stylish restored diner serving a wide variety of classic comfort foods. $–$$

BRUNSWICK

The Great Impasta
42 Main Street
Tel: 207-729 5858
A small storefront serving – true to its name – pasta of all types. $–$$

CAMDEN

Camden Harbor Inn
83 Bayview Street
Tel: 207-236 4200
Fine continental dining overlooking Camden harbor. $$$–$$$$
The Belmont
6 Belmont Avenue
Tel: 207-236 8053
New American wizardry, in a peaceful setting. $$$
Hi Bombay
31 Elm Street
Tel: 207-230 0434
When you just can't look at another lobster, this relaxed Indian spot serves up curries and tandoor-roasted meats. $–$$
Sea Dog
43 Mechanic Street
Tel: 207-236 6863
A brew pub situated in a former wool mill. $

CAPE NEDDICK

Cape Neddick Inn
Routes 1 and 1A
Tel: 207-363 2899
Ambitious seasonal cuisine in a neo-traditional setting, north of York Beach. $$$–$$$$

CAPE PORPOISE

Cape Porpoise Lobster Company
15 Pier Road
Tel: 207-967 0123/
800-967 4268
Oceanfront lobster shanty cooks up ocean-fresh lobsters and fried clams. Seasonal. $

CASTINE

The Pentagoet Inn
Main Street
Tel: 207-326 8616
A *prix-fixe* dinner party in a turreted Victorian inn. Reservations are required. **$$$**
Castine Inn
Main Street
Tel: 207-326 4365
Regional delicacies served in a dining room painted to depict the town. Dinner only. **$$**
Dennett's Wharf
Sea Street
Tel: 207-326 9045
Casual harborside seafood. **$$**

DEER ISLE

Pilgrim's Inn
Route 15A
Tel: 207-348 6615
An exquisite *prix-fixe* menu served in a rustic barn. **$$$$**

FREEPORT

Harraseeket Inn
162 Main Street
Tel: 207-865 9377
Fabulous local produce, seafood, and game. The buffets are especially renowned. More casual fare – hamburgers, steamers, and simple fish dishes – are on offer in the tavern room, which has a hunting lodge-style ambiance. **$$–$$$**
Harraseeket Lobster Company
Main Street
South Freeport
Tel: 207-865 3535

Seafood basics in the rough: lobster dinners, fried clams, and other fried seafood. Next to the town landing in South Freeport. Picnic tables outside for al fresco munching in fair weather. **$–$$**
Freeport Inn & Cafe
Route 1
Tel: 207-865 3106
Simple soups, salads, and sandwiches, plus all-day breakfasts, in this small spot south of the shopping district. **$**

GARDINER

A-1 Diner
Route 201
Tel: 207-582 4804
A 1946 Worcester diner, south of Augusta, serving the standards. **$**

GEORGETOWN

Robinhood Free Meetinghouse
Robinhood Road
Tel: 207-371 2188
An 1855 Greek Revival meetinghouse near Bath transformed into a simple yet elegant temple of classic and fusion cuisine. Think American bistro fare blended with Italian, Chinese, Thai, and Caribbean influences. The chef's signature dessert is "Obsession in Three Chocolates". **$$$–$$$$**

GREENVILLE

Greenville Inn
Norris Street
Tel: 207-695 2206

Bountiful dinners accompanied by giant popovers in an opulent mansion overlooking Moosehead Lake. **$$$**

KENNEBUNKPORT

White Barn Inn
Beach Street.
Tel: 207-967 2321
A beautifully appointed barn serving stellar nouvelle cuisine. **$$$$**
Windows on the Water
Chase Hill
Tel: 207-967 3313
A modern restaurant known for its inventive treatments of lobster, which may appear in half-a-dozen succulent guises. Reservations essential. **$$$$**
Kennebunkport Inn
Dock Square
Tel: 207-967 2621
Delightful regional cuisine with French accents. **$$$–$$$$**
Cape Arundel Inn
Ocean Avenue
Tel: 207-967 2125
Ocean views and an interesting menu. **$$$**
Grissini
27 Western Avenue (Route 9).
Tel: 207-967 2211
Fine contemporary northern Italian fare – such as grilled lamb with Tuscan white beans, gnocchi (potato dumplings), and grilled salmon served on sweet potato polenta – in a casually upscale room. **$$**

KINGFIELD

One Stanley Avenue
Tel: 207-265 5541
The indigenous foods of Maine, artfully prepared. **$$–$$$**
The Herbert
Main Street
Tel: 207-265 2000
Hearty regional dishes served in an airy Victorian dining room. **$$**
Longfellow's
Main Street
Tel: 207-265 4394
A casual riverside cafe with good dishes and good prices. **$**

Restaurant Guidelines

Prices are approximate, but for a three-course meal for one (excluding beverages, tax, and tip), the following guidelines may prove helpful:
$$$$ = over $40
$$$ = $28–40
$$ = $15–28
$ = under $15
Meal tax varies from state to

state, but it is customary to tip 15 to 20 percent on the pre-tax total.
Credit cards The more expensive establishments generally accept credit cards, but call ahead to check just in case.
Reservations Most restaurants, except for the clearly casual, appreciate reservations (some require them).

KITTERY

Warren's Lobster House
Route 1
Tel: 207-439 1630
On the water just north of
Portsmouth, a local institution
serving lobster and other seafood.
Hefty salad bar, too. **$$**

The Friendly Toast
Bridge Street
Tel: 207-439 2882
Funky cafe overlooking the river
serving playful roadhouse food,
plus creative vegetarian options.
Breakfast available all day. **$**

LITTLE DEER ISLE

Eaton's Lobster Pool
Blastow Cove
Tel: 207-348 2383
Water views and fresh-off-the-boat
seafood. **$$$**

NORTHEAST HARBOR

Asticou Inn
Tel: 207-276 3344
Yankee standards and welcome
interlopers, in a grand old dining
room overlooking the sea. **$$$$**

Redfield's
Main Street, 04662
Tel: 207-276 5283.
A summery café serving all three
meals, New American-style. **$$$**

OGUNQUIT

Arrows
Berwick Road (off Route 1)
Tel: 207-361 1100
Adventurous (and exquisite)
international cuisine in an English-
country-style farmhouse. Dinner
only. **$$$$**

Barnacle Billy's
Perkins Cove
Tel: 207-646 5575
Classic seafood at a great location,
right on the water. **$$$**

Ida Reds
Route 1
Tel: 207-646 0289
An upscale bistro next to the

Restaurant Guidelines

Prices are approximate, but for a
three-course meal for one
(excluding beverages, tax, and
tip), the following guidelines may
prove helpful:
$$$$ = over $40
$$$ = $28–40
$$ = $15–28
$ = under $15
Meal tax varies from state to

Playhouse, serving often-
dramatically constructed
contemporary dishes. **$$$**

PORTLAND

Back Bay Grill
65 Portland Street
Tel: 207-772 8833
Sophisticated decor, sensuous New
American dishes. **$$$**

Street & Company
33 Wharf Street
Tel: 207-775 0887
Fresh fish and seafood served in
the pan right on one of the dozen
copper-topped tables. You can
choose a vegetarian alternative if
you must, but seafood is the
reason to be here. **$$–$$$**

Cotton Street Cantina
10 Cotton Street
Tel: 207-775 3222
A lively spot serving creative
preparations that get their soul
from the flavors of South America,
Mexico, and the Caribbean. **$$**

Cafe Uffa!
190 State Street
Tel: 207-775 3380
An eclectic bistro emphasizing
vegetarian dishes, as well as fish.
Microbrews, too. **$–$$**

RANGELEY

Country Club Inn
Mingo Loop Road
Tel: 207-864 3831
Traditional white-tablecloth fare in
a glassed-in dining room with lake
and mountain views. Reservations
required. **$$$–$$$$**

state, but it is customary to tip 15
to 20 percent on the pre-tax total.
Credit cards The more expensive
establishments generally accept
credit cards, but call ahead to
check just in case.
Reservations Most restaurants,
except for the clearly casual,
appreciate reservations (some
require them).

ROCKLAND

Jessica's
2 S Main Street (Route 73)
Tel: 207-596 0770
European bistro-style cuisine, such
as pasta, risotto, and paella,
served in four cozy dining rooms in
a Victorian house. Located at the
far southern end of town. **$$**

The Waterworks
Lindsey Street
Tel: 207-596 7950
A former waterworks-turned-funky
pub serving comfort food, ranging
from roast turkey and fish 'n' chips,
through grilled sausages to
meatloaf, and microbrews. **$–$$**

ROCKPORT

Marcel's at the Samoset Resort
220 Warrenton Street
Tel: 207-594 0774
Million-dollar views, with eclectic
cuisine priced to match. From rack
of lamb and Chateaubriand to more
contemporary fare with French and
Italian influences. **$$$$**

Sail Loft
Rockport Harbor
Tel: 207-236 2330
Upmarket seafood classics served
baked, sautéed, and fried with an
ocean view. Lots of lobster choices.
$$$–$$$$

ROCKWOOD

The Birches
(Off Route 15)
Tel: 207-534 7305
Seafood, steaks, and pasta

overlooking Moosehead Lake at this north woods resort. **$$$**

SEARSPORT

Nickerson Tavern
Route 1
Tel: 207-548 2220
Superb regional cuisine (dinner only) in a former sea captain's home. **$$$**

SOUTHWEST HARBOR

The Claremont
Clark Point Road.
Tel: 207-244 5036.
The formal dining room of this venerable 1884 inn has an ambitious modernist menu. Jackets are required for men; "corresponding attire" for women. **$$$**

Beal's Lobster Pier
Clark Point Road
Tel: 207-244 7178
A good old classic wharfside lobster shack. **$**

STONINGTON

Bay View Restaurant
Seabreeze Avenue
Tel: 207-367 2274
Great at-the-source seafood feasting. **$$**

WISCASSET

Le Garage
Water Street
Tel: 207-882 5409
Regional American fare in a picture-perfect town. **$$$**

Squire Tarbox Restaurant
Route 144
Tel: 207-882 7693
A colonial farmhouse serving home-raised delicacies, including farm's own goat cheese. Dinner only. **$$$**

YORK AREA

York Harbor Inn
Route 1A, York Harbor
Tel: 207-363 5119
Well-considered continental/regional fare with a seafood focus in a "big night out" room. **$$$–$$$$**
The Restaurant at Dockside Guest Quarters
Harris Island Road
(Off Route 103), York
Tel: 207-363 2868
From fried clams and steamed lobsters to "swordfish Pacific Rim" and pesto chicken – all with a water view. **$$$**
Mimmo's
Route 1A, York
Tel: 207-363 3807
An unprepossessing café with an exuberant Tuscan chef. **$$**

Maine Festivals

Spring
March may be the beginning of spring in other states, but Maine is still celebrating winter when Rangeley plays host to the annual **Sled Dog Races** (tel: 207-864 5364).

Summer
Portland kicks off the summer season with the **Old Port Festival** (tel: 207-772 6828) in early June, while later in the month, Wiscasset hosts its **Strawberry Festival** (tel: 207-882 7184).
 Other summer celebrations of Maine food include **Rockland's Lobster Festival** (tel: 800-562 2529) in late July, and the mid-August **Wild Blueberry Festival** (tel: 207-255 6665) down east in Machias.
 Also in late June, Maine shows off its distinctive on-the-water craft, both improvised and historic, at the **Great Kennebec Whatever Week** (tel: 207-623 4559) – including a river race of homemade rafts – and during **Windjammer Days** (tel: 207-633 2353) in Boothbay Harbor.

In July and August, musicians assemble in Hamilton for the **Sebago-Long Lake Chamber Music Festival** (tel: 207-583 6747), while the **Bar Harbor Music Festival** (tel: 207-288 5744) comes to Mount Desert Island.

Fall
Several towns honor the season's colors in October with **Fall Foliage Festivals**, including events in Camden (tel: 207-236 4404), Boothbay (tel: 207-633 4743) and York (tel: 207-363 4422).
 Portland toasts the season in a different way at the annual **Maine Brewer's Festival** (tel: 207-767 5424).

Winter
For two December weekends, the Kennebunk area hosts holiday crafts fairs with tree-lighting and caroling during the annual **Christmas Prelude** (tel: 207-967 0857).
 In January, all of the cross-country ski areas thumb their noses at winter throughout the statewide **Ski Fest** events (tel: 800-754 9263).

Culture

CLASSICAL MUSIC

Portland Symphony Orchestra (tel: 207-842 0800; 20 Myrtle Street, Portland).
Performs year-round except during September.

MUSIC FESTIVALS

Bowdoin Summer Music Festival (tel: 207-725 3895; Brunswick) hosts a popular and renowned six-week series of concerts.
Kneisel Hall Chamber Music Festival (tel: 207-374 2811; Route 15, Blue Hill) has a developed a fine reputation for its summer concerts.

THEATER

Portland Performing Arts Center (tel: 207-761 0591; 25A Forest Avenue, Portland) is a multi-purpose venue offering space for music, dance, and theater. Also in Portland, check the local newspapers for anything mounted by the **Portland Stage Company** (tel: 207-774 0465). **Ogunquit Playhouse** (tel: 207-646 5511; Route 1, Ogunquit) stages musicals, theater, and plays during the summer only. It's one of the oldest playhouses in the US.

ART GALLERIES

Bayview Gallery (tel: 207-773 3007, 800-244 3007; 75 Market Street, Portland) represents preeminent Maine artists.

Nightlife

LIVE MUSIC

Left Bank Bakery and Cafe (tel: 207-374 2201; Route 172, Blue Hill) brings folk music to the already-musical town.

GAY & LESBIAN VENUES

Le Club (tel: 207-646 6655; 13 Main Street, Ogunquit) primarily caters for a seasonal gay clientele. Ogunquit has an growing number of gay-friendly establishments; look for the rainbow flags. **Underground** (tel: 207-773 3315; 3 Spring Street, Portland) is the city's gay and lesbian club.

LATE-NIGHT VENUES

It doesn't have to be late to pop into the **Sea Dog Tavern & Brewery** (tel: 207-236 6863; 43 Mechanic Street, Camden), which features its own microbrews in a lively setting within a former wool mill.

Sunday River in Bethel is a hoping kind of place (both slopeside and in town) during ski season. Check out the **Sunday River Brewery** (tel: 207-824 4253; Route 2) and **Bumps Pub** (tel: 207 824 3000; on the mountain), which both have rock bands.

DANCING

Zootz Nightclub (tel: 207-773 8187; 31 Forest Avenue), for the college set, and **Granny Killam's** (tel: 207-761 5865; 55 Market Street), for post-college crowd, are two of Portland's better dance clubs.

Outdoor Activities

BIKING

When the snow melts after winter, the Sunday River Ski area turns into the **Sunday River Mountain Bike Park** (tel: 207-824 3000), where bikers can ride the lifts up and then bike down.

Boston-based **Bike Riders' Tours** (tel: 800-473 7040) is one of several companies offering bicycle tours in the state of Maine. Their week-long Penobscot Bay trip stops off in Camden, Islesboro and Castine.

CANOEING, KAYAKING, AND RAFTING

With more than 2,000 coastal islands and their protected waters, Maine has become a center for sea kayaking. The **Maine Island Kayak Company** (tel: 800-796 2373), based at Peaks Island near Portland, runs a range of sea-kayaking trips and instructional courses.

H2Outfitters (tel: 207-833 5257), on Orr's Island near Brunswick, offers one-day sea kayaking classes, as well as multi-day trips.

The Kennebec, Dead, and Penobscot Rivers offer some of New England's most challenging

Kayak Tours

A tour with a difference... Guided sea-kayaking excursions are conducted in the Acadia area by two Bar Harbor-based companies:
National Park Kayak Tours Tel: 207-288 0342
Coastal Kayaking Tours Tel: 207-288 9605

whitewater rafting. **North American Whitewater Expeditions** (tel: 800-727 4379) organizes Maine river rafting trips for novices through experts. The Allagash Wilderness Waterway, a 92-mile (150-km) corridor of lakes and rivers from Baxter State Park to the Canadian border, is another canoeing and rafting destination.

Outfitters in this area include **Allagash Canoe Trips in Greenville** (tel: 207-695 3668), **Mahoosuc Guide Service**, based in Newry (tel: 207-824 2073), and **North Country Outfitters** in Rockwood (tel: 207-534 2242).

For more sedate paddling excursions, the **Maine Audubon Society** (tel: 207 781 2330) offers guided canoe trips and rentals in Scarborough Marsh, the state's largest salt marsh.

On Mount Desert Island, **National Park Canoe Rentals** (tel: 207-244 5854) has canoes for hire on Long Pond.

FISHING

The Rangeley area is a popular destination for those who fly-fish. For ocean fishing excursions, **Devils Den** (tel: 207-761 4466) runs half- and full-day trips from Portland. In Kennebunkport, **Chick's Marina** (tel: 207-967 2782) offers fishing cruises for up to six people.

HIKING

Baxter State Park (tel: 207-723 5140) in Maine's North Woods draws thousands of hikers annually who tackle the day-long climb to the summit of **Mount Katahdin**, the state's highest peak (5,267 feet, or 1,755 meters). Eighteen mountains in the park are taller than 3,000 feet (900 meters).

SAILING

The Camden area is Maine's center for windjammer cruising. The **Maine Windjammer Association** (tel: 800-

Scenic Tours in and around Portland

Bus 1 takes passengers round the Eastern and Western Promenades and the rest of downtown Portland.
Bikes Forest City Mountain Bike Tours operate guided two- to six-hour tours of Portland, South Portland, Cape Elizabeth and elsewhere. 51 Melbourne Street, Portland. Tel: 207-780 8155.
Cruises Casco Bay, to the east of Portland town, is the starting point for cruises to Maine's islands.
Casco Bay Lines (tel: 207-774 7871) runs mail/delivery motorboats that you can hop on for cruises of various lengths up to just under two hours. From the Ferry Terminal at 56 Commercial Street at Franklin Street.
Eagle Tours, Long Wharf, Commercial Street (tel: 207-799 6498) runs trips to Eagle Island and Portland Head Light.

807 9463), headquartered in Blue Hill, represents a number of Camden-based windjammers that offer multi-day excursions.

Do-it-yourself sailors can contact **Manset Yacht Service** (tel: 207-244-4040), near Acadia National Park, to arrange sailboat rentals. Boats can also be hired on Sebago and Long Lakes: try **Mardon Marine** (tel: 207-693 6264) or **Sun Sports Plus** (tel: 207-693 3867), both in Naples.

SKIING

Maine's largest areas for downhill skiing are:
Sunday River in Bethel (tel: 207-824 3000, 800-543 2754).
Sugarloaf/USA in Kingfield (tel: 207-237 2000/800-843 5623).
Saddleback in Rangley (tel: 207-864 5671).

Bethel is also home to several cross-country ski centers including: **The Bethel Inn Ski Center** (tel: 207-824 2175).

Island Ferries

Maine State Ferry Service runs ferries from the mainland to most of Maine's major islands. Tel: 207-596-2202.
Marine Atlantic operates a car and passenger ferry from Portanld and Bar Harbor to Yarmouth, Nova Scotia and Canada. Tel: 800-341-7981.

Carter's Cross Country Ski Centers (tel: 207-539 4848).
Sunday River Inn Ski Touring Center (tel: 207-824 2410).

Other Nordic skiing spots include the **Harris Farm Cross Country Ski Center** in Biddeford (tel: 207-499 2678).

Shopping

WHERE TO SHOP

Between the towns of Freeport and Kittery, Maine's cornered the market in outlet stores *(see also page 153)*. You'all also find outlet stores on Route 1 between Kittery and Wells.

If heavy foot traffic is any indication of good shopping, it's readily apparent that the Dock Square area in Kennebunkport offers it in spades.
Portland's Old Port Exchange area, a dense few blocks along Fore and Exchange Streets, is great for browsing and buying.

SHOPPING MALLS

Maine Mall (tel: 207-774 0303), 5 miles (8 km) south of Portland, has almost 150 stores, including large anchor department stores.

BOOKS

DeLorme's Map Store (tel: 207-846 7000; Yarmouth) stocks an outstanding range of Maine and New England specialty maps, as well as travel guides.
Owl and Turtle Boookshop (tel: 207-236 4769; 8 Bay View Street, Camden) has two floors of Maine maritime and children's books.
Port in a Storm (tel: 207-244 4114; Main Street, Somesville, near Acadia National Park), regardless of the weather, is one of the best bookstores on the Maine coast.

ANTIQUES

You can often find silver for the price of flatware at flea markets, if you know what you're looking for. Route 1 through Searsport is lined with semi-permanent seasonal flea markets, as well as the more traditional antiques shops. Bargain hunters should do well here.

CHINA AND GLASS

Stein Gallery Contemporary Glass (tel: 207-772 9072; 195 Middle Street, Portland) make modern functional and decorative glassware.

Gifts and Souvenirs

For those must-have mementos, downtown Boothbay Harbor (along with Camden and Bar Harbor, situated further to the north) is absolutely chock-a-block with shops that will draw the money from your pockets like magnets to steel.

ARTS AND CRAFTS

Handworks Gallery (tel: 207-374 5613; Main Street) and **North Country Textiles** (tel: 207-374 2715), both on Main Street in Blue Hill, are just two of many shops in town that carry excellent hand-made crafts. Don't miss **Rackliffe Pottery** (tel: 207-374 2297; Route 172) and **Rowantrees Pottery** (tel: 207-374 5535; Union Street), also both in Blue Hill.

A Stain on Maine

In the cemetery at Bucksport, Maine, the tombstone of the town founder and judge Colonel Jonathan Buck bears a peculiar dark blemish, which is shaped like a woman's leg. Allegedly, the mark is impossible to remove, and the perpetrator is believed to have been a defendant who was sentenced for witchcraft.

Although you may visit studios by only appointment, many alumni of the **Haystack Mountain School of Crafts** (tel: 207-348 2306; off Route 15 south of Deer Isle) have settled in the area and have their own studio/shops.

Stop in at **Blue Heron Gallery & Studio** (tel: 207-348 6051; Church Street, Deer Isle) which sells Haystack faculty work. **Deer Isle Artists Association** (no phone; Route 15, Deer Isle) mounts revolving shows of area artists.

Edgecomb Potters (tel: 207-882 6802; Route 27) and **Sheepscot River Pottery** (tel: 207-882 9410; Route 1) are both located in Edgecomb and sell distinctive pottery. Sheepscot also offers a wide variety of other hand-crafted goods.

Children

THEME PARKS

Palace Playground (tel: 207-934 2001; Old Orchard Street, Old Orchard Beach) features an old carousel and Ferris wheel and lots of other rides.

ZOOS

Maine Aquarium (tel: 207-284 4512; Route 1, Saco) features all the underwater creatures you'd expect to see here (sharks, seals, and penguins), plus some land-roamers too.
Acadia Zoo (tel: 207-667 3244; Route 3, Trenton) is small but it will occupy the kids.

JOURNEYS BY STEAM TRAIN

Belfast & Moosehead Lake Railroad (tel: 207-948 5500; Unity) operates two scenic trains: one passes along a river, another by villages. Kids will particularly like the open-air cars.
Seashore Trolley Museum (tel: 207-967 2800; Log Cabin Road, Kennebunkport) offers a 4-mile trolley tips aboard one of their restored antiques.
Maine Coast Railroad (tel: 207-882 8000; Route 1, Wiscasset) travels to Newcastle on vintage trains.
Boothbay Railway Village (tel: 207-633 4727; Route 27, Boothbay) offers just a 1½-mile narrow-gauge steam train ride, but it's picturesque as it travels through a re-created New England village.

MUSEUM

Children's Museum of Maine (tel: 207-828 1234; 142 Free Street, Portland) is one of the best in New England. Highly interactive, it will keep even the most boisterous youngsters occupied for hours – hauling in traps on a lobster boat, broadcasting the news, making stained glass, and more. Admission is free on Friday 5–7pm.

Further Reading

Not all the books cited are currently in print, but it can be fun tracking them down in New England's atmospheric secondhand bookshops.

History and Culture

Battles of the United States, by Sea and Land by Henry B. Dawson. *New York, 1858.*
A Description of New England by Captain John Smith. Boston, 1865.
The Flowering of New England by Van Wyck Brooks. New York, 1936.
New England: Indian Summer, 1865–1915 by Van Wyck Brooks. New York, 1940.
New England Frontier: Puritans and Indians by Alden T. Vaughan. Boston, 1965.
The New England Mind: From Colony to Province by Perry Miller. Cambridge, 1953.
Nooks and Corners of the New England Coast by Samuel Adams Drake. New York, 1875.
The Spread of New England Settlement and Institutions to the Hill Country of Northern New England by Harold Fisher Wilson. New York, 1967.

Landscape and Natural History

These Fragile Outposts: A Geological Look at Cape Cod, Martha's Vineyard and Nantucket by Barbara B. Chamberlain. New York, 1964.
A Guide to New England's Landscape by Neil Jorgensen. Barre, VT, 1971.

Architecture

Cityscapes of Boston: An American City through Time by Robert Campbell and Peter Vanderwarker. Boston, 1992.
Preserving New England by Jane Holtz Kay and Pauline Chase-Harrell. New York, 1986.

Fiction

Contemporary New England Stories by Michael C. Curtis, ed. Old Saybrook, CT, 1992.
String Too Short to B*e Saved: Recollections of Summers on a New England Farm* by Donald Hall. Boston, 1979.
Imagining Boston: A Literary Landscape by Shaun O'Connell. Boston, 1990.

Other Insight Guides

More than 190 *Insight Guides* cover every continent. In addition, a companion series of more than 100 *Insight Pocket Guides* provides selected, carefully timed itineraries for the traveler with little time to spare and include a full-size fold-out map. And more than 100 *Insight Compact Guides* provide ideal on-the-spot companions, with text, maps and pictures all carefully cross-referenced.
Titles which highlight destinations in New England include:

Insight Guide: Boston (above) is a lavishly illustrated companion to the present book, and *Pocket Guide: Boston* provides recommendations and a full-size city map.

Boston, Cape Cod, and *Martha's Vineyard & Nantucket* are covered in detail by three Compact Guides.

Feedback

We do our best to ensure the information in our books is as accurate and up-to-date as possible. The books are updated on a regular basis, using local contacts, who painstakingly add, amend and correct as required. However, some mistakes and omissions are inevitable and we are ultimately reliant on our readers to put us in the picture.

We would welcome your feedback on any details related to your experiences using the book "on the road". Maybe we recommended a hotel that you liked (or another that you didn't), as well as interesting new attractions, or facts and figures you have found out about the country itself. The more details you can give us (particularly with regard to addresses, e-mails and telephone numbers), the better.

We will acknowledge all contributions, and we'll offer an Insight Guide to the best letters received.
Please write to us at:

Insight Guides
APA Publications
PO Box 7910
London SE1 1WE
Or send e-mail to: **insight@apaguide.demon.co.uk**

ART & PHOTO CREDITS

Picture Spreads

INSIGHT GUIDE New England

Cartographic Editor **Zoë Goodwin**
Production **Linton Donaldson**
Design Consultants
Carlotta Junger, Graham Mitchener
Picture Research
Hilary Genin, Monica Allende

Maps Colourmap Scanning Ltd.
© 2002 Apa Publications GmbH & Co.
Verlag KG (Singapore branch)

Index

Numbers in italics refer to photographs

✺ INSIGHT GUIDES

The world's largest collection of visual travel guides

Insight Guides – the Classic Series that puts you in the picture

Alaska	China	Hungary	Munich	South Africa
Alsace	Cologne			South America
Amazon Wildlife	Continental Europe	Iceland	Namibia	South Tyrol
American Southwest	Corsica	India	Native America	Southeast Asia
Amsterdam	Costa Rica	India's Western	Nepal	Wildlife
Argentina	Crete	Himalaya	Netherlands	Spain
Asia, East	Cuba	India, South	New England	Spain, Northern
Asia, South	Cyprus	Indian Wildlife	New Orleans	Spain, Southern
Asia, Southeast	Czech & Slovak	Indonesia	New York City	Sri Lanka
Athens	Republics	Ireland	New York State	Sweden
Atlanta		Israel	New Zealand	Switzerland
Australia	Delhi, Jaipur & Agra	Istanbul	Nile	Sydney
Austria	Denmark	Italy	Normandy	Syria & Lebanon
	Dominican Republic	Italy, Northern	Norway	
Bahamas	Dresden	Italy, Southern		Taiwan
Bali	Dublin		Old South	Tenerife
Baltic States	Düsseldorf	Jamaica	Oman & The UAE	Texas
Bangkok		Japan	Oxford	Thailand
Barbados	East African Wildlife	Java		Tokyo
Barcelona	Eastern Europe	Jerusalem	Pacific Northwest	Trinidad & Tobago
Bay of Naples	Ecuador	Jordan	Pakistan	Tunisia
Beijing	Edinburgh		Paris	Turkey
Belgium	Egypt	Kathmandu	Peru	Turkish Coast
Belize	England	Kenya	Philadelphia	Tuscany
Berlin		Korea	Philippines	
Bermuda	Finland		Poland	Umbria
Boston	Florence	Laos & Cambodia	Portugal	USA: On The Road
Brazil	Florida	Lisbon	Prague	USA: Western States
Brittany	France	Loire Valley	Provence	US National Parks: East
Brussels	France, Southwest	London	Puerto Rico	US National Parks: West
Budapest	Frankfurt	Los Angeles		
Buenos Aires	French Riviera		Rajasthan	Vancouver
Burgundy		Madeira	Rhine	Venezuela
Burma (Myanmar)	Gambia & Senegal	Madrid	Rio de Janeiro	Venice
	Germany	Malaysia	Rockies	Vienna
Cairo	Glasgow	Mallorca & Ibiza	Rome	Vietnam
Calcutta	Gran Canaria	Malta	Russia	
California	Great Britain	Mauritius, Réunion		Wales
California, Northern	Greece	& Seychelles	St Petersburg	Washington DC
California, Southern	Greek Islands	Melbourne	San Francisco	Waterways of Europe
Canada	Guatemala, Belize &	Mexico City	Sardinia	Wild West
Caribbean	Yucatán	Mexico	Scandinavia	
Catalonia		Miami	Scotland	Yemen
Channel Islands	Hamburg	Montreal	Seattle	
Chicago	Hawaii	Morocco	Sicily	
Chile	Hong Kong	Moscow	Singapore	

Complementing the above titles are 120 easy-to-carry Insight Compact Guides, 120 Insight Pocket Guides with full-size pull-out maps and more than 100 laminated easy-fold Insight Maps

Boston Subway

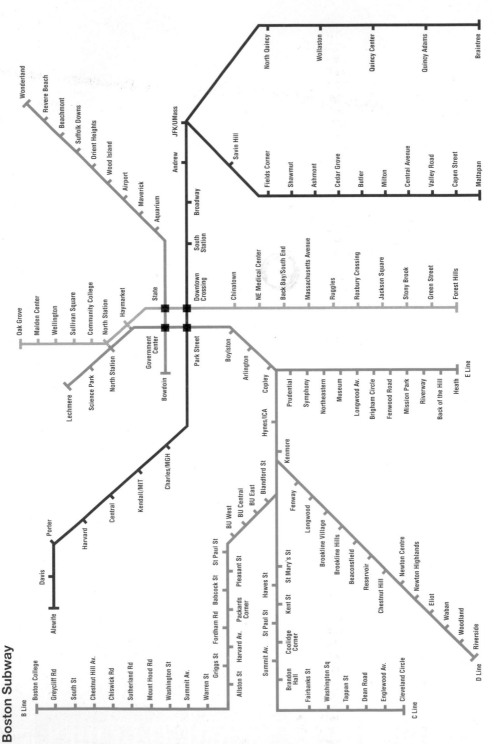